THE TWO KOREAS AND THE GREAT POWERS

This book explores Korea's place in a rapidly changing world in terms of multiple levels and domains of interaction pertaining to foreign policy behaviors and relations with the four regional/global powers (China, Russia, Japan, and the United States). The synergy of global transformations has now brought to an end Korea's proverbial identity and role as the helpless shrimp among whales, and both North Korea and South Korea have taken on new roles in the process of redefining and projecting their national identities. Synthetic national identity theory offers a useful perspective on change and continuity in Korea's turbulent relationships with the great powers over the years. Following a review of Korean diplomatic history and competing international relations theoretical approaches, along with a synthetic national identity theory as an alternative approach, one chapter is devoted to how both Koreas relate to each of the four powers in turn, and the book concludes with a consideration of inter-Korean relations and potential reunification.

Samuel S. Kim is an adjunct professor of political science and senior research scholar at the Weatherhead East Asian Institute, Columbia University, New York. He previously taught at the Foreign Affairs Institute, Beijing, China, as a Fulbright professor (1985–86) and at the Woodrow Wilson School of Public and International Affairs, Princeton University, Princeton, New Jersey (1986–93). He is the author or editor of twenty-two books on East Asian international relations and world order studies, including *China, the United Nations and World Order* (1979); *The Quest for a Just World Order* (1984); *China and the World* (ed., 1984, 1989, 1994, 1998); *North Korean Foreign Relations in the Post–Cold War Era* (ed., 1998); *Korea's Globalization* (ed., 2000); *East Asia and Globalization* (ed., 2000); and *The International Relations of Northeast Asia* (ed., 2004). He has published more than 150 articles in edited volumes and leading international relations journals, including *American Journal of International Law, Asian Perspective, Asian Survey, China Quarterly, International Interactions, International Organization, Journal of East Asian Studies, Journal of Peace Research, World Policy Journal,* and *World Politics.*

Books Written under the Auspices of the Center for Korean Research, Weatherhead East Asian Institute, Columbia University, 1998–2006

Samuel S. Kim, ed., *North Korean Foreign Relations in the Post–Cold War Era* (New York: Oxford University Press, 1998).

Samuel S. Kim, ed., *Korea's Globalization* (New York: Cambridge University Press, 2000).

Laurel Kendall, ed., *Under Construction: The Gendering of Modernity, Class, and Consumption in the Republic of Korea* (Honolulu: University of Hawaii Press, 2001).

Samuel S. Kim, ed., *The North Korean System in the Post–Cold War Era* (New York: Palgrave, 2001).

Charles K. Armstrong, ed., *Korean Civil Society: Social Movements, Democracy and the State* (London: Routledge, 2002).

Samuel S. Kim, ed., *Korea's Democratization* (New York: Cambridge University Press, 2002).

Samuel S. Kim, ed., *Inter-Korean Relations: Problems and Prospects* (New York: Palgrave Macmillan, 2004).

Samuel S. Kim, *The Two Koreas and the Great Powers* (New York: Cambridge University Press, 2006).

THE TWO KOREAS AND THE GREAT POWERS

SAMUEL S. KIM

Columbia University

CAMBRIDGE UNIVERSITY PRESS
Cambridge, New York, Melbourne, Madrid, Cape Town, Singapore, São Paulo, Delhi

Cambridge University Press
32 Avenue of the Americas, New York, NY 10013-2473, USA

www.cambridge.org
Information on this title: www.cambridge.org/9780521660631

First published 2006
Reprinted 2007

Printed in the United States of America

A catalog record for this publication is available from the British Library.

Library of Congress Cataloging in Publication Data

Kim, Samuel S., 1935–
The two Koreas and the great powers / Samuel S. Kim.
p. cm.
Includes bibliographical references and index.
ISBN 0-521-66063-7 (hardback) – ISBN 0-521-66899-9 (pbk.)
1. Korea (South) – Politics and government. 2. Korea (North) – Politics and government. 3. United States – Foreign relations – 21st century. 4. East Asia – Foreign relations. 5. World politics – 21st century. I. Title.
JQ1725.K565 2006
327.519 – dc21 2005037957

ISBN 978-0-521-66063-1 hardback
ISBN 978-0-521-66899-6 paperback

For
Helen,
with Gratitude,
Joy, and
Love . . .

Contents

Tables and Figures

Tables

Figures

Preface

The Korean peninsula, although situated at the crossroads of Northeast Asia, has often been home to political entities that sought isolation from the world outside. In the twentieth century, however, Korea's attempts to maintain itself as the "hermit kingdom" were overthrown in succession by Japanese colonization, the World War II settlement, the beginning of the Cold War, the end of the Cold War, and the intensification of globalization. Because of the course of international history following World War II, on the Korean peninsula today there are two Korean states, whereas for the 1,269 previous years there had been only one. North and South Korea as we know them today do not exist as entities entirely of their own making but rather as two incomplete nation-states with national identities crafted in the cauldron of Cold War conflict and galvanized in the post–Cold War age of globalization.

With a synthetic interactive approach to studying foreign relations as its starting point, this book explores how the identities of North and South Korea have evolved in relation to the Big Four of Northeast Asia: China, Japan, Russia, and the United States. Just as for individuals there can be no definition of the self without reference to some other, so with nation-states there can be no development of national identity without reference to the set of other actors in world politics. For the two Korean states, these referents include the Confucian empire-cum-socialist experiment, China; the former colonial occupier, Japan; the formerly meddlesome and now cautious friend to all, Russia; the South Korean savior and North Korean nemesis, the United States; and, perhaps most important, the mirror against which each Korea most closely judges itself – the other Korea across the thirty-eighth parallel.

As regional and international politics interact on the Korean peninsula, the synergy of momentous global transformations – democratization, the end of the Cold War and its superpower rivalry, and globalization – has now brought Korea's proverbial identity and role as the helpless shrimp among whales decisively to an end. Even though Korea's search for a national identity has been unusually tumultuous because of the vast gap between role capabilities and role commitments, South Korea today is no longer a pawn but a pivotal player in Northeast Asian economics, security, and culture. North of the demilitarized zone, the other Korean state has survived, despite a rapid succession of external shocks on top of a series of seemingly fatal internal woes. In fact, not only has North Korea, the weakest of the six main actors in Northeast Asia, continued to exist, but it has also catapulted itself as a primary driver of Northeast Asian geopolitics through its strategic use of nuclear brinkmanship diplomacy.

In North and South Korea, we have two countries that hearken back to bygone historical eras even as they herald the coming of new ones in Northeast Asia. Through the lens of the Korean peninsula, we can examine how Northeast Asia has evolved in the post–Cold War world from a region firmly entrenched in East–West conflict to one with a broader range of possible alliances and antagonisms, and we also can forecast possible futures for the regional order, including issues of security conflict, economic cooperation, cultural assertion, and Korean reunification. Through the lens of the Big Four of Northeast Asia, it becomes clear how North and South Korea are integral to these processes, and how they have been and will continue to be defined as nation-states in the context of regional history and ongoing processes. There is much movement and fluctuation in Korean foreign relations, but by looking at how national identity interacts with military, economic, and functional foreign policy goals, it is the intention in this book to pin down these trajectories and locate them in a space to which all global citizens can relate.

It is somewhat embarrassing to admit that this book has had a gestation period of almost a decade. A study of this nature and duration owes a great deal to the contributions of many people who have participated in the conception of the work, as well as in the individual and collective remedies to the many problems and shortcomings.

From the very beginning, the research and writing of this book has been closely keyed to and shaped by my teaching of a graduate course in Korean Foreign Relations for the past twelve or so years in the Department of Political Science at Columbia University. This experience served as a kind of force multiplier, providing not only the primary reason and audience, but also an ideal testing laboratory and an invaluable opportunity to try out some of the ideas embodied in the book. In a real sense, then, this book is an offspring of this course (as my lecture notes and many discussions with my students provided first-cut materials and ideas to further my research and rewriting). So my thanks go to many serious students in the course for their contributions to the shaping of the book.

Without field interviews of many different kinds, this study would have lost a vital primary source for delineating the motivational and behavioral dimensions of the many contentious issues involved in the relations of the two Koreas with the Big Four. From May to June 1998 and from early to late June 2000, I conducted field research in Seoul and Beijing, as well as conducted many interviews with current and former government officials on a confidential basis in order to broaden my understanding of behind-the-scenes internal debates on many controversial political, military, and diplomatic issues. Unfortunately, my contacts with North Korean diplomats were limited to only two closed executive – Track I.5 – meetings in New York and a few visits by North Korean "NGO" delegations to Columbia's Center for Korean Research. I have liberally taken advantage of my position as chair of the (monthly) Contemporary Korean Affairs Seminar (1994–present) in conducting "informal interviews" – the functional equivalent of my extensive field interviews in the United States, as it were – either before or after the formal seminar presentations of the participants. The keynote seminar speakers were more or less divided evenly between Americans and South Koreans: former U.S. government officials or ambassadors and then-current South Korean ambassadors to the United States and prominent Koreanist scholars and journalists. This book has been immeasurably enriched by the many informal interviews with those keynote seminar speakers: Donald Gregg, William Gleestein, Thomas Hubbard, Wendy Sherman, Charles Kartman, Phillip Yun, Charles Pritchard, Robert Gallucci, Desaix Anderson, Mitchell Reiss, Lee Hong koo, Park Soo Gil, Yang Sung Chul, Marcus Noland, Nicholas Eberstadt, Bruce Cumings, Kathy Moon, Victor Cha, John Merrill, Leon Sigal, David Steinberg, Steve Linton, Chong Sik Lee, Myung Soo Lee, Choi Jang Jip, Don Oberdorfer, Selig Harrison, David Kang, Chung-in Moon, Ilpyong Kim, Manwoo Lee, Sonia Ryang, Seungsook Moon, Scott Snyder, C. Kenneth Quinones, Lee Sook-jong, and Cameron Hurst.

I have benefited from the critical reading and helpful comments of a number of individual friends and colleagues in the fields of Korean studies and international relations. James Seymour, John Feffer, Jack Snyder, and Matt Winters all read parts of the manuscript with helpful comments and suggestions for substantive improvement. In the course of the peer review and vetting process at Cambridge University Press, three anonymous readers provided critical and perceptive comments and suggestions for the final revisions of the manuscript for publication.

During the preparation of this work, I was greatly assisted by the overall facilities and congenial atmosphere provided by the Weatherhead East Asian Institute (WEAI) and the Department of Political Science, Columbia University, and want to express my thanks to my area studies and international relations colleagues for their continuing support and encouragement. The WEAI's research atmosphere was most congenial to my particular project because each academic year it attracts a dozen visiting scholars and professional Fellows from China, Japan, South Korea, and Taiwan to interact with resident faculty members in East Asian area studies drawn from political science, history, sociology, and economics through numerous brown-bag noon lecture series, colloquia, Weatherhead Policy Forum, faculty research lunches, and so on.

As befits a project so long in the making, I have received considerable research help from a number of my graduate student research assistants in recent years – Joon Seok Hong, Abraham Kim, Ji In Lee, Emma Chanlett-Avery, Erik Tollesfson, and Janice Yoon. I would like to thank them all for their diligent library or online research tasks. Above all, I am most grateful to Matthew Winters, who read my next-to-last draft with care and insight that would amaze anyone unacquainted with him; as a graduate student, he is already endowed with the critical, conceptual, and analytical power of an established international relations scholar.

The McCune-Reischauer romanization system is used throughout this book, with some familiar exceptions for well-known place names (e.g., Pyongyang, Seoul, Pusan) and personal names (e.g., Syngman Rhee, Park Chung Hee, Kim Dae Jung, Kim Il Sung, Kim Jong Il, Kang Sok Ju) that would otherwise be difficult to recognize.

It was a pleasure to work with Cambridge University Press in the production of this book. I am particularly grateful to Frank Smith, social science editor, for his support and encouragement and for his role as an invaluable navigator throughout the publication process. Special thanks are due to Cathy Felgar and for the publisher's efficient steering of the manuscript through the various stages of production.

As always, without the unflagging forbearance, support, and music of my wife Helen, the most significant other – yes, she is a professor of music, not political science – this project would never have come to fruition. By participating in every step of this long and seemingly endless journey of revisions and updates, and by providing me the chance to share its opportunity costs with a collaborative spirit, she sufficiently prodded me to finish this project before it finished me. Hence, this is as much her book as it is mine.

Because the two Koreas still remain in many ways moving targets on turbulent and indeterminate trajectories, I am reluctant to declare the manuscript complete. Nonetheless, I do so now – without a sense of completion but with a deep sigh of relief and a deep sense of gratitude to the many individuals who helped me along the endless road. The usual disclaimer still applies: I alone am responsible for whatever local, inter-Korean, regional, and global errors in fact or interpretation may remain in the book.

CHAPTER 1

Introduction: Korea and the Great Powers in a Changing World

> A shrimp gets crushed to death in the fight between whales.
>
> – *An old Korean saying*

> Historically, we Koreans have lived through a series of challenges and have responded to them. Having to live among big powers, the people on the Korean Peninsula have had to cope with countless tribulations. For thousands of years, however, we have successfully preserved our self-respect as a nation as well as our unique culture. Within the half-century since liberation from colonial rule, and despite territorial division, war, and poverty, we have built a nation that is the 12th largest economic power in the world.
>
> – *President Roh Moo-hyun's Inaugural Address, February 25, 2003*[1]

The Three Koreas Revisited

The previous old Korean saying pithily captures the conventional realist wisdom about the security predicament of the weak in the region of the strong. Indeed, there is no mistaking the extraordinary ramifications of great-power rivalry for Korea's place in world affairs. For more than a century, and especially between 1894 and 1953, the Korean peninsula became a highly contested terrain that absorbed and reflected wider geopolitical struggles and even sanguinary wars involving, to varying degrees, imperial Japan, czarist Russia, the Soviet Union, Qing China, the People's Republic of China (PRC), and the United States – variations on the Big

[1] An English text available at http://english.president.go.kr/warp/app/en_speeches/view?group_id= en-ar. . . .

Four of contemporary Northeast Asian international relations.[2] During this period, except in the Korean War (1950–53), an aggressive, imperial Japan was at the forefront of hegemonic wars in a quest to extend the Japanese hegemony over Korea to the entire Asia-Pacific region – the Sino–Japanese War of 1894–95 to gain dominance in Korea, the Russo–Japanese War of 1904–5 for mastery over Manchuria and Korea, the Sino–Japanese War of the 1930s, and the Pacific War of 1941–45 (World War II in the Asia Pacific). In the process, Korea as the hermit kingdom was conquered, colonized, liberated, divided, and devastated by civil-cum-international war, spawning a three-stage mutation of Korea's stunted national identity as a shrimp among whales from Chosun (Yi) Korea (1392–1910) to Colonial Korea (1910–45) to Divided Korea (1945–).

Soon after the eclipse of Japanese control over the peninsula came the Korean War, by any reckoning an event beyond compare. More than any other international event since the end of World War II, the Korean War served as the most important determinant in shaping the character not only of the two Koreas, but also of great-power politics in Northeast Asia (NEA) and beyond. Although fueled by escalating political tensions within Korea from 1947 to 1950, and although the idea of initiating the war came directly from Kim Il Sung, in actuality it was a great-power war fought on Korean soil. The United Nations (UN) also involved itself in the war through so-called police action, with sixteen member states dispatching combat troops of varying sizes and incurring casualties of varying magnitude.[3]

The Korean War served as the chief catalyst for a quadrupling of U.S. defense expenditures; for the proliferation of a series of bilateral defense treaties with Japan, South Korea, Taiwan, South Vietnam, the Philippines, and Thailand; and for an ill-conceived and short-lived multilateral security organization, the South East Asia Treaty Organization (SEATO). Yet, as diplomatic historian William Stueck argues, the greatest paradox of the Korean War was how the conflict devastated Korea, militarized the Cold War, and subsequently threatened to escalate out of control, but in the end functioned as a proxy war for what could have been an even more destructive great-power war in Europe – that is, as a substitute for World War III.[4] Its aftereffects were felt for decades as the Cold War played out on the Korean peninsula.

Particularly significant, but not sufficiently acknowledged, is the role of the Korean War in the creation of Cold War identity in NEA and beyond.

[2] For a multidimensional and multidisciplinary analysis of contemporary Northeast Asian international relations, see S. S. Kim (2004e).

[3] For a detailed breakdown of the number of participating member states' troops and war casualties, see Ministry of National Defense (2000: 355–56).

[4] Stueck (1995: 3, 370).

For both Koreas, the experience of the Korean War initiated a decisive shift in identity politics from the competition of multiple identities to the dominance of the Cold War identity. As a consequence, the collective identity of Korea as a whole nation was weakened radically.[5] Although the Korean War accelerated and completed the process of Cold War identity construction, decades later the end of the Cold War, as well as the collapse and transformation of the communist world, failed to turn inter-Korean identity politics around.[6]

The United States, too, owes to the Korean War the crystallization of its Cold War identity, which in turn gave birth to an American strategic culture that thrived on a Manichaean vision of global bipolarity and the omnipresent communist threat. Similarly, until the latter half of the 1980s, Soviet strategic culture was anchored in and thrived on its own Cold War identity. The simplicity of a stark bipolarized worldview provided an indispensable counterpoint for the quest for superpower identity and security in the region dominated by American hegemony. Soviet geopolitical conduct seems to make no sense, except when viewed as the drive to assume a superpower role and acquire equal status with the United States to compensate for its siege mentality and to legitimize its authoritarian iron hand at home. Indeed, the United States was the Soviets' "significant other," the dominant international reference actor, to be envied, emulated, and at times cajoled for condominial collaboration. It is worth noting in this connection that some of the U.S.–USSR rivalries during the Cold War had more to do with the promotion of national identity as status competition than with the promotion of any identifiable "national interest."

As for China, although its troops suffered huge casualties in the Korean War, Beijing succeeded in forcing the strongest nation on earth to compromise in Korea and to accept China's representatives as equals at the bargaining table. No one in the West would ever again dismiss China's power as U.S. General Douglas MacArthur had in the fall of 1950. Indeed, the Korean War confirmed for the national self and "significant others" that China could stand up against the world's antisocialist superpower for the integrity of its new national identity as a revolutionary socialist state.

For Japan, the Korean War turned out to be a blessing in disguise because Tokyo reaped maximum economic and political benefits. By the end of the war, Tokyo had regained its sovereignty and had skillfully negotiated a new mutual security treaty that provided for U.S. protection of Japan, while allowing Tokyo to escape the burden of joint defense. Without becoming involved in the bloodshed or material deprivation, Japan was able to reap the benefits of a war economy that had been imbued

[5] C. S. Chun (2001: 132). [6] C. S. Chun (2001: 142).

with new potential as a logistical base for the United States and as a key manufacturing center for war supplies.[7] The Korean War and the resulting globalization of antagonistic Cold War identities throughout Asia and Europe have also made it possible for Tokyo to avoid coming clean on its imperial past (thus planting the seeds of post–Cold War identity conflicts in NEA). Emblematic of this phenomenon was the reemergence of Kishi Nobusuke as prime minister in 1957; Nobusuke was the former head of the Manchurian Railroad, a Minister of Munitions in the Tojo government, and a signatory of the 1941 declaration of war against the United States. The return to power of such a person as prime minister was a turn of events that would have been unthinkable in the German context.

Thanks to the end of the Cold War and the other global transformations of the past two decades – globalization and the "third wave of democratization" – South Korea is no longer the marginal shrimp but now a pivotal player in Northeast Asian economics, security, and culture. After South Korea had already taken on a new economic and political identity as a newly industrialized country (NIC) and a newly democratized country (NDC), President Roh Moo-hyun pledged in his inaugural address of February 23, 2003 to devote his "whole heart and efforts" to bringing the Age of Northeast Asia to fruition "at the earliest possible time." Roh also challenged South Koreans to embrace the growing regionalism in NEA and to play a leading role as the hub of a wheel with collaborative spokes integrating its neighbors into a single unit, a wheel ready to roll on the road of a globalized economy. More recently, in a speech on March 22, 2005, Roh presented his most striking articulation and projection of Korea's future role that "Korea will play the role of a balancer, not only on the Korean peninsula, but throughout Northeast Asia."[8]

North of the demilitarized zone, the other Korean state has survived, despite a rapid succession of external shocks – the crumbling of the Berlin Wall, the end of both the Cold War and superpower rivalry, the demise of the Soviet Union and the international communism at its epicenter – on top of a series of seemingly fatal internal woes, including spreading famine, deepening socialist alienation, and the death of its founder, the "eternal president" Kim Il Sung. In fact, not only has North Korea, the weakest of the six main actors in the region, continued to exist, but it has also catapulted itself as a primary driver of Northeast Asian geopolitics through its strategic use of nuclear brinkmanship diplomacy.[9] From this

[7] The United States spent nearly $3 billion in Japan for war and war-related supplies from 1950 to 1954. See J. E. Woo (1991: 33–34).

[8] An English text available at http://english.president.go.kr/warp/app/en_speeches/view?group_id=en-ar. . . .

[9] S. S. Kim (1995).

transformed geopolitical landscape emerges the greatest irony of the region: today, in the post–Cold War world, each of two incomplete Korean nation-states seems to command greater security sovereignty than was ever enjoyed by a unified Korean state.

For six decades now, two Koreas have existed where there had been only one for more than 1,000 years previously. None of the other countries divided by the Cold War had known such extensive national unity, and yet along with China, the division of Korea has the distinction of having survived the deterioration and dismantling of the bipolar world that had given that division birth and had more generally defined most of the history of the latter half of the twentieth century. Both North Korea (the Democratic People's Republic of Korea, or DPRK) and South Korea (the Republic of Korea, or ROK) still proclaim sovereignty over the whole of the Korean peninsula. Yet, over the years, each has also developed mechanisms that allow it to function as a "normal" nation-state in the world community. Like conjoined twins attached at the hip, each half of Korea has operated with the knowledge that both its every move and its national identity are reflected in its ideologically opposed doppelganger.

The foreign relations that define the place of North and South Korea in the world community today are therefore the product of the trajectories that the states have chosen to take – or were forced to take – given their Cold War identity and politics. In addition, the choices of the Korean states are constrained by the international environment in which they interact, given that NEA is a region in which four of the world's great powers – China, Japan, Russia, and the United States – uneasily meet and interact. North and South Korea each remain entangled with one of the Big Four through a Cold War alliance: the DPRK to China and the ROK to the United States. Despite the historical identity of Korea as a shrimp among whales, both the DPRK and the ROK have found a new capacity for taking initiatives that would not have been possible during the Cold War years. The synergy of momentous global transformations – democratization, the end of the Cold War and its superpower rivalry, and globalization – has now brought Korea's proverbial identity and role as the helpless shrimp among whales decisively to an end.

The simultaneous potential for new initiatives and lingering regional and global constraints became manifest when South Korean President Kim Dae Jung and North Korean Chairman Kim Jong Il embraced each other at an inter-Korean summit in Pyongyang, symbolically signaling their acceptance of each other's legitimacy. The summit was most remarkable because it was initiated and executed by the Koreans themselves in the absence of any external shock or great-power sponsorship. The summit seemed to have brought the two Koreas down from their respective hegemonic unification dreamlands to a place where peaceful coexistence of two separate states was possible. While in the wake of the summit Pyongyang proclaimed publicly for the first time that "the issue of unifying the differing systems in the north and the south as one may be *left to posterity to settle slowly in the future*,"[10] South Koreans have been increasingly wary of a German-style unification by absorption and more supportive of engaged interaction with the North, as demonstrated in the "Sunshine Policy" under the Kim Dae Jung administration and the "Policy of Peace and Prosperity" under the Roh Moo-hyun administration. Since the summit, the two countries have arranged family reunions, increased trade, and developed tourism to Mt. Kumgang in North Korea. Although Kim Dae Jung proclaimed frequently that he did not expect Korean reunification on his watch or in his lifetime, the gradual and functional pathway to a peaceful reunification of Korea seems more apparent today than ever.

In October 2002, only two years after the Pyongyang summit, in a dramatic although not necessarily surprising turn of events, North Korean leaders were depicted by the Bush administration as having revealed to U.S. interlocutors that they had a highly enriched uranium (HEU) nuclear program under development. This "admission" has led to a series of trilateral and six-party talks involving the Big Four and both Korean states. From the beginning of the talks, the United States expected its South Korean ally to fall in line and support its all-or-nothing demands on North Korea. But the ROK has taken a more moderate position, trying to temper U.S. and DPRK belligerence toward one another and working with China and Russia on more flexible, compromise proposals. Such an alignment of stability-centered interests – with the ROK, China, and Russia all working together – would hardly have been imaginable during the Cold War, yet the fact that the same set of Cold War players are involved indicates a certain sense of *plus ça change, plus c'est la même chose* (the more things change, the more they stay the same).

Although the nuclear standoff has been the focus of attention regarding North Korea in Washington and consequently in the U.S. press, Seoul – the presumed prime target of any North Korean nuclear weapons – has continued to pursue functional linkages with the DPRK and has played down the standoff. For the Roh Moo-hyun administration, a government elected in part because of a platform that promised to distance Korea from the United States, the desired international image of North Korea is that of the 2000 summit, not that of the 2002 nuclear revelation. The contrast between these two events and between their legacies reflects the multiple levels at which Korean foreign relations occur.

[10] *Rodong Sinmun [Worker's Daily]*, June 25, 2000, p. 6; emphasis added.

This highlights with particular clarity that the stability of Korean national identities is not exclusively or even largely a domestic phenomenon, but rather is closely keyed to and conditioned by the stability of the Northeast Asian environment.

Korean Identity in the Regional Environment Old and New

In the early years of the new millennium, there is something both very old and very new in the regional security complex surrounding the Korean peninsula. What remains unchanged and unchangeable is the geographical location of the Korean peninsula, tightly enveloped by the three big neighboring powers. As Jules Cambon wrote in 1935, "The geographical position of a nation is the principal factor conditioning its foreign policy – the principal reason why it must have a foreign policy at all."[11] Of course, geography matters in the shaping of any state's foreign policy, but this is especially true for the foreign policies of the two Koreas and their three neighboring powers. A glance at the map and the geopolitical smoke from the latest (second) U.S.–DPRK nuclear standoff suggests why NEA is one of the most important yet most volatile regions of the world. It is hardly surprising, then, that each of the Big Four has come to regard the Korean peninsula as the strategic pivot point of NEA security and therefore as falling within its own geostrategic ambit.[12] The Korean peninsula, divided or united, shares land and maritime borders with China, Russia, and Japan, uniquely situating it within the geopolitics of NEA. Crowded by all four great powers, Korea's unique place in the geopolitics of NEA remains at once a blessing, a curse, and a Rorschach test.

From China's geostrategic perspective, Korea has been a *cordon sanitaire* against Japanese continental expansionism. Lying in the path of Russia's southward expansion in search of an ice-free port, Korea has been a major focus of strategic interest for Russian foreign policy in the Far East. For Japan, Korea served not only as an indispensable corridor for continental expansionism – or as a threat of continental retaliation, "a dagger pointed at the heart of Japan," in the words of Meiji oligarch Yamagata Aritomo[13] – but also as a major source of agricultural supplies for Japanese industrialization and militarization. For the United States, Korea was initially a backwater in which it had to accept Japanese surrender, later transformed into a frontline domino state, standing against communist expansion.

In the age of great-power rivalry at the end of the nineteenth century, Korea had found itself at a loss. Locating itself in an East Asian regional

[11] Cited in Pastor (1999: 7). [12] See Eberstadt and Ellings (2001).
[13] Green (2001: 113).

order and not in a larger international community, Korea deferred to China, with which it maintained a (tributary) relationship, when the West came knocking at the door. Korea preferred to remain a Confucian hermit kingdom, isolated from the "barbarian" outsiders. Despite having been subject to numerous invasions and occasional occupations during its 2,000 years of recorded history, Korean civilization possessed and maintained a distinct one-nation identity. When Japan forced China, through treaty, to enter the world of modern nation-states, Korea's entrance was not far behind. But its existence as an independent nation-state was short lived because Japan exercised increasing control over the country, relieving China of influence in the Sino–Japanese War of 1894–95, doing the same to Russia in 1904–5, and then beginning full colonization of Korea in 1910.

Without the chance to conceive of itself as a modern nation-state before the onset of colonization, Koreans did not do well in forming a cohesive national identity during the colonial period. The March First Uprising of 1919 symbolized a nascent awareness of national identity, but its suppression forcibly transformed the Korean nationalists into a movement of exiles abroad and underground at home. The Korean Provisional Government in Shanghai quickly became embroiled in intense factional conflict, and the Korean communist movement also degenerated into factional strife. The Korean Communist Party (KCP), founded in April 1925, suffered so many defeats that its checkered life was brought to an end by 1931.[14]

On the eve of liberation in 1945, the Korean nationalist movement was fragmented, frustrated, and without a charismatic leader to herald the returning nationalists from abroad. The exile movement suffered from protracted combat fatigue and had been factionalized to such an extent that it would have been extremely difficult, if not impossible, for any one nationalist leader to unify the newly liberated country.[15] Except for the negative anti-Japanese identity that was shared by all, the nationalist exiles returned home with a set of mutually competing foreign sources of legitimacy; the groups were, in varying degrees, Americanized, Russianized, Sinicized, Communized, or Christianized. Given these divided and divisive identities, Kim Il Sung in the North – and to a lesser extent Syngman Rhee in the South – was driven to link his legitimacy to the national political mythology by exaggerating and even falsifying his national revolutionary background abroad.[16] Just as no single national movement formed before or during colonization, neither did one precipitate after liberation. This was reinforced by the division of the country into zones controlled by the USSR and the United States.

[14] D.-S. Suh (1967: 117–41). [15] S. S. Kim (1976); C. S. Lee (1963).
[16] J. A. Kim (1975: 287, 338).

The Korean division along the thirty-eighth parallel was initially imposed as part of an ad hoc U.S. zonal plan proposed by Harry Truman on August 15, 1945 – to which the Soviet Union agreed the next day – for dividing up Japanese troop surrender arrangements in the wake of Japan's unconditional surrender on that same day (the biggest national holiday, the Day of Liberation [*Kwangbok chol*]). The hardening of the division was a direct consequence of early postwar superpower conflict. The first blood of the Cold War was spilled in Korea with the outbreak of the Korean War in June 1950, and at the end of its three years, the war's fatalities would number several million. The war had the impact of restructuring national, regional, and global systems; it had the decisive catalytic effect of institutionalizing the rules of the Cold War zero-sum game, thereby congealing patterns of East–West conflict across East Asia and beyond.[17] The 37,000 U.S. troops stationed on South Korean soil today (to be reduced to some 25,000 as of 2008) serve as a reminder of Korea's role in the Cold War and also indicate the extreme local legacies of that global conflict. The lesson to be acknowledged is that a country's foreign relations are never limited to domestic sources but are products of both regional and global environments, even for a self-defined hermit kingdom like Korea.

In fact, Korea has a long history of being at the center of the Northeast Asian region. For centuries, NEA has comprised China, Korea, and Japan, with only brief interruptions due to the Mongol and Manchu invasions. Therefore, through the various incarnations of regional order – from the Sinocentric world of the Middle Kingdom, to the Japanese imperial world, to the Cold War world, to the post–Cold War era of U.S. hegemony – Korea has remained central, although historically this has not meant that ties were particularly deep.[18] Japan's imperialism and later economic power, Russia's rivalry with Japan and headquartering of a world socialist movement, China's ascendancy at the end of the twentieth century, and the U.S. role as global hegemon have all assigned identities to Korea as these processes worked to define the region and the world.

Nonetheless, NEA is more than a geographical referent. Although geographical proximity is important, defining East Asia or especially NEA in these terms alone is more problematic than may be apparent because any strictly "geographical" approach would hide rather than reveal the critical role of the United States in Northeast Asian international relations and especially geopolitics.[19] If NEA as an international region is

[17] Jervis (1980).

[18] For a collected volume addressing Korea's role in each era, see Armstrong et al. (2006).

[19] The common use of "East Asia" and "Northeast Asia" as one and the same had to do with the fact that Asia, in general, and East Asia, in particular, are so overwhelmingly Sinocentric. As a result, the concept of East Asia "has conventionally referred only to those states of Confucian heritage." See Ravenhill (2002: 174).

defined in both geographical and functional terms (i.e., in terms of the patterned interactions among its constituent member states) – as it is in this study – it encompasses China, the two Koreas, and Japan as core states, with the addition of the Russian Far East, and it also involves the United States as the extraterritorial, lone superpower. NEA is said to hold vital importance in America's security and economic interests, and the U.S. role remains a crucial component (perhaps the most crucial) of the regional geostrategic and geoeconomic equations. The United States, by dint of its deep interest and involvement in Northeast Asian geopolitics and geoeconomics, provides more than 80 percent of the 100,000 troops deployed in the Asia-Pacific region, concentrated mostly in Japan and South Korea.[20]

Accordingly, the world's heaviest concentration of military and economic capabilities is in this region: the world's three largest nuclear weapons states (the United States, Russia, and China), one seminuclear state (North Korea), three threshold nuclear weapons states (Japan, South Korea, and Taiwan), the world's three largest economies on a purchasing power parity basis (the United States, China, and Japan),[21] and Asia's three largest economies (Japan, China, and South Korea). It was in NEA that the Cold War turned into a hot war, and the region was more involved in Cold War politics than any other region or subregion without nonaligned states. Even with the end of the Cold War and superpower rivalry, the region is still distinguished by continuing, if somewhat anachronistic, Cold War alliance systems linking the two Koreas, Japan, China, and the United States in a bilateralized regional security complex.

As this might suggest, for several reasons, the divide in NEA between regional and global politics is substantially overlapped, if not completely erased. First, the region is "strategic home" to three of the five permanent members of the UN Security Council, which are also three of the five "original" nuclear weapons states that are shielded by the two-tiered, discriminatory Nuclear Non-Proliferation Treaty (NPT) regime. Second, Japan, Greater China, and South Korea alone accounted for about 25 percent of world gross domestic product (GDP) in 2000.[22] As of mid-2005, NEA

[20] In the latest Quadrennial Defense Review (QDR) Report, "Northeast Asia" and "the East Asian littoral" are defined as "critical areas" for precluding hostile domination by any other power. See United States Department of Defense, *Quadrennial Defense Review Report*, September 30, 2001, p. 2 (hereafter cited as *QDRR 2001*) at http://www.defenselink.mil/pubs/qdr2001.pdf.

[21] According to the purchasing power parity (PPP) estimates of the World Bank (which are not unproblematic), China, with a 1994 GDP just less than $3 trillion, had become the second largest economy in the world, after the United States. By 2003, China's ranking as the world's second largest economy remained the same, but its global national income (GNI)/PPP more than doubled to $6,435 billion. See *Economist* (London), January 27, 1996, 102; World Bank (1996: 188); World Bank (2004: 256).

[22] See Ellings and Friedberg (2002: 396).

is home to the world's four largest holders of foreign exchange reserves: Japan ($825.0 billion), China ($711.0 billion), Taiwan ($253.6 billion), and South Korea ($205.7 billion).[23] In addition, Japan remains the world's second largest financial contributor to the United Nations and its associated specialized agencies. Finally, the rapid rise of China's economic power – the country has sustained the world's fastest economic growth in the post–Cold War era – and related military power has sired many debates among specialists and policy makers over how much influence Beijing actually exerts in NEA and what this means for U.S. interests or emerging Northeast Asian order.[24]

With the overarching superpower conflict and overlay gone, local and regional dynamics are becoming ever more salient, and the two Koreas are experiencing greater latitude in the shaping of their regional security environment and policies. But the same cannot be said in the economic domain, where all East Asian states – including the two Koreas but more the South than the North – are participating in an East Asian economic regionalism, based on the shared embrace of economic development and well-being, as well as the shared sense of vulnerability associated with the processes of globalization and regionalization. Greater regional cooperation is one of the few available instruments with which East Asian states can meet the double challenge of globalization from above and localization from below. Operating in a regional context, the East Asian states can "Asianize" their individual responses to globalization in a politically viable form.

Nonetheless, NEA is not without its share of territorial and maritime disputes in varying degrees of intensity: China–Russia border (low), China–North Korea border (low), China–Tajikistan border (low), China–Japan maritime (the Diaoyu/Senkaku islands) (moderate), Japan–Russia maritime (the Northern Territories) (moderate), Japan–South Korea maritime (Tokdo/Takeshima Islands) (moderate), North Korea–South Korea (the Northern Limit Line on the Yellow/West Sea) (low), and China versus six other East Asian states on the Spratly Islands (low).[25] With the entry into force of the UN Convention on the Law of the Sea (UNCLOS) in 1994, the enlarged exclusive economic zones (EEZs) pose the clear and present danger of a new pattern of maritime conflict in the region.

Furthermore, in the late 1990s, the volcano of potential security eruption in the North seemed to have become more active than ever before. An unstable or collapsing North Korea, given its proximity to Seoul (in

[23] Edmund L. Andrews, "Shouted Down: A Political Furor Built on Many Grudges," *New York Times*, August 3, 2005, p. C1.

[24] See Buzan and Foot (2004); Johnston (2004); Goldstein (2005); Deng and Wang (2005); Shambaugh (2004/05; 2005); Sutter (2005).

[25] See J. Wang (2003: 385).

rocket sights within 3 minutes) and inordinate asymmetrical military capabilities, could have extraordinary refractory ramifications for great-power politics in NEA and beyond. The necessity of coping with North Korean security or insecurity behavior in multiple and mutating forms, aided and abetted by America's rogue-state demonization strategy, has become an integral part of both the NEA security problem and the NEA security solution.

Yet, there has also been an underemphasized peace in NEA. Despite periodic tension escalations on the Korean peninsula, there has not been a single intrastate or interstate war during the post–Cold War era. Part of the answer to the question of recent, relative peace in NEA lies in the rise of China as a responsible regional power that has transformed not only Chinese foreign policy, but also in the process the geopolitical and geoeconomic landscape of Asia, including NEA. Within the wheel of emerging East Asian regionalism, China serves as the hub power and has managed to radiate a series of cooperative bilateral and biminilateral (minimultilateral) spokes.[26] The combined interactive effects of (1) the globalization pressures that sharply increase the costs of the use of force; (2) China's successful settlement of territorial disputes with most of its neighbors, with the corresponding sense of enhanced state sovereignty; (3) the demise of ideological conflict; and (4) the substantial accomplishment of China's status drive as a great power all augur well for the peace and stability of the East Asian region and beyond.

At still another level of generalization, as a result of the uneasy juxtaposition of continuity and discontinuity, there is emerging in place of the clarity, simplicity, and apparent discipline of bipolarity a new Northeast Asian regional order with multiple complexities and uncertainties that is of indeterminate shape and content. The structural impact of power transition and globalization seems to have accentuated the uncertainties and complexities of great-power politics in the region. The centripetal forces of increasing economic interaction and interdependence are grating against the centrifugal forces of historical and national identity animus and differing notions of conflict management in NEA. In the absence of superpower conflict, the foreign policies of the two Koreas and the Big Four are subject to competing pressures, especially the twin pressures of globalization from above and localization from below. All are experiencing the wrenching national identity difficulties in adjusting to post–Cold War realignments, and all are in flux regarding their national identities and how these relate to the region as a whole.

As a consequence of the uncertainty surrounding these identity adjustments, the security situation of the NEA region is vastly more complex

[26] S. S. Kim (2004d).

than any other region of the world, and in subsystemic terms, the region is almost undoubtedly multipolar, despite the existence of global unipolarity. This is the only region where so many combinations and permutations of two, three, four, two-plus-four, and three-plus-three power games can be played in both regional and global arenas. In one sense, the region is as much under the sway of unipolarity as anywhere else, given the unchallenged hegemony of the United States and its aggregate structural power.[27] However, given the emergence of China as a nuclear power in the 1960s, as a political power in the 1970s, and as an economic power in the 1990s, along with the rise of Japan as an economic superpower in the 1980s, the region is more multipolar than is any other. Complicating matters is the fact that the Korean peninsula is divided, so the Big Four cannot address the threats and opportunities inherent in the peninsula without paying heed to inter-Korean relations, and the seemingly local and bilateral relations between the two Korean states are, in reality, part of the nexus of great-power politics.

Assessing the future of the region, some have suggested that the Korean peninsula could become the pivot point of Sino–U.S. relations, whereas others have focused on the intricacies and dangers of a Beijing–Seoul–Pyongyang strategic triangle involving three sets of asymmetrical mutual interests and perceptions. Still others have imagined an emerging Sino–Russian strategic partnership as "the beginning of a new quadrilateral alignment in East Asia in which a 'continental' Russo-Chinese bloc balances a 'maritime' American-Japanese bloc," with the Korean peninsula caught in the middle.[28] Regardless of which scenario most accurately reflects the trajectory of NEA, the unifying characteristic that the Korean peninsula is at the center of each – a consequence of geography – cannot be mistaken. What will determine which, if any, of these paths is followed is the way in which the participant countries come to define themselves in East Asia vis-à-vis their neighbors.

Since the end of the Cold War, the foreign policy makers of the ROK and the DPRK have had to consider these alternative worlds in which conflict no longer takes place along a clear East–West divide. With so little regionalism in NEA[29] – given the paucity of regional organizations and the painful memories of historical and national identity enmity – it is difficult for a state that has fallen from the Cold War world order to feel that it has landed in any sort of firm international society.[30] At the same time, the way that the great powers have all had their eyes focused on

[27] On post–Cold War unipolarity, see Krauthammer (1991); Wohlforth (1999).

[28] Brzezinski (1997); Bedeski (1995); Garver (1998).

[29] For the most comprehensive study of Northeast Asian regionalism, see Rozman (2004).

[30] On the idea of an international society that defines the rules and norms by which a system of states operates, see Bull (1977).

the Korean peninsula – and still do – imparts a power to the two Korean states that might not otherwise be reconcilable with their capabilities. For more than a century, Korea has had a variety of opportunities and capacities to be an agenda setter, a spoiler, or simply a conduit. Whereas in premodern times Chinese culture spread to Japan through Korea, today Japanese culture spreads to China in the reverse direction. With astounding economic growth in Japan in the 1980s and in China in the 1990s, Korea is positioned as the third leg of a hypothetical Northeast Asian free trade zone, high-tech industrial belt, or (when Russia is involved) energy corridor.

South Korea has recently taken on a new leadership role in a somewhat unexpected domain, one that deals inherently with national identity: culture. One way that NEA has become a defined region is via the growth of international media conglomerates, which has led to the export of Korean television and film to hungry markets in Taiwan and China, where other sources have either dried up or have been found politically incompatible. Korean fashion styles have likewise become common on the streets of Shanghai and Taipei. The future status of Korean cultural production, however, will depend on the growth of China's and Taiwan's own cultural production industries. The prominence of the "Korean wave" will decline, but the contents of Korean culture will become ingrained in the everyday life of those cultures where it is now popular. On a grander scale, we cannot discount the impact that growing cultural awareness and transculturation can have on regional cultural cooperation and understanding.[31]

This burgeoning economic and cultural regionalism with its shared identity component, however, is often overshadowed by conflict among national identities. This paradox is explained in part by the fact that the Korean peninsula's geographic centrality has aided and abetted the competitive foreign policies of North and South Korea, which are linked to their respective struggles for national identity and state legitimacy, and are conceived under the microscope of the Big Four. So, the received wisdom about the traditional Korean security predicament as a helpless shrimp has not since the late 1980s been as reliable a guide in explaining epochal peninsular and regional developments. Neither are the major theories of international relations (neorealism and neoliberalism) much help, if they are taken to be encompassing. To the contrary, Korea demonstrates the contingencies that exist in the application of international relations theory and the need for a synthetic theory that recognizes the contingent nature of relations among states and peoples.

So, scholars and policy makers alike, as they seek to divine the shape of things to come in Korea's international life, are challenged by a rather

[31] J. S. Park (2006).

unique and complex cocktail of regional characteristics: high capability, abiding animus, deep albeit differentiated entanglement of the Big Four in Korean affairs, North Korea's recent emergence as a nuclear loose cannon, the absence of multilateral security institutions, the rise of America's unilateral triumphalism (or "new imperialism"), growing economic integration and regionalization, and the resulting uncertainties and unpredictability in the international politics of NEA. Regional cooperation to alleviate the security dilemma or to establish a viable security community is not impossible, but it is more difficult to accomplish when the major regional actors are working under the long shadows of historical enmities and contested political identities. The next section assesses what theories of international politics might be useful in assessing the possible futures of NEA. It argues for a break from the tradition of grand systems-level theorizing and a more direct incorporation of domestic-level national identity issues into explanations of the international relations behavior of individual states.

Theoretical Perspectives on Korea–Great Power Relations

For many area specialists and policy pundits, international relations (IR) theorizing may seem like a misguided, irrelevant, or unreal exercise, especially when IR theories have been so inept at explaining, let alone predicting, the momentous transformations that occurred in world politics in the late 1980s and early 1990s.[32] This is no less true for the field of Korean foreign policy because IR theory seems preprogrammed for great-power conflict or cooperation.[33] As if to further compound the matter, there is the consensus, at least in the United States, that theory building and policy making remain disconnected.[34] Much of IR theorizing is

[32] For a trenchant critique of realism's explanatory and predictive failures with reference to the collapse of the Soviet Union and the end of the Cold War, see Deudney and Ikenberry (1991); Gaddis (1992/93); Kegley (1994); Kratochwil (1993); Lebow (1994); Lynn-Jones and Miller (1993).

[33] Most studies on small states focus on external systemic variables impacting and shaping small states' policies and behaviors. They analyze the power of small states within alliances and the influence of small allies on their great-power allies within tight or loose bipolar systems, paying little attention to the dynamics of domestic politics in the shaping of their alliance behavior. The near consensus in the literature can be summarized as follows: (1) small states are more sensitive and more vulnerable to structural constraints than great powers; hence, the primacy of external systemic factors in the shaping of small state behavior; (2) small states can still play a role in world politics only in the bipolar international system – that is, the higher the superpower rivalry and tension, the greater the leverage of small states – the "power of the weak" paradox; and (3) small states are more likely to bandwagon with, rather than balance against, an aggressive great power. See Morrison and Suhrke (1979); Rothstein (1968); Vital (1967); Handel (1981); Paul (1994); Schou and Brundland (1971); Walt (1987); Elman (1995).

[34] See Tanter and Ullman (1972); George (1993).

perceived in the American policy community as an endless "mirror, mirror on the wall, who is the fairest of them all" beauty contest of, by, and for the chosen few, with little if any inclination to communicate with policy specialists or area specialists. The theory/practice gap can be bridged, if not completely eliminated, Alexander George argues, by developing "policy-relevant theory."[35] Policy makers and policy specialists, regardless of whether they realize it, inevitably draw on certain theory-related assumptions and perspectives in the decision-making process. As Harold and Margaret Sprout once sharply pointed out, a "perspective-less book" on IR is the rarest item in any library, and the choice is not between "an explicitly stated perspective and an implicit, concealed, or disguised perspective, bootlegged in by the back door, so to speak. . . . [In] assessing a particular chosen perspective, the relevant question to ask is not whether it is right or wrong, but whether it contributes more than other perspectives to a better understanding of the subject at hand."[36] Ultimately, the *raison d'être* of any theoretical approach is a commitment to seek truth, not parsimony; that is, theories should be accepted or rejected on the basis of their ability to be consistent with the evidence.[37] What follows is a critical assessment of the explanatory ability of the three dominant IR theoretical paradigms – neorealism, neoliberalism, and constructivism – followed by an argument for synthetic interactive explanations as a more suitable alternative framework.

Realist Perspectives

Modern IR theory was born with the Cold War in the wake of World War II. Realist perspectives, which cast states as unitary actors and privilege the pursuit of material power over any altruistic or ideological motives, proved dominant for much of the Cold War. When realism appeared to be ceding ground to other perspectives, Kenneth Waltz published his landmark *Theory of International Politics*, and neorealism was inaugurated.[38] This structural theory is said to have given classical realism the kind of theoretical rigor and parsimony that such traditional realists as Hans Morgenthau and others had long promised but never quite delivered. Waltz's deductive theory conceptualized international politics as a system composed of a structure and units in which the structure acts as a constraining and disposing force, producing a systemwide consistency in foreign policy behavior. State behavior is then constrained, almost to a fault, by the international distribution of aggregate state power. Balance-of-power theory is seen as the most essential political

[35] George (1993). [36] Sprout and Sprout (1971: 13); emphasis in original.
[37] Vasquez (1992: 841). [38] Waltz (1979).

theory of international politics, and bipolarity is a key system-defining and system-stabilizing element of world politics.

The parsimony of neorealism allows no room for the internal attributes of states because behaviors of similarly situated states are similarly determined and thus predictable. It is only "to the extent that dynamics of a system limit the freedom of its units [that] their behavior and the outcomes of their behavior become predictable."[39] As a system theorist, Waltz elegantly simplifies and synthesizes classical realism by replacing the first image (human nature) with the third image (anarchy), while continuing to ignore the second image (regime attributes and domestic dynamics). Structural realism offers a macrostructural explanation to replace the unit-level account of classical realism, and the units are rendered undifferentiated and lacking in identity. The impact of macrostructural variables, nonetheless, is conceptualized in deterministic rather than dynamic and probabilistic terms. In the quest for a parsimonious and deductive metatheory, Waltz seems to have reconceptualized the dynamics of the international system as mechanical, "clocklike" general laws.[40] Parsimony in *Theory of International Politics* was purchased at the expense of the multilayered thinking in Waltz's earlier work, *Man, the State, and War.*[41]

Neorealism, therefore, provides a permissive cause for why wars can occur (i.e., anarchy) but does not specify the proximate causes that determine when and which wars do occur, causes that seem more likely to deal directly with intermediate, second-level characteristics. Waltz and his realist followers would respond by saying that structural realism is a systems theory of world politics, not a foreign policy theory, and that as such the theory should not concern itself with the character of the units making up the system.[42] But this distinction is logically and operationally flawed: although the character of units is excluded from structure, it is, by definition, part of the system. As Barry Buzan succinctly points out, "system = units + interaction + structure."[43] Besides, Waltz himself implies in a number of places in *Theory of International Politics* that his structural balance-of-power theory leads to "many expectations about behaviors and outcomes." For example, in a self-help system, states that do not help themselves will fail to prosper or "states will engage in balancing behavior, whether or not balanced power is the end of their acts."[44] If this is not a theory of foreign policy, what then is? Yet even so, it is a theory of foreign policy that has little concern for the actual foreign policies of the states involved: the way that they choose to express themselves through action in the international system and with reference to their neighbors in that system.

[39] Waltz (1979: 72). [40] Almond and Genco (1977). [41] Waltz (1959).
[42] See Wohlforth (1994/95). [43] Buzan (1991: 153). [44] Waltz (1979: 118, 128).

Waltz also overestimates the degree of anarchy and underestimates the degree of order in the international system because he treats anarchy and order as an either/or condition, whereas they are better seen as poles on a continuum.[45] Even in times of stability the international system provides only the context within which a state may act. How each state actually behaves in a given situation depends on a host of other factors, such as its own definition of the international situation (which may not correspond with the reality of the international structure), its perceptions of national interests (which seem to change more rapidly than do shifts in the configuration of power), its negotiating skills and resources, and so on. In short, the state is a pivot, not a billiard ball, adjusting between domestic and international pressures, as well as between and among competing internal pressures.[46]

One of the most problematic features of the so-called structural balance-of-power theory has to do with its conception of power in world politics. The traditional military-strategic notion of power pays too much attention to a state's aggregate power (i.e., its power potential as inferred from its as-yet-nonconverted resources and possessions) and too little to more dynamic, interactive, and interdependent notions of power in issue-specific domains or relationships – power "as the ability to prevail in conflict and to overcome obstacles" or power "conceived in terms of control over outcomes."[47] Waltzian structural realism exactly fails to distinguish between aggregate structural power and usable issue-specific power, and as Alexander George reminds us, "The distinction is often critical for understanding why powerful states do less well in military conflicts and trading disputes with weaker states than with strong states."[48] In fact, Thucydides' long-standing realist maxim, "the strong do what they have the power to do, the weak accept what they have to accept," does not always hold in asymmetrical international negotiations between strong and weak states.[49] Consider the North Korean case – how a small and weak state was able to obtain almost everything it wanted from the lone superpower during the nuclear negotiations of 1993–94; the DPRK was able to mobilize its tactical bargaining power against the massive aggregate capabilities of the United States.[50] The literature on asymmetric conflicts shows that weaker powers have engaged in wars against stronger adversaries more often than not, and big powers frequently lose wars in asymmetric conflicts (e.g., the Vietnam War).[51] According to a recent study, weak states were victorious in nearly 30 percent of all asymmetric wars in the approximately 200-year period covered in the *Correlates of War* data set. More tellingly, weak states

[45] Vasquez (1992: 854). [46] See Putnam (1988); J. Snyder (1991: 317).
[47] Deutsch (1988: 20); Keohane and Nye (1977: 11). [48] George (1993: 111).
[49] Thucydides (1978: 402). See Habeeb (1988). [50] See S. S. Kim (1997b).
[51] See Mack (1975); Paul (1994); Christensen (2001).

have won with increasing frequency over time.[52] Weaker states have also initiated many brinkmanship crises that fell short of war, a strategy that North Korea has employed repeatedly.[53]

Modified realism in the form of "balance-of-threat theory," as expounded by Stephen Walt,[54] is a better fit for explaining the security behaviors of the two Koreas because it focuses on the alliance behaviors of great powers and small states. Although accepting the core assumptions of realism, balance-of-threat theory modifies balance-of-power theory by predicting that states will primarily balance against threats rather than against power alone. Threats are defined as a function not only of power (albeit the most important factor), but also of geographic proximity, offensive power, and aggressive intentions.[55] In Walt's balance-of-threat theory, threat perception is conditioned mainly by whether perceived intentions of other states are aggressive or not. In this process of defining a state's perceptions on other states' threats and intentions, historical experience could play a significant role. While the traditional balance-of-power theory focuses on state capabilities alone, balance-of-threat theory gives further consideration to the process of identity-cum-threat (enemy or friend) formation.

The balance-of-threat theory, however, seems fairly indeterminate because it catalogues no less than four independent variables without providing an *a priori* aggregate weighting formula. Balancing behavior is also said to be more common than bandwagoning behavior, which is confined to especially weak and isolated states. In other words, the theory would predict that North Korea as a weak and isolated state would bandwagon with rather than balance against the most threatening state.

As the realist state encounters the turbulence of domestic politics in the post–Cold War era, more scholars have been shifting their attention away from conventional concerns about great-power wars and superpower rivalry toward domestic and societal sources of international conflict. The current position of domestic societal-level explanatory variables at the center of the study of international conflict is a belated acknowledgment of and response to their long neglect in the literature, to the growing empirical anomalies of structural realism, and to the increasing salience of the "black-hole syndrome" affecting many weak or failing states.[56] A new breed of Young Turks espousing neoclassical (neotraditional) realist theories of foreign policy typically allows significantly more latitude for the role of individual leaders, although they continued to posit power – traditionally conceived – as the central variable.[57]

[52] Arreguin-Toft (2001: 96). [53] Lebow (1981). [54] Walt (1987).
[55] Walt (1987: 264–65). [56] Levy (2001); Holsti (1996).
[57] See Rose (1998); Zakaria (1998); Christensen (1996); Wohlforth (1993); Schweller (1998).

This is not to say that balance-of-power or balance-of-threats realism has lost all its relevance and salience in NEA geopolitics surrounding the Korean peninsula. With a strong China and a strong Japan trying to balance each other for power and influence, and with the constant attention and sometimes interference of the United States and Russia, the Northeast Asian geopolitical field resembles the multipolarity of Europe in the nineteenth-century age of great European powers. China is also widely recognized as the nearest competitor to the hegemonic United States, and the contest is becoming increasingly even on China's home turf. The proactive conflict management role played by China in Asia and in the second U.S.–DPRK nuclear standoff, in particular, should be taken as representative of the "soft" balance between the United States and the PRC.

The idea that Northeast Asian politics around the Korean peninsula closely match the image of a multipolar world has found special resonance in Moscow, at least since the mid-1990s. It is said to be the foreign policy concept most vigorously advanced by Foreign Minister Yevgeni Primakov as an overriding guide to Russian foreign policy. The eight-point DPRK–Russia Moscow Declaration of August 4, 2001, issued at the end of the second Putin–Kim summit in Moscow, speaks volumes about the emerging multipolar world order.[58] Tellingly, Primakov argued that in NEA two types of multipolar systems are vying for primacy: on the one hand, the old classical multipolar system within which Russia can attempt to balance the United States and China, and on the other hand, the new contemporary multipolar system based on multilateral cooperation and interdependence within which Russia can and should become part of any negotiated solution and achieve its foreign policy goals through cooperation with other powers.[59]

Of all three variants of realism, a neoclassical realist theory of foreign policy, which emphasizes the role of leadership change, seems to be the best fit for explaining the changing foreign policy behaviors of the two Koreas and the Big Four, especially in South Korea and the United States, in post–Cold War years. However, better theoretical logics might be found in some of the paradigms that have grown out of the response to realism.

Liberalist Perspectives

During the 1980s, neorealism's main competitor for the position of lead paradigm in international relations was neoliberal institutionalism.

[58] For an English text of the Moscow Declaration, see Korean Central News Agency (KCNA), August 5, 2001, at www.kcna.co.jp/index-e.htm.

[59] Sokov (2002: 135).

Classical international liberalism – as compared with classical realism – argued that domestic politics matter and that different regime types will interact in different ways with one another. Classical liberalism also argued that commerce would reduce the risk of war by creating interdependencies between countries.[60] Scholars such as Robert Keohane and Joseph Nye revived the interdependence argument in the 1970s.[61] Then, neoliberal institutionalism developed in the 1980s, taking neorealism's primary assumptions as its own but drawing different conclusions from them. Neoliberalism disputed neorealism's claim that states could not cooperate with each other because of relative gains concerns, by arguing that states care about absolute gains and, given a long shadow of the future, can cooperate to achieve welfare improvements.[62] In the early 1990s, several rational choice models demonstrated that the neorealist–neoliberal debate was one over special cases of more generalized models in which relative gains mattered in some circumstances but not in others.[63] Therefore neoliberalism might more clearly be seen as a variant within the neorealist paradigm rather than as an alternative to it.

Other scholars in the neoliberal tradition have looked explicitly at domestic politics – at the patterns of different regime types and the constraints imposed on leaders by domestic political actors.[64] These theories claim that a state's foreign policy behavior, in general, and its war-prone behavior, in particular, depend more on its particular type of national government or social system than on the structure of the international system. Democratic peace theory has gained much ascendancy in the international relations literature, with both empirical data and a variety of theories as to why democracies fight only very rarely with each other while still fighting wars in general.[65] The new emphasis on domestic politics and ideology came as no surprise to area specialists. Even a cursory review of the literature on Chinese foreign policy suggests that the overwhelming majority of Chinese foreign policy specialists focus on a variety of domestic factors in the search for a fitting explanatory model.[66] It is

[60] The classic statement of trade liberalism is Angell (1913).

[61] See Keohane and Nye (1977).

[62] See Axelrod (1984); Keohane (1984); Oye (1985); Baldwin (1993).

[63] See Powell (1991, 1994); Niou and Ordeshook (1994).

[64] Bueno de Mesquita and Lalman (1992) present a formal model with *realpolitik* and domestic constraints versions; in empirical testing, the latter easily proves more fruitful and accurate than the former. See also Rosecrance and Stein (1993); Kapstein (1995); J. Snyder (1991).

[65] See Doyle (1983a, 1983b); Russett (1993); Russett and Oneal (2001) for contributions to the democratic peace theory. The domestic politics matter is not necessarily a new claim. Proceeding from sharply divergent premises, Kant, Wilson, and Lenin all situated the causes of war and the conditions for peace in the nature of the social and political systems of the state.

[66] See S. S. Kim (1998c: 3–31) for a review.

worth noting, however, that a second image (domestic regime) theory with ideology as the key determinant has been critiqued in the field of Soviet foreign policy studies because it seems to imply an unbroken continuity of Soviet foreign policy from the 1917 revolution to the 1991 fall of the empire, something that is empirically not true.[67] More recently, Robert Litwak sharply argued that it is regime intention (leadership) more than regime type that is the more accurate and critical indicator of a country's decision to go nuclear.[68] There can be little doubt that the Bush Doctrine has delivered a serious body blow to the democratic peace theory. What structural realist or Kantian liberal would have predicted in 2000 that, within a year or so, George W. Bush would launch a preventive war against Iraq or emerge in many parts of the world, including both Koreas, as the most disliked American president ever?

Constructivist Perspectives

Beyond an inclusion of new domestic variables, the post–Cold War period also gave increased momentum to an entirely different current in international relations theorizing: constructivism. The new school of constructivist scholars challenges the acultural and ahistorical bases of neorealism and its claim to universality. Constructivism posits that international politics is "socially constructed," which implies that the fundamental structures of world politics are social rather than strictly material and that these ideational structures shape not only state behavior, but also state identities and interests.[69] In effect, states are concerned with the meaning of their actions, not merely the material reasons for or results of them. As Max Weber put it, "We are *cultural beings*, endowed with the capacity and the will to take a deliberate attitude towards the world and lend it *significance*."[70] So, foreign policies are concocted with a concern for the meaning of the policies.

Unlike primordialists, social constructivists argue that national identity is formed and changed through repeated interactions with significant international reference groups. The identity of a state (national identity) provides a cognitive framework for shaping its interests, preferences, worldviews, and consequent foreign policy actions. A state actor in the international system understands other states based on the identity it ascribes to them and often responds accordingly. Hence, the distribution of identities of relevant states, rather than the international power

[67] Wallander (1996). [68] Litwak (2003: 11).

[69] Wendt (1995: 71–72). See also Wendt (1987, 1992, 1994, 1999); Ruggie (1998); Jepperson, Wendt, and Katzenstein (1996).

[70] Quoted in Ruggie (1998: 856); emphasis in the original.

structure (structural realism) or international regimes (neoliberal institutionalism), best explains and predicts whether international cooperation is possible. Collective memory of the past is central to the constructivist thesis.[71]

Although constructivism spawned several contending approaches all keyed to the level at which state identities and interests are produced and reinforced (e.g., systemic or structural constructivism, normative constructivism, and domestic-social constructivism), it seems useful to describe the theory in the terms of Alexander Wendt, who has put forth the most comprehensive constructivist theory of international politics. Indeed, Wendt is to constructivism what Waltz is to neorealism (structural realism). In *Social Theory of International Politics* (1999), Wendt presents a "structural idealist" theory of international politics by situating his approach between mainstream neorealism and neoliberalism, on the one hand, and postmodern critical theory, on the other hand. Because culture supervenes on nature, any analysis of world politics should begin with culture, contrary to neorealism and neoliberalism, and only then move to power and interests.[72] It is more sensible to begin our theoretical inquiry with the distribution of ideas in the international system and "then bring in material forces rather than the other way around."[73] All the same, Wendt rejects the "idea *all* the way down" thesis that he says is associated with a "thicker, more radical constructivism."[74]

In a cultural theory of international politics, according to Wendt, a fundamental determinant that helps shape state interests and capabilities, as well as behavioral tendencies in the international system, is whether states view each other as (Hobbesian) enemies, (Lockean) rivals, or (Kantian) friends, thus echoing his famous pronouncement in 1992, "Anarchy Is What States Makes of It."[75] State interaction at the systemic level changes state identities and interests, and state *realpolitik* self-help behavior is therefore a function not of anarchical international structure but of how states identify who their friends and enemies are and, in part, how they identify themselves. In short, a state's *realpolitik* behavior is socially learned from social interaction with other states.[76]

The basic idea of Wendt's structural idealist theory – he also characterizes his approach as a "cultural theory of international politics" or a

[71] "Collective memory, by its very nature, impels actors to define themselves intersubjectively. Shaped by past struggles and shared historical accidents, collective memory is both a common discriminating experience and a 'factual' recollection of the group's past 'as it really was'." See Cruz (2000: 276).

[72] Wendt (1999: 193). [73] Wendt (1999: 371).

[74] Wendt (1999: 371); emphasis in original.

[75] The main title of Wendt's 1992 article in *International Organization*. See Wendt (1992).

[76] Wendt (1992, 1994).

"theory of the international system as a social construction" – is summarized as follows:

> identities and their corresponding interests are learned and then reinforced in response to how actors are treated by significant Others. This is known as the principle of "reflected appraisals" or "mirroring" because it hypothesizes that actors come to see themselves as a reflection of how they think Others see or "appraise" them, in the "mirror" of Others' representations of the Self. If the Other treats the Self as though she were an enemy, then by the principle of reflected appraisals she is likely to internalize that belief in her own role identity vis-à-vis the Other.[77]

Shared knowledge is all about ideas, and "this dependence of social structure on ideas is the sense in which constructivism has an idealist ('idea-ist') view of structure."[78] Shared understandings, expectations, and knowledge define social structures, constituting actors and the nature of their relationships, whether conflictual or cooperative. Therefore, a *security dilemma* is considered a social structure composed of intersubjective understandings by which states are so distrustful of each other that they define interests predominantly in egotistical or self-help terms. Conversely, a *security community* is considered a social structure in which shared knowledge is based more on trust and cooperation.[79]

Therefore, on one level, constructivism strives to demonstrate the way that a social environment constitutes actors with identities and interests, and provides meaning to certain material capabilities. At the same time, it also emphasizes how "agency and interaction produce and reproduce structures of shared knowledge over time."[80] If a state engages in hostile action such as military buildup, it can threaten other states and compel them to arm as well. But if a state conducts policies of reassurance, as the Soviet Union did at the end of the Cold War, it can move a hostile structure toward one of cooperation. Structure and agency thus is a two-way street of mutual interaction and influence. Because past actions have created a structure in which a state currently finds itself, practice and process are important. As Wendt notes, "*History matters.*"[81] As is argued here and throughout the book, a historical identity – or the quest to craft an identity for history – also matters.

[77] Wendt (1999: 327). This strikes me as a restatement of the famous statement made in 1928 by W. I. Thomas, the dean of American sociologists: "If men define situations as real, they are real in their consequences." Some two decades later, Robert K. Merton declared that the Thomas statement has now become "a theorem basic to the social sciences." See Thomas (1928: 572); Merton (1949: 179).

[78] Wendt (1995).

[79] Wendt (1995). Wendt's understanding closely echoes Hedley Bull's notion of the rules that define the "anarchical society" (Bull, 1977).

[80] Wendt (1995: 76). [81] Wendt (1995: 77); emphasis in original.

To explain the behavior of specific states, constructivists draw on the power of ideas and norms, the sometimes visible remnants of historical experience. A state's experience of colonialism, national liberation, or political change through revolution can leave lasting traces on its identity, interests, and behavior. Strategic cultures develop within states, such that they choose to use force or not, and to use it in particular ways, based on historically rooted strategic preferences that are context specific and not determined precisely by objective changes in the strategic environment.[82] Constructivism returns agency to the state such that states are not merely mechanical balancers, but rather they act – as rational units or because of domestic interests – because they have notions of how they should be acting.

There is little doubt that Wendt has provided a rich "structural ideaist" understanding of international politics at the systemic level. Nonetheless, Wendtian systemic constructionism suffers from a "too much, too little" problem – too much discourse on ontology, epistemology, and postmodern critical theory at the highest level of systemic abstraction; too much dense postmodern prose, which Robert Gilpin and others have accused of giving a bad name to social science; and too little in the way of country-specific empirical case studies.[83] Not unlike Waltz, Wendt defensively argues that his main concern – and objective – "has been with international politics, not foreign policy."[84] Even more surprisingly, Wendt claims that explaining identities and interests is not his main goal because *Social Theory of International Politics* is all about explaining the international system – a "systems theory" approach to IR – rather than explaining the *behavior* of individual states. Wendt declares, "Like Waltz, I am interested in international politics, not foreign policy."[85]

Toward Synthetic Interactive Explanations

The theoretical/analytical perspectives reviewed previously command varying degrees of explanatory power. The complex and evolving relations between Korea and the great powers in a rapidly changing post–Cold War world cannot be explained adequately without reference to material, institutional, and historical/ideational factors. That is to say, realism, liberalism, and constructivism each offer insights into the various dimensions and interactive effects in various issue areas regarding the place of Korea in world politics. To fully capture the dynamic interplay

[82] Johnston (1995).
[83] For country-specific case studies of the interplay between national identity and foreign policy, see Dittmer and Kim (1993); Prizel (1998); Hopf (2002).
[84] Wendt (1999: 371). [85] Wendt (1999: 11).

of local, regional, and global forces requires more synthetic interactive explanations than any of these theories offers alone.

In general, there has been such a move away from monocausal, single-level explanations toward multifaceted and multidimensional approaches to international conflict analysis in the post–Cold War era.[86] The progressive decay of the Westphalian sovereignty-bound world order, combined with the twin pressures of globalization from above and without and localization from below and within, makes it all the more important that we take a synthetic, multidimensional approach to the study of specific countries within international politics. The synthetic interactive approach directly addresses the important, yet understudied, gaps between the different cultures of academe and government and between theory and practice in international relations.[87] As Peter Katzenstein and Muthiah Alagappa, among others, argue, "analytical eclecticism," as opposed to theoretical parsimony, is the more promising, yet underexplored, way of capturing and explaining the complex links and interactions among the power, interests, and norms underlying Asian international relations.[88]

For example, in a work aiming at a general theory of war, Robert Jervis relies on a combination of insights from other theories. He observes that the most developed states in the international system – the United States, Western Europe, and Japan – form what Karl Deutsch called a "pluralistic security community."[89] Constructivists explain this in terms of changed ideas and identities; liberals point to democracy and economic interest; realists stress the role of nuclear weapons and American hegemony. Jervis's own explanation combines the high cost of war, the gains from peace, and the values that are prevalent within the security community; it is therefore a unification of the most persuasive elements from the other theories.[90] Alastair Johnston, the foremost bridge builder between IR theory and area studies (Chinese foreign policy, in particular), offers a similarly interactive explanation for the rise of China's cooperative status quo behavior by combining liberal institutionalism and social constructivism.[91] Similarly, in seeking to answer the question of why pessimistic realist "back to the future" predictions have failed to materialize, Amitav Acharya – combining constructivist, traditional liberal, and liberal institutionalist insights, respectively – argues that "Asia is increasingly able to manage its insecurity through shared regional norms and rising economic interdependence, and growing institutional linkages."[92]

[86] See S. S. Kim and A. Kim (2004). [87] George (1993).
[88] Katzenstein and Okawara (2001/02); Alagappa (1998: 61–62). [89] Deutsch (1967).
[90] Jervis (2002). [91] See Johnston and Evans (1999); Johnston (2003).
[92] Acharya (2003/04: 150).

These works do not claim that every variable holds equal weight, nor do they simply go from insight to insight without having a central analytical framework to provide guidance. Rather, they look across levels of analysis and examine both material and ideational factors, and they refuse to deny that coherent insights from incommensurable theories might be relevant. As Muthiah Alagappa explains, "The significance of analytical eclecticism is in the interface of the different insights in framing and explaining an issue or problem. Analytical eclecticism is not a general theory or tradition but an approach to explanation that builds on the insights of other theories."[93]

National Identity Redefined and Applied

A more integrated and synthetic theory – a virtual window to the real world, as it were – would help us better describe, explain, and predict both Koreas' foreign policy behavior toward the Big Four and across time. In other words, the ultimate concern – the dependent variable – in this study is the foreign policy behavior of the two Korean states. As Alastair Johnston points out, "there is no sense, then, in analyzing images, perceptions, worldviews, doctrines, norms, and other ideational variables unless this is part of a broader research program that links these to the behavior of individuals, groups, organizations, states, and systems."[94] As a point of departure, then, synthetic national identity theory as suggested here is a useful yet underused analytical, eclectic path to synthetic interactive explanations of behavioral change and continuity in Korea's turbulent relationship with the great powers over the years.

The literature of Korean foreign policy studies has largely remained marred by overly idiographic and particularistic conceptual frameworks lacking generalizable insights. All the same, most of the IR theoretical approaches examined in the preceding pages demand an either-or (internal or external) causality choice – either domestic level factors or the international system as the determinant in framing foreign policy – and require varying degrees of modification to fit the North and South Korean cases, especially the former. Any single-country developmental foreign policy theory, as James Rosenau argues, "must synthesize idiographic and nomothetic knowledge, that is, the most salient aspects of a country's uniqueness as well as the dynamics it shares with other countries."[95] As John Ikenberry and Michael Mastanduno observe, "the 'value-added' in social science explanation often results from the interplay of

[93] Alagappa (2003: xiii). [94] Johnston (1995: 171).
[95] Rosenau (1987: 64; 1994). For a similar line of reasoning for single-country developmental foreign policy theory, see also Snyder (1984/85).

general theoretical insight and deep knowledge of the particular political and cultural circumstances of a state or region."[96] There are several reasons why a synthetic national identity framework provides a better "fit" than any other IR theoretical perspective in tracking and explaining Korean foreign relations with the Big Four over time.

For the two Koreas, there is an unusual array of significant others in the shaping of national identity.[97] First, Korea – a place with over two millennia of recorded history – was in 1945 simultaneously liberated and divided into two states, resulting in two separate systems, two incomplete nation-states, and two distinct identities. Such partial states and divided nations are primed for zero-sum, often violent politics of national identity mobilization aimed at maximizing exclusive security and legitimacy. The politics of competitive legitimation and delegitimation on the divided Korean peninsula started in August 1945 with the two Koreas taking separate state-making, identity-forming, and legitimacy-seeking paths under the sponsorship of the two competing superpowers. This was the beginning of a legitimation-cum-identity crisis that continues to impact both the domestic and international politics of divided Korea. The sources of the crisis have remained more or less the same in both Koreas: (1) a leadership and succession problem from within (legitimation challenge); (2) a threat, actual or perceived, from the other Korea (national identity challenge); and (3) twin security dilemmas of allied entrapment or abandonment from without (security challenge). Politics unfold in all three separate but mutually interdependent and interpenetrable domains – domestic, international, and inter-Korean – calling for a synthetic, multilevel theory.[98] This means that each of the two Koreas has no choice but to accommodate the other as an alter ego in the construction or reconstruction of a one-nation identity. An identity reconciliation, or at least the peaceful coexistence of identity differences, is a necessary condition for establishing a long peace on the Korean peninsula, because the identity differences between the two Koreas are too deeply rooted to be merged into one common one-nation identity.[99]

Second, as discussed previously, the Big Four stand out as the most significant others in the making and unmaking of Korean national identity over the years. Even today, in a post–Cold War world, the two Koreas cannot fully escape the constraints and opportunities imposed by the United States, China, Japan, and Russia – in that order – in any successful enactment of their preferred national identities in world politics. What

96 Ikenberry and Mastanduno (2003b: 422).

97 See Bleiker (2004, 2005); S. S. Kim (1991, 1998b); D. C. Kim and C. I. Moon (1997); C. S. Chun (2001); Rozman (2002c).

98 See S. S. Kim (1991a); Dittmer and Kim (1993a); Kim and Dittmer (1993).

99 Bleiker (2005: xliii).

complicates the analysis is that the shifting roles of the Big Four in Korean affairs have much to do with the wrenching national-identity difficulties that North and South Korea share, with practically all states trying to adjust to a world in which conflict no longer takes place along an East–West divide. Both Koreas, albeit more for the North than the South, face the daunting challenge of balancing the Big Four to capture a special place in a rapidly changing world. Without the support of one or more of the Big Four, the ROK and the DPRK find the Korean peninsula too small an arena for national-identity validation or enactment.[100]

Third, globalization and East Asian regionalism have unleashed forces that both pluralize and stabilize Korea's historical national identity. Paradoxically, contemporary globalization is having a pluralizing impact on identity formation alongside a greater determination to hold onto national identity as a defense mechanism against the alternative collective regional or global identities that the new global space has spawned. In the post–Cold War era of globalization, then, both Koreas are now faced with a new challenge of synthesizing the traditional national identity with a new regional and global identity, while ridding themselves of any lingering residues of Cold War identity. Faced with these challenges, South Korea is far better positioned and prepared to manage the forces of globalization and East Asian regionalism in its identity politics than is North Korea.[101]

Despite its conceptual and operational ambiguity, the concept of national identity, when synthetically reformulated, has much to offer as a road map for exploring the place of Korea in world politics over the years – especially the changing relations with the Big Four. At the very least, national identity is an important factor in explaining otherwise inexplicable twists and turns in Pyongyang's – and Seoul's – international *démarche.* Rather than examining Korean foreign relations strictly in the material terms of strategic state interests, balance of power, nuclear arsenals, and conventional force capabilities, it is important to question how instances of conflict and cooperation might be redefined in terms of conflicting and commensurable identities. This is not to say, however, that force ratios and trade levels do not matter, but rather that the contours of North and South Korean foreign relations are defined because of the confluence and interaction of multiple logics. Moreover, national identity will have different degrees of salience in different issue areas, meaning that the use of any one theory is contingent on the strategic environment under discussion. This coming together of different theoretical components on a continuum of relevance is what is meant by the synthetic interactive explanation. As a bridging concept, national identity

[100] Rozman (2002c). [101] See S. S. Kim (2000d).

suggests a cross-cultural comparative framework through which Korea-centric empirical richness can be combined with international relations theoretical rigor by linking the symbolic and behavioral dynamics of a nation-state in its interaction with the world at large.

National identity analysis, like other parts of the constructivist research program, is not without its limitations, of course. There is a remarkable lack of consensus on how to define and operationalize identity.[102] Although it is unlikely that a single definition of identity will suffice for the diverse manifestations of identity politics in international relations, it is important to note how the lack of a single prevalent definition has limited the accumulation of knowledge about the influence of collective identities on the behaviors and practices of individuals and groups. Many scholars implicitly assume that identities vary only in extremes and that particular identities either exist or not.[103] In place of this dichotomous treatment, it is important to see the ways in which identities can overlap – even identities that must be reconciled against one another due to cognitive dissonance – or be situationally contingent.

Erik Erikson originally introduced the concept of identity to explore the growth of a sense of individual human identity in the course of the life cycle, the possible distortions this development might undergo, and the circumstances under which an identity crisis might arise.[104] Absent an identity, there is only anomie. Barrington Moore captures this important dimension of group identity when he argues that "membership in a group can save the individual from the anxieties of carving out his or her own meaningful place in the world, especially when the realistic chances of doing so are tiny."[105]

Out of this concept of group identity comes that of *national* identity, a concept that was introduced in the course of the behavioral revolution in political science in the late 1950s and 1960s, but has remained relatively barren since then.[106] The reasons for the lack of development in the scholarly study of national identity may derive to some degree from the concept's seeming elusiveness and the difficulty of operationalizing national identity variables, although Erikson argued that the concept of identity was indeed applicable to nations: "In nations, too, my concepts would lead me to concentrate on the conditions which heighten

102 For a more elaborate discussion, see Johnston et al. (2001). It is worth noting in this connection that identity is no more elusive than other international relations concepts, such as power and security. As Muthiah Alagappa points out, "Security is now used with more than 30 different adjectives." See Alagappa (1998: 11).

103 Johnston et al. (2001). 104 Erikson (1946, 1956, 1959, 1965, 1968, 1974).

105 Moore (1978: 488).

106 Binder (1971). The discussion in this section on the synthetic national identity theory draws heavily on, but somewhat alters, my collaborative work with Lowell Dittmer. See Dittmer and Kim (1993a, 1993b).

or endanger a national sense of identity rather than a static national character."[107]

For the purposes of this study, the concept of national identity draws on the Durkheimian notion that a social entity has a life of its own and organizational needs distinguishable from the sum of its constituent parts.[108] National identity, then, is made manifest in the characteristic collective behavior of the national system as a whole, in interaction with other subnational, national, and international systems, flowing from the totality of shared attributes and symbols of a solidarity political group known as a "nation-state." National identity is formed by the relationship between nation and state that is obtained when people who identify themselves as members of a particular nation also identify with the state under which they are governed. National identity is not only what the nation-state is (as represented by its core values and symbols), but also what the nation-state *does* (via its role performance in domestic and foreign policy).

In the international system, the state ends up being both the substantive expression and also the agent of a national identity, and the state defines itself by what roles it plays – by self-categorization in alignment with positive reference groups and in opposition to negative reference groups in the international arena. It is important to understand the developmental processes of national identity growth and change in terms of a continuous bargaining process in which all national identities are contested in a distinct but changing international environment. Thus, national identity enactment entails an ongoing negotiating process through the cycles of international life to enhance physical and psychological survival, security, and well-being. In the course of this process, the self attempts, especially in those problematic moments of ambiguity, to secure an identity that others do not bestow, while others attempt to bestow an identity that the self does not appropriate.

A mature national identity consists of a well-structured hierarchy of ideas and symbols that remain coherent over time. These ideas and symbols must be integral to the people sharing the collective identity, embracing common core values and substantive goals. Once firmly established, a national identity anchored in mutually enhancing and complementary national roles may be expected to provide a basis for reasonably stable and predictable behavior under various contingencies. As the agent of national identity, a state is expected by its citizens to act at home and abroad to safeguard the integrity of the national essence. If, however, the nation-state in question has difficulties in establishing a national identity

107 Erikson (1968: 198).

108 This makes the usage here different from that of Sidney Verba (1971), who restricts the term to a group of individuals who are selected as falling within the decision-making scope of the state.

or in projecting its role conception based on that identity, its behavior is likely to be erratic. A national identity crisis signals that the political and social system can no longer effectively project a self-image because it has lost its integrating and legitimating force. In times of crisis, the need to construct national identity can drive state behavior that defies neorealist predictions for when states will use force. Hence, the stability of national identity is also closely keyed to and shaped by the stability of the "intermestic" environment.[109] In other words, national identity both reflects and effects its domestic and external environment, while serving as an independent and dependable variable.

The dovetailing of identity and legitimacy is crucial here. Jürgen Habermas, the key theorist of legitimacy, notes that a legitimation crisis "is directly an identity crisis."[110] Habermas argues that such crises arise from unresolved steering problems in a social system when the social structure allows fewer possibilities for problem solving than are necessary to maintain the system. The penalty for this failure of system performance is the withdrawal of political legitimation. The threat of such a crisis has dominated the thinking of both North and South Korean systems over the years. The ROK, given the major gains it has made in international political and economic relations, today has less of a sense of impending crisis. In the DPRK, however, the sense of legitimacy crisis may have increased since the end of the Cold War and the falling away of socialist allies.

However, legitimacy and national identity are not synonymous. Certainly, a crisis of legitimacy may imply a crisis of national identity, but in most cases, a crisis of identity need not imply a crisis of legitimacy. In the case of divided Korea, however, the quest for national identity and the quest for political legitimacy are substantially overlapping and mutually complementary, as the politics of competitive legitimation – the intensive status competition between North and South Korea – are played out in changing domestic and international environments. As a result, the performance of the competitive legitimation and national identity mobilization of the two Koreas may vary in different domains of polity and over time as their capabilities shift. Moreover, legitimacy can wax and wane in response to a shifting balance between the performance effectiveness level of the government in domestic and foreign policy, on the one hand, and the general support, compliance, and cooperation of the people, on the other hand. Political stability is closely keyed to the amount of legitimacy surplus at a government's disposal. All the same, when national identity and legitimation are blocked in one domain, they seek to compensate in another.

[109] Prizel (1998: 2). [110] Habermas (1973: 46).

Nationalism is collective identity par excellence. It has also become a principle of modern political legitimation that no political leadership can do without. Ernest Gellner argues that nationalism is "a theory of political legitimacy, which requires that ethnic boundaries should not cut across political ones."[111] Similarly and somewhat more cautiously, Ernst Haas deems national identity a necessary but not sufficient condition for legitimacy: "Legitimate authority under conditions of mass politics is tied up with successful nationalism; when the national identity is in doubt, one prop supporting legitimacy is knocked away."[112] In an age of ethnonationalism, he who defames the national identity threatens his mandate to govern. The history of modern nationalist movements supplies ample evidence to suggest that nationalism is one of the most powerful legitimizing forces of our age. Little wonder, then, that Kim Il Sung in the North – as to a lesser extent Syngman Rhee in the South – was driven to link his legitimacy to the national political mythology by exaggerating and even falsifying his national revolutionary background abroad.[113] Successful nationalism – that is, effective national identity mobilization – is a requirement for coping with domestic legitimation deficits. Viewed in this light, national security is and becomes a close function of national identity, as governments define others as friends or enemies as a means of developing and reinforcing their own *raison d'être.*

As noted previously, national identity can be conceptualized as a critical link integrating the study of relevant aspects of political culture, role theory, *realpolitik* and idealpolitik perspectives on national interest and purpose, and long-term case-specific continuities amid historical flux. National identity is a necessary precondition for ensuring a measure of behavioral prognosis and predictability in domestic and international politics alike. What is crucial here is the fact that national identity enactment is situation specific. In terms of national security, both threats to and opportunities for the enhancement of security serve as catalysts for identity mobilization. The greater the intensity and exclusivity of national identity, the greater the animus toward the negative reference group, and the more competitive and conflictive the policies directed at the negative outgroup. As others have noted, there exists a mutually complementary relationship – "a strong dialectical relationship" – between the definition of national identity and the formulation and implementation of foreign policy goals.[114] Although external threats tend to provoke a greater concern with identity, international opportunity – the opening of the Western frontier to American "manifest destiny," for example, or the Soviet rise

[111] Gellner (1983: 1). [112] Haas (1986). [113] J. A. Kim (1975: 287, 338).
[114] Prizel (1998: 2).

to international leadership in the wake of the destruction of the Axis powers – may also have a major impact on national identity.

National identity enactment is more salient in the military and security domain than in other issue areas.[115] As Barry Buzan put it, "National identity is a central component of the security problematique whether or not it lines up with the state."[116] National security and national identity can be seen as mutually complementary and interdependent in two ways: (1) a stable or congealed national identity makes for internal coherence and unity of the nation-state, promoting effective national identity mobilization and responses to external threats; and (2) identities appropriated to other states better facilitate recognition of and response to those external enemies and threats.[117]

Historically, war has performed a critical role in the transformation of national identity, generating crises of both self-inclusion and self-definition. The resort to collective violence can sharpen an us/them dualism in its most absolutist form. As the historian Michael Howard observes, "No nation, in the true sense of the word, could be born *without* war," and "no self-conscious community could establish itself as a new and independent actor on the world scene without an armed conflict or the threat of one."[118]

In contrast to this use of and concern with national identity in the field of security, in political economy the national identity variables are notable mostly for their absence. Trade between South Korea and China has grown remarkably over the past two decades, and economic interaction between North and South Korea has recently shown remarkable resilience in the face of the DPRK's nuclear standoff with the United States. Foreign direct investment (FDI) from the ROK to the DPRK may come to resemble that between Taiwan and the PRC in the sense that the practical components of identity – having the same language and the same traditions – come to weigh more heavily than those parts of identity involved in legitimacy competition. However, the Pyongyang regime has been known to erase national origin indicators on goods and aid coming from the ROK. Given this variation in the relevance and application of national identity, a synthetic interactive explanation takes account of the contingent nature of national identity and tries to identify those situations in which it is more or less salient.

The relationship between domestic politics and international behavior is also cast slightly differently in a synthetic interactive approach. Synthetic theory postulates that domestic societal factors are generally more important than external systemic ones in the formation of national

[115] Katzenstein (1996); Hopf (1998, 2002); Desch (1998); Kowert (1999).
[116] Buzan (1991: 72). [117] Kowert (1999). [118] Howard (1979: 102).

identity, whereas external systemic factors generally take precedence in determining the outcomes of national identity enactments. As most dramatically illustrated by the sudden shift of Soviet identity from superpower donor to Third World supplicant, successful national identity enactment may vary over time as a nation's capabilities shift and its status changes. In addition, globalization has changed the way national identity operates in international relations. The previously unquestioned and direct links between identity, nation, and state are now less clear. Sovereignty seems far from absolute in the era of globalization, and supranational institutions are an increasingly prominent feature of the global landscape. This is symbolic of a marked decrease in state capacity for effective territorial control and national identity mobilization. State leaders no longer enjoy the hegemonic power to remold national identity with a minimum of external interference or competition. Korea provides an interesting case in this regard because both Korean states persist in having a holistic "Korean" identity, despite the combination of more than a half-century of division *and* the advent of globalization.

Globalization has also blurred the divide between the local and the international, and between "domestic" and "foreign" affairs, making political space more decentered and multidimensional.[119] It has also obfuscated self/other relations, especially in the wake of the end of the Cold War and the demise of East–West conflict. In the 1990s, both the agency and the scope of "threat," as well as the sources and effects of security, have become more complex and diverse than ever before. If national identity has the dual security functions of enhancing internal coherence (sameness) while sharpening external distinctiveness (difference),[120] contemporary globalization has greatly complicated the task of identifying the external positive and negative reference groups – our friends and our enemies – in a rapidly changing world. Globalization also reflects and affects the rapid rise and fall of the "effective state" and the rapid change in the status ranking of the state in the world system, as it waxes and wanes in its power to attract the identification of its citizenry. This phenomenon may be expected to rise with the increasing globalization of electronic media and the growing mass public forgetfulness of history and imagined tradition.

Historically, the construction of national identity has been closely keyed to and shaped by place – to wit, who "we" are has often been defined by "where" we are in the world.[121] But contemporary globalization is having a pluralizing impact on identity formation, detaching identities from particular times, places, and traditions.[122] With "post-international relations"

[119] Held (1995); Rosenau (1996); McGrew (1997). [120] Kowert (1999).
[121] Scholte (1996: 43). [122] Held (1995: 124).

becoming characterized by more borderless interactions, people's identities are being reconstituted and renegotiated not only by the nation-state, but also by substate localization and supranational globalization processes.[123]

Thus, globalization has brought about greater complexity and multidimensionality to self/other relations. Collective identities are experiencing both denationalization and renationalization at the same time, giving rise to multiple identities. National identity has by no means disappeared, as some advocates of the "hyperglobalization" school would have us believe, although it is no longer as robust as many (neorealist) advocates of the "globaloney" school argue. Instead, national identity is only one of a number of collective identities that people can embrace, especially those in multinational states. This is because the nation-state is not the only or even the most important experienced reality in their psychocultural consciousness and in historical time. In fact, what we encounter now is a new phenomenon of "identity surfing," as multiple group memberships and multiplying social interactions sire multiple identities. In the sea of multiple collective identities based on many loyalties – ethnic, gender, religious, cultural and linguistic, regional, and even brand loyalty – individuals are able to slide from one group identification to another.[124] Under conditions of contemporary globalization, collective identity is said to be inevitably "*en route* rather than *rooted*."[125]

This is not to say that identity is infinitely malleable; identity change occurs as a result of repeated social interactions. In the age of globalization, the scope, intensity, speed, sheer number, modalities, and impact of human relations and transactions have radically increased regionally and globally, eroding the boundaries between hitherto separate economic, political, and sociocultural entities throughout the world. As a consequence, the speed of identity change has accelerated even as collective identities are being constructed, deconstructed, and reconstructed anew in our global neighborhood.

It is paradoxical then that national identity in its apparent solidity continues to play such a central role in the realm of security. Wars of ethnonational identity mobilization – internal state-making wars – have emerged as the primary species of regional conflict in the post–Cold War era and are the basis for most of the post–Cold War UN peacekeeping operations.[126] Although globalization has created a new social space for the construction of various alternative collective identities, it has also provoked a greater sense of threat to national identity. So, globalization has,

[123] Krause and Renwick (1996); Scholte (1996).
[124] Barber (1995); Kowert (1999). [125] Scholte (1996: 69); emphasis in original.
[126] See Wallensteen and Axell (1993); Wallensteen and Sollenberg (2001).

in a way, made identity a source of armed conflict.[127] This threat prompts a greater determination to hold onto national identity as a defense mechanism against alternative collective identities that the new global space has spawned. Indeed, as national space has increasingly disappeared, some people have clung ever more frantically to the imagined certainties and comfort of national identity. North Korea, in fact, can be cited as a prime example of this reaction being realized at a state level.

For better or worse, then, the nation-state remains a pivotal pillar of global and territorial construction of collective identity.[128] Likewise, states still command the loyalty of their citizens, still have control over material resources (one third to one half of GDP), and still define the policies and rules for those within their jurisdiction. Far from making states functionally obsolete or irrelevant, globalization has in effect redefined what it takes to be a competent and effective state in an increasingly interdependent and interactive world. Globalization is a double-edged sword in this respect: it threatens both minimalist and maximalist states, and provides an opportunity for competent and adaptable states.[129]

In sum, the following assumptions and claims of identity theory might usefully be kept in mind during the explorations of the places in the world occupied by North and South Korea that comprise the rest of this book[130]:

- All identities, from an individual nuclear family to the global system, comprise a series of relationships with positive or negative reference groups; national identity is a relationship, not a possession.
- The construction of national identity begins with the establishment of the categories of self and other as mutually conflictive, yet interdependent; although identity begins in differentiation, it cannot be confirmed and legitimized without internalizing the mores, symbols, and behavioral patterns of significant others.
- The more closely the inclusion–exclusion criteria of expressed national identity comport with the constituent emotional and symbolic elements of popular national self-image, the firmer the national identity and the more predictable the state's foreign policy behavior. People with the same or shared identification generally tend to pool their resources to act in concert for the enhancement of their common identity. Similarly, the greater the intensity and exclusivity of national identity, the greater the animus toward the negative outgroup, which results in more competitive and conflictive policies directed at the outgroup.

127 See V. Cha (2000b: 220). 128 Scholte (1996: 64–65).
129 See World Bank (1997, 1999); S. S. Kim (2000a).
130 This formulation of identity theory draws on, but alters, the expositions of Bloom (1990); Connolly (1991); Erikson (1963); Hoover (1975); Norton (1988); Weigert, Teitge, and Teitge (1986); Dittmer and Kim (1993a, 1993b); Wendt (1994).

- National identity enactment in international relations is situation specific; threats to security and opportunities for its enhancement function as catalysts for identity mobilization.
- A national identity enacts itself by assuming and projecting various national roles in international relations. National identity enacts itself in the form of the presentation of national role conceptions and role performance, and is tested in the course of a nation-state's interactions with significant others. The self often attempts to secure an identity that others do not bestow, while avoiding the appropriation of identities that others do bestow.
- Just as individuals in modern society have multiple identities and multiple social roles, so do nation-states in international life have multiple identities and multiple international roles.

Structure of the Book

This book explores Korea's place in a rapidly changing world over the years, with primary temporal focus on the post–Cold War era (1989–mid-2005) and in terms of multiple levels and domains of interaction pertaining to foreign policy behavior and relations with the four regional/global powers (China, Russia, Japan, and the United States). The working premise of this book is that peace and stability on the Korean peninsula remain in large part a function of the behavior of the two Koreas and their relationships with the Big Four, and that synthetic national identity theory offers a useful analytical framework for tracking behavioral change and continuity in Korea's turbulent relationships with the great powers over the years.

After briefly reviewing Korean diplomatic history and the competing theoretical approaches to the study of international relations and foreign policy, this introductory chapter lays out a synthetic conception of national identity as an alternative yet underused way of understanding the consistency and commensurability of North and South Korean behavior at the domestic, inter-Korean, and international levels, with special attention to Korea–great power relationships. The chapter also identifies the relevance of doing so both for the Korea specialist and for the student of international relations, suggesting the importance of using IR theory to investigate the peculiarities of the Korean situation, while also using the Korean context to pinpoint theoretical weaknesses and lacunae.

That being said, however, the book shies away from the common approach of international relations of posing and testing one or more hypotheses. The primary objective – and methodology – is not to join the seemingly endless theoretical "beauty contest" of, by, and for the chosen few with little, if any, inclination to communicate with policy specialists, let alone area specialists, by reaffirming or rebutting any hypothesis. Rather, on the basis of historical and comparative analysis of Korea–great power relations, the purpose is to arrive at some conclusions about the changing identities and roles of the two Koreas in world politics. Jack Snyder's suggested triple requirement for the advancement of the study of Soviet foreign policy – richness, rigor, and relevance – seems no less compelling in assessing how to advance the study of Korea's place in the world community,[131] but I assign the pride of place to the following prioritized order: empirical richness, policy relevance, and theoretical rigor in the form of analytical eclecticism. In other words, I take an empirical-inductive approach rather than a logical-deductive approach.[132]

The synthetic concept of national identity provides a guide in this empirical-inductive sense for the discussions in subsequent chapters on the changing national identities and roles in Korea's relations with the great powers over the years. In addition, the focus on national identity and Korea–great power relations will help address questions of both theoretical and real-world concern, such as

- How constant or changeable is Korean foreign policy over time?
- How unique or common are North and South Korean foreign policy behaviors compared with each other?
- What are the key determinants or sources of the two Koreas' foreign policy behaviors? How are they affected by historical legacies, changes in balances of power (global and local), and changes in patterns of economic, social, and cultural relations with the Big Four?
- How well do the two Koreas – and the Big Four – cope with wrenching national identity difficulties in the post–Cold War world?
- What are the trends in the levels of conflict and cooperation in the foreign relations of both Koreas? To what extent and in what specific ways can the Big Four meet the post–Cold War challenge of preventing, controlling, restraining, or encapsulating the Korean conflict?
- Will the two Koreas become one? What are the roles of the Big Four in the Korean reunification process?

Chapter 2 addresses Korea's relationship with China, its oldest "international" relationship but – like its relationships with the other members of the Big Four – one that saw tremendous change in the post–Cold War years. Between China and North and South Korea there has been a constant stream of attempts to enact national identity against one

[131] Snyder (1984/85). For a similar line of reasoning for single-country developmental foreign policy theory, see Rosenau (1987, 1994).

[132] For the comparative advantages of the empirical-inductive approach over the logical-deductive approach, see Alagappa (1998: 14–15).

another: from Korea's striving to be the more Confucian state during the late nineteenth century to China's paradoxical retention of the Cold War pact with its junior socialist ally in the face of remarkably disparate interactions favoring South Korea. With the recent development of a Chinese identity as a responsible regional power, new opportunities have arisen for South Korea to collaborate with China in initiating and maintaining Northeast Asian economic integration and institutions.

Russia, whose relationship with the Koreas is considered in Chapter 3, has most consistently been the state undertaking great power intrigue on the Korean peninsula. The Korean imperial court and the post–World War II Pyongyang regime have tried to manipulate or abrogate Russian and Soviet interest in Korea with varying degrees of success. Today, it is too easy to lose sight of post-Soviet Russia in the great power balancing of the two Koreas. With the coming of Vladimir Putin's presidency in March 2000, Moscow now has a stronger central government; a purposeful foreign policy to use ties with Beijing, Pyongyang, and Seoul for leverage; and a new initiative for developing energy resources for the economic development of the Russian Far East as part of emerging Northeast Asian geoeconomic integration. Russian interests in reaping economic gains on and through the Korean peninsula have made Moscow an active player in both North and South Korea. Post-Soviet Russia's desire to maintain the trappings of a great power also make it possible that it will line up with a North Korea being pursued by the hegemonic United States.

The Korean–Japanese relationship, reviewed in Chapter 4, has been turbulent. There is no denying that modern Chinese and Korean nationalism defined themselves largely in opposition to Japan, nor that there remains a high degree of historical and national identity animus and mutual distrust between Japanese and Koreans and also between Japanese and Chinese. Indeed, what seems unique to NEA (although perhaps similar to Southeast Asia) is the immense distrust of Japan shared in varying degrees by Koreans, Chinese, and Russians.[133] Japan forced Korea into the world of modern nation-states, only then to colonize it and try to convert its people into second-class Japanese citizens. Tensions between Japan and both Koreas have simmered since the end of World War II. Although South Korea and Japan united in an uneasy alignment because of their key roles in the U.S. containment of communism, Japan and North Korea have long been unable to normalize their relations because of a variety of threats and scandals that involve both true security issues and seemingly nonnegotiable threats to national identity and legitimacy.

As addressed in Chapter 5, the United States has played as important a role on the Korean peninsula as it has anywhere else in the post–World

[133] D. C. Kim and C. I. Moon (1997).

War II world. From haphazardly determining the border that has become the sixty-year dividing line of the peninsula, to preventing Kim Il Sung from realizing his "magnificent obsession" of military reunification in 1950, to denying North Korea the development of a nuclear program, the United States has had much to do with determining the way Korea's place in the world community as a whole has been situated. The U.S. role, however, has not been immutable, and the new boundaries of the post–Cold War world have allowed opportunities for Korea, particularly for the ROK, to define itself apart from the United States and without the baggage of a hegemonic ally.

Finally, the book concludes with a chapter examining inter-Korean relations in conjunction with Korea–Big Four relations and at the possibilities and limitations for reunification. After various fits and starts in the 1970s and early 1990s, the late 1990s and early twenty-first century have yielded unforeseen interactions between the ROK and the DPRK, as well as between the two Koreas and the Big Four. These new interactions are indicative of the national identity variation that has become possible in the post–Cold War era. Inter-Korean economic relations have grown from almost nothing to sizeable proportions, whereas tourism to North Korea and the reunion of separated families have brought the first substantial contact between relatively large numbers of North and South Koreans since the Korean War. Although these signs are remarkable and fortuitous, they are not deterministic indicators of an imminent reunification. Much distance remains to be traveled before North and South Korea will complete the path to reunification. On this path, the external world dominated by the Big Four is likely to be neither uninvolved nor left unaffected by virtue of the place of the two Koreas in the world community.

CHAPTER 2

China and the Two Koreas

Past experience, if not forgotten, is a guide for the future.
(Qianshi bu wang, houshi zhi shi)
– *An old Chinese saying*

The China Factor

There is no mistaking the importance of the PRC in post–Cold War Korean foreign relations. The combined weight of history, culture, geography, demographics, military power, political status, and, most recently, market power virtually guarantees that China will be acknowledged as a major player. Consider China's potential trump cards in Korean affairs: (1) demographic weight as the world's most populous country (nineteen times the population of the two Koreas); (2) continental size, as the world's second largest country, forty-four times the size of the Korean peninsula, and territorial contiguity in the sharing of a 1,360-km-long border with almost the entire northern stretch of the Korean peninsula; (3) modernizing military manpower with the world's largest armed forces (but reduced to 2.25 million by 2004) and the world's third largest nuclear weapons stockpile; (4) veto power in the UN Security Council; (5) new economic status as the world's second largest economy (with its gross national income at $5.6 trillion in 2002 and $6.4 trillion in 2003, measured in PPP[1]), the world's fastest growing economy (with per capita GDP passing the $1,000 level in 2003)[2], the world's third largest trading

[1] World Bank 2003 Statistics. Available at http://www.worldbank.org/data/databytopic/GDP_PPP.pdf. Note that 2003 GNI statistics are not kept in PPP but are measured with the atlas method. Thus this number is the GDP PPP measured in international dollars.

[2] World Bank 2003 GNI, Per Capita Statistics. Available at http://www.worldbank.org/data/databytopic/GNIPC.pdf.

power – with trade reaching $1.15 trillion in 2004, up 36 percent from 2003 – after the United States and Germany but ahead of Japan, the world's largest recipient/destination of FDI (at $60.6 billion in 2004),[3] and the world's second largest holder of foreign exchange reserves at $609.9 billion at the end of 2004; and (6) traditional Confucian cultural influence with strong historical roots.

Not surprisingly, Chinese strategic analysts regard the Korean peninsula as a vital strategic shield, as well as the "core problem" (*hexin wenti*) of Northeast Asian security.[4] Even the looming conflicts in the South China Sea and the Taiwan Strait pale in comparison to the potential escalation of military tensions and political instability on the Korean peninsula.[5] When China looks at its 850-mile-long (1,360 km) porous border with North Korea, it remembers the route by which imperial Japan launched its invasion of the Chinese mainland in the 1930s and also the U.S. intervention in the Korean War, where, in late 1950, General Douglas MacArthur's forces crossed the thirty-eighth parallel and approached the Chinese border.

Because the Korean peninsula is the dangerous flash point where four of the world's five major regional/global powers – the United States, Russia, China, and Japan – uneasily meet and interact, China's Korea policy is closely intertwined with its regional and global policy. Today, of these four major powers, China is the only one with a full-fledged and multifaceted two-Korea policy. Sino–ROK relations in political, economic, cultural, and perceptual terms have grown by leaps and bounds since the early 1990s. According to a major public opinion survey conducted by the ROK Ministry of Information in 1996, to cite one example, 47.1 percent of South Koreans chose China as Korea's "closest partner for the year 2006," in striking contrast with only 24.8 percent for the United States.[6]

Yet, during the Cold War China's identity as a regional power was deeply ambivalent.[7] Although much of China's external relations pivots around the Asia-Pacific region as a whole, Beijing had seldom defined its place in Asian international relations, as is evident by a rocky past with most of its Asian neighbors – including India, Indonesia, and Vietnam – during the Cold War years. Although the identity continues to develop, China can

[3] In 2003, for the first time, China overtook the United States as the world's largest recipient/destination of FDI. Although FDI into the United States declined to $40 billion in 2003 from $72 billion in 2002 and $167 billion in 2001, FDI into China declined only slightly to $53 billion in 2003 from $55 billion in 2002. See Laurent Frost, "China Overtakes U.S. as Investment Target," The Associated Press, June 28, 2004. For 2004 figure, see *People's Daily Online*, January 25, 2005.

[4] D. Song (1998: 35). [5] W. Hu (1995); X. Zhang (1998).

[6] J. H. Chung (2001: 784). [7] S. S. Kim (1992).

be said with certainty to have become an important regional and global economic power in the post–Cold War era. As early as 1991, the World Bank singled out post-Mao China as having garnered an all-time global record by doubling output per capita in the shortest period (1977–87).[8] Its GDP growth rate from 1990 to 2001 was nearly four times the world average; China easily won the global sweepstakes in economic growth rate and ranking, with the nearest peer competitor being the tiny city state of Singapore. China's trade has exploded, from only several million dollars in the 1950s, to $20 billion in 1978, to $1.15 trillion in 2004, and trade as a percentage of GDP (a widely used measure of both integration into the global economy and trade dependence) has more than doubled every decade, from 5.2 percent in 1970 to 44 percent in 2000, compared with 11 percent for North Korea, 18 percent for Japan, 19 percent for India, and 21 percent for the United States in 2000. In 2004, the rate of China's foreign trade dependence witnessed a steep rise, reaching an all-time high of 70 percent.[9] In the post-Mao era, from 1978 to 2004, China's foreign trade volume has registered a whopping fifty-eight-fold increase. As a result, China's economy at the end of 2004 is now 3.5 times more integrated into the global capitalist economy than that of Japan (20%) or the United States (19.4%). By 2004, China, with $1.15 trillion of trade for the year, had already emerged as the world's third largest trading country and also as the largest trade partner with such key Asian countries as South Korea ($79.4 billion), Japan ($210 billion, including Hong Kong), Taiwan ($60 billion), and a number of Southeast Asian countries. Within less than a decade, China seems well poised to surpass Germany as the world's second largest trading country.[10] In 2004, China's newborn economic status was recognized with an invitation to join the annual G7 meeting of the world's seven largest advanced industrial economies, with the expectation that membership might become permanent.[11]

Nonetheless, there are some limits on and downsides to China's economic power. China's more than $1.1 trillion foreign trade in 2004 entailed a processing trade value of more than $600 billion; about 60 percent of Chinese exports and 50 percent of Chinese imports involved trading in products for which components and materials came from overseas and the finished products were exported to foreign countries. The relentlessness with which China has pursued foreign capital has meant that it

[8] World Bank (1991: 12). [9] *People's Daily Online,* January 10, 2005.

[10] Nicholas Lardy's prediction in 2002 that within a decade (i.e., by 2012) "China's trade is likely to surpass that of Japan and Germany, making China the world's second largest trader" is off the mark by eight years as far as Japan is concerned, and China seems well positioned to surpass Germany as the world's second largest trading nation by 2006, if not sooner. See Lardy (2002: 176).

[11] See Elizabeth Becker, "Guess Who's Invited to Dinner," *New York Times*, September 23, 2004, pp. C1, C9.

has not always pursued sustainable development. Local officials have pursued FDI instead of native investment and have contributed to significant lost tax revenues because of subsidies given to foreign corporations. With fast development have come externalities such as land and air pollution, shifting tax structures, and bad bank loans. Despite the impressive quantitative leap, the structural weaknesses and problems of China's foreign trade are evident in the fact that its high-tech exports accounted for only 28 percent of its total exports in 2004, compared with 44 percent for the United States and 39 percent for Japan. Moreover, more than one-seventh of the total antidumping investigations from 1995 (when the World Trade Organization [WTO] was born) to June 2004 had been filed against China. China faced more antidumping cases than any other nation in the world from 1995 to 2004, that is, for ten years in a row.[12]

Since 1989, the Chinese government has announced a succession of large peacetime increases in military spending. The rate of increase in Chinese military expenditures grew substantially in the late 1990s and early twenty-first century (by 19.4% in 2001 and 17.6% in 2002).[13] The International Institute for Strategic Studies (IISS) in London estimates China's actual military expenditure in 2001 at $US46 billion, 2.6 times the official defense budget of $17.4 billion, whereas the Stockholm International Peace Research Institute (SIPRI) estimates $27 billion for the same year, 1.6 times the official figure.[14] The increased defense expenditure in recent years, according to China's National Defense White Paper 2002, has been incurred primarily because of increased expenses for personnel, the military social security system, maintenance, cooperation with the international community in antiterrorism activities, and high-technology equipment.

Despite concerns in the United States and Japan about China's increased military expenditures, an alarmist interpretation is not justified. The Chinese defense burden remains relatively light by SIPRI's measure, and the military expenditure/GDP ratio is lower than that of all major powers and neighboring countries (with the exception of Japan). This defense burden does not appear to have reached a level at which the Chinese economy is being militarized to balance against U.S. power. Military expenditures are not only simple functions of external threats and opportunities, but are also determined by considerations such as technological innovation cycles, organizational interests, and bureaucratic

[12] *People's Daily Online*, January 10, 2005.

[13] These official figures are cited in China's National Defense White Paper 2002. For a full text in English, see The PRC State Council's Information Office, "China's National Defense in 2002," in FBIS-CHI-2002-1209 December 9, 2002 (Internet version).

[14] IISS (2001); SIPRI (2002).

rivalries. There is every indication that Chinese leaders are determined not to repeat the Soviet strategic blunder of placing an unbearable defense burden on the economy.

There is a double paradox at work in the heated rise-of-China debate. Although today's China is more integrated into the world community and exhibits greater levels of cooperative (status quo) behavior within that community than ever before by most available indicators, the core premise of the contending approaches of containment, engagement, and constrainment (*congagement*) is that China as a dissatisfied revisionist (non–status quo) power is operating outside the global community on a range of international norms, thus posing the most difficult questions and challenges for the future of regional and global orders.[15] Although the People's Liberation Army (PLA) has been involved in nine wars and armed conflicts – fought for ideological reasons and for the protection of national sovereignty and territorial integrity – most of those actions were taken in the 1950s and 1960s, and no war involving China took place in the 1990s, reflecting the demise of the ideological basis for war and the peaceful settlement of territorial disputes with Russia, Mongolia, Central Asian countries, Burma, Pakistan, and Vietnam.[16]

Nowhere is China's status quo behavior more evident than in its two-Korea policy in the post–Cold War era. This policy suggests a subtle but significant transformation of China's national identity from a system-transforming revisionist challenger to a system-maintaining status quo actor in contemporary world politics. With the most recent reconstruction of Chinese identity as a *responsible* regional power, new opportunities have arisen for South Korea to collaborate with China in promoting East Asian economic institutions and integration, as well as in seeking via bimultilateral consultations peaceful resolution of the issue of North Korea's nuclear program. There is no mistaking that on balance Beijing enjoys a much more positive image in the perceptions of the South Korean elite and public than does the United States. China has become an independent variable and a means to diversify Seoul's foreign policy options, to reduce dependency on the U.S.–ROK alliance (thus diminishing if not completely erasing its dependent identity), to secure external support for inter-Korean reconciliation, and to enhance South Korean economic development (especially now that Beijing has already become South Korea's top trade partner and the top destination of South Korea's FDI).

Throughout the years, there has been a constant stream of attempts between China and Korea to readjust and reenact national identity against one another, from Korea's striving to be the more Confucian

[15] See Johnston (2004). [16] See Y. Ji (2001b: 119–20); Johnston (1998).

tributary state during the late nineteenth century to China's paradoxical retention of the Cold War security pact with its junior socialist ally in the face of remarkably disparate interactions favoring South Korea. The blossoming of Sino–ROK relations since the mid-1980s seems made to order for David Mitrany's "working peace system"[17] or China's diplomatic axiom of *qiutong cunyi* (seeking common ground while preserving differences). This means in effect that both Beijing and Seoul have sought common ground in economic identity (e.g., Beijing's post-Mao reform and opening identity and Seoul's identity as a newly industrialized country), while preserving their respective political identity differences. China's ideational justification for shifting from a one-Korea policy to a two-Koreas policy is based on the Five Principles of Peaceful Coexistence, which overlapped with Seoul's *Nordpolitik*, calling for the normalization of relations with all countries irrespective of ideological differences. This shift reflected and effected a relatively smooth transition from Cold War to post–Cold War identity in South Korea.

The successful conclusion of normalization talks in a short period of time stands out as a textbook case of the peaceful coexistence of identity differences or multiple identities. It is worth noting in this connection that one major sticking point in the home stretch of Sino–ROK normalization talks in mid-1992 was Seoul's request that Beijing acknowledge its past "aggression" in the Korean War. The South Korean negotiators recognized that this was an unrealistic request but nonetheless made it for the historical record and to ensure domestic considerations. The Chinese negotiators responded that there was no "past issue" to discuss and that any such acknowledgment, let alone an apology, was out of the question. The final PRC–ROK normalization treaty – issued in the form of a six-point communiqué – is silent on the past, as if there were no past relationship of any kind. In short, the Sino–ROK normalization was possible not because of converging or common political identity but despite political or ideological identity differences, whereas Sino–DPRK relations suffered strains and stresses despite the seemingly shared socialist identities.

Weight of the Past

It is essential here to step back and reassess the "circumstances directly encountered, given, and transmitted from the past." Given the vast scale of Chinese and Korean history and the long history of Sino–Korean relations, we must ask to which period or tradition the "weight of the past" refers and how it influences, if at all, the various dimensions of foreign policy thinking and behavior in Seoul, Pyongyang, and Beijing. Richard

[17] See Mitrany (1966) for the classic statement of functionalism.

Neustadt and Ernest May, among others, have called our attention to the dangers of international conflict escalation when policy makers resort instinctively or conveniently to the use of a particular historical analogy or a particular war experience to cope with new conflicts in a new setting.[18] We should therefore be wary of deducing from China's vast and ambiguous past any specific lessons or guides for its future behavior. What follows is thus not an argument in support of historical or cultural determinism, but only a broad outline of some salient historical experiences transmitted, if not directly learned, from the past.

Despite the half-century of interruption from the late nineteenth century to the end of World War II, the Sino–Korean relationship is almost as old as the Korean nation. The Korean state's jurisdiction has had a high level of contiguity with its own nation since 676 – when the first united Korean nation-state was established by the Silla Dynasty (57 B.C. to 935 A.D.) – and as such remains one of the world's most concordant nation-states. Ensconced in the vast protective cocoon of the Sinocentric world order – *Pax Sinica* – throughout its history, traditional Korea, known as the hermit kingdom, had no foreign relations of which to speak. Its relations with China, a subordinate relationship structured and symbolized by the so-called tribute system, constituted the sum total of Korean relations with the outside world. Tributary relations, which began as early as the fifth century, were regularized during the Koryo dynasty (918–1392) and became fully institutionalized during the Chosun (Yi) dynasty (1392–1910).[19]

The Sino–Korean tributary relationship incurred Korea's deficit financing. The total value of China's imperial gifts was about one-tenth that of the Korean tributary goods.[20] China's help in repelling the Japanese (Hideyoshi) Invasion (1592–98) greatly increased Beijing's request for tributary gifts, especially silver and gold. Thus, Korea served as an exemplary tributary state throughout this period, maintaining this relationship with China longer than any other country. The tributary relationship was expressed in terms of the Confucian concept of *sadae chui* (literally, "serving the great" but expressive of a broad Confucian notion of great-power chauvinism), which became the institutionalized expression of traditional Korea's "foreign relations." The tribute system proved to be a *sine qua non* for establishing and maintaining political legitimacy at home, explaining its long duration: "To live outside the realm of Chinese culture was, for the Korean elite, to live as a barbarian."[21] As late as the early 1880s, few Koreans regarded their country as equal to or

[18] Neustadt and May (1986); Vasquez (1987); Khong (1992).
[19] H. J. Chun (1968: 90, 99); C. J. Lee (1996: 1). [20] H. J. Chun (1968: 105).
[21] Eckert (1991: 226–27).

independent of China.[22] Given the ideological supremacy of *sadae chui*, national identity and nationalism could not rise in traditional Korea.

The opening of Korea during the heyday of imperialism in the second half of the nineteenth century instantly transformed the hermit kingdom into a vortex of great-power rivalry. Concurrent with the Korean opening were the collapse of the traditional Chinese world order, the rise of Japanese imperialism, and the rise of Korean antipathy and mistrust toward China; these had the combined effect of finally putting an end to centuries of Sino–Korean tributary relations. The amity characteristic of traditional Sino–Korean tributary relations was rapidly replaced by mutual distrust, suspicion, and even antagonism, and the Treaty of Shimonoseki to terminate the Sino–Japanese War of 1894–95 officially ended Sino–Korean suzerain relations.[23]

China became a highly contested terrain where the emerging Korean politics of competitive legitimation was to occur even during the Japanese colonial period. With the Chinese nationalist (Kuomintang) government supporting the Korean Provisional Government in Shanghai and the Korean Restoration Army on the one hand, and the Chinese Communist Party (CCP) at Yan'an supporting the North China Korean Volunteer Army and the Northeast Anti-Japanese United Army (in which Kim Il Sung served as a division commander) on the other hand, the seeds for Korea's division and the fratricidal politics of competitive legitimation and delegitimation were already planted during the second Sino–Japanese War (1937–45).[24] The Korean War (1950–53) exerted a profound and lasting influence on the construction and enactment of China's identity as a great socialist power, and on the formulation and application of the CCP's basic lines during the Mao era. As explained in Chapter 1, war is the single greatest catalyst for a new national identity. In reviewing fifty years of Chinese diplomacy, Beijing still calls the Korean War a war of aggression launched by the imperialists to strangle the new People's Republic. The Chinese performance in Korea is still publicly exalted as "a world miracle in which the weak vanquished the strong," even as "the signing of the Korean armistice rewrote the history of Chinese diplomatic negotiations which [prior to the coming of the PRC] had always ended with sacrifice of China's national interests."[25] By successfully forcing the strongest nation on earth to compromise in Korea and to accept China's representatives as equals at the bargaining table, Beijing successfully overcame its identity as the "Sick Man of Asia."

[22] K. H. Kim (1980: 341). [23] C. J. Lee (1996: 3).

[24] C. J. Lee (1996: 3); C. S. Lee (1963: 129–79); D. S. Suh (1988: 11–29); S. S. Kim (1976).

[25] *Renmin ribao*, September 3, 1999, p. 1.

The Sino–Soviet Treaty of Friendship, Alliance, and Mutual Assistance (signed on February 14, 1950) received a shot in the arm by China's intervention in the Korean War, consolidating the Moscow–Beijing axis on a foundation of shared values and shared fears. The entry of the United States into the Korean War helped Mao answer with ease and clarity his perennial question for the Chinese revolution and helped China "unite with real friends in order to attack real enemies."[26] Indeed, the Korean War confirmed for the national self and "significant others" that China could stand up for the integrity of its new national identity as a revolutionary socialist state against the world's antisocialist superpower.

The idea of initiating the war came directly from Kim Il Sung, who began lobbying for a Soviet-backed invasion as early as March 1949, with the assurance that it would take no more than three days to "liberate" the South, leaving the United States no time to intervene. Stalin rejected this plan on the grounds that it was not necessary, that North Korean forces could cross the thirty-eighth parallel only as a counterattack, that the Chinese Civil War was still unresolved, and that the North Korean military was still weak and ill prepared.[27] It was not until May 1950 that "the Soviet dictator explained to Mao Zedong that it was now possible to agree to the North Koreans' proposal 'in light of the changed international situation.'"[28] The victory of the Chinese Communist Party and the establishment of the PRC in October 1949, the successful test of the Soviet atom bomb in 1949, and the withdrawal of American troops from South Korea in June 1949 all contributed to Stalin giving the final go-ahead, on the condition that Mao Zedong agreed.

Because of the Korean War, the Sino–Soviet alliance was at once strengthened in the short run and weakened in the long run. An eventual split became the unavoidable consequence of growing equality in the Sino–Soviet alliance. The widening gap between Beijing's rising demands and expectations, and Moscow's inability and unwillingness to satisfy them, undermined the alliance. The Korean War had a decisive catalytic effect in enacting the rules of the Cold War game and in congealing patterns of East–West conflict across East Asia and beyond. It was the Korean War that brought about such defining features of the Cold War as high military budgets, a militarized North Atlantic Treaty Organization (NATO), the globalization of competing alliance systems, and the dangerous pattern of East–West confrontation in world affairs.[29] Yet, by dint of its timing, its course, and its outcome, "the Korean War served in many ways as a substitute for World War III."[30]

[26] Z. Mao (1965: 13). [27] Barzhanov (1995); Weathersby (1995, 1999).
[28] Weathersby (1999: 93). [29] See Jervis (1980). [30] Stueck (1995: 3).

Despite or perhaps because of the extreme dependence on the Soviet Union in the preparation of North Korea's invasion of South Korea, a balance of great-power influence shifted from Moscow to Beijing, due in no small measure to the Chinese intervention in October 1950. The deepening Sino–Soviet conflict gave Kim Il Sung more leverage opportunities and space than could be realistically considered under the Sino–Soviet alliance. The Soviet army that had successfully maneuvered Kim Il Sung into power failed to return, while the Chinese "volunteers" intervened to rescue the fledgling socialist regime on the verge of collapse and stayed on until 1958, marking the end of Soviet domination and the beginning of Chinese influence.

The newly established PRC almost single-handedly rescued Kim Il Sung's regime from extinction, but at inordinate material, human, and political costs. In addition to more than 740,000 casualties[31] – including Mao's son – China missed the opportunity to "liberate" Taiwan, was excluded from the United Nations for more than two decades, and lost twenty years in its modernization drive. However, China's performance in Korea was also a source of heightened stature and influence in world politics. Sino–DPRK relations were consolidated in November 1953 when Kim Il Sung led a large delegation to Beijing and negotiated agreements for long-term military, economic, and cultural cooperation. Beijing promised $200 million in aid for reconstruction during the next three years, only $50 million less than committed by Moscow.[32] In addition, Chinese troops remained in North Korea for five years following the war, helping with reconstruction projects. During the long Cold War years, Chinese leaders reiterated the immutability of their "militant friendship" with North Korea. Premier Zhou Enlai and People's Liberation Army Marshall Zhu De used the metaphor of the closeness of "lips and teeth" to describe the strategic importance of Korea to China as a buffer state against hostile external powers.[33] The militant revolutionary "alliance sealed in blood" (*xiemeng*) during the Korean War, formalized in a 1961 treaty, sustained China's one-Korea (pro-Pyongyang) policy for more than three decades.

During most of the Cold War, Beijing had virtually no ideological or strategic space in which to deviate from this special relationship with Pyongyang. However, with the ascendancy of Deng Xiaoping as China's paramount leader at the historical Third Plenum in December 1978 and his inauguration of "an independent foreign policy line" in 1982, Beijing's one-Korea policy began to be "deideologized," if not completely

[31] According to one official Chinese estimate, combat casualties were more than 360,000 (including 130,000 wounded) and noncombat casualties were more than 380,000. See A. Zhang (1994: 137).

[32] Stueck (1995: 362).

[33] Lampton and Ewing (2004: 45) and Spurr (1988: 62–63).

decoupled from the great-power dynamics. The interplay between China and the two Koreas became more complex, variegated, and multidimensional, with some highly paradoxical consequences. To accurately assess the place of the Korean peninsula in Chinese foreign policy thinking and behavior – the place of the PRC in the politics of competitive legitimation on the divided Korean peninsula – has never been more involved than it is today. Nonetheless, China has produced the most advanced and coherent triangle of relations with the two Korean states; it is the only country in the region with a successful two-Korea policy.

The Making of a Triangular Relationship

On August 24, 1992, after more than four decades of Cold War adversity and an overlapping decade of expanding informal relations, the PRC and the ROK signed a joint communiqué in which each agreed to recognize the other and establish full diplomatic relations "in conformity with the interests and desires of the two peoples." In a single stroke, a newly legitimated East Asian state officially known *Da Han Min Guo*, or simply *Hanguo* (ROK), was established, and *Nan Chaoxian* (South Korea) left Beijing's diplomatically correct lexicon.[34] This shift from the familiar one-Korea policy to a two-Korea policy stands out as one of the most momentous changes in China's post–Cold War foreign policy.[35]

Rather than being a foreign policy "crisis" – characterized by surprise, high stakes, short response time, and a limited number of options and participants in the decision-making process – China's Korea policy evolved by fits and starts during the long Deng decade (1978–92). It passed through several phases, shifting by installments from the familiar pro-Pyongyang one-Korea policy through a one-Korea *de jure* / two-Korea *de facto* policy to, finally in August 1992, a two-Korea *de facto* and *de jure* policy. The 1992 decision was the culmination of a process of balancing and adjusting

[34] For the official Chinese text of the joint communiqué, see Liu and Yang (1994: 2611–12). It is emblematic of the politics of divided Korea – the politics of competitive legitimation and delegitimation – that Seoul and Pyongyang use different words for "Korea" in Korean – *Chosun* (*Chaoxian* in Chinese) in the North and *Hanguk* (or *Hanguo* in Chinese) in the South. South Korea and North Korea in English seem normatively neutral, but not so *Chosun* and *Hanguk* in the politics of everyday life in divided Korea. This is also a reminder of the Chinese capacity to live with contradictions because the Chinese text of the joint communiqué still adheres to *Chaoxian* in referring to the Korean peninsula (*Chaoxian bandao*, not *Hanguo bandao*) and the Korean people (*Chaoxian minzu*, not *Hanguo minzu*). See Liu and Yang (1994: 2612).

[35] When asked by South Korean President Kim Dae Jung during his official state visit to China in November 1998 to identify the most difficult challenge he faced during his decade-long service as China's Foreign Minister, Qian Qichen said it was the establishment of Sino–ROK diplomatic relations. See *The Korea Times*, November 13, 1998 (Internet version).

post-Mao foreign policy and its multiple identities to changing domestic, regional, and global circumstances.

The Korean peninsula has consistently been viewed as a significant element of China's security environment. In addition, South Korea was seen as a fitting – if unspoken – model for China's state-led development strategy, as well as a potential source of support for China's modernization drive. Increasingly, South Korea has also been seen as a potential partner in countering American economic pressure and Japanese economic hegemony in East Asia. Finally, China has been intent on seeing a Korea – divided or united – that posed no challenge to the legitimacy of the PRC as a socialist and multinational state. Beijing applied, gradually, a "maxi-mini" approach, a real, if unstated, axiom of maximizing China's rights and interests, while minimizing its responsibilities and costs.[36] Indeed, Beijing's decision to recognize and establish full diplomatic relations with the ROK underscores a foreign policy shift from ideological to material national interest.

The demise of the global Sino–Soviet–U.S. Cold War triangle also shifted China's strategic environment. During much of the Cold War, China's regional policy was a stepchild of its global superpower policy. The turning points in Chinese foreign policy, although instantly reverberating throughout the entire region, implicated the United States and/or the Soviet Union. In the post-Tiananmen period, and especially after the collapse of the Soviet Union in December 1991, however, Chinese foreign policy became more Asiacentric. This acknowledgment allowed for changes to its policies toward both North and South Korea.

The Expanding Circle of Seoul's Nordpolitik

The first change to China's near abroad external security environment originated with South Korean President Roh Tae Woo's *Nordpolitik*. Previously, both presidents Park Chung Hee and Chun Doo Hwan tried forms of *Nordpolitik* in different, less congenial external strategic contexts without much success. For instance, Park's "Special Foreign Policy Statement Regarding Peace and Unification" pronouncement on June 23, 1973, called for the normalization of relations with all countries irrespective of ideological differences and, above all, the dual and simultaneous entry formula for UN membership of the two Koreas. But the policy did not lead to any significant outcomes in the ROK's foreign relations.

South Korea's winning bid in 1981, in the wake of the Kwangju uprising, for the 1988 Summer Olympics in Seoul surely boosted Chun Doo Hwan's lagging political support and legitimacy at home. This allowed

[36] S. S. Kim (2001).

him to launch a major diplomatic offensive in January 1982 to shore up the country's domestic and external base of legitimacy. A new flexible foreign policy, coupled with "economic diplomacy," was designed to globalize Seoul's foreign relations and to rectify its international identity as a dependent Third World client regime. As an acknowledgment of the PRC's concerns, beginning in the early 1980s, South Korean leaders deliberately excluded Taipei from their official state visits. Successful resolution by the PRC and ROK of a 1983 hijacking of a Chinese airliner and of a 1985 naval mutiny by Chinese sailors, followed by cooperation during the 1986 Asian Games, spurred a surge of bilateral communication and the normalizing of civilian aviation. Yet, despite these informal contacts, this series of events did not lead to official recognition by China.

With the administration of President Roh Tae Woo, *Nordpolitik* was officially inaugurated and vigorously pursued. Inspired by West German *Ostpolitik*, the policy called for the improvement of inter-Korean relations as well as South Korea's relations with socialist countries in conformity with the principles of equality, respect, and mutual prosperity. *Nordpolitik* was proclaimed in a special six-point presidential declaration on July 7, 1988, just two months prior to the 1988 Seoul Olympic Games, another event around which the ROK and the PRC would build functional cooperative links.

The first five points in Roh's proclamation had to do with building a functional "working peace system"[37] on the Korean peninsula through functional cooperation (e.g., promoting exchanges of visits, helping separated families, opening doors for inter-Korean trade). The sixth and final point outlined a strategy of engagement with China: "To create an atmosphere conducive to durable peace on the Korean peninsula, we are willing to cooperate with North Korea in its efforts to improve relations with countries friendly to us . . . we will continue to seek improved relations with the Soviet Union, China and other socialist countries."[38] To a certain extent, *Nordpolitik* reflected Seoul's confidence in the competition between the two Koreas, almost overconveying a message to Pyongyang and Beijing: "If you can't beat us, join us."

The 1988 Olympics in Seoul were a watershed event in this regard, accelerating cross-bloc functional cooperation between Seoul and both Moscow and Beijing. Of the four East Asian NICs, South Korea was viewed as a fitting model for China's state-led development strategy. Beijing even adopted Seoul's developmental slogans and projections as Deng Xiaoping pronounced that China's per capita gross national product (GNP) would reach $1,000 by the year 2000, a figure Park Chung

[37] See Mitrany (1966). [38] T. W. Roh (1992: 306).

Hee had often used for predicting South Korea's per capita GNP by 1980.[39]

As a reciprocal gesture to Beijing's participation in the 1988 Seoul Olympic Games and as a means of gaining more credibility for its engagement strategy, the South Korean government refused to follow the lead of the United States, Japan, Europe, and some international organizations in imposing sanctions or announcing official condemnation of the Chinese government for the 1989 Tiananmen incident. To the contrary, the Roh government went to extraordinary lengths to promote tourism to China, which had been badly hurt by the Tiananmen carnage. It also supported the 1990 Asian Games in Beijing by providing $15 million in advertising revenues and other substantial donations.

The instruments of Seoul's *Nordpolitik*-cum-engagement policy included economic exchange and cooperation (i.e., trade and investment), sports, and myriad informal contacts via international intergovernmental and nongovernmental organizations and conferences. Indirect Sino–ROK trade began slowly and stealthily from a near-zero base (about $40,000 in 1978). By 1984, it was $434 million – approaching the level of China's trade with North Korea ($498 million). After the 1988 Olympic Games, the figure rose to $3.1 billion in 1989 (about 80 percent of Seoul's total trade volume with all socialist countries at the time) and to $4.4 billion in 1991, more than seven times the level of Sino–DPRK trade in the same year (Table 2.1). One inevitable outcome of rapidly growing Sino–ROK trade was Beijing's decision in October 1990 to agree on the establishment and exchange of trade offices between the Korean Trade Promotion Association (KOTRA) and the Chinese Chamber of Commerce. This move marked a significant shift from indirect trade to open and direct trade, as well as a shift from the one-Korea policy to a two-Korea policy *de facto* if not *de jure.*

To the extent that it was possible, Seoul extended its engagement strategy to multilateral forums and organizations, particularly Asia-Pacific Economic Cooperation (APEC), Association of Southeast Asian Nations (ASEAN), and many of the specialized agencies of the UN system. Doing so enabled the ROK to maintain informal contacts and exchange views with China. South Korea played a major role in the behind-the-scenes negotiations for membership of all three "Chinese" applicants – Beijing, Taipei, and Hong Kong – in the then twelve-member APEC in August 1991. In his first trip to Seoul, Chinese Foreign Minister Qian Qichen expressed his appreciation for Seoul's role in performing delicate diplomatic surgery keyed closely to Beijing's party line.

[39] Cumings (1984: 246–47). China's GNP per capita finally surpassed the projected goal of $1,000 in 2003.

Table 2.1. China's Trade with North and South Korea, 1990–2004

Year	Exports to North Korea	Imports from North Korea	Total North Korean-Chinese Trade (Balance)	Change in North Korean-Chinese Trade	Exports to South Korea	Imports from South Korea	Total South Korean-Chinese Trade (Balance)	Change in South Korean-Chinese Trade
1979	N/A	N/A	N/A	N/A	15	4	19	N/A
1980	374	303	677 (+71)	N/A	73	115	188 (−42)	+889%
1981	300	231	531 (+69)	−22%	75	205	280 (−130)	+49%
1982	281	304	585 (−23)	+10%	91	48	139 (+43)	−50%
1983	273	254	527 (+19)	−10%	69	51	120 (+18)	−14%
1984	226	272	498 (−46)	−6%	205	229	434 (−24)	+262%
1985	231	257	488 (−26)	−2%	478	683	1,161 (−205)	+168%
1986	233	277	510 (−44)	+5%	621	699	1,320 (−78)	+14%
1987	277	236	513 (+41)	+1%	866	813	1,679 (+53)	+27%
1988	345	234	579 (+111)	+13%	1,387	1,700	3,087 (−313)	+84%
1989	377	185	562 (+192)	−3%	1,705	1,438	3,143 (+267)	+2%
1990	358	125	483 (+233)	−14%	2,268	1,553	3,821 (+715)	+22%
1991	525	86	611 (+439)	+26%	3,441	1,000	4,441 (+2,441)	+16%
1992	541	155	696 (+386)	+14%	3,725	2,650	6,375 (+1,075)	+44%
1993	602	297	899 (+305)	+29%	3,928	5,150	9,078 (−1,222)	+42%
1994	424	199	623 (+225)	−31%	5,462	6,200	11,662 (−738)	+28%
1995	486	64	550 (+422)	−12%	7,401	9,140	16,541 (−1,739)	+42%
1996	497	68	565 (+429)	+3%	8,539	11,377	19,916 (−2,838)	+20%
1997	531	121	652 (+410)	+15%	10,117	13,572	23,689 (−3,455)	+19%
1998	355	57	412 (+298)	−37%	6,484	11,944	18,428 (−5,460)	−22%
1999	329	42	371 (+287)	−10%	8,867	13,685	22,552 (−4,818)	+22%
2000	451	37	488 (+414)	+32%	12,799	18,455	31,254 (−5,656)	+39%
2001	571	167	738 (+404)	+51%	13,303	18,190	31,493 (−4,887)	+1%
2002	467	271	738 (+196)	+0%	17,400	23,754	41,154 (−6,354)	+31%
2003	628	396	1,024 (+232)	+39%	21,900	35,100	57,000 (−13,200)	+39%
2004	799	585	1,384 (+214)	+35%	29,585	49,763	79,348 (−20,178)	+39%

Unit: US$1 million.
Source: Ministry of Foreign Trade and Economic Relations, People's Republic of China. Available at http://www.moftec.gov.cn/moftec/official/html/statistics_data; 1996 Diplomatic White Paper Ministry of Foreign Affairs and Trade, Republic of Korea, p. 348; 1997 Diplomatic White Paper, pp. 396, 400; 1998 Diplomatic White Paper, pp. 481, 486; 2000 Diplomatic White Paper, p. 496; 2001 Diplomatic White Paper, p. 483; 2002 Diplomatic White Paper, p. 497; www.mofat.go.kr.

The Closing Circle of Pyongyang's One-Korea Angst

Although the PRC–ROK relationship was growing at the informal level to no small degree during the 1980s, the Sino–DPRK relationship in that decade reflected a shifting mixture of shared values and interests and growing policy cleavages. During the Cold War, North Korea's geostrategic importance and its proximity to China and the Soviet Union made it easier for Pyongyang to cope with the twin abandonment/entrapment security dilemmas. With the rise of the Sino–Soviet dispute in the late 1950s and the eruption of open conflict between the two countries in the 1960s, Kim Il Sung opted for a strategy of making virtue out of necessity by manipulating his country's relations with China and the Soviet Union in a flexible and self-serving manner. He took sides when necessary on particular issues, always attempting to extract maximum payoffs in economic, technical, and military aid but never completely casting his lot with one over the other.

The long shadow of the Korean War assured the continuity of a "militant friendship" between China and North Korea at the level of policy pronouncements until at least the late 1980s. Beijing applied its maxi-mini strategy, compensating for its comparative disadvantage against the USSR in economic and military aid by giving increased political and symbolic support. Despite its obvious misgivings, Beijing did not wait too long before endorsing Kim Il Sung's father-to-son succession arrangements, which were made public in October 1980, the first ever dynastic succession in the communist world. A flurry of secret visits in the first half of the 1980s offers circumstantial proof of Beijing's tacit support of North Korea's *fait accompli* succession.[40]

The two states, however, were on separate and increasingly path-dependent trajectories. If the central challenge of post-Mao Chinese foreign policy was how to make the world congenial for its resurgent modernization drive via reform and opening to the capitalist world system, Pyongyang's top priority was to contain, isolate, and destabilize South Korea in the seemingly endless pursuit of absolute legitimation and Korean reunification on North Korean terms. The 1983 Rangoon bombing (in which 17 members of President Chun Doo Hwan's delegation were killed) and the 1987 midair sabotage of a Korean Air jetliner (which claimed the lives of all 115 people aboard) dramatize the vicious circle. To maintain a measure of political leverage through nuisance value, and

[40] (1) Deng Xiaoping and Hu Yaobang's secret visit to North Korea in April 1982, during which they met Kim Jong Il; (2) Defense Minister Geng Biao's visit to Pyongyang in June 1982; (3) Kim Jong Il's secret visit to China in June 1983, the one and only overseas trip he had made between 1980 (when his official inauguration as heir apparent became known) and 2000; and (4) Hu Yaobang's visit to Sinuiju in May 1985, during which Hu held discussions with both Kim Il Sung and Kim Jong Il. B. C. Koh (1985: 272–73).

to extort economic and military concessions from Beijing and Moscow, Pyongyang also seemed compelled to demonstrate its fragility, unreliability, unpredictability, and its "tyranny of the weak" skills to force its allies to take a principled stand.

In the late 1980s and early 1990s, rapid progress in Moscow–Seoul relations, culminating in Soviet–ROK normalization in 1990, combined with an equally rapid decompression of Moscow–Pyongyang relations and a sudden end to the superpower conflict, produced paradoxical consequences for China's post–Cold War foreign policy. On the one hand, these momentous changes meant the sudden diminution of China's global status and influence and a consequent identity crisis stemming from the widening contradiction of its status as a regional power with global aspirations. On the other hand, Beijing sensed new openings for compensatory diplomacy and renewed national identity enactment. The ending of Cold War bipolarity not only took the sting out of the long-standing ideological and geopolitical Sino–Soviet rivalry over North Korea, but also dissipated Pyongyang's leverage in both Moscow and Beijing. The decisive Soviet tilt toward Seoul provided an escape for the PRC from the entrapment of its one-Korea policy or at least a convenient cover for its own shift from a one-Korea to a two-Korea policy two years later. As two PRC scholars aptly put it, "It has been China's practice to let Moscow take the lead in approaching Seoul while it avoided lagging too far behind."[41]

Negotiating Sino–ROK Normalization

A number of the crucial events in the chronology of normalization between China and South Korea occurred external to either state. Events in the Soviet Union and at the United Nations were particularly relevant. Mikhail Gorbachev's changes to the foreign policy of the Soviet Union were key factors in the reshaping of China's strategic context in several ways: Gorbachev ended Cold War bipolarity, effected Sino–Soviet renormalization, and established Soviet–ROK normalization. By addressing nearly all Chinese and American security concerns through a series of unprecedented unilateral actions, Gorbachev altered beyond recognition the strategic *raison d'être* of the Sino–Soviet–U.S. triangle that had long dominated Chinese foreign policy decisions.

Crucial to Beijing's own quest for absolute international legitimation – its one country/two systems formula – was disconnecting Pyongyang's quest for absolute international legitimation. This problem had to be overcome before Beijing could start normalization talks with Seoul, and the solution would ultimately come through the United Nations. In 1990

[41] Jia and Zhuang (1992: 1140).

and 1991, Beijing seized several opportunities to assure Pyongyang that their "traditional friendship" and "revolutionary loyalty" would endure many generations, while responding to Seoul's repeated diplomatic prodding with the familiar refrain, "Conditions are not ripe." Progress was not being made. But against this backdrop, Seoul's all-out campaign for UN membership offered a solution.

The China factor was certainly one of the major determinants – perhaps the most crucial one – in the reversal of Pyongyang's long-standing opposition to the separate-but-equal UN membership formula. After the entry of the two Koreas into the United Nations in September 1991, Sino–ROK contacts were both accelerated and elevated to the foreign ministerial level, with the United Nations or other multilateral forums providing a convenient venue for talks on issues of common concern. Immediately after the two Koreas gained UN membership, the Chinese and South Korean foreign ministers – Qian Qichen and Lee Sang Ock – met for the first time in New York to discuss bilateral relations (Table 2.2). These meetings were preliminary, and China resisted normalization talks until April 1992, when "conditions" finally became ripe for Beijing.[42]

Clearly, UN membership for both Koreas seven months earlier was the major proximate factor that enabled Beijing to overcome Pyongyang's one-Korea angst and Taipei's two-China "flexible (dollar) diplomacy." The stepping up of Sino–North Korean military cooperation was the price Beijing had to pay for gaining Pyongyang's grudging acceptance of China's two-Korea policy and a shift from its absolute legitimation-via-reunification strategy to a Stalinist "socialism in one country" strategy. The state of inter-Korean relations also turned out to be a proximate factor facilitating the initiation of normalization talks. The seven-month period from September 1991 to April 1992 witnessed a remarkable finale of inter-Korean talks at the prime ministerial level: the Agreement on Reconciliation, Nonaggression, and Exchanges and Cooperation Between the South and the North (December 13, 1991), and the Joint Declaration of the Denuclearization of the Korean Peninsula (January 20, 1992).

Another unspoken causal assumption underlying Beijing's decision was the matter of Chinese leadership in shaping a new order in East Asia after the demise of the Soviet Union, a point repeatedly stressed by South Korean interlocutors. Having lost the vaunted leverage in the strategic Cold War triangle with which to magnify its leverage in global politics, Beijing started mending fences with its Asian neighbors. Against this backdrop, Beijing managed to establish or renormalize its official diplomatic

[42] Author's interview with former ROK Foreign Minister Lee Sang Ock, Seoul, May 1998.

Table 2.2. Chronology of Sino–ROK Normalization Talks, October 1991–August 1992

Date (mm/dd/yy)	Place	Beijing's and Seoul's Positions/Actions
10/02/91	New York	First Qian-Lee Talks: at UN General Assembly annual meeting, Foreign Minister Qian held his first talks with ROK Foreign Minister Lee; Lee raised issue of bilateral relations; Qian showed interest only in improving functional cooperation.
11/14/91	Seoul	Second Qian-Lee Talks: at ministerial meeting of APEC in Seoul, Lee raised issue of starting normalization talks; Qian said conditions were not yet ripe.
04/13/92	Beijing	Third Qian-Lee Talks: at ESCAP conference in Beijing, Qian approaches Lee proposing normalization talks.
05/14–16/92	Beijing	PT-I: First round of preliminary talks. PRC's only precondition is principle of one China; ROK responds with one-Korea principle; Impasse.
06/02–04/92	Beijing	PT-II: ROK presents four demands: (1) maintaining "the highest unofficial relations" with Taipei; (2) China's apology for intervention in Korean War; (3) promise of China's help on the North Korean nuclear issue; (4) promise of China's "equidistance policy" toward both Koreas. China's response: (1) apology is out of the question; (2) promise of help in resolving the North Korean nuclear weapons issue.
06/20–21/92	Seoul	PT-III: Both parties agree on language of joint communiqué; China agrees to ROK's request for Roh's state visit.
07/29/92	Beijing	Formal and final meeting: both parties penciled in their initials; Roh's state visit and summit meeting with President Yang Sangkun is agreed on.
08/24/92	Beijing	Joint Communiqué is signed by Qian and Lee and publicly issued on establishment of formal diplomatic relations.

Source: Author's field interviews in Seoul and Beijing, May/June 1998.

relations with all Asian neighbors, including Indonesia, Singapore, India, Vietnam, Uzbekistan, Turkmenistan, Kyrgyzstan, and Kazakhstan, leaving only South Korea out of the expanding diplomatic circle. To recognize Seoul – with the partial goal of further isolating Taiwan – became an integral part of China's Asiacentric foreign policy orientation.

China's domestic political forces were equally divided between conservative leaders opposed to formal diplomatic ties and senior policy advisors in favor of normalization. The opposition relied on the following assumptions and arguments: (1) China's switch to a formal two-Korea policy would provide powerful ammunition for advocates of a two-China policy; (2) PRC–ROK normalization would be perceived as a betrayal of China's junior socialist ally and might consequently accentuate Pyongyang's siege mentality and contribute to, if not precipitate, the collapse of the North Korean system; and (3) Beijing could have its cake and eat it too by continuing its present one-Korea *de jure* and two-Koreas *de facto* policy. The pronormalization arguments advanced by senior foreign policy advisors, including Foreign Minister Qian Qichen, were (1) given Moscow's growing influence in South Korea, Beijing could not afford to procrastinate if it did not want to forfeit Chinese influence on the Korean peninsula; (2) there were limits to South Korean patience, and normalization talks had to be completed before the end of President Roh's tenure in December 1992; (3) Beijing could not afford to wait for Japan–DPRK and U.S.–DPRK normalization because the prospects for such recognition were not too bright; and (4) Pyongyang could not accuse Beijing of socialist betrayal because China remained supportive of North Korea in many other ways. The logic of Beijing's maxi-mini strategy was made evident in Qian's secret report to the CCP's Foreign Affairs Leading Small Group. Qian reportedly argued that full normalization of relations with Seoul would have the effect of "downing four birds with one stone": (1) increasing Taiwan's diplomatic isolation, (2) strengthening Beijing's economic cooperation with Seoul, (3) diminishing Pyongyang's endless requests for aid, and (4) enhancing Beijing's bargaining power to defuse the mounting "Super 301" pressure from the United States concerning unfair trade practices.[43]

Not surprisingly, Deng Xiaoping had to intervene to settle the matter. Deng saw the value of a new "Korean connection" in his campaign to rekindle China's reform and open policy,[44] and he believed "that the ROK government and Korean business community would be willing and able to provide capital and technology" to further the reform process. Undoubtedly, a new Korean connection would also stimulate ROK–Japan and ROK–Taiwan economic competition for the Chinese market, enabling Beijing to obtain more favorable trade and investment terms from all three parties.

Compared with the complicated and protracted normalization and renormalization negotiations with Tokyo, Washington, and Moscow,

[43] See the report by Tokyo's KYODO in English in FBIS-China, September 15, 1992, p. 12.
[44] P. Chang (1993: 170).

PRC–ROK normalization negotiations proceeded without major obstacles. As shown in Table 2.2, it took only three two-day sessions – three rounds of preliminary talks – to iron out the details of the agreement. In the meeting of April 13, 1992, Qian and Lee agreed on the basic rules of the game: (1) normalization negotiations had to be confined to diplomatic channels; (2) complete secrecy had to be maintained throughout the talks; and (3) in the event of any press leakage, both parties were to immediately deny it. This was designed primarily to respect North Korea's expressed preferences and to prevent Pyongyang from exercising its negative power.

Qian assured Kim Il Sung that PRC–ROK normalization would help accelerate Pyongyang's own normalization talks with Tokyo and Washington, serve to stabilize the situation on the Korean peninsula, and contribute to North Korea's system maintenance. He managed to obtain Kim's grudging understanding, if not full acceptance, of China's normalization decision.[45] Once Beijing obtained Kim Il Sung's understanding, normalization talks gained momentum for rapid finalization.

One major sticking point in the talks was Seoul's request that China acknowledge its past aggression in Korea. South Korean negotiators recognized that this was an unrealistic request but made it nonetheless, for the purpose of placing it on historical record and for domestic political reasons. Chinese negotiators responded that there was no "past issue" to discuss and that any such acknowledgment, let alone an apology, was out of the question.[46] Although not specified in the joint communiqué, Beijing is said to have promised Seoul support on the North Korean nuclear issue.[47] Seoul returned the favor by promptly severing diplomatic ties with Taipei and turning over Taiwan's $1.7 billion embassy complex in Seoul to the PRC, something that may well be regarded as a functional equivalent to Seoul's $3 billion aid to Moscow for the 1990 Soviet decision.

In short, the Sino–ROK normalization was made possible by the mutual acceptance and recognition of differences in political identity following China's long-standing Five Principles of Peaceful Coexistence and Seoul's *Nordpolitik*, which called for the improvement of inter-Korean relations as well as South Korea's relations with socialist countries in conformity with the principles of equality, respect, and mutual prosperity and irrespective of political and ideological identity differences. Ironically, but not surprisingly, China and the DPRK have had greater difficulties in

[45] C. J. Lee (1996: 125) and author's field interviews in Seoul and Beijing in May–June 1998. All field interviews were conducted on a confidential – background – basis.

[46] Author's interview with Lee Sang Ock, then ROK Foreign Minister, Seoul, June 4, 1998.

[47] Shortly before the Sino–ROK joint communiqué was issued, a high-ranking Beijing diplomatic source disclosed that North Korea had promised to China that it would abandon the development of nuclear weapons. See *JoongAng Ilbo* (Seoul), August 26, 1992.

adjusting their socialist identities in the post–Cold War (and post-Socialist) world.

New Challenges of the Beijing–Seoul–Pyongyang Triangle

If Beijing's two-Korea decision represented the greatest triumph of Seoul's *Nordpolitik* and one of the two greatest blows to Pyongyang's identity politics, China was left faced with multiple challenges on bilateral, regional, and global fronts. The making of the two-Korea decision did not come to a sudden end; it marked the beginning of a process of implementing the decision on a variety of issues over time. Nonetheless, the main challenge has remained the same – how to translate China's preference for the peninsula status-quo-cum-stability by maintaining a "special relationship" with Pyongyang, while promoting and expanding "normal state relations" with Seoul.[48] As ways of capturing the multifaceted and mutating nature of the new Beijing–Seoul–Pyongyang triangle in the postnormalization period (1992–mid-2005), we need to look closely at Sino–Korean relations in three separate but mutually interrelated issue areas: military/strategic, economic/functional, and national identity.

Military and Security Issues

Beijing often pursues several mutually competitive goals on multiple fronts. With regard to Korea, these goals include maintaining peace and stability on the peninsula, promoting economic exchange and cooperation, helping the North Korean regime survive, preventing dominance of Korea by any external power, halting the flow of both North Korean refugees and South Korean Christian missionaries into Jilin Province, stopping the rise of ethnonationalism among ethnic Chinese Koreans, and preventing the formation of any anti-China coalition in East Asia. The single greatest challenge to these goals and to smooth management of the new triangular relationship with the ROK and the DPRK has been Pyongyang's security (or insecurity) behavior, from its nuclear brinkmanship to its missile programs. The euphoria of 1990–92 was greatly overshadowed by the first U.S.–DPRK nuclear standoff of 1993–94; the Taepodong missile crisis of 1998–99; and, beginning with the coming of the hardline Bush administration, another U.S.–DPRK standoff involving Pyongyang's nuclear programs.

Coping with the U.S.–DPRK Nuclear Confrontation

North Korea's nuclear brinkmanship in 1993–94 – billed in the West as the first nuclear proliferation crisis of the post–Cold War era – became

[48] D. Song (1998: 37).

an instant security challenge for Chinese and South Korean foreign relations. Although Seoul was more or less sidelined, the nuclear issue confronted Beijing with a new set of dangers and opportunities for the management of China's two-Korea policy. Paradoxically, it was the threat of a Chinese veto on any draft sanctions resolution in the Security Council that enabled Pyongyang to obtain what it had been seeking from the beginning – direct bilateral confrontation-cum-negotiation with the United States. High-level talks between the North Koreans and the Americans in Geneva, growing out of former President Jimmy Carter's shuttle diplomacy in the heat of the nuclear crisis in June 1994, resulted in the landmark U.S.–DPRK Agreed Framework of October 21, 1994. As if to take chief credit for the breakthrough, China highly praised Carter's "fruitful mediation" as showing that "dialogue is better than confrontation."[49]

Rodong Sinmun [Worker's Daily], the official organ of the Korean Workers' Party (KWP), seemed determined to refute the notion that Beijing's behind-the-scenes diplomacy had anything to do with the Agreed Framework, which was quickly dubbed "the biggest diplomatic victory by the DPRK": "We held the talks independently with the United States on an independent footing, not relying on someone else's sympathy or advice, and the adoption of the DPRK–U.S. Agreed Framework is a fruition of our independent foreign policy, not someone's influence, with the United States finally accepting our proposal."[50]

Beijing was neither willing nor truly able to play a decisive role in reshaping Pyongyang's nuclear behavior during the first U.S.–DPRK nuclear standoff. Post-Tiananmen China in the early 1990s was afflicted with twin legitimation crises at home (the Tiananmen carnage of June 1989) and abroad (the collapse of transnational communism at its epicenter). The threat of international sanctions, especially U.S.-sponsored sanctions against a socialist regime, thus provoked a sovereignty-bound "sound and fury" response.[51] As one Security Council representative put it, "[Chinese representatives] used the North Korean debate as a case to illustrate a deeper point – if you can't force the North Koreans to do what you want, how do you imagine you could ever force the Chinese to do anything?"[52]

From Beijing's *realpolitik* maxi-mini perspective, the 1994 U.S.–DPRK Agreed Framework was seen as a window of opportunity for improving economic conditions in North Korea, for bolstering the legitimacy of the

49 *Renmin ribao*, June 22, 1994, p. 6.
50 *Rodong Sinmun [Workers's Daily]* (Pyongyang), December 1, 1994.
51 For a trenchant attack on U.S. "sanctions diplomacy," see *Renmin ribao*, July 15, 1994, p. 6.
52 S. S. Kim (1999: 56).

Kim Jong Il regime, and for enhancing the prospects of political stability. The Agreed Framework would go some way in alleviating the imbalance of power between the two Koreas.[53] Nonetheless, China refused to join the Korean Peninsula Energy Development Organization (KEDO), the multinational consortium for the implementation of the Agreed Framework. Adhering to the mini-maxi line, China refrained, "We can be of greater help being outside than inside the KEDO."[54] With Chinese help, Pyongyang demonstrated to the entire world that sanctions would be accepted as a declaration of war and, as such, a no-win proposition for all parties concerned.

All this has changed in the heat of the second U.S.–DPRK nuclear confrontation in early 2003. Given the contrasts between China's behavior in the two U.S.–DPRK nuclear standoffs, what explains the differences between Chinese attitudes and behavior in 2003–05, when Beijing was devoted to preventive diplomacy, and a decade earlier, when it preferred to take a passive, risk-averse, "who me?" stand. There were multiple catalysts for the shift, including regional factors, U.S. strategic and military policy and behavior, North Korean responses, China's own enhanced geopolitical and economic leverage, the steady rise of regional and global multilateralism in Chinese foreign-policy thinking and behavior, and the creeping unilateralism under the Clinton administration that then turned into rampant runaway unilateralism under the Bush administration. In short, the unique confluence of both proximate and underlying factors – greater danger, greater stakes, and greater leverage – explains why Beijing was spurred into action in early 2003.[55]

Although popular consensus is that the second nuclear crisis began with the North Korean confession in October 2002 that it had an HEU program, in reality the ingredients of a high-pressure standoff between the United States and the DPRK had been brewing for more than a year and a half before that media maelstrom. Growing security concerns have served as a strategic catalyst for Beijing's uncharacteristically proactive and hands-on conflict management (CM) diplomacy. The first of these concerns is over possible United States recklessness in trying to resolve the North Korean nuclear challenge through military means. In addition, China worries that the crystallization of certain regime security conditions could lead North Korea to calculate that lashing out (to preempt America's preemptive strike, as it were) would be a rational course of action, even if victory were impossible. Alarming to Beijing, for instance,

[53] Garrett and Glaser (1995).
[54] Author's interview with Dr. Choi Young-jin, Deputy Director of the KEDO, New York, April 22, 1998.
[55] For a detailed analysis along this line, see S. S. Kim (2004b).

was the Bush administration's dispatch of the aircraft carrier Carl Vinson to the Pacific in the wake of Pyongyang's withdrawal from the Nuclear Non-Proliferation Treaty (NPT) on January 10, 2003. Then, in March of the same year, the Pentagon sent twelve B-1 and twelve B-52 bombers to Guam for the explicit purpose of "sending a message" to North Korea.[56]

Although Beijing's security wish list with respect to North Korea includes at least five "no's" – no nukes, no refugees, no collapse, no instability, and no war – and although these are all related, the greatest priority has remained "no war." Peace and stability on the Korean peninsula, which is a key contributor to peace and stability within China, remains first and foremost among Chinese strategic concerns. In short, growing fears at the potential for aggressive action by the United States and North Korea as they engage in mutual provocation – which could trigger, either inadvertently or by design, another war in China's strategic backyard – have served as a kind of force-multiplier in catapulting Beijing into hands-on CM diplomacy.

While swings in U.S. foreign policy have provided proximate causes for China's proactive CM diplomacy, China's concern over regional destabilization is motivated to no small degree by an underlying cause: the combination of economic and political gains that it made in the past decade and the clear and continuing threat to them. After spending the 1990s advancing these goals, China wants to protect the gains it has made.

A solution imposed by Washington, furthermore, would change the military situation so as to constitute major geostrategic gains for the United States at the expense of China. Beijing has strong incentives, therefore, to prevent any military resolution of a Korean crisis or conflict. However, China's policy shift, abrupt as it may seem, must be understood in the context of China's changing role in world politics and its chosen identity as a responsible great power. The implications of these dynamics reach much further than the immediate crisis on the Korean peninsula.

Beijing's assumption of a proactive CM role in mediating a highly sensitive and volatile regional dispute in its strategic backyard reflects and effects the greater confidence and leverage with which the new leader – President Hu Jintao – has taken command of a more multilateral Chinese diplomacy in Northeast Asia. So China's proactive mediation-as-conflict-management diplomacy has been shaped by the Northeast Asian regional context, the level of risk inherent in the aggressive Bush Doctrine, reactions in North and South Korea to U.S. policy, its own enhanced geopolitical and economic factors, and the changing strategic priorities and calculus of the new leadership.

[56] Barbara Starr, "U.S. Orders 24 Long-Range Bombers to Guam," CNN. Available at http://www.cnn.com/2003/US/03/04/n.korea.bombers/.

Although it has defined its conflict management role as "active mediation," China has in fact assumed the multiple and mutually complementary roles of initiator, host, facilitator, prodder, consensus-builder, go-between, broker, and deal-maker in the on-again, off-again six-party process. With its conflict management resources, both diplomatic and economic, China has clearly made a heavy investment in forwarding the six-party process toward a negotiated solution or at the very least in averting its collapse. China's mediation-cum-CM diplomacy required from the very beginning shuttle/visitation diplomacy – and aid diplomacy – to bring the DPRK to a negotiating table in Beijing. From early 2003 to late 2005, senior Chinese officials have stepped up shuttle/visitation diplomacy on a quarterly basis. Moreover, these visits have been conducted at levels senior enough to require meetings with Chairman Kim Jong Il, serving notice to Washington that direct interaction with the Chairman is the shortest way toward progress in the six-party process.

Caught in diplomatic gridlock and against the backdrop of being labeled as an "outpost of tyranny" by the second-term Bush administration, Pyongyang raised the ante of its own brinkmanship diplomacy with a statement on February 10, 2005, that it had "manufactured nukes for self-defense to cope with the Bush administration's evermore undisguised policy to isolate and stifle the DPRK" and that it was therefore "compelled to suspend participation in the [Six-Party] talks for an indefinite period."[57]

Against this ominous backdrop, Beijing intensified a two-sided mediation diplomacy. On one side, China sustained its shuttle diplomacy with North Korea by sending senior party official Wang Jiaru to Pyongyang in mid-February 2005 – shortly after the February 10 announcement – and subsequently by hosting DPRK Prime Minister Pak Bong-ju and Vice Foreign Minister Kang Sok Ju for additional consultation in March and April. On the other side, Beijing resisted pressure from Washington to impose economic sanctions on Pyongyang, while Seoul stepped in to support Beijing's mediation diplomacy. A combination of Chinese efforts to entice the North Koreans back to a fourth round of talks and an increasing convergence of the positions of Beijing and Seoul played a critical role in laying the basis for opening the "New York channel," a working-level dialogue between U.S. and North Korean officials in New York in May and June 2005, with the United States and the DPRK offering each other assurances designed to end "a war of words" and to lay the groundwork for a return to the negotiation table.[58]

[57] For an English text of the DPRK Ministry of Foreign Affairs' statement of February 10, 2005, see KCNA, February 10, 2005, available at http://www.kcna.co.jp/item/2005/200502/news0211.htm.

[58] Snyder, Cossa, and Glosserman (2005: 7–8).

The Chinese are reported to have made an exceptional effort in the fourth round of talks – the most important and extended round to date – mobilizing a professional work force of about two hundred experts from nine departments or bureaus in the Ministry of Foreign Affairs. These diplomats spent all day and night working on successive drafts of a joint statement of principles, pulling together the lowest common denominator among views laid out by the six parties in the behind-the-scenes negotiations, which included an unprecedented half-dozen bilateral meetings between U.S. and DPRK diplomats.[59]

To a great extent, Pyongyang's decision to rejoin the six-party talks after a thirteen-month hiatus can be attributed to the synergy of Chinese and South Korean mediation diplomacy that was aimed at providing a face-saving exit from the trap of mutual U.S.–DPRK creation. This was particularly important in the wake of the Bush administration's characterization of Kim Jong Il as a "tyrant" and Condoleeza Rice's labeling of North Korea as an "outpost of tyranny." Beijing, Seoul, and Moscow have been prodding the Bush administration to stop using this kind of language and to map out detailed economic and security incentives as quid pro quo for North Korea's nuclear disarmament. Indeed, the implicit withdrawal of vilifying rhetoric was important in Pyongyang, as made evident in an official statement of the DPRK Ministry of Foreign Affairs: "... the U.S. side at the contact made between the heads of both delegations in Beijing Saturday clarified that it would recognize the DPRK as a sovereign state, not to invade it and hold bilateral talks within the framework of the six-party talks and the DPRK side interpreted it as a retraction of its remark designating the former as an 'outpost of tyranny' and decided to return to the six-party talks."[60]

The "words for words" and "action for action" approach that North Korea advocated as its negotiating stance and that China implied as group consensus in the Chairman's statement at the end of the third round of talks also provided an exit with voice for Pyongyang, if not for Washington. China was the most critical factor in achieving a group consensus in the form of the Joint Statement of Principles issued by the participants in the fourth round of six-party talks process on September 19, 2005, the first ever successful outcome of the on-again, off-again multilateral dialogue of more than two years. This was a validation of the negotiated approach to the second nuclear standoff on the Korean peninsula that both Pyongyang and Washington have at various times resisted.

[59] See Edward Cody, "China Tries to Advance N. Korea Nuclear Talks," *Washington Post*, July 31, 2005, A23 and "China Show Off Newfound Partnership at Six-Party Talks," *The Korea Herald*, August 5, 2005.

[60] "Spokesman for DPRK Foreign Ministry on Contact between Heads of DPRK and US Delegations," KCNA, July 10, 2005.

Assessment of the effectiveness of China's mediation-as-conflict-management in the second U.S.–DPRK nuclear standoff requires an understanding of China's own characterization of its role. Chinese Vice Foreign Minister Wang Yi has described its role as "active mediation."[61] Mediation-as-conflict-management is an intrinsically triangular diplomatic process because the parties to the conflict seek to position themselves in reference both to each other and to the mediator, while the mediator seeks to guide them both toward a negotiated solution that neither is able to make alone, or to persuade them to engage in direct, bilateral negotiation.[62] Viewed in this light, any third-party mediation between a unilateral America and a unilateral North Korea is bound to be a daunting challenge; it may be doubly so for China. Indeed, the greatest challenge for Beijing's mediation-as-conflict-management diplomacy is how to navigate between a rock and a hard place: between allied abandonment, with the potential for instability or even collapse in North Korea, and allied entrapment, with the danger of being caught in conflict escalation not of its own making.

Despite the challenges involved, throughout the second nuclear standoff the United States has had unrealistically high expectations that China would join the Bush administration's "tailored containment" and push the North Korean regime toward nuclear dismantlement via "complete, verifiable, irreversible, dismantlement" (CVID). But Beijing's leverage in Pyongyang is not as great as some U.S. foreign policy makers and pundits believe. Nonetheless Chinese diplomats have indeed managed, by tempting the North Koreans with many kinds of aid, to influence behavior coming out of Pyongyang. First, China brought the DPRK to the six-party talks, overcoming North Korea's principled insistence on direct bilateral negotiation with the United States, or at least altering that stand. This was made possible by a "*qiutong cunyi*" formula (seeking common ground while preserving differences) of allowing "bilateral talks within the six-party talks framework" for the much-delayed and much-anticipated fourth round of talks. Chinese diplomats are reported to have played a key behind-the-scenes CM mediation role in facilitating the U.S.–DPRK bilateral contacts in May to June 2005 that led to the fourth round of the six-party talks lasting twenty days in two sessions (July 26–August 7, September 13–September 19), compared to three to four days for the first three rounds of talks. A strengthened relationship is a necessary prerequisite for coaxing out of Kim Jong Il whatever concessions possible to support and sustain the six-party talks process.

61 "Wang Yi Explains PRC Stand on DPRK Nuclear Issue in Interview with Reporters," Xinhua, June 22, 2004 in FBIS-CHI-2004-0622.

62 Crocker, Hampsen, and Aall (2004: 23).

While China's influence in North Korea is somewhat limited, Beijing still has a far greater ability to effect change in Pyongyang than in Washington. One constraint on China's leverage over Washington is its economic relationship with the United States. The PRC stands in a position of extremely high trade dependency on the United States. The fact that the United States "is currently the only country with the capacity and the ambition to exercise global primacy" means that it is the only country "that can exert the greatest strategic pressure on China," according to Wang Jisi, Dean of the School of International Studies at Peking University. Wang adds that "China's political, economic, social, and diplomatic influences on the United States are far smaller than the United States' influences on China."[63]

The other key constraint on China's influence over U.S. policy is the inflexibility of the American CVID stance. The stubborn U.S. insistence on CVID, albeit slightly modified for tactical reasons at the fourth round of talks, reflects a fundamentalist quest for absolute security. It is the product of a Manichean worldview that makes judgments about good and bad, with no shades of gray. Viewed in the context of Pyongyang's historical anxieties, CVID is nothing short of an evil-state strangulation (regime-change) strategy.

Above all, Beijing was the primary mover and linchpin of the six-party process to achieve a "*qiutong cunyi*" agreement, in the form of the Joint Statement of Principles, as a group consensus and a roadmap for future progress.[64] Chinese diplomats are reported to have been even-handed to a fault in producing five successive drafts of a possible joint statement designed to seek common ground – or split the differences – between the U.S. and North Korean positions during the second and final phase of the fourth round of talks. By September 17, 2005, China's fifth and final draft of a possible Joint Statement became acceptable to all five parties other than the United States, thus reaching a breakthrough or breaking point in Beijing's CM efforts. Paradoxically, to paraphrase Mao's famous statement, China's leverage grows from the barrel of America's self-inflicted troubles. As Wang Jisi aptly put it, "So long as the United States' image remains tainted, China will have greater leverage in multilateral settings."[65]

China has come to a point in its CM mediation that it feels it can challenge the Bush administration openly. First, Beijing is taking advantage of the global wave of anti-Americanism (or anti-Bushism) and of widespread disbelief in U.S. intelligence about weapons of mass destruction, both issues related to the Iraq war. Second, China feels increasingly confident that the emerging Northeast Asian coalition of the willing is

[63] J. Wang (2005: 39, 47). [64] Snyder (2005). [65] J. Wang (2005: 43).

moving away from the Bush administration's approach and toward the Chinese incremental "peace by pieces" approach or the mutually reciprocal "words for words" and "action for action" approach. Finally, Beijing's open challenge reflects its concern that the six-party talks could collapse if the CVID formula were not dismantled at least in part.

Sino–DPRK Alliance Interaction

For better or worse, the DPRK is the only country with which the PRC "maintains" – whether in name or in practice – a Cold War security pact. Yet, in light of China's evenhanded behavior in the second nuclear standoff, one can question the meaningfulness of the 1961 PRC–DPRK Treaty of Friendship, Cooperation, and Mutual Assistance.[66] The most oft-quoted description of China–DPRK relations is "as close as lips to teeth," but recently this has been quoted in contrast to China's actual attitudes toward its ally. As South Korea has become an increasingly attractive economic partner and as North Korea has become an increasingly unpredictable neighbor, China has somewhat distanced itself from the DPRK, although with a conscious desire to avoid committing the Soviet fallacy of premature allied abandonment. In essence, the PRC is caught between the belief that the 1961 treaty is an unusable Cold War relic and the notion that it is a symbol of the special socialist relationship between China and North Korea.[67]

Relations between the Korean People's Army (KPA) and the PLA have declined precipitously in terms of the frequency, level, and substance since the days of the Korean War and, in particular, since the death of Kim Il Sung in 1994. Although regular military-to-military visits continue, the close cooperation seems to have given way to symbolism and ceremony. Many of the PLA visits to North Korea in recent years have been described as "goodwill delegations."[68] Similarly, the strained relationship is also reflected in an appreciable decline in the frequency and level of mutual visits by political leaders in the post–Kim Il Sung years. For more than a decade – until the mid-2000 – neither Jiang Zemin nor Kim Jong Il found it politically important or convenient to negotiate the short distance between Beijing and Pyongyang (an hour by plane) for a summit meeting.[69] In contrast, there were many summit meetings between South Korean and Chinese leaders during this period; there was even a visit to Seoul by all seven members of Politburo

[66] During the initial stages of the DPRK nuclear standoff, a noted scholar from the China Academy of Social Sciences actively called for a revision of the treaty, asking for the nullification of the security alliance between the PRC and DPRK to avoid being pulled into a war; see J. Shen (2003).

[67] J. Shen (2003: 58). [68] Scobell (2004a: 8). [69] T. H. Kim (1999: 306–08).

Standing Committee of the Chinese Communist Party, the most powerful organ of the Chinese political system. Since 1997, China has pursued a new security concept that calls for basing international security on multilateral dialogue and on pledges by states to foreswear the use of military threats, coercion, and intervention in the internal affairs of other states. In particular, this new security concept criticizes bilateral and multilateral military alliances as relics of the Cold War that undermine rather than enhance international security.[70] China is seeking to enhance its international influence by redefining its national identity as a responsible great power; by improving its foreign political, diplomatic, economic, and military relationships; by settling border disputes with neighboring states; and by increasing its role in and contribution to regional and global multilateral institutions. For China, the alliance with North Korea serves mostly as a mechanism for monitoring its neighbor's unpredictable behavior and for retaining some relevant level of influence.

With these changes, the China–DPRK alliance has begun to serve an ironic security function: it best provides security by working to ensure that the DPRK does not undertake rash or destabilizing actions. China certainly has an interest in preventing the collapse of North Korea, given the refugee situation that would develop inside China in the case of such an event. Although the present-day Sino–DPRK relationship is not as close as it once was, neither Beijing nor Pyongyang has shown any interest in formally modifying the treaty. Unlike the 1961 Soviet–DPRK treaty, the Sino–DPRK treaty cannot be revised or abrogated without prior mutual agreement (Article 7).[71]

Still, Beijing let it be known, if only informally at first, that it would not support Pyongyang if North Korea attacked South Korea. During Jiang Zemin's state visit to South Korea in 1995, a Chinese Foreign Ministry spokesperson stated that the alliance does not commit Chinese troops to defending North Korea. On other occasions, the formulation has been that Beijing's support would not be provided if the North launched "an unprovoked attack," that the treaty does not require the dispatch of Chinese military forces, or that China was not willing to intervene "automatically." With seeming impunity, Beijing projects a strategic posture of calculated ambiguity, letting it be known to all that the treaty commitment to Pyongyang could be interpreted as Chinese leaders choose and that it does not consider the treaty an *ipso facto* hard-and-fast commitment.[72] Even while distancing itself from the treaty, China has undertaken foreign

[70] J. Shen (2003: 57).
[71] For the Chinese and Korean texts of the treaty, see Liu and Yang (1994: 1279–80); J. S. Lee (2001: 318–20).
[72] McVadon (1999: 280).

policy actions to reassure the DPRK. In October 2000, at the same time that PRC Prime Minister Zhu Rongji was visiting Seoul to elevate Sino–ROK relations from a "cooperative partnership" to a "full-scale cooperative partnership," Defense Minister Chi Haotian was in Pyongyang to celebrate the fiftieth anniversary of China's entry into the Korean War – the "War to Resist America and Aid Korea," in Beijing's lingo – and to reaffirm Sino–DPRK military ties. In September 2001, PRC President Jiang Zemin made a three-day official visit to Pyongyang, the first such visit in more than a decade by a Chinese head of state. In part, the visit was to repay two successive visits by Kim Jong Il (one to Beijing in May 2000 and the other to Shanghai in January 2001).

Sino–ROK Security Interaction

In terms of coming into alignment with Seoul, it was in 1999 in Beijing that China and South Korea held their first ever talks between defense ministers. Seoul requested broader Sino–ROK security cooperation, including joint PRC–ROK military exercises, a joint maritime search-and-rescue exercise, exchanges of naval port calls, the establishment of multilateral arms control and disarmament dialogue to prevent the proliferation of weapons of mass destruction, and a return visit by Chinese Defense Minister Chi Haotian. Not surprisingly, Beijing responded with the maxi-mini strategy: (1) it accepted Seoul's invitation for Chi's return visit, (2) it warned Seoul against enhancing military ties with the United States, (3) it warned about the danger of American hegemony, and (4) it danced away from Seoul's request for Beijing's help or response on the other issues. Beijing remains unwilling to participate with Seoul in joint exercises, even in basic areas such as search and rescue or humanitarian operations, nor in the exchange of naval port calls by each other's ships.

There remains some need of definition in Sino–ROK relations. On the eve of President Kim Dae Jung's state visit to China in November 1998, Chinese and South Korean negotiators were engaged in a last-minute tug-of-war over how to define and what to include in the "partnership" agreement to be signed by their leaders at the conclusion of the Jiang–Kim summit meeting in Beijing. There were intense behind-the-scenes negotiations centered on and mired in what modifying adjective to use to characterize "partnership" (e.g., "strategic," "comprehensive," "good, friendly"). After the two parties hit many rough spots, the South Korean side wanted to describe the new relationship as a "partnership without any modifier," whereas the Chinese side insisted on putting "cooperative" ahead of "partnership." "The negotiations went through childbirth pains," according to Park Jie-won, the chief presidential spokesperson for the Blue House in Seoul, as the negotiators eventually agreed to call it a "cooperative partnership."[73]

Security discourse in South Korea distinctly avoids painting the rising China as a menace. The ROK's Defense White Paper generally devotes four to five pages to briefly outlining China's military modernization and ROK–PRC military exchanges, showing no trace of security concern. In striking contrast, the corresponding Japanese publication devotes about three dozen pages to China's various weapons programs and military policy, in not-so-subtle terms.[74] In 1999, Seoul decided not to participate in the U.S. theater missile defense (TMD) program out of deference to Beijing, creating some degree of ire in Washington. Although the United States often discusses TMD in terms of the North Korean threat, as evidenced in the second round of six-party talks on the nuclear standoff, Seoul's stance on North Korea's nuclear and missile programs is increasingly in line with that of Beijing rather than Washington. In fact, according to public opinion surveys South Koreans describe U.S. unilateralism as a "critical threat" to South Korea's vital interests and are more concerned about it than about "the rise of Japanese military power" or the emergence of "China as a world power."[75]

It is abundantly clear that South Korean support for the Bush administration's North Korea policy has flagged substantially, partly due to Seoul's interest in maintaining constructive and fruitful relations with a rising China and partly due to the transformation of Seoul's approach to North Korea, catalyzed by a "regime change" in South Korean domestic politics (i.e., the Kim Dae Jung and Roh Moo-hyun administrations in 1998 and 2003). The "special allied relationship" between the United States and the ROK has been most threatened by a lack of agreement on the nature of the North Korean threat and on what constitutes an appropriate conflict-management approach.

In March 2005 President Roh warned that Seoul may not side with the United States and Japan against China and North Korea.[76] President Roh, while criticizing the traditional idea that Seoul should seek triangular security cooperation with Washington and Tokyo, asserted in a recent interview with a local Internet newspaper that South Korea needs a multiparty security regime that would include China, not contain it, in the interests of a lasting peace on the Korean peninsula and in Northeast Asia.[77] The Roh government's position on the North Korean nuclear

[73] *The Korea Herald*, November 13, 1998 (Internet version). For a more upbeat assessment, see "Sino–ROK Partnership Toward New Century Introduced," *Beijing Review*, 41: 48 (November 11–15, 1998), p. 6.

[74] See *East Asian Strategic Review* (2000: 67–69, 77–79, 83–88, 104–07, 139–41, 191–93).

[75] Chicago Council on Foreign Relations (2004: 11). [76] *Chosun Ilbo*, Mar. 22, 2005.

[77] Ryu Jin, "Roh Seeks N-E Asian Security Regime," *The Korea Times*, October 21, 2005.

crisis is far closer to that of China than that of the United States. Just as Beijing is having to cope with twin security dilemmas of one kind (wanting neither allied abandonment nor allied entrapment), Seoul is experiencing twin security dilemmas of another kind. While no longer fearing allied abandonment of its own security interests in Washington's pursuit of a separate deal with Pyongyang, Seoul's main security dilemma is now centered on allied entrapment in the Bush administration's evil-state strangulation strategy sucking South Korea into a military conflict escalation not of its own making.

In a summit meeting in Seoul in mid-November 2005, President Roh Moo-hyun and Chinese President Hu Jintao said cooperation between South Korea and China had entered "a new stage" and agreed to set up a hotline between the two countries' foreign ministers, to establish a regular discussion channel between vice foreign ministers, to expand military cooperation, and to double bilateral trade to US$200 billion by 2012. The latest move by Seoul to build closer security and economic ties with Beijing is reported to leave U.S. officials and some South Korean officials nervous.[78]

Economic and Functional Issues

For China, from the national interest perspective of post-Mao reform and opening, the South Korean economy represented opportunities to be more fully exploited, whereas North Korea's economic troubles posed a burden to be lessened, albeit without damaging geopolitical ties or causing system collapse. It is a dubious blessing that China, in the wake of the 1990 Soviet–ROK normalization, has become, *faute de mieux*, North Korea's biggest trading partner and economic patron. In the process of the geopolitical and geoeconomic transformations of the early post–Cold War years, a highly asymmetrical Beijing–Seoul–Pyongyang triangular economic relationship emerged.

Sino–ROK Economic Relations

Since the 1992 normalization decision, China and the ROK have been busily making up for lost time in the economic sphere. As part of its *Nordpolitik* policy, Seoul was willing and able to accommodate Beijing's economic interests and preferences to the point of sacrificing its own short-term economic interests, allowing almost continuous trade deficits from 1987 to 1992. As shown in Figure 2.1, trade increased by double-digit percentage points during every year of the 1990s and early

[78] "Korea-China Cooperation 'Reaches New Stage,'" *Chosun Ilbo*, November 16, 2005.

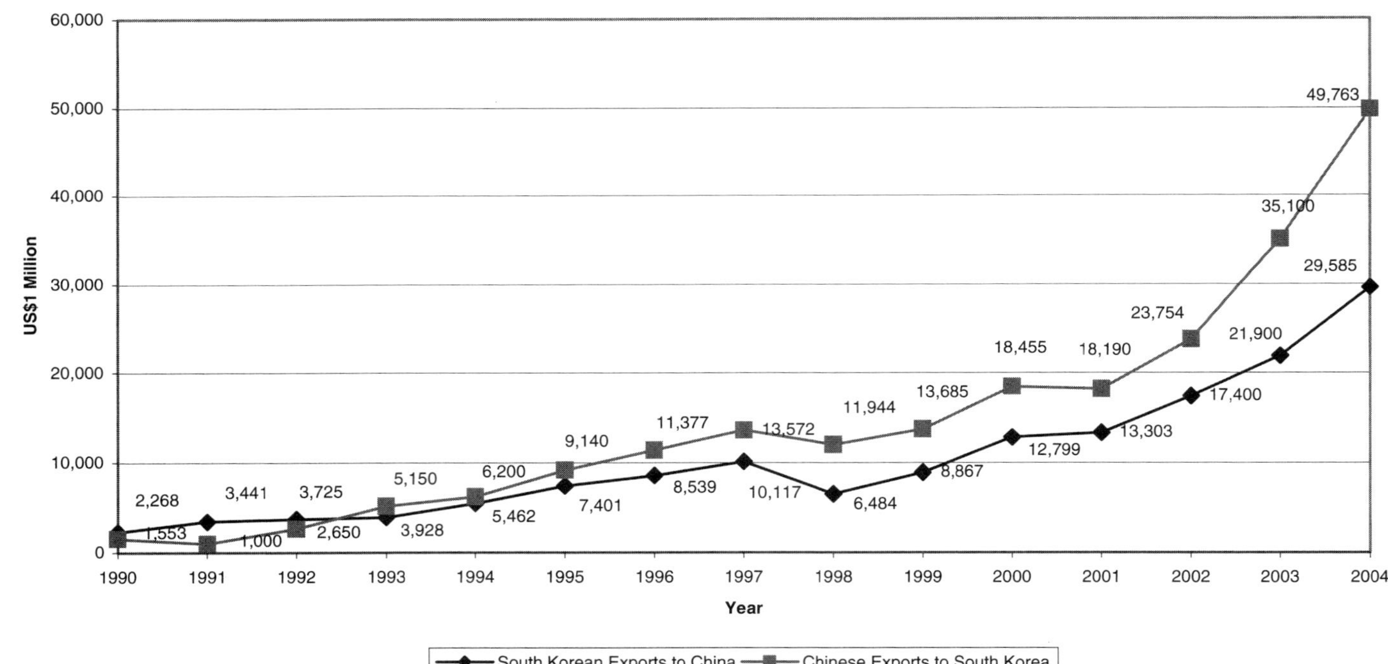

Figure 2.1. China's trade with South Korea, 1990–2004.
Source: 1996 Diplomatic White Paper Ministry of Foreign Affairs and Trade, Republic of Korea, p. 348; 1997 Diplomatic White Paper, pp. 396, 400; 1998 Diplomatic White Paper, pp. 481, 486; 2000 Diplomatic White Paper, p. 496; 2001 Diplomatic White Paper, p. 483; 2002 Diplomatic White Paper, p. 497. Available at www.mofat.go.kr

twenty-first century except two. In 2003, China emerged as South Korea's largest export market and began competing with the United States to be the ROK's largest overall trade partner. A 48-percent rise in exports to $35.1 billion accounted for a startling 98 percent of South Korea's GDP growth in 2003. Without China as an export market, South Korea's economic growth would have been virtually flat.[79] With a 42-percent rise in exports to nearly $50 and a 39-percent increase in total foreign trade ($79.4 billion) in 2004, China has emerged as the largest trading partner of South Korea. In their first summit meeting in Beijing in July 2003, two new leaders – presidents Hu Jintao and Roh Moo-hyun – pledged to strive to increase their annual trade volume to $100 billion in five years (i.e., by 2008), but at current growth rates this mark might well be reached by the end of 2005.

This increasingly interdependent relationship extends beyond trade to include investment as well. In 2000, China officially surpassed the United States as the most popular destination for South Korean outward foreign direct investment (OFDI). As shown in Table 2.3 and Figure 2.2, investment underwent an amazing eighteen-fold increase from 2000 to 2004. By the end of 2004, South Korea's investment in China had increased from $4.5 billion in 2003 to $17.2 billion, a whopping 283-percent increase. This level is high enough that some might even consider it dangerous if China institutes stricter foreign capital controls or chooses to nationalize foreign investments, for instance. Fortunately for South Korea, this does not appear to be a probable future path for PRC economic policy.

South Korea, however, did experience its first major economic shock due to its growing interdependence with China in 2003. Beijing's announcement that it would try to reign in its overheated economy at the end of April led to a drop of nearly nine percentage points in the Korean Composite Stock Price Index (KOSPI), as overseas investors sold more than $600 million in Korean stocks.[80] South Korean economic dependence on exports to China for growth – instead of domestic consumption – indicates the potential losses that the ROK could suffer as the PRC economy slows down.

The initial political logic of Seoul's *Nordpolitik* has been overlaid, if not completely replaced, with the new logic of enhancing national competitiveness in the global marketplace. South Korea's economic competitiveness has continued to slide since 1991. By the mid-1990s, many South Korean firms came to depend on exports to China as providing a significant stimulus for South Korean industry because South Korean companies had seen profits fall with declining demand in developed countries

[79] Snyder (2004). [80] Snyder (2004).

Table 2.3. Chinese–South Korean FDI Relations, 1989–2004

Year	Amount of South Korean FDI into China	Amount of South Korean FDI into China (percent change)	Amount of Chinese FDI into South Korea	Amount of Chinese FDI into South Korea (percent change)
1989	6			
1990	16	+167%		
1991	42	+163%		
1992	141	+236%		
1993	622	+341%		
1994	821	+32%	6	
1995	1,237	+51%	11	+83%
1996	1,679	+36%	7	−36%
1997	907	−46%	7	0%
1998	896	−1%	8	+14%
1999	482	−46%	27	+238%
2000	931	+93%	76	+181%
2001	983	+6%	70	−8%
2002	1,980	+101%	249	+256%
2003	4,489	+127%	50	−80%
2004	17,200	+283%	1,165	+2,230%

Unit: US$1 million.
Source: Keum (1996: 581); 1997 Diplomatic White Paper, Ministry of Foreign Affairs and Trade (MOFAT), Republic of Korea (ROK), pp. 405, 408; 1998 Diplomatic White Paper, pp. 491, 493; 2000 Diplomatic White Paper, pp. 503, 505; 2001 Diplomatic White Paper, pp. 489, 491; 2002 Diplomatic White Paper, pp. 498, 499; www.fdi.gov.cn.

and global product competitiveness rapidly deteriorated due to skyrocketing labor costs at home. Seoul's exports to China acted as a catalyst for export-driven development; South Korea was indebted to China for helping it through a recession in the early 1990s.[81]

Thus, in both trade and investment, the development of close ties between China and South Korea have led to conditions of interdependence and increasingly intense competition. As Albert O. Hirschman argues in his classic work *National Power and Foreign Trade*, trade has an "influence effect": as one country becomes dependent on trade with another country, the latter state has increasing influence in the policy design of the former state. With increased gains from trade comes increased vulnerability to this effect, and a state can avoid these vulnerabilities only if it is has alternate markets at its disposal.[82] Although U.S. geopolitical investments in South Korea make it unlikely that China would

[81] *Tong-A Ilbo* (Seoul), August 24, 1994, p. 5. [82] Hirschman (1980: Chapter 1).

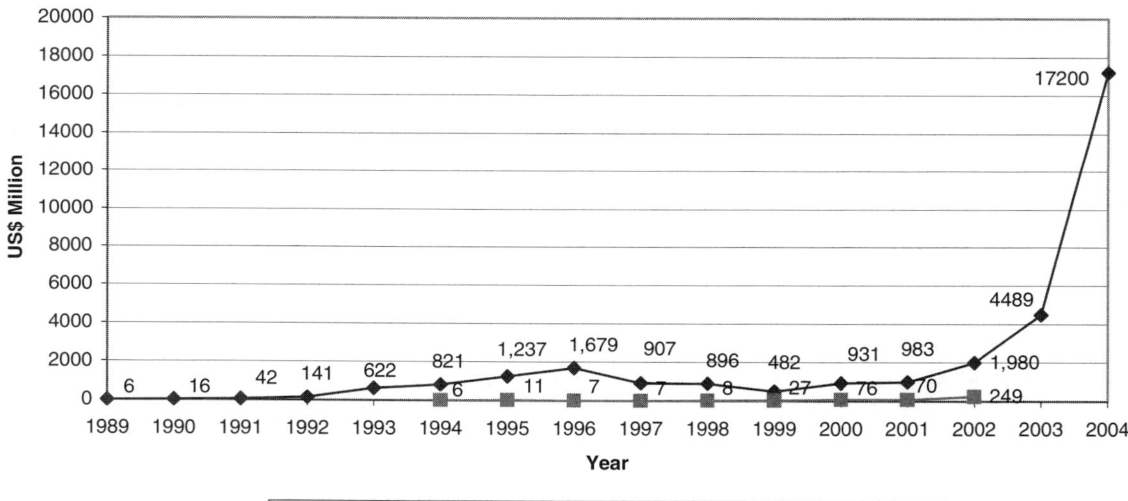

Figure 2.2. Amount of Chinese–South Korean FDI, 1989–2004.
Source: Keum (1996: 581); 1997 Diplomatic White Paper, Ministry of Foreign Affairs and Trade, Republic of Korea, pp. 405, 408; 1998 Diplomatic White Paper, pp. 491, 493; 2000 Diplomatic White Paper, pp. 503, 505; 2001 Diplomatic White Paper, pp. 489, 491; 2002 Diplomatic White Paper, pp. 498, 499.

be able to shift ROK policy substantially, Hirschman's admonition on the relationship between trade and policy influence should not be taken lightly.

Today, South Korean firms are increasingly seeking to target the more than 100 million people in China's urban middle class with per capita incomes of more than $5,000. The greatest interest among South Korean businesses currently appears to be in the telecommunications and electronics sectors. The Chinese mobile phone market has been a site of competition for Japanese and Korean high-tech firms, and China's demand for semiconductors and computers has also increased dramatically since the mid-1990s. Korean firms are experiencing "China fever" as they eagerly try to maximize exports of high-end consumer technology goods, as well as steel and petrochemicals. This trade has not been frictionless in terms of international economics; of the twenty-three antidumping lawsuits filed by Chinese business, eighteen were targeted against Korea.[83] The Chinese Ministry of Foreign Trade and Economic Cooperation (MOFTEC) instituted its first ever temporary antidumping measures in April 2000 against Korean and Japanese stainless steel imports. Since then, MOFTEC, in conjunction with the State Economic and Trade Commission (SETC), has approved antidumping measures on South Korean polyester chips, fiber products, and chemical products.[84] On the Korean peninsula, despite the enthusiasm for the Chinese market, Korean companies have become worried about copyright infringement and intellectual property rights issues within China.

As this competitive angle indicates, not only has China become a source of South Korea's export-driven growth, but it is also rapidly catching up as a competitor, chipping away at Seoul's export market share in third countries, especially in the United States and Japan, and competing for access to valuable natural resources. Whereas projections in the late 1990s suggested that Korean products remained more competitive than Chinese products in international markets,[85] evidence from the beginning of the twenty-first century indicates that Chinese competition is eroding Korean market share as Chinese manufacturers are closing the technology gap with Korean products. As Chinese technology improves, firms will be less willing to invest in a Korean manufacturing sector that they see as prone

[83] Snyder (2003c: 113–17).

[84] See China Facts and Figures 2002, "China Imposes Anti-dumping Duties on Imported ROK-made Products," Xinhua News Agency, February 10, 2003. Available at http://www.china.org.cn/english/international/55347.htm. The tariffs on chemical products were later removed. "Chemical Anti-Dumping Charge Dropped," *People's Daily Online*, November 29, 2003. Available at http://english.peopledaily.com.cn/200311/29/eng20031129_129312.shtml.

[85] Estimates and projections by the Bank of Korea in Seoul. See *The Korea Herald*, March 14, 2000 (Internet version).

to frequent strikes, cumbersome regulations, and political and social instability.[86] Chinese investors have in fact begun investing in strategic industrial sectors in Korea as a method of gaining Korean technology and expertise. A survey among major *chaebols* shows that 43 percent now believe that the technological gap between the ROK and the PRC in major industrial fields has been reduced to about four to five years, whereas 27 percent believe that the gap is only one to three years, and 10 percent believe that there is no difference in technological levels between the two countries.[87] A report written by the Korea Institute of Science and Technology Evaluation and Planning (KISTEP) benchmarked U.S. technological excellence in 99 fields at 100, while giving Korea a score of 65.1 and China 52.5; this puts Korea 5.8 years behind the United States and only 2.1 years ahead of China.[88] Korean textile exports dropped to a thirteen-year low in 2003 because of competition from China.[89] When the international Multi-Fiber Agreement quota system ends at the beginning of 2005, an event that will lead to a tremendous amount of relocation to China by clothing manufacturers, Korean apparel exports are likely to be even more severely diminished by Chinese competition. At the same time, Chinese manufacturing is driving up the cost of natural resources on world markets, contributing to both absolute and relative costs of manufacturing in Korea. Although the new Chinese openness was once a boon to Korean manufacturers, it is now becoming a threat to their continued viability.

South Korean firms, however, have sought to retain a foothold in the Chinese auto assembly market. At the end of 2002, just as China was surpassing Korea to become the sixth largest auto producer in the world, Korean automobile manufacturers rushed to invest in China as a means of capturing market share.[90] These investments allowed Hyundai and Kia to announce record production levels for 2004.[91] Indeed, a recent survey indicated that 40 percent of small and medium-size Korean firms were looking to move production overseas; 80 percent of those firms are planning to relocate to China.[92] There has also been some friction because a number of small South Korean companies that jump started their entry into the China market made a poor impression due to a host of managerial problems. They lacked a basic understanding of the local business culture, relied excessively on ethnic Koreans to solve the language problem, targeted rural areas to exploit the cheap labor, and lacked knowledge

86 *The Korea Herald*, November 6, 2003. 87 Snyder (2004).
88 *Chosun Ilbo*, September 29, 2004. 89 Snyder (2004). 90 See Snyder (2003a).
91 Snyder (2004).
92 According to a 2004 survey conducted by KFI, 43.7 percent of Korean firms expressed they would in the next five years increase investment in China and decrease their investment in Korea. Yonhap News Agency (hereafter cited as Yonhap), July 7, 2004.

Table 2.4. Sino–ROK Exchange of Visitors, 1992–2004

Year	South Korean Visitors to China	% Change	Chinese Visitors to South Korea	% Change	Total	% Change
1992	43,000	N/A	45,000	N/A	88,000	N/A
1993	110,585	+157%	99,957	+122%	210,542	+139%
1994	233,675	+111%	140,985	+41%	374,660	+78%
1995	404,421	+73%	178,359	+27%	582,780	+56%
1996	532,332	+32%	199,604	+12%	731,936	+26%
1997	584,487	+10%	214,244	+7%	798,731	+9%
1998	484,009	−17%	210,662	−2%	694,671	−13%
1999	820,120	+69%	316,639	+50%	1,136,759	+64%
2000	1,033,250	+26%	442,794	+40%	1,476,044	+30%
2001	1,297,746	+26%	482,227	+9%	1,779,973	+21%
2002	1,722,128	+33%	539,466	+12%	2,261,594	+27%
2003	1,560,581	−9%	513,236	−5%	2,073,817	−8%
2004	2,340,000	+50%	410,000	−20%	2,750,000	+33%

Source: Korean National Tourism Organization. Available at http://www.knto.or.kr.

about real estate value and manpower costs. These points of contention have become smoother in recent years.

Sino–ROK Sociocultural Interaction

The economic growth in China and its increasingly close relations with South Korea are both apparent in the increase in tourism between the two countries (Table 2.4). When the South Korean government started a no-visa service for Chinese tourists visiting Cheju Island in April 1998, the number of Chinese visitors increased by 50 percent from the previous year. By the end of 1999, the Chinese were the third largest national group among tourists, behind Japanese and Americans. In 2001, there were for the first time more Chinese visitors (442,794) to South Korea than Americans. Koreans are likewise choosing to travel to China. With more than one-fourth of all South Korean overseas travelers choosing China as their destination, reaching a level of 1.72 million visitors in 2002, only Japan – the preferred destination for 30 percent of Korean travelers – receives more Korean visitors. The number of visitors fell slightly in 2003 to 1.56 million, a result of the SARS (severe acute respiratory syndrome) disease scare in China that devastated the tourism industry for several months (a 9 percent decline for 2003), but rose again sharply by 50 percent in 2004, as shown in Figure 2.3. However, China and Korea

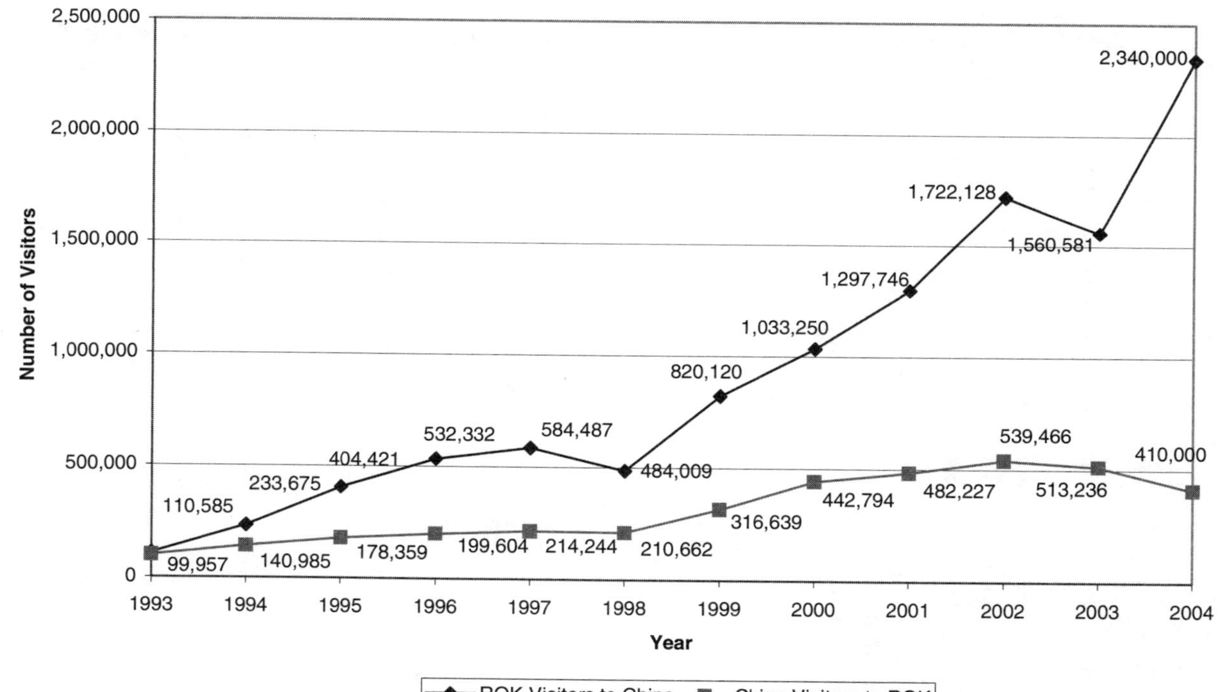

Figure 2.3. Sino–ROK exchange of visitors, 1993–2004.
Source: Korean National Tourism Organization. Available at http://www.knto.or.kr.

in the early twenty-first century are exchanging ten times as many tourists as they were in the early 1990s. This tourism is providing both a mutual source of revenue and also a reaffirmation of the growing investments between the two countries.

Overall, China's ascendancy in the region has quickly made hollow South Korean President Roh Moo-hyun's ambition to make Korea the economic hub of NEA. In his inaugural address in February 2003, Roh declared: "In this new age, our future can no longer be confined to the Korean peninsula. The Age of Northeast Asia is fast approaching. Northeast Asia, which used to be on the periphery of the modern world, is now emerging as a new source of energy in the global economy." He further noted, "Koreans have lived through a series of challenges and have responded to them. Having to live among big powers, the people on the Korean peninsula have had to cope with countless tribulations. . . . Within the half-century since liberation from colonial rule, and despite territorial division, war, and poverty, we have built a nation that is the 12th largest economic power in the world." Referencing the divisions of the past as a contrast, Roh called explicitly for South Korea to see the future of growing regionalism in NEA, to embrace this future, and to play a leading role in defining it.[93]

Yet, it has been China that has stepped forward to provide the leadership in defining NEA as an economic region. It is toward China that countries both inside and outside the region turn when thinking regionally about East Asia. This should not be surprising, given China's economic status as the world's fastest-growing economy. Most recently, China has become the world's third largest trading nation, after the United States and Germany but ahead of Japan. In short, there has been a major transformation of NEA, as South Korea has gone from having no diplomatic relations and only minimal economic relations with the PRC to being both a prime collaborator in the region and a key international competitor.

Sino–DPRK Economic Relations

On the northern half of the Korean peninsula, China's economic role has also undergone significant changes since the end of the Cold War and the reformatting of the international system. China's continued economic engagement with the DPRK speaks to the multiple roles of economic ties in international relations, but the growth in disparity between China's economic relations with the ROK and with the DPRK indicates the true trajectory of Chinese political economy in NEA. Although Sino–ROK

[93] Roh Moo Hyun, "Address at the 16th Inaugural Ceremony: A New Takeoff Toward an Age of Peace and Prosperity." Available at http://www.korea.net/government/president/news/xcontent.asp?color=BP&cate=01&serial_no=20030225003.

trade and investment are clear components of a global economic order, it is equally clear that Sino–DPRK economic relations are remnants of a Cold War ideological life support system, one that has little place in the globalization era.

As an indication of the ways that Sino–DPRK trade is closely keyed to and determined by turbulent geopolitical activities, the percentage of North Korean foreign trade belonging to China has fluctuated greatly over the years: (1) 25 to 60 percent (with an absolute value around $100 million) in the 1950s; (2) about 30 percent in the 1960s until 1967, when the ratio declined to around 10 percent in the wake of the Cultural Revolution; (3) about 20 percent in 1973 (to the level of $300–$600 million); and (4) a decline to the 10 to 20 percent range in the 1980s, although its total value had risen to $3 to $4 billion. In the first post–Cold War decade, the 1990s, the ratio started at 10.1 percent in 1990 but increased dramatically to around 30 percent in 1991 and stayed at this range until 1998, even as its total value began to decline from $899 million in 1993 to $371 million in 1999. In the early years of the twenty-first century, Sino–DPRK trade registered several sequential increases in percentage of total trade (Table 2.2).

In general, North Korea has become increasingly cut off from the rest of the world, although it is sadly far from self-sufficient. If we look at trade as a percentage of GDP – a widely used measure of a country's integration into the global economy – in 2000, this figure stood at 11 percent for North Korea, compared with 44 percent for China, 18 percent for Japan, 21 percent for the United States, and 73 percent for South Korea. North Korea's ratio has actually declined from about 20 percent in 1990, whereas Beijing's trade/GDP ratio more than tripled from 13 percent in 1980 to 44 percent in 2000 – and 70 percent in 2004.[94] In comparative perspective, North Korea's total trade with China in 2000 ($488 million) represented 20 percent of its overall foreign trade but only about 0.1 percent of China's global trade, and it was equivalent to only 0.15 percent of South Korea's global trade and 1.6 percent of South Korea's trade with China.

The second notable aspect of Sino–DPRK economic relations is that the trade is characterized by chronic and substantial deficits for North Korea, amounting cumulatively to $5 billion from 1990 to 2004. Because North Korea does not have high-value products to export and because its primary exportable commodities are losing competitiveness,

[94] The 2000 figures for China, Japan, South Korea, and the United States are based on the World Bank (2001: 236–39); the figures for North Korea are based on the report issued by South Korea's National Statistics Office in late December 2001 and summarized in *Korea Now* (December 29, 2001), p. 8; and The Economist Intelligence Unit, *Country Profile 2001: South Korea and North Korea* at http://www.elu.com/schedule. See also *People's Daily Online*, January 25, 2005, for the 2004 data.

it seems unlikely that Pyongyang will be able to remedy the situation. Although China remains North Korea's largest trade partner, Beijing allows Pyongyang to run large annual deficits. China's role in North Korea's trade would be even larger if barter transactions and aid were factored into the calculations.

There are several tactics China has employed in its behind-the-scenes diplomatic efforts in the economic arena. Beijing has been applying pressure on Pyongyang to lift its collapsing economy through reform and opening to the outside world. Beijing also followed Moscow's lead in 1993, in demanding hard currency cash payments in trade as another way of coaxing Pyongyang to get its act together in foreign trade. It soon became clear, however, that Pyongyang would be unable or unwilling to meet such demands. Consequently, China was forced to waive North Korea's debt in "friendship prices" for oil and food, becoming in the process a leading provider of humanitarian assistance. China's aid to North Korea is generally estimated at one-fourth to one-third of China's overall foreign aid.

Indeed, Sino–DPRK economic relations seems to resemble the description by Mao's Foreign Minister Huang Hua (at the Sixth Special Session of the General Assembly in 1974) of the global capitalist economic system of the early 1970s as an "interdependence between a horseman and his mount,"[95] except that it is not easy to see whether Beijing or Pyongyang is the horseman. In Tom Hart's pithy characterization, it is "a mutually grating, reluctant patron-proud mendicant relationship" in which such "cooperation" as can be observed is "chiefly in the form of Chinese grants and subsidies, plus classic protestations of traditional good neighborliness and party-to-party solidarity."[96]

Paradoxically, Pyongyang's growing dependence on Beijing for economic and political survival has also bred mutual distrust and resentment. Pyongyang has taken a sleight-of-hand approach, privately asking for more and more aid, even as North Korean diplomats habitually deny that they have ever asked for or received any Chinese aid.[97] In every high-level meeting between the two governments, according to one Chinese scholar, the North Korean request for economic aid dominates the agenda.[98] For Beijing, a multitasking strategy is made palpably evident in its "humanitarian aid," which is designed to lessen flows of refugees to China, to delay

[95] S. S. Kim (1979: 265). [96] Hart (2001: 255–56).

[97] In a closed executive session in New York in May 1998 involving two high-ranking North Korean ambassadors (Ambassadors Li Hyong-chol and Li Gun) and a dozen U.S. government analysts and private scholars, including this author, Ambassador Li Hyong-chol categorically denied any Chinese aid, saying: "If we wanted Chinese aid, we could get one million tons of grain from China tomorrow but it would come with an unacceptably heavy price of 'dependence.'"

[98] Y. Ji (2001a: 391).

a possible North Korean collapse, and to enhance China's own leverage in Pyongyang and Seoul.

Despite being Pyongyang's external life support system, especially since November 2002 when the United States halted monthly delivery of heavy fuel oil, China does not, to its frustration, receive as much North Korean gratitude as it would like nor does it wield as much leverage as Washington would believe, precisely because Pyongyang knows that China's aid is in its own self-interest.[99] As one senior Chinese leader said to a visiting U.S. scholar in the context of expressing China's opposition to any economic sanctions on North Korea, "We can either send food to North Korea or they will send refugees to us – either way, we feed them. It is more convenient to feed them in North Korea than in China."[100] Thus, Beijing is cautious to a fault for fear of provoking and/or causing collapse in the North by withholding too much aid because that event would bring a host of destabilizing social, economic, and political consequences.

North Korea's dependency on China for aid has grown unabated and has even intensified in the face of Washington's rogue state strategy. Recent estimates of China's aid to North Korea are in the range of 1 million tons of wheat and rice and 500,000 tons of heavy fuel oil per annum, accounting for 70 to 90 percent of North Korea's fuel imports and about one-third of its total food imports. With the cessation of America's heavy fuel oil delivery in November 2002, China's oil aid and exports may now be approaching nearly 100 percent of North Korea's energy imports.[101] As a way of enticing Pyongyang to the six-party talks in late August 2003, President Hu Jintao promised Kim Jong Il greater economic aid than in previous years. The Chinese government has extended indirect aid by allowing private economic transactions between North Korean and Chinese companies in the border area, despite North Korea's mounting debt and the bankruptcy of many Chinese companies resulting from North Korean defaults on debts.

In 2003 and 2004, Sino–North Korean trade reached a new all-time high of just more than $1 billion in 2003 (up 39 percent from 2002) and $1.4 billion in 2004 (an increase of 35 percent from 2003), demonstrating the paradoxical effect of the second U.S.–DPRK nuclear standoff, which has accelerated Pyongyang's economic isolation due to the reinforced sanctions by Washington and Tokyo, while deepening North Korea's dependence on Beijing and Seoul for trade and aid. As shown in Table 2.5, there is great volatility in Sino–DPRK trade, reflecting and effecting Beijing's economic coaxing/coercive diplomacy. The first half of 2003 shows the coercive aspect of Beijing's economic relations

[99] Snyder (2000/2001: 530). [100] Quoted in Lampton and Ewing (2004: 70).
[101] Shambaugh (2003: 46).

Table 2.5. China's Trade with North Korea by Half-Year, 2001–03

	01–06/2001	07–12/2001 (% change)	01–06/2002 (% change)	07–12/2002 (% change)	01–06/2003 (% change)	07–12/2003 (% change)
Imports	24,655	142,142 (+477%)	103,904 (−27%)	166,959 (+61%)	107,764 (−35%)	287,782 (+167%)
Exports	284,124	286,536 (+1%)	221,131 (−23%)	246,178 (+11%)	270,064 (+10%)	357,931 (+33%)
Volume	308,779	428,678 (+39%)	325,035 (−24%)	413,137 (+27%)	377,828 (−9%)	645,713 (+71%)

Unit: US$1,000.
Source: Chinese Customs Statistics and KOTRA (Korean Trade Association).

with Pyongyang, whereas the second half shows the coaxing aspect, with China's imports from North Korea registering a whopping 168-percent increase on a semiannual basis. North Korea's dependence on China in trade (and aid) was greatly deepened owing to the reimposition of economic sanctions as well as the overall sharp decline in North Korea's trade with Japan. As an incentive to coax Pyongyang to be more flexible and forthcoming at the second round of six-party talks in February 2004, Beijing is reported to have delivered about $US50 million in aid to North Korea, including heavy fuel oil and the promise of a glass factory near Pyongyang.

Beijing's pressure on Pyongyang to lift the collapsing economy by its own *juche*-bootstraps has been persistent since China began its own reforms. Yet, Pyongyang has issued mixed and contradictory signals and statements about post-Mao Chinese socialism. In six informal summit meetings between 1978 and 1991, Deng Xiaoping repeatedly urged Kim Il Sung to develop the North Korean economy through reform and opening. This only provoked Kim Il Sung's testy retort, "we opened, already," in reference to the Rajin-Sonbong Free Economic and Trade Zone.[102] In September 1993, however, Kim Il Sung reportedly told a visiting Chinese delegation that he admired China "for having achieved brilliant reforms and openness," while continuing to build "socialism with Chinese characteristics," and that the Chinese experience would become "an encouraging factor for us Koreans."[103]

Despite this pressure for reform, in an odd turn of events, China had much to do with the recent derailment of the Sinuiju Special Autonomous Region (SAR) in northern North Korea, a special economic zone that was to have operated according to more market-based rules. According

[102] Economist Intelligence Unit (EIU), *Country Report: South Korea and North Korea* (1st Quarter, 1999), p. 40.

[103] *North Korean News*, No. 702 (September 27, 1993), p. 5.

to Pyongyang, Sinuiju was to be a complex of finance, trade, commerce, industry, technology, recreation, and tourism. But the Chinese saw it as the likely home of gambling, money laundering, and other illegal businesses; they did not want it on their border and therefore arrested Yang Bin, the Dutch-Chinese tycoon who had been designated Chief Executive of Sinuiju SAR. Beijing saw Sinuiju as a likely point of friction between itself and Pyongyang and, in fact, had urged the North Korean regime in 1998 to locate the SAR on the border with South Korea. Nonetheless, Pyongyang is pushing ahead with the opening of Sinuiju, and Beijing will likely have to undertake new responsive measures to ensure that it takes a desirable shape.[104] Although the nuclear challenge from Pyongyang is grabbing headlines, it is perhaps the changing economic role of China on the Korean peninsula that will have the most lasting impact. Chinese economic relations with North Korea are defined by aid from Beijing designed to keep the Pyongyang regime afloat so China has a strategic buffer and so the number of refugees will be limited; however, Chinese economic relations with South Korea are becoming increasingly important and integrated in a global context. With such proximity, competition and tension often follow, and that seems to be the case regarding China's position on the Korean peninsula. The ability of the Seoul and Beijing regimes to channel these energies into constructive projects and into defining – together – a regional economic order will determine the long-run impact of China's new role and power on the southern half of the peninsula.

Managing Identity Politics

One of the overlapping sets of Pyongyang–Beijing–Seoul relations is a triangle of human movement, involving in 2004 flows of hundreds of thousands of refugees (or "illegal immigrants" in Chinese eyes) from North Korea to northeast China, about half a million Chinese middle-class tourists to South Korea, about 135,000 Chinese-Korean (*Chosonjok*) illegal migrant workers from China to South Korea, and more than 2.3 million South Korean tourists to China. Against this backdrop, the North Korean "refugee" question and a dispute over the origins of the ancient kingdom of Koguryo have brought into sharp relief Beijing's abiding concerns about the possibility of a North Korean collapse leading to Korean reunification by Southern absorption.

For Seoul and Pyongyang, the mythological birthplace of the Korean nation – the Paektu Mountains (*Changbaishan* in Chinese) and the Chongji Lake – is located on the Jilin–North Korean border. Not

[104] M. Liu (2003: 370–72).

surprisingly, then, the birthplace of the Korean nation has turned into a primary battleground for the politics of competitive national identity enactment and legitimation. It has also become a magnet for the DPRK's refugees/defectors, security agents and spies, and the ROK's Christian missionaries, Buddhist humanitarian workers, businesspeople, tourists, and journalists. For China, the center-periphery disparity – thinking nationally but acting locally – in the implementation of the two-Korea decision has been made particularly evident in the northeastern region.

In the late 1990s, some hundreds of thousands of North Korean "food refugees" are reported to have used the porous Sino–DPRK border as a kind of revolving door each year, moving into and out of China in search of food. Estimates of the number of North Korean refugees in China vary widely, ranging from 7,000 to 8,000 by the Chinese government to 10,000 to 30,000 by the South Korean government, 50,000 by the U.S. Committee for Refugees, 100,000 by most common scholarly estimates, and 300,000 by the South Korean press.[105] In the five years or so following 1995, the famine-related death toll is estimated at between 1.5 and 2 million. For a somewhat longer period (and including multiple-cause deaths), UN High Commissioner for Refugees (UNHCR) reports put the number of famine-related deaths at between 2 and 3.5 million, whereas U.S. Committee for Refugees and the Hopkins School of Public Health give more modest figures.[106] Perhaps the most striking feature in the refugees' demographics is the very large proportion of women (some three-fourths or 75.5 percent of the total refugee population).[107]

The interplay of several separate but interrelated "push" and "pull" factors led to an explosive increase in the illegal migration of North Koreans to Northeast China in the latter half of the 1990s: (1) the deepening North Korean economic crisis accompanied by the Great Famine of 1996–99; (2) the easing of government control and an explosive growth in corruption among North Korean officials, including frontier guards; (3) the porous Sino–DPRK border coupled with many more opportunities for business or employment in Northeastern China, with the resulting population of some 2 million Korean-Chinese (the world's largest or now the

[105] J. H. Shim (1999: 11); Natsios (2001); Lankov (2004b). There is no agreement on the exact numbers of the North Korean refugees in Northeast China at a given point in time partly because of the lack of reliable statistics and partly because the number continues to change. A large-scale study conducted by South Korean sociologists in China between November 1998 and April 1999, when the famine was at its peak, estimates that between 143,000 and 195,000 refugees then took shelter in Northeast China, whereas Andre Lankov (2004b: 859) writes that the number of refugees decreased from 2001 to 2003 and at any given moment, about 100,000 North Koreans resided illegally in China. The South Korean press often mentions 300,000 North Korean refugees in China.

[106] Seymour (2005, 2006). [107] Good Friends (1999); Lankov (2004b: 860).

world's second largest Korean diaspora); (4) the bourgeoning presence in Northeast China of South Korean tourists, businesspersons, humanitarian nongovernmental organizations (NGOs), and missionaries in the wake of the 1992 Sino–ROK normalization; and (5) the relaxation of post-Mao China's grip on the floating population of some 100 million.[108]

The status and maltreatment of North Korean food refugees in Northeast China has already become a bone of contention between Beijing and South Korean human rights and humanitarian NGOs. Faced with a burgeoning North Korean refugee population in the region, Beijing has abandoned its policy of "benign neglect" and has instead stepped up search-and-arrest operations, imposing heavy fines of 3,000 to 50,000 yuan (a fortune in Chinese terms) against those who shelter refugees and forcibly repatriating refugees back to North Korea. In April 1999, a nationwide petition launched by South Korean NGOs and religious groups associated with the Christian Council of Korea requested that the United Nations grant official refugee status to North Korean refugees in China. Beijing's point man in Seoul – Chinese Ambassador Wu Dawei – entered the fray by attacking South Korean and international concerns over the human rights situation as "neointerventionism," infringing on Chinese (and North Korean) state sovereignty. His statements provoked an anti-Chinese rally in front of the Chinese Embassy in Seoul on September 8, 1999.

Against this ominous backdrop, in 1999, the plight of the "NK-7" – seven starving members of a North Korean family, ranging in age from thirteen to thirty – captured the public imagination and prime time media coverage in Seoul. The tragic odyssey started when the NK-7 risked their lives by crossing the Tumen River into China and then entered Russia, only to be arrested by Russian border guards. Thanks to a mass media frenzy and a major global NGO conference in Seoul, the office of the UNHCR intervened and acknowledged them as bona fide refugees. At the same time, the hapless NK-7 told a Russian television crew that they would be killed if repatriated back to their homeland and that they preferred to remain in Russia even if it meant going to prison. The case of the NK-7 crossed a firewall, becoming an instant *cause celebre*. Seoul launched a flurry of diplomatic activities on their behalf, but to no avail. Moscow decided to disengage itself from the NK-7 imbroglio by sending them back to China as illegal immigrants rather than accepting them as refugees. Beijing, in turn, lost no time in forcibly repatriating them back to North Korea.

For Beijing, a "red line" of state sovereignty was crossed, and China had to repatriate them as illegal immigrants in accordance with the 1960

[108] Lankov (2004b).

Sino–DPRK Criminal Extradition Treaty. The bottom line seemed clear enough – to grant refugee status to North Korean escapees would open a floodgate of massive refugee exodus. Meanwhile, UN High Commissioner Ogata Sadako sent a letter to the Chinese government protesting the violation of the 1951 Refugee Convention (of which both China and Russia are signatories) and urging China to refrain from additional deportations of North Korean refugees in the future.[109] The response of Tokyo and Washington has been one of "total silence." True to form, Pyongyang has taken a two-handed approach, exerting pressure on Beijing to crack down and repatriate "illegal immigrants" in accordance with the mutual extradition treaty, while asking for Seoul's economic aid in deterring the further defection of DPRK citizens.

In 2002, the refugee issue again took center stage as a wave of North Korean refugees began storming foreign embassies in China in hopes of gaining asylum. First, in March, a group of twenty-five refugees rushed past Chinese guards to get into the Spanish embassy in Beijing. After several days of negotiations, China allowed the ROK to sponsor their transit to Seoul through a third country (the Philippines). The group attracted much international attention and was able to take advantage of Beijing's sensitivity to international opinion in its attempt to win the bid for the 2008 Summer Olympics. In June, however, China offended South Korean public opinion by entering the ROK embassy to remove an asylum seeker. But the PRC amended its policy over the summer, such that in September a group of fifteen people who had sought refuge in the German embassy and a group of twenty-one who had made their way into the South Korean embassy in Beijing were allowed to travel to the ROK through Singapore and the Philippines, respectively.[110] With increased security and better monitoring, China was able to cut down on the number of refugees attempting to defect to the ROK through Western embassies, but 2002 nonetheless saw some sixty North Koreans transported out of China to South Korea.

China is pursuing a two-track policy, quietly transferring those refugees who successfully enter diplomatic compounds to South Korea, while increasing the ruthlessness of its enforcement of border controls and repatriation policies for refugees who are caught in the border areas, away from the public spotlight. China continues to deny the UNHCR access to border areas or suspected North Korean refugees, and by practicing

[109] Article 1 of the 1951 Refugee Convention defines a "refugee" as anyone who is outside of his or her own country and unable or unwilling to return home due to a well-founded fear of persecution for reasons of race, religion, nationality, membership in a particular social group, or political opinion.

[110] See BBC News, "Deal Reached on Korean Refugees," December 5, 2002. Available at http://news.bbc.co.uk/2/hi/asia-pacific/2238041.stm.

refoulement – the return of refugees to the DPRK despite risks of persecution – it continues to violate the UN conventions on refugees that it has signed. (The opposition to this policy is indicated by rumors of hunger strikes involving upward of 100 detained North Koreans.) China claims that this repatriation is based on a bilateral treaty with the DPRK, but it is unclear to which treaty Beijing refers. In June 2004, the PLA sent a delegation to Pyongyang to sign the PRC–DPRK Border Protection and Cooperation Agreement, which turned over administrative border duties from the People's Armed Police to the PLA. This protocol was probably aimed in part at increasing pressure on Pyongyang to enforce control on its side of the border.

The more secure China's central leadership and the lower its anxiety about domestic instability, the less likely it is to see these externally generated problems as a serious threat, and the more likely it is to adopt a flexible posture in addressing them. Most recently, therefore, a relatively secure CCP has on balance demonstrated considerable flexibility and pragmatism in its handling of Koreans seeking asylum. At least when high-profile cases have been involved, China, relying on quiet diplomacy and face-saving solutions (e.g., sending Korean refugees to a third country rather than permitting them to go directly to the ROK), has thus far been able to accommodate international pressure for humanitarian treatment, while avoiding blatant affronts to Pyongyang and minimizing the danger that such incidents could trigger domestic debates about the legitimacy of foreign intervention in the case of human rights violations within a sovereign state, specifically one led by a repressive communist regime.[111]

In some ways, Beijing's management of the Hwang Jang-yop affairs in early 1997 exemplifies China's balancing act in inter-Korean politics. In an unprecedented but exceptional trilateral tug-of-war over the case of Hwang Jang-yop, the highest-ranking North Korean leader ever to announce his intent to defect to South Korea, Beijing was forced to take its first mediating role between the niggling South and the defiant North in a highly publicized and politicized defection/asylum case. Remarkably, Beijing managed to escape from the predicament. First, after weighing image costs and benefits – Seoul's legal position, espousing accepted international law principles, that Hwang should be allowed to go to the country of his choice, along with China's own status and reputation as one of the Perm Five on the Security Council and a responsible great power – Beijing decided to let Hwang go. Then, Beijing managed to reduce Pyongyang's anger by allowing Hwang a respectable interlude in China and by "deporting" Hwang to a third country (the Philippines),

[111] For more information and analysis, see Seymour (2006).

thus showing compliance with its own domestic law of not granting political asylum. At the same time, China blocked the United States and Japan from assuming any role in the resolution of this inter-Korean crisis in Beijing (and in global prime time), even as it extracted Seoul's promise not to take "political advantage" of the Hwang Jang-yop affair.

Particularly significant, but neither widely nor sufficiently acknowledged, is Seoul's changing identity and approach to the North Korean refugee crisis. By the logic of Cold War identity, North Korean refugees would have met an enthusiastic welcome in the South, as was the case in the 1980s, when successful defections were very rare. But in recent years, especially since the coming of the Kim Dae Jung administration in 1998, Seoul's approach to the refugee problem has been driven by a set of pragmatic considerations (e.g., Seoul's manifest unwillingness to create a diplomatic row with Beijing, the reluctance to bear heavy welfare costs for North Korean refugees in the South, and the determination not to undermine or destabilize the North, leading to a hard crash landing).[112]

President Kim Dae Jung's Sunshine Policy as applied to the refugee issue seems to be paying off in the form of an increasingly pragmatic approach from Pyongyang. Despite occasional assertions and reports of executions of apprehended refugees/defectors in the Western press, the majority of the defectors who are apprehended by border guards or extradited from China are detained for only a short term, normally a week or two. The fact that an astonishing 40 percent of them somehow managed to return to China after their release from detention is proof positive of North Korea's pragmatic and reciprocal approach.[113]

Another aspect of the refugee/defector issue is a burgeoning illegal immigrant population in South Korea. The postnormalization years of the 1990s witnessed a dramatic increase in the number of Chinese visitors to South Korea, with many of them overstaying their time limit in the ROK. Ethnic Koreans (Korean-Chinese) from the Jilin province took advantage of both their bilingual skills and South Korea's labor shortage to engage in illegal commercial activities and factory work.[114] More than half the 200,000 illegal foreign workers in South Korea are Korean-Chinese. Many have found themselves cheated by Korean employers and have sought shelter in Korean churches to make ends meet while avoiding Korean immigration authorities.

In addition, the 1990s saw the presence of some 370,000 migrant workers from South and Southeast Asia and China. In striking contrast to Tokyo's policies toward foreign migrant workers, Seoul shied away from any policy of ethnic preference toward Korean-Chinese migrant workers, even though they comprise the largest single group of foreign migrant

[112] Lankov (2004b: 865, 873). [113] Lankov (2004b: 870–71). [114] C. J. Lee (1996: 166).

workers. To give preferential treatment to diasporic Koreans from China would be to establish a dangerous precedent for other would-be entrants of Korean descent.[115] Few people in South Korea seem willing or able to recognize the inherent conflict between the ideals of ethnonational brotherhood and the harsh realities of mistreatment of ethnic Chinese-Korean workers.[116]

The evolving tension between nationalism and globalism was manifest when the ROK Ministry of Justice announced in 1998 plans for a special law that would accord 6 million ethnic Koreans abroad legal status virtually equal to that of Korean citizens at home. The main objective of this proposed legislative plan, according to the ministry, was to give overseas Koreans a stronger sense of belonging as members of the Korean community and to provide them with more opportunities to contribute to the economic development of their motherland. Not only would this nationalistic legislative sleight of hand directly contradict the spirit and letter of President Kim Dae Jung's professed globalism, but it would create legal and diplomatic disputes with the host countries of overseas Koreans, most of whom (about 60 percent, or 3.1 million) are by birth or naturalization bona fide citizens where they are now domiciled. China, as well as Uzbekistan and Kazakhstan, lost no time making known through diplomatic channels their strong displeasure with the law and the likelihood of trouble ahead.

Against this backdrop, the Ministry of Foreign Affairs and Trade expressed opposition to the proposed legislation for fear that it might create serious diplomatic and legal disputes with China and some other foreign countries. The government drastically revised the dual-citizenship bill to accommodate Beijing's concerns, and a revised bill passed by the National Assembly in 1999 extended benefits only to those overseas Koreans who emigrated after the establishment of the ROK in 1948. But President Kim Dae Jung instructed the Cabinet to establish "supplementary measures" to include ethnic Koreans in China and the former Soviet Union so it would grant them virtually the same legal status as other overseas ethnic Koreans. The law was declared unequal and unconstitutional by the Constitutional Court, which ordered its amendment by December 2003 to put an end to the dispute that had lasted for five years. On February 9, 2004, the National Assembly passed the Law on Ethnic Koreans Abroad, which allowed South Korean citizenship for first-generation ethnic Koreans in China and Russia who had moved there before the establishment of the ROK in August 1948. So far, this is another situation in which neither China nor Russia has done much to press the issue.

[115] K. H. Moon (2000). [116] K. H. Moon (2000: 148–50).

Since 2002, China has, however, pushed the envelope with regard to a particular cultural-historical issue. Partly in response to a 2001 North Korean request to the UN Scientific, Educational and Cultural Organization (UNESCO) seeking to add mural paintings produced in the kingdom of Koguryo (37 B.C.–667 A.D.) to the World Cultural Heritage list, in February 2002, China established a five-year Northeast Asian History project. In 2004, that project issued a report in which it disputed centuries of conventional scholarship and claimed that Koguryo was not a Korean kingdom but rather a Chinese vassal that had used the Chinese language and absorbed Chinese culture. The PRC also requested UNESCO recognition for Koguryo-era castles and tombs on its territory. (In its heyday, Koguryo stretched from the middle of the Korean peninsula into Northeast China; about two-thirds of its territory was in present-day Manchuria.) Beijing deleted references to Koguryo from government histories of Korea on official web sites and then, because of protests from the South Korean government, deleted all pre-1948 Korean history.

China's motives for claiming Koguryo as its own seem to revolve largely around the possibility of territorial disputes over Manchuria in the event of Korean reunification or North Korean collapse. With more than 2 million *Chosonjok* living in contemporary Manchuria, Beijing wants to forestall any claims on the territory as belonging to a contemporary Korean state. The ceding of any Chinese territory to Korea would be fuel for China's 55 other ethnic minorities and a blow to Beijing's One People policy. The rewriting of history, however, galvanized South Korean civil society and forced the Seoul government to act. Any attempt by an outside power, such as China, to deny that Koguryo is part of Korean history can be seen as a denial of Korean nationhood, an act of aggression that threatens the very existence of Korea as a human collectivity. North Korea has not offered any direct criticism, but the newspaper of *Chosen Soren*, the pro-North Korean General Association of Korean Residents in Japan, described China's attempt to incorporate the history of Koguryo into its own history as a serious distortion.[117]

In August 2004, China and South Korea reached a five-point "verbal understanding" after nine and a half hours of negotiations. The two sides agreed to make joint efforts to prevent the dispute over history from developing into a political issue. Then, in September, an arm of the Chinese Education Ministry acknowledged that it was a "managerial mistake" to say that the Koguryo kingdom was an ancient local government of China. For the time being, at least, China relaxed its claim to this part of Korean history.

[117] K. S. Nam (2004: 9–11).

Conclusion

In the 1980s, Beijing's reform and opening and Seoul's *Nordpolitik* converged to bring about the transformation of Sino–Korean relations. With the successful completion of normalization talks in 1992 came the metamorphosis of Sino–Korean relations from two sets of competing Cold War alliance systems to a more complex, multifaceted triangular relationship. Throughout the 1990s, China reformatted its foreign policy, deciding to play the role of the responsible great power. With its economic growth and regional economic integration, China has become the hub of East Asia, radiating its influence outward in concentric circles, affecting Korean peninsular affairs in particular. The paradox is that the Sino–ROK normalization and the new status of the PRC have come about with neither the disassembly of the remaining Cold War alliance systems in the region – the Sino–DPRK, U.S.–ROK and U.S.–Japan pacts – nor the improvement of the security situation on the Korean peninsula.

Beijing has made it known that its primary interest in Korean affairs is the maintenance of "intermestic" (domestic and near abroad) stability. China sees the regional common interest as promoting the peaceful coexistence of the two Korean states on the peninsula rather than having to cope with chaos in the wake of system collapse in the North. The evolution in Beijing's thinking is evident in the difference between its disinterested stance during the 1994 nuclear crisis and its proactive conflict management diplomacy during the second U.S.–DPRK nuclear standoff. Not only has China found a positive role that it can play in regional geopolitics, but it also has realized the necessity of playing such a role to prevent the Sword of Damocles from falling on its three primary strategic goals and demands: preservation of domestic stability and legitimacy, promotion of a peaceful and secure external (especially near abroad) environment free of threats to China's sovereignty and territorial integrity, and cultivation of its status and influence as a responsible great power in the Asia-Pacific region and beyond. Indeed, the dangerous potential confrontation between an ally once characterized "as close as lips to teeth" and the global hegemon, the United States, is currently the dominant threat to the fourth-generation PRC leadership's single greatest "intermestic" challenge of establishing a stable, orderly, and healthy society.[118]

This evolution of Chinese behavior has led to a subtle and significant change in the foreign policy behavior of South Korea. Whereas for years the ROK lived under the shadow of allied abandonment, fearing a U.S. departure that would leave Seoul exposed to North Korean

118 Y. Wang (1999).

provocations, the movement in China's foreign policy stances has made China an independent variable for the ROK, enabling Seoul to pursue a more independent foreign policy. The fear of allied abandonment has been transformed into a fear of allied entrapment as the United States under the Bush administration pursues its provocative, nonnegotiable policies with regard to North Korea. Increased convergence of stability-centered concerns and interests between Seoul and Beijing has allowed the ROK to create distinctions between its policies and those of the United States while simultaneously doubling Beijing's leverage over Washington and Pyongyang for the conflict management of the second U.S.–DPRK nuclear standoff.

When the ROK and the PRC realized that they had more in common than they had believed, Pyongyang was more or less sidelined. The odd man out, it was all too preoccupied in the 1980s and 1990s with the first ever socialist dynastic succession at home and the increasingly untenable quest for absolute, one-Korea international legitimation. At the very moment when the DPRK might have followed China's cue to change its historical pattern of behavior and become more outwardly oriented, it instead continued to count on its rusty mutual defense pact with the PRC while whispering criticisms of the reform path that the post-Mao Chinese leadership was pursuing.

Of course, China is not without complicity in the matter. Beijing does still try to maintain a difficult two-Korea balancing act, tipping its hat to the North Koreans with substantial amounts of aid, while deepening its economic, diplomatic, and political linkages with South Korea. The momentum of this two-Korea policy is what has enabled Beijing to play a leadership role during the second nuclear standoff because it is one of only two countries (along with Russia) in the six-party talks to have normal diplomatic relations with all five other players. For a country trying to demonstrate its new, pragmatic, responsible great-power diplomacy, the second nuclear standoff represents an opportunity for China to exploit.

At the same time, however, the nuclear situation on the Korean peninsula represents a great danger to China. As South Korean and Japanese companies relocate their manufacturing bases to China, and as the PRC's economy becomes increasingly integrated in – indeed begins to take a leadership role in – East Asia, China desperately needs to prevent political instability in its backyard that could yield social instability spilling over its borders. China's ascent into the hub of East Asia – in contrast to President Roh Moo-hyun's inaugural attempt to claim that role for South Korea – means that it must protect its spokes from injury. China's role as the responsible great power is not only a national identity issue, but also a practical one for the world's fastest-growing economy and third largest trading power.

The Korean peninsula, then, is an issue of central interest to China and is demonstrative of the surprising ways in which international politics can shift. Through its decision to normalize relations with South Korea and to maintain an anachronistic defense pact with North Korea, China has created both opportunities and concerns for itself in its quest for regional leadership and recognition as a responsible great power. Growing economic linkages with South Korea have been coeval with sustained aid-giving to North Korea, and whereas China's diplomatic presence has freed South Korea from some of the strictures of the alliance with the United States, Chinese ties to North Korea have created certain restrictions for the PRC. It is clear that the evolution of the Korean peninsula and indeed the evolution of NEA as a notional region will remain intimately related to, and perhaps dependent on, the contours of the Seoul–Beijing–Pyongyang triangle of relations.

Although the transformation of relations to a stable triangle was an outgrowth of the interaction of domestic and external factors, as well as the underlying and proximate causes, what really mattered in the end was political leadership in Beijing. Political leadership mattered in the sense that the paramount leader Deng in Beijing – and to a lesser extent President Roh Tae Woo in Seoul – played a determinative role at the starting and ending points in the incremental decision-making process between 1978 and 1992. The prime motive of Seoul's *Nordpolitik*, in which Beijing's recognition was the ultimate prize, was initially more political than economic, whereas Beijing sought multiple goals such as economic benefits, alleviating Pyongyang's one-Korea angst, enhancing its influence in Korean affairs, and expanding and diversifying its foreign policy options by eyeing East Asia as the center of Chinese power and influence.

To explain the Sino–ROK normalization in terms of national identity theory is to argue that in the long Deng decade (1978–92) both Beijing and Seoul made remarkable adjustments in their respective national identities and role conceptions to establish a better congruence between foreign policies and emerging trends in world politics. Pyongyang, in contrast, has remained, at least until mid-2002, smugly ensconced in the cocoon of the socialist hermit kingdom. Indeed, post-Mao China can be seen as drawing on a variety of national identities and roles to readjust its foreign policy to the changing domestic, regional, and global circumstances. For the fiftieth birthday of the PRC, Beijing floated no less than fifty officially sanctioned political slogans. This does not mean China has fifty national identities or roles, but it certainly suggests that China has more than a single identity to enact and that there is now growing difficulty in the prioritization of these multiple identities.

In implementing the two-Korea decision in the postnormalization period, China and South Korea had to work in an uncertain and complex strategic setting where contradictory historical, ideological, geostrategic, and geoeconomic factors were at work. China's two-Korea policy and South Korea's one-China policy are necessarily a balancing act, reflecting and effecting their respective basic principles and interests, as well as their consecutive and simultaneous participation, in multiple games on the bilateral, regional, and global chessboards, with all their complexities and variations.

With the demise of the Sino–Soviet competition over North Korea, there emerged a more complex geoeconomic and geostrategic triangle involving three sets of asymmetrical mutual interests and perceptions – Beijing–Seoul, Beijing–Pyongyang, and Seoul–Pyongyang. On the first and second sides of the triangle, Beijing sought to maintain its traditional geostrategic ties with North Korea even as it promoted new geoeconomic ties with South Korea. On the third side of the triangle, the most turbulent and contentious domain at least until the 2000 inter-Korean summit, Beijing tried hard to keep out of harm's way by following a strategy of calculated ambiguity and equidistance during the first U.S.–DPRK nuclear standoff of 1993–94. But symbolic of the changes in the PRC–ROK–DPRK triangle, Beijing has been centrally and crucially involved in the second U.S.–DPRK nuclear standoff and has worked to bring both sides to the negotiating table and succeeded in the fourth round of six-party talks in crafting the Joint Statement of Principles (on September 19, 2005) as a group consensus and roadmap for moving forward the six-party process from the agreed-upon Joint Statement to a coordinated "action for action" and "commitment for commitment" implementation process.

The Beijing–Pyongyang–Seoul triangular relationship faces several major challenges ahead. First, there is the challenge of implementing the two-Korea decision. The fact that China and the two Koreas have come to interact with each other in more channels, with more depth and complexity, and in more arenas than ever before has brought about some serious managerial problems for all parties involved. More and different actors or interests now comprise different aspects of the Beijing–Seoul–Pyongyang triangular relationship. As Beijing and Seoul's integration with the outside world widens and deepens in tandem with Pyongyang's economic crisis, new domestic and international groups with varying sets of interests will strive to "participate" in the remaking and unmaking of the triangular relations.

Like it or not, China's two-Korea policy cannot be contained in a bilateral framework. The capacity of Beijing and Seoul to initiate and implement parallel policies and structures toward each other regarding foreign trade and investment, maritime and fishery disputes, North Korea's nuclear weapons and missile programs, human rights issues, and Korean reunification is constrained as well by the norms and practices of important domestic groups; Northeast Asian regional and global regimes; and the United States, Japan, and Russia. Consider the extent to which North Korean high-profile defectors and low-profile food refugees/defectors have made a crash landing on the Beijing–Seoul–Pyongyang triangular relationship in recent years. Of course Beijing, Seoul, and Pyongyang cannot separate their foreign policy thinking and strategies from their overall definition of and response to a new Northeast Asian regional order.

The second challenge ahead is that China and the two Koreas, like all other states in the turbulent post–Cold War world, are confronted with the relentless twin pressures of globalization from without and above and localization (*glocalization*) from within and below. The prime force for nationalistic behavior in the post-Tiananmen era is not any sense of an imminent military threat from an external power but the leadership's resolve to enact China's national identity as an up-and-coming great power in the Asia-Pacific region, so as to make up for growing domestic social, environmental, and security deficits.

Third and finally, all states in the post–Cold War world, especially multinational states such as China and divided nations such as the two Koreas and China, have to cope with wrenching national identity difficulties. Although commanding a rather unique position as the only major power that maintains good relationship with both Koreas, Beijing has the daunting task of managing the primal reality that China and Korea remain the last two Cold War legacies of divided polity. Given the growing chasm between the two halves of Korea, any scenario of Korean reunification poses troubling implications for China's own unification drive. Although Beijing stresses the fundamental differences between the Chinese and Korean cases, the two-Korea policy can only underscore the fact that the two Chinas, too, are going their separate ways.

CHAPTER 3

Russia and the Two Koreas

> To industrialize our country, the primary issue before us is to learn from the Soviet Union. . . . we must set going a tidal wave of learning from the Soviet Union on a nationwide scale, in order to build up our country . . . 'follow the path of the Russians.'
>
> – Renmin ribao [People's Daily], *14 February 1953*[1]

> One cannot say that, as it stands, the post-1991 Russian Federation is really a nation-state. It is more a bleeding hulk of empire: what happened to be left over when the other republics broke away.
>
> – *Geoffrey Hosking, 1997*[2]

> And all our decisions, all our actions must be designed to secure Russia a place among strong, economically developed and influential countries in the foreseeable future. . . . I believe that Russia's return to the community of rich, developed, strong, and respected countries of the world must be our fundamental goal.
>
> – *Vladimir Putin, 2003*[3]

The Russia Factor

What is most striking about the new identity and role of Russia in Korean affairs is not that there have been no situation-specific turns and twists – for indeed there were many, as we discuss later in the chapter – but that in the transition from the Cold War to post–Cold War era Moscow, more than Washington, Beijing, or Tokyo, started with a bang and ended

[1] *Renmin ribao* [*People's Daily*], February 14, 1953. [2] Hosking (1997: 484–85).
[3] Putin (2003: 1, 8).

with a whimper. Although Soviet Russia played an integral part in the competing Cold War alliance systems in East Asia and beyond (e.g., its acceptance of a U.S. proposal for the Korean division in August 1945, its Sovietization and sponsorship of the establishment of the Democratic People's Republic of Korea [DPRK] in 1948, its support of Kim Il Sung's initiation of the Korean War in 1950, and the USSR–DPRK security pact in 1961), its sudden decline and demise also ushered in the post–Cold War era, but it did so with many paradoxical consequences.

The precipitous and traumatic decline of Russia from great-power status to that of a poor state – and the lack of a widely accepted "national" identity – explains the turbulence of Russia's foreign policy in general and Korea policy in particular in the post–Cold War era. The continued decline of the Russia Federation in the 1990s occurred concurrently with the rise of China, and the trajectory of the DPRK in the 1990s mirrored that of the former socialist superpower. So far, however, North Korea has avoided the USSR's ultimate demise, while South Korea has continued its march of integration into the global economy and liberal democracy. Considering Russia, China, the DPRK, and the ROK together, it is obvious that the most extreme swings in national power in the last quarter of the twentieth century have occurred in NEA.

The 1990s were tough on Russia in particular, and the country underwent major declines in nearly all dimensions of power. Until the early 1970s, the communist economies kept pace with their capitalist adversaries, but the Soviet economy floundered in the face of relentless globalization pressures: its state-run enterprises and heavy industry could not compete in the rapid development world of information technology and flexible production. Having produced 7 percent of the world's GNP in 1980, Russia was producing only 1.5 percent in 2001. Between 1990 and 2001, a period of global economic boom, Russia's annual GNP averaged a negative growth rate of 3.7 percent, an average worse even than that of the DPRK.[4] Concurrently, China's economy was on the rise, more than tripling from 3.3 percent of global GNP in 1980 to 10.7 percent in 1997. An even greater swing in industrial power occurred in the period from 1980 to 1997, with USSR/Russia's share of global industrial production declining from 9.0 percent in 1980 to 1.8 percent in 1997 (as China's share rose from 3.0 percent in 1980 to 15.3 percent in 1997), as shown in Table 3.1. In short, it is in NEA that a rising China, a declining post-Soviet Russia, a rising South Korea, and a declining North Korea have brought about the greatest swings in economic power in the last half-century.[5]

[4] See World Bank (2003a: 238–39).

[5] The concern for such major power transitions led many realists in the early 1990s to make dire "back to the future" predictions that East Asia was primed for the revival of

Table 3.1. Changing USSR/Russia's Shares of Global GNP and Industrial Production in Comparative Perspective, 1980–97

	1980	1990	1995	1997
Shares of Global GNP (%)				
USSR/Russia	7.0	5.6	1.9	1.7
USA	22.3	22.5	20.8	20.6
China	3.3	6.6	10.7	10.7
Japan	8.0	9.0	7.7	7.7
Shares of Global Industrial Production (%)				
USSR/Russia	9.0	7.0	2.0	1.8
USA	18.7	17.4	16.9	16.6
China	3.0	8.0	14.1	15.3
Japan	7.3	8.7	7.1	6.9

Source: Adapted from Paviatenko (1999: 20–21).

Russia's federal government at the end of the 1990s collected less than 9 percent of its GDP in revenue, a ratio too small to sustain a national government whatever its condition.[6] The Russian military, which long held the top position in the accounting of number of soldiers on active duty (some 4.3 to 5 million in its heyday), by 1995 had declined to under 2 million members and had fallen from having one-fourth of the world's military strength in 1950 to having only 6 percent in 1995.[7] Further cuts reduced Russian force levels to 961,000 military personnel in 2005. Beyond the decline in internal capabilities, today's Russia, like Lenin's Russia, finds itself largely without military allies.[8]

Although these figures are such that some might dismiss Russia's power or influence, it remains a contender for the category of world power. The Russian landmass is the largest in the world, and its population is the sixth largest. Its military, although diminished, is still the fifth largest in the world in terms of manpower, and only the United States spends more money on its military. Russia is one of the five permanent members of the UN Security Council, and its nuclear arsenal makes it the only country capable of removing the United States from the planet. Because oil prices have risen since 1999, so has Russia's economic growth; Russian

a classical great-power rivalry that would be more prone to instability and conflict than were bipolar systems. For realist analyses along this line with some variations, see Betts (1993/94); Friedberg (1993/94, 2000); Buzan and Sigal (1994).

6 In the United States, where the share of GDP spent on national government is among the lowest of advanced countries, it is still nearly 20 percent. Legvold (1999: 171).

7 Pastor (1999: 21). 8 Legvold (1999: 173).

GDP grew by 8.2 percent in 2003 and 7.2 percent in 2004 on the back of four straight years of rising oil prices. Yet, rather than assuring the country, these points of strength compound its sense of identity crisis: how can a nation with so much lethal power be undergoing a process that some have described as Third Worldization?

Robert Legvold argues that the collapse of the Soviet Union "was less the disintegration of a state than the decolonization of the last empire."[9] Similarly, Robert Jervis points out that the collapse of the Soviet Union was akin to a major military defeat – such as those proposed by realist power transition theory – but without a victorious power to take over the country, fill the power vacuum, and provide new rules.[10] This prevailing uncertainty in Russia spread throughout the Northeast Asian region. The cumulative effect of the fading of the Cold War, the collapse of the Soviet Union, and the demise of the Soviet threat reflected the end of old certainties and the beginning of more complex, shifting, and diffuse patterns of power and influence in the region. The shifting roles of the Big Four in Korean affairs have a lot to do with the wrenching national identity difficulties that practically all states have encountered in trying to adjust to a world in which conflict no longer takes place along an East–West axis. For Russia this has meant both crisis, because of its departure from is central position, and also opportunity, because of its new need and capacity to define its place in NEA.

Because of the power of geography, Russia had no choice but to define a place for itself in NEA. No matter what political, military, economic, or ideological disagreements exist, a shared border usually means a common stake in good relations. This is particularly true for a Russia concerned primarily about Europe and wanting mostly to maintain a status quo on its Far Eastern flank. In fact, Russia's failure to specify its interests in resolving the Korean "nuclear crisis" of 1993–94 resulted in a decrease in Russian prestige on the Korean peninsula.[11]

A crisis of self-definition may occur at any time in a nation's development when the consensually agreed-on national developmental trajectory is thrown open to fundamental question. Such a crisis is likely to erupt at three different junctures: when the chosen developmental "road" conspicuously fails, when it succeeds beyond expectations, and when it is challenged by a convincing alternative.[12] The USSR was faced with both its own failure and the success of the United States. Because who we are depends on where we are going, if we have been moving toward a dead end, then a fundamental rethinking is called for. This was the case with

[9] Legvold (1999: 158). [10] Jervis (1991/92: 41). [11] Toloraya (2003a: 26).
[12] Dittmer and Kim (1993a: 29–30).

regard to the Soviet Union after the death of Brezhnev, and it became essential during the Gorbachev and Yeltsin eras.

Undertaking this thinking with regard to contemporary NEA situates Russia in a markedly different environment from that known to any previous Russian leader during the past three centuries. First, in contrast to its immediate neighbors – China, Japan, and the two Koreas – Russia found itself at the beginning of the post–Cold War period in a state of precipitous socioeconomic, political, and military decline. Even in 1905, when defeated by Japan, Russia remained notably more powerful than either the underdeveloped and incompetent China or the soon-to-be-colonized Korea. Second, Russian military capability in East Asia was severely diminished at the start of the 1990s. The Pacific Fleet, for example, which was the largest of the four fleets in the Soviet Navy, deploying the most surface ships, was aging and lacked funds to operate. Third, even if Russia desired to continue the Soviet role of great power patron-protector to North Korea, its ability to do so was much reduced. It lacked the wherewithal to service the DPRK's dependence on imports of energy and heavy industrial equipment. This factor alone could account for the withering of Moscow's influence in Pyongyang, but the Kremlin compounded it with an intense policy of pro-Westernism in the early 1990s.

This is perhaps the first time in its history when Russia has been forced to identity itself and its national interests.[13] In doing so, different segments of Russian society have referred to one of three incompatible worldviews.[14] Conservative nationalists, the most militant Communists, and the so-called Eurasianists believe that the Russian Federation should try to restore a union including as many former Soviet republics as possible. Others adopt an idea that was prevalent in the prerevolutionary period – Russia as the union of Great Russians, White Russians (Belarussians), and Little Russians (Ukrainians), an idea of Slavic unity closely identified with Soviet dissident author Aleksandr Solzhenitsyn and involving ambitions to include other areas with Russian populations, such as northern Kazakhstan. Its supporters reflect back on the great age of Russian identity after the Napoleonic wars, when Russian music, painting, and most notably Russian literature flowered.[15] A third vision integrates the Russian-speaking diaspora into the federation and allows, perhaps, some non–Russian-speaking autonomies – such as Tuva or Tataristan – to separate from the Russian state.

Beyond these visions, it is important to note that expansion in the East has been a traditional trope of Russian behavior when things have not gone well in Europe. Following the Russo–Turkish war of 1878, Russia reoriented itself toward Central Asia and the Far East; the USSR repeated

[13] Prizel (1998: 6). [14] Tolz (1998). [15] See Prizel (1998: 168).

this pattern in the late 1980s, in the face of the crumbling and ultimate collapse first of its holdings in Eastern Europe and then of the USSR itself.[16] Frustration with the realities of Russia and ambiguity concerning Russia's role in Europe created in the Russian psyche a strong dependence on military power to compensate for the sense of inferiority vis-à-vis the West, although most Russian nationalists viewed expansion as a way of affirming Russia's status as a great European power.[17]

When identity is blocked in one domain, it seeks to compensate in another. In the case of post-Soviet Russia, many Russians are humiliated by the sudden disintegration of the Soviet Union and blame the West for it. They are inclined to seek compensation in arguments about the exceptional civilizational role of Russia. The question of civilizational identity has become the central issue of nearly all political debates; all public and political figures, as well as all people of any standing in today's Russia, are forced to state clearly their position on this issue. Different answers to the questions "Who are we?" and "Where are we going?" divide Russian society no less deeply than do social inequality and political sympathies or idiosyncrasies.[18]

Russian exceptionalism is also said to stem from two ineluctable geographical facts: even post-Soviet Russia has the largest territory in the post–Cold War world, and Russia is the only truly Eurasian continental power. That is, even in an era of globalization, size matters in the mobilization and projection of Russia's identity as a great power. It expresses as well Moscow's inability and unwillingness to define its identity as anything but a great power. No matter how weak it was at the moment, Russia continued to identify itself internally and externally as a great power, and "great powers seldom operate under the same rules and constraints as lesser powers."[19] Nonetheless, the lack of a clear, coherent, or widely accepted national identity has lain at the core of Russia's foreign policy fluctuations in the post–Cold War era.

In a rare piece by a Russian scholar addressing Russia's national identity crisis, Sergei Kortunov, a national security adviser in the Putin administration, argues, "Political decisions on which the country's future for many years to come depend cannot be based merely on pragmatism even if they look absolutely correct and the only possible ones for the time being. I should say that there is a direct cause-and-effect connection between the practically zero economic growth and a practically non-existent national identity."[20] Kortunov believes that Russia must either embrace its identity as a former imperial power or else resolve itself to forget about national identity in favor of lingering in the antinational Soviet past. With an

[16] See Hauner (1992). [17] Prizel (1998: 172–73). [18] Podberezsky (1999: 34).
[19] Suny (1999/2000: 149). [20] Kortunov (2003: 97).

almost primordialist faith in the Russian empire, he asserts that the Soviets deprived Russia of its "civilizational and liberatory mission," making it a scarecrow for a world that feared communist expansion.[21] As the three visions of Russia imply, however, there is little civilizational or ideational consensus in Russia.[22]

Increasing unity and direction seem to have come to Russia since the appointment-cum-election of Vladimir Putin to the presidency in March 2000. Since Putin took office, Russia's GDP has increased by 20 percent, capital investment by more than 30 percent during the first three years of his presidency, and exports by one-fourth during that same time period. In particular, Russia has emerged as a major fuel and energy exporter in the world, something that gives it particular influence in energy-strapped NEA. For the first time in half a century, Russia ceased to be an importer of grain and became an exporter in 2002. Mobile phone usage has doubled every year, and an estimated 10 million people in Russia today use the Internet.[23]

However, the Russian Federation's economic foundation is still shaky and very weak; most sectors of the economy are not competitive. The political system has not developed much in fifteen years of democratic experience, and the state apparatus is inefficient. Despite the return of 7 million ethnic Russians from the former Soviet republics, the Russian population is shrinking because of a simultaneous decrease in the birth rate and increase in the death rate, notably among men. The Chechen rebellion, associated terrorism, and other separatist movements pose a threat to internal security. Two provisos are therefore essential in considering Russia's role in Korean peninsular affairs. First, Russian foreign policy – more so than that of other countries – must be seen as in flux. In addition, of the Big Four (China, Russia, Japan, and the United States), Russia is the country that has the least material leverage in Korean affairs, although this is not to say that it is not angling for more.

The common strand connecting diverse groups in post-Soviet Russia is that they attempt to use foreign policy as a tool to advance their vision of Russia's national identity. The dialectical process of sorting out future leadership in Russia, therefore, will ultimately shape the country's world outlook.[24] In terms of Korea, this has meant, since 1999 or early 2000, a two-Korea policy that has established a stable "equal involvement" balance between the ROK and the DPRK (as compared with a hesitant "equidistant" policy). Moscow views Seoul as a potential pillar of support for its economic resurgence and integration into NEA, while eyeing Pyongyang as the key to its diplomatic and geopolitical resurgence. Russia seems to

[21] Kortunov (2003: 100–02). [22] See Podberezsky (1999: 50–51). [23] Putin (2003: 6).
[24] Prizel (1998: 11).

have perceived a "pivotal role" for itself when the Sunshine Policy started in 1998 and even more so when the second U.S.–DPRK standoff over nuclear weapons began in late 2002.[25]

This interpretation, however, is not indisputable. Nikolai Sokov argues, from a close reading of basic Russian documents on foreign and national security policy, that Russia does not have a long-term policy toward the Korean peninsula. He believes that Russian policy exists only with respect to the external aspects of the situation on the peninsula – nonproliferation problems or international consequences of various scenarios of unification – and points out that no politically relevant interest groups in Russia associate themselves with either of the two Koreas. As far as Russia is concerned, the main actors in NEA are the great powers: the United States, China, and Japan. In addition, Russia is reactive rather than proactive, and it apparently lacks a set of goals with regard to Korea. Russia therefore desires to be on the inside track of any negotiations regarding the peninsula and is generally supportive of the status quo; it does not perceive a military threat coming from the peninsula.[26]

Indeed, it would seem accurate to describe Soviet policy toward the Korean peninsula during the Cold War as "derivative."[27] The USSR viewed its interactions with North and South Korea vis-à-vis the other major powers in the world, so these interactions have traditionally been situated within broader swaths of Russian foreign policy. This past, however, is not a reason to assume that Russo–Korean interactions are the same today. In fact, because of diminished national power and its desire to enact a national identity via foreign policy, Russia may be taking a new approach to the Korean peninsula in the post–Cold War world. Rather than the persistence of Russian indifference, today what might limit Russia's involvement on the Korean peninsula is instead Korean preferences for interacting with the other members of the Big Four. The stability and sustainability of Russia's preferred national identity as a great power is closely keyed to and shaped by two factors: the support of Russia's significant others, and the material and ideational resources undergirding Moscow's foreign policy in general and its Korea policy in particular.

Weight of the Past

The course of Russo–Korean history followed a sinusoidal wave of development in which three different Russias (Imperial Tsarist Russia, Soviet Russia, and post-Soviet Russia) have interacted with and affected three different Koreas (Chosun Korea, Colonial Korea, and Divided Korea).

[25] Bazhanov (2005). [26] Sokov (2002). [27] S. H. Joo (2003).

Imperial Russian intrigue in Chosun Korea began in the mid-nineteenth century and reached its zenith in the final decade of that century. Then, Japan obtained ascendancy, in part through the military defeat of the Russian Empire, and Russia would remain clear of the colonized Korean peninsula until the Soviet Union's mid-twentieth-century entrance on the northern half of the peninsula, an event that helped create the third Korea: divided Korea. Today, post-Soviet Russia faces a still-divided Korea. The earlier history is helpful in explaining Korea's trajectory into Japanese colonialism, whereas the latter history is to no small degree responsible for the continued bifurcation of and conflict on the peninsula.

During the age of Western imperialism in East Asia, many countries expressed suspicion about Russia's designs on Korea. As early as 1856, a French admiral advised Paris that France should act to take a hold on the Korean peninsula before Russia could encroach there. The Russians were interested in the peninsula's warm-water ports – a traditional Russian concern. As Czar Nicholas II once instructed his foreign minister: "Russia absolutely needs a port free and open throughout the whole year. This port must be located on the mainland (southeast Korea) and must certainly be connected with our possessions by a strip of land."[28] Russia came to share a common border with Korea for the first time in 1860 when it acquired the Maritime Province from China in the Peking Treaty. Japan began to worry about Russian encroachment, both on Japanese territory and on the Korean peninsula; their worries were intensified by a Russian expedition to Tsushima, the island that traditionally mediated Korean–Japanese relations. By 1864, the Koreans themselves were asking the French to keep the Russians off Korean territory, offering to loosen restrictions on Catholicism if they would do so. The French were not willing to help.[29]

After the signing of the Treaty of Kanghwa with Japan in 1876, the Japanese offered their services in countering a Russian threat to Korean territorial integrity, but the Koreans refused the offer until China urged them to pursue closer ties with Japan.[30] Russian interest in Korea, therefore, propelled Korea closer to Japan in the late 1870s. Following a rise in anti-Japanese sentiment in the 1880s, inspired by Japan's participation in a progressive coup attempt, the Korean court turned toward Russia as a possible protector from both declining China and aggressive Japan.[31] The Russians, however, were mostly interested in protecting their interests in Manchuria from any threat emanating from or traveling through

[28] Quoted in S. S. Cho (1967: 49). [29] K. H. Kim (1980: 41, 79–80, 89–91, 45–46).
[30] K. H. Kim (1980: 300). [31] C. I. Kim and H. K. Kim (1967: 61–63).

the Korean peninsula, although Czar Nicholas II did express the traditional interest in a warm-water port on the Korean peninsula.[32]

When Japan used its victory over China in the Sino–Japanese War of 1894–95 to reap enormous territorial gains and new regional privileges in the Treaty of Shimonoseki, Russia joined with Germany and France to stage the Triple Intervention, forcing Japan to return the Liaotung (Liaodong) peninsula to China and to honor, for the time being, Korea's independence. In addition, Russia renewed its interest in the Far East and began an expansionary period. Japanese intrigue in Seoul in 1896 led to the smuggling of the Korean king into the Russian legation, which began a brief period of Russian ascendancy in Korea. By 1898, the Russians were out of favor with the Koreans, and, beginning with the naval battle of Inchon on the first day of the Russo–Japanese War in 1904, the Russians also were out of Korea, leaving Japan ascendant on the peninsula for the next four decades.[33] In the Russian Far East, there was occasional talk of a "yellow peril" created by Korean and Chinese migrants, and after Stalin became head of the USSR, he deported some 180,000 Koreans to the Central Asian republics because of paranoia about Japanese spies. Some 20,000 ethnic Koreans died in the Soviet Union in the 1930s, either because of the forced relocation or from forced labor and imprisonment.[34] In 1993, the Russian Parliament recognized the illegality of this repression and affirmed the right of Koreans in Russia to national development and equal opportunity in the exercise of their political freedoms.[35]

The fact that North Korea is beyond compare on Stalinism, that it has been most frequently called a Stalinist state, and that it has gained the dubious distinction of being the one and only country in the post–Cold War era still offering a postmortem imprimatur of the late Soviet dictator Joseph Stalin,[36] speak directly to the shadow of the Soviet past for the northern half of the Korean peninsula. However, contrary to some widely held contemporary views that were ready-made for the politics of competitive legitimation and delegitimation in later years, the initial decision for a zonal plan – to draw a line at the thirty-eighth parallel for dividing up Japanese troop surrender arrangements – was not a secret

[32] S. H. Chang (1974: 303) and S. H. Joo (2003).

[33] C. I. Kim and H. K. Kim (1967: 83, 85, 88–91, 94–96, 102).

[34] V. Li (2000b: 349–446); Wishnick (2001a). [35] Wishnick (2004).

[36] As late as 1996, for example, the Soviet "revisionists" were condemned in North Korea because they branded "loyalty to Stalin as a personal idolatry . . . The counterrevolutionary maneuvers perpetrated by those traitors, who debased Stalin, who had fostered the younger Soviet Union into a great power, blotting out all of his prestige and achievements, were the meanest act of betrayal which is beyond imagination." *Rodong Sinmun [Worker's Daily]*, November 3, 1996. For a more detailed analysis of the place of Stalinism in the North Korean system, see Armstrong (2001).

deal made at the Yalta Conference (in the manner of the infamous Taft-Katsura deal of 1905)[37] but wholly an American decision taken during a night-long session of the State-War-Navy Coordinating Committee on August 10–11, 1945. Two young military officers (Colonels Charles H. Bonesteel III and Dean Rusk) were given only thirty minutes to find on a map an appropriate place to divide Korea and selected the thirty-eighth parallel because it would place the capital city of Seoul in the U.S. occupation zone. The day after the plan was communicated to the Soviets, Stalin sent a message to Truman: "I have received your message with the General Order No. 1. Principally I have no objections against the contents of the order."[38]

Nothing stood in the way of Soviet troops marching down to the southern end of the Korean peninsula in mid-August 1945; they had entered Korea almost a full month before American forces, with the entire peninsula its for the taking. A combination of geopolitical considerations may explain why Stalin accepted the American zonal plan without objections. First, Stalin may have interpreted the zonal plan as a sphere-of-influence redux in East Asia because Russia and Japan had conducted secret negotiations early in the twentieth century on the possible division of Korea along either the thirty-eighth or the thirty-ninth parallels.[39] Second, Stalin's main geopolitical interests at the time were more in Manchuria and Northern Japan than in Korea. Third, Stalin probably desired to continue Allied cooperation, or at least not to alienate the United States by occupying the whole peninsula in mid-1945, because Japan was the key focus of Soviet interest in terms of a postwar settlement. Whatever the real reason, Stalin permitted joint divisional action in Korea at a time when he had the military power to grab the whole peninsula.

The hardening of the ad hoc division of Korea was a direct consequence of early postwar superpower conflict. When Russia reentered the Korean peninsula in August 1945, memories of imperial Russia did not have much impact on Korean opinions. Soviet occupation authorities accomplished the Sovietization of North Korea in a relatively short time period, taking full advantage of the lack of resistance to their presence or programs.[40] During the Soviet occupation period (1945–48), the politics of everyday life were largely devoted to building the Soviet-style party, military, and governmental infrastructures needed for the founding of the KWP (August 28–30, 1946), the KPA (February 8, 1948), and the DPRK (September 9, 1948).

[37] In 1905, the United States, in a secret agreement between Prime Minister Katsura and Secretary of War Taft, officially approved Japan's suzerainty (hegemony) over Korea in return for a Japanese disavowal of any claims on the Philippines.

[38] Quoted in S. S. Cho (1967: 55). [39] S. S. Cho (1967: 49).

[40] See D. S. Suh (1988: 59–73).

One thing seems clear enough – that Kim Il Sung could not possibly have risen in informal politics as *primus inter pares* without Soviet support. The first constitution of the DPRK (1948) formalized the outcome of the informal politics of the occupation period and was patterned after the Soviet (Stalin) Constitution. As Dae-Sook Suh put it, "All administrative directives and decisions by the Soviet occupation authorities were executed through Kim, making him the pivotal link between the Korean people and the occupation forces."[41] There is no easy or simple answer as to why the Soviet occupation authorities picked Kim as the Soviet man in Pyongyang. One factor might have been Soviet determination to pick a man without past factional entanglements. Kim Il Sung was one of a few communists who had not only escaped Japanese arrest but had also avoided getting himself trapped in the old factional strife.[42] Several major political groups were contending for power in the north of Korea after liberation: (1) the domestic noncommunist nationalists; (2) the most numerous domestic communist group, which mostly was operating in Seoul where they believed their political future was to be decided (a major strategic blunder); (3) the Yan'an group of returned revolutionaries from China; (4) the Soviet-Korean group, composed of Soviet-Koreans who returned home with Soviet military forces; and (5) the partisan group – also known as the Kapsan group – made up of Kim Il Sung's own guerrilla fighters who were with him in Manchuria. The domestic communist and Yan'an groups were not united in supporting a single political leader, whereas the Kapsan partisan group and those Soviet-Koreans who returned to Korea as regular members of the Soviet army were united in supporting Kim Il Sung. Moreover, Kim Il Sung's control of military and security forces meant that no other group had real power.[43]

Kim had retreated into the Soviet Far East to evade the pursuing Japanese forces in March 1941, and he was trained in the Soviet Union for four and a half years (1941–45). He could speak a little Russian and was perceived as a man of swift action, according to Hwang Jang-yop.[44] Emerging from a fractured and muddied political scene in the Soviet occupation period, and taking full advantage of it, Kim Il Sung had demonstrated the resilience, resourcefulness, tenacity, and absolute opportunism of a formidable guerrilla fighter turned into a superb politician with a Machiavellian/Stalinist sense of timing and sensitivity to the changing correlation of domestic and external political forces. He maneuvered masterfully to control the agenda of informal politics and to gradually and

[41] D. S. Suh (1988: 72).
[42] Scalapino and Lee (1972: 326). For a similar argument, see McCormack (1993: 22–23); Wada (1992).
[43] D. S. Suh (1988: 73). [44] *Chosun Ilbo*, June 15, 1998 (Internet version).

methodically smash all rival political groups for two and a half decades, understood as the first consolidation cycle in the DPRK.[45]

It is now abundantly clear, since the post–Cold War opening of important archival materials in the former Soviet Union in 1992–94, that the outbreak of the Korean War on June 25, 1950, was not the first salvo in a well-planned communist expansionism controlled from the Kremlin, as many traditionalists argued, nor was it primarily a civil conflict with only marginal involvement by the Soviets, nor was Kim Il Sung driven to war by South Korea's recurring provocations, as the revisionists would have us believe.[46] The idea of initiating the war came directly from Kim Il Sung, who began lobbying for a Soviet-backed invasion as early as March 1949, with the assurance that it would take no more than three days to "liberate" the South, leaving the United States no time to intervene. Stalin rejected this plan on several grounds: it was not necessary because North Korean forces could cross the thirty-eighth parallel only as a counterattack, the Chinese Civil War was still unresolved, and the North Korean military was still weak and ill prepared.[47] Central to Stalin's strategic thinking in the face of Kim Il Sung's repeated entreaties in 1949 was the determination to avoid any military confrontation with the United States. Only in May 1950 did Stalin explain to Mao Zedong that it was now possible to agree to the North Koreans' proposal "in light of the changed international situation."[48]

The changes in the international situation from March 1949 to May 1950 included (1) the victory of the Chinese Communist Revolution and establishment of the PRC in October 1949; (2) the Soviet testing of an atom bomb in 1949; (3) the withdrawal of American troops from South Korea in June 1949; and (4) the perceived weakening of American resolve indicated, for instance, by Secretary of State Dean Acheson's exclusion of the Korean peninsula from the American defense perimeter in the Asia-Pacific region in January 1950. Stalin gave the final go-ahead on the basis of Soviet geopolitical interests and his short- and long-term estimates of the U.S. strategic posture in East Asia. But the necessary condition was Mao Zedong's consent. Stalin calculated that Kim Il Sung's

[45] For a more detailed analysis, see S. S. Kim (2000c).

[46] The new Soviet archival materials on the Korean War became available in 1992–93. Then, in July 1994, Russian President Boris Yeltsin presented South Korean President Kim Young Sam with a collection of documents from the Presidential Archive, the still-closed Kremlin repository that holds the Soviet records of greatest sensitivity. In 1995, the Wilson Center's Cold War International History Project (CWIHP) in Washington, DC, obtained a larger set of documents from the same archive. For a detailed study of these newly available archival materials, see Bajanov (1995); Weathersby (1995, 1996, 1999). For a review of the traditionalist literature, see H. J. Kim (1990, 1994). For the most influential revisionist work, see Cumings (1981, 1990).

[47] Bajanov (1995); Weathersby (1995, 1999). [48] Weathersby (1999: 93).

victory would produce multiple geostrategic benefits: enlarging the Soviet security zone, providing a springboard against Japan, testing American resolve, intensifying the hostility between Beijing and Washington, and forcing a diversion of U.S. military forces from Europe to Asia.[49]

The Korean War brought about several unexpected and paradoxical consequences for both Soviet foreign policy and Soviet–DPRK relations. First, the Sino–Soviet alliance formally forged on February 14, 1950 was at once strengthened in the short run and weakened in the long run. The irony is that the Sino–Soviet split became the unavoidable consequence of growing equality in the alliance. The widening gap between Beijing's rising demands and expectations and Moscow's inability and unwillingness to satisfy them undermined an alliance rooted in shared values and shared fears. Second, the Korean War, more than any other postwar international event, had a decisive catalytic effect in enacting the rules of the Cold War game, bringing about high military budgets, a militarized NATO, the globalization of competing alliance systems, and the dangerous pattern of East–West confrontation in world affairs.[50] Yet, by dint of its timing, its course, and its outcome, "the Korean War served in many ways as a substitute for World War III."[51]

The third consequence of the Korean War was that the balance of influence on the Korean peninsula shifted from Moscow to Beijing, due in no small measure to the Chinese intervention on October 25, 1950. The deepening Sino–Soviet conflict gave Kim Il Sung more leverage opportunities and space than could be realistically considered under the Sino–Soviet alliance. The Soviet army that had successfully maneuvered Kim Il Sung into power failed to return, whereas the Chinese "volunteers" intervened to rescue the fledgling socialist regime on the verge of collapse and stayed on until 1958, marking the end of Soviet domination and the beginning of Chinese influence. Fourth, Kim Il Sung's daring attempt at the reunification-by-war scenario not only resulted in a fratricide claiming millions of lives, but also sealed Korea's fate as a divided polity – two separate, unequal, and incompatible systems moving on two divergent tracks.

From the late 1950s on, Kim Il Sung successfully exploited the emerging Sino–Soviet rift, gaining for himself independence from either of the two large socialist states. Moscow and Beijing tried to offset the other's influence in North Korea with generous economic and military assistance. For a time, Pyongyang sided with Mao against the USSR, then tilted toward Moscow in the late 1960s, during the years of Mao's destructive Great Proletarian Cultural Revolution. Thereafter, North Korea adapted

[49] Goncharov, Lewis, and Xue (1993: 152, 214). [50] See Jervis (1980).
[51] Stueck (1995: 3).

adroitly to his two patrons, whose enmity continued through the 1970s and most of the 1980s. Moscow's aim was to keep Pyongyang from slipping too close to China; the Soviets did not want a new war attempting to reunify Korea.[52] Soviet diplomatic representatives in Pyongyang became accustomed to finding themselves severely isolated in a hostile environment. It is likely that Soviet leaders believed they labored under a permanent, built-in disadvantage when compared with the PRC with regard to predominant influence in Korea. Nonetheless, because the DPRK proved a useful partner in confronting the United States and clear insulation against U.S. troops in South Korea, the USSR continued to provide Pyongyang with the technology and products that it requested. But Moscow viewed North Korea as a functional buffer rather than as a useful ally.[53]

The threat of war on the Korean peninsula was noticed regularly in Moscow. In the early 1960s, when Beijing was ascendant in Pyongyang's strategic thinking, Nikita Khrushchev came to disfavor Kim Il Sung, concerned that the radical fever that infested Beijing and Pyongyang at the time would set the Far East afire in war. Leonid Brezhnev likewise feared a second war in Korea and deemed it important to bring Pyongyang back from its newfound relationship with the PRC. Perceiving North Korea as a strategic ally, a Far Eastern outpost in the overall picture of the Soviet Union's confrontation with the United States, Moscow increased its military and material aid and spared no effort to praise all that Kim Il Sung was doing.[54]

In the mid-1980s, as the Soviet Union was descending onto the path to dissolution, Kim Il Sung visited Moscow for the first time since the late 1960s in an attempt to renew relations. This move was motivated by the improvement of Sino–American relations at a time of U.S.–Soviet tensions. Konstantin Chernenko rewarded Kim's unrelenting anti-Americanism with a substantial aid package: North Korea's debt was deferred, advanced military equipment to upgrade North Korea's air force and air defenses was provided, and Soviet technicians were to help with the transfer of new technology pertaining to conventional and nuclear power generation. When Gorbachev succeeded Chernenko, he continued the commitment to the DPRK, while Pyongyang granted the USSR airspace for military flights to and from Vietnam and agreed to greater naval cooperation, including joint naval operations in the Sea of Japan, as well as Soviet access to the port of Wonsan.[55]

A few years later, however, Gorbachev decided to participate in the Seoul Olympic games and then began the normalization of Soviet–ROK

[52] Rubinstein (1997: 157). [53] Sokov (2002). [54] See Bazhanov (2005).
[55] Rubinstein (1997: 158).

relations. Consular relations were established; permanent trade offices were opened in the respective capitals; a direct sea link was inaugurated between Vladivostok and Pusan; the Soviet press wrote positively on South Korea's economic accomplishments and prospects; trade expanded; and Kim Young Sam, coleader of the Democratic Liberal Party, visited Moscow. To encourage Moscow's disengagement from Pyongyang – and as part of the price for rapid recognition – Seoul started dispensing a $3 billion aid package for the Soviet Union a month after South Korean president Roh Tae Woo made his first official visit to Moscow.

The Making of a Triangular Relationship

Most of post–World War II era was bleak in terms of relations between Soviet Russia and South Korea. For four decades from 1948 to 1988, there was virtually no contact, only the Cold War politics of mutual demonization. Although during the 1970s – when the Cold War was no longer so hot and Third World politics was in its peak – small Third World countries (mostly from Africa) could establish official diplomatic relations with both Korean states, the Soviet Union could not compromise its role as leader of the socialist bloc by recognizing South Korea. The period did lead to an increasing number of diplomatic recognitions for Pyongyang, and consequently, to an intensification of Park Chung Hee's sense of insecurity and siege mentality. This perception was exacerbated by Sino–U.S. rapprochement, the U.S. defeat in Vietnam, and the threatened withdrawal of U.S. troops from South Korea. By mid-1976, Seoul was recognized by ninety-six countries, and ninety-three recognized Pyongyang (Table 6.2).

The Soviet Union would likely have enjoyed benefits from recognition of Seoul, given that the DPRK was not a particularly close ally. The USSR needed North Korea, however, to check the U.S. military presence in NEA and also to remain somewhat neutral in the Sino–Soviet dispute. Moscow therefore adhered to Pyongyang's preference against cross-recognition of the two Korean states. It went so far as to avoid postal or telegraph links with the ROK, and in its official press to refer to South Korea as a "puppet terrorist dictatorship" and a "land of poverty and terror." Seoul responded by labeling the Soviet Union an "evil empire," describing it as responsible for the division of the Korean nation and the establishment of the northern Stalinist regime and as the source of the worldwide "red menace."[56]

By the late 1980s, the situation was changing rapidly in both Moscow and Seoul. Moscow could no longer afford to ignore the rising economic power of South Korea, and simultaneously the fear of communism was

[56] Lankov (2004a).

dying out in an increasingly democratic and prosperous South Korea. The convergence of four momentous events – the rise of Mikhail Gorbachev and perestroika in the USSR (1985), the inauguration of *Nordpolitik* by President Roh Tae Woo in South Korea (July 1988), the staging of the twenty-fourth Olympic Games in Seoul (September 1988), and the Sino–Soviet renormalization (May 1989) – combined to provide the necessary and sufficient synergy for the Soviet–ROK normalization process to proceed with all deliberate speed from 1988 to 1990.

The Gorbachev years yielded "new thinking" in the Soviet Union, including a new revolutionary concept of security that transcended both Marxist class struggle and the Western realist notion of struggle for power among nations.[57] The proposition, advanced by Foreign Minister Eduard Shevardnadze at the 1988 UN General Assembly plenary session, was that a voluntary transfer of certain sovereign rights to the world community was the surest and cheapest way of enhancing national and global security. Gorbachev expounded a Soviet proposal for a comprehensive security system in an unusual newspaper article in September 1987. "The idea of a comprehensive system of security," Gorbachev asserted, "is the first project of a possible new organization of life in our common planetary home. In other words, it is a pass into a future where the security of all is a token of the security of each."[58] Moscow withdrew its troops from Afghanistan, agreed to remove medium-range missiles deployed in Asia, and unilaterally reduced its armed forces. Sino–Soviet relations underwent rapprochement – leading to renormalization in May 1989 – and the East Asian region no longer faced an imminent danger of being sucked into a Sino–Soviet armed conflict.

An even greater impact of the Gorbachev challenge was seen on the Korean peninsula. At first, it did not seem like it would be so. In a July 1986 speech in Vladivostok – his first major statement on Soviet Asia policy – Gorbachev reiterated Soviet support for the DPRK and for North Korea's proposal for a nuclear-free zone on the Korean peninsula. In 1987–88, officials became acutely aware that the Korean problem posed a major obstacle to superpower cooperation in the East Asia, to the establishment of an Asian security system, and to Moscow's participation in international economic cooperation.[59] Beginning in 1988, therefore, Gorbachev took a series of steps that would have a profound impact on the Korean peninsula. In March 1988, the USSR consciously created a loophole in the ban on Soviet travel to South Korea, allowing ethnic Koreans from Sakhalin

[57] For a detailed analysis, see Wishnick (2001b: ch. 6). It should be noted that much of Gorbachev-era new thinking can be traced to the economic difficulties besetting the Soviet Union: the USSR needed to retrench itself globally or face domestic implosion. See S. H. Joo (2000b, 2003) and, more generally, Brooks and Wohlforth (2000/01).

[58] Gorbachev (1987: 16). [59] Bazhanov (2005).

to visit their homeland via third countries. Then, in August 1988, 6,000 Soviet athletes and tourists, accompanied by the Bolshoi Chorus and the Moscow Philharmonic, traveled to Seoul for the 1988 Summer Olympics, despite Moscow's earlier support of a plan for Pyongyang to cohost the event.[60]

The 1988 Seoul Olympiad was a watershed in the acceleration of cross-bloc functional cooperation between Seoul and Moscow, as well as between Seoul and Beijing. Against repeated North Korean demands, Mikhail Gorbachev authorized Soviet participation. The Soviet media broadcast images of South Korea that definitely did not match the official description of the country as an impoverished Third World dictatorship. The Soviet press, increasingly free from censorship, began to extol the economic achievements and prosperity of the capitalist South at a time that Soviet citizens were increasingly disappointed with their own system and looking for positive models elsewhere. During the September games, Gorbachev delivered a speech while traveling across Siberia in which he made it clear that the Soviet Union intended to develop a relationship with South Korea. Following the games, in consideration of Politburo preferences to move slowly, Gorbachev decided to expand nonofficial trade and open consular relations with Seoul.[61] At the same time, Hungary became the first Communist country to establish regular diplomatic relations with Seoul.

With the doors open, newly elected South Korean President Roh Tae Woo announced in July 1988 his *Nordpolitik*, a major policy initiative aimed at improving inter-Korean relations by expanding South Korean political, economic, and cultural ties with the Soviet Union, China, and other socialist states, and urging Japan and the United States to develop better relations with North Korea. Gorbachev in turn formulated a new Asia-Pacific strategy; one of the most interesting and groundbreaking ideas was Soviet recognition of Seoul, which became a key component of Gorbachev's "new thinking" in Asia policy.[62] Soviet interest in Korea shifted from a passive desire to avoid an unwanted confrontation with the United States to a more active solicitation of South Korean support for Soviet Far Eastern development, including greater integration of the Soviet economy with that of the North Pacific Triangle. In 1989, the USSR and the ROK exchanged trade representatives.

Gorbachev and Roh held their first ever meeting in San Francisco in June 1990; Gorbachev pledged to open diplomatic relations, whereas Roh promised aid for the faltering Soviet economy. In early September, Soviet Foreign Minister Eduard Shevardnadze went to Pyongyang to inform Kim Il Sung of Soviet plans to normalize ties with Seoul; he could meet only

[60] Wishnick (2004). [61] Lankov (2004a). [62] Ellison (2001: 165).

with North Korean Foreign Minister Kim Yong Nam for talks that he later described as among the most difficult of his career. On September 30, 1990, the Soviet Union established formal diplomatic relations with South Korea, becoming the first great power with a two-Korea policy. In December 1990, Roh Tae Woo traveled to Moscow to meet with Gorbachev. Pyongyang referred to normalization as "disgusting, nauseating, and unseemly."[63]

When the Kremlin announced in 1990 that it would normalize relations with Seoul, the DPRK said in a memorandum that normalization would imply an end to the DPRK–USSR alliance and that North Korea would have "no other choice but to take measures to provide for ourselves some weapons for which we have so far relied on the alliance."[64] The North Koreans even threatened to retaliate against the Soviet Union by supporting Japanese claims to the South Kuril Islands, and they began referring to ROK–USSR relations as "diplomacy purchased by dollars."[65] Moscow responded by admonishing the DPRK that no matter how hard the USSR tried to help its neighbor, it would be difficult to solve its problems until the confrontation and arms race underway on the Korean peninsula ceased and until the North shed its semi-isolation from economic contacts with the majority of developed countries.[66]

South Korean motivations for opening relations with the USSR were more political than economic. Seoul hoped that Moscow would use its leverage in Pyongyang to push forward inter-Korean dialogue. Indeed, the Soviet–ROK normalization influenced North Korea to open a dialogue with the South at the prime minister level, resulting in two major inter-Korean accords, the Agreement on Reconciliation, Nonaggression, and Exchanges and Cooperation between South and North Korea – better known as Basic Agreement – and the Joint Declaration of the Denuclearization of the Korean peninsula. Moscow's motivations, in contrast, were largely economic; South Korea was willing to provide a $3 billion loan for economic cooperation. In a report to the Supreme Soviet about his visit to South Korea, Gorbachev asserted:

> We have to pay special attention to the experience of South Korea, which has overcome underdevelopment and reached the stage of industrial development within a short period of time. We all know that South Korea was a dictatorial country not too long ago. If the Soviet Union and South Korea can combine the potential power of each country for beneficial and future-oriented economic development, we can certainly establish a creative and efficient model of economic cooperation.[67]

[63] Bazhanov and Bazhanov (1994: 792).
[64] Quoted in Mack (1993: 342). See also Sokov (2002).
[65] Lankov (2004a); *Rodong Sinmun [Worker's Daily]*, October 5, 1990, p. 2.
[66] Bazhanov (2005). [67] *Pravda*, November 22, 1991, quoted in I. J. Kim (1994: 89).

The flurry of diplomacy and change did not end with normalization. Gorbachev visited Cheju Island in April 1991 and announced his support for Korean entry into the UN, for inter-Korean dialogue aimed at reducing peninsular tensions, and for nuclear inspections in North Korea. The Soviet–ROK normalization also led directly to Sino–ROK normalization in 1992. In fact, Gorbachev-era "new thinking" in the Soviet Union led to the complete rearrangement of three crucial strategic triangles in NEA – the ROK–USSR–DPRK triangle, the ROK–PRC–DPRK triangle, and the PRC–USSR–U.S. triangle – repositioning Korea in the global community for the twenty-first century.

After the dissolution of the Soviet Union, Russian President Boris Yeltsin visited South Korea and presented twenty-three economic projects that the Russian Federation and the ROK could develop jointly, including natural resources exploration, cooperation in science and technology, tourism, and the construction of infrastructure such as roads and ports. Yeltsin also asked for more active Korean investment to help the troubled Russian economy. In the ROK–Russia treaty of November 1992, Presidents Roh and Yeltsin affirmed "their conviction that the development of friendly relations and cooperation between the two countries will contribute not only to their mutual benefit but also to the peace, security and prosperity of the Asian and Pacific region and throughout the world."

New Challenges of the Moscow–Seoul–Pyongyang Triangle

At its birth, post-Soviet Russia announced that it was to initiate "a completely fresh policy of unrestrained partnership and integration with the West."[68] President Boris Yeltsin and his foreign minister Andrei Kozyrev actively courted the United States, West European countries, and their allies Japan and South Korea. The remaining communist states – North Korea, Cuba, and Vietnam – were shocked by the virulent anticommunism of the new Russian leaders, particularly when these leaders joined Western states in condemning the human rights records of Cuba and the DPRK. To the Kremlin of the early 1990s, the pure Stalinism of the North Korean system appeared particularly odious.[69]

Although foreign policy makers tried to deny it, the Russian Federation's initial foreign policy orientation had much continuity with the Gorbachev era. In terms of the Korean peninsula, this included continued distancing from North Korea and engagement with South Korea, although the anticommunist tinge was obviously new. In the mid-1990s,

[68] *Moscow News*, January 2, 1992, quoted in Bazhanov (2005). [69] Bazhanov (2005).

however, as reforms encountered ever-greater difficulties and as the public grew disappointed with liberal democrats, Yeltsin had to become more conservative in foreign policy. The tensions of the 1993–94 nuclear standoff between the United States and the DPRK also made Russia realize that it could play a larger role in Northeast Asian relations if it had leverage in Pyongyang. This attitude was encouraged by then opposition leader Kim Dae Jung, who supported a general rapprochement of the great powers with the DPRK.

With Vladimir Putin taking control of the Russian government, Moscow has embraced a more equidistant two-Korea orientation. Putin identifies the Asia-Pacific region as equally important with the West in the pursuit of Russia's national identity goals at home and abroad. Today, the Kremlin has four goals for the Korean peninsula: (1) to reduce tensions, making sure that a new war does not erupt in Korea; (2) to prevent the spread of weapons of mass destruction (WMD) because they are likely to produce a nuclear arms race in the Asia-Pacific region; (3) to use Korea to the benefit of Russia's economy, especially modernization of its Far East; and (4) to restore Russian influence and strengthen Moscow's position in NEA as a whole.[70]

Political and Diplomatic Issues

Moscow–Seoul Normalization

Russia made its intention to look to the southern half of the Korean peninsula clear, beginning with Foreign Minister Andrei Kozyrev's March 1992 Asia trip to China, Japan, and South Korea; the omission of North Korea from the itinerary was deliberate, signaling Moscow's interest in comprehensive diplomatic and economic ties with the ROK. Not only did the Kremlin want to develop cooperative ties with South Korea, but Yeltsin viewed such cooperation with the ROK as a component of a strategy of increasing openness with China.[71] Furthermore, as part of an interesting triangular relationship between Russia, Japan, and the ROK in the 1990s, the Kremlin was ready to play "the Korean card" to put pressure on Japan. South Korea, meanwhile, consciously looked to the Russian connection as a counterbalance to Japanese – and also U.S. – influence in the region.

Given these conflicting and shifting goalposts, relations between South Korea and Russia were far from completely smooth in the 1990s. Despite the Yeltsin government's decision not to renew the Russo–DPRK defense treaty, its existence was an issue for South Korea in the early 1990s because Seoul demanded that Moscow renounce the military clauses in

[70] Bazhanov (2005). [71] Wishnick (2004).

the alliance treaty. This led instead, in 1993, to the Russian Foreign Ministry denouncing such interference. Early in the life of the Russian Federation, South Koreans had also hoped to achieve justice in the case of the Korean Air Lines (KAL) passenger plane that had been shot down over Sakhalin in 1983. But they were bitterly disappointed when a special state committee in Russia concluded that Moscow could not be held responsible. The Russians, however, were interested in being compensated for embassy property in Seoul that the Park Chung Hee government had nationalized in 1970.

Nonetheless, during Yeltsin's November 1992 visit to Seoul, Russian and South Korean leaders signed the Treaty on Principles of Relations between the Russian Federation and the ROK. The treaty states that relations between the two partners are based on shared commitment to ideals of freedom, democracy, human rights, and a market economy. Although claiming that the treaty was not intended to be detrimental to North Korean interests, Yeltsin did acknowledge that concluding the treaty allowed Russia to alter certain aspects of policy toward the DPRK, including the cessation of deliveries of offensive weapons and nuclear equipment and the end of the mutual defense clause of the 1961 treaty. Yeltsin couched these changes in the context of improving inter-Korean relations.[72] The new proximity between Russia and South Korea was reinforced during Kim Young Sam's 1994 visit to Moscow, where Kim expressed support for ongoing reforms in Russia and for its future membership in APEC.

In the late 1990s, Russia–ROK relations cooled noticeably; very few high-level diplomatic exchanges occurred. Then, in September 2004 Roh Moo-hyun held a summit meeting with Russian President Vladimir Putin. Roh had already visited Beijing, Tokyo, and Washington before traveling to Moscow, however, indicating the relative ranking of Russia in South Korean foreign policy. Although both security and economic issues were on the agenda, Roh's main focus was on securing energy resources in Russia. The role of Russia as a supplier of energy resources is likely to play a major role in the future relations between Russia and South Korea.

Moscow–Pyongyang Renormalization

The political relationship between Moscow and Pyongyang was defined during the Cold War by the 1961 Mutual Defense and Cooperation Treaty. When the Soviet Union dissolved, Russia initially agreed to honor the USSR's extant treaties and commitments, although they would be susceptible to renegotiation. Russian President Boris Yeltsin sent a personal

[72] Wishnick (2004).

envoy to Pyongyang to explain Russia's policy and to probe North Korea's. The North Koreans considered the 1961 treaty "outdated." Not only did Pyongyang not object to termination of the treaty, but the North Korean regime also dismissed Moscow's reassurances that the Russian nuclear umbrella still covered North Korea, implying a revision of Pyongyang's concept of national security.[73]

The DPRK might not have recognized all the implications of its nonchalance, however. The decision in 1992 not to renew the treaty – which would expire in 1996 – meant an end to Russian military aid, and it quickly became clear that Pyongyang was not happy with the lower status of its relations. The DPRK expressed that it had been "betrayed and damaged in a material sense" by its former mentor, and some officials hinted that the dismal North Korean economic situation of the mid-1990s was caused by the "abrupt cessation of Soviet (Russian) aid and the withdrawal of its military shield." Left alone, North Korea "had no other choice but to pour all our scarce resources into military programs, especially because Americans and their South Korean puppets used the opportunity to immediately increase pressure on the DPRK." North Korea wanted Russia to compensate it for this "damage," at least partially, by repairing and modernizing enterprises built in North Korea by the USSR during the Cold War.

In general, security relations between Russia and the DPRK have evolved through three stages in the post–Cold War world.[74] In the first half of the 1990s, Russia's "short-sighted" or "romanticist"[75] foreign policy put heavy emphasis on relations with the West, meaning that Russia was estranged from North Korea and increasingly close with South Korea. However, during the first U.S.–DPRK nuclear standoff, Russia predictably followed the U.S. line but was then excluded from the settlement. Combined with other factors, this lack of respect for a blatantly pro-ROK Russia inaugurated a new stage of Moscow–Pyongyang relations in which Russia moved toward a role more akin to that of a balancer on the Korean peninsula.

The slight against Russia was aggravated in 1996 when the United States and South Korea proposed holding four-party peace talks on the Korean peninsula that would include China but not Russia. Russian officials believed they were getting few benefits from partnership with China and normalization with South Korea, although North Korea did not demonstrate any interest in having Russia as a party to the talks either. In fact Pyongyang, unimpressed with Russian complaints, suggested that instead of advocating six-party talks, Russia should have concentrated on

[73] Rubinstein (1997: 164). [74] S. H. Yang, W. S. Kim, and Y. H. Kim (2004).
[75] Vorontsov (2002: 48).

"demanding the withdrawal of the American military from South Korea and on disrupting U.S. schemes for NMD" (national missile defense).[76] Russia was forced to try its hand in applying pressure on Seoul, stressing the coincidence of Russian and South Korean national interests and pointing out that Russia is virtually the only power honestly desiring the reunification of Korea.[77] But these pressures were ineffectual.

Russia's exclusion from the four-party talks on Korea was widely criticized in Moscow's policy circles, prompting a debate about Russia's Korea policy among government officials and scholars; the Russian parliament (Duma), in a constant battle with Yeltsin, took the opportunity to hold hearings and condemn the government's Korea policy.[78] The exclusion from the four-party talks implied that even the modest concept of Russia as a "regional power in a U.S.-led world" did not appear to be valid.[79]

Internal upheaval such as this inspired Pyongyang to look past Russia's anticommunist stance in the early 1990s and maintain hope that the former friend might come back to its senses. In a remarkable show of self-restraint, Pyongyang refrained from denouncing or refuting the anticommunist tendencies of Moscow. They were aided in this effort by the presence of a small but vocal group of North Korea supporters in Russian domestic politics. Russian communists often praised *juche* ideology, the achievements of the DPRK in its socialist construction, and its pursuit of an independent foreign policy. Nationalist Vladimir Zhirinovsky was even more eloquent in praising Pyongyang and was rewarded with lavish treatment when he visited Pyongyang in the mid-1990s. North Korean patience paid off as the Yeltsin government, frightened by the 1995 parliamentary elections that saw a large gain in Communist Party representation, agreed to restore a working relationship with the DPRK, accepting arguments that expansion of links with Pyongyang was advantageous to all countries in East Asia.[80]

More particularly, the government admitted that restoration of ties to North Korea would be advantageous to Russia, which had lost influence in East Asia by ceasing to be a conduit to North Korea. Yeltsin's one-sided pro-ROK policy had cost Russia strategic influence on the peninsula, and a restoration of the ability to influence Pyongyang – if possible – would be welcomed by all.[81] Work began on a new treaty to replace the alliance treaty of 1961, and the Kremlin proposed – but never realized – an international conference on the Korean peninsula. The administration's hands were held to the fire by members of parliament who took

[76] The DPRK Report, NAPSNET, No. 22, p. 1.
[77] The DPRK Report, NAPSNET, No. 2, p. 6. [78] Wishnick (2002). [79] Sokov (2002).
[80] Wishnick (2002). [81] S. H. Joo (2003); Bazhanov (1996).

a trip to North Korea in 1996, headed by the Duma Speaker. Even with these pressures, it took from the 1996 until 2000 to complete the treaty renormalizing relations between Russia and North Korea. The treaty lacks a clause obligating prompt military intervention and is said to be an absolutely normal interstate agreement that complies with international law and is not directed against third countries.

The opinion, held across the political spectrum, that Russia had lost influence in East Asia by downgrading relations with North Korea coincided with a rising conservative sentiment among the Russian elite – and in Russian society as a whole – a result of the great difficulties with the process of reform. Initial attempts at rapprochement with the DPRK were made within the boundaries of a two-track policy approach supported by Foreign Minister Yevgeni Primakov, who became prime minister in 1998; relations with the ROK were not considered in pursuing new relations with Pyongyang. The attempt to keep relations with North and South Korea separate did not meet with much success, however. Russia did best when it combined its approach and included both Korean states. As those favoring an equal engagement policy asserted, it was best for Russia to "walk on both legs" in Korea.[82] The creation of a single Korea policy from a discrepant, bifurcated policy was in part the result of domestic changes in South Korea. When he was elected ROK president in December 1997, Kim Dae Jung viewed Russia in a different light from his predecessors. He looked forward to opportunities to integrate Russia into regional structures, including those related to North Korea.[83] In May 1999, Kim Dae Jung visited Boris Yeltsin in Moscow and received the latter's endorsement of the Sunshine Policy, while also putting to rest a 1998 Russo–ROK spy scandal.[84] Economic discussions dominated the agenda, however. Russia's president changed at the end of 1999 with Yeltsin's surprise resignation, and the new Russian president, Vladimir Putin, traveled to the ROK a year later in early 2001. In this meeting, Putin worked to establish some distance between South Korea and the newly inaugurated Bush administration in the United States on issues such as missile defense and the U.S. withdrawal from the 1972 Anti-Ballistic Missile (ABM) Treaty. Pyongyang, of course, was displeased with the warm Russian reception and the announcement of plans for Russo–ROK cooperation in military matters.

But, overall, the improvement in Russo–North Korean relations accelerated in the late 1990s. The spring 1999 NATO air war against Yugoslavia over the fate of Kosovo found Pyongyang and Moscow both condemning U.S. intervention. The growing distance between Washington and Moscow warmed North Korean hearts. Pyongyang also demonstrated

[82] See Toloroya (2002: 151). [83] Wishnick (2002). [84] Bazhanov (2005).

sympathy with Russian authorities over the conflict in Chechnya, saying that Moscow had every right to fight separatists and terrorists to restore order and unity in the country. In typical North Korean fashion, representatives from Pyongyang blamed the United States and other "imperialist forces" for "stirring up troubles in hopes of driving Russia out of oil-rich regions."[85]

During Vladimir Putin's administration, Russia shifted course with regard to North Korea almost immediately, embarking on a third stage of post–Cold War relations with Korea. Within one month of assuming the presidency after Yeltsin's New Year's Eve 1999 retirement, he dispatched his foreign minister to Pyongyang to cement the new treaty on which the two countries had been working since 1997; it was signed in February 2000. The Treaty of Friendship, Good Neighbourliness and Cooperation between Russia and the DPRK provides new legal grounds for bilateral relations and includes neither an automatic military intervention clause nor support for the DPRK's reunification formula. It does contain a "mutual contact" clause, which might be subject to different interpretations in a crisis situation because the treaty does not clarify what "contact" means nor what measures may (or may not) be taken after "contact." The clause is essentially Russia's attempt to increase its influence over North Korea and to establish its right to intervene in a crisis without having an automatic arrangement that might jeopardize its security.[86] The section on the resolution of inter-Korean problems references the UN Charter and the upholding of international law. For the DPRK, this was the first time that the state had signed onto a treaty that stressed adherence to the UN Charter and universal norms of international law.[87] Russian public opinion supported the treaty as restoring balanced relations between Moscow and North and South Korea.[88]

In May 2000, Putin made the decision to become the first Russian head of state to visit the DPRK. His visit was the first of a foreign leader personally invited by Kim Jong Il, the first international summit in Pyongyang after Kim came to power, and the first to produce an international document signed by Chairman Kim.[89] The summit came despite North Korea's expressed preference for Communist Party candidate Gennady Zyuganov in the March 2000 presidential elections. The Russian public received the visit as a logical step; Moscow had managed to improve relations with virtually every state in the Asia-Pacific region with the sole exception of North Korea. Pyongyang's moves toward more openness and reform may also have aided the Russian decision. Putin described Kim Jong Il in the most favorable terms, as a "well informed ... totally modern man

[85] The DPRK Report, NAPSNET, No. 22, pp. 2–3. [86] S. H. Joo (2003).
[87] Toloroya (2002: 153). [88] Wishnick (2004). [89] Toloroya (2002: 154).

whose assessment of the situation in the world is objective."[90] The two men "developed a great deal of personal chemistry, mutual respect, and understanding. Some even say that they became 'true friends.'"[91]

Russo–DPRK relations were completely renormalized. During the summit, Putin and Kim agreed to actively promote economic, scientific, cultural, and technological exchanges. Moscow declared its eagerness to become a principal mediator between the DPRK and the ROK, suggesting new economic cooperation that included both Koreas and Russia. Putin's visit to the DPRK sent a signal to the United States and other players in Northeast Asian politics that Russia intends to be involved in Korea and to compete economically with other countries on the Korean peninsula. In fact, Putin has relayed Pyongyang's messages to the West and to Seoul on a number of occasions, and he has been willing to add his own positive appraisals of Kim Jong Il. Russia has spoken up on behalf of the DPRK in international settings; has offered to mediate between North Korea and either South Korea, Japan, or the United States; and has suggested compromise solutions regarding the nuclear standoff. For the domestic audience, Putin's initial trip to the DPRK also demonstrated a Russian commitment to the economic development of the Russian Far East.[92]

Kim Jong Il returned Putin's visit in August 2001 in a bizarre 6,000-mile train trip across Russia to Moscow that inconvenienced thousands of Russian rail travelers along the way – it took more than a year just to organize it. This was part of Kim Jong Il's coming-out party, evidenced also in 2000 by a May visit to China, a June inter-Korean summit, and an October visit to Pyongyang by U.S. Secretary of State Madeleine Albright. In Moscow, Putin and Kim confirmed their positions on the preservation of the ABM Treaty and on the promotion of global security. The Kremlin even agreed to include in the declaration a statement in which "the DPRK explained its position that withdrawal of American troops from South Korea presents a pressing important problem in the interest of providing peace and security on the Korean peninsula and in Northeast Asia." However, Putin inserted contingent language into the declaration regarding the restructuring of Soviet-built enterprises.[93] Not even during the decades of fraternal friendship based on socialist internationalism did North Korean and Soviet leaders enjoy such a high degree of interpersonal trust and credibility as President Putin and Chairman Kim Jong Il appear to share.[94]

Since these mutual visits, Kim Jong Il has stayed in close touch with Russian representatives in Pyongyang and has made visits to the Russian

[90] Quoted in S. H. Joo (2003). [91] Mansourov (2004: 275). [92] Bazhanov (2005).
[93] Wishnick (2002). [94] Mansourov (2004: 278).

Far East to examine the implementation of Russian economic programs.[95] In August 2002, Putin and Kim held a third summit in Vladivostok.[96] There Putin allegedly assured Kim Jong Il that Moscow would not support any U.S. efforts to impose a so-called "Iraqi scenario" on North Korea and that Russia would not join any anti-DPRK international coalition. Moreover, Russia would try to help the DPRK distance itself from the so-called "axis of evil" and to get out of the U.S.-sponsored international isolation.[97] This is known as the "Putin formula." In connection with the events in Iraq, the Russian president stated: "In recent times – and there have been many crises recently – Russia has not once permitted itself the luxury of being drawn directly into any of these crises," and Putin also promised to do everything within his power "to prevent Russia being dragged into the Iraq crisis in any form."[98]

New North Korean policy toward Russia can be best described as "old wine in new bottles." It is based on shared geopolitical interests, especially with respect to hardline U.S. policy and U.S. military presence on the peninsula. It is reinforced by personal chemistry and close ties between Chairman Kim Jong Il and President Putin, and is cemented by interlocking institutional networks connecting North Korean and Russian bureaucracies at the central and local levels.[99] Although Russia is not yet ready to extend economic aid to its former ally, many believed that Moscow can at least become more active diplomatically in competing for influence on the peninsula. Russian analysts believe that greater Russian presence in North Korea could be useful to Pyongyang and to the peace process on the peninsula because reinforced contacts with Russia will help the DPRK feel more self-confident, and consequently, encourage it to behave in a more flexible manner with other states.[100]

Military and Security Issues

Security concerns are the most immediate issue for Russia. Russia's 1997 "Concept of National Security," which repeats almost word for word a 1993 statement of military doctrine, expresses a deep concern with any large concentration of forces in the vicinity of Russia. This provision in particular might be applied to U.S. troops in the ROK, to Chinese

[95] S. H. Joo (2003).

[96] It is worth noting in this connection that no other great power can match Russia's summit diplomacy with both Koreas in the first four years of Putin's presidency – three summit meetings with Kim Jong Il (July 2000 in Pyongyang, August 2001 in Moscow, and August 2002 in Vladivostok) and two summit meetings with South Korean presidents (Kim Dae Jung in February 2001 in Seoul and Roh Moo-hyun in September 2004 in Moscow).

[97] Mansourov (2004: 278). [98] Quoted in Zhebin (2005: 150).

[99] Mansourov (2004: 282–84). [100] The DPRK Report, NAPSNET, No. 24, p. 6.

military forces at near abroad, or to implosion or explosion in the DPRK with spillover effects on Russia's Far East. However, the Russian defense ministry in a 1996 statement did not seem to weight the Korean peninsula with any degree of alarm, preferring to see it as the one zone of safety along the Russian border.[101] Given the renormalization of relations with the DPRK, Russia has viewed the nuclear stand-off, the stalled Korean peace process, and Korean reunification as areas in which it can play a supportive, if not leading, role, largely as a means by which Russia can increase its own stature in the global community and play out the role of a great power.

Moscow's motivations are both security and status oriented. After the starry-eyed beginnings of the post-Soviet era, it has been realized in Russia that the North Korean regime will not necessarily collapse in the immediate future and that collapse, if it does happen, may actually create greater security risks. Russia desires both to guarantee its security and to regain influence and prestige, and it is showing its flag wherever possible to these ends. It hopes to become closer with new partners and also to return to former allies that were recklessly abandoned in the immediate post–Cold War years. Because Moscow created Kim Il Sung's regime and spent considerable time and money nourishing it, North Korea seems like a natural partner with which to restore links. This is an argument about perceptions and sentiments, claiming that although leaders come and go, people's memories and friendships endure. Russia also believes that it can restore its influence in the ROK by rekindling its leverage with the DPRK.

These sentiments contrast with Moscow's policy toward North Korea in the early 1990s. When Pyongyang announced in March 1993 that it would withdraw from the NPT – a treaty that Gorbachev had succeeded in convincing North Korea to sign in December 1985 – and also that it would no longer allow International Atomic Energy Agency (IAEA) inspections of its nuclear waste processing facilities, Russia suspended its 1991 agreement to provide North Korea with three 660-megawatt light water reactors (LWRs) and suffered considerable financial losses as a result. When Yeltsin made the decision to halt construction on the $4 billion reactors, the project was almost complete, and the North Koreans refused to compensate the Russian firms for their work.[102] Yeltsin also publicly admonished Pyongyang for withdrawing from the NPT, leading the North Koreans to publicly accuse Russia of dumping nuclear waste into the Sea of Japan.[103] Yeltsin further enraged Kim Il Sung in 1994 by threatening to support international sanctions against North Korea if it persisted in its attempts to acquire nuclear weapons capability.

[101] Sokov (2002: 133). [102] Wishnick (2002); S. H. Joo (2000a). [103] Wishnick (2002).

Despite all this support for the U.S. zero tolerance policy on nuclear proliferation, Russia found itself excluded from the Agreed Framework solution to the 1993–94 nuclear standoff. Despite Russia's previous involvement in the North Korean energy sector, KEDO, established in 1995, decided to construct two South Korean LWRs in North Korea. Moscow rejected a secondary role refining waste from the South Korean reactors, claiming that Russia was being penalized for its participation in the NPT, while the parties to the Agreed Framework were being motivated by their commercial interests – a violation of the NPT.[104]

A majority of Russian experts believe that Pyongyang never completely halted work on its military nuclear program, despite signing the Agreed Framework in 1994. They believe that the North merely slowed the pace of its research and development work and hid its efforts more thoroughly. At the same time, officials at the Russian Ministry of Atomic Energy, despite having seen U.S. satellite images, are not convinced that North Korea has an atomic bomb because unlike Pakistan and India it has not conducted a test. (Russian experts do believe, however, that the DPRK continues to develop chemical and biological weapons, something not emphasized by the United States.) The South Asian tests, in fact, may have spurred North Korean persistence in pursuit of nuclear weapons. One Russian Foreign Ministry official quoted a high-ranking North Korean diplomat as saying in 1998 that Pyongyang had drawn two lessons from the Indian and Pakistani tests: (1) if huge India believed it necessary to add the nuclear element to guarantee its own national security, then tiny North Korea should be even more attentive to this need; and (2) the world reaction to the South Asian tests shows that the "offenders," instead of being punished, may reap additional fruit from projecting a nuclear image.[105]

One of the concessions that Putin granted to Kim Jong Il during his July 2000 summit trip was a joint declaration in which the Russians stated their belief that North Korea's missile programs were purely peaceful and therefore not threatening to anyone.[106] Under the Yeltsin administration, in contrast, Russia had made its displeasure known at North Korea's 1998 Taepodong missile test. The Russian government requested an official explanation from North Korea, noting that the trajectory of the missile had taken it through Russia's exclusive economic zone. North Korean representatives adamantly defended "the unquestionable right of a sovereign state to test and produce missiles for any purpose, including for space exploration and the protection of the Motherland,"

[104] Wishnick (2004). [105] The DPRK Report, NAPSNET, No. 12, May 1998, pp. 1–2.
[106] Bazhanov (2005).

citing the missile programs of the Big Four.[107] The Putin administration's acceptance of the DPRK's missile program is also difficult to gel with Russia's support for nuclear-free Korean peninsula, as well as its welcoming of Pyongyang's self-imposed moratorium on missile testing that began in September 1999 and was extended in 2002. Putin, grabbing global prime time headlines, did reveal that the North Korean leader pledged to eliminate his country's Taepodong missile program – a key rationale for U.S. NMD – if developed countries provided access to rocket boosters for peaceful space research. Putin also managed to put Kim Jong Il's "satellites for missiles" offer on the agenda of the G-8 summit meeting in Japan. Kim Jong Il later retracted the offer, calling it "a joke" and saying, "[The joke] must be a headache for the United States. It is reluctant to give us money, but it has to stop our scientific development. It must be a big headache."[108] Such interpretation of Kim Jong Il's remarks has been disputed by Georgi Toloraya, Deputy Director-General of the First Asian Department of Russia's Foreign Ministry. Toloraya claims that Kim Jong Il informed South Korean journalists in August 2000 that he had told Putin "we will not develop missiles if the U.S. would agree to launch satellites for us." He then mentioned the irony of the situation, observing that the United States or Japan would never seriously take him up on his offer. Kim's use of the word "irony," according to Toloraya, was later misinterpreted as "joke" by hostile media.[109]

The Putin government's sanguinity with regard to North Korea missiles is not necessarily echoed in the Russian military. The General Staff of the Russian Armed Forces is paying close attention to North Korean efforts to develop its nuclear and missile potential and has described the programs as "directly affecting . . . Russia's national security, as well as regional and global stability." Russian military officials believe that North Korean nuclear missile ambitions – as well as those of India, Pakistan, and Israel – should be checked through stronger international agreements, through the creation of nuclear weapon-free zones, and through full implementation of the Comprehensive Test Ban Treaty.[110] It is unclear how the military feels about the April 2001 agreement by Russia to resume military cooperation with North Korea, limited to upgrading weapons supplied during the Soviet era.[111]

Meanwhile, Russia has looked to Seoul to join Moscow in opposition to the U.S. plan for NMD and TMD. A joint communiqué following a 2001 meeting between Kim Dae Jung and Putin clearly accomplished

[107] The DPRK Report, NAPSNET, No. 19, August 1999, p. 1.
[108] For a full English text of the interview, see Foreign Broadcast Information Service (FBIS), *Daily Report/East Asia (DR/EA)*, August 13, 2000.
[109] Toloraya (2003: 40); Meyer (2006).
[110] The DPRK Report, NAPSNET, No. 21, December 1999, p. 1. [111] Wishnick (2002).

this, although not explicitly so. Kim said, "The ABM treaty is a cornerstone of strategic stability and an important foundation for international efforts on nuclear disarmament and non-proliferation."[112] This did not sit well with the Bush administration, creating a rift in the U.S.–ROK alliance. After several awkward attempts to dispel any notion of disagreement between Seoul and Washington, and after a disastrous summit meeting with George W. Bush in Washington, Kim Dae Jung resolved the crisis in the old-fashioned way (in the manner of Kim Young Sam), with a major shake-up of his cabinet, replacing key officials, including the Foreign Minister and the Unification Minister. When Kim Jong Il went to Moscow in August 2001, he likewise affirmed his support of the ABM Treaty from which the United States subsequently withdrew.

Although the DPRK is interested in updating its armaments with new Russian technology, it is the ROK that has made the weapons deal with the Russian Federation. In December 2002, the ROK agreed to accept $534 million worth of Russian weaponry as part of a loan repayment plan. The agreement stipulated that by 2006 the ROK would purchase six types of Russian weapons, paying half by forgiving debt that Moscow owes to Seoul and the other half in cash.[113] President Roh Moo-hyun later agreed to write off 30 percent of the Soviet debt (approximately $660 million). North Korea, meanwhile, purchases $10 million in spare parts each year for Soviet-made weapons and has collaborated with India in attempts to improve the life and quality of the weapons.[114] Russia has repeatedly denied requests to purchase more modern weapons systems because of the DPRK's preference for paying in empty credit rather than with hard currency.[115] Pyongyang, meanwhile, is full of complaints about Russian arm sales to South Korea, whereas no new weapons flowed to North Korea. Whereas the Yeltsin administration's refusal to sell weapons to the North Koreans on the grounds that it might hinder cooperation with South Korea was met with protests in the Duma, Putin's two-track approach has yielded less criticism.

Recognizing that Pyongyang's security fears revolve around the United States, Russia often criticizes the Bush administration's hard-line approach toward North Korea and urges the United States to solve DPRK–U.S. disputes through peaceful means. In regard to the second U.S.–North Korea nuclear standoff, the Russian deputy foreign minister stressed that pressure on Pyongyang would only worsen the situation and argued that it was necessary to understand the root causes of the issue. The speaker of the Duma blamed the United States for North Korea's resumption of its nuclear program, pointing out that the United States

[112] Quoted in S. H. Joo (2003). [113] S. H. Joo (2003).
[114] The DPRK Report, NAPSNET, No. 4, p. 6. [115] Wishnick (2004).

had failed to fulfill its promises to build nuclear reactors for the DPRK and had included North Korea as part of the "axis of evil."[116] Despite some differences on this issue within the Russian foreign policy establishment, today Moscow supports "transformation" of the North Korean system, not "regime change." In the early 1990s, many pro-Western Russians anticipated and even hoped for the early collapse of what they considered to be an odious Stalinist regime in Pyongyang. More recently, however, many Russian analysts have seen the collapse of the North Korean regime as neither inevitable nor as desirable as was first assumed.[117]

At the same time, Russia conducted war games that anticipated possible implications of a U.S. attack on the DPRK – refugees or radioactive fallout. With the U.S. war against Iraq, the Russians were alarmed that the United States might actually act on some of its threats against North Korea.[118] If Moscow were to join a united front with Washington against Pyongyang or to participate in any coalition of willing against North Korea, we are told, "this would add nothing to the perception of Russia as a world power – or even of Russia as a regional power capable of defending its own interests. On the contrary, it would result in the most adverse consequences for Moscow's international position, including in countries of the so-called 'near abroad.'"[119] Thus, status (identity) and security are inextricably linked in Russia's Korea policy. This has led Russia to coordinate closely with China on its stance on the nuclear talks. After Putin met with Jiang Zemin and Hu Jintao, the leaders issued a declaration calling for a nuclear-free Korean peninsula and the normalization of relations between the United States and North Korea.

In general, Russia seeks a multinational arrangement for Korean peace and security, and supports the notion that Korean questions should be resolved by the Koreans themselves if possible. Russia opposes neither U.S.–North Korean bilateral talks nor four-way talks among the United States, China, and North and South Korea, although the latter make Moscow feel sidelined. Russia asserts, however, that the United States alone cannot untie the "Korean knot" but must rely on a multilateral approach to creating lasting peace and security in NEA. Russian policy makers believe that Pyongyang is genuinely interested in reform but is isolated and paranoid; they argue that renewed friendship and trust between Russia and North Korea will help Pyongyang regain self-confidence and engage South Korea in a constructive way.[120]

Russia was a serious supporter of the six-party talks on the nuclear standoff. According to Alexander Zhebin, Russia was invited to join the six-party talks at Pyongyang's insistence: "Some observers considered it a

[116] Zhebin (2005). [117] Meyer (2006); Bazhanov (2000b: 219–20).
[118] Bazhanov (2005). [119] Zhebin (2005: 147). [120] S. H. Joo (2003).

foreign-policy 'failure' that Russia was not invited to the trilateral meeting in Beijing in April 2003, so when the DPRK decided to ask Russia to take part in the six-party talks on August 27–29, 2003, in Beijing, this was welcomed in Russia as 'a positive step' with certain feeling of relief."[121] At times, however, the Russians oversold their case, as when a deputy foreign minister declared, "Without taking Russia's interest into account, [resolution of nuclear crisis] is almost impossible."[122] Russia has tried to build up its relevance by enhancing its leverage in Pyongyang, mostly by proposing to involve North Korea in its plans to develop a Northeast Asian energy network. The North Korean regime, however, usually detects the transparency of such schemes. Russia's inclusion in the six-party talks is the first time since the dissolution of the Soviet Union that Russia has been included in multilateral talks regarding the Korean peninsula.

The on-again, off-again nuclear talks have allowed Russia to engage its goal of working with both North and South Korea. In January 2003, South Korean officials asked Moscow to persuade North Korea to rescind its decision to withdraw from the NPT. Putin sent his deputy foreign minister to Pyongyang to deliver a message to Kim Jong Il on how to resolve the nuclear crisis. The proposed package included nuclear-free status for the Korean peninsula, a security guarantee for the DPRK, and a resumption of humanitarian assistance and economic aid to North Korea.[123] The proposal never got off the ground, and both the United States and the ROK view China as the real key player in terms of influencing the Pyongyang regime. The three-party and six-party talks on the nuclear issue have all therefore been held in Beijing. Remembering its exclusion from the 1994 Agreed Framework and from KEDO, Russia offered to build a nuclear power plant in North Korea as part of an effort to diffuse the crisis, and a Russian power company proposed constructing a power line from Vladivostok to Chongjin.[124]

Once the six-party talks got underway in August 2003, Moscow proposed a package solution in close alignment with Beijing's approach. Russia's package solution is based on the principles of a stage-by-stage process and a parallel synchronized implementation of coordinated measures by the concerned parties.[125] Russian officials have spoken out repeatedly for a peaceful, negotiated resolution of the crisis. They have warned against the dangers of a military solution. They have rejected sanctions or other pressure as counterproductive. They have opposed referring the North Korean nuclear issue to the UN Security Council. Russian observers have warned that pressure is likely to backfire by backing Pyongyang into a corner and increasing its sense of insecurity. Russian

[121] Zhebin (2005: 143). [122] Quoted in Wishnick (2004). [123] S. H. Joo (2003).
[124] Wishnick (2004). [125] Zhebin (2005: 144).

officials have touted the benefits of adopting a policy of reassurance toward North Korea rather than a policy of pressure. Moscow has volunteered to help provide North Korea with international security guarantees and energy assistance.[126]

Although Russia remains steadfast in its goal to keep the Korean peninsula nuclear free, the Russian Far East remains a possible origin for nuclear technology and material taken from military bases by underemployed scientists. Many Russian nuclear submarine bases are located near North Korea, providing opportunity for infiltration. In particular, North Korean agents might seek to purchase small pieces of equipment or software – items that would be difficult to detect. Several agents have been caught trying to purchase Russian radioactive materials and the schedules for decommissioning nuclear submarines.[127]

Russia wants to see further development of the six-party talks into an Asia-Pacific multinational conference, a proposal that dates back to the Brezhnev era when the Soviet Union first called for the creation of an Asian collective security system. Gorbachev reintroduced the idea of collective security in Asia.[128] Early proposals during the Yeltsin administration included the creation of an Asia-Pacific center for conflict prevention and a research institute on security problems. But the birth of APEC in 1989 and the ASEAN Regional Forum in 1993 mean that the East Asian regional organizations already exist, and existed before Russia was in a position to pursue its suggested conference. When the nuclear talks began in April 2003, Russia also suggested that those could be used as a forum for discussing a range of Korean issues – particularly inter-Korean issues – rather than just the DPRK's nuclear program.

Sensing that its strategic importance for Russia is growing under President Putin, Pyongyang hopes that Russia will be able to assist it in solving a set of problems by providing or creating (1) *de facto* protection against possible military threats from the United States; (2) Russian backing in bargaining with Washington over nuclear and missile matters; (3) U.S. interest in accommodating North Korean demands and requests as a means of countering the increase in Russian influence with the DPRK; (4) renewed Russian military aid, including spare parts for existing weapons and hardware, as well as new, more technologically advanced armaments; (5) Russian participation in the modernization of industrial facilities built by the Soviet Union during the early Cold War period; (6) reliable long-term deliveries of Russian oil and gas; (7) competitive sentiments within China through which Pyongyang might extract additional aid and political concessions from Beijing; and (8) greater interest

[126] Meyer (2006). [127] Wishnick (2004). [128] S. H. Joo (2003).

in cooperation with the DPRK among the countries of the former Soviet Union.

Russia's involvement in the six-party talks in 2003–05 was cautious but committed. Although China played the frontline role, ensuring that the talks got off the ground and continued, Russia also came to play an important supporting role. Ranking Russian diplomats described China as "a locomotive" driving the six-party dialogue, whereas Russia's role was to play "whisper diplomacy."[129] Russia and China did work to coordinate strategically during summit meetings in early 2004; both countries stated their desire to keep North Korean nuclear weapons free.[130] In 2003, Russia abstained from an IAEA vote about whether to send the North Korean nuclear issue to the UN Security Council, effectively announcing its support for the six-party format and for continued negotiation. During the third round of talks, Russia joined with China and South Korea in offering to supply energy – in the form of fuel oil – to North Korea in exchange for the DPRK halting any further development of its nuclear programs. Throughout the talks, Russia continued to supply modest food aid to North Korea and to have meetings with North Korean representatives.

Economic and Functional Issues

During the last years of Gorbachev's reign, as the Soviet Union recognized the need for retrenchment, and then during all Yeltsin's rule, as Russia tried to reestablish its independent identity in the world, ideology became increasingly irrelevant, geopolitics became secondary, and economics became the prime mover driving Russia's relations with the two Koreas. This is not to say that the three are unrelated. For instance, the development of the Siberian coast is a major national objective for Russia, but Moscow fears undertaking such development without peace in Korea. Stability and international cooperation in neighboring areas are seen as necessary for Russia's own development.[131] Gorbachev recognized at an early date that South Korea provided a model to follow in terms of developing a modern industrial economy and joining the global economy.[132]

In 1990, the Soviet Union was doing $2.2 billion worth of trade with the DPRK and $890 million with the ROK. One year later, trade with the DPRK had plummeted by 84 percent to $365 million, whereas that with the ROK had ballooned to $1.2 billion. This marked the beginning of the trend that would define post-Soviet Russo–Korean trade, as shown

[129] Y. Bin (2004). [130] See Y. Bin (2004). [131] The DPRK Report, NAPSNET, No. 6, p. 5.
[132] I. J. Kim (1994).

in Figure 3.1. From 1995 to 2002, Russian trade with North Korea was always less than $100 million of goods exchanged annually. Trade with the ROK generally increased, with some setback at the time of the Asian Financial Crisis of 1997–98, and in 2004 stood at $6 billion with a healthy $1.3 billion surplus in favor of Russia. Yet, although Russia is the ROK's eighteenth largest overall trading partner, it is the DPRK's fourth largest trading partner.

To achieve its economic objectives in NEA, we are told, Moscow has no choice but to play its role as a great power in peacefully resolving the U.S.–DPRK nuclear standoff. Yet, Moscow's leverage over Pyongyang is limited because Russia does not provide the large-scale economic assistance needed to help the North Korean regime survive. Russia's annual bilateral trade with North Korea was only $210 million in 2004 (up from $119 million in 2003), far less than North Korea's annual trade with South Korea or China. If the nuclear crisis is resolved, however, Russia may become more important as a provider of electricity and/or natural gas to North Korea, although the realization of these projects, especially the more expensive ones, may depend on funding from South Korea and other external sources.[133]

Russo–ROK Economic Relations

As the trade figures suggest, early in the Russian Federation's new existence, South Korea was a bright spot in the Asia-Pacific for the withered former superpower. Korean companies, interested in Russian natural resources and military and space technology, tried to keep a high profile in the Russian market. Some explored opportunities for major investment, and Moscow in turn solicited Korean capital and pressed for resumption of the $3 billion loan that had been frozen by Seoul after the collapse of the USSR. Yeltsin succeeded in reopening the credit line, making it appear as if Russo–ROK economic relations were going to greatly accelerate.[134] Within a few years, however, Moscow decided to postpone the payments due on the loan. Seoul newspapers called it "an act of arrogance beyond our understanding and patience."[135] Seoul froze the remaining half of the loan, and the opposition party attacked the government for making mistakes in foreign and economic policy. Russians, in turn, claimed frustration with the fluctuations in Seoul's behavior in the economic sphere and with the alleged dishonesty of some Korean businessmen. In 1994, a compromise was reached in which Russia agreed to transfer and sell weapons to Seoul as partial payment of the outstanding Soviet debt. The initial euphoria had been lost, however, and the

[133] Meyer (2006). [134] Bazhanov and Bazhanov (1994: 789–90).
[135] Quoted in Bazhanov (2005).

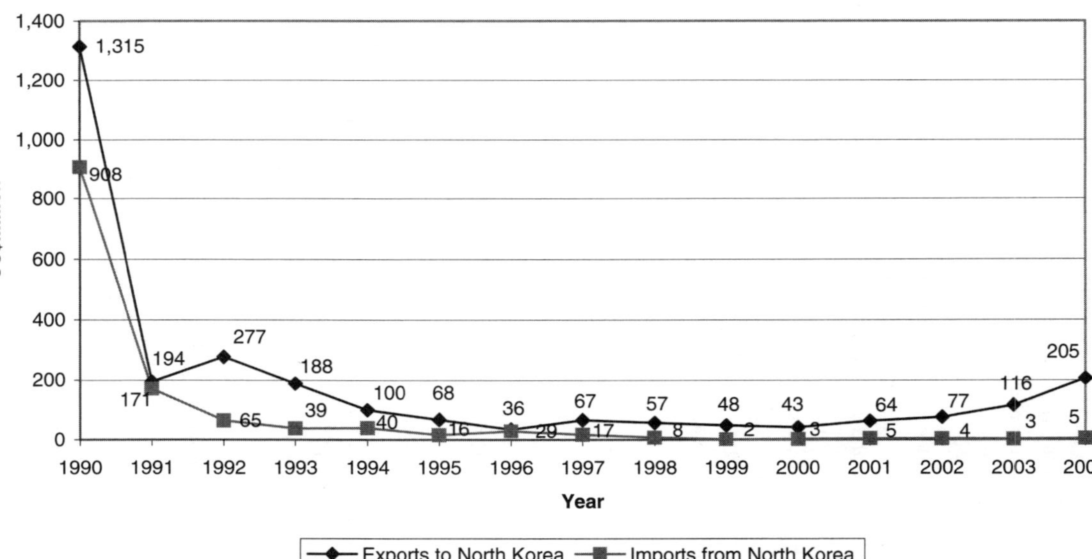

Figure 3.1. Russia's trade with North Korea, 1989–2004.
Source: 1997 Diplomatic White Paper Ministry of Foreign Affairs and Trade (MOFAT), Republic of Korea (ROK), pp. 396, 401; 1998 Diplomatic White Paper, pp. 481, 486; 2000 Diplomatic White Paper, p. 497; 2001 Diplomatic White Paper, p. 484; 2002 Diplomatic White Paper, p. 497. Available at www.mofat.go.kr and KOTRA at www.kotra.or.kr.

promise of the early 1990s that bilateral trade would reach $10 billion within a few years has not been materialized.Russia and South Korea complement each other structurally and technologically. Russia lacks – and will lack for decades to come – an effective consumer goods sector, especially in the Far East. Korea easily could become the primary supplier of consumer goods, given that Chinese goods have a bad (and declining) reputation in Russia, while Japanese goods are too expensive. Korean electrical appliances, cars, clothes, textiles, and other products are therefore well positioned to gain an increasing share of the Russian market. There is no emerging market comparable to the 145 million people in Russia looking for modern manufactured goods.[136]

In the Roh–Putin summit of 2004, Russia outlined a four-point project to develop the political economy of its Far East region: (1) construct and develop the Iron Silk Road by linking the Trans-Siberian Railway (TSR) and the Trans-Korean Railway (TKR); (2) develop gas pipelines; (3) link the Russian electric grid to that of other regional powers; and (4) link its information and technology network to other countries in the region, following the development of transportation infrastructures for crude oil, gas, and electricity. All four projects are designed to boost Russia's national interest and regional economic development, based on the so-called Northeast Asian United Energy Market concept. The plan runs the risk, however, of stimulating regional conflict, particularly between China and Japan, which are both in need of energy imports.[137] Roh had to admit, following the summit, that the visit to Russia had failed to produce a tangible agreement on South Korea's participation in Russian oil, gas, and other natural resource sectors.[138]

From the summit, the two countries did agree to collaborate on some space technology programs. This agreement will allow South Korea to develop its own rocket to launch satellites and will also put a South Korean astronaut in space on a Russian spacecraft by the end of 2007. Russia is hoping to take advantage of a synergy effect with South Korea's semiconductor and electronics resources.[139]

Although the trade between Russia and South Korea is fairly substantial and has great potential, it is limited in kind. On the Korean side, 95 percent of the trade is controlled by the twenty largest Korean

[136] The DPRK Report, NAPSNET, No. 6, p. 8.

[137] Kwon Won-soon, "Summit to Promote Energy Cooperation," *The Korea Times*, September 17, 2004.

[138] "Putin Hopes to Enhance Cooperation with S. Korea on Energy, Space," Yonhap, September 22, 2004.

[139] "Roh Visits Space Center to Show Will to Develop Space Technology," Yonhap, September 22, 2004; "Russia to Send S. Korea Joint Satellite Project Proposal," Yonhap, September 22, 2004.

companies.[140] On the Russian side, much Russo–ROK trade has been via "shuttles," that is, small-time Russian traders who collectively purchase $400–$500 million worth of consumer goods annually in the ROK and bring them back to Russia for resale.[141] South Korea exports petrochemical products, transport machinery, fabrics and textiles, household electrical products, wireless devices, electronics, and foot products to Russia, and it imports mostly raw materials, such as steel and iron – including scrap iron – nickel, aluminum, coal, and oil. Russia has the world's largest reserves of natural gas and the second largest coal reserves, and it is believed to hold the world's second largest amount of petroleum. The Russian economic presence in Korea is almost unnoticed to a layperson, whereas the Korean presence in Russia is highly visible: Korean-made consumer goods are the focus of large-scale advertisement campaigns that include huge billboards in downtown Moscow and St. Petersburg. South Korean cars are now a familiar sight on the roads of virtually any Russian city, as 22 percent of all foreign cars in Russia are Hyundai and Daewoo. Hyundai is the number one import carmaker in Russia, outdistancing such global brands as Toyota and General Motors. Samsung Electronics, which entered the Russian market in 1999, posted more than $1.5 trillion won in sales in 2003 and has become the top brand in color televisions, microwaves, and DVD players.[142]

Although South Korea exports products with a high value-added content to Russia, the trade balance has heavily favored Russia since 1999, as Table 3.2 and Figure 3.2 indicate, largely because of inflated energy prices. But the numbers are ultimately quite small: the combined trade numbers account for just more than 2 percent of Russia's foreign trade and just less than 1 percent of South Korea's. Despite Russia's interest, the ROK retains its traditional orientation toward the United States and is regionally far more interested in China than in Russia.

The ROK also has been hesitant – particularly in the early and mid-1990s – to invest in Russia because of the lack of legal protections; South Korean investors have preferred to place their bets on China, it seems. As indicated in Table 3.3 and Figure 3.3, only in 1995 and 1996 did OFDI flows to Russia top $50 million, and then they plummeted to a paltry $3 million in 1999 in the wake of the Russian financial collapse of 1998. In 2004, there was a striking 800 percent increase in OFDI to Russia – from $10 million in 2003 to $90 million in 2004 – perhaps a result of investment opportunities related to soaring oil and gas prices on world markets. Russia possesses about 30 percent of the world's known gas deposits, and

[140] Sokov (2002). [141] The DPRK Report, NAPSNET, No. 6, p. 10.

[142] Seo Jee-yeon, "Energy Cooperation Tops Roh-Putin Summit," *The Korea Times,* September 17, 2004.

Table 3.2. Russia's Trade with North and South Korea, 1989–2004

Year	Exports to North Korea	Imports from North Korea	Total North Korean-Russian Trade (Balance)	Change in North Korean-Russian Trade	Exports to South Korea	Imports from South Korea	Total South Korean-Russian Trade (Balance)	Change in South Korean-Russian Trade
1979					4	7	11 (–3)	N/A
1984					42	3	45 (+39)	N/A
1985					42	16	58 (+26)	+29%
1986					68	50	118 (+18)	+103%
1987					133	67	200 (+66)	+69%
1988					178	112	290 (+66)	+45%
1989					392	207	599 (+185)	+107%
1990	1,315	908	2,223 (+407)		370	520	890 (–150)	+49%
1991	194	171	365 (+23)	–84%	580	640	1,220 (–60)	+37%
1992	277	65	342 (+212)	–6%	490	370	860 (+120)	–30%
1993	188	39	227 (+149)	–34%	970	600	1,570 (+370)	+83%
1994	100	40	140 (+60)	–38%	1,230	960	2,190 (+270)	+39%
1995	68	16	84 (+52)	–40%	1,900	1,410	3,310 (+490)	+51%
1996	36	29	65 (+7)	–23%	1,810	1,968	3,778 (–158)	+14%
1997	67	17	84 (+50)	+29%	1,535	1,768	3,303 (–233)	–13%
1998	57	8	65 (+49)	–23%	999	1,114	2,113 (–115)	–36%
1999	48	2	50 (+46)	–23%	1,590	637	2,227 (+953)	+5%
2000	43	3	46 (+40)	–8%	2,058	788	2,846 (+1,270)	+28%
2001	64	5	69 (+59)	+50%	1,929	938	2,867 (+991)	+1%
2002	77	4	81 (+73)	+17%	2,200	1,100	3,300 (+1,100)	+15%
2003	116	3	119 (+113)	+47%	2,500	1,700	4,200 (+800)	+27%
2004	205	5	210 (+200)	+76%	3,671	2,339	6,010 (+1,332)	+43%

Units: $US1 million.
Source: 1997 Diplomatic White Paper Ministry of Foreign Affairs and Trade (MOFAT), Republic of Korea (ROK), pp. 396, 401; 1998 Diplomatic White Paper, pp. 481, 486; 2000 Diplomatic White Paper, p. 497; 2001 Diplomatic White Paper, p. 484; 2002 Diplomatic White Paper, p. 497; www.mofat.go.kr; KOTRA at www.kotra.or.kr.

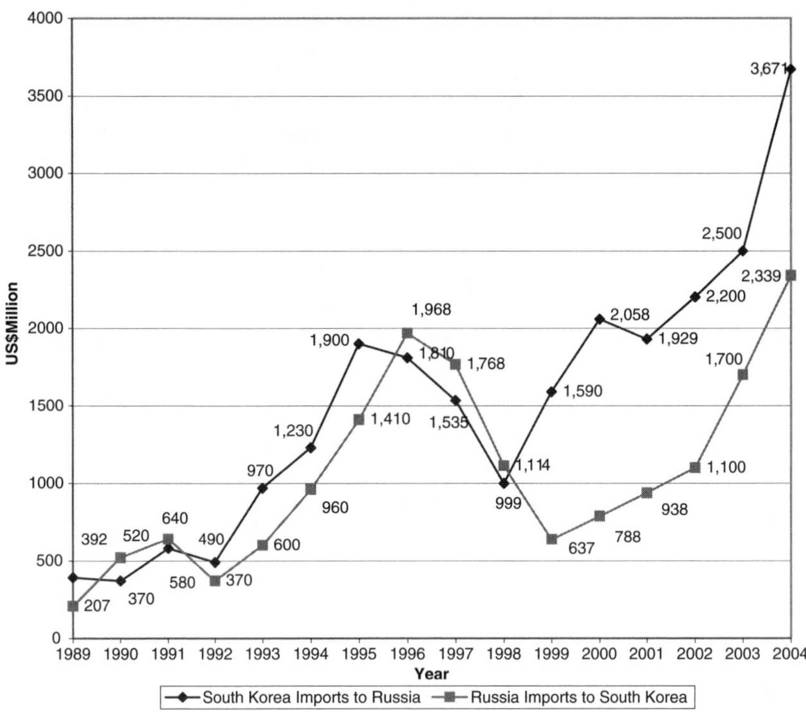

Figure 3.2. Russia's trade with South Korea, 1989–2004.
Source: 1997 Diplomatic White Paper Ministry of Foreign Affairs and Trade (MOFAT), Republic of Korea (ROK), pp. 396, 401; 1998 Diplomatic White Paper, pp. 481, 486; 2000 Diplomatic White Paper, p. 497; 2001 Diplomatic White Paper, p. 484; 2002 Diplomatic White Paper, p. 497. Available at www.mofat.go.kr and KOTRA at www.kotra.or.kr.

many of its rich gas fields are located in Eastern Siberia, not far from Korea. Just as Putin decided to commercialize Russian territory in the Russian Far East and Siberia, South Korean investors developed plans for gas development in Russia. Seoul wants to participate in a gas field project in the Irkutsk-Kovicta area of Siberia in conjunction with China and Russia, to develop oil and gas fields in Sakhalin, to join Russia's converged gas development project in East Siberia, and to jointly research and develop mineral resources in East Siberia.[143] In 2004, South Koreans invested some $90 million in Russia, but this constituted only 0.6 percent of the ROK's OFDI of $5.7 billion in 2004. In late 2004, the president of the Russian Union of Industrialists and Entrepreneurs expressed his

[143] "Roh to Focus on Energy Provision in Talks with Putin," Yonhap, September 17, 2004.

Table 3.3. Russian–South Korean FDI Relations, 1989–2004

Year	Amount of South Korean FDI into Russia	Amount of South Korean FDI into Russia (Percent Change)	Amount of Russian FDI into South Korea	Amount of Russian FDI into South Korea (Percent Change)
1990			0.2	N/A
1991			0.7	+250%
1992			1.5	+114%
1993	5	N/A	0.9	–40%
1994	36	+620%	1.4	+56%
1995	52	+44%	1.0	–29%
1996	72	+38%	1.7	+70%
1997	34	–53%	0.6	–65%
1998	35	+3%	1.8	+200%
1999	3	–91%	0.7	–61%
2000	10	+233%	0.7	0%
2001	21	+110%	N/A	N/A
2002	47	+124%	N/A	N/A
2003	10	–79%	N/A	N/A
2004	90	+800%	N/A	N/A

Units: US$1 million.
Source: 1997 Diplomatic White Paper, Ministry of Foreign Affairs and Trade (MOFAT), Republic of Korea (ROK), pp. 406, 409; 1998 Diplomatic White Paper, pp. 492, 494; 2000 Diplomatic White Paper, p. 504; 2001 Diplomatic White Paper, p. 490; 2002 Diplomatic White Paper, p. 498; Ministry of Commerce, Industry and Energy (MOCIE), Export-Import Bank of Korea. Available at http://www.koreaexim.go.kr/kr/file/publication/200502_1.pdf.

dissatisfaction and called on South Korean businessmen to increase investments in Russian economy.[144] Investment flows in the other direction have been entirely negligible: very little capital enters the ROK from Russian sources. The financial relations between the two countries are simply not that deep or developed.

There are numerous industries in which Korean investment would be particularly welcome in Russia: retail stores, restaurants, hotels, business centers, housing, electrical appliance and car factories, communications, transportation, maritime products, and so on. Russia is also interested in developing Far Eastern agriculture for export to Korea and China. The Kremlin hopes to see a dramatic rise in South Korean investment in the near future. A high official in the Russian government noted in the late 1990s that "huge Korean companies have already established a solid

[144] "Business Union Leader Calls on South Korea to Increase Investments," ITAR-TASS, September 22, 2004.

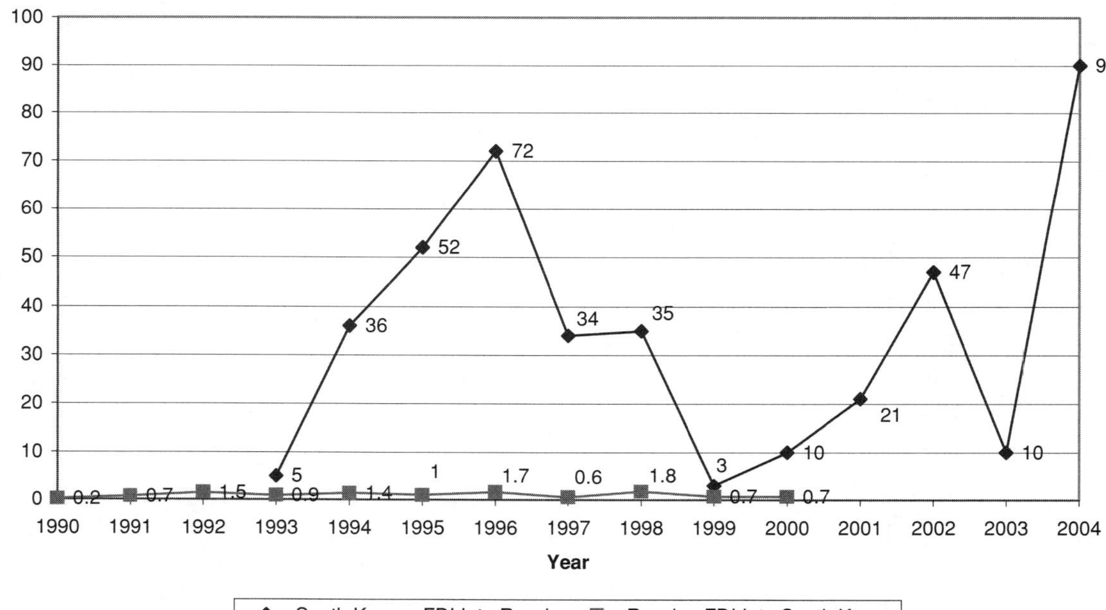

Figure 3.3. Amount of Russian–South Korean FDI, 1989–2004.
Source: 1997 Diplomatic White Paper, Ministry of Foreign Affairs and Trade (MOFAT), Republic of Korea (ROK), pp. 406, 409; 1998 Diplomatic White Paper, pp. 492, 494; 2000 Diplomatic White Paper, p. 504; 2001 Diplomatic White Paper, p. 490; 2002 Diplomatic White Paper, p. 498.

presence in our country. There are also numerous agreements between Moscow and Seoul, laying the proper foundation for cooperation."[145] South Korean trust in the stability and good prospects of the Russian market remain lacking.

For instance, the collapse of the ruble in 1998 – following the Asian Financial Crisis – resulted in a nearly complete end to the purchase of foods and ready-made garments that used to be the pillars of Korean export to Russia. Hundreds, if not thousands, of Far Eastern petty traders who specialized in bringing consumer goods from Korea to Vladivostok or Khaboreovsk lost their jobs. In a single year, the pattern of import into the region changed completely – from finished goods to the equipment for the production. In particular, Russia began importing cloth for the production of garments.[146]

Although South Korea is not importing much Russian capital, it is importing a fair amount of Russian labor. From the late 1990s, Korea has been home to many illegal Russian workers; Russian call girls are the most notorious, but there are also numerous manual laborers from Russia and other post-Soviet republics. Korean companies now employ a large number of Russian scientists and engineers. Their presence is not widely known, but more than 1,000 Russian specialists now work in Korea.

South Korea is also sending its citizens to Russia. As indicated in Table 3.4 and Figure 3.4, the number of South Koreans visiting Russia has more than doubled in the last decade. In 2003, of the 43,000 South Koreans who went to Russia, more than 20,000 were tourists, more than 11,000 were traveling for business purposes, and more than 3,000 went to study or conduct research. Today, South Koreans form one of the most prominent groups of overseas students in Russian universities.

Ultimately, all eyes are on the energy sector insofar as future Russo–ROK economic relations are concerned. Importing more than 70 percent of its oil from the Middle East, South Korea has sought energy cooperation as a means of diversifying the energy supply and meeting rising demand. Increases in oil prices in 2004 and China's rapidly increasing demand for oil imports emphasized the need for South Korea to reduce its dependence on oil by increasing consumption of natural gas and other alternative energy sources, and also to broaden the geographic range of energy imports. Another alternative use of the Russian market is to develop Russo–Korean strategies in such sectors as food products and textiles to cope with the increasing influx of cheap Chinese products.[147]

[145] The DPRK Report, NAPSNET, No. 9, p. 6. [146] Kovrigin (2003: 103).
[147] Seo Jee-yeon, "Energy Cooperation Tops Roh-Putin Summit," *The Korea Times*, September 17, 2004.

Table 3.4. Russia–ROK Exchange of Visitors, 1993–2004

Year	South Korean Visitors to Russia	% Change	Russian Visitors to South Korea	% Change	Total	% Change
1993	20,370	N/A	116,821	N/A	137,191	N/A
1994	27,713	+36%	153,777	+32%	181,490	+32%
1995	29,372	+6%	155,098	+1%	184,470	+2%
1996	30,429	+4%	157,401	+1%	187,830	+2%
1997	30,328	0%	136,841	–13%	167,169	–11%
1998	18,306	–40%	135,401	–1%	153,707	–8%
1999	26,837	+47%	127,892	–6%	154,729	+1%
2000	44,989	+68%	155,392	+22%	200,381	+30%
2001	54,762	+22%	134,727	–13%	189,489	–5%
2002	38,846	–29%	165,341	+23%	204,187	+8%
2003	42,983	+11%	168,051	+2%	211,034	+3%
2004	52,942	+23%	156,876	–7%	209,818	–1%

Unit: Individuals.
Source: Korea National Tourism Organization. Available at http://www.knto.or.kr.

Russo–DPRK Economic Relations

Ironically, while Russia was angling with South Korea in the mid-1990s for loans and debt relief, Russia's logic for continuing to pursue relations with the DPRK in the same period revolved around hopes of receiving payments on debts owed to Moscow by Pyongyang. Pyongyang had announced its refusal to repay a 4 billion ruble loan, when Yeltsin announced his intention not to renew the 1961 treaty and to halt weapons and technology transfers. Although Russia has traditionally been North Korea's main supplier of equipment, petroleum products, timber, coal, fish, and marine products, approximately 70 percent of North Korea's estimated $4 billion debt to Russia originates from unpaid-for weapons.[148]

In the wake of President Putin's visit to Pyongyang, North Korea is becoming increasingly active in economic contacts with Russia, which was exactly what Putin had hoped would result from the summit meeting. DPRK authorities have requested Russian assistance in the reconstruction of a number of facilities built by the Soviet Union in the 1950s and 1960s. The problem is that the DPRK does not have money to pay for the services, insisting on barter deals and low-interest credits instead. However, the Russian government, as it faces persistent economic and financial hurdles, cannot agree to such conditions. Barter is unlikely because of the Russian market economy and the fact that government authorities

[148] Rubinstein (1997: 173).

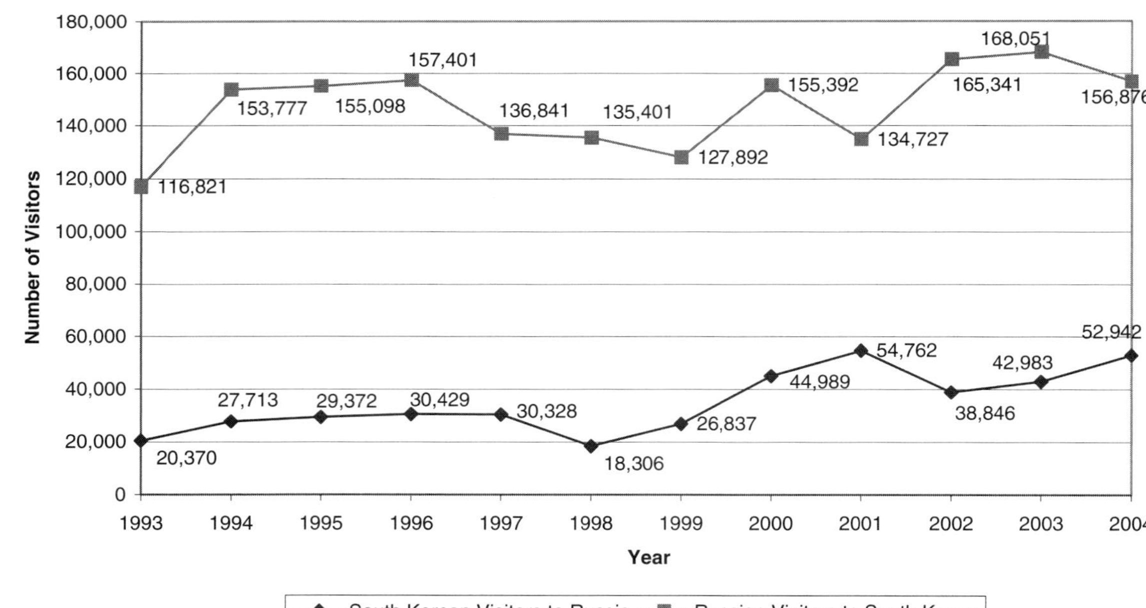

Figure 3.4. Russian–South Korean exchange of visitors, 1993–2004.
Source: Korea National Tourism Organization. Available at http://www.knto.or.kr.

cannot force Russian companies to accept goods they do not need or want – although there were reports of a developing intra-Russian barter economy in the mid-1990s.[149] The DPRK has presented a list of goods it could export to Russia in exchange for Russian goods and services, but Russian officials say that most of the items on the North Korean list are of no interest to Russian companies. One possible way out of the predicament is to have South Korean banks and firms provide credits to the DPRK to exchange for Russian technical assistance. Perhaps the most revealing part of the DPRK–Russia Moscow Declaration of August 4, 2001 is embodied in point five: "In order to carry out a series of bilateral plans, the Russian side confirmed its intention to use the method of *drawing financial resources from outsiders* on the basis of understanding of the Korean side."[150] In other words, Moscow and Pyongyang are now looking to Seoul, Washington, and Tokyo to foot the bill.

Attempts are currently being made to find interested parties in the ROK. Meanwhile, Pyongyang has asked Russian authorities to allocate logging areas for the DPRK in the Russian Far East. Russia needs help with its timber industry, particularly given increased demand from China, and North Korean wages are very low. There was even some speculation in the Russian media following the summit that Putin had allowed Pyongyang to write off $50 million of its debt by providing free labor to timber camps in the Russian Far East.

The presence of approximately 12,000 North Korean workers in the Russian Far East has created problems not only because they have sought political asylum, but also because they have become involved in illegal activities such as smuggling and drug trafficking.[151] The Russian press has also reported North Korean involvement in counterfeiting and poaching. In addition to the migrant workers from North Korea, the Russian Far East saw the return in the 1990s of ethnic Koreans who had been forcibly relocated under the Stalin regime. Native Russians met the returning Koreans with hostility.

Nonetheless, Russia is the only country that might be able to absorb a North Korean workforce that is increasingly without jobs in North Korea. At the regional level, cooperation is growing between North Korea and the Russian Far East; since the Soviet period, North Korean workers have been involved in timber projects in the Russian Far East, and more recently, they have been active in construction, agriculture, and forestry. North Korean workers help fill a labor shortage in a region experiencing a population outflow, particularly of working-age

149 See Woodruff (1999).

150 For an English text of the Moscow Declaration, see KCNA, August 4, 2001; emphasis added.

151 The DPRK Report, NAPSNET, No. 26, pp. 2–3. See also Wishnick (2002, 2004).

inhabitants. In April 2001, Moscow and Pyongyang apparently agreed in principle to settle the pestering debt issue through a labor-for-debt swap deal, whereby North Korea would cover $5.5 billion in Soviet-era debt during the next thirty years by supplying workers who would toil unpaid in Russian labor camps across Siberia. About 90 percent of Pyongyang's debts to Moscow was covered in such a manner in 2000, to the tune of $50.4 million.[152] At this rate, it would take 109 years to pay off Pyongyang's debts to Moscow.

On the whole, DPRK–Russian economic ties do not look very promising, and the development of serious investment and trade relations will likely need to involve South Korea. Russians complain that the DPRK still wants to build economic relations "along the lines of the old Soviet–DPRK model of getting things free-of-charge." On a brighter note, cultural cooperation has resumed in recent years. Russian performing artists are again touring in Pyongyang, and North Korean students can again be found in Russian schools.[153]

Russo–DPRK–ROK Economic Relations

Disappointed with the results of bilateral economic cooperation with both the ROK and the DPRK, Russia began to consider multilateral projects involving both Koreas. In part, this was related to the sense that Russia generally had lost influence in the region by losing leverage in Pyongyang. Moscow is very desirous of three-way economic cooperation that would combine Russia's technical knowledge, North Korean labor, and South Korean capital. Russia wants to use South Korean investors' capital to modernize factories in North Korea that were built with the support of the Soviet Union and are in need of repairs and upgrading. South Korea, however, is not interested in pouring money into such investment because the goods produced by these plants are unlikely to be competitive on international markets. South Korean business is under the presumption that the North Korean industrial plants will have to be completely overhauled in the event of Korean reunification.[154]

At the summit meeting with Kim Jong Il, Putin energetically championed three-way economic projects, especially modernization of the inter-Korean railway such that it could be connected with the 9,288-kilometer Trans-Siberian Railroad to form an "Iron Silk Road." The $3 billion project would ensure rapid transport of freight from Europe to South Korea's southern ports, such as Pusan and Kwangyang, via Moscow, Kazakhstan, Siberia, and North Korea. In fact, the reconnection of some inter-Korean rail was one of the most material agreements reached at the

152 AFP, August 4, 2001. 153 Toloroya (2003: 28). 154 S. H. Joo (2003).

inter-Korean summit of June 2000, and significant work has been accomplished in the interim. Seoul has generally embraced the idea of restoring inter-Korean rail links and tying them into regional systems. Kim Dae Jung went so far as to call the project "*de facto* Korean unification." Furthermore, the completion of these rail links might change some opinions in South Korea about the possibilities for collaboration with North Korean industry because the transaction costs will be lowered. Shipping goods from South Korea to Europe over the rail line rather than by sea will reduce shipping charges, and it will shorten transportation time from 40 to 15 days. Russian officials estimate that the connection would lead to a tenfold rise in shipping along the Trans-Siberian, from 45,000 containers per year to 500,000 to 600,000.[155]

Moscow's role in the Iron Silk Road project is crucial, and Russia has embraced its role with gusto so far. The project picked up immediate speed with Putin's election as president, and he has held five summits with leaders of either North or South Korea during which the railroad has been discussed. During the August 2001 Moscow summit with Kim Jong Il, Putin signed an accord pledging Russian financial support of North Korea's part of the reconstruction of the severed inter-Korean railways. By the end of 2004, the ROK had finished work on its rail links, but the DPRK had not done likewise on its side of the demilitarized zone (DMZ).[156] Nonetheless, the two countries held a rail-joining ceremony in October 2004. In fact, the rail in North Korea is weak, and accidents are possible, such as the April 2004 explosion at Ryongchon that killed 161 and injured more than 1,000 people. The current railway in the North does not guarantee punctuality, speed, safety, or effectiveness, making it unsuitable for use as an international route.[157]

Russia has provided a conduit through which Seoul and Pyongyang can cooperate on the project. Russian support for railroads in North Korea is not new; until the 1980s, the Soviet Union assisted North Korea's railways with some $145 million, as well as building factories for locomotives. According to one Korean official, this has more to do with economics than politics because Russia wants to regain the glory it had under the Soviet Union through more integration into the global economy.[158]

Two attempts at natural gas line projects linking Russia and South Korea through North Korea (and to the benefit of North Korea) unfortunately have not come to fruition. In the early 1990s, an agreement was

[155] Wishnick (2004).

[156] "'Iron Silk Road' Project to Make Progress with Roh's Russia Visit," Yonhap, September 17, 2004.

[157] B. M. Ahn (2004).

[158] "Roh, Putin 'Refrained' from 'Directly' Mentioning DPRK's Nuclear Issue," *The Korea Times*, September 22, 2004.

reached to build a 6,600-kilometer pipeline from Yakutia, but then Seoul decided the project would be unprofitable and attention shifted to a 4,000-kilometer gas pipeline from the Irkutsk region. The field at Irkutsk is estimated to be able to supply up to 20 million tons of gas to Russia, the two Koreas, and China for thirty years, covering half of all energy requirements for the DPRK and the ROK at a price one-fourth less than today.[159] However, the 2003 feasibility study for the project suggested a pipeline through China and then across the East Sea to South Korea in order to avoid expensive construction costs and instability in North Korea. South Korean officials have explicitly stated that if pipelines come through North Korea, the rights to control the gas supply may be interrupted, costs may be higher, and the process may be more complicated. In contrast, Seoul expects energy projects in Russia to help resolve tensions over North Korea's nuclear development program. Shortly after Roh was inaugurated in February 2003, his national security adviser suggested in an interview with the *Financial Times* that Russian gas could be provided to North Korea as part of a peaceful resolution of the nuclear dispute.[160]

Russia continues to pursue the energy angle for its own economic gain. The Russian energy strategy, adopted in May 2003, involves a substantial reorientation of Russian energy exports from Europe to NEA, reflecting a European desire to avoid dependence on gas imports from Russia and also Putin's desire to diversify Russian export markets.[161] In addition to the considered pipelines, a third project would involve not only shipping oil from East Siberia with the principal destination of China, but possibly also to the Korean peninsula and Japan. In addition, there are coal deposits in Siberia – and Mongolia – that could be developed with Korean investment. But South Korea will need to generate some $30–$40 billion of investment in exchange for work for South Korean companies and a stable supply of energy for Korea.[162] The ROK is also regarded as a strategic partner for developing metal ore, timber, fertilizer, cotton, and gold projects in Siberia.

The Tumen River Area Development Programme (TRADP), established in 1991 under the UN Development Programme (UNDP) with the involvement of both Koreas, China, Mongolia, and Russia, has been another disappointment. The goal was to develop a "new Hong Kong" – a global trade, transportation, and communications gateway – by using Russian natural resources, Chinese and North Korean labor, and Japanese and South Korean finances and technology. Although technocrats in Moscow energetically lobbied for the project, representatives

[159] Bazhanov (2005).
[160] "Roh to Focus on Energy Provision in Talks with Putin," Yonhap, September 17, 2004.
[161] Wishnick (2004). [162] The DPRK Report, NAPSNET, No. 6, p. 8.

of Primorskii Krai, the Russian province on which the North Korean land borders, opposed it, citing the presence of large numbers of Chinese on Russian territory and the possibility that Beijing was aiming to annex Russian land. Moscow was forced to temper its enthusiasm. Because of domestic Russian concerns, Japan's refusal to participate until relations with the DPRK have been normalized, and the two nuclear standoffs on the Korean peninsula, the whole project has been a significant nonstarter in the region.

In 1996, Russia and North Korea signed an investment agreement envisioning Russian investment in the Rajin-Songbong free trade zone. Although letters of intent were signed between various European countries and North Korea over the course of the 1990s, very little actual investment has occurred in the zone. Russian investment is supposed to be coordinated with activity in the Nakhodka Free Economic Zone – a South Korean industrial complex in Russia, the establishment of which Moscow and Seoul had repeatedly discussed until Kim Dae Jung finally agreed in 1999 to provide up to $1 billion of investment. But Russian obstacles to the development of the Nakhodka zone have limited cooperation in Rajin-Songbong as well. In 1997, North Korea undertook the unprecedented move of leasing the entire territory to the Russian Kontsern Industriya Company for fifty years, but when foreign companies did not come forward to sublease, the Russian firm defaulted on its end of the deal. Little Russian investment has occurred since then. In February 2002, Russia did agree, however, to help modernize Rajin's port and telecommunications infrastructure as a means to facilitate Russian cargo shipments to South Korea, Japan, China, Canada, and Australia.[163]

The integration of the Russian Far East into the Northeast Asian regional economy is a worthwhile task because economic decline in that part of Russia might easily lead to security challenges for both North and South Korea. Russia is afraid that economic instability in the region will lead to decreased interaction with the two Korean states. Russia has therefore been increasingly active in ASEAN. For instance, in 1997, Prime Minister Primakov launched a drive to include the Korean peninsula in the agenda of the ASEAN Regional Forum (ARF), ASEAN's security regime, and when the organization established a mechanism for regular meetings of deputy foreign affairs ministers to discuss security matters, the first such meeting was held in Moscow. ASEAN is viewed in Moscow as an emerging regional pole, on par with China, India, or Japan. Russia has also supported North Korean participation in international regimes. Moscow came out in favor of Kim Dae Jung's idea that Pyongyang should join APEC as a "guest."[164]

[163] Wishnick (2004). [164] S. H. Joo (2003).

Conclusion

Historically, Russia was the state most consistently undertaking great-power intrigue on the Korean peninsula. Both the Korean imperial court and the post–World War II Pyongyang regime tried to manipulate or abrogate Russian and Soviet interest in Korea, with varying degrees of success. Today, Russian interest in reaping economic and status gains on and through the Korean peninsula has made Moscow an active player on both sides of the DMZ. In search of an identity in a globalizing world where it is no longer a recognized superpower, Russia is looking for places in which to reenact its identity as a great Eurasian continental power, and the contours of the Korean peninsula make that a likely locale in which Russia might try to do so. A potential danger of this kind of status drive is that post-Soviet Russia's desire to maintain the trappings of a great power could have Moscow lining up with a North Korea being pursued by the hegemonic United States.

However, as Robert Legvold points out, predicting Russia's future is nearly impossible. Russia maintains an ambiguous and evolving relationship with other great powers, particularly the United States, and its relationship with the new neighboring states is likewise unsettled. These factors generate an immense spectrum of possibilities, ranging from a moderate Russia increasingly well integrated into the external order to an alienated and increasingly combative state. This, to no small degree, is a question of how Russia will define its place and role in NEA. The worst option would be a broken and collapsed Russia, a turbulent vortex in the international system. Not since 1918 have Russian politics and the Russian national identity been in such flux. Imperial collapse has been so complete that for the first time in its history Russian nationhood must be reconsidered and reconstructed.[165]

In this task, Russia confronts a changed international system. Relations among the major powers of the world do not revolve around active strategic rivalry but instead involve cooperative and multilateral undertakings in the name of world order. (Events such as the 2003 U.S. war against Iraq, however, demonstrate that not every undertaking is cooperative and multilateral.) The indisputable leader of the current international system is the United States. Both Russia and North Korea are undoubtedly more interested in their relations with the United States than in their relations with each other. Although North Korea has welcomed greater Russian participation in inter-Korean relations, as Pyongyang's behavior in the second nuclear standoff indicates, dialogue with the United States is viewed as the central component of North Korean security.

[165] Legvold (1999: 187).

That said, the Kremlin's interest in Korea – Russia's enactment of a great-power identity – has already made a significant contribution to the reduction of tensions on the peninsula. Because of Russian brinkmanship diplomacy, Pyongyang agreed to enter the United Nations simultaneously with South Korea, China followed the path to normalization of relations with South Korea, and the DPRK agreed to sign the Basic Agreement and the denuclearization agreement of December 1991. Russians have also objected audibly to the U.S. opinion that the DPRK is an "aggressive" state. In fact, most Russians reject the idea of any dangers posed to the United States by North Korean missiles, given the comparative number of missiles at the disposal of Washington. A common belief in Russia is that the DPRK is a militarily weak state that faces overwhelmingly powerful opponents and truly must fear for its own survival. Therefore, its efforts are viewed as defensive in nature. In the wake of the NATO-led war in former Yugoslavia, Russians were predicting that it was only a matter of time before the United States took action against North Korea.[166] Needless to say George W. Bush's hardline policy toward Pyongyang has driven Moscow and Pyongyang to have closer ties.

Pro-Pyongyang lobbyists in Russia continue to praise the "outstanding achievements" of the North Korean regime. The pro-DPRK contingent includes Russian Communist Party functionaries, who see the DPRK as an ideological friend, and nationalists, who see North Korea as an available geopolitical partner in opposition to the United States and Japan. The North Korean economy, although a basket case, is nonetheless connected to the Russian economy. The DPRK has a natural orientation toward interaction with post-Soviet Russia and, in fact, requires huge quantities of Russian technology, equipment, and spare parts, while it is in turn ready to supply various raw materials.

Russia's ability to influence North Korea is to no small degree related to its struggle to adjust its national identity. Back in the early 1990s, Russia concentrated on becoming a respected, democratic member of the Western community. The United States and Europe were seen as the main political and ideological allies of postcommunist Russia, the principal source of economic aid, and the model for Russian development. This drove the Russian Federation and the DPRK apart. Yet with difficulties in consolidating Western-style reforms and the threat of NATO expansion, Russia became disillusioned with the West and began to emphasize security concerns in its foreign policy, which became increasingly conservative and nationalistic. In this milieu, North Korea found more favor and solidarity with the Kremlin. The Korean peninsula became central

[166] The DPRK Report, NAPSNET, No. 20, October 1999, p. 1.

in Russian sights in terms of status, and Russia's involvement in – but perhaps not yet its influence over – North Korea began to renew itself.

Although Russia has tried to achieve greater balance in its relations with North and South Korea, it has not achieved equidistance: Russo–ROK economic relations have developed much more quickly than ties between Russia and North Korea for the simple fact that Moscow stands to gain much more from improved ties with Seoul. Although the Kremlin wants to foment a belief in its unbiasedness and consequent trilateral cooperation, it lacks the economic resources to subsidize Pyongyang's participation. To the contrary, Moscow hopes to recover as much as possible of Pyongyang's $4 billion in Soviet-era debt and to earn forgiveness of the USSR's debt to Seoul. At times, it seems, economics trumps identity pursuits. Vladimir Putin burst onto the international stage with promises of railway and gas line projects, but Russia's economic weakness and its limited economic ties with South Korea have circumscribed Moscow's participation. Progress is more likely to occur regionally, as Japan, South Korea, and China collaborate with Russia on projects in North Korea.

Russia has tried to contribute to the Korean peace process by serving as an honest broker – suggesting the creation of a multilateral security mechanism in NEA – and by facilitating trilateral economic projects. Russia has earned prestige for its neutral stance, consistency, and sincerity.[167] Russia's influence, however, is still marginal because it does not have material leverage over North Korea and is likely to gain it only through large provisions of economic and military aid.

[167] S. H. Joo (2003).

CHAPTER 4

Japan and the Two Koreas

The Japan Factor

A phrase that has been used frequently to describe the character of Japan–Korea relations over the years is "so near, yet so far."[1] Indeed, distance seems to make Japan's political heart grow fonder. Japan and Korea are so close geographically (in the case of South Korea), ideologically, and developmentally, yet they are so far apart in myriad other ways. Of the Big Four, Japan is beyond compare on Northeast Asian identity politics because Tokyo serves as a clear and present reminder of (wounded) national identity for Korea and China, and as a lightening rod for domestic politics in Seoul, Pyongyang, and Beijing. Of the Big Four, Japan has been the most significant negative other in the making of modern Korean national identity and nationalism.

As one of a few true nation-states – the state's jurisdiction coincides perfectly with its own nation (homogenous people) – Japan should have escaped the wrenching national identity difficulties that have afflicted so many states old and new. Yet, by a more synthetic notion of national identity, the state defines and differentiates itself not only essentially by what it *is* – what the Japanese refer to as *kokutai* (national essence) – but also behaviorally by what it *does* in international relations.

Some of the manifest symbolic and behavioral anomalies in Japanese foreign policy cannot be fully explained by realist and liberal theories. In fact, Walter Lippman once famously described the dangers that can arise when a gap is created in which a state's foreign policy commitments exceed its available power resources. However, Japan has spent most of

[1] In Japan, Korea is often characterized as "*chikakute toi kuni*" (a country that is both close and far) and the Koreans refer to Japan in identical terms, "*kapkpkodo mon* nara" (a country that is close yet far). See B. C. Koh (1998: 33).

the latter half of the twentieth century suffering from a "reverse Lippman gap": its available power resources have consistently outpaced its international commitments and its potential influence. By most conventional measures, Japan is one of the world's great powers: its economy is the second largest in the world on the basis of conventional GDP if not PPP, its defense budget of $42.8 billion is the world's fifth largest, and its technological capabilities are exceeded only by those of the United States. Japan's armed forces are among the largest and most well equipped in the world, replete with the latest state-of-the-art weapons systems, and there is little doubt that Japan could develop a formidable nuclear arsenal on short notice.[2] Japan is also the world's second largest foreign aid donor in absolute terms[3] and the second largest contributor to the UN budget.[4] Yet, neither on the world stage nor in East Asia has contemporary Japan been able to seize a place such that it is recognized and regarded as a global great power.

The gap between Japan's economic power and political influence can be explained by the heavy burdens of geography, history, and national identity, including historical international role, that lie upon the country. As Jules Cambon argued, "The geographical position of a nation is the principal factor conditioning its foreign policy – the principal reason why it must have a foreign policy at all."[5] As a relatively small, resource-poor island state ranking fifty-ninth in the world in terms of territorial size, but having the world's ninth largest population (127 million people), Japan is almost entirely dependent on imports for its oil and natural gas and for more than half its food supply. Most of Japan's trade with the outside world takes place along lines of communication that stretch for thousands of miles, through the South China Sea, Southeast Asia, the Indian Ocean, and the Middle East, areas of conflicting sovereignty claims and doubtful stability.[6]

Prior to 1945, Japan sought to confront resource scarcity by engaging with the outside world from a position of strength, building a powerful military and creating a vast empire in Asia, including the occupation and colonization of Korea. This strategy, however, ultimately proved disastrous, bringing Japan into conflict with much of the rest of the world and resulting in its devastating defeat in World War II. This imperial period created a historical burden under which contemporary Japan operates

[2] Harrison (1996).

[3] With aid measured as a percentage of GNI, the United States, Italy, and Japan rank twenty-seventh, twenty-sixth, and twenty-fifth, respectively, among twenty-seven rich countries. See UNDP (2005: 278).

[4] Japan's ODA was $8.8 billion in 2003 and its assessed contribution to the UN regular budget in 2004 was $280 million (19%), making it the second largest contributor to UN coffers, behind the United States ($363 million or 24% of total UN budget).

[5] Cambon (1935), cited in Pastor (1999: 27).

[6] Berger (2004: 138–39).

today and from which there seems to be no easy exit. Japanese imperial expansion between 1890 and 1945 left behind bitter memories in much of East Asia, particularly in Korea, which was under Japanese colonial rule for thirty-five years, and in China, where it is estimated that 20 million people died following the Japanese invasion that began in the early 1930s in Manchuria and then expanded to China proper in 1937. This history created a widespread and enduring perception that Japan is by nature a militaristic and aggressive nation that, if given the opportunity, could easily revert to its expansionist ways. The unrepentant stance of prominent right-wing Japanese politicians and opinion leaders exacerbates such fears, and throughout the Northeast Asian region, any steps taken by Japan to expand its military or to take on a larger security role tend to be greeted with suspicion and trepidation. Thanks to another round of disputes over history textbooks and territorial boundaries in early 2005, Tokyo seems to have accomplished a diplomatic mission impossible by siring a united Northeast Asian front – involving China and the two Koreas – against Japan's renewed bid for permanent membership on the UN Security Council.[7]

This history creates a zone of contestation with regard to Japan's national identity. Japan is often accused – with some justification – of suffering from "historical amnesia" regarding its modern history.[8] However, this is not so much historical amnesia as it is selective remembering and forgetting.[9] Japan has not made a clean and decisive break with its past in the way that Germany did following the conclusion of World War II. Because of this "who me?" historical revisionism-cum-escapism, Japan is often described as being *in* Asia but not *of* Asia, and Japan has not in fact had a satisfactory definition of its place in Asia since it joined the Western international order in the mid-nineteenth century, at a time when the West meant civilization and Asia meant barbarism.[10] History and national identity interact with one another in such a way that Japan is consistently searching for a national identity and trying to establish a global identity without first addressing its problematic East Asian identity.

Failure to do so has the potential to initiate a spiral of nationalist conflict. For instance, the Japanese Society for History Textbook Reform – which authored controversial history textbooks in 2004 – consists of nationalist academics who allegedly are "deeply concerned by the very

[7] See *Chosun Ilbo* (Seoul), April 1, 2005; Joseph Kahn, "If 22 Million Chinese Prevail at U.N., Japan Won't," *New York Times*, April 1, 2005; and "China Vows to Vote Against Contentious UNSC Expansion Plan," *People's Daily Online*, June 22, 2005. From day one of its UN membership and participation in September 1991, North Korea has maintained its principled stand of opposition to Japan's bid for permanent membership on the UN Security Council.

[8] See Hicks (1997); Buruma (1994); Chang (1997).

[9] See Gong (1996).

[10] See Tamamoto (1991).

serious state of history education in Japan." Fujioka Nobukatsu, the vice chairman of the organization, argues that Japan is currently "educating our children using unsubstantiated, wartime, enemy propaganda.... In actuality, there is no evidence proving that Japanese war crimes were any worse than war crimes committed by other nations." Demands from China and South Korea in response to the textbooks are consequently played off by the Japanese political elite as being anti-Japanese rhetoric, which then ignites Japanese nationalism, moving the population further toward supporting rearmament and a nationalist foreign policy.[11]

Japan has gone through five post–Cold War periods of pursuing a great-power identity. Beginning in the 1950s, many Japanese believed their country would become the third superpower, and in the late 1980s, as the Soviet Union collapsed and Japan was at the height of its economic bubble, it appeared that superpower status might not be far off. Japan expected to be able to speak boldly at the G-7 summits and the United Nations, use its economic power to help redefine the international financial architecture, and stand tall as the inspiring representative of the East Asian alternative model of capitalism. (Nonetheless, throughout this time period, Japan played only a passive role on the Korean peninsula, as compared with the active roles played by the United States, Russia, and China.) Japan's ascent seemed to continue in the early 1990s, when the isolation of China following the Tiananmen Square protests and crackdown encouraged Japan to aspire to regional leadership as well. However, in the mid-1990s, as relations soured with several great powers and also with its neighbors, Japan initiated its third phase of post–Cold War international relations. Its economic bubble had burst, and its political leadership did not present a clear vision for the country. Rather than being an agent leading globalization, Tokyo saw itself as a victim of globalization.[12] Japan's hopes for either superpower status or regional leadership seemed unlikely to be realized. In the late 1990s, Japan attempted both to enter the great-power balancing game being played out between the United States and China and to grab the mantle of regional leadership by establishing an Asian Monetary Fund in the wake of the Asian Financial Crisis of 1997–98. The United States rebuffed both moves, preferring to control both global political and global economic interactions. Finally, in the early twenty-first century Japan's political right wing began to pursue a new strategy for leverage by boosting national military power and rearming. Diet (the Japanese parliament) approval of the national anthem and flag, which had been relegated to unofficial use

[11] Norimitsu Onish, "In Japan's New Texts, Lessons in Rising Nationalism," *New York Times,* April 17, 2005/IV/p. 3.

[12] Grimes (2000).

after the war, signified a new determination to seek a great-power national identity.[13]

Because of this varied trajectory, there is no scholarly consensus on how to characterize Japan's post–Cold War foreign policy. Initially, Japan was seen as a reactive state, responding to the course of world history rather than shaping it.[14] In the late 1990s, it was suggested that Japan was becoming a "reluctant realist," defined by the muscular, nationalist foreign policy being advocated by Japanese conservatives.[15] In contrast, Japan was also described as a "cautious liberal," eschewing military power in favor of diplomacy and cooperation.[16] Post-1945 Japanese leaders, for instance, secured access to outside markets through nonmilitary means – diplomacy, trade, and foreign aid – and tried to maintain diplomatic and trade relations with all nations as much as possible.[17]

The history of Korean–Japanese relations might be best described in terms of quasicrises. A quasicrisis, according to Chung-in Moon, is kindled when external events are perceived to inflict severe vulnerability to core national values or interests that cannot be managed within the existing policy framework unless prompt, explicit, and remedial countermeasures are taken. This stands in contrast with a real crisis, in which core national interests actually are deprived. International quasicrisis involves mostly nonmilitary, nonsecurity values such as economic well-being, political integrity, national prestige, or identity. Decision time is constrained, and major decision makers must play a role in reaching a resolution. Otherwise, a quasicrisis can escalate to an acute crisis situation through spill-over effects in security and military dimensions.[18]

In analyzing the bargaining that surrounds such quasicrises, we might look to asymmetrical bargaining theory.[19] This theory argues that the aggregate structural power of a stronger state does not always translate into issue-specific power. Thinking in terms of capacities for asymmetrical bargaining may help explain the seeming anomaly of a small state – whether North or South Korea – outmaneuvering or prevailing over its larger adversary or negotiating partner (Japan) on some issues on some occasions.

In NEA – in contrast with Western Europe and North America – the centrifugal forces of identity politics struggle against the centripetal forces of growing regional economic interdependence. The liberal ideals motivating Japanese national security policy have therefore been tempered by a pragmatic or incremental realism. Japan remains strategically liberal but is willing to consider the tactics of *realpolitik*. In recent years,

[13] On the five stages of Japanese post–Cold War foreign policy, see Rozman (2002a: 75).
[14] Calder (1988). [15] Green (2001). [16] Berger (2004). [17] Berger (2004: 138–39).
[18] C. I. Moon (1991). [19] See Habeeb (1988).

the realist train of thought has led, for instance, to an increased willingness to expand Japan's military capabilities and to support the use of force. However, these realist moments in Japan's foreign relations are not viewed with favor by other East Asian countries, and particularly not by Korea.

Aiding the realist strains in Japanese foreign policy has been the stance of the United States. Since the end of the Cold War and particularly under the administration of George W. Bush, the United States has been doing everything in its power to encourage and even accelerate Japanese rearmament as an integral part of an American grand strategy for global hegemony. For example, in August 2004, Secretary of State Colin Powell stated baldly in Tokyo that if Japan ever hoped to become a permanent member of the UN Security Council, it would first have to get rid of its pacifist constitution. Since the early 1990s, the Japanese government has launched a stealth program of incremental rearmament. Since 1992, it has enacted twenty-one major pieces of security-related legislation, nine of them in 2004 alone. On February 19, 2005, Japan and the United States signed a new military agreement, which for the first time had Japan identify security in the Taiwan Strait as a "common strategic objective."[20]

In addition to the real pressures from the United States that create distance between Japan and its East Asian neighbors, Japanese leaders have continued to engage in domestic symbolic politics that the rest of East Asia – and particularly the collective colonial memory in Korea – finds neoimperialistic or insulting. In 1995, on the fiftieth anniversary of the end of the Pacific War, the Diet issued a watered-down resolution of apology, which was coupled with many prefectural assembly resolutions that essentially rationalized the path of colonization and war that Japan had taken. Prime Minister Koizumi Junichiro has visited the Yasukuni Shrine in Tokyo every year since becoming prime minister in April 2001, ostensibly to honor the nation's war dead. Although these war dead include, for instance, more than 1,000 convicted war criminals from World War II, attention has centered on the fourteen Class A war criminals, mostly top Japanese military leaders – including Japan's wartime prime minister, General Hideki Tojo – who were convicted by the Allies at the Tokyo trials after the war's end. These nationalist stances generally meet with public approval. Bookstores in Japan in the late 1990s showcased an unprecedented display of assertive writings on how Japan should stand up for its national interests.[21] More than 60 percent of the Japanese public supports a constitutional change that would remove the

[20] On the U.S. pressure on Japan in the post–Cold War period and during the George W. Bush administration, see Johnson (2005).

[21] Rozman (2002a: 85).

pacifist clauses; a whopping 90 percent of Diet members younger than age fifty want such a constitutional revision.[22] Yet, interestingly enough, no less than five former prime ministers – Miyazawa Kiichi, Murayama Tomiichi, Hashimoto Ryutaro, Mori Yoshiro, and Kaifu Toshiki – have publicly expressed their opposition to such shrine visitations and have asked Koizumi to refrain from visiting the Yasukuni Shrine to avoid further damaging Tokyo's ties with its Northeast Asian neighbors.[23] Likewise, Emperor Akihito has snubbed repeated calls from right-wingers to visit the Yasukuni Shrine.

In 2000, when a national commission established to revise middle school history textbooks called for only minor changes that nonetheless met with little sympathy inside Japan, Chinese and Korean observers were shocked. What had been seen as extreme views rationalizing the occupation of Korea and the invasion of China were suddenly being countenanced by the mainstream in Japan. In addition, and in opposition to the United States, the mainstream press carried an article saying that Japan had suffered a "holocaust" during World War II, describing the two atomic bombs dropped on Japan as the greatest war crimes ever committed. The same article asked how Japan can be an independent country while Okinawa is still occupied.[24]

The question of national identity in East Asia is ultimately a struggle between the past and the future. Koreans, in both the North and the South, see Japan as an imperialist power, and proclaim the escape from Japanese domination as the foundation of their nation building and of their process of forming and enacting national identity.[25] In the face of regional memories such as these, it is perhaps not surprising that Japan has attempted to form its national identity on a global stage. Japan's shared global identity also originates in its consistent alignment with the West during the Cold War. In contrast, Japan's regional identity could be brought to the fore if its common Confucian heritage with the other countries of East Asia – an alternative to Western culture – were to be emphasized. Because nationalist appeals have so much political weight at home, the process of finding a stable mix of global, regional, and national elements in one national identity will be gradual.[26]

National identity conflicts are less salient in the economic domain. Despite Japan's difficulties in coming to terms with its imperial past in a way that is acceptable to its Northeast Asian neighbors, economic and social interaction with China and South Korea has increased. Japanese exports to China jumped 70 percent between 2001 and 2004 and provided, in fact, the main impetus for a Japanese economic recovery. Some

[22] Green (2000). [23] D. C. Kang and J. Y. Lee (2005). [24] See Rozman (2002a: 87).
[25] Rozman (2002a: 90); Hahm and Kim (2001); S. S. Kim (1976). [26] Rozman (2002a).

18,000 Japanese companies now have operations in China. In 2003, Japan passed the United States as the top destination for Chinese students going abroad for a university education. In terms of Eurasian diplomatic engagement with Russia, Japan also seemed ready, in the late 1990s, to meet with success. Supporting Russia's entrance as a full member of the G-8 and APEC to sooth its ruffled feathers after the loss of its superpower status, Japan held several summits with Russia. However, the two countries did not resolve their long-running territorial dispute over the Southern Kurile Islands (Northern Territories); hence, relations have cooled once again to a state of cold peace.

With regard to relations with Korea, there is a string of overlapping contrasts: public versus private, words versus deeds, and promise versus performance. Perceptions are crucial in determining the long-term impacts of interactions across the East Sea. Whereas some argue that a "nuanced realism" can explain Korean–Japanese relations,[27] it seems more likely that relations have mirrored Allen Whiting's description of Sino–Japanese relations in which "high-level acrimonious exchanges between the two capitals . . . belied official affirmations of friendship and endangered the basic relations."[28] Although Korea, like China, admires Japan as an economic model that deserves at least some emulation, and although it has a strong desire to acquire transfers of technology, these are secondary to a deep, historically based distrust that repeatedly surfaces in the relationship.

In Korea, there is a significant amount of what Allen Whiting, referring to the Chinese case, calls "war recall"; this might be expanded in the Korean case to "colonial/imperial recall."[29] That is, in response to events such as political statements of Japanese leaders, historical textbook publications, visits to the Yasukuni Shrine, activities by Japanese right-wing groups, and visits by Japanese leaders, there is an almost knee-jerk reaction from Korean political leaders, civil society protests, or the media, a reaction that brings historical events to the fore in discussing contemporary interactions with Japan. Therefore, even as Japan–ROK relations have become closer than ever in terms of economic ties, security cooperation, and political and cultural linkages, the two countries have nonetheless engaged in acrimonious disputes over fishing and territorial boundaries and over the interpretation of history because of the historical sensitivity of these issues.

Colonial/imperial recall is triggered each year on the anniversary of the anticolonial March 1 (1919) independence movement and on liberation day, August 15, the two biggest South Korean national holidays. In addition, there are dynamic triggers in the form of new events, such

[27] V.D. Cha (1999a). [28] Whiting (1989: 20). [29] Whiting (1989).

as those mentioned previously. Japanese politicians and academics have often been careless in their remarks, leading to aggravation in Korea. This interference in Korean affairs and direct threat to Korea's national identity clearly inspires colonial/imperial recall among ordinary Koreans.

The year 2005 was supposed to be a great year for South Korean–Japanese relations because Seoul and Tokyo had agreed to call it the "Korea–Japan Friendship Year" to mark and celebrate the fortieth anniversary of the 1965 ROK–Japan Normalization Treaty.[30] The two countries also initiated talks to pave the way for a free trade agreement (FTA). Yet, hopes for better bilateral relations were suddenly dashed by the escalating historical/territorial tensions and controversies over a high school history textbook to be published with the support of a right-wing nationalist scholars' group known as the Society for Composing a New Textbook on History, and more seriously, over the disputed Tokdo (Dokdo) Islands – Takeshima in Japanese – triggered by the Shimane prefecture assembly's passage on March 16, 2005, of a local ordinance designing February 22 as "Takeshima Day." The conflation of the history textbook issue and the Takeshima Day declaration, coupled with Japanese ROK Ambassador Takano Toshiyuki's public statement that the Tokdo/Takeshima Islands are "historically and legally Japan's territory," pushed Tokyo–Seoul relations to a critical tipping point. On March 17, the Roh government announced a new doctrine for dealing with Japan in which seeking an apology and compensation from the former colonial power for its wartime atrocities took center stage. The Japan Doctrine, announced in a National Security Council meeting, called Japanese moves "a second dispossession of the Korean Peninsula that denies the history of Korean liberation."[31] On March 31, Seoul took its "diplomatic war" with Japan to the United Nations, where it began lobbying to block Japan's bid for a permanent seat on the UN Security Council.

The most important variable in the shaping of Japan–Korea relations remains the relative salience of Japan's imperial past as it is being played out in domestic coalition politics and acted out in foreign policy. Underlying these national identity concerns are five long-term characteristics of Japanese–Korean relations: (1) the Japanese colonial legacy, which was the crucible of modern Korean nationalism and national identity in both Koreas[32]; (2) the existence of more than 650,000 "Zainichi" Koreans

[30] The twenty years it took after the end of World War II and the Japanese colonial era for Japan and South Korea to normalize relations is significant given that the two countries shared the United States as a common ally. Despite a dozen rounds of normalization talks, Japan and North Korea have not reached a normalization agreement.

[31] *Chosun Ilbo*, March 17, 2005.

[32] Kim Il Sung and Syngman Rhee, for instance, had nothing in common in terms of political background, ideology, or worldview *except* a shared anti-Japanism.

residing in Japan – two-thirds of whom are ROK nationals and one-third of whom have an allegiance to the DPRK; (3) Japan's seeming inability or unwillingness to come clean with its imperial past and wartime atrocities; (4) festering historical-cum-territorial animosities and suspicions; and (5) abiding ethnic animosities, especially between Japanese and Koreans.[33] The key proximate variable is the interaction between the dynamic international triggers and domestic politics as structured and exploited by political leaders in Japan and both Koreas. As Robert Jervis suggests, "Domestic politics may dictate that a given event be made the occasion for change in policy; bargaining with the bureaucracy may explain what options are presented to the national leaders; the decision maker's predisposition could account for the choice that was made; and the interests and routines of the bureaucracies could explain the way the decision was implemented."[34] Before looking at some of the proximate issues that have engaged Japanese–Korean passions, it is important to review the history that defines so many of the underlying antagonistic national identity conflicts.

Weight of the Past

The relationships between the two Korean states and Japan carry some of the heaviest historical baggage in contemporary international relations. In the late nineteenth century, in a series of starts and stops, Japan succeeded in drawing Korea out of the traditional Sinocentric East Asian world order and into the system of Western international relations based on sovereign nation-states. This was part of a broad challenge that Meiji Japan presented to the traditional supremacy of China in East Asia, arising at the same time that Chinese supremacy was being challenged by Western imperialism.[35] In the early twentieth century, Japan colonized Korea; independence came only with the conclusion of World War II. As described previously, the memories of the colonial period resonate strongly in contemporary Korean–Japanese relations.

Even before the advent of modernity in East Asia, Toyotomi Hideyoshi's invasions of the Korean peninsula in the 1590s held a substantial purchase on the Korean imagination. The Japanese had occupied almost all of Korea, were widely regarded as marauders, and were repelled only with Chinese help. Korea therefore maintained arm's length relations with Japan following the conclusion of a trade agreement in 1609, an

[33] For an argument that ethnic hatreds are the most likely source of future military clashes in East Asia, see Berger (2000: 405–06).

[34] Jervis (1976: 16–17).

[35] The twin challenges to the traditional East Asian world order are organizing themes of Key-hiuk Kim's classic *The Last Phase of the East Asian World Order* (1980).

agreement that would serve as the sole basis for Japanese–Korean relations for the next 250 years.[36] Through the Tokugawa period that preceded the Meiji restoration in Japan, Korean relations with its neighbor proceeded with little Chinese involvement. In contrast to the *sadae chui* ("serving the great") relationship that Korea had with China, foreign relations with Japan were defined as *kyorin* ("neighborly relations"). The Korean king and the Japanese shogun treated each other as equals and dealt with each other through the medium of Tsushima, an island between Japan and Korea.[37]

This began to change in the face of the Meiji restoration and Japan's opening to the West. Although Japan continued to maintain the same type of relations with Korea, using Tsushima as an intermediary, national opinion regarding Korea became more interested and expansionist, with some intellectuals claiming a traditional tributary role for Korea vis-à-vis Japan. In the 1860s, Chinese observers of Korea began to make note of Japan's aspirations on the peninsula.[38] Japan, watching Russian and British interest in Tsushima and various parts of coastal China grow, knew that if it was going to take a dominant role on the Korean peninsula it would have to hold off Western powers who wanted to stake their own claims there. Therefore, for example, Japan offered to mediate between the United States and Korea over the U.S. inquiry into a missing merchant ship, the *USS General Sherman*. Japan's expansionism was motivated in part by its desire for security: by taking Korea, Japanese intellectuals believed, the homeland might be made more secure against Western aggression.[39] One high-ranking Japanese official observed, "France will not let Korea survive long. Russia is watching its moves, and the United States has its own designs."[40]

In 1871, Japan and China signed the first East Asian treaty based on Western international law. With the door open, Japan also began revising its relations with Korea, first ending the tradition of conducting relations through Tsushima. Following its 1874 expedition in southern Taiwan, a clear challenge to China and a warning to Korea, Japan began taking bold actions in Korea that led quickly to the Treaty of Kanghwa in February 1876.[41] The treaty declared Korea an "autonomous state," terminating traditional relations between Japan and Korea in favor of Westernized relations.[42] Interactions between Korea and Japan increased markedly in the wake of the treaty.

These interactions, however, were far from universally positive. A mutiny with an anti-Japanese character led to Japan demanding an

[36] K. H. Kim (1980: 15–16). [37] On Tsushima, see K. H. Kim (1980: 17–20).
[38] K. H. Kim (1980: 71–72). [39] K. H. Kim (1980: 102–09).
[40] Quoted in K. H. Kim (1980: 129). [41] K. H. Kim (1980: 193–94, 200–03).
[42] K. H. Kim (1980: 253).

indemnity, while two years later the Japanese were on the other side of the fence, involved in an attempted coup by Korean progressives. China responded to the coup with military force, and Japan, at the end of the event, again demanded reparations from Korea.[43] The Tonghak Rebellion of 1894 served as a catalyst for the Sino–Japanese War. During the war, the Japanese occupied the royal palace in Seoul, remodeling the Korean government and instituting detailed reform measures that covered almost all aspects of Korean life.[44]

Japan's ambitions were set back when Russia, France, and Germany intervened to alter the terms of the settlement reached with China in the Treaty of Shimonoseki and then again in 1896, when the Russians provided refuge to the king so he could rule free from Japanese influence. Japan's surprise victory in the Russo–Japanese War of 1904–05, however, left Japan unchallenged on the peninsula.[45] By a combination of diplomatic intrigue and military maneuver, Japan not only brought Korea into the international sphere of sovereign state relations, but also brought Korea increasingly under Japan's direct control.

The Japanese cabinet declared that Japan was "to take possession of the real powers of protection in political and military matters of Korea and to promote the development of [Japanese] economic rights and interests in Korea."[46] Japan claimed that the Korean peninsula was "a dagger pointing at Japan's heart." Obtaining support from the United States and Britain, Japan pursued protectorate status over Korea, achieving in a November 1905 treaty "control and direction of the external relations of Korea" and the stationing of a resident-general in Seoul to manage diplomatic affairs and to have personal audience with the Korean emperor, as the king had become.[47] Despite Korean contention that the treaty was not legitimate, the Japanese began installing advisers in every Korean government office. Within two years, Russia and Japan reached agreement that would allow for Japan's official annexation of Korea.[48] This annexation then took place under a treaty signed on August 22, 1910, by Korean Emperor Sunjong and the Japanese government. Opposition to Japanese rule was squelched with brutal efficiency, and the economic and strategic needs of the Japanese home islands, rather than the interests of the Korean population, dictated the course of Korean economic and social development.[49] The exploitation of Korea

[43] C. I. Kim and H. K. Kim (1967: 34–38, 46–54).
[44] C. I. Kim and H. K. Kim (1967: 80–81). [45] C. I. Kim and H. K. Kim (1967: 88–91, 102).
[46] Quoted in C. I. Kim and H. K. Kim (1967: 122–23).
[47] C. I. Kim and H. K. Kim (1967: 125, 131). [48] C. I. Kim and H. K. Kim (1967: 141–43).
[49] There is considerable debate over the extent of the benefits brought by Japanese rule. For a balanced overview, see Myers and Peattie (1984).

on the political and economic level was exacerbated by popular Japanese feelings of superiority vis-à-vis Koreans and other Asians on the societal level.

Issues from the earliest days of colonization linger to our times. The Tokdo/Takeshima islands, a small cluster of rocky islets in the East Sea, have been administered by South Korea since 1953 and are currently occupied only by a South Korean police unit. Nonetheless, Japanese interests have made use of a 1905 declaration to lay claim to the islands, which are rich in fishing. The name of the sea in which the islands lay is also a point of contention. To Japan, it is known as the Sea of Japan, and this is the way that it usually is known on Western maps, despite the fact that precolonization Western maps call it the Sea of Corea or the East Sea of Korea, as do historical Chinese maps. Indeed, the spelling of Korea with a "K" is sometimes alleged to be a Japanese invention from the colonial period so that Korea would follow Japan in alphabetical listings in the Roman alphabet.

In a very real way, modern Korean national identity – and nationalism – was forged in the crucible of Japanese colonial domination of Korea. The March 1, 1919, uprising against colonial rule and oppression is regarded by many as the founding moment of the modern Korean nation. It holds a similar place in Korean national mythology, as does the May 1, 1919 Chinese uprising in China's national history. When the ROK was formed after the war, many of its most revered figures were former leaders of the anti-colonial movement. The symbols of the new country also drew actively on anti-Japanese symbols. For instance, a national monument was erected in honor of An Chung-gun – the Korean assassin of the first Japanese Consul General of Korea, Ito Hirobumi – and his image was widely used on Korean currency. This produced in Korea a powerful association between patriotism and anti-imperial, anti-Japanese sentiments. It also created a deep and lasting gulf between the ways the Japanese and their neighbors understand each other.

Japanese control during the colonial period was as coercive as it was comprehensive. Imperial Japan tried to erase entirely any elements of Korean national identity: the use of the Japanese language was made universal and mandatory from the first grade in elementary schools and public places; the adoption of Japanese names was required; and the worship of the Shinto state religion was mandated. The colonial police intruded extensively into every aspect of society and suppressed attempts at resistance, often brutally.

In 1931, when Japan expanded militarily into Manchuria, Korea became an invaluable source of mineral resources, cheap labor, and hydroelectricity. The Japanese referred to the role of Korea in their imperial plans with slogans such as "Chosen as a base of war supplies" and

"Chosen as a base of penetration."[50] The colonial government invested heavily in railways, ports, roads, and communications infrastructure, while also guaranteeing political stability. These two factors proved the necessary incentives for Japanese conglomerates (Zaibatsu) to invest in colonial Korea. By the mid-1930s, Zaibatsus were the largest capital investors in Korea and spearheaded industrial expansion.[51]

With the intensification of the Pacific War, hundreds of thousands of Koreans were conscripted to support the Japanese war machine and even more were forced into labor conscription programs, which abruptly transported nearly 20 percent of the rural population to low-skill mining and factory jobs in northern Korea, Manchuria, Sakhalin, and Japan under subhuman working conditions. The number of Koreans in Japan alone at the time of Japanese surrender in August 1945 was more than 2 million. Korean immigrant workers in Japan were typically relegated to menial tasks and hard manual labor and generally occupied the lowest rungs of the social hierarchy.[52] They were subject to discrimination and persecution, as in the wake of the great Kanto earthquake of 1923, when thousands of resident Koreans were hunted down and killed by Japanese militias.

In addition, Korean women were forced into the Japanese military in World War II as sex slaves. Many survivors have testified to being tricked and forced into slavery. The surviving women in Korea and throughout Asia, including in China and the Philippines, are still fighting for compensation, but Tokyo has never apologized and has refused compensation. The issue still sparks public anger in Korea and other Asian countries captured by the Japanese during the war. The estimated number of comfort women ranges from 100,000 to 300,000. Because Japan alone among the countries of Asia had successfully industrialized and learned to compete with the Western powers on an equal or near-equal footing, Koreans, Chinese, and other Asian peoples were viewed as superstitious and backward. These feelings of superiority were translated into everyday discrimination against Koreans in the education and labor markets. All Koreans were the object of social discrimination and relegation to the lowest strata of society. Today, *Zainichi* (literally "residing in Japan") is the euphemism for Koreans that live in Japan. Most Zainichi Koreans are second- or third-generation Koreans who still hold either North or South Korean allegiance and suffer much discrimination by Japanese policies and society. Until recently, Japan required them to adopt Japanese names as part of naturalization, and many are still ineligible for Japanese citizenship.

[50] J. E. Woo (1991: 30). [51] J. E. Woo (1991: 31–33).
[52] See Bridges (1993: 8); Weiner (1994); V. Cha (1999a: 19).

Despite or perhaps even because of this stained imperial past, following the war Japanese education emphasized postwar Japan as a defeated nation that suffered from aggression by great Western powers and that received two atomic bombs at Hiroshima and Nagasaki. The role of Japan as aggressor and tormentor in East Asia was not discussed. Japan's conservative elites had every reason to avoid a serious pursuit of the issue of responsibility for the war – many members of Japan's postwar leadership were directly implicated in the expansion of Imperial Japan (including the Emperor himself), the war against the United States, and wartime atrocities (far more so than in Germany) – whereas Japan's leftist opposition had its own strategic political reasons for portraying the Japanese people as the innocent victims of war. Japanese conservatives argued that the U.S. occupation had dealt a near-lethal blow to the Japanese sense of national pride and that restoring the population's sense of pride in the nation's past was vital if Japan was to once again become a great nation-state. Conservatives also tended to link the history issue to national security because they argued that a strong sense of national identity was the critical psychological component needed for a successful national security policy. Therefore, the Liberal Democratic Party (LDP) government worked to purge Japanese textbooks of views that were overly critical of postwar Japan and to avoid any reference to the invasion of China or to atrocities that had been committed by the Japanese imperial forces.

Beyond these domestic reasons for revisionist history, Japan's geostrategic environment in the 1940s and 1950s encouraged only a limited confrontation with the issue of accepting responsibility for the war and colonialism. Three factors in particular made the structure of the Cold War in Asia very different from that of Europe: the relative looseness of the U.S.-led coalition, the paucity of democracies in the region, and the deep divisions among the Communist nations in Asia. As a result, the United States created a system of bilateral security relations with various Asian countries instead of a single, multilateral framework as in Western Europe. This so-called hub-and-spokes arrangement placed the United States at the center of regional politics. For virtually every one of its regional allies, including South Korea, Japan, and the Philippines, bilateral diplomatic dialogue with the United States was the single most important point of contact with the larger international system. One consequence of the hub-and-spokes arrangement was that the pressure for political dialogue between the U.S. allies in Asia was much weaker than was the case in Western Europe. As long as the United States was willing to subordinate justice and international reconciliation to the larger goal of defending against Communism, there was little structural reason for Asian nations, including Japan, to pursue the regional issues of historical injustice. The Federal Republic of Germany, in contrast, was already in the 1940s and

1950s compelled to seek reconciliation with its Western neighbors (mostly France).[53]

When the Korean War erupted in June 1950, Japan was not involved militarily, yet it reaped maximum economic and political benefits. Japan was still under U.S. occupation and was economically fragile at the start of the war; by the end of the war, the country had regained its sovereignty, and its economy had been imbued with new potential. Japan served as a logistical base for the U.S. forces and also became a key manufacturing center for war supplies. The United States spent close to $3 billion in Japan for war and war-related supplies from 1950 to 1954.[54] Without becoming involved in the bloodshed or material deprivation, Japan was able to reap the benefits of a war economy. The postwar U.S. commitment to protect Korea buttressed the U.S. commitment to Japan. The Japanese skillfully negotiated a mutual security treaty that provided for U.S. protection of Japan while allowing Tokyo to escape the burden of joint defense and also to transfer human and material resources that might otherwise be spent on defense into the promotion of its economy.

In Korea, Syngman Rhee objected vehemently to the benefits accruing to Japan as a result of the Korean War. Rhee became particularly enraged at American suggestions that aid given to Korea should be spent on Japanese goods; he did not want Korea to be an economic appendix of the Japanese recovery. Rhee called instead for aid to be used on nurturing Korean industries and the Korean economy. U.S. estimates of procurements of Japanese goods by Korea had to be revised downward to assuage the South Korean government.[55]

The geostrategic situation that emerged in NEA after the Korean War also allowed Japan to deflect scrutiny of its domestic politics. This resulted in the quick reintegration into Japanese politics of individuals directly implicated in the expansion of Imperial Japan, the war against the United States, and wartime atrocities. Emblematic of this phenomenon was the reemergence of Kishi Nobusuke, who was the former head of the Manchurian railroad, a Minister of Munitions in the Tojo government, and a signatory of the 1941 declaration of war against the United States. Although he was held briefly as a Class A war criminal after the war, Kishi returned to active politics in the 1950s and became prime minister in 1957, a turn of events that would have been unthinkable in the German context.[56] Japan's conservative leadership, who gathered together under the umbrella of the LDP after 1955, favored a narrative of the origins of the Pacific War that was largely exculpatory in nature, stressing the defensive motives behind the expansion of the empire and neglecting

[53] See Berger (2003). [54] J. E. Woo (1991: 33–34). [55] J. E. Woo (1991: 34–36).
[56] See Berger (2005a).

for the most part the issue of Japanese wartime atrocities. These conservatives believed strongly that the American occupation, together with the Japanese left, had used the history issue to deal a near-lethal blow to the Japanese sense of self. Restoring the population's sense of pride in the nation's past was vital if Japan was to become a great power again.

In the 1950s, Japan began to seek reconciliation with its neighbors through bilateral negotiations with other Western-aligned Asian states, beginning with the Republic of China (Taiwan) in 1952, followed by Burma in 1954, the Philippines in 1956, Indonesia in 1958, South Vietnam in 1959, South Korea in 1965, and Malaysia in 1967. Japanese negotiators were able to hammer out ambiguously worded agreements in which it offered economic development assistance that could be interpreted as reparations without officially having to acknowledge them as such. In the late 1960s and early 1970s, the Sino–Soviet split even encouraged Chinese Communist leaders to bury the issue of a Japanese apology and compensation for suffering during the war in return for economic aid and investment. The desperate need of these countries for funds, their limited leverage vis-à-vis Japan, and the recognition of Japan as a key member of the U.S.-led alliance to contain communism in Asia, all strongly encouraged these governments to settle for limited reparations instead of holding out for more. Fierce popular protests in South Korea forced the Japanese government to offer more strongly worded expressions of remorse and larger sums of aid, but in the end the harshly authoritarian government of Park Chung Hee was able to bring the protestors under control.

Although the normalization agreement with Seoul was reached in 1965, the fierce inter-Korean rivalry of the 1950s and the 1960s left no room for a fitting independent Japanese role in inter-Korean "diplomacy" during that time. Inter-Korean relations were essentially war by other means and were severely limited by the security challenge the two Koreas posed to each other and to the complex but stable balance of power among their great power patrons, the United States, China, and the Soviet Union. Japan's insertion into the deadlocked inter-Korean relations would thus have upset the unforgiving zero-sum calculations of the rival Koreas and their great power allies, making any Japanese initiative potentially costly and unsettling.[57]

The last Cold War decade of the 1980s was a turning point in bringing the historical issues back into Japan–Korea relations. As the Cold War world structure began to unravel with the coming of the Gorbachev revolution in Soviet foreign policy, issues of national identity construction and enactment became increasingly salient. In 1985, Nakasone Yasuhiro became the first postwar Japanese prime minister to pay an official visit to

[57] C. S. Kang (2004).

the Yasukuni Shrine, which is dedicated to the spirits of the war dead as described previously. Periodic visits to the shrine by high-ranking government officials have since served as an on-again, off-again dynamic trigger, setting in motion the politics of historical enmity between Japan and its Northeast Asian neighbors (China and South Korea). These other East Asian governments, freed of the constraints imposed by the East–West conflict and increasingly wealthy and prosperous in their own right, no longer felt as dependent as they once had on Japanese support. Therefore, as foreign policy issues other than security – trade, the environment, defense, human rights – gained in importance, it became more important to discuss history. At the same time, the pluralization of politics and toppling of dictatorships in South Korea created political space where such sentiments could be voiced without fear of repression. The end of the Cold War was to establish a New World Order in East Asia by breaking down the extant bipolar hierarchies and relational patterns, but it did so only to a limited extent, and more important, it did so with the revelation of older and deeper wounds that have now become constant points of reference in Korea–Japan relations. In short, both Japan and the two Koreas are now faced with the daunting challenge of changing or shifting their national identities from a Cold War to a post–Cold War footing.

New Challenges of the Tokyo–Seoul–Pyongyang Triangle

Political and Diplomatic Issues

Postwar political relations between Japan and the two Korean states have a twisted history. It took fourteen years for Tokyo and Seoul to achieve diplomatic normalization, whereas Tokyo and Pyongyang continue to negotiate over the issue. Despite forty years of "normalized" relations, national identity issues today call into question the "normalcy" of Japan–ROK relations. Despite the defining influence of the Cold War in NEA, the weight of history and the weight of national identity enactment command special resonance and saliency in the examination of Tokyo's political and diplomatic relations with both Seoul and Pyongyang. The clash of competing national identities seems made to order for providing a useful analytical framework for examining the current and future course of Japan–Korea relations as well.

The Long Road to Japan–DPRK Normalization

From the time it regained its sovereignty until the end of the Cold War, Japan made little effort to normalize ties with North Korea. There was little political or economic gain to be had by establishing official diplomatic relations with Pyongyang, and it appeared that the lack of political relations was not impacting the economic ties that did exist. Japan was firmly enmeshed in the U.S. alliance structure in East Asia and did not want to upset the balance by pursuing relations with the communist DPRK. So, Japan had only a small incentive to deviate from the policy of nonrecognition. In addition, in 1955, the General Association of Korean Residents in Japan (*Chongryun* in Korean or *Chosen Soren* in Japanese) established itself as a pro-North Korean organization and thereby became a *de facto* embassy for Pyongyang, representing North Korean interests in Japan through lobbying and occasional protest activities.

Once Japan had signed the 1965 normalization treaty with South Korea, Pyongyang had less desire to pursue normalization, given its opposition to cross-recognition of the two Korean states and its insistence on regarding diplomatic ties as a component of international legitimation. With a debt of hundreds of millions of dollars owed to Japan from trade relations, Pyongyang also lacked the incentive to find itself at a bargaining table where it might be called on to pay such a debt (estimated at $530 million incurred, with Pyongyang initially defaulting from 1972 to 1975). In the 1980s, North Korea sponsored several terrorist strikes against South Korean targets; these ensured that Japan kept the door firmly shut on the possibility of normalization.

In the late 1980s, the confluence of the Gorbachev revolution in Soviet foreign policy, Seoul's *Nordpolitik,* and Beijing–Moscow renormalization began to undermine the deep structure of Cold War politics in NEA in general and on the Korean peninsula in particular. In July 1988, newly elected South Korean President Roh Tae Woo announced *Nordpolitik,* a major policy initiative aimed at improving inter-Korean relations by expanding South Korean political, economic, and cultural ties with the Soviet Union, China, and other socialist states. It also urged Tokyo and Washington to develop better relations with North Korea. When Gorbachev formulated a new Asia-Pacific strategy, one of the most interesting and groundbreaking ideas was Soviet recognition of Seoul, which was achieved in 1990, paving the road to Sino–ROK normalization two years later. The United States had relaxed its rigid North Korea policy in 1988, creating space for its allies to undertake more independent foreign policies toward the DPRK. North Korea, in turn, was watching the financial and political support of its socialist allies recede. In the late 1980s and early 1990s, Japan was viewed as being on a trajectory to surpass the United States as the largest economy in the world and so seemed a ripe target for a North Korean state badly in need of support in the form of foreign capital and technology transfer. Japan indeed wanted to be sure that it was in place to play a leadership role in the new Northeast Asian order.

Tokyo and Pyongyang, in fact, had shared a reaction to the Soviet–South Korean summit meeting held in San Francisco in June 1990. The DPRK was shocked by the defection of the socialist superpower from its one-Korea policy and sought to compensate for the diplomatic setback with its own surprise normalization. Japan, shocked by the success of Seoul's *Nordpolitik* and its ability to reach out to the USSR and the PRC, felt compelled to act in the name of regional leadership.

Given the ups and downs of inter-Korean diplomacy, the possibility of either a Korea suddenly reunified under terms favorable to increasingly powerful South Korea or a desperate North Korea lashing out with WMD seemed more than likely. Japan therefore found it increasingly difficult to be a bystander in inter-Korean relations that now had the potential to directly impact Japan, and to be the driving force of new and uncertain international relations throughout the Asia-Pacific region. Japan had to contemplate the possibility of another destructive inter-Korean war, which would this time probably involve Japan directly, or else the uncertain ramifications of a sudden reunification.[58]

Therefore, on September 28, 1990, the leaders of Japan's ruling LDP delegation, headed by Kanemaru Shin, joined with the Japan Socialist Party (JSP) delegation, led by Tanabe Makoto, and the DPRK's KWP to sign a joint declaration agreeing to hold normalization talks. The most important initiator was Kanemaru Shin, a noted "kingmaker" in Japanese/LDP politics, who was schmoozed by Kim Il Sung in a private one-on-one meeting to sign onto the controversial eight-point joint declaration, which stated that Japan should compensate North Korea not only for the damage caused during the colonial rule, but also for the "losses suffered by the Korean people in the forty-five years" since World War II. The Japanese Ministry of Foreign Affairs then ran a rearguard delaying action for years. The joint declaration led to eight rapid-fire rounds of normalization talks between January 1991 and November 1992. The first two rounds were held in Tokyo and Pyongyang, respectively, and the next six rounds were held in Beijing. As Table 4.1 details, the talks floundered on disputes about history, reparations, abductions, and nuclear weapons. Pyongyang demanded that Japan undertake a display of public contrition for its colonization of Korea and also pay reparations for damages sustained during the colonial period. Japan rejected most of Pyongyang's demands and made its own regarding the return of Japanese Red Army plane hijackers, visits to Japan of Japanese women married to North Koreans, and the cessation of North Korea's nuclear and missile programs.

The strange case of Yi Un-hye became a focal point and ultimate stumbling block for the talks. At the third round of talks, the Japanese

[58] See C. S. Kang (2004: 99–101).

Table 4.1. Chronology of Japan–DPRK Normalization Talks, 1991–2004

Date and Place	Comment
01/29/91 Pyongyang	**First round talks** between Foreign Vice Minister Chon In-Chol (DPRK) and Ambassador Nakahira Noboru (Japan): Chon and Nakahira note historical significance of meeting. **DPRK** states need for (1) an explicit official apology, (2) compensation re: reparation between former belligerents and property claims, and (3) declaration that the 1910 treaty of annexation between Japan and Korea and all other treaties "imposed... were illegal and thus null and void." **Japan** says Japan–DPRK negotiations must not adversely affect Japan–ROK relations; it will not accept any ideas of compensation and reparations, and raises "international issues" (e.g., NPT compliance and inter-Korean relations). Japan also broaches issues of DPRK debts exceeding 70 billion yen to Japan, status of DPRK-oriented Korean residents in Japan, and Japanese wives of North Korean nationals.
03/11–03/12/91 Tokyo	**Second round talks** begin with DPRK stating its principal goal to hear Japan's response to DPRK's arguments laid out during first round. **Japan** refutes DPRK's claims from first round and adds new issues, including limiting DPRK's jurisdiction to northern part of peninsula (DPRK refuses) and return of seven former Japanese Red Army members who hijacked a Japan Air Lines plane to North Korea in 1970. **DPRK**, in turn, dismisses Japanese arguments, and progress is at a standstill, although DPRK notes during a news conference that there is a "general climate of mutual respect and friendship" and looks toward third round talks for forward movement.
05/20–05/22/91 Beijing	**Third round talks** begin with **DPRK** stressing diplomatic normalization as first and foremost agenda item before resolving other issues. **Japan** is caught off guard and has three preconditions: DPRK (1) accepting nuclear inspections, (2) resuming inter-Korean talks, and (3) agreeing to simultaneous entry of the two Koreas into the United Nations. Raises new sensitive issue re: Yi Un-hye, a Japanese woman allegedly kidnapped by North Korea and a tutor to Kim Hyon-hui, who blew up a Korean Air passenger plane in 1987. Japan rejects DPRK's push for dealing with diplomatic normalization first, angering the North Korean delegation, but the "new" issue irks DPRK the most, claiming that it is a fiction created by ROK. Third round ends without agreement on next meeting date.
08/31–09/??/91 Beijing	**Fourth round talks** are plagued by the Yi Un-hye issue, causing a 1.5-day delay in meeting, and "resolved" by having "working-level" talks. Two of Japan's conditions are close to being met: the UN membership issue and resolving differences over a nuclear safeguards agreement. **Japan** expresses regret at the unilateral postponement of inter-Korean prime ministerial talks. **DPRK** denounces Japan's remarks as interfering in internal affairs and says Japan can never evade its responsibility of paying compensation. DPRK agrees to seriously consider

(cont.)

Table 4.1 (cont.)

Date and Place	Comment
	Japan's proposal rewording DPRK's jurisdiction; says that complete resolution of the Japanese wives issue hinges on normalization, but would consider individual cases based on progress.
11/18–11/??/91 Beijing	**Fifth round talks** start with the UN admission issue settled, as ROK and DPRK entered as UN members simultaneously in September. Inter-Korean prime ministerial talks have also resumed. **Japan** urges DPRK to sign IAEA safeguards agreement without further delay. **DPRK** charges Japan for being too partial to ROK regarding this issue; continues to argue for compensation, stating it is "international practice" (e.g., Germany– Japan rejects this). Jurisdictional issue is discussed without resolution; however, DPRK brings some information re: 32 Japanese wives. Japan requests more information. Both sides maintain status quo on Yi Un-hye issue.
01/30–02/??/92 Beijing	**Sixth round talks** open in a new milieu. Several developments have made DPRK "cocky" and "on the offensive." DPRK and ROK signed two major agreements in December 1991; in January, DPRK upgraded diplomatic contacts with the United States, and on the first day of the talks, DPRK also signed a full-scope IAEA safeguards agreement. **DPRK** states that it has satisfied all preconditions and challenges Japan to move quickly toward diplomatic normalization; Japan still has its doubts. DPRK continues attacks on Japan re: "comfort women," the illegality of the 1910 annexation and other treaties, and compensation, and says that normalization will lead to full information and resolution of Japanese wives issue. DPRK proposes an "antidomination clause" for a future DPRK–Japan treaty; **Japan** responds that the UN Charter renders this unnecessary. "Working-level" consultations continue re: Yi Un-hye.
05/13–05/15/92 Beijing	**Seventh round talks** begin with some notable developments, including the change of the head of the DPRK delegation – with the passing of Chon In-Chol, Yi Sam-no takes the helm. **DPRK** continues to push compensation issue linking it to human rights, conscience, and reason; also makes a veiled threat about "serious consequences" if Japan continues to raise the Yi Un-hye issue. **Japan** stresses the difficulty of establishing diplomatic relations with DPRK without the effective implementation of the IAEA safeguards agreement and inter-Korean declaration on denuclearization.
11/05/92 Beijing	**Eighth round talks** last only half a day due to North Korean intransigence on the Yi Un-hye issue. **Japan** stresses that DPRK should dispel all suspicions re: nuclear weapons and allow Japanese wives to visit Japan on humanitarian grounds. **DPRK** stresses a need to "settle the past" as a core issue, including compensation, and calls on Japan to stop raising "artificial barriers" to the talks, such as the nuclear issue. DPRK delegation walks out on the Yi Un-hye issue, with no agreement to future meeting date.

Table 4.1 (cont.)

Date and Place	Comment
04/04–04/08/00 Pyongyang	**Ninth round talks** resume after an eight-year hiatus, gaining momentum from the U.S.–DPRK Berlin Agreement in 1999. Two issues continue to dominate the following three rounds: (1) settlement of the colonial past, and (2) the alleged abduction of ten Japanese nationals by North Korean security agents during the 1970s and 1980s.
08/21–08/25/00 Tokyo	**Tenth round talks** saw **Japan** advancing for the first time a proposal of "economic cooperation" of $300 million and a loan of $200 million, in lieu of "compensation," to the DPRK. **DPRK** makes a concession of sorts by no longer demanding "reparations" from Japan, settling for "compensation."
10/30–10/31/00 Beijing	**Eleventh round talks** open in the context of Japan having announced on October 6 its decision to donate 500,000 tons of rice to DPRK through the World Food Program (WFP), but talks last only two days. Japanese negotiators put forth a $9-billion "economic aid" package with 60% in grants and 40% in loans as *quid pro quo* for DPRK's moderation of the missile threat and resolving the abduction issue. DPRK finds this unacceptable and talks collapse.
09/17/02 Pyongyang	**First Koizumi–Kim Summit** opens with both sides giving ground on bilateral issues, overcoming two large obstacles to normalization. Kim claims responsibility for abduction of Japanese nationals and apologizes, with information on those abducted and assurances that it will never happen again. In a joint declaration released after the historic summit, Japan expresses "deep regrets and a heartfelt apology" toward DPRK, and DPRK ensures that abductions of Japanese citizens will never occur again. An agreement is reached that "compensation" be made through grants, low-interest loans, and economic cooperation. Kim promises to extend missile-testing moratorium.
10/29–10/30/02 Kuala Lumpur	**Twelfth round talks** reveal that a wide chasm exists between the two parties, and both sides fail to make any significant progress re: two major issues – the abductees and DPRK's nuclear weapons program. **Japan** says that there would be no normalization without Pyongyang agreeing to send the children of Japanese abductees to Japan and halt its nuclear program and dismantling its medium-range Nodong missiles. Talks end without agreeing on next round of normalization talks.
05/22/04 Pyongyang	**Second Koizumi–Kim Summit** opens with Kim allowing the families of the five former Japanese abductees to go to Japan for a family reunion. Japan requests further information on the remaining ten missing Japanese, and Kim promises a new investigation. Koizumi emphasizes need to resolve DPRK nuclear weapons and missiles issue, and Kim reiterates DPRK's position to maintain nuclear deterrent and counterbalance to U.S. threat and pressure while acknowledging ultimate goal of a nuclear-free Korea. Moratorium on missile testing reassured. Koizumi promises 250,000 tons of food, $10 million in medical assistance, and no economic sanctions as long as DPRK adheres to Pyongyang Declaration.

delegation demanded information about Yi Un-hye, a Japanese resident of Korean descent who was allegedly kidnapped by the North Koreans to serve as a trainer for Kim Hyon-hui, the North Korean agent who planted a bomb aboard a KAL flight in November 1987 that destroyed the plane over the Andaman Sea. The North Korean delegation denied any knowledge of the woman in question and described the allegation as a South Korean invention. The fourth round of talks was interrupted by a day-and-a-half delay because the North Koreans were insulted that the issue was continuing to be raised. The two sides agreed to working-level consultations on the matter, but when the Pyongyang delegation walked out with finality during the eighth round of talks, it was because the Yi Un-hye issue had again come to the fore.

After the eight rapid-fire rounds of talks in the early 1990s, both North Korea and Japan backed away from holding any additional talks. With the signing of the 1994 Agreed Framework between the United States and North Korea, Pyongyang began probing whether Japan might welcome additional talks, but it received only a lukewarm response. LDP leader Watanabe Michio failed to restart the talks, and the 1995 and 1996 editions of Japan's White Paper on Defense still listed North Korea as the "major destabilizing factor" with regard to East Asian security. In the late 1990s, the United States, China, the ROK, and the DPRK gathered for the Four-Party Peace Talks. These talks were an attempt to initiate a series of confidence-building measures as a first step to replace the 1953 armistice agreement that had effectively ended the Korean War. Japan supported the talks, despite being unhappy about its exclusion from them. When the Four-Party Talks became bogged down, LDP leader Mori Yoshiro, sensing a diplomatic opening, proposed a six-party security forum consisting of the two Koreas, Japan, China, Russia, and the United States.[59] The six-party scheme received diplomatic support from South Korea and, not surprisingly, Russia, but the proposal languished.[60]

On August 31, 1998, North Korea launched a Taepodong-1 missile over Japan. The event was at once a strategic surprise, a crisis, and perhaps even a blessing in disguise in terms of legitimating a growing born-again, rising sun nationalism in Japan. The missile launch was a complete surprise to the international community, initially summoning anything but a united response from Tokyo, which was shocked; Seoul, which gave no response; and Washington, which gave a delayed and mixed response. In early September, the Japanese government announced its decision to halt its involvement with KEDO, and to freeze its food and other humanitarian

[59] For details, see Kang and Kaseda (2000).

[60] During his tenure, South Korean President Kim Dae Jung voiced support at various times for the six-party talks proposal.

support to North Korea.[61] These unilateral actions alarmed Seoul, which was trying to sustain its Sunshine Policy, and also Washington, which wanted to protect its own engagement policy for the sake of regional stability. The United States and the ROK were ultimately able to persuade Tokyo to withdraw the suspension of its commitment to KEDO. As a result of the incident, in April 1999, the three countries established the Trilateral Coordination and Oversight Group (TCOG) to coordinate future policy.

In anticipation of a second missile test, the United States negotiated the Berlin Agreement of September 1999 with the DPRK. Both parties agreed in principle that Washington would lift its sanctions on North Korea in exchange for Pyongyang's suspension of the Taepodong-2 firing, while the two countries would accelerate normalization talks. Prodded by Seoul and Washington, and always anxious not to lag too far behind the United States, the Japanese government lifted its ban on charter flights in November, sent a multiparty delegation led by a former prime minister to Pyongyang in December, agreed to resume negotiations to restore bilateral ties, and lifted the remaining sanctions on North Korea.

Following this agreement, three new rounds of talks were held from April to October 2000 in Tokyo, Pyongyang, and Beijing respectively. The ninth round of talks in April involved discussions of Japan's colonial history and North Korea's abduction of Japanese citizens during the 1970s and 1980s. Japan suspected that North Korea had abducted eleven Japanese citizens from coastal towns across the archipelago and in Europe. In August, at the tenth round of talks, North Korea reportedly agreed to stop demanding "reparations" and to discuss "compensation" instead; Japan offered a $200 million loan and $300 million of "economic cooperation" aid – as opposed to "compensation." Japan also emphasized the importance of solving the abduction issue, as the chief Japanese negotiator pointed out that any normalization treaty to come out of the talks would need the approval of the Diet, which would not be forthcoming without public support that would be contingent on resolution of the abduction issue. At the eleventh round of talks, Japan offered 500,000 tons of rice[62] and a very large economic package as a *quid pro quo* for North Korea's moderation of the missile threat and satisfactory resolution of the abduction issue.[63] North Korean negotiators rejected the offer, and

[61] In addition, the Japanese government revoked its permission to North Korea's Air Koryo for nine chartered flights between Pyongyang and Nagoya and decided not to permit any further chartered flights. Tokyo then threatened to impose additional unilateral sanctions on Pyongyang if the North Koreans tested another missile over Japanese territory.

[62] The rice would have been from Tokyo's own reserves of Japanese rice, which at the time was twelve times more expensive than Thai or Chinese rice, such that the total value amounted to 120 billion yen (more than $1 billion).

[63] V. Cha (2001a).

the talks collapsed in only two days, without discussion of the date for the next round of normalization talks.

These normalization talks again fell apart because of their failure to resolve two major issues: North Korea's demand for compensation and Japan's demand for accountability on the abduction of Japanese citizens. North Korea persisted in its denial of any knowledge about the abduction issue, while refusing to accept the Japanese proposal to offer economic aid rather than reparations. In view of the uncompromising positions taken by both sides on these issues at the normalization talks, it became evident that the settlement of these thorny issues would require a high degree of political compromise between Tokyo and Pyongyang, probably achieved as a package deal rather than through the piece-meal approach.

Koizumi Junichiro was inaugurated as Japanese prime minister in April 2001. Despite the Japanese sinking of a North Korean spy ship in December 2001, under Koizumi's leadership the year 2002 witnessed significant progress in relations between Japan and North Korea. Japanese and North Korean Red Cross delegations met in Beijing in April and agreed that North Korea would conduct a "serious investigation" into "missing" Japanese, and in mid-August, the first details of abducted Japanese citizens began to emerge from North Korea. In addition, Pyongyang expressed a willingness to accept Japan's economic aid instead of insisting on "reparations." Against this background, Japan announced on August 30, 2002, that Koizumi would visit North Korea on September 17 for a summit meeting with Kim Jong Il. Koizumi's decision apparently reflected the prime minister's determination to normalize relations with North Korea, and the historic visit aroused high expectations for a normalization breakthrough. The United States, in contrast, on learning about the surprise visit, is said to have put inordinate pressure on Japan not to move too fast on normalization talks.[64]

In Pyongyang, at the first ever Japanese–North Korean summit, both sides gave ground on bilateral issues. Kim Jong Il acknowledged North Korea's responsibility for abducting Japanese nationals and offered an apology – indeed, the mother of all confessions of a high normative order. Providing information about new abductees about whom Japan had not asked, North Korea revealed that out of thirteen abductees, eight had died and five were still alive. Koizumi demanded that North Korea continue its investigation into the cases, return those who were alive, and take measures to prevent such activities in the future. Kim pledged not to engage in such an act again, saying that Pyongyang had already punished those responsible. The talks ended with a joint declaration in which Japan promised "economic assistance" in the form of grants, long-term

[64] Harrison (2005a).

soft loans, and humanitarian assistance via international organizations, while North Korea promised compliance with international law, pledging to take appropriate measures so that regrettable incidents that took place under the abnormal bilateral relationship would never happen in the future. Both countries agreed to fulfill "all related international agreements" pertaining to nuclear issues on the Korean peninsula.

According to a public opinion poll conducted by the *Mainichi Shimbun* in the wake of the summit, Koizumi's diplomatic initiative was supported by the Japanese, with 54 percent of the public supporting the renewal of normalization talks. However, three-fourths of the respondents said Japan should not hurry to establish diplomatic ties with Pyongyang, and the reaction to Koizumi's visit to Pyongyang was far from wholly positive because many Japanese were shocked to learn that eight of thirteen abductees had died after being taken to North Korea. There were angry reactions from the relatives of the abduction victims who resented Koizumi's "hasty" decision to resume normalization talks without securing adequate information concerning the circumstances surrounding the deaths of the eight abductees or making necessary arrangements for the return of the surviving five abductees and their families to Japan. Nearly 74 percent of surveyed Japanese remained dissatisfied with Kim Jong Il's apology, and only 7 percent believed that the summit reflected a genuine change in the character and intention of the DPRK regime.[65]

To placate enraged public opinion, Japan dispatched an official delegation to collect further information concerning the fate of the Japanese abductees. Pyongyang told the Japanese team that all eight had died from "illness and disasters" and had not been the victims of foul play. However, there were inconsistencies in the North Korean story that further aggravated Japanese families. The Koizumi government arranged for the five surviving abductees to return to Japan for a two-week visit in October. Before the end of their visit, Japan announced that it had decided to extend the stay of the five abductees indefinitely so as to enable them to decide their future freely.

Following the summit, the twelfth round of Japanese–North Korean normalization talks were held in Kuala Lumpur, Malaysia, on October 29–30, 2002. At these talks, it quickly became evident that there was a wide chasm between Japan and North Korea on several key issues. The North Korean delegation rejected Japan's demand for the settlement of the abduction issue, contending that it had been resolved at the Pyongyang summit when Kim Jong Il offered an apology with a promise to prevent recurrences. Furthermore, North Korea insisted that it was cooperating with Japan in investigating details surrounding the deaths of

[65] H. N. Kim (2005).

the eight deceased abductees. North Korea also accused Japan of breaking its promise to return the five abductees to Pyongyang after a two-week home visit in Japan and demanded that Japan keep its promise to pave the way for the resolution of the issue; the Japanese delegation denounced Pyongyang's "criminal act of kidnapping." Japan was also insistent that North Korea maintain the tenets of the Pyongyang Declaration, submit to its responsibilities under the NPT, and not target Japan with its Rodong missiles. In response to North Korea's desire to discuss economic cooperation as a priority issue, Japan replied that economic aid would come only in the aftermath of the normalization of Tokyo–Pyongyang diplomatic relations. The talks adjourned without agreement on the next round of normalization talks.

Much of the abductions controversy and the twelfth round of negotiations came at the same time as the reemergence of the North Korean nuclear issue. So, when Japan–DPRK relations became stalemated after the Kuala Lumpur meeting, there was little external intervention to push them forward. In 2003, therefore, there was no movement in the normalization talks. In fact, Japan, because of domestic political pressure, became increasingly anxious about and mired in the abduction issue. Despite Japan's concern about North Korea's nuclear program, the issue of the roughly two dozen Japanese citizens abducted by North Korean agents in the 1970s for espionage training has now come to threaten to dominate Japanese policy toward North Korea, to the exclusion of all else.[66]

In early 2004, it became clear that Japan was taking preliminary steps toward the imposition of economic sanctions against North Korea. This led Pyongyang to indicate its willingness to be more flexible on the abduction issue. In fact, Pyongyang agreed to allow a Japanese delegate to come to North Korea to pick up eight family members of the abductees who had returned to Japan. Koizumi, desiring to normalize diplomatic relations with North Korea before the end of his tenure as prime minister in 2006, indicated that his visit to Pyongyang should not be ruled out as an option.

On May 22, 2004, Koizumi visited Pyongyang to hold talks with Kim Jong Il, a second Koizumi–Kim summit in the short span of less than two years. Kim agreed to allow the families of five former Japanese abductees to go to Japan for a family reunion and promised a new investigation into the fate of other abductees. Koizumi emphasized the importance of a comprehensive solution to pending security issues, including Pyongyang's development of nuclear weapons and missiles. Kim reiterated North Korea's position that Pyongyang had to maintain a nuclear

[66] D. C. Kang (2005b: 107).

deterrent but also stated that his goal was to achieve a nonnuclear Korean peninsula. In addition, Kim reassured Koizumi that the North would maintain a moratorium on missile firing tests. For these diplomatic victories, Japan paid richly. Koizumi promised Kim 250,000 tons of food and $10 million worth of medical assistance through international organizations. He also pledged that Japan would not invoke economic sanctions as long as North Korea observed the terms of the joint declaration from the first summit. In return, Pyongyang merely allowed five children of the repatriated abductees to go to Japan with the prime minister.

Most Japanese believed that Koizumi had paid too high a price at the second summit, although they gave him high marks for bringing home the family members of the five surviving abductees. According to an opinion survey conducted by the *Yomiuri Shimbun*, 63 percent of the respondents said they supported Koizumi's second visit to Pyongyang, but 70 percent said they were not satisfied with the results. Specifically, 56 percent of the respondents did not approve of Koizumi's pledge to provide North Korea with food and medical assistance. Public opinion also asserted that Koizumi should not have given away the bargaining lever of economic sanctions for such small gains.[67]

The Japanese Diet took matters into its own hands and, in an attempt to pressure North Korea to make concessions, in June 2004 enacted a law to ban certain foreign ships from making port calls in Japan. It was designed to prohibit the entry of North Korean ships suspected of being engaged in illegal trafficking of money, drugs, counterfeit currencies, and equipment and supplies used in the production of strategic weapons. At August 2004 working-level talks, the North Korean delegation refused to address the abductees issue in any new way and was not ready to engage Japanese negotiators on the nuclear issue either. Without a breakthrough in resolving either the (remaining) abduction issue or Pyongyang's nuclear weapons program, the Koizumi government decided not to resume normalization talks.

It might appear puzzling that Japan has tried as hard as it has to normalize relations with North Korea. After all, what could it expect to gain from the process? In the first place, nonnormalized relations with North Korea stick out as a reminder of Japan's imperial past, and although there has been a recent surge of nationalism in Japan, there is still a desire among the Japanese public to wipe its World War II slate completely clean. Economically speaking, Japan is worried that it might not be able to compete effectively on a Korean peninsula where other major powers – China and Russia – have established diplomatic ties with both North and South Korea. In addition, there is a concern among some influential leaders

[67] H. N. Kim (2005).

of the LDP and among Foreign Ministry officials that the collapse of North Korea would create enormous economic, political, and humanitarian problems for Japan. This last concern contributes to the possibility that DPRK–Japan normalization of relations might be a component of a solution to the North Korean nuclear standoff.

The Japan–ROK Normalization Process

An ROK mission was established in Tokyo in January 1949, a year and a half before the outbreak of the Korean War and at a time when the U.S. occupation force was still in charge of Japan. The normalization process began officially in October 1951 – still some six months before Japanese sovereignty was restored – and would last until 1965. Although Japan and South Korea today have had normalized relations for four decades, the process of normalization was neither automatic nor smooth, and was completed because of a confluence of Cold War security imperatives and domestic political needs in Tokyo and Seoul. Many of the same issues of historical interpretation and national identity that plague the Japan–DPRK normalization talks were also once responsible for derailing various incarnations of the Japan–ROK normalization talks. Despite having normalized relations, some of these same issues linger today.

During the 1950s, Japan was not inclined to moderate its opinions to assuage Korean sensibilities. In 1953, during the third round of normalization talks, for example, Kubota Kanichiro, the chief Japanese delegate, engaged in an acrimonious exchange in which he flatly declared (1) that the U.S. repatriation of Japanese nationals from Korea, disposition of Japanese properties to Koreans, and establishment of an independent Korean state (ROK) prior to the peace treaty with Japan had violated international law; (2) that Japan's occupation of Korea for thirty-six years was actually beneficial to the Korean people; and (3) that Japan had actually contributed to the Korean economy by carrying out such infrastructure projects as reforestation, irrigation, and port and railway construction. He also stated that had Japan not taken control of Korea, either China or Russia would have done so, adding that the Koreans would have suffered far more under Chinese or Russian occupation than they did under Japanese rule. His remarks so enraged the South Korean delegates that the talks were suspended for four and a half years.[68]

The delay during the 1950s was due in part to the manipulation of national identity by the South Korean government of Syngman Rhee. Following the third round of normalization talks, the Rhee government publicized Kubota's statements and his subsequent apology, fueling

[68] Cumings (1997: 319); C. S. Lee (1985: 24–25).

an atmosphere of mutual distrust and enmity.[69] The United States regarded Rhee's approach to Japan as "completely recalcitrant... since he always seemed to suggest a negotiating stance that would guarantee failure."[70]

In the late 1950s, *Chongryun*, the North Korea-aligned organization of Koreans in Japan – in conjunction with Pyongyang – began pressuring the Japanese government to repatriate its members who wanted to leave Japan for North Korea. In 1959, Japan decided to repatriate 51,325 Zainichi Koreans to North Korea, and another 22,801 made the journey in 1961.[71] When the repatriation process was completed, 88,611 Zainichi Koreans had been sent to North Korea. This served as a serious blow to South Korea's pursuit of absolute, one-Korea legitimation and as a big propaganda victory for Pyongyang. According to the ROK's official diplomatic history, Japan's 1959 decision was described as having created "the most difficult deadlock situation," emblematic of Seoul's defeat in the legitimacy war with North Korea.[72] In the early 1960s, the talks between Japan and South Korea were reinvigorated. This turn of events was aided in the first place by Park Chung Hee's rise to power in the ROK. Park was a graduate of the Japanese Military Academy and a Japonophile who embraced Meiji Japan's strategic axiom, "Strong Army, Prosperous Economy." Park believed that there was a need to establish a new basis of legitimation – performance-based legitimation – and also a need for a massive infusion of Japanese capital and technology that would allow Korea's economy to take off. Within the Park regime, there were many Koreans who had willingly learned from Japan in the 1930s and were ready to do so again.[73]

In the international sphere, the United States also took a renewed interest in seeing a normalization of relations between its two allies in the mid-1960s. With the onset of the Vietnam War and the rising threat from China, the need to push Tokyo–Seoul normalization became increasingly urgent, even as the war provided a bonanza for the South Korean economy similar to the role that the Korean War had played in Japan's economic takeoff. The breakthrough is said to have come in 1964, "after years of urging" on the part of the United States, such as personal letters from John Kennedy to the leaders of both Japan and South Korea, according to one report from the U.S. embassy in Tokyo.[74] The final eighteen months of normalization talks witnessed the United States giving Seoul and Tokyo added exhortations and incentives to reach a prompt settlement as a way of consolidating the Japan–Korea axis in response to

[69] Macdonald (1992: 129). [70] Cumings (1997: 318).
[71] Lee and DeVos (1981: 106–07). [72] Ministry of Foreign Affairs (1979: 28).
[73] Cumings (1997: 319). [74] Macdonald (1992: 134); Woo (1991: 86).

heightened Cold War tensions in the region.[75] Related to this pressure to normalize relations, Seoul was also able to squeeze a large amount of aid out of Washington – about $1 billion – for ROK participation in the Vietnam War from 1966–69; this accounted for as much as 19 percent of South Korea's total foreign exchange earnings over those three years.[76]

Finally, the underlying similarity and complementarity of Korean and Japanese economic interests was a major factor driving normalization. Korea had much to gain through technology transfer and human capital imports from Japan, while Japan lacked for nearby markets because of the off-limits nature of China and the Soviet Union. Park Chung Hee understood that to launch an export-driven developmental strategy it would be necessary to take advantage of what Japan had to offer.

In April 1965, Korean and Japanese representatives initialed agreements on all outstanding issues in the normalization negotiations. On June 22, 1965, the Treaty on Basic Relations Between Japan and the Republic of Korea was signed, along with five other agreements dealing with (1) fishery, (2) property claims and economic cooperation, (3) the legal status of Korean residents in Japan, (4) cultural property and cultural exchanges, and (5) peaceful settlement of disputes. Despite a long battle over the course of the remaining summer months, in which Park Chung Hee's cabinet resigned and Park declared martial law in South Korea, the ROK National Assembly ratified the treaty on August 14.

Article II of the treaty reads, "It is confirmed that all treaties or agreements between the Empire of Japan and the Empire of Korea on or before August 22, 1910 are already null and void." This article was a compromise between Seoul's insistence that the treaties in question were null and void *ab initio* and Tokyo's claim that they were nullified by Japan's defeat in World War II and the conclusion of the San Francisco peace treaty. The Japanese Diet, after the signing of the treaty, insisted that earlier treaties had been legally valid and signed on the basis of mutual agreement but had ceased to be in effect with the establishment of the Republic of Korea in 1948. Because of the imprecise wording, disputes linger today, such as on the Tokdo/Takeshima Islands.

As for recognizing the South Korean government, Article III confirms that "the Government of the Republic of Korea is the only lawful Government in Korea as specified in Resolution 195 (III) of the United Nations General Assembly." This article, too, lends itself to varying interpretations. It can support Seoul's claim that it is the only lawful government on the entire Korean peninsula – although that claim virtually vanished with Kim Dae Jung's Sunshine Policy – or Tokyo's interpretation that UN

[75] V. Cha (1999a: 28–34), [76] Macdonald (1992: 110); J. E. Woo (1991: 93–96).

General Assembly Resolution 195 (III) limits the jurisdiction of the ROK to the southern half of the peninsula where UN-monitored elections were held in 1948.

Under the terms of the Agreement on Economic Cooperation and Property Rights, Japan extended a $300 million grant, a $200 million loan, and private commercial credits worth at least $300 million to the Korean government, and it arranged for the resolution of outstanding property claims.[77] The Japanese government insisted that these payments were not to be understood as reparations or compensation for past injustices, flatly contradicting public statements being made by the Korean negotiators. In somewhat contradictory terms, the Japanese government did insist that demands for compensation had been resolved under the terms of the agreement and that the Japanese government was under no legal obligation to recognize such claims. The Korean government, in contrast, argued that although it had relinquished the right to compensation, the treaty did not apply to individual Korean citizens.

The differences in interpretation of the agreement have helped ensure that the history issue would remain a chronic source of bilateral tension between Japan and South Korea. Throughout the Cold War and beyond, Japanese policy makers claimed that the compensation and colonial guilt issue had been resolved by the 1965 treaty, and they simultaneously espoused a sanitized version of modern Japanese history that ignored or downplayed the suffering inflicted on the Korean people.

Normalization had an immediate effect in the economic realm. Within three years of normalization, South Korea had emerged as Japan's second largest export market, after the United States. In addition, Japan became one of the two most important sources – along with the United States – of both public and private loans for the ROK. By 1973, Japan surpassed the United States as the main source of FDI in South Korea, accounting for 60 percent of all inward FDI on a cumulative basis. These continuing economic relations, however, have been punctuated by a series of unresolved historical-cum-territorial disputes and political tensions stemming from internal political dynamics in both Tokyo and Seoul.

The high point of ROK–Japan relations came in the late 1990s. During a summit trip to Japan in October 1998, President Kim Dae Jung issued a joint statement with Prime Minister Obuchi Keizo, in which the Japanese government offered a clear and forthright apology for the pain and suffering that its colonial rule had inflicted on the Korean people. Perhaps more important, Kim Dae Jung (more than any Korean leader before him) suggested that Korea was willing to accept such an apology

[77] This $800 million package was offered to South Korea at a time when its total exports were only $200 million.

and use it as the basis for an improved bilateral relationship.[78] In return for softening demands for an apology, Korea received $3 billion in aid from Japan, continuing the pattern of exchanging Japanese money for Korean circumspection. Subsequently, both sides undertook a number of steps designed to further reconciliation between the two peoples. In 1999, amidst much fanfare, South Korea lifted its ban on the import of Japanese cultural products. Japan in turn offered aid and compensation to Korean victims of the World War II atomic bombings and to Korean veterans of the Imperial Army, two groups that had previously been barred from receiving aid on the basis of their nationality. Likewise, a new debate was initiated in regard to granting resident Koreans in Japan increased civil rights, possibly including the right to vote in local elections. The two sides intensified joint planning and training between their armed forces.

Developments in the spring and summer of 2001 suggested that even under favorable conditions, attempts at reconciliation can be undermined by the lack of sustained leadership. Conservative scholars in Japan, under the directorship of Nishio Kanji, produced a draft textbook offering a decidedly revisionist view of modern Japanese history that downplayed or ignored the negative aspects of Japan's period of imperial expansion and the atrocities committed by its forces during World War II. After requiring only relatively minor revisions, the Japanese Ministry of Education then approved the use of the textbook in Japanese schools, sparking sharp criticism from South Korea and the PRC. Soon thereafter, Prime Minister Koizumi Junichiro undertook a controversial visit to the Yasukuni Shrine dedicated to the Japanese war dead, making good on a promise to conservatives in his party at the price of further antagonizing Japan's neighbors. Military-to-military talks between Japan and Korea were suspended, the ban on Japanese cultural items was reimposed, and the South Korean Ambassador was temporarily recalled to Seoul for "consultations."[79]

As if this were not trouble enough, a fishing dispute flared up between Japan and the ROK when Tokyo announced on June 19, 2001, that it would ban South Korean fishing vessels from waters near the Russian-held Kurile Islands off northern Japan, claiming that the area was in Japan's EEZ. Seoul, however, argued that its vessels were allowed to fish around the Kuriles under a fisheries accord reached with Moscow in December 2000. In protest, Tokyo declared a ban on South Korean fishing in the waters off the coast of Sinriku until the Korean government promised not to send its fishing boats into the waters off the Kuriles. The Japanese

[78] For the text of the statement and initial press reactions, see *Asahi Shimbun* and *Yomiuri Shimbun*, October 8, 1998, p. 1.

[79] See *The Korea Herald*, August 15, 2001.

government's hardline stance was clearly tied to its ongoing territorial dispute with Russia over the Kuriles, but this national identity enactment came at the expense of Korean fishermen.

Efforts to patch Japanese–Korean and Sino–Japanese relations accelerated in the wake of the September 11 terrorist attacks on the United States. As close U.S. allies, both Japan and South Korea came under pressure to cooperate closely on how to provide a regional response to the terrorist threat. Of particular concern was to defuse possible regional tensions arising from Japan's unprecedented dispatch of war ships to the Indian Ocean in support of the U.S. military campaign in Afghanistan. In addition, the two countries were acutely aware of the need to orchestrate policy on the thorny issue of North Korea, which was defined as part of the new "axis of evil" and seemed to be headed toward becoming the primary target of a second round of the U.S. war on terror. Koizumi visited both South Korea and China to try to resurrect normal relations. In Korea, Koizumi reiterated previous apologies for Japanese past misdeeds and paid his respects to Korean freedom fighters celebrated at a museum in Seoul. The two sides agreed to renew cooperation on a wide range of issues, including joint historical research, counterterrorism, and fishing rights.[80]

After several years of relatively normal relations, South Korean President Roh Moo-hyun urged Tokyo to continue its process of grappling with its past. On March 1, 2005, in a speech commemorating the March 1 uprising against Japanese colonial rule eighty-six years earlier, Roh urged Japan to offer a heartfelt apology and to settle its past history with Koreans, including paying compensation if necessary for real reconciliation to take place. On March 17, the Roh government announced a new doctrine for dealing with Japan in which seeking an apology and compensation from the former colonial power for its wartime atrocities took center stage. Roh's aggressiveness was a clear response to the emerging sovereignty dispute over the Tokdo/Takeshima Islands. Some Koreans saw the introduction of the Takeshima Day bill in the Shimane prefectural legislature as an insult intended to coincide with the celebration of the March 1 holiday in South Korea. The bill also came at the same time as a new controversy over textbooks was ballooning, part of which pertained directly to the history of the Tokdo Islands. In an ROK National Security Council meeting, the Japanese moves were described as "a second dispossession of the Korean Peninsula that denies the history of Korean liberation."[81]

Japan's claim to the uninhabited islands dates to the Russo–Japanese War of 1904–05, when Japan gave them the name Takeshima. However,

[80] See *Asahi Shimbun,* October 22, 2001, p. 3. [81] *Chosun Ilbo,* March 17, 2005.

a January 1946 edict from U.S. occupation forces commander Douglas MacArthur excluded Takeshima from the area of Japanese sovereignty, implying that South Korea became an independent state possessing territory that included the Takeshima/Tokdo Islands. After years of having ignored the islands, despite the *de facto* occupation and control of Tokdo by South Korean police since 1953, Japan has turned them into a tinderbox of controversy and the object of a war of national identities.[82] In short, the controversy over Tokdo has recently been escalated to an international quasicrisis.

The Roh government made several moves that internationalized this bilateral dispute. It declared that South Korea would work to block Japan's latest bid for permanent membership in the UN Security Council.[83] The National Security Council announced a maritime drill to prepare responses to contingencies in and around the East Sea. The Defense Ministry published a revised edition of the 2004 Defense White Paper, stating that the country's armed forces had bolstered their naval, aerial, and submarine patrols in maritime security areas, including Tokdo; the original Defense White Paper had not mentioned Tokdo. As if these measures were not sufficient, on August 28, 2005, the South Korean government released a total of 35,000 pages of 156 records about the Japan–ROK normalization talks, along with a new claim that Japan is now *legally* responsible for its past war crimes, thus reversing its previous assertion that Japan remains *morally* responsible for its harsh colonial and war crimes.

What is rather unique about South Korean identity politics and response vis-à-vis Japan, compared with the anti-American (anti-Bush) case as fully discussed in Chapter 5, is that it transcends domestic political, regional, and ideological cleavages and affirms once again the proposition that Japan's seeming inability or unwillingness to come clean with its colonial and imperial past – at least in deeds if not always in words – serves as a constant war recall trigger for the total mobilization of national identity politics in South Korea.

Military and Security Issues

In both 1993–94 and 2002–05, there was a nuclear standoff on the Korean peninsula involving the United States and the DPRK. Given the decadal

[82] It is worth noting that this is not the only territorial/history dispute faced by Japan. To the south, Tokyo is engaged in a sovereignty dispute with China over the Diaoyu Islands (known in Japan as the Senkaku Islands) and competing development of offshore gas fields in the East China Sea. In the north, it has the thorny issue of the Russian-held Northern Territories, known in Russia as the Southern Kurils.

[83] China, in fact, seems poised to do the heavy lifting in terms of blocking Japan's ascent to permanent member status. Colum Lynch, "China Fights Enlarging Security Council," *Washington Post*, April 5, 2005, p. A15.

déjà vu, a comparison of Japan's reactions provides insight into the trajectory of Japan's thinking on security issues vis-à-vis the Korean peninsula. Whereas in 1994 the Japanese Diplomatic White Paper (Bluebook) saw the nuclear issue as one to be settled between the United States and the DPRK with only peripheral Japanese support, the 2004 Diplomatic Bluebook describes the existence of a North Korean nuclear programs as a "direct threat" to international and East Asian peace and security, and it ranks the issue in Japan's top security concerns, along with Iraq and the alleged proliferation of WMD. Whereas Japan's diplomacy at the end of the Cold War was focused on Russia and the United States and the definition of the Japanese role in the new international order, today Japan seems ready to consider the Korean peninsula on its own terms and with reference to a particular set of regional end goals.

Japan–DPRK Security Interaction

During the Cold War, there was very little security interaction between Pyongyang and Tokyo. Japan was securely ensconced in the protective shield of the U.S.–Japan alliance system, in which the United States did all the heavy lifting while Japan pursued a free ride policy that fits more closely with "mercantile realism" than with structural realism (neorealism).[84] Because North Korea's development of missile and nuclear programs was not yet known, Japan had little interest in interacting with the DPRK. Pyongyang, at home in its own ideological alliances with the Soviet Union and China, had no compelling strategic or ideological reason for diplomatic normalization with Japan. Tokyo pursued a policy of separating economics from politics, and Pyongyang pursued an equidistant "maxi-mini" strategy in the course of the protracted Sino–Soviet conflict as a way of maximizing its aid-seeking leverage without casting its lot explicitly with either Moscow or Beijing.

However, as the DPRK's ballistic missile and nuclear programs began surfacing in the early years of the post–Cold War era, Japan may have been the one country that was more alarmed than was South Korea. Although the Kim Young Sam government in Seoul was concerned by the advancing ballistic missile and nuclear capabilities in the North, ordinary South Korean citizens did not appear overly concerned or threatened. The Japanese, however, having suffered the twin blows of Hiroshima and Nagasaki on the eve of their surrender during the last days of World War II, felt a degree of atomic angst they had perhaps never felt during the Cold War.[85]

[84] See Heginbotham and Samuels (1998) for the mercantile realism interpretation of Japan's foreign policy. For a greater elaboration of the logic of mercantile realism, see Gilpin (1981).

[85] C. S. Kang (2004).

Japanese fear became palpable during the nuclear crisis of April 1994, when North Korea removed spent fuel rods from its nuclear reactor in Yongbyon and refused to segregate rods that could provide evidence of a plutonium-based nuclear weapon program.[86] Japanese leaders let out a sigh of relief when the crisis was defused by former U.S. President Jimmy Carter's June 1994 visit to Pyongyang, where Carter's meeting with Kim Il Sung paved the way for the signing of the U.S.–DPRK Agreed Framework in October 1994.[87] The 1995 Diplomatic Bluebook, issued after the conclusion of the Agreed Framework, placed Japan at somewhat of a distance from the North Korean nuclear issue. Japan saw its main roles as cooperation in the newly established international consortium providing energy to the DPRK, as well as diplomatic cooperation with the United States and the ROK.

The next year's analysis from Japan referenced a possible resumption of the normalization negotiations that had been suspended since 1992 and asserted that policy toward North Korea was shaped in light of two considerations: (1) to rectify the anomalous relations between the two countries after World War II, and (2) to contribute to peace and stability on the Korean peninsula. In May 1995, following North Korea's first ever request for food aid, Japan provided emergency rice and humanitarian assistance. But economic assistance would only come, the Bluebook said, after successful normalization negotiations, indicating a clear separation between "humanitarian assistance" and "economic assistance" that might be construed as reparations or compensation for past deeds.

The period covered by 1997 and 1998 Bluebooks saw a more detailed elaboration of Japanese policy in general, as well as additional talk of normalizing DPRK–Japan relations. First, however, the Asian Financial Crisis in 1997 caused a shift in Japan's attention away from the DPRK. Then, the August 1998 North Korean missile launch over Japan and the suspected cases of North Korean abduction of Japanese nationals led to the complete suspension of discussion regarding normalization talks and humanitarian aid. The missile launching had a psychological impact on the Japanese equivalent to the Sputnik shock that affected the American people in 1957.[88]

Indeed, Japan wasted no time in responding to the Taepodong-1 launch. On September 1, 1998, Chief Cabinet Secretary Nonaka Hiromu issued a statement that "this action directly affects Japan's security and . . . presents a very serious situation of concern" and that "Japan must

[86] For a comprehensive discussion of the 1994 nuclear crisis, see Sigal (1998). See also Kihl and Hayes (1997).

[87] For the specific details of the Agreed Framework, see Chapter 5.

[88] Yoichi Funabashi, "The Question of What Constitutes Deterrence," *Asahi Shimbun*, February 15, 1999.

reconsider its policy toward North Korea . . . and take stringent responses in a firm manner."[89] The concrete measures Japan would take included (1) consulting with the United States and the ROK, (2) pursuing the option of raising the issue in the UN General Assembly, (3) suspending all negotiations with North Korea on diplomatic normalization, (4) not extending food and other humanitarian assistance to North Korea, and (5) suspending Japan's contribution to KEDO.[90] Although additional measures were introduced in the next several days (e.g., the cancellation of permission for charter flights between Japan and North Korea and a letter sent to the president of the Security Council), by late October Japan had partially lifted its sanctions on North Korea by signing a "KEDO Executive Board resolution concerning the cost-sharing of the light water reactor project." Nonaka cited three reasons for Japan's decision to resume cooperation with KEDO: (1) Japan saw no realistic alternatives to KEDO and the Agreed Framework, (2) Japan's response to the missile test was having concrete effects, and (3) the appeal from Washington and Seoul for the resumption of Tokyo's cooperation with KEDO.[91]

The Taepodong shock also galvanized the Japanese government into action on long-term plans. Tokyo decided to develop and deploy its own spy satellite system to improve its ability to monitor – independently of the United States – developments on the Korean peninsula and elsewhere in the Northeast Asian region.[92] In March 1999, Defense Agency Director General Norota Hosei told a Diet defense panel that Japan had the right to make preemptive military strikes if it felt a missile attack on Japan was imminent.[93] Japan therefore decided to acquire midair refueling aircraft to enable its Air Self-Defense Force (ASDF) to conduct long-range strike missions. Tokyo viewed this as important because of Japan's vulnerability linked to its lack of offensive military capacities that could deter or counter North Korean attacks, capabilities that are possessed by the

[89] Japan Ministry of Foreign Affairs, "Announcement by the Chief Cabinet Secretary on Japan's Immediate Response to North Korea's Missile Launch" (Tokyo: September 1, 1998).

[90] Japan withheld its signature on a cost-sharing agreement regarding the LWR project. Under the agreement, Japan's share of the estimated $4.6 billion cost of the project would be $1 billion (about 22 percent), whereas South Korea would contribute about 70 percent of the total cost of building two LWRs.

[91] Japan Ministry of Foreign Affairs, "Press Conference by the Press Secretary" (Tokyo: October 23, 1998), pp. 2–3.

[92] The satellite system was billed as "multipurpose" and was not included in the official defense budget. The decision to acquire the satellites required the Japanese government to override a Diet resolution of 1969 that limited the use of space technology to nonmilitary activities. C. S. Kang (2004: 107). Two satellites were launched in March 2003.

[93] C. S. Kang (2004: 107). It has come to light recently that Japan had contemplated possible preemptive strikes against North Korean military sites in 1994.

United States and, to a lesser extent, South Korea. Domestic political support increased for the revised U.S.–Japan Guidelines on Defense Cooperation, despite lingering concerns about entrapment. The new guidelines allowed Japan during crises to supply U.S. forces with nonlethal material assistance and to open civilian ports and airfields, and they also allowed new missions for Japan's Self-Defense Forces (SDFs), such as the resupply of U.S. warships during a crisis, the evacuation of civilians and U.S. military personnel from dangerous situations, the removal of mines from the high seas, or the enforcement of UN sanctions. Japan also agreed to cooperate with the United States on a joint project to develop a TMD system. Finally, the Japanese government authorized the Japanese Navy and Coast Guard to pursue unidentified ships entering Japanese territorial waters and to use force against them if necessary.

These last instructions resulted, in December 2001, in an armed clash between an unidentified ship – later confirmed to be of North Korean origin – and the Japanese Coast Guard and Maritime SDFs. The incident resulted in the sinking of the then-unidentified ship and the death of all fifteen crew members. Remarkably, this incident – the first deliberate and open use of force by the Japanese armed forces since 1945 – met with general public approval, which would have been all but unthinkable ten years earlier.

The historic inter-Korean summit meeting of June 2000 drastically changed the milieu in East Asia, and Japan's relationship with the DPRK improved as normalization talks materialized in April, August, and October. The dramatic summit diplomacy gave some comfort to the Japanese regarding the prospect of a more reasonable and responsible North Korea. Food aid through the World Food Program (WFP) resumed, and the issues of visitations by Japanese nationals living in North Korea and the investigation of "missing" Japanese citizens were broached.

Then, in the wake of the October 2002 revelation about North Korea's HEU nuclear weapon program and the outbreak of the new nuclear standoff, Japan readily agreed to increase funding and research support for the missile defense project. Not surprisingly Japan, as compared with Europe and Canada, had few misgivings regarding the implications of deploying a ballistic missile defense system.[94] Simultaneously, however, the Koizumi government made it clear that Japan would work for the dismantling of North Korea's nuclear weapons program through a peaceful diplomatic approach. Too much pressure on the North could lead the Kim Jong Il regime to take unpredictable actions, and Japan wanted to avoid the renewal of war on the Korean peninsula because Japan would be embroiled in the conflict either directly or indirectly through the

[94] C. S. Kang (2004: 108).

security arrangement with the United States. At the U.S.–Japan Security Consultative Committee meeting in Washington in December 2002, Japan and the United States urged North Korea to give up its nuclear weapons program in a "prompt and verifiable fashion." In addition, they expressed "serious concern" over Pyongyang's ballistic missile programs and urged Pyongyang to terminate all missile-related activities. They also urged Pyongyang's full compliance with the Biological Weapons Convention and Chemical Weapons Convention. Japan indicated its willingness to support the U.S. plan to convene a multilateral forum on the North Korean nuclear issue.

North Korea's official media accused Japan of blindly following the United States in pursuing a hostile policy toward North Korea. *Rodong Sinmun [Worker's Daily]* declared that the Korean peninsula's nuclear issue "is not an issue for Japan to presumptuously act upon" because it is a "bilateral issue to be resolved between the U.S. and North Korea." The newspaper slammed the door on Japan by saying that "Japan is not a party concerned with the resolution of the Korean Peninsula's nuclear issue and has no pretext or qualification to intervene."[95] In addition, referencing national identity issues, it criticized Japan for using "various pretexts and excuses to shelve the liquidation of its past and deliberately slackened normalizing relations" with North Korea.

In the spring of 2003, North Korea escalated tensions further on the Korean peninsula by reactivating its graphite-moderated nuclear reactor at Yongbyun and test-firing an antiship missile on the eve of President Roh Moo-hyun's inauguration in late February. Pyongyang also attempted to intercept a U.S. reconnaissance plane and launched another antiship missile in early March. In response to these incidents, Koizumi expressed his view that "the Pyongyang Declaration has been breached" at least partially, if not in its entirety. In testimony before a parliamentary standing committee, Chief Cabinet Secretary Fukuda Yasuo warned North Korea that the test-firing of a long-range missile or the reprocessing of spent nuclear fuel for weapons-grade plutonium would constitute crossing the "red line" and would nullify the Pyongyang Declaration. At a May 2003 U.S.–Japan summit meeting in Crawford, Texas, both Bush and Koizumi declared their determination not to tolerate North Korea's nuclear weapons program. Koizumi also stated that Japan would "crack down more vigorously" on illegal activities involving North Korea or pro-Pyongyang Koreans in Japan. Following the summit, Japan agreed to become one of eleven nations participating in the U.S.-led Proliferation Security Initiative (PSI) to interdict WMD shipments to and from countries such as North Korea.

95 "Japan Intervention in Nuclear Issue 'Ineffective' – North Korean Radio," BBC-AAIW, January 27, 2003.

That the emphasis is on the DPRK and not terrorism is indicated by the fact that the 2003 Diplomatic Bluebook lists North Korea ahead of the war on terror and weapons of mass destruction as Japan's greatest diplomatic concern.

In the summer of 2003, the Japanese parliament passed three "war contingency bills" that would give the Japanese government new power to cope with armed attacks on Japan. Such contingency legislation had first been discussed among Japanese conservatives some 40 years earlier but was shelved because of the possibility that it would violate Article 9 of the Japanese constitution. The threat posed by North Korea and international terrorism, however, enabled the Koizumi government to win the support of the main opposition party, the Democratic Party of Japan (DPJ), for the enactment of this special legislation. The legislation enables Japan to deploy the SDF swiftly by suspending numerous restrictions hindering its effective mobilization and operation.

These measures generally met with support among the Japanese population, indicating the extent to which North Korea's behavior had led to a change in Japanese attitudes regarding the national military. According to an opinion survey conducted by the *Mainichi Shimbun* in December 2003, more than 50 percent of the respondents indicated that they regarded North Korea as a threat to Japan's security, whereas only 24 percent regarded China as a threat. Regarding the North Korean nuclear issue, only 5 percent of the respondents believed that progress would be made in 2004. Pertaining to Japan's food aid to North Korea, 64 percent maintained that Japan should suspend the aid to North Korea, whereas 26 percent supported offering such aid to the North.[96]

According to Japan's 2004 Diplomatic Bluebook, the official "basic policy" concerning North Korea revolves around two main issues: the abduction issue and the security issue (i.e., nuclear and missile issues). The Bluebook goes on to say that the Pyongyang Declaration, which was signed by the leaders of the DPRK and Japan at the Japan–North Korea summit meeting in September 2002, serves as a foundational starting point for resolving these issues. Following the comprehensive resolution of these two matters, Japan would "thereby normalize relations with North Korea in a manner that would contribute to the peace and stability of Northeast Asia."[97] Japan's approach in this regard is similar to that of the United States: Tokyo wants to resolve all outstanding issues before diplomatic normalization rather than establishing diplomatic relations as a first step toward resolving the outstanding issues.

With regard to the nuclear issue, Japan has (1) called for CVID of the North Korean nuclear programs, (2) agreed that discussions on North

[96] H. N. Kim (2005). [97] Japan Ministry of Foreign Affairs (2004: 25).

Korea's security concerns and energy assistance could be advanced within the six-party talks after the DPRK agreed to CVID, and (3) asserted that there is no change in Japan's basic positions of settling outstanding issues based on the Pyongyang Declaration and the normalization of relations in a peaceful manner.[98] Japan has also continued to pursue defensive military measures, such as an effective missile defense system. Starting in 2004, Japan began to procure and deploy Patriot Advanced Capability missiles to shoot down enemy missiles shortly before they hit targets in Japan and a Standard Missile system to intercept enemy missiles before they enter the earth's atmosphere. Japan initially committed to spend $1 billion to procure these advanced interceptor missiles, and by 2007, plans to deploy a functionally layered antimissile defense system at a total cost of $7 billion. Some hawkish Japanese leaders have advocated the acquisition of cruise missiles (e.g., Tomahawks) for possible preemptive strikes against North Korean missile sites in case of an imminent attack.

An alternative interpretation of this Japanese armament – and indeed of the entire U.S.–Japan alliance – is possible. In this analysis, although Japan talks about North Korea, the real object of its rearmament is China.[99] If this is the case, it is a secret well kept among Japan's policy elite because the majority of the Japanese population believes in the North Korean threat and in the preparation of a military response.

North Korea has been easy to demonize in part because of national identity issues, such as the abductions issue. During the six-party talks on the nuclear issue, Japan has taken opportunities to discuss the abduction issue with North Korean representatives. During the second round of six-party talks, there were bilateral consultations in which the Japanese side underscored the importance of resolving the issue, strongly calling for the unconditional return of all family members of the abductees and a full account and whereabouts of the ten nationals whose fates are not known. The North Korean side, however, responded that all five former abductees in Japan should be returned to North Korea as originally agreed on and that ultimately the problems between Japan and North Korea "should be resolved one by one in line with the Japan-DPRK Pyongyang Declaration."[100] Japan denied the North Korean demand. The five former abductees and their family members are back in Japan for good and are actively seeking more information on the deaths of eight abductees; this is close to proof positive that Tokyo is becoming a prisoner of its own domestic politics.

[98] Japan Ministry of Foreign Affairs (2004: 27).
[99] For an analysis along these lines, see Johnson (2005).
[100] Japan Ministry of Foreign Affairs (2004: 31).

Alongside resolution of the abduction issue, there is no question that reduction of Pyongyang's military threat remains atop the list of Japanese priorities. Japanese security planners, however, are also concerned that a marked deterioration of political stability in North Korea or a military miscalculation by Pyongyang would invite great-power intervention, affecting Japanese interests on the peninsula.[101] Japan therefore has an interest in restraining the United States, especially in a world in which the Bush administration has outlined a national security strategy based on preventive war. The Koizumi administration, for example, warmly welcomed the Bush administration's October 2003 offer of a security guarantee for the DPRK.[102]

Japan–ROK Security Interaction

Despite, or perhaps because of, having the United States as a common ally, South Korea and Japan had limited direct bilateral military ties during the Cold War.[103] Neither Tokyo nor Seoul made much of an effort to promote direct bilateral security ties. The South Koreans, well protected by the United States, harbored bitter memories of Japanese colonialism, whereas the Japanese, also well protected by the United States, were reluctant to get involved in entangling commitments.[104] Although the end of the Cold War did not alter many South Koreans' negative perception of Japan and did not fundamentally transform Japan's circumspect attitude toward alliances, it did change both the context and conditions for strategic calculus in Tokyo and Seoul.

With the end of the Cold War and the demise of the Soviet threat, the U.S. military deployment in NEA came into question. The East Asian Strategic Initiative of April 1990 was a U.S. blueprint for a force reduction in East Asia to be implemented in two phases: 1990–92 and 1992–95. Neither Seoul nor Tokyo knew of the other's intentions. In its 1990 Defense White Paper, the South Korean defense ministry stated

101 Akaha (2002). 102 Samuels (2004: 324).

103 Victor D. Cha (1999a) argues that during the Cold War the dynamics of South Korea–Japan security cooperation worked in the context of a quasialliance system through the mutual fears of allied abandonment (by the United States), despite historical enmity. That is, the dynamics of Korea–Japan security cooperation in the context of a quasialliance system is explained in terms of the perceived level of U.S. military commitment to their respective security. Yet, specific cases of Japan–ROK bilateral security cooperation are rare and spotty. Moreover, in analyzing Japan–ROK relations Cha makes the mistake of "putting all his eggs in one basket" in the sense that he tries to explain too much with a single variable: the policies of the United States. See T. R. Yoon (2006) for an elaboration of "net threat theory" along these lines rebutting Chan's neorealist theory of quasialliance.

104 For more on Japan's entanglement-averse strategic culture during the Cold War, see Berger (1993).

that a Japanese military buildup could be a negative factor affecting South Korea's national security, and South Korea became particularly concerned over debates in the Japanese Diet about the use of the SDF for peace-keeping operations abroad, in light of the 1991 Persian Gulf War. The South Korean foreign minister, Choi Ho Joong, expressed his concern that the dispatch of Japanese troops would be "the starting point of the remilitarization of Japan," and the 1991 Defense White Paper depicted the SDF as being "transformed into offensive forces for the purpose of forward defense."[105]

Seoul's normalization of relations with both Moscow and Beijing contributed to the creation of an uncertain environment for Tokyo. Some Japanese believed that the rapidly improving relations between Seoul and Moscow might put additional pressure on the more frigid and fragile Japan–Soviet ties by giving Moscow a "South Korea card" to play against Tokyo. Many more were concerned when Seoul–Beijing normalization came, and the South Korean press and other opinion leaders expressed a view that the South Koreans and the Chinese could form a bloc to check the power of Japan.[106]

These uncertainties forced South Korea and Japan to undertake a series of confidence and security building measures (CSBMs), albeit in fits and starts. Initially, these measures were seen as a response to uncertainties about each other's strategic calculus in the transformed post–Cold War security environment. However, the rise of the North Korean threat in the mid-1990s has since served as the primary catalyst and driver of the bilateral military contacts. Pyongyang's on-again, off-again brinkmanship strategy has dampened if not erased the anxiety felt by South Korea and Japan about each other.[107] The emergence of the clear and present danger presented by North Korea's nuclear and missile programs has simply overwhelmed the vague and amorphous threat posed to each by the other.

In 1993, training exchange programs between the South Korean Navy and Japan's SDF were initiated. The following year, South Korean naval vessels made their first port call in Japan, and Japanese vessels made a reciprocating visit to South Korea in 1996. More important, beginning in 1994, an institutionalized annual meeting of the South Korean defense minister and the Japanese defense agency chief, supported by working-level talks, has been held.[108] The two militaries held their first joint exercises in 1998, and Japanese and South Korean peace-keeping forces now serve side by side in East Timor.

By all accounts, the greatest wave of security cooperation between South Korea and Japan resulted from President Kim Dae Jung's summit

[105] Kang and Kaseda (2000: 96–97). [106] Kang and Kaseda (2000: 96–97).
[107] Kang and Kaseda (2000). [108] Kang and Kaseda (2000: 99–101).

meeting with Prime Minister Obuchi Keizo in Tokyo in October 1998. The South Korean leader lauded Japan for its prosperity and its diplomatic and security policy based on the peace constitution, and he urged a "forward-looking partnership."[109] The Japanese leader, in turn, praised South Korea's deepening democratization and economic development, and, for the first time in writing, he extended Japan's "sincere apology" and expressed "poignant remorse" for the misdeeds perpetrated during Japanese imperial rule in Korea. Most important, the two leaders publicly acknowledged that they shared common security interests and agreed to expand direct security cooperation. In May 1999, three hotlines were hooked up to link the South Korean defense ministry with the Japanese defense agency. In August of that year, the first joint naval "search and rescue exercise" – involving three Maritime SDF destroyers, two ROK Navy destroyers, and aerial and intelligence support engaging in joint formation training and tactical maneuvers – occurred, as Japan, South Korea, and the United States urged North Korea to abandon its plan to test-launch a Taepodong-2 missile.

The 2004 Japanese Bluebook notes the installment of the new administration under President Roh Moo-hyun in 2003 and the advancement of the "Peace and Prosperity Policy" toward North Korea that follows on Kim Dae Jung's "Sunshine Policy."[110] According to the report, the "amicable relations" that had developed under the Kim administration through increased cultural exchange and the joint hosting of the 2002 World Cup "have been maintained and strengthened."[111] The document also notes that the North Korean issue has created opportunities for bilateral and multilateral cooperation, such as the ASEAN Plus Three Summit involving Japan, the ROK, and China.

However, even with these recent advances in ROK–Japan relations, as Japan seeks to increase its contribution to international security both regionally and globally, issues of history and national identity promise to become more salient than ever. The recent row over the Tokdo Islands is evidence of this. Confronted by a hostile, nuclear-armed North Korea and participating in the broader War on Terror spearheaded by the United States, Japan has been compelled to undertake unprecedented measures to bolster its security. It has dispatched naval forces to provide rear-area support for the U.S.-led military campaign in Afghanistan, launched reconnaissance satellites over North Korea, permitted its maritime forces to engage in fire fights with unidentified vessels lurking in Japanese territorial waters, and even provided armed soldiers to aid in the perilous reconstruction of Iraq. This expansion of Japanese commitments is worrisome for South Korea, which reinforces the tenuousness of

[109] *Asahi Shimbun,* October 9, 1998. [110] Japan Ministry of Foreign Affairs (2004: 3).
[111] Japan Ministry of Foreign Affairs (2004: 7).

the security cooperation between the two states. South Korea has found a partner in China in responding to Japanese behavior that stirs the colonial memory. The two countries have been allied in opposition to Japan's latest bid for a permanent seat on the UN Security Council, and Beijing has increasingly supported Seoul playing a "balancing role" in Northeast Asian geopolitics. Until Japan fully and forcefully confronts the historical issues related to its imperial past, it seems unlikely to have truly normal relations with either North or South Korea.

Economic and Functional Relations

Until the twentieth century, the only external power that really had an impact on the Korean economy was China. But Japan's radical reformatting of Korean society during the colonial period involved significant changes to the Korean economy. Imperial Japan imposed its own logic of the economic division of labor and specialization, emphasizing agriculture in the South as a major source of food supply for Japan and concentrating on the development of rich natural resources (e.g., coal, ferrous and nonferrous metals, nonmetallic resources), heavy industry, and hydroelectric power in the North as a major source of raw materials, semifinished manufactures, and war goods. The interior of the North, however, remained underdeveloped compared with its coastal regions, which were connected by sea to the Japanese imperial economic network.[112]

Revisionist scholarship on economic development in Korea has focused to a great extent on the beneficial effects of this Japanese colonial project and the perceived continuities between South Korea's growth strategy before and after World War II.[113] However, there are several major reasons to rebut the revisionist claim of beneficial continuity in South Korea: (1) the economic record at the time of Japanese colonialism was not as strong as the revisionists would have us believe and, more seriously, the end of Japanese rule in 1945 was followed immediately by fifteen years of severe social conflict, war, policy drift, and a modest economic record; (2) the continuity argument is based on a deterministically technocratic bias because it is the political leaders, not the bureaucracy, that makes policy; (3) much of the Japanese-financed capital stock was destroyed or depreciated from 1945 to 1953; and (4) with the exception of labor repression, there occurred a reversal of the social legacies of Japanese colonialism, such as increased attention to human capital and land reform, which only became possible because of political independence from Japanese rule.[114]

[112] Hughes (1999: 118). [113] See Cumings (1984); J. E. Woo (1991); Kohli (1994).
[114] Haggard, Kang, and Moon (1997).

Table 4.2. Japan's Trade with North and South Korea, 1962–89

Year	Japan's Exports to North Korea	Japan's Imports from North Korea	Total Japan–North Korea Trade (Balance)	Change in Japan–North Korea Trade	Japan's Exports to South Korea	Japan's Imports from South Korea	Total Japan–South Korea Trade (Balance)	Change in Japan–South Korea Trade
1962					109	24	133 (+85)	N/A
1963					159	25	184 (+134)	38%
1964	12	18	30 (−6)	N/A	110	38	148 (+72)	−20%
1965	18	13	31 (+5)	3%	175	45	220 (+130)	49%
1966	5	21	26 (−15)	−16%	294	65	359 (+229)	63%
1967	6	30	36 (−23)	40%	443	85	528 (+358)	47%
1968	21	34	55 (–13)	53%	623	100	723 (+523)	37%
1969	24	32	56 (−8)	2%	754	113	867 (+641)	20%
1970	26	31	57 (−5)	2%	809	234	1,043 (+575)	20%
1971	32	27	59 (+5)	4%	954	262	1,216 (+692)	17%
1972	104	34	138 (+70)	134%	1,031	410	1,441 (+621)	19%
1973	111	66	177 (+45)	28%	1,727	1,169	2,896 (+558)	101%
1974	277	99	376 (+178)	112%	2,621	1,380	4,001 (+1,241)	38%
1975	199	59	258 (+140)	−31%	2,434	1,293	3,727 (+1,141)	–7%
1976	106	65	171 (+41)	−34%	3,099	1,802	4,901 (+1,297)	31%
1977	139	61	200 (+78)	17%	3,927	2,148	6,075 (+1,778)	24%
1978	203	98	301 (+105)	51%	5,982	2,627	8,609 (+3,355)	42%
1979	310	137	447 (+173)	49%	6,657	3,353	10,010 (+3,304)	16%
1980	414	165	579 (+249)	30%	5,858	3,039	8,897 (+2,818)	−11%
1981	319	127	446 (+192)	−23%	6,374	3,503	9,877 (+2,871)	11%
1982	344	137	481 (+207)	8%	5,305	3,388	8,693 (+1,917)	−12%
1983	360	116	476 (+244)	−1%	6,328	3,404	9,732 (+2,924)	12%
1984	280	131	411 (+149)	−14%	7,640	4,602	12,242 (+3,038)	26%
1985	274	161	435 (+113)	6%	7,560	4,543	12,103 (+3,017)	−1%
1986	204	154	358 (+50)	−18%	10,869	5,426	16,295 (+5,443)	35%
1987	238	218	456 (+20)	27%	13,657	8,437	22,094 (+5,220)	36%
1988	263	293	556 (−30)	22%	15,929	12,004	27,933 (+3,925)	26%
1989	216	267	483 (−51)	−13%	17,449	13,457	30,906 (+3,992)	11%

Units: US$1 million.
Source: Cha (1999: 235–37).

Regardless of the impact of Japan's colonial economic policy, post-1945 economic relations between Japan and Korea have proceeded in fits and starts, often linked to larger geopolitical, geostrategic, and national identity issues. Today, in the post–Cold War era, Japan's policy toward the peninsula is driven by two goals: (1) the promotion of continued economic recovery and growth in South Korea, and (2) the support of the process of domesticating North Korea.

Japan–DPRK Economic Relations

Hatoyama Ichiro, who became the Japanese prime minister in 1955, first stimulated postwar economic ties between Tokyo and Pyongyang. But only in November 1962 did Japan and North Korea begin direct cargo shipments, on a very small scale. Trade agreements were signed two years later, in July 1964, but the impact was small. As Table 4.2 indicates, economic relations between North Korea and Japan were modest throughout the 1960s and made a large jump forward in the early 1970s.

The increase in trade in 1972 and 1974 was due in part to the recognition by Tokyo's leftist governor Minobe Ryokichi of *Chongryun* – the civil society organization of pro-Pyongyang Koreans in Japan – as North Korea's *de facto* representative in Japan. The group was granted tax-free status.[115] At trade fairs in Pyongyang, the North Korean hosts purchased all Japanese products on display and ordered more, but they were not forthcoming with payments for the goods. When North Korea defaulted in 1972 on payments to the Kyowa Bussan Trading Company – comprised of twenty large Japanese firms – Japan's Ministry of International Trade and Industry (MITI) suspended all export credits in 1974. This led to an immediate decline in trade, although there was a revival at the end of the decade. By 1975, Japanese creditors claimed nearly 80 billion yen in unpaid notes. In 1983, the Japanese government ceased underwriting trade insurance for Japanese firms doing business in the DPRK. Finally, in October 1986, the Japanese government provided 300 billion yen in compensation for losses incurred by Japanese firms that had traded with North Korea.[116] Despite the lack of payments, limited trade, usually worth no more than $500 million, continued between Japan and North Korea. After North Korea announced its Law on Joint Ventures in 1984, a Mitsui Trading Company subsidiary backed a gold mine venture with North Korean residents of Japan, and an Osaka-based firm established a cement factory in North Korea in 1990.[117]

Remarkably, in 1993, Japan became North Korea's second largest trading partner after China and soon thereafter temporarily became its largest

[115] Samuels (2004: 319). [116] Hughes (1999: 135–36, 141). [117] Hughes (1999: 132).

Table 4.3. Japan's Trade with North and South Korea, 1990–2004

Year	Japan's Exports to North Korea	Japan's Imports from North Korea	Total Japan–North Korea Trade (balance)	Change in Japan–North Korea Trade	Japan's Exports to South Korea	Japan's Imports from South Korea	Total Japan–South Korea Trade (balance)	Change Japan–South Korea Trade
1990	194	271	465 (−77)	N/A	18,574	12,638	31,212 (+5,936)	N/A
1991	246	250	496 (−4)	+7%	21,120	12,360	33,480 (+8,760)	+7%
1992	246	231	477 (+15)	−4%	19,460	11,600	31,060 (+7,860)	−7%
1993	243	222	465 (+21)	−3%	20,020	11,560	31,580 (+8,460)	+2%
1994	188	297	485 (−109)	+4%	25,390	13,520	38,910 (+11,870)	+23%
1995	282	306	588 (−24)	+21%	32,610	17,050	49,660 (+15,560)	+28%
1996	249	265	514 (−16)	−13%	31,449	15,767	47,216 (+15,682)	−5%
1997	197	269	466 (−72)	−9%	27,907	14,771	42,678 (+13,136)	−10%
1998	175	219	394 (−44)	−15%	16,840	12,238	29,078 (+4,602)	−32%
1999	147	202	349 (−55)	−11%	24,142	15,862	40,004 (+8,280)	+38%
2000	207	257	464 (−50)	+33%	31,828	20,466	52,294 (+11,362)	+31%
2001	249	226	475 (+23)	+2%	26,633	16,506	43,139 (+10,127)	−18%
2002	135	234	369 (−99)	−22%	29,856	15,143	44,999 (+14,713)	+4%
2003	92	172	264 (−80)	−28%	36,313	17,276	53,589 (+19,037)	+19%
2004	89	164	253 (−75)	−4%	46,144	21,701	67,845 (+24,443)	+27%

Units: US$1 million.
Source: International Monetary Fund (1992: 247, 304; 1993: 247, 305; 1994: 265, 326; 1995: 269–70; 1996: 275, 342; 1997: 342, 347; 1998: 289, 349); MOFAT (1998: 396; 401; 1999: 481, 486; 2001: 497; 2002: 483–84; 2003: 497). Available at www.mofat.go.kr and KOTRA at www.kotra.or.kr.

partner. But as Table 4.3 and Figure 4.1 show, overall trade volume soon began to decline, largely due to the severe deterioration of North Korea's economy sparked by the withdrawal of Soviet and Chinese support in the late 1980s and early 1990s. Although Japan is a major trading partner for the DPRK, the latter ranks ninety-eighth among the markets for Japan's exports (behind Slovenia and Kazakhstan) and ranks sixty-fourth among sources of Japan's imports (behind Sri Lanka and Costa Rica). Crabs, clams, and other seafood make up almost half of the North's exports to Japan, followed by woven apparel, vegetables, and electrical machinery. Japan also imports coal and other minerals from the DPRK. Japan sends primarily vehicles, animal hair/yarn and fabrics, and machinery to North Korea. Although the *South China Morning Post* optimistically predicted that "a surge of Japanese investment in North Korea" would result from Prime Minister Koizumi's September 2002 visit to Pyongyang,[118] the Japanese press reported widespread skepticism in the Japanese business community.

By mid-2003, bilateral trade was at its lowest level in a decade. More stringent Japanese port controls have led in part to the acceptance of fewer shipments from North Korea, but more to the point, Japanese firms that had been commissioning manufacture – textiles and electrical machinery – from North Korean plants found the DPRK too risky and Chinese alternatives too attractive.[119] Although trade levels continue to decline, the concurrent shrinking of the North Korea economy may mean that trade with Japan – particularly exports, which generate hard currency – is relatively more important to North Korea today than it was in the 1980s.

The largest part of Japan–DPRK trade by far has involved either businesses established by North Korean citizens living in Japan or illegal narcotics traffic, and the two often intersect. More than 100 Chongryun joint ventures were created in the wake of the 1984 North Korean Joint Ventures Law. Many of the Chongryun "patriotic plants" in North Korea have failed or found their finances under investigation by the Japanese government. Recently, a number of local governments have decided to reconsider their policy of making Chongryun facilities either partially or entirely exempt from fixed-asset taxation.[120] Meanwhile, a Japanese government crackdown on drug smuggling has caused much of the North Korean narcotics traffic to be rerouted through China.[121] In June 2003, Japan ordered its customs and immigration services and its coast guard to expand safety inspections and searches for illicit contraband on North

118 *South China Morning Post,* September 18, 2002.
119 Manyin (2003); Samuels (2004: 320). 120 *The Japan Times,* June 30, 2003.
121 *The Tokyo Shimbun,* November 25, 2003.

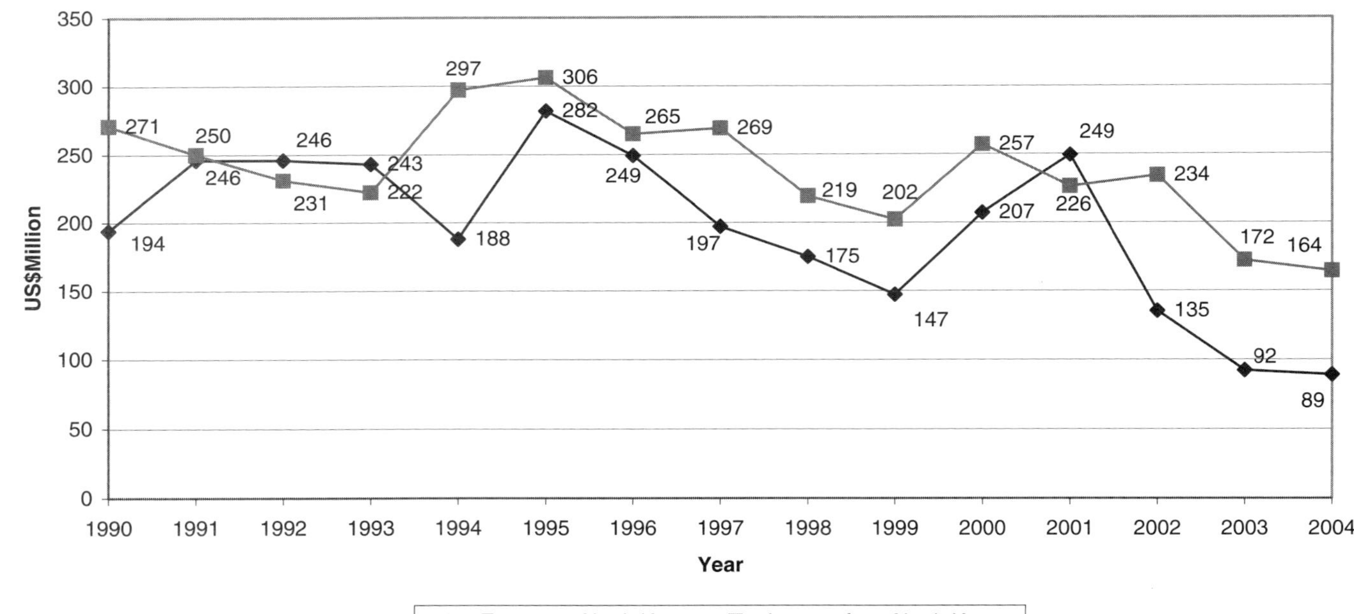

Figure 4.1. Japan's trade with North Korea, 1990–2004.
Source: International Monetary Fund (1992: 247, 304; 1993: 247, 305; 1994: 265, 326; 1995: 269–70; 1996: 275, 342; 1997: 342, 347; 1998: 289, 349); MOFAT (1998: 396; 401; 1999: 481, 486; 2001: 497, 2002: 483–84, 2003: 497). Available at www.mofat.gokr and KOTRA at www.kotra.or.kr.

Korean cargo and passenger ships. North Korean ships had made 1,300 calls at Japanese ports in 2002. Between January and August 2003, North Korean port calls were down by 25 percent, and of 120 North Korean ships inspected in Japan, 70 percent were ordered to halt operations or otherwise received safety warnings, as compared with a general average of 10 percent for all countries' shipping.[122] The Mangyongbong 92-passenger cargo ferry, suspected of being used by North Korea for clandestine activities, suspended its regular several-times-per-month service for seven months in 2003 due to the suddenly strict inspection regime. Interestingly, however, trade has fallen rather than increased since North Korea resumed the Mangyongbong ferry service.

There have also been periodic, highly visible crackdowns on illegal exports from Japan. Japan has enacted and is enforcing a law that restricts exports to North Korea of items that may be used in the development of nuclear weapons. In April 2003, for instance, Japanese authorities filed criminal charges against Meishin, a trading company run by a pro-Pyongyang Korean resident in Japan that allegedly tried to ship electronic control devices that can be used in the production of strategic weapons to North Korea. A shipment of the devices from Meishin was seized by Hong Kong customs officials at Japan's request. The shipment was reported to be destined for North Korea via Hong Kong and Thailand.[123]

When Pyongyang failed to respond to Japanese requests for quick and thorough action on the abduction issue, Prime Minister Koizumi indicated at the end of 2003 his intention to consider imposing sanctions on North Korea. Although Koizumi maintained that his government was not considering immediate economic sanctions against North Korea, his chief cabinet secretary did not rule out possible sanctions in the future "if North Korea makes things worse." North Korea's reactions to this possibility were negative; a spokesman for the North Korean Foreign Ministry denounced it as a "wanton violation" of the Pyongyang Declaration, warning that Japan would be responsible for "all consequences to be entailed by its foolish moves."[124]

The amended Law on Liability for Oil Pollution Damage, which took effect March 1, 2005, amounts to a *de facto* economic sanction on the DPRK. The new law bans from Japanese ports all foreign vessels weighing more than 100 tons without proper liability insurance regarding oil spills. Most DPRK freighters are not covered by the required "Protection and Indemnity Insurance," and they will in effect be banned from Japanese ports. According to the Japanese Transport Ministry, 73 percent of foreign vessels that entered Japanese ports in 2003 were insured and

[122] Nanto and Chanlett-Avery (2005: 26–28). [123] H. N. Kim (2005).
[124] "DPRK Slashes Japan's Foreign Exchange Bill," Xinhua News Agency, January 31, 2004.

met insurance requirements, but only 2.5 percent of the 982 DPRK vessels that visited Japanese ports in 2004 had such coverage.[125] It is unclear how effective these independent sanctions against North Korea will be; they could, in fact, result in China gaining much more influence over North Korea. Some commentators have begun complaining that Japan is forsaking the influence that it does have in Pyongyang. Amid the declining Japan–North Korea trade, the value of trade between China and North Korea tripled in the four years from 2001 to 2004, and now amounts to one-half of North Korea's overall trade, whereas Japan and North Korea are trading only one-fifth as much as at their peak of economic relations in 1980. Japan simply cannot effectively sanction the DPRK without China's support.

The combination of illegal trade and remittances from Korean permanent residents in Japan means that Japan is a significant source – indeed one of the only sources – of North Korea's foreign exchange. North Korea has been in need of foreign reserves ever since moves by Moscow in 1990 and then by Beijing in 1992 to hard currency regimes of trade with the DPRK. North Korea also lost, with the collapse of communism, subsidized export markets and cheap imports of indispensable commodities such as food and oil. Although the exact amount of remittances from Chongryun is unknown, the total appears to be in the neighborhood of $100 million per year (some press reports estimate that it is ten times that amount), and it has declined sharply to around $30 million since the burst of Japan's economic bubble of the early 1990s and the death of Kim Il Sung in 1994.[126] A number of Chongryun credit unions that were the source of many remittances went bankrupt with the decline in the Japanese economy and have come under the control of the Japanese government.[127]

The Japanese government also stepped up an investigation of the finances of the pro-Pyongyang organization and its affiliated credit unions beginning in 2001. In February 2004, partly in response to growing public anger over the abduction issue, the Japanese Diet, led by a group of young LDP members, amended the Foreign Exchange and Foreign Trade Control Law to allow the government to halt all trade, stop all cash remittances, and stop transportation links to enemy countries.[128] Official money transfers between Japan and North Korea fell by 34.5 percent in 2004. In addition, Tokyo reportedly has drawn up contingency plans that would bar banks from remitting funds to North Korea, and would also deny landing rights to the crew and passengers of ferries between Japan and North Korea (with an exception for Korean permanent residents of Japan) if North Korea tests a nuclear device.[129]

[125] D. C. Kang (2005a). [126] Eberstadt (1996). [127] Manyin (2003: 14).
[128] Green (2001: 117). [129] Nanto and Chanlett-Avery (2005: 26–28).

In general, Japan's role is potentially critical in the crisis over North Korea's nuclear weapons programs. Most important, Japan has promised to North Korea, using the 1965 Japan–South Korean normalization agreement as a model, a large-scale economic aid package in recognition of the "tremendous damage and suffering" Japan inflicted during its colonial rule of Korea from 1910 to 1945. The aid package would go into effect after the two countries agree to normalize relations, and Japan now links normalization to a resolution of the abduction and nuclear issues. Japanese officials are reportedly discussing a package on the order of \$5–\$10 billion, an enormous sum for the North Korean economy, the total GDP of which is estimated to be in the range of \$20 billion. There is some fear, however, that a payment of this size would serve to prolong Kim Jong Il's regime artificially without inducing any behavioral changes, or possibly that the funds would be redirected to the North Korean military. To capture the money, Pyongyang has moved away from demands that the package be labeled as "reparations" or "compensation" and has also backed off from its periodic insistence that Japan provide compensation for harms allegedly inflicted since 1945.

It is possible that Japanese negotiators will try to obtain restitution of approximately 80 billion yen (about \$667 million) that North Korean enterprises owe Japanese banks from deals carried out in the 1970s and 1980s.[130] Although resolution of the debt problem is not the major obstacle to normalization, in May 2003, the Japanese government announced that it could legally invoke a complete trade ban with the DPRK. The government cited not only Japanese law, but also a bilateral treaty with the United States. Japanese law allows the government to restrict trade if it affects the healthy development of Japan's economy, so the government concluded that a Japanese failure to comply with U.S. sanctions against North Korea would seriously undermine the U.S.–Japan relationship and hence Japan's economy.

There has been little indication of how the normalization of relations would impact financial flows to the DPRK, and this may ultimately be of more importance to North Korean economic development than are trade flows. The most likely initial source of such financial flows would come from DPRK-friendly residents of Japan. Although Chongryun is the most active group doing business with North Korea, its resources are extremely limited, and its political clout has shrunk to near zero. In the event of normalization, Korean residents of Japan will play a role as middlemen for large firms, and local governments and business groups in the coastal areas near North Korea are expected to increase their investment in the DPRK. But here, too, resources are very limited and, in fact, declining. Japanese investors have shown only limited interest

[130] Manyin (2003: 9–10).

in multilateral regional development programs, such as the UN Development Programme's TRADP.[131] Substantive increases in the form of direct investment would have to come from large Japanese firms and financial institutions, but this is likely to depend on resolution of the DPRK debt issue. Ultimately, North Korea will have to prove a more attractive location for investment than China.

Japan's economic relations with North Korea extend beyond trade and investment. North Korea's first ever public aid-seeking diplomacy came in May 1995 when Pyongyang sent a delegation to Tokyo. In a humble request to a longtime enemy, the DPRK, trying to violate its policy of self-reliance as little as possible, said, "We would like to ask Japan to lend as much rice as possible for a certain period of time." Against the warnings of ROK President Kim-Young Sam, Japan and South Korea decided to give food aid in coordination with one another. Since then, Japan has provided more than 1 million metric tons of humanitarian food aid to North Korea, mostly through the UN WFP. Most of the aid (valued at $1.45 billion) was sent to North Korea free of charge, whereas 350,000 tons were provided on a long-term loan basis.[132] The pattern of Japanese aid reflects developments in the political relationship between Tokyo and Pyongyang; shipments began in 1995 and 1996 when relations warmed and then were suspended after the Taepodong missile launch over Japan in 1998 and the spy ship incident in 2001. In the face of North Korea's unwillingness to give up its nuclear weapons program, the Koizumi government announced that it had ruled out the possibility of extending any additional food aid to North Korea beyond that agreed on at the Pyongyang summit. In August 2004, Japan shipped the first half of the food aid and medical supplies to North Korea from the humanitarian aid package promised by Koizumi at the summit, including 125,000 tons of food aid (worth $40 million) and $7 million of medical supplies to be distributed through international organizations. The aid was designed to encourage Pyongyang to come up with a reciprocal gesture of goodwill at the forthcoming bilateral working-level talks in Beijing.

Japan's 2004 Diplomatic Bluebook notes that 2003 marked a "significant turning point" for Japan's Official Development Assistance (ODA) because Japan's basic ODA policy was revised for the first time in eleven years. The document says that ODA

> is provided as an element of diplomacy, [and] can neither be understood nor supported, unless it contributes to Japan's security and prosperity. Recently, various issues such as humanitarian ones (poverty, hunger, refugees and disasters), global ones (the environment and water), conflict and terrorism in

[131] Hughes (1999: 133). [132] H. N. Kim (2005).

> particular have become more serious. The ODA Charter states, therefore, that Japan's initiative in making full use of ODA to resolve these issues will not only benefit Japan in a number of ways, for example through further advancement of friendly relations and promotion of people-to-people exchanges and through improvement of Japan's position in the international arena, but also, will lead to the stability and development of developing countries, which is vital for Japan as it is heavily dependent on overseas countries for resources and energy.[133]

North Korea is notable for its absence in this description of ODA. While posing as one of Japan's greatest potential threats, the DPRK is also a country that continues to face various humanitarian issues that have been present since the mid-1990s. Japan, which has provided aid to North Korea in the past, states that its ODA priority is in Asia but makes no mention of North Korea in light of the changes to its ODA policy.

Japan–North Korea bilateral trade and economic relations have declined surprisingly since the end of the Cold War. Although the levels of trade between the countries pale in comparison to those between Japan and South Korea, Japan is an extremely important source of goods and capital for the DPRK. Japan also stands poised to be a major underwriter for economic reforms in North Korea. In terms of engaging North Korea since the October 2002 nuclear revelation, Japan's possible economic aid has acted as the biggest bunch of carrots dangling before Pyongyang in trying to ensure peace and stability in NEA and also to improve inter-Korean relations.

In recent years, however, Japan has put in place several laws that limit North Korea's ability to engage in either legal or illegal trade with Japan. The problem is not an economic one; rather, the question of abductions weighs heavily on Japanese engagement. Many Japanese citizens feel an emotional involvement in the fate of the abductees, driven not only by a genuine sense of horror at the actions of the North Korean government, but also nurtured for political gain by the LDP.[134] Although the ongoing nuclear issue is also relevant for Japan's normalization of economic and political relations with North Korea, it is really the abductions around which public imagination crystallizes. The abductions are yet another national identity issue providing a wedge in Japan–Korea relations and preventing the expansion of contacts. Pyongyang, however, prefers to accuse Japan of acting as the "shock brigade" for the U.S.-led "psychological warfare and blockade operation" in regard to its implementation of sanctions.[135] Until political issues can be settled, it is unlikely that there will be any major changes in Japan–DPRK economic relations.

[133] Japan Ministry of Foreign Affairs (2004: 204).
[134] Samuels (2004: 331–32). [135] *The Age* (Melbourne), June 25, 2003.

Japan–ROK Economic Relations

Almost from the founding of the ROK, the United States sought to achieve rapprochement between capitalist South Korea and Japan. NSC 5506 explicitly called for a reduction of the U.S. financial burden in Japan by increasing Japan's trade with the other free nations of Asia. President Syngman Rhee, however, vehemently opposed using the Korean economy to prop up Japan in any way. As mentioned previously, he became particularly enraged at American suggestions that aid given to Korea should be spent on Japanese goods, arguing that aid should be used on nurturing Korean industries and the Korean economy.

In the late 1950s, Rhee attempted to balance the amount of imports from Japan with the amount of goods the ROK exported, but substantial underground trading between the two countries indicated the natural economic attraction between the two neighbors. It was the diplomatic stalemate concerning repatriations that prevented greater economic ties between the two countries in the 1950s. Whereas Rhee argued that Japan should pay $2 billion in repatriations, the Japanese claimed that they should receive compensation for properties left behind in Korea after colonialism. Only with the rise of Park Chung Hee as chief of state did these dynamics change.

By 1963, imports from Japan had reached $162 million – 30 percent of total ROK imports. If aid is included in the measure of imports, then more than 70 percent of South Korea's imports were emanating from Japan. Tokyo gave numerous forms of credit to Seoul in the first half of the 1960s, including $40 million in short-term credit in 1962, $18 million in grain purchases, and $37.4 million in suppliers' credit. Japanese firms also played a key role in developing links between the two countries. Companies such as Nippon Koei identified projects in South Korea early in the 1960s and built lasting relationships. Besides direct contributions to economic projects, it is reported that Japanese firms also funded two-thirds of Park Chung Hee's budget ($66 million).[136] In the early 1960s, these Japanese contributions to South Korean growth catalyzed calls by the Korean government to normalize relations to cover the current debt to Japan, as well as to encourage future economic transfers.

From the 1965 normalization agreement, South Korea received a total of $800 million from Japan: $300 million in grants, $200 million in government loans, and $300 million in commercial credit. Park Chung Hee happily accepted the funds and used a large proportion of the grants to build Pohang Steel. The 3.5 percent loans were used for infrastructure projects, including power plants, railroads, and communication facilities.

[136] J. E. Woo (1991: 85–86).

The commercial credit went into financing plant exports from Japan (e.g., power facilities). Nippon Koei, for instance, won several contracts to build hydroelectric dams in Korea.

As indicated in Tables 4.2 and 4.3, Japan–ROK trade has grown steadily since normalization in 1965. The only major decline in trade was in the wake of the 1997–98 Asian Financial Crisis (AFC); trade levels took four years to recover from the AFC. In fact, Japan was instrumental in helping prop up the stricken South Korean economy. The AFC ended up boosting economic ties: Japan–ROK trade, which declined by 10 percent in 1997 and 32 percent in 1998, bounded back with a 38 percent increase in 1999 and a 31 percent increase in 2000. In June 1999, South Korea eliminated the discriminatory import diversification tax that had barred many imports from Japan. By 2004, total trade stood at $67.8 billion, an increase of 133 percent from 1998.

With this steady growth in trade, the South Korean bilateral trade deficit with Japan has also grown steadily. The ROK has never once exported more to Japan than it has imported, although Korean products compete with those from Japan in steel, consumer electronics, shipbuilding, and other key areas. With Japan as the major source of South Korea's capital goods and technology imports, Seoul finds itself in a paradoxical position of generating more and more bilateral trade deficits with Japan to generate more and more trade surpluses with other countries. Some South Koreans believe that Japan, through its investments and transfers of technology, purposely shaped Korea's industrial structure in such a way as to require huge amounts of imports of Japanese capital goods and machinery and to inhibit Korea from upgrading to the highest types of technology.[137]

Japan is a global leader in environmental technology, particularly in the air pollution control sector. Because Japan does not have an official environmental-technology transfer program for Korea, technology transfer and investment between the two countries has been arranged mainly between the countries' private sectors. However, competition between private companies in the two countries has limited the transfer of technology. The ROK wants regional environmental cooperation to be a channel for environmental-technology transfer through exchanges of experts and information and the implementation of joint projects. The development of environmental cooperation in NEA may facilitate technology transfer among countries through joint projects, and also by the adoption of binding technologies and effluent standards for emission control. To this end, Korea also participates in broad regional cooperation led by Japan in the Environment Congress for Asia and the Pacific (ECO-ASIA) and

[137] Rozman (2002b: 14).

Table 4.4. Japanese–South Korean FDI Relations, 1989–2004

Year	Amount of South Korean FDI into Japan	Amount of South Korean FDI into Japan (Percent Change)	Amount of Japanese FDI into South Korea	Amount of Japanese FDI into South Korea (Percent Change)
1989	10	N/A		
1990	17	+70%	236	N/A
1991	12	−29%	226	−4%
1992	28	+133%	155	−31%
1993	9	−68%	286	+85%
1994	96	+967%	428	+50%
1995	103	+7%	418	−2%
1996	57	−45%	255	−39%
1997	99	+74%	265	+4%
1998	24	−76%	504	+90%
1999	108	+350%	1,750	+247%
2000	140	+30%	2,448	+40%
2001	95	−32%	772	−68%
2002	92	−3%	1,403	+82%
2003	51	−45%	541	−61%
2004	328	+543%	2,250	+316%

Units: US$ 1 million
Source: Keum (1996: 581); MOFAT (1998: 405, 408; 1999: 491, 493; 2001: 503, 505; 2002: 489, 491; 2003: 498–99); Ministry of Commerce, Industry & Energy (MOCIE).

the Acid Deposition Monitoring Network in East Asia (EANET) forums. Although promoting further cooperation, Korea is trapped in a dilemma of its own making: it seeks Japan's financial and technological contributions for effective environmental cooperation, but at the same time it tries to restrain Japanese leadership in regional environmental politics. In addition to technology transfer, Korea also seeks the niche market in Japan for its intermediate-level technologies.

Complementing these imports of Japanese technology has been FDI from Japan. As shown in Table 4.4 and Figure 4.2, Japanese FDI into the ROK topped $2.25 billion in 2004, as compared with only $328 million of OFDI from the ROK into Japan. Japanese FDI into Korea has grown even as Japanese investors have increasingly turned toward China as the best country in which to invest for production.

The rise of China has generally made both Tokyo and Seoul more Asiacentric – or Sinocentric – in their foreign economic relations in the post–Cold War era. Whereas China has replaced Japan as South Korea's largest trade partner, China has replaced South Korea as Japan's second largest trade partner.

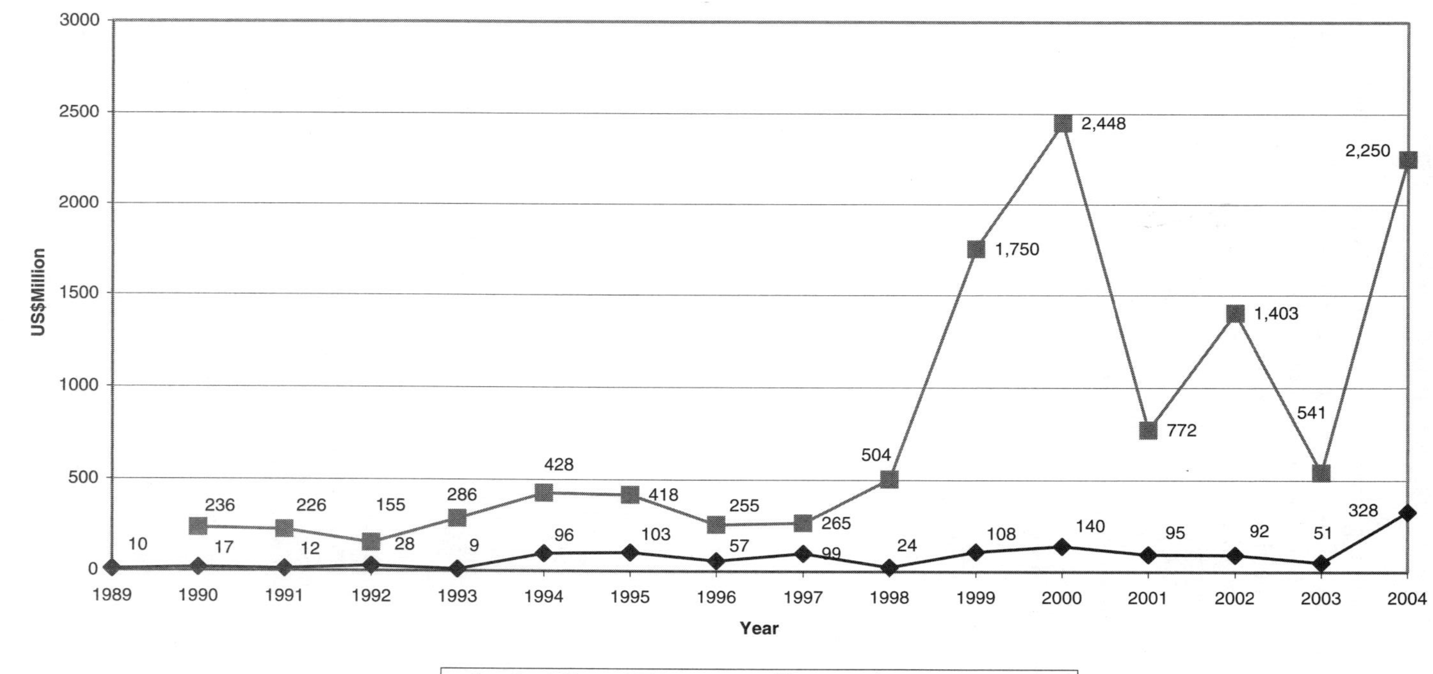

Figure 4.2. Amount of Japanese–South Korean FDI, 1989–2004.
Source: Keum (1996: 581); MOFAT (1998: 405, 408; 1999: 491, 493; 2001: 503, 505; 2002: 489, 491; 2003: 498–99); Ministry of Commerce, Industry & Energy (MOCIE).

As part of this growing interest in forwarding Asian economic integration, a possible Japan–Korea Free Trade Agreement (JKFTA) has been on the table since October 1998. At a Tokyo summit meeting, Prime Minister Keizo Obuchi and President Kim Dae Jung signed "The Joint Declaration of the New Japan–ROK Partnership for the 21st Century," which had as its goal the building of a future-oriented relationship on the basis of the spirit of reconciliation and friendship. A study group was established in December 1998 under the initiative of two major research institutes – the Institute of Developing Economies (IDE) in Japan and the Korea Institute for International Economic Policy (KIEP) – to further explore the economic feasibility and desirability of an FTA between the two countries. The respective studies of the two institutes concluded that a bilateral FTA would have a positive impact on both economies in the long run and would be an effective mechanism to further advance the economic relations between Japan and Korea.

In March 2002 in Seoul, Prime Minister Koizumi Junichiro and President Kim Dae Jung agreed to launch a new joint study group composed of representatives from government, business, and academia. The purpose of the group was to reexamine the feasibility and desirability of establishing the JKFTA and also the potential scope of the FTA and some basic elements of individual issues related to the FTA. In Tokyo, a year later, in June 2003, at a summit meeting between Koizumi and President Roh Moo-hyun, it was decided to launch the FTA negotiations at an early date. These talks began in December 2003, although they derailed in 2004 because of disagreement over how far Tokyo should go to reduce and remove import tariffs on agricultural products. Japan had hinted that it might open about 50 percent of its market to South Korean agricultural goods, but South Korea said the low market access would defeat the purpose of an FTA. Tokyo, in turn, has cited flagrant examples of Korean discrimination against Japanese products. The dispute over the Tokdo Islands has stalled the resumption of the talks.

This endeavor in pursuit of an FTA on the part of Japan and South Korea is allegedly not intended to undermine their long-standing policy of supporting the multilateral trading system. Rather, the two countries are seeking to enhance freer trade and more open, transparent economies as complementary measures to global trade liberalization and the multilateral trading system as a whole. In a 2003 policy pronouncement, Roh emphasized that South Korea must make a determined effort to sign FTAs to expand its markets and facilitate the growth of its economy. In addition to Japan, the ROK is engaged in free trade negotiations with Canada, Singapore, the four-member European Free Trade Association, and the ten-member ASEAN. The Ministry of Foreign Affairs and Trade says that studies are also under way with India, Mexico, Russia, and the South American MERCOSUR market, as well as with the United States and China.

There is a threat of great losses to Japan if the FTA with South Korea is not achieved. A report by the Institute of Developing Economies shows that scrapping the proposed FTA could result in Japan's GDP losing about 10 percentage points of growth over a decade, translating into a loss of $443 billion in national income. The Japanese institute also predicts a decline in local interest in South Korean cultural products, such as television dramas and songs, which could result in $1.9 billion in earning losses for the Japanese economy. Anti-Japanese sentiment could also hinder South Korean acceptance of Japanese cultural products, resulting in another $17.7 billion in lost gains over an extended period.

Despite these threats to economic growth, a surprising trend in the ROK–Japan trade data is the seeming lack of effect that periodic national identity clashes have had on trade flows. Despite the diplomatic *Sturm und Drang* that surrounds Japanese textbooks and visits to the Yasukuni Shrine, there do not seem to be lasting economic effects of these issues coming to the fore in Japan–Korea relations.

In the row over the Tokdo Islands, however, Seoul has suggested that there could be an economic impact if the dispute is not resolved. The islets, although uninhabited, are surrounded by rich fishing grounds, and there are reports of gas and oil as yet unexplored in the area. In response to Japan's Takeshima Day declaration, President Roh warned on March 23, 2005 that "the South Korean government has no choice but to sternly deal with Japan's attempt to justify its history of aggression and colonialism and revive regional hegemony," and cautioned that "there could be a hard diplomatic war . . . that may reduce exchanges in various sectors and cause economic difficulty." Of the possibility, Roh said, "we do not have to worry much about it . . . we are determined to take the hardship on our shoulders if we really have to."

Beyond these economic interactions with South Korea, Japan has been a strong supporter of multilateral efforts to stabilize and improve inter-Korean relations since the nuclear crisis of 1994. Japan has contributed to and participated in a number of aid programs (e.g., the rice shipments to North Korea) and developmental schemes, and its generous contribution to KEDO stands out for both its financial and political significance. Whereas Tokyo has tended in most cases to follow cues coming from Seoul and Washington, with KEDO Japan took a prominent role in the organization and readily agreed to a large financial contribution of around $1 billion. If and when the North Korean economy undergoes major reforms, it is likely that they will require a close coordination of assistance between Japan and South Korea, suggesting another place where Tokyo can take the lead in diplomatic economics.

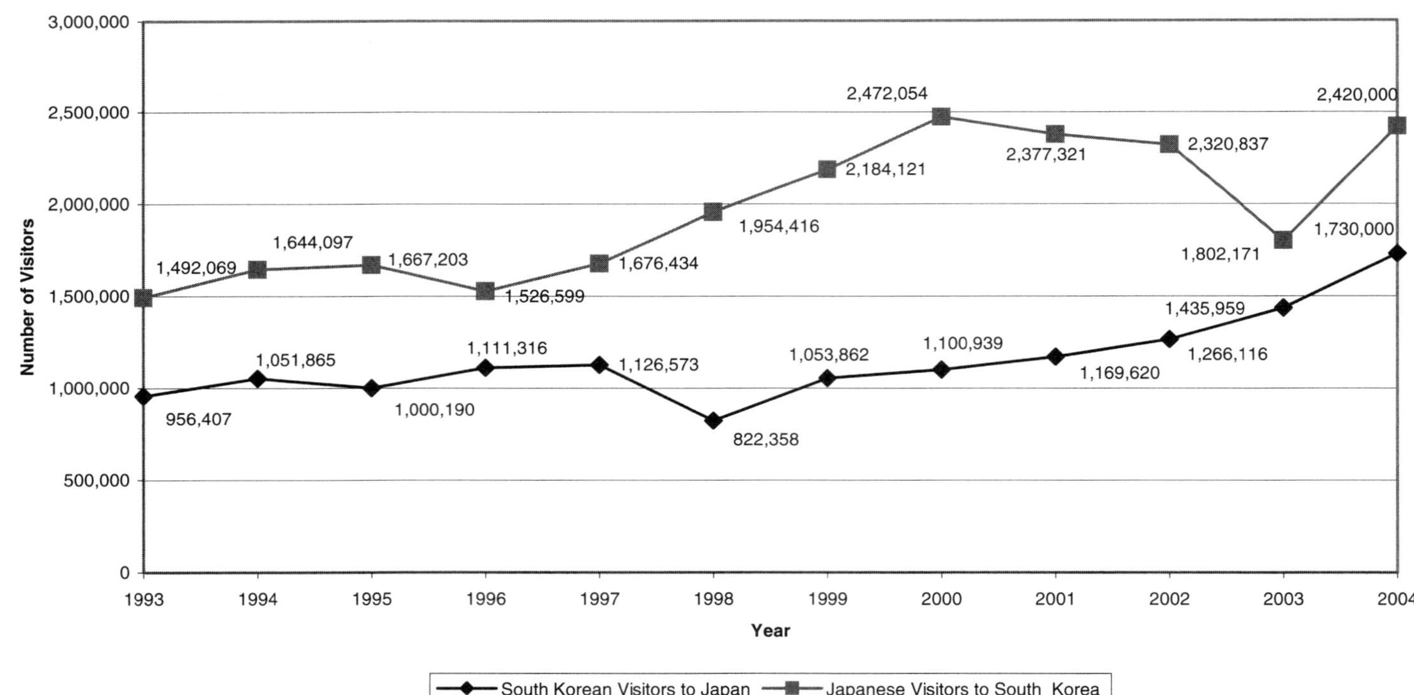

Figure 4.3. Japan–ROK exchange of visitors, 1993–2004.
Source: Korea National Tourism Organization. Available at http://www.knto.or.kr.

Table 4.5. Japan–ROK Exchange of Visitors, 1993–2004

Year	South Korean Visitors to Japan	Percent Change	Japanese Visitors to South Korea	Percent Change	Total Visitors	Percent Change
1993	956,407	N/A	1,492,069	N/A	2,448,476	N/A
1994	1,051,865	+10%	1,644,097	+10%	2,695,962	+10%
1995	1,000,190	−5%	1,667,203	+1%	2,667,393	−1%
1996	1,111,316	+11%	1,526,599	−8%	2,637,875	−1%
1997	1,126,573	+1%	1,676,434	+10%	2,803,007	+6%
1998	822,358	−27%	1,954,416	+17%	2,776,774	−1%
1999	1,053,862	+28%	2,184,121	+12%	3,237,983	+17%
2000	1,100,939	+4%	2,472,054	+13%	3,572,993	+10%
2001	1,169,620	+6%	2,377,321	−4%	3,546,941	−1%
2002	1,266,116	+8%	2,320,837	−2%	3,586,953	+1%
2003	1,435,959	+13%	1,802,171	−22%	3,238,130	−10%
2004	1,730,000	+20%	2,420,000	+34%	4,150,000	+28%

Unit: Individuals.
Source: Korea National Tourism Organization. Available at http://www.knto.or.kr.

Japan–ROK Cultural and Social Interaction

In recent years, there has been a South Korean culture boom – *hallyu* (Korean wave) – in Japan. Korean soap operas, such as *Winter Sonata,* and Korean movies have become very popular. Similarly, Japanese culture has been increasingly popular in South Korea and also increasingly available, thanks to legal changes originating from the Kim–Obuchi Tokyo summit of October 1998, when Seoul agreed to eliminate, in stages, barriers on the importation of Japanese cultural products. South Korea agreed to and then completed removal of the barriers by the time the two countries jointly hosted the World Cup soccer tournament in 2002. Now, Japanese entertainers are seen on Korean TV, and young Koreans like to listen to Japanese pop songs called J-pops on their MD (minidisc) players. The two countries are well connected by the Internet, and there is increasing communication between the two through e-mails and chat rooms using automatic translation software. A tourist boom is also occurring, especially as Japanese flock to Korea; 2002 was designated a year of "citizens' exchanges" (Figure 4.3 and Table 4.5). The current level of exchange and familiarity is unprecedented in the history of Japan–Korea relations.[138]

Yet, despite these cultural interactions, there is a constant simmering distrust among Japanese and Korean citizens. A 1990 poll in the *Asahi*

[138] Takahashi (2005).

Shimbun found that 23 percent of Japanese respondents disliked South Korea, and 61 percent said they were indifferent. At the same time, a nationwide opinion survey by Seoul's *Dong-A Ilbo* found that 66 percent of those polled said they disliked Japan; the degree of antipathy was particularly high among the young and best educated respondents – 70 percent of those in their 20s and 70 percent of university graduates said they disliked Japan.

There was a boom in positive sentiment in 2002, a result of Korean–Japanese dialogue and the joint sponsorship of the World Cup: public opinion polls revealed that unprecedented numbers of Koreans and Japanese held a positive image of the other country, with 79 percent reported as feeling that the relationship between the two nations was headed in a good direction.[139] However, the Tokdo Islands dispute has revived antipathy toward Japan. Whereas a 2004 South Korean poll found that 39 percent of the respondents said the United States was the most threatening country to Korea and only 7.6 percent of those surveyed counted Japan as most threatening, in an April 2005 poll, 37.1 percent of respondents said that they believed Japan was the greatest threat to Korea, with 28.6 percent selecting North Korea and 18.5 percent selecting the United States. Only 3.5 percent of respondents believed that Seoul should cooperate more with Japan than other countries in matters of national defense.[140]

Conclusion

The history of relations between Japan and Korea is one of mutual distrust. From the sixteenth-century invasions of Korea by Toyotomi Hideyoshi to the twentieth-century annexation and colonization of the peninsula, post–World War II relations have been built with significant baggage attached to them, hampering otherwise obvious cooperation on political and economic issues. In the early twenty-first century, the national identity conflict in East Asia retreated for a moment, only to return with a vengeance. With the threat of terrorism pressing for inter-Asian cooperation, leaders at the APEC summit in the fall of 2001 agreed to put the history issue aside for the time being. The Korean–Japanese dialogue and the two countries' joint sponsorship of the World Cup soccer tournament in the spring of 2002 resulted in public opinion polls revealing that unprecedented numbers of Koreans and Japanese held a positive image of each other's country, with 79 percent reported as feeling that

139 *Asahi Shimbun*, July 6, 2002, p. 2.
140 Ahn-sung Kyoo, "Survey Shows Japan is Seen as Leading Threat," *JoongAng Ilbo*, April 18, 2005.

the relationship between the two nations was headed in a good direction.[141] On the level of popular culture, a type of "Korean wave" took hold in Japan. Even the Japanese emperor commented on the fact that the imperial household historically had its roots in Korea.[142] This period of camaraderie was short lived, however, as indicated by the reignited textbooks controversy and the dispute over the Tokdo Islands in 2005.

The 1990s witnessed an alarming increase in the number of pronouncements and actions by Japanese political leaders with distinctly nationalistic and militaristic overtones attempting to justify Japan's past aggressions against its neighbors. These include everything from revisionist Japanese history textbooks, visits by Japanese politicians to the Yasukuni Shrine, one-sided views of territorial disputes such as those over the Tokdo Islands, tacit promises to cooperate with the United States in military action against China over Taiwan, and refusals to admit to the sickening catalog of Japanese atrocities against China and Korea before 1945. Japan's claims of apology are virtually meaningless given Japan's propensity to say one thing and mean something quite different, and then to repeat the same noxious offense: another visit to the Yasukuni Shrine, another new textbook that raises the ire of Korea and China. Simultaneously, Japan has been rebuilding its military and expanding its domain of operation.

Regardless of what may be occurring in the international political environment of NEA, the most important variable in shaping Japan–Korea relations remains the relative salience of Japan's imperial past as it is played out in domestic coalition politics and acted out in foreign policy. As political actors in Tokyo – and elsewhere in Japan, as the Tokdo Islands flap demonstrates – manipulate nationalist sentiment for their own ends, Korean popular opinion becomes agitated, and Korean politicians begin a countercyclical spiral of agitation as they decry the Japanese actions for *their* own ends. Without the Cold War communist threat to keep the U.S. allies in line, it is possible that we have not yet begun to plumb the depths of national identity conflict and crisis that might emerge between Korea and Japan.

Paradoxically, Japan is both driving Seoul to a closer embrace of Beijing and yet worried that a reunified Korea will be aligned with China. Japan fears a militarized united Korea – particularly one with nuclear weapons – yet it is militarizing its own society in a classic manifestation of the security dilemma. Japan speaks of increased economic integration in NEA, yet acts to reduce its contact with North Korea, antagonizes Russia over territorial

141 According to survey results reported in the *Asahi Shimbun,* July 6, 2002, p. 2.
142 Howard French, "Japan Rediscovers its Korean Past," *New York Times,* March 11, 2002.

issues, and implicitly backs a containment policy for China.[143] Although it is hard to believe that Japan wants to antagonize its neighbors intentionally, domestic nationalism is distinctly having this effect by producing foreign policy that interacts acerbically with national identity wounds in all other Northeast Asian countries. Paradoxically, although Chinese and Koreans are constantly being criticized for dwelling too much on the past and too little on the future, "it is the Japanese who may be least able to come to terms with it [the imperialist past], as it needs to in order to 'renter Asia.'"[144]

In contrast, there is nothing certain in any sort of Beijing–Seoul alliance, and there is no telling where Pyongyang's provocative security behavior can drive Seoul–Tokyo relations. Policy makers in the ROK might decide that overlooking national identity issues is the prudent thing to do as a strategic hedge against the economic might of China. Or a North Korean nuclear test of some sort might quickly revive the Japan–ROK quasialliance. Given the difficulty of measuring and operationalizing national identity angst, it is difficult to assess the extent to which the walls going up between Japan and South Korea and between Japan and North Korea can be brought down, or what might lead to this turn of events. But it is clear, both in theory and from the historical evidence, that when Japan and the two Korean states do get past the national identity issue, they can cooperate in a mutually beneficial way across a number of functional domains. Policy makers in Pyongyang, Seoul, and Tokyo must all keep this in mind as they look toward the future.

143 See Japan's latest Defense White Paper, which gives greater place to the rise of China as the foremost security challenge.
144 Rozman (2003: 539).

CHAPTER 5

The United States and the Two Koreas

If men define situations as real, they are real in their consequences.

– *W. I. Thomas*[1]

Our . . . goal is to prevent regimes that sponsor terror from threatening America or our friends and allies with weapons of mass destruction. Some of these regimes have been pretty quiet since September the 11th. But we know their true nature. North Korea is a regime arming with missiles and weapons of mass destruction, while starving its citizens. . . . States like these, and their terrorist allies, constitute an axis of evil, arming to threaten the peace of the world.

– *George W. Bush, January 29, 2002*[2]

The modern imperialists are pursuing a more crafty policy of aggression and war, styling themselves a guardian of peace and freedom. Its good example is the slogan of anti-terrorism put up by the U.S. This nature of modern imperialism also finds a manifestation in the fact that it seeks to launch an undisguised armed invasion of those progressive and anti-imperialist independent countries.

– *Korean Central News Agency, October 20, 2002*[3]

The U.S. Factor

Without a doubt, the United States remains the most dominant external actor on the Korean peninsula. Although U.S. primacy at almost any point

[1] Thomas (1928: 572).

[2] George W. Bush, State of the Union Address, January 29, 2002. Available at http://www.whitehouse.gov/news/releases/2002/01/20020129–11.html.

[3] "Vigilance Against Imperialists' Vicious and Crafty Nature Called for," KCNA, October 20, 2002, online edition. Available at http://www.kcna.co.jp.

on the globe is widely accepted, the description is particularly apt: history, geopolitics, and geoeconomics all drive U.S. interest in NEA, and Korea's location at the strategic crossroads of the region makes it a natural place for the United States to concentrate its concern. By dint of what it is and what it does, Washington is seen in both Seoul and Pyongyang, albeit for different reasons, as having become part of both the Korean problem and the Korean solution. Nonetheless, in the conception and conduct of foreign policy, the United States, as the world's only superpower, is impacted on and shaped by the changing dynamics of its domestic politics and regional and global interests, even as local and regional factors have gained greater saliency in the foreign relations of both Koreas in the post–Cold War era.

Although the United States might seem to be at great geographic distance and disadvantage, the Pacific Ocean has increasingly become something akin to an "American lake" since the end of World War II.[4] This means that the United States acts in Korea (and also in Japan) as if it were a *de facto* neighbor. Because the U.S. economy is increasingly dependent on trade and financial transactions with China, Japan, and Korea – the three core states of NEA and also (as of the end of 2004) America's third, fourth, and seventh largest trading partners, respectively – the United States sees a need to ensure stable and consistent relations among the countries of NEA to prevent any severe market fluctuations that might reverberate in the United States or, worse, any severing of market connections caused by armed conflagration or regime change. Even more significantly, China, Japan, and South Korea stand out respectively as America's first, second, and sixth largest trade deficit generators and as the world's second, first, and fourth largest holders of foreign exchange reserves, as of the end of 2004.

Politically and militarily, the concern in East Asia changed from the perceived Soviet threat after World War II to possible Sino–American rivalry in the region. For more than a half-century, therefore, the United States has focused its attention on East Asia as primed for great-power conflict and hegemonic rivalry (the received neorealist wisdom even in the early post–Cold War era[5]), and thus a site of looming armed conflict. Korea has been, with Japan, one of two main sites for forward U.S. military deployment in the region – although belatedly, given that the United States had withdrawn troops from the peninsula prior to the Korean War.

[4] Hayes, Zarsky, and Bello (1986).

[5] Betts (1993/94); Friedberg (1993/94); Buzan and Segal (1994). Through the prism of "offensive realism," John Mearsheimer pessimistically predicts China's emergence as a regional hegemon in NEA as the most dangerous scenario the United States might face in the early twenty-first century, warning and prodding Washington to do what it can to reverse or slow the rise of China. See Mearsheimer (2001: 401–02).

The DPRK's attempts to develop WMD have raised the ante for the United States, forcing it to concentrate efforts and interests on the peninsula.

During the Cold War, friction in the U.S.–ROK relationship was kept suppressed. Although the United States was not always pleased with the behavior of particular South Korean leaders, and although South Korean civil society sometimes lashed out at the U.S. presence for its support of military dictatorship, by and large a veneer of allied unity was maintained. This was due in no small measure to the fact that Washington and Seoul had shared a Cold War anticommunist identity. In the post–Cold War era, however, the alliance seems far less united, and the two countries openly drifted apart on a number of issues. Even South Korea started shedding the residues of its Cold War identity in tandem with the normalization of relations with Gorbachev's Soviet Union and post-Mao China.

This is part of a broader trend for the United States in reconstructing its post–Cold War national identity as a lonely unilateral superpower. As Samuel Huntington observed in 1999 in a trenchant critique of creeping U.S. unilateralism, "On issue after issue, the United States has found itself increasingly alone, with one or a few partners, opposing most of the rest of the world's states and peoples. . . . On these and other issues, much of the international community is on one side and the United States is on the other."[6] Although Huntington spoke of tendencies present in the 1990s during the presidential administration of Bill Clinton, it was not until the election of George W. Bush that U.S. unilateralism became a fully refurbished national identity, as well as a fully deployed weapon of American exceptionalism. Although some see imperial continuity between Clinton and Bush, claiming that the differences between the two have been greatly exaggerated for partisan reasons,[7] the Bush administration's hardline fundamentalist ideas have actually taken Washington and the world at large by storm, radically reorienting American foreign policy. In the process a new trinity of neoconservative fundamentalism, a Manichaean worldview, and blinding hypernationalism has driven the United States toward a new and dangerous (un)diplomatic and fiscal train wreck.[8] Indeed, one is hard-pressed to come up with another instance in American diplomatic and presidential history when such a sudden and drastic strategic wrong turn has done so much damage to Washington's international image, reputation, and security partnerships, in this case with Europe and South Korea, in such a short time and with so little to show for it.

In its first two years, guided by runaway unilateralism-cum-exceptionalism, the Bush administration decided to trash multilateral treaties and

[6] Huntington (1999: 41). [7] Bacevich (2002).
[8] Falk (2003); Hoffmann (2003); Ikenberry (2004); Gurtov and Van Ness (2005).

treaties in the making, one after another: the ABM treaty, the Biological Weapons Convention, the Comprehensive Test Ban Treaty, the Land Mine Treaty, the Kyoto Protocol, the treaty to establish the International Criminal Court (ICC), the Geneva Conventions, and a draft treaty on international small arms sales. In May 2002, the Bush administration took the unprecedented step of "unsigning" the Rome Statute of the International Criminal Court by informing the UN Secretary-General of its decision not to be party to the treaty, claiming that the United States had no legal obligation arising from President Clinton's signature on December 31, 2000. In short, the Bush administration exemplifies in extreme form the notion of American exceptionalism that is often presented as an aspect of a newly minted U.S. national identity and international persona.

This turn away from multilateralism and international cooperation was enacted suddenly but had deep roots in conservative think tanks and among the career policy makers in the Bush administration. In 1992, at the end of the George H. W. Bush administration, a draft of the Defense Planning Guidance (DPG), an internal set of military guidelines rewritten every few years, was produced by Paul Wolfowitz at the Department of Defense. The 46-page document argued that the United States should work to prevent the emergence of a new superpower, should actively promote U.S. values, and should be prepared to take unilateral action to support its interests. The draft assumed that the most important of America's unique qualities was its military dominance. Despite a controversy that erupted when the draft was leaked to the *New York Times* and the *Washington Post*, a revised DPG came to be known as "Dick Cheney's masterwork" (he was Secretary of Defense at the time). The Cheney draft retained the idea that unilateral military action, the preemptive use of force, and the maintenance of a U.S. nuclear arsenal strong enough to deter the development of nuclear programs elsewhere were now appropriate U.S. policies.[9] Many have found echoes of the 1992 DPG in the 2002 *National Security Strategy of the United States of America*; one analyst described it as "the final avatar of Cheney's 1992 defense draft."[10]

Faced with criticisms after the leak, Lewis (Scooter) Libby, Paul Wolfowitz's protégé and top assistant, who held the title of principal deputy undersecretary of defense for strategy and resources in 1992, reformulated the logic of the DPG to read something like the following:

> The main point shouldn't be to block rival powers, but rather for the United States to become so militarily strong, so overwhelming that no country would dream of ever becoming a rival. America should build up its military lead to

[9] Hoffmann (2003: 28). [10] Hoffmann (2003: 30).

> such an extent that other countries would be dissuaded from even *starting* to compete with the United States. The costs would be too high; America's military technology would be so advanced, its defense budget so high that no one else could afford the huge sums necessary to embark on a long-term military build-up that, even if successful, would still not catch up to the United States for thirty years or more. Thus the United States would be the world's lone superpower not just today or ten years from now but permanently.[11]

As National Security Adviser and then as Secretary of State, Condoleeza Rice has been an enthusiastic supporter of dismantling international treaties and organizations from the start of Bush's presidency. Rice published an article in *Foreign Affairs* at the beginning of the 2000 election season that presaged the ideological shift. The article trashed the international community in the name of "promoting the national interest" and attacked the Clinton administration as having "often been so anxious to find multilateral solutions to problems that it has signed agreements that are not in America's interest."[12] Rice also presaged the coming of Bush's "axis of evil" by singling out three "rogue regimes" (Iraq, North Korea, and Iran) as America's major challenges.[13] Although the Clinton administration had enacted a semantic shift from "rogue states" to "states of concern" in June 2000, the Bush administration, both during the campaign and after the 2000 election, preferred the old terminology.

In September 2000, the neoconservative think tank Project for the New American Century (PNAC) issued a policy report entitled "Rebuilding America's Defenses: Strategies, Forces and Resources for a New Century." The document was written by individuals who now hold senior positions in the Bush administration, including Vice President Dick Cheney and Defense Secretary Donald Rumsfeld. The PNAC document supports a "blueprint for maintaining global U.S. pre-eminence, precluding the rise of a great power rival, and shaping the international security order in line with American principles and interests." It also describes the ability of the United States to "fight and decisively win multiple, simultaneous major theater wars" as a "core mission." Clearly, the foreign policy of the Bush administration was not a scramble policy dreamed up in the months after the 2000 election but rather a long-desired set of grand strategies.[14]

One claim about this set of policies is that they have succeeded in creating an American empire. Although the word imperialism has long remained verboten in American political and intellectual discourse, except among the left-wing thinkers and revisionist historians in the Vietnam War era,[15] the debate on American empire is now back in the

[11] Mann (2004: 212); emphasis in original. [12] Rice (2000: 48). [13] Rice (2000: 60–61).
[14] See Mann (2004).
[15] The dean of this revisionist school, William Appleman Williams, argued that America's genuine idealism had been subverted by the imperial pursuit of power and capitalist

news and on the agenda of a "new world order." Thanks to the radical strategic reorientation of the Bush administration, the old left-wing epithet "American imperialism" has suddenly become a term of conceptual and strategic approbation on the right, triggering a debate – and a burgeoning literature – on American empire involving hawkish neoconservative columnists, as well as international relations scholars of all ideological and theoretical stripes. It is equally striking, and no coincidence, that a number of major studies of American empire have been published during the Bush years.[16] This is further testimony to the extent to which the Bush administration broke from its predecessor, appropriating a newly minted identity as the "ABC" (All But Clinton) administration.

At issue in the debate over American empire is U.S. global domination – its nature, logic, and consequences. American primacy is taken as a point of departure for the debate such that there is little doubt or disagreement that the United States is the one and only military superpower with global reach; it has military contingents in forty countries, naval bases in ten. The U.S. defense budget for FY2003 was $405 billion (up from $322 billion for FY 2001), which accounted for 41 percent of the total global defense expenditures ($997 billion) and is larger than the defense budgets of the next twenty-three countries combined.[17] Most of these countries are America's formal or *de facto* allies. The United States is also a global economic superpower, with its GDP of $10.4 trillion in 2002 accounting for 32.5 percent of global GDP.[18] Although measurement is difficult, the United States is widely acknowledged as a cultural, educational, and scientific superpower with no peer competitor in sight. In short, America commands multidimensional global power that is disproportionate to a country with less than 5 percent of the world's population.

Critics who believe that there is an existent or emerging American empire describe a wildly inflated sense of American power; unacceptably high economic, political, and image costs; the corrosive effect of empire on democracy; and the clear and present danger to international law, international institutions, and even alliance partnerships that have secured U.S. national interests since World War II. The bottom line for these critics is that American empire is not sustainable. The imbalance between military power and political and economic power leads Washington to follow the slippery road of overemphasizing the use of

greed. Although Williams recognized "informal expansion," he paid too much attention to economic imperialism and too little to cultural imperialism. See Williams (1961, 1980).

16 See Bacevich (2002); Johnson (2004); Ferguson (2004); Mann (2003); Barber (2003); Todd (2003); Kupchan (2002); Kagan and Kristol (2002).

17 IISS (2004: 353–58). See also "World Wide Military Expenditures." Available at http://www.globalsecurity.org/military/world/spending.htm.

18 UNDP (2004: 184–87).

brute force, turning the quest for empire into hyperactive militarism, which then merely increases resistance to the imperialist adventure at home and abroad.[19]

Some centrist critics argue that the United States is not an empire because the core feature of imperialism remains political power and control: whatever else "empire" may be, it must, to deserve the name, include political dominance. Despite an unequal relationship between the United States and weaker countries that can be conducive to exploitation, these critiques argue, the term "imperialism" or "empire" is misleading in the absence of formal political control. Moreover, countries can, and often do, escape U.S. domination simply by asking the United States to leave, as the Philippines did.[20] Paul Kennedy's response to such a formalistic argument of denial is worth noting: "So, call it as you prefer; ladies and gentlemen, but if it looks like an empire, and acts like an empire, and increasingly quacks like an empire, well, perhaps you know what it is?"[21]

The hawkish neoconservative pundits[22] trumpet their own vision of "benevolent imperialism," describing an era of global rule organized around the bold unilateral exercise of military power as a liberal force that promotes democracy and undercuts tyranny, terrorism, and WMD proliferation. Such a strategy of liberal empire requires emancipation from the constraints of international law and organizations, they argue; instead, absolute security can be pursued, not so subtly, through empire.[23] For example, Max Boot of the *Wall Street Journal* argues that the problem has not been excessive American global ambition and assertiveness but rather insufficient global ambition and assertiveness. Boot attacks the George H. W. Bush administration for having followed a classic *realpolitik* policy in the early 1990s and the Clinton administration for having been scandalously irresolute in the assertion of U.S. power. Writing in late 2001, Boot confidently predicted: "Once we have deposed Saddam, we can impose an American-led, international regency in Baghdad, to go along with the one in Kabul. With American seriousness and credibility thus restored, we will enjoy fruitful cooperation from the region's many opportunists, who will show a newfound eagerness to be helpful in our larger task of rolling up the international terror network that threatens us."[24]

British historian-provocateur Niall Ferguson (who has recently decamped from Oxford University to New York University) and

[19] Eland (2002); Barber (2003); Falk (2003); Hoffmann (2003); Mann (2003); Todd (2003); Johnson (2004).
[20] Ikenberry (2004); Schell (2003). [21] Kennedy, Perle, and Nye (2003: 14).
[22] Kagan (1998); Krauthammer (2001); Boot (2001); Mallaby (2002).
[23] Eland (2002); Chace (2002). [24] Boot (2001: 27).

Canadian human rights scholar Michael Ignatieff join the neoconservative trumpery of "benevolent imperialism." Ferguson argues that the United States is indeed an empire and has been for a long time but that it is a liberal empire that upholds rules and institutions and underwrites public goods by maintaining peace. He sees the challenge not as too much liberal empire but rather that the world might not get enough. Ferguson's case for the virtues of American imperialism rests on the dubious claim that the post–Cold War world faces a stark choice – a new global order anchored in America's liberal empire or a world of decentralized, competing states resulting in chaos.[25] For Ignatieff, the United States is said to have no choice but to exercise its imperial power, and how it does so will shape the emerging world order.[26] The case for liberal empire, according to Ignatieff, "is that it has become, in a place like Iraq, the last hope of democracy and stability alike."[27]

After the September 11, 2001, terrorist attacks, it became clear that the White House was going to frame its response to the attacks in terms that incorporated the radical neoconservative vision of a future global order. The Bush administration seized the opportunity provided by the attacks to shift the focus of the U.S. response from the al Qaeda presence in Afghanistan to "the axis of evil" countries that had essentially no connection with Osama bin Laden but were definitely standing in the way of moving forward the project of American empire.[28] Echoing President William McKinley, who initiated the first attempt at American empire at the end of the nineteenth century, President Bush flatly declared in his West Point Address that "America has no empire to extend or utopia to establish."[29] Where McKinley had expanded the Spanish-American War – begun in April 1898 over the question of Cuba and the alleged sinking of the *USS Maine* in the Havana harbor – into the so-called "Splendid Little War," Bush has similarly used the rhetoric of the War on Terror to again expand the global reach of the United States. McKinley rationalized his actions to a group of Protestant clergymen in August 1898 by saying "that there was nothing left for us to do but to take them all, and to educate the Filipinos, and uplift and civilize and Christianize [sic!] them."[30]

In the wake of this expansion of U.S. activity around the globe, there has been a resurgence of nationalism on the Korean peninsula. Korean nationalism, having arisen historically as an ideology of anti-imperialism and anticolonialism, has fostered ethnic unity among Koreans and has also served as one of the key determinants in the shaping of inter-Korean

[25] Ferguson (2004). [26] Ignatieff (2003a, 2003b). [27] Ignatieff (2003a: 54).
[28] Falk (2003).
[29] See "President Bush Delivers Graduation Speech at West Point." Available at http://www.whitehouse.gov/news/releases/2002/06/print/20020601–3.html.
[30] Quoted in Michael and Taylor (1964: 295).

relations and the relationship of both Koreas with the United States. When President Bush proclaimed in his 2002 State of the Union speech that North Korea was part of the "axis of evil" along with Iraq and Iran, North Koreans were not the only ones who were enraged. South Koreans were equally angry. Anti-U.S. sentiment had been growing in the ROK since a Korean speed skater was stripped of his gold medal at the 2002 Winter Olympics, and Bush's "evil" epithet needlessly fueled it.[31] Anti-imperialist nationalism is even more pronounced in North Korea, which stresses the importance of ethnic identity in the struggle for national survival. Despite different political systems, both North and South Korea still prioritize ethnic one-nation identity and nationalism, and the public branding of the DPRK as evil in some ways reinvigorated a sense of kinship between the North and the South.[32]

The use of the word "imperialist" to describe the United States and its leaders appears almost daily in official North Korean pronouncements. The term not only conveys Pyongyang's view of Washington, but also aptly conjures up North Korea's self-image and seige mentality. For North Korea, imperialism connotes aggression and expansion of one actor into the sphere of another to take control or impose authority. Ever since the Korean War, North Korea has viewed the United States as interfering in Korean affairs with hostile intentions. The end of the Cold War has only exacerbated Pyongyang's fear and sense of insecurity, which the hardline policy of the Bush administration has further fueled. *Juche*, the guiding principle of the North Korean state, reflects its identity as a "go it alone" state in international relations, and its constant use of the term "imperialist" to describe the United States reflects its view of the United States as a threat to this ideal.

Nonetheless, both despite and in conjunction with this decrying of U.S. imperialism, the United States has become central in Pyongyang's strategic thinking and behavior alternately as a mortal threat or an external life support system, and sometimes as both. With the demise of the Soviet Union, unreliable aid from China, and increasingly close PRC–ROK relations, the United States has become *faute de mieux* the functional equivalent of China and the Soviet Union in Pyongyang's perspective. However, whereas the DPRK's specialty during the Cold War was playing its allies Moscow and Beijing off against each other to reap economic, technical, and military aid, now it must seek to achieve the same aid – and also international legitimacy, investment, and trade – from a single adversary that is increasingly inclined to use force rather than favor.[33]

Since August 1945, the United States has been so closely involved in the Korean peninsula that it could take no action there without significant

[31] Shin and Chang (2004). [32] Shin and Chang (2004). [33] See Manning (2002: 82).

consequences, especially in the security dimension. The United States, by virtue of its historic involvement in the Korean peninsula and its mutual security treaty with its South Korean ally, cannot avoid playing the leading role in Korea. The irony is that the United States is today the most important country for both Korean states; it is perhaps more intimately tied to the pursuit of peace in Korea than it is in the Arab–Israeli conflict.[34] In short, America's post–Cold War identity as the world's sole superpower and the Korean post–Cold War one-nation ethnonational identy have come to grate against each other; this identity conflict is fueled by the (second-image) dynamics of domestic politics in Washington, Pyongyang, and Seoul.

Weight of the Past

Korea began the nineteenth century with a grudge against the West. Christianity had made inroads among Korean commoners in the late eighteenth and nineteenth centuries, and the imperial court cracked down on this Western religion and culture that was seeping in from China, where Jesuit missionaries resided. When Western ships began appearing in Korea, the Koreans wanted nothing to do with them and tried to pursue a policy of isolation. After some initial forays, the United States was only too happy to oblige Korea, leaving the peninsula for the Japanese. The United States would return to the peninsula only at the conclusion of World War II and then, at first, with only a seeming modicum of interest.

Commodore Matthew C. Perry famously opened Japan in 1854, and Japan responded by signing a commercial treaty with the United States within four years. In Korea, however, such gunboat diplomacy took a different turn. In 1866, a U.S. merchant ship, the *USS General Sherman*, sailed up the Taedong River in defiance of local officials who proclaimed that foreign commerce and Western religion were outlawed in Korea. Engaging in battle with Korean government forces, the entire 24-man crew was killed when the ship ran aground near Pyongyang. The North Koreans today have a plaque marking the alleged site of the incident, while official history and part of Kim Il Sung's hagiography claim that his great-grandfather, Kim Ung U, led the attack on the *General Sherman*.[35] When the United States inquired after the ship, they were referred to the Chinese imperial court. Angered, the Americans vowed to "go up to 'Ping yang' river at the proper season and inflict proportionate punishment."[36] In 1871, the United States approached the Korean peninsula with a squadron of five ships. Although the Koreans eventually forced

[34] Barry (1996). [35] Armstrong (1998: 32).
[36] Drake (1984: 107). See also Cumings (1997: 97).

U.S. retreat, they suffered some 350 fatalities in doing so, solidifying isolationist mentality on the peninsula.[37]

One cannot ignore the fact that the *USS General Sherman* incident occurred in Pyongyang, present-day North Korea. North Koreans have not forgotten about the incident because it proudly serves as useful propaganda. Although the historical accuracy of the assertion that Kim Ung U led the attack is questionable, it reflects the North Korean need to construct a national identity around the Kim family. The *USS General Sherman* episode also foretells the Korean perception of Americans as imperialists intent on mercantilism and proselytization, and the American perception of Koreans as violent, closed-off hermits. Such perceptions can and do last and matter. Of course, beginning with the peninsular division in 1945, the path of the two Korean states have diverged: North Korea still maintains its hostility toward the outside world, but South Korea has opened up to the world and has succeeded in becoming a major player in the era of globalization.[38]

When Japan began its attack on the East Asian Sinocentric order in the 1870s, China urged Korea to align itself with the United States as one means of resisting Japanese expansionism. China wanted Korea to follow a balance-of-power strategy and said that the United States would be the best ally because it was, one Chinese intellectual suggested, "the only Western power that has never sought selfish gains."[39] When the *USS Ticonderoga* arrived in Korea to negotiate a treaty, the Chinese took the initiative to mediate. In doing so, they completed the opening of the hermit kingdom to the outside world, which had begun with Korea's signing of the Treaty of Kanghwa with Japan (1876). Continuing the superimposition of the Western system of international relations on the East Asian world order, the treaty with the United States was signed at Inchon in May of 1882, inaugurating Korea's official relations with the West and over 122 years of U.S.–Korean relations (interrupted, however, by Japan's imperial interregnum of 1905–45).[40] The Chinese – and to a lesser extent the Koreans – believed that this treaty with the United States (and similar treaties with France, England, and Germany) would protect Korea against Japanese encroachment.

The Korean king was interested in strengthening U.S.–Korea ties and requested American advisers and instructors, but the United States did not show much interest. Because China was facing a number of problems with Western imperialism and Japanese aggression, and Japan clearly

[37] See K. H. Kim (1980: 51–62). According to Bruce Cumings, about 650 Koreans died. See Cumings (1997: 97).

[38] For more on South Korea and globalization, see S. S. Kim (2000a).

[39] K. H. Kim (1980: 211–12, 285, 295).

[40] K. H. Kim (1980: 301–02, 328).

could not be trusted, U.S. disinterest drove the Korean court to pursue closer relations with Russia.[41] The United States had little involvement in Korea in the 1890s and then turned its back on Korea completely with the dawn of the twentieth century. In 1900, soon-to-be-elected President Theodore Roosevelt said that he would "like to see Japan have Korea" as a check on Russia.[42] During Roosevelt's presidency, the United States tacitly would acknowledge Japan's predominance in Korea in exchange for tacit acknowledgment of U.S. interests in the Philippines, an agreement often referred to as the Taft–Katsura Agreement. When Korea appeared at The Hague Peace Conference of 1907, the United States did not support its delegates' call for independence, nor did it interfere or even protest when Japan completely annexed Korea in 1910.

At the end of World War II, U.S. involvement in Korean affairs resumed, and the Korean people had positive expectations. The United States was perceived as having had no colonial or imperialistic involvement in Korea, and the United States had been an important operational base for exiled Korean nationalists, including Syngman Rhee. Traditional American values, as embodied in the Declaration of Independence and the Wilsonian principle of national self-determination, captured the national imagination of Koreans and were seen as legitimizing by many Korean nationalists.[43] Finally and most important, the United States was the leader of the Allied Powers that had defeated the hated enemy state, Japan. Hence the United States was depicted by many Koreans as the national savior, with all the goodwill, responsibility, and promise that such symbolism entails.[44]

Paradoxically enough, Korea was liberated and divided at one and the same time, with the United States playing the determinative liberating and dividing roles. In fact, the most lasting legacy of U.S. involvement with Korea in 1945 is the division of the Korean peninsula and the Korean people. As Gregory Henderson has famously said,

> No division of a nation in the present is so astonishing in its origin as the division of Korea; none is so unrelated to conditions or sentiment within the nation itself at the time the division was effected; none is to this day so unexplained; in none does blunder and planning oversight appear to have played so large a role. Finally, there is no division for which the U.S. government bears so heavy a share of the responsibility as it bears for the division of Korea.[45]

During the war, the administration of Franklin D. Roosevelt had advocated international trusteeship for postwar Korea to protect the interests

[41] C. I. Kim and H. K. Kim (1967: 44, 61–62).
[42] Quoted in C. I. Kim and H. K. Kim (1967: 125, n14).
[43] President Wilson refused to follow up on his fourteen-point declaration of national self-determination in Korea around the March First (1919) demonstrations.
[44] S. S. Kim (1980/81). [45] Henderson (1974: 43).

of the nations directly concerned with the peninsula and to forestall potential conflict. It was believed that a neutral Korea would best serve peace and stability in Asia and also would require Soviet–Chinese consent.[46] Viewed as a future trusteeship, Korea was refused representation at the founding UN Conference in San Francisco in the spring of 1945. In August 1945, however, the presence of Soviet troops on the Korean peninsula forced the Truman administration to make a snap decision about how to treat Korea. The division of the peninsula into two zones of occupation came about when two young army colonels, Charles H. Bonesteel (who would later command UN forces in Korea) and Dean Rusk (who would later be Secretary of State), assigned to the Policy Section, Strategy and Policy Group of the Operations Division of the War Department, were given thirty minutes to determine an appropriate place to split the peninsula between the United States and Soviet Union.[47] The nearest U.S. troops were 600 miles away in Okinawa, but the Soviets already had entered northern Korea. The issue for them was how to quickly create a surrender arrangement that the Soviets would accept, while preventing their seizure of Korea. They chose the thirty-eighth parallel because it was a nearly even split of the peninsula and would keep the capital city of Seoul on the U.S. side.[48]

After making its way through the chain of command, the plan was signed by President Harry S. Truman on August 14 and communicated to General Douglas MacArthur the next day as part of General Order Number One, which also arranged for the United States to accept Japanese surrender in Japan and the Philippines and for the Soviets to accept surrender in Manchuria. Although many in the administration expected Stalin to reject the plan, because the Soviets had not received any American warning not to enter Korea and were in a superior military position from which they could occupy the entire peninsula before any American troops could get there, he accepted the proposal without question on August 16. Stalin's willingness to accept the surrender arrangement, for whatever reasons, made possible the American occupation of southern Korea.

In his memoirs, President Truman portrayed the decision to divide Korea at the thirty-eighth parallel as the consequence of military convenience and expediency in accepting the Japanese surrender.[49] Nonetheless, he considered it a great success to have been able to obtain Stalin's agreement on the matter. Although a few suspected that the decision to divide Korea was made at the wartime conferences at Yalta or Potsdam, Truman's account is essentially accepted by most scholars. It is tempered

[46] Matray (1985: 19). [47] W. S. Lee (1982: 83). See also Cumings (1981: 120–21).
[48] See Hart-Landsburg (1998: 40–41). [49] Truman (1955: 445).

with the implicit understanding that U.S. options were limited by the political and strategic realities and that this was therefore the best that could be done.[50] Stalin, in turn, was apparently motivated by his desire to maintain Allied harmony so as not to arouse too much reaction to the Sovietization of Eastern Europe, his hope to partake in the Japanese occupation or have equal voice in it, and his confidence that trusteeship could lead to a pro-Soviet Korea.

As the Soviets consolidated authority in the north, a massive flow of refugees began. The Soviets labeled these refugees wealthy landlords and Japanese collaborators, but in truth they were of all social strata. By mid-1947, 1.8 million refugees had fled south, and another 3 million would flee in the early months of the Korean War in 1950. These 4.8 million refugees translate today into around 10 million families separated between North and South Korea. The departure of these people from North Korea sadly made it easier for the Soviet-sponsored Koreans to capture political power in the north.[51]

General Order Number One was not intended to produce a permanent political division of Korea – it was an order about accepting Japanese surrender – but within three years it had achieved political division. The U.S. goal was to negotiate a unified trusteeship over the peninsula, but it was unable to reach a compromise with the Soviet Union. Balancing the State Department's concern with U.S. prestige in the postwar world and the War Department's desire to redeploy U.S. troops in Korea elsewhere, the United States decided to seek the establishment of a Korean government in its zone of occupation. In August 1948, the ROK was proclaimed in the South, and a month later the DPRK was proclaimed in the North. In December of that year, based on the fact that the UN Temporary Commission on Korea (UNTCOK) had been able to observe elections only in the South, the UN General Assembly adopted a resolution recognizing the ROK government as the lawful government for the peninsula. On January 1, 1949, the United States extended recognition to the ROK, and 37 other countries quickly followed. Only the countries of the Soviet bloc extended recognition to the DPRK. Thus began the long, competitive battle for diplomatic recognition and hence legitimation between North and South Korea. U.S. troops remained on the peninsula until June 1949 to guarantee stability, whereas the Soviet military had left Korea by the end of 1948.

Six months after the last troops left South Korea, U.S. Secretary of State Dean Acheson addressed the National Press Club, describing

[50] For alternative and more critical interpretations, see Harrison (2002) and S. S. Cho (1967).

[51] W. S. Lee (1982: 187–86). Cumings (1981: 55–61).

the American defense perimeter in Asia. In this January 1950 speech, Acheson's perimeter excluded both Korea and Formosa.[52] According to Acheson, if an attack were to occur beyond the defense perimeter, it would initially be up to the people attacked to resist it and then to the United Nations to respond collectively. The exclusion of Korea from the defense perimeter became the focus of scholarly criticism. Acheson's assertion reflected administration confidence that South Korea would not face outright aggression, but more likely subversion, the best response to which was the development of local strength and self-reliance.[53] Acheson also seemed to be sending a signal to the Chinese communists, now installed in Beijing, that the administration sought friendship. Whatever the United States intended to impart through Acheson's remarks, what came across to Moscow, Beijing, and Pyongyang was that it did not want to be involved in armed conflict in China or Korea.

The Korean War began in June 1950. There are four contending interpretations of its origins. The traditional approach has seen the war as a product of Stalin's strategy for the worldwide spread of communism; in this recounting, Kim Il Sung is a puppet and the perpetrator. The revisionist school, at the other end of the spectrum, argues that the United States and the ROK bear responsibility for the war; in this version of events, Syngman Rhee is the puppet and the perpetrator, attempting to facilitate an expansion of the U.S. empire. The neotraditionalist school reconceives Kim Il Sung – and not Stalin – as the instigator of the war. The neorevisionist school moves away from pointing fingers at any individual and blames protracted class struggle on the peninsula as the cause of the war.[54] Among these four views on the origins of the Korean War, evidence revealed with the opening of the Soviet archives in the early 1990s demonstrates that the neotraditionalist school is closest to the truth. Soviet documents establish that Kim Il Sung had made plans for an all-out military attack on the South by early 1949. At this time, he began making repeated requests for a meeting with Stalin and met with him in Moscow in March 1949. The Soviet ambassador, however, counseled Stalin that an attack was not advisable, and the Soviet Central Committee made an official decision against attacking in 1949. In January 1950, Kim Il Sung proposed a new plan for invasion, and Stalin responded by urging that the North continue military preparations. Kim traveled to Moscow again in April 1950. At this time, Stalin suggested that international conditions had changed in such a way as to make an attack possible but required Kim to receive Mao Zedong's blessing before proceeding. Kim Il Sung met with Mao in mid-May of 1950, and the war began on June 25.[55]

[52] Acheson (1950). [53] Matray (1985: 218). [54] H. J. Kim (1994).
[55] Goncharov, Lewis, and Xue (1993); H. J. Kim (1994).

The KPA advanced rapidly down the peninsula. Nearly all U.S. forces had been removed from Korea, and it was clear that the ROK would not be able to hold back the communist forces on its own. Truman later said in his memoirs that the decision to intervene in Korea was the toughest decision of his presidency but that he considered Korea "a symbol of the strength and determination of the West" in the Cold War.[56] Apparently, three factors dominated in this case: the strategic threat to Japan, the credibility of the Atlantic alliance, and the effectiveness of the United Nations' collective security system. Truman gave MacArthur permission to transfer munitions from Japan to the ROK Army and to use air cover to protect the evacuation of U.S. citizens. Meanwhile, the United States went to the UN Security Council on June 27 and obtained a resolution in support of rolling back the DPRK forces. The USSR undoubtedly would have vetoed the resolution, but the Soviet ambassador was boycotting the Security Council meeting as a means of protesting the failure to turn China's seat over to the Chinese communists. U.S. combat troops arrived in Pusan on July 1. Fighting from a perimeter around Pusan and beginning with the famous amphibious assault at Inchon, U.S. and ROK forces reclaimed Seoul and most of South Korea before capturing Pyongyang in mid-October.

Kim Il Sung appealed to Mao and Stalin, and by October 25, the Chinese People's Volunteers Force under the command of General Peng Dehuai had intervened in the war, halting the U.S. advance up the peninsula. Soviet MiG fighters – their crews masquerading as Chinese or Korean pilots – ended U.S. strategic air superiority around the same time. By the end of 1950, each side held territory approximately equivalent to what it had held at the beginning of the war. Although combat continued until July 1953, the ROK and the DPRK emerged from the war with largely the same geographic boundary they had begun with, except for the addition of a 2.5-mile-wide DMZ. The armistice signed on July 27 did not include an ROK signature: only the DPRK, the PRC, and the UN Command were signatories to it, a result of ROK President Syngman Rhee's all-out opposition to truce talks.

After thirty-seven months of fighting, the United States had suffered 137,250 casualties – 36,940 killed in action, 92,134 wounded, 3,737 missing in action, and 4,439 prisoners of war.[57] The South Koreans lost 400,000 troops, with a huge civilian loss as well; and combined North Korean and Chinese casualties were close to 2 million. Property damage

[56] The outstanding analysis of Truman's decision to intervene in Korea is in Paige (1968). In addition to providing the most detailed account available of the first week of the war, Paige reviews various propositions as to the causes of Truman's actions and their appropriateness to the crisis.

[57] Ministry of National Defense (2003: 8).

on both sides of the DMZ was enormous.[58] The destructive U.S. bombing of North Korea left almost nothing standing anywhere in the country. The war, therefore, left North Koreans with enormous fear, resentment, and hatred of the United States, which has been exacerbated by the continued presence of UN forces in South Korea.[59] The war was the defining event of North Korean identity formation. Whereas the 1950 invasion etched into the minds of the American policy maker and public an image of North Koreans as aggressive communists that must be deterred and stopped at any cost, North Koreans view the U.S. intervention in the Korean War and subsequent military presence on the Korean peninsula as yet another example of great-power interference in Korean affairs. Fifteen years after the end of the Cold War, the United States and North Korea remain technically at war and mired in ideological conflict.

The 1953 truce was not expected to last long, yet it has held for over 50 years. The institutions produced by the truce also endure. The Military Armistice Commission (MAC) composed of officers of both sides served as virtually the only point of formal U.S.–DPRK contact from 1953 to the late 1980s and is still in place today. The Neutral Nations Supervisory Commission (NNSC), consisting originally of Sweden, Switzerland, Czechoslovakia, and Poland (the latter two are no longer members since the fall of communism), endures as well.

The Korean War served as the great catalyst for the creation of Cold-War identity for the two Koreas as well as for the United States. For both Koreas, the war experience triggered a decisive shift in identity politics from multi-identity competition to Cold War identity as dominant, with the consequences of weakening the collective ethnonational identity as one whole.[60] The United States also owes to the Korean War the crystallization of its Cold War identity, which in turn gave birth to an American strategic culture that thrived on a Manichaean vision of global bipolarity and the omnipresent communist threat. While the Korean War accelerated and completed the process of Cold War identity construction, decades later the end of the Cold War and the collapse and transformation of the communist world failed to turn inter-Korean identity politics completely around.[61] In short, the Korean War set the future course not only for the Korean peninsula but also for much of the Cold War.

The way the politics of the war were conducted also enacted the rules of the Cold War game and congealed patterns of East–West conflict across East Asia and beyond.[62] High military budgets, a militarized NATO, and the globalization of competing alliance systems were all formed in the crucible created by the Korean War. The war effectively crystallized

[58] Barry (1996: 69). [59] I. Y. Chun (1977: 77–84). [60] C. S. Chun (2001: 132).
[61] C. S. Chun (2001: 142). [62] Jervis (1980).

East–West conflict into a rigid strategic culture dependent on a Manichean vision of stark bipolarity. The war also had important consequences for the cohesion of the communist bloc. The Sino–Soviet alliance formally forged on February 14, 1950, was both strengthened in the short run and weakened in the long run by the Korean War. Whatever the perceptions of Third World neutrals, the Chinese intervention significantly elevated the PRC's stature with the Soviet Union. However, the Sino–Soviet split became the unavoidable consequence of growing equality in the Sino–Soviet alliance.[63] In East Asia, the balance of great-power influence gradually shifted from the Soviet Union to the PRC.

U.S. forces, under the banner of the UN command, have remained in South Korea since the conclusion of the war, and the size of the U.S. Forces Korea (USFK) footprint has changed only a few times in the past five decades. In 1971, the Nixon Administration withdrew a division. Then, in 1976, Jimmy Carter announced during the U.S. presidential campaign that he would incrementally withdraw U.S. forces from Korea, given the ROK's growing economic edge over the DPRK. Coupled with a force modernization program, Carter implemented his plan during his term until a February 1979 announcement that troop withdrawals would halt because of growth in North Korean military strength in the late 1970s. Today, the U.S. presence, and especially the behavior of U.S. troops in South Korea, remains a contentious issue for U.S.–ROK relations.

New Challenges of the Washington–Seoul–Pyongyang Triangle

Political and Diplomatic Issues: The Long Road to Normalization

By the end of the Cold War, the United States had a working relationship with China. Then, the second term of Bill Clinton's presidency would bring about rapprochement with Vietnam, two decades after the end of the U.S. conflict with that country. Few, however, predicted a quick normalization of relations with North Korea in the post–Cold War years. The intensity of the Stalinist state's political position made such an outcome seem unlikely; after all, Pyongyang rhetorically disparaged "cross-recognition" of the two Koreas as a move toward perpetual division of the peninsula. Furthermore, the predictions of Pyongyang's probable collapse made a pursuit of normalization seem like a waste of time. Nonetheless, by the late 1990s, as Clinton was preparing to leave office, normalization seemed to be on the table, only to be scuttled by new "nuclear revelations" that sent Pentagon planners and State Department strategists scrambling toward their alternate scenarios for resolving a new standoff that thoroughly obscured any progress toward normalization.

[63] See Stueck (1995: 370).

In the early twenty-first century, the U.S.–DPRK relationship is one of a kind. With the fall of the Soviet Union, North Korea is the longest-running political, military, and ideological adversary for the United States, and vice versa. No other bilateral relation in contemporary international affairs approaches this sixty-year history of mutual enmity, animosity, and provocation fueled and sustained by seemingly immutable antagonistic Cold War identities.

From the end of the Korean War in 1953 until the late 1980s, there was no formal diplomatic contact of any kind between the United States and the DPRK. In 1973, the first North Korean diplomats arrived in New York to staff the DPRK's permanent *observer* mission to the United Nations, but they failed to make a dent in the frozen Cold War enmity between Washington and Pyongyang. The following year, the DPRK Supreme People's Assembly sent a letter to the U.S. Congress proposing that the Korean Armistice be replaced with a U.S.–DPRK peace treaty. In 1975 and again 1976, Secretary of State Henry Kissinger, in fact, was a voice in favor of some recognition of North Korea. He called for cross-recognition according to which the United States and Japan would recognize North Korea in exchange for the Soviet Union and China extending diplomatic relations to South Korea.[64] Despite its policy of demonizing the United States, Pyongyang continued to propose bilateral talks aimed at establishing official ties under U.S. Presidents Gerald Ford and Jimmy Carter. In April 1983, Egyptian President Hosni Mubarak visited Pyongyang and was asked to communicate such a proposal to Washington. The United States, however, continued to rebuff North Korean suggestions of talks that excluded South Korea. In January 1984, North Korea offered its "Tripartite Conference Proposal," suggesting, in a letter to the administration and Congress sent through the Chinese premier, that the two Koreas and the United States negotiate as equal partners to arrive at a formal peace treaty to end the state of hostilities. This would then lead to American troop withdrawal and initiate North–South dialogue for unification. However, as formulated by Pyongyang, there would be two sets of negotiations: one between the United States and DPRK to replace the Armistice, and the other between the two Koreas on arms reduction and a nonaggression pact. The United States responded with support for the ROK's appeal for inter-Korean bilateral talks and also indicated that it would welcome genuine four-power talks, including China.[65]

With the winding down of the Cold War and the consequent strategic transformation taking place throughout the world, the Reagan administration launched what was termed a "modest initiative" to start a dialogue with North Korea. Recognizing that Pyongyang's increasing isolation was

[64] Barry (1996: 78). [65] Clough (1987: 190–92).

a dangerously destabilizing factor in NEA, Reagan authorized the State Department in the fall of 1988 to hold substantive discussions with North Korean representatives in neutral settings and allowed nongovernmental visits from North Korea in academics, culture, sports, and a few other areas. He also ended the almost-total U.S. ban on commercial and financial transactions with North Korea by allowing certain exports on a case-by-case basis.[66] The George H. W. Bush administration, however, did not continue the initiative.

In the early 1990s, the collapse of the Eastern Bloc and the Soviet Union were the major issues of concern for Presidents Bush and Clinton in the United States. There was a need to secure nuclear weapons in Belarus, Kazakhstan, and Ukraine and more broadly to facilitate the transition to democracy and capitalism in the postcommunist countries. The policy toward North Korea was one of ignorance at worst and containment at best. Minimal steps were taken to counter North Korean aspirations for nuclear weapons, and there was a standing commitment to avoid any sort of *quid pro quo* agreement with the presumably failing communist regime.

On March 12, 1993, however, the DPRK gave the ninety-day legal notice that it was withdrawing from the NPT, which it had signed in December 1985. The withdrawal was a response to the demand by the IAEA – backed by the threat of an application for UN sanctions – for special inspections permitting unlimited access at any time or place (the first such request ever made by the IAEA). The announcement of withdrawal created an instant atmosphere of crisis in Seoul, Tokyo, Washington, Vienna, and New York, while 149 countries "issued statements denouncing Pyongyang's intended withdrawal."[67] Over the course of 1993, tensions rose between the United States and North Korea, as the DPRK allegedly tampered with IAEA seals on its nuclear facilities and as the UN Security Council considered sanctions. UN sanctions were forestalled by the threat of a Chinese veto, and the Security Council instead passed a mild resolution in May of that year. U.S.–DPRK talks began in New York in June and led quickly to U.S. acceptance in principle of the most important component of North Korea's demands: the provision of LWRs. The DPRK had succeeded in reducing the options available to the IAEA (which could only refer the matter to the Security Council), the Security

[66] Testimony of Mark Minton, director of the Office of Korean Affairs, before the Senate Foreign Relations Committee, Subcommittee on East Asian and Pacific Affairs, Washington, DC, September 12. 1996.

[67] Wit, Poneman, and Gallucci (2004: 27). This book, written by three American participants, easily stands out as the most authoritative and comprehensive account of the first North Korean nuclear crisis. Wit was in the State Department and Poneman in the National Security Council, while Gallucci was American chief negotiator in Geneva during the first North Korean nuclear crisis.

Council (which could only muster a resolution without the teeth of sanction), and the United States (which was forced into direct, bilateral negotiations with Pyongyang). The Clinton administration, meanwhile, was hampered further by its need to attempt to bring Seoul, Tokyo, Beijing, Moscow, the IAEA, the Security Council, and the U.S. Congress together in a united front strategy against Pyongyang.

Despite the U.S. agreement on the principle of supplying North Korea with two LWRs, the agreement stalled in the hammering out of details, dragging on for almost a year. In May 1994, Pyongyang began removing nuclear fuel rods from the Yongbyon reactor without the presence of IAEA inspectors. As the matter appeared before the UN Security Council, the DPRK declared that "U.N. sanctions will be regarded immediately as a declaration of war,"[68] and China again tied the hands of the UN Security Council with a veto threat and a reassertion of its commitment to the 1961 mutual security treaty with the DPRK. By June, the United States was considering military action and, in fact, apparently came remarkably close to attempting a military solution.[69] The Clinton administration's continuation of the containment policy had failed, and alternatives had not been readied. Former U.S. President Jimmy Carter went to Pyongyang and received Kim Il Sung's personal pledge to freeze the DPRK's nuclear program. Somewhat embarrassed, the Clinton administration had no choice but to negotiate with Pyongyang, and it began a four-month process that led to a written agreement, officially known as the US-DPRK Agreed Framework.

As Clinton's Secretary of Defense William Perry recalls regarding the appearance of the possibility of negotiation, "We were about to give the president a choice between a disastrous option – allowing North Korea to get a nuclear arsenal, which we might have to face someday – and an unpalatable option, blocking this development, but thereby risking a destructive nonnuclear war."[70] Although some hardline opponents of this North Korean policy cried out "appeasement," the fact is that in the absence of the Agreed Framework that resulted from the negotiations, North Korea might today have 50 to 100 nuclear weapons, rather than 1 or 2 or possibly 6 to 8 nuclear bombs.[71]

The Agreed Framework realized in October 1994 inaugurated a period of limited engagement between the United States and the DPRK. As

[68] *The Pyongyang Times,* June 18, 1994, p. 2.

[69] Sigal (1998: 132); Oberdorfer (1997: 323–26).

[70] Carter and Perry (1999: 123–24). A footnote for this statement explains that Ashton Carter was not present for the meeting referred to here, so Perry "tells this story himself." See also Perry (2002: 121).

[71] The figure of 50 to 100 nuclear weapons is Perry's extrapolation. See William J. Perry, "It's Either Nukes or Negotiation," *Washington Post,* July 23, 2003, p. A23.

a supposed solution to the North Korean nuclear issue, the document called on the United States and North Korea to implement four conditions. To deal with the energy crisis in North Korea, the United States was to facilitate the construction of two LWRs, with the first one scheduled for completion by 2003, in exchange for a written agreement with the DPRK on the peaceful use of nuclear energy. Also, the DPRK was to freeze and dismantle the graphite-moderated reactors under construction. In addition, the United States would ensure the supply of heavy fuel oil at a rate of 500,000 tons annually. To deal with the DPRK's pursuit of nuclear weapons for security purposes, the United States also pledged that it would not use or threaten to use nuclear weapons against North Korea (i.e., negative security), and the DPRK was expected to engage in dialogue with the ROK. In the pursuit of effective international regimes, the DPRK was to come into compliance with the NPT and the requirements of the IAEA. Finally, the two countries were to move toward full normalization of political and economic relations, beginning with reduced barriers to trade and investment within three months of the signing of the Agreed Framework.

Pyongyang was very positive in its assessment of the document. North Korea's chief negotiator, Kang Sok Ju, described it as "a very important milestone document of historical significance" that would resolve the nuclear dispute with finality. The official news media in the DPRK called the accord "the biggest diplomatic victory" and went to great lengths to describe it as an end achieved by the DPRK on its own – that is, without pressure or assistance from China. "We held the talks independently with the United States on an independent footing, not relying on someone else's sympathy or advice, and the adoption of the DPRK-U.S. agreed framework is a fruition of our independent foreign policy."[72]

The Agreed Framework, therefore, served as a roadmap for moving U.S.–DPRK relations toward normalization, starting with the establishment of liaison offices in Pyongyang and Washington (similar to the pathway that Sino–American rapprochement took to full normalization), but because of the half-hearted implementation of the agreement on the part of the United States, very little progress was made. The lack of seriousness with which the United States was going to treat the Agreed Framework was made manifest when the U.S. General Accounting Office stated that the Agreed Framework should properly be described as "a nonbinding political agreement" or "nonbinding international agreement" rather than an internationally binding legal document.[73] North Korea, of course,

[72] *Rodong Sinmun [Worker's Daily]*, December 1, 1994.

[73] See "Nuclear Nonproliferation – Implications of the U.S./North Korean Agreement on Nuclear Issues," GAO Report to the Chairman, Committee on Energy and Natural Resources, U.S. Senate, October 1996 (GAO/RCED/NSIAD-97-8).

had anticipated that the signed agreement would be treated as a legally binding treaty and has since perceived itself as suffering from a double standard of expectations regarding implementation.

Implementation of the Agreed Framework became politically less feasible in the United States when the Republican Party regained control of Congress in the midterm elections of November 1994. The Clinton administration was unwilling to expend the political capital necessary to take on Congress over an unpopular issue such as the North Korean nuclear program. In fact, it is questionable whether the Clinton administration ever anticipated implementing the Agreed Framework. Many experts in 1994 were predicting the collapse of the DPRK within six months or three years. Insofar as the agreement was implemented, therefore, it was only by fits and starts.

Despite the subversive scuttling of the Agreed Framework, another front opened up in the arena of U.S.–DPRK diplomatic relations within two years. In April 1996, the United States and South Korea agreed during a summit meeting on Cheju Island to promote a two-plus-two formula involving the DPRK and China for four-party peace talks. Presidents Clinton and Kim Young Sam proposed the peace talks even while privately predicting that North Korea would collapse within two to three years.[74] Pyongyang had made a two-plus-zero proposal for replacing "the outdated armistice system" with "a new peace arrangement system" in April 1994 before the completion of the Agreed Framework.[75] The United States, however, refused to respond to any proposal that excluded South Korea. In fact, the South Korean line was that a peace process should be an inter-Korean process, but Clinton was willing to expend political capital in demanding a more flexible policy from Seoul because he wanted to demonstrate progress on the North Korean issue before the November 1996 election.[76]

The talks were almost scuttled in September 1996 when a North Korean spy submarine ran aground and South Korea began a massive manhunt for the North Korean commandos that had escaped into remote mountain areas. Over the course of a week, the North Koreans were hunted down and killed. South Korea demanded an apology from Pyongyang and received in late December an expression of "deep regret" that was sufficient for the purpose of allowing the peace talks to proceed.

[74] Green (1997). See also Associated Press, "North Korea Collapse Predicted," March 6, 1997.

[75] *The Pyongyang Times*, May 7, 1994.

[76] On the day of the U.S.–ROK joint announcement, for example, *Wall Street Journal* noted that "any movement in the 43-year Korean stalemate would be an election-year boost for Clinton." *Wall Street Journal*, April 16, 1996, p. A1.

When preliminary talks began in August 1997 in New York, however, the parties could not agree on which topics the peace talks would cover. U.S. and South Korean officials proposed establishment of permanent peace mechanisms, as well as measures to build confidence and ease tension in the Korean peninsula; the North Koreans, however, insisted that any further discussion must focus on the withdrawal of U.S. troops from South Korea. North Korea also insisted on negotiating a separate peace treaty with the United States, demanding that South Korea and the United States guarantee massive food aid and ease economic sanctions before the full peace talks began. The South Korean leadership was highly sensitive to Pyongyang's attempt to marginalize Seoul and negotiate exclusively with the United States. Kim Young Sam's administration opposed economic aid to North Korea unless Pyongyang agreed to Seoul's conditions for the peace talks and even slowed down the flow of humanitarian aid being provided in response to the North Korean famine.

Therefore, North Korea was not happy with the peace talks, South Korea was not happy with the peace talks, and China was not happy with the peace talks. Beijing believed that the United States had acted prematurely and put both Pyongyang and Beijing in the spotlight unprepared, not knowing what was being asked of them, much less what response they should give to avoid being trapped in negotiations destined to work to their disadvantage. Beijing, therefore, took a neutral position, opposing Pyongyang's demand that the negotiations focus on U.S. troops in South Korea and a U.S.–North Korean peace treaty and refusing to support the joint U.S.–ROK proposal that the talks address confidence-building measures. Instead, Beijing advanced its familiar bilateral line – that the four countries should discuss the improvement of bilateral relations.[77]

Despite these inauspicious beginnings, the peace talks went through three preliminary rounds in New York and then moved to Geneva. The talks progressed slowly, but by 1998 there were beginning to be signs of possibilities for some form of conclusive agreement. They were guided along in part by the election of Kim Dae Jung as South Korean President at the end of 1997. But the four-party peace talks suddenly became greatly overshadowed by a trio of North Korean provocations: a series of submarine incursions into South Korean territorial waters, suspected underground nuclear construction at Kumchang-ri, and the launching of a three-stage Taepodong-1 missile over Japan in late August 1998. The combined – if never explicit – conclusion of both the United States and South Korea was that more immediate issues than a permanent peace treaty needed addressing.

[77] *The Korea Herald* (Internet version), August 23, 1997.

The missile test and the suspicions about the restarting of plutonium processing were accompanied by North Korean rumblings about abandoning the Agreed Framework. In response, Clinton drafted his former Secretary of Defense, William Perry, to conduct a thorough review and assessment of U.S. policy toward North Korea. The Perry process marked the beginning of a sustained effort at the highest levels of the Clinton administration to achieve a larger breakthrough in relations with North Korea. The Perry Report was issued in October 1999. It notes the centrality of the Agreed Framework and calls for a two-track approach of step-by-step comprehensive engagement and normalization with a concurrent posture of deterrence. The report also stresses that during the process of exploring policy options, a policy of regime change and demise – "a policy of undermining the DPRK, seeking to hasten the demise of the regime of Kim Jong Il " – had been considered and rejected.[78]

The Congressional Republicans responded to the Perry Report with immediate attack, encapsulated in the report of the North Korea Advisory Group, chaired by Representative Benjamin Gilman of New York. This report described the Clinton administration's policies as inadequate and claimed that the DPRK was undeniably a larger threat than it had been before the Agreed Framework was signed.[79] Despite this prominent negative response, the issuance of the Perry Report and the implementation of some of its recommendations led to a lessening of the tense atmosphere and to substantive steps in both U.S.–DPRK relations and inter-Korean relations. These steps, of course, remained far short of those that might be necessary for normalization of relations.

Although North Korea's desire to normalize relations with the United States is not entirely of recent vintage – Kim Il Sung claimed in a 1977 interview with *Le Monde* that he was willing to normalize relations with the United States, provided that the United States took the initiative – it is important to question Pyongyang's earnestness in desiring normalization. Given the North Korean habit of manipulating major powers to gain maximum security and economic benefits, some have speculated that the historic inter-Korean summit of June 2000 was a concession to Washington aimed at speeding up normalization talks for the purpose of gaining access to bilateral and multilateral aid and FDI. In part, the summit was fulfillment of the clause in the Agreed Framework that called for a revival of North–South dialogue. At the same time, the United States announced additional relaxation of long-standing trade sanctions against the North in June 2000 in return for the DPRK reaffirming its moratorium on additional missile tests. The inter-Korean summit, therefore, contributed to progress in U.S.–DPRK relations so that quasisummit meetings were held

[78] Perry (1999). [79] North Korea Advisory Group (1999).

first in Washington between President Clinton and DPRK Vice Marshal Jo Myong-Rok in early October, and then in Pyongyang between U.S. Secretary of State Madeline Albright and Kim Jong Il later that month.

Although the North Koreans were hoping for a presidential visit to Pyongyang, Jo's U.S. visit resulted in the U.S.–DPRK Joint Communiqué of October 12, 2000, as well as Albright's official state visit beginning on October 24. The Communiqué stated *inter alia* that the two sides "are prepared to undertake a new direction in their relations" and that "as a crucial first step, the two sides stated that neither government would have hostile intent toward the other and confirmed the commitment of both governments to make every effort in the future to build a new relationship free from past enmity."[80] The countries pledged to develop mutually beneficial economic cooperation and exchanges, to resolve the missile issue, and to strengthen the Agreed Framework for the purpose of fundamentally improving bilateral relations. The declaration was couched almost entirely in bilateral terms, moving further away from the moribund multilateralism of the four-party peace talks.

The quasisummit meetings in October and the communiqué, in fact, together represented some progress toward a missile accord. Several former Clinton administration officials – most notably, Albright and the Special Coordinator for North Korean Affairs, Ambassador Wendy Sherman – believed that a missile agreement was within reach in the waning weeks of the Clinton presidency but that a presidential visit to Pyongyang would have been required to achieve it.[81] However, the DPRK hesitated over on-site verification requirements in late 2000 at the same time that George W. Bush was elected president of the United States, leading to a period of noninteraction as the Bush administration searched for a North Korea policy while systematically "unilateralizing" nearly all other components of U.S. foreign policy. Less than three weeks after the Bush administration assumed office, Kim Dae Jung dispatched Minister of Foreign Affairs and Trade Lee Joung-binn to Washington. Lee briefed the new Secretary of State, Colin Powell, on ROK policy toward the North, sought a renewed U.S. endorsement of the Sunshine Policy, and lobbied for a meeting between President Bush and President Kim at the earliest possible time. Although Secretary Powell offered a broad endorsement of ROK policy, he also said that specific U.S. policies regarding the DPRK were under review by the new administration. Bush was less kind when he conferenced with Kim Dae Jung. The president voiced open skepticism about

[80] For the text of the joint communiqué, see U.S. Department of State, Office of the Spokesman, "U.S.-D.P.R.K. Joint Communique," October 12, 2000. Available at http://www.armscontrol.org/Events/commique.asp.

[81] Pollack (2003).

the trustworthiness of Kim Jong Il and whether the North was "keeping all terms of all agreements." Some of Bush's remarks, in fact, proved to be a sharp and humiliating rebuke to Kim, and the ROK president reportedly took ample offense. North Korea wasted little time in reacting to the meeting by canceling ministerial-level talks scheduled for Seoul the following week and harshly criticizing "hostile" U.S. policy. Pyongyang reiterated that it was "fully prepared for both dialogue and war."

All of this said, however, North Korea's manifest desire to normalize relations with the United States had much to do with the changing correlation of geostrategic forces in the early post–Cold War years – such as failure of the Third World as a viable alternative (and thus the inefficacy of Pyongyang's campaign for diplomatic recognition and leadership in the Non-Aligned Movement), the collapse of the Soviet Union, and the triumph of Seoul's *Nordpolitik* in gaining diplomatic recognition from Moscow and Beijing. Under Bush, the non- or underimplementation of the Agreed Framework continued, as shown in Table 5.1, and Pyongyang began to openly express its concern as the 2003 deadline for the delivery of a LWR approached. On February 20, 2001, a DPRK Foreign Ministry spokesman said, "If [the United States] does not honestly implement the agreed framework, . . . there is no need for us to be bound to it any longer. We cannot but consider the existence of the Korean peninsula Energy Development Organization (KEDO) as meaningless under the present situation when no one can tell when the LWR project will be completed."[82] On June 18, 2001, the same source warned, "The agreed framework is in the danger of collapse due to the delay in the LWR provision."[83] Nonetheless, the terrorist attacks of September 11, 2001, reaffirmed the diminished U.S. policy priority attached to engaging North Korea and strengthened the administration's predisposition to view Pyongyang as a looming danger rather than a negotiating partner.

It cannot be gainsaid that there was a great deal of foot-dragging over the implementation of the Agreed Framework. The expectation – in Seoul no less than in Tokyo and Washington – that Pyongyang would collapse before the KEDO construction program was completed was commonplace. Yet, the delay was not all on one side, and neither were some North Korean actions designed to maintain the mutual confidence necessary for the work to go forward. Six months were wasted on "identity argument" as to what the reactor type was to be called, and then a deliberate labor dispute shut down the construction until workers from Central Asia were brought in by KEDO to substitute for the DPRK workforce. Over and above these problems, the 1996 submarine incident hardly represented a conciliatory gesture. The biggest problem of all had a lot

[82] KCNA, February 22, 2001. [83] KCNA, June 18, 2001.

Table 5.1. Implementation Status of the Agreed Framework (as of the end of 2002)

Agreed Framework Provisions	Implementation Status
The U.S. agrees to provide two light water reactor (LWR) power plants by the year 2003 (article 1.2).	Four years behind schedule in 2002. There was no delay in South Korean or Japanese provision of funds. The delay was U.S. implementation and construction.
The U.S. agrees to provide formal assurances to the DPRK against the threat or use of nuclear weapons by the U.S. (article 2.3.1).	Not implemented. The U.S. maintains that military force is an option on the peninsula. The U.S. continues to target North Korea with nuclear weapons as in the December 2001 "Nuclear Posture Review."
The DPRK agrees to freeze its nuclear reactors and to dismantle them when the LWR project is completed (article 1.3).	Compliance until December 2002.
The DPRK agrees to allow the IAEA (International Atomic Energy Agency) to monitor the freeze with full cooperation (article 1.3).	Compliance until December 2002.
The U.S. and the DPRK agree to work toward full normalization of political and economic relations, reducing barriers of trade and investment, etc. (article 2.1).	Limited lowering of U.S. restrictions on trade. No other progress toward normalization or a peace treaty. U.S. State Department continues to list North Korea as a terrorist state.
The U.S. and the DPRK will each open a liaison office in the each other's capital, aiming at upgrading bilateral relations to the ambassadorial level (articles 2.2, 2.3).	Not implemented.

Source: Cha and Kang (2003: 137).

to do with North Korea's alleged HEU program. The Clinton administration probably knew about the HEU program but did not consider it either a violation or a significant violation of previous understandings.[84]

The only context in which Bush seemed to care about North Korea was vis-à-vis NMD; the DPRK served as the poster child for why the United

[84] Selig Harrison's heated debate with Robert Gallucci and Mitchell Reiss in the recent pages of *Foreign Affairs* seems relevant here in illustrating the ambiguity of both American intelligence and Pyongyang's counterclaims. See Harrison (2005a, 2005b) and Reiss and Gallucci (2005).

States needed to deploy a system, given that it – unlike Iraq or Iran – was alleged to have the long-range missile capacity to threaten U.S. interests and perhaps the United States itself. With Bush's declaration of an "axis of evil" in his January 2002 State of the Union address, the administration's refusal to certify in March 2002 that the DPRK was acting in accord with the Agreed Framework (which threatened U.S. funding of KEDO), and finally Pyongyang's alleged revelations of October 2002 regarding a HEU program, Pyongyang and Washington found themselves at loggerheads. After a long delay, Assistant Secretary of State James Kelly went to North Korea in early October under the guise that Pyongyang had agreed to comprehensive policy discussions. Nothing in the public depiction of the purposes of the Kelly visit even remotely hinted at an impending confrontation in Pyongyang, and there is no reason to believe that U.S. officials had conveyed advance hints to the DPRK that the assistant secretary was coming to Pyongyang to deliver a stern message and little else. By most accounts, Kelly wasted little time on diplomatic niceties, making clear that U.S. intelligence findings regarding the North Korean HEU nuclear program precluded any possible forward movement in U.S.–DPRK relations. Other accounts suggest that the North sought to hold the United States accountable for the nullification of the Agreed Framework. In addition, North Korean officials interviewed by Don Oberdorfer

> never denied seeking to enrich uranium in secret facilities, but portrayed their actions as a response to the Bush administration's hostility. . . . [O]ur interlocutors said North Korea has adopted a "neither confirm nor deny" policy about whether the program existed before Bush took office. They would also "neither confirm nor deny" whether North Korea already possesses a nuclear weapon.[85]

In the summer of 2003 (following the fall 2002 meeting between the United States and the DPRK in Pyongyang), the Defense Department's Operations Plan 5030, containing various scenarios for antagonizing and intimidating North Korea, was leaked to the press,[86] while the PSI was announced in May 2003, organized around the idea of being able to intercept ships and planes believed to be carrying illicit weapons material. These strategic documents proved anathema to Pyongyang; both DPRK officials and the North Korean media had long and assiduously followed the U.S. security policy debate and documents. For instance, after the nuclear standoff unfolded in October 2002, North Korean statements regularly cited President Bush's inclusion of the North in the "axis of evil" and the administration's preemption doctrine as virtual declarations of war that justified the DPRK's withdrawal from the NPT.[87]

[85] Don Oberdorfer, "My Private Seat at Pyongyang's Table," *Washington Post*, November 10, 2002, p. B3.

[86] See Auster and Whitelaw (2003). [87] Pollack (2003).

By the end of the first term of the Bush administration, virtually all former U.S. ambassadors to the ROK and special envoys to the DPRK had openly criticized the administration's approach to North Korea: Donald Gregg, James Laney, Stephen Bosworth, William Perry, Wendy Sherman, and Charles Kartman. Charles Pritchard, who resigned as the State Department's special envoy for North Korean nuclear issues in August 2003, said, "We've gone, under [Bush's] watch, from the possibility that North Korea has one or two weapons to a possibility – a distinct possibility – that it now has eight or more. And it's happened while we were deposing Saddam Hussein for fear he might get that same capability by the end of the decade."[88]

If normalization is to come about, security guarantees seem to be a necessary if not a sufficient precursor. The centrality of the survival-driven security dilemma is evidenced in comments by Pritchard regarding the 2000 U.S. diplomatic trip to North Korea:

> I am struck by what Kim Jong-il, North Korea's leader, said to Madeleine Albright, former US secretary of state, in October 2000. He told her that in the 1970s, Deng Xiaoping, the Chinese leader, was able to conclude that China faced no external security threat and could accordingly refocus its resources on economic development. With the appropriate security assurances, Mr. Kim said, he would be able to convince his military that the US was no longer a threat and then be in a similar position to refocus his country's resources.[89]

In a 1999 interview, William Perry offered a similar assessment: "We do not think of ourselves as a threat to North Korea. But I fully believe that they consider us a threat to them, and therefore, they see [the Taepodong-1] missile as a means of deterrence."[90]

Without U.S. engagement, North Korea seems destined to receive neither the international aid that it needs nor the international recognition that it covets. More to the point, without engagement, the DPRK is likely to maintain its bunker mentality, evidenced by pronouncements such as this one from August 2003:

> The Bush administration openly disclosed its attempt to use nuclear weapons after listing the DPRK as part of 'an axis of evil' and a target of 'preemptive nuclear attack.' This prompted us to judge that the Bush administration is going to stifle our system by force and decide to build a strong deterrent force

[88] Quoted in David Sanger, "Intelligence Puzzle: North Korean Bombs," *New York Times*, October 14, 2003, p. A9.

[89] Charles Pritchard, "A Guarantee to Bring Kim into Line," *The Financial Times*, October 10, 2003.

[90] Public Broadcast Service interview, Washington, DC, September 17, 1999, as provided by NAPSNet, September 30, 1999. Available at http://www.nautilus.org/archives/pub/ftp/napsnet/special_reports/Perry_Albright_Press_Briefing.txt.

to cope with it. Hence, we determined to possess that force. . . . It is a means for self-defense to protect our sovereignty.[91]

The failed pattern seems to be the one in which the U.S. demands that Pyongyang abandon its weapons programs before the United States decides whether to be benevolent. Washington's security assurances and economic inducements have helped convince South Korea, Taiwan, Brazil, Argentina, South Africa, Ukraine, Belarus, and Kazakhstan to abandon nuclear armament. Only in Pakistan have they failed.[92] South Korea gave up its nuclear program in the 1970s in exchange of more and better security assurances from the United States. Under the Nunn-Lugar aid program, Russia has dismantled many of its weapons, and Ukraine – which had possession of some 1,900 former Soviet nuclear warheads – agreed to get rid of them all in exchange for security assurances, economic support, and energy assistance.[93] These successes should serve as inspiration for a policy of positive inducements and should indicate the importance of providing meaningful security guarantees to replace those associated with the possession of nuclear weapons. The United States seems to be hampered from giving such guarantees and promises of aid, however, by what it sees as Pyongyang's repeatedly use of "blackmail."

Military and Security Issues

U.S.–DPRK Security Interactions

The U.S. foreign policy strategy toward the Korean peninsula and toward East Asia in general has already changed several times in the post–Cold War era. In 1990, a report from the Department of Defense defined the role of the United States as that of "regional balance, honest broker and ultimate security guarantor." Even if the Soviet threat declined substantially, the United States would stay involved to check the "expansionist regional aspirations" of "second tier states."[94] In 1992, with the dissolution of the Soviet Union, the United States decided to reduce force commitments in East Asia, but this decision was reversed in 1995, in part because of a desire to rejuvenate the U.S. leadership role in the region and in part because "it is cheaper to base the forces in Asia than in the United States."[95]

In the early post–Cold War years, the U.S. policy toward North Korea was one of deterrence, but it was clear that this policy could not deal with the clear and continuing danger of a hard landing by the DPRK.

[91] KCNA, August 29, 2003. [92] Sigal (1998: 4, 254).
[93] See Hayes (2003); Sigal (1998: 254, 305n). [94] U.S. Department of Defense (1990).
[95] Nye (1995: 98).

So, in 1996, the United States shifted to a "deterrence-plus" posture. The hallmark of deterrence plus was a process of dialogue and functional confidence building; without propping up the North Korean system, the United States would shift from a reactive to an active role in inter-Korean affairs.[96] Deterrence plus proved difficult to implement given that the hard-landing scenario of North Korean regime collapse and accompanying political and economic anarchy was the least desirable but the most likely outcome, whereas any type of soft landing was seen as desirable but unlikely.[97]

Throughout the 1990s and into the twenty-first century, the nuclear card has consistently been a very potent lever for North Korea. The DPRK has striven to use its nuclear weapons program as an all-purpose, fungible, cost-effective instrument of foreign policy. For Pyongyang, the nuclear program is a military deterrent, an equalizer in national identity competition with South Korea (which lacks nuclear weapons), a bargaining chip for extracting concessions from the United States and from China, and an effective insurance policy for regime survival. A little international uncertainty surrounding nuclear capabilities has gone a long way for North Korea.

With reference to its nuclear weapons program, asymmetric conflict and negotiation theory explain the logic of some parts of the threat that North Korea presents. Weak states can display bargaining power disproportionate to their aggregate structural power if they occupy territory of strategic importance to the more powerful state or if the field of play is the weak actor's home turf.[98] In 1994, North Korea was able to successfully employ an asymmetric negotiating strategy with the United States and thereby shape the Agreed Framework. When the United States failed to implement the Agreed Framework to Pyongyang's satisfaction, the DPRK returned to these tactics of negotiation first in 1998 by making missile technology and proliferation an issue with the Taepodong-1 launch, and then in late 2002 and early 2003, by the lighting of "three long nuclear fuses": the seeking of equipment to process uranium, the production of plutonium at the Yongbyon facility, and the resumption of construction on the reactors frozen by the Agreed Framework.[99]

The events that began in October 2002 with the alleged North Korean admission that it had a secret HEU program are often referred to as the "second nuclear crisis" on the Korean peninsula. The description of the situation as a crisis, however, is not clarifying so much as it is misleading. A crisis is defined by surprise, high stakes, a short response time, limited

[96] Laney (1996). [97] Drennan (1998b).
[98] Habeeb (1988: 130–33); Barston (1971); S. S. Kim (1997b); J. J. Suh (2006).
[99] Leon V. Sigal, presentation at Columbia University, February 26, 2003.

options, and limitations on the number of decision makers involved – criteria not met in this case. In the first place, the Bush administration had been aware of the program for four months; hence, there was no element of surprise involved other than Pyongyang's surprisingly open "confession." Despite the North's coming clean, the Bush administration did not go into crisis mode. Finally, the "crisis" had been long in the making, given the U.S. refusal to implement in a timely fashion the various provisions of the 1994 Agreed Framework and also given Bush's denunciations of Kim Jong Il and North Korea during his presidential campaign and, most famously, during his 2002 State of the Union address.[100] More to the point, it now appears that Washington raised the HEU issue as a result of growing alarm over the conciliatory approach that Seoul and Tokyo had been taking with regard to Pyongyang. With North and South Korea moving ahead with plans for railroad links and for the development of a new economic zone at Kaesong in North Korea, and with Japanese Prime Minister Koizumi Junichiro visiting Pyongyang to discuss normalization of relations – a visit that Japan had been quietly exploring for more than nine months without telling the United States – Washington sought to rein in its allies and regain control over the direction of negotiations in NEA.[101]

During the 2000 campaign season, a July report produced by the Republican Congress denounced Clinton administration policy toward North Korea as "appeasement" and demanded an extensive overhaul.[102] Condoleeza Rice's early 2000 article in *Foreign Affairs* on "promoting the national interest" likewise suggested that the U.S. policy was not being aggressive enough in confronting the DPRK. These documents were followed by the September 2000 publication of a neoconservative manifesto for the new American century, some of the contributors to which (e.g., Paul Wolfowitz) would soon join the Bush administration.[103] After Bush's election, a series of radical shifts in America's military doctrine

[100] When the new ROK president Roh Moo-hyun met with Bush, he is said to have told Bush regarding Kim Jong Il, "Yeah, he's a bad guy, but we don't have to say it in public," making the point that turning the nuclear dispute into a personal confrontation, the way the Bush administration had done with Saddam Hussein and Iraq, could undercut any chance of diplomatic success in disarming North Korea. David E. Sanger, "U.S. Is Shaping Plan to Pressure North Koreans," *New York Times*, February 14, 2005, p. A1.

[101] Harrison (2005a: 101–02).

[102] See House Policy Committee, the House of Representatives, U.S. Congress, "Clinton-Gore North Korea Aid: Evidence Shows False Premise for Appeasement," April 11, 2000; "Clinton-Gore North Korea Aid Will Provide Plutonium for Nuclear Bombs," April 14, 2000; and "Clinton-Gore Aid to North Korea Supports Kim Jong-il's Million Man Arms," July 27, 2000.

[103] *Rebuilding America's Defenses: Strategy, Forces and Resources for a New Century, A Report of the Project for the New American Century*, September 2000. Available at http://www.newamericancentury.org/RebuildingAmericasDefenses.pdf.

made it increasingly evident that this was more than mere rhetorical posturing: the Quadrennial Defense Review of September 2001 called for a paradigm shift from threat- to capability-based models; the Nuclear Posture Review, submitted to Congress on the last day of 2001, lowered the threshold for the use for tactical nuclear weapons and listed North Korea as one of seven target states; and the Bush doctrine of preemption, first proclaimed at West Point in June 2002 and then officially enunciated and codified in *The National Security Strategy of the United States of America* in September 2002, was exercised in Iraq in March 2003 with perverse and self-defeating consequences.

North Korea pays very close attention to these public policy pronouncements, and it is not far fetched to say that the DPRK's willingness in October 2002 to confess having a nuclear program was inspired by the bellicosity it found in these official U.S. policies. While Colin Powell was saying in June 2002 that the United States would be ready to meet with the DPRK "any time, any place, without precondition," Robert Gallucci claims that the North Koreans interpreted this as a willingness on the part of Washington "to meet to accept North Korean surrender."[104] In fact, as the United States moved toward talks with the DPRK, Powell inserted various behavioral preconditions, such as getting out of the proliferation business, providing for North Korean children, moving to a less threatening conventional weapons posture, and coming into full compliance with the NPT. In August, the administration demanded that improvements be seen in relations between North Korea and Japan. Also, it should be noted that elements of the Nuclear Posture Review explicitly contradicted the Agreed Framework's negative nuclear security provision under which the United States assured North Korea that it was not a target of U.S. nuclear weapons. Instead of providing such assurances, the review explicitly endorsed the targeting of the DPRK. With the second nuclear standoff, the United States has declared the Agreed Framework "effectively dead."[105]

To resolve the nuclear standoff that began in October 2002, the DPRK Ministry of Foreign Affairs issued a comprehensive and authoritative statement detailing its version of what had actually occurred in the Kelly–Kang exchanges behind the scenes a few weeks earlier, and also describing the "grand bargain" offered by the North Korean negotiators to U.S. Assistant Secretary of the State James Kelly:

> The DPRK, with greatest magnanimity, clarified that it was ready to seek a negotiated settlement of this issue on the following three conditions: firstly, if

[104] "Bush's Hard Line with North Korea," *New York Times*, February 14, 2002.
[105] CBS News, "Powell: U.S.–N. Korea Nuclear Deal Dead," October 20, 2002. Available at http://www.cbsnews.com/stories/2002/10/21/world/main526243.shtml.

> the U.S. recognizes the DPRK's sovereignty; secondly, if it assures the DPRK of nonaggression; and thirdly, if the U.S. does not hinder the economic development of the DPRK.... If the U.S. legally assures the DPRK of nonaggression, including the nonuse of nuclear weapons against it by concluding... a treaty, the DPRK will be ready to clear the former of its security concerns.[106]

There were no explicit calls for financial compensation from the United States. Subsequent North Korean pronouncements essentially adhered to the proposals outlined in the October 25 statement.

Some have taken the DPRK's initial stance as an indication that the North Korean nuclear program is not as advanced as others fear. As noted by the Central Intelligence Agency (CIA) in an unclassified November 2002 estimate provided to Congress, the construction of a centrifuge facility was not initiated "until recently.... Last year the North began seeking centrifuge-related materials in large quantities.... We recently learned that the North is constructing a plant that could produce enough weapons-grade uranium for two or more nuclear weapons per year when fully operational – which could be as early as mid-decade."[107] At the least, the intelligence community believed that North Korea still confronted daunting obstacles to building an enriched-uranium weapon, or even to acquiring the production capabilities that might ultimately permit such an option.

In reality, it is easier to make use of low enriched uranium (LEU) to plutonium LWRs. The production of HEU in the necessary quantity sufficient to produce nuclear weapons requires the continuous operation of numerous centrifuges over a sufficiently long period of time. Richard Garwin, a nuclear scientist, has estimated that 1,300 high-performance centrifuges would have to operate full time for three years to make the 60 kilograms of fissile material needed for a basic nuclear weapon. Given North Korea's limited electricity and limited machine capabilities, it seems unlikely that the country has produced more than a negligible amount of the HEU that the United States accuses it of producing.[108] The South Korean government, in fact, has said as much, declaring that it "has no conclusive evidence that North Korea has a nuclear weapons program based on highly enriched uranium (HEU)."[109]

[106] See KCNA, "Conclusion of Non-Aggression Treaty between DPRK and U.S. Called for," October 25, 2002. Available at http://www.kcna.co.jp/item/2002/200210/news10/25.htm. See also O'Hanlon and Mochizuki (2003) for a "grand bargain" proposal from an American perspective.

[107] CIA Report to the U.S. Congress on North Korea's Nuclear Weapons Potential, November 19, 2002. Available at www.fas.org/nuke/guide/dprk/nuke/CIA111902.html.

[108] Harrison (2005: 130); Pollack (2003: 30–33).

[109] Yonhap, "ROK Unification Minister Notes No 'Direct Evidence' of DPRK HEU Program," October 21, 2004.

However, Pakistan announced in February that its key nuclear physicist, Abdul Qadeer Khan, had confessed to secretly transferring nuclear technology to North Korea, as well as to Iran and Libya. His confession backed Washington's claim that Pyongyang has an HEU program. The DPRK has responded by consistently denying the use of uranium in its nuclear weapons drive and has accused the United States of orchestrating Khan's "false" confession as an excuse to launch an Iraq-style military attack against it. This debate about the technical probabilities of North Korea actually having a nuclear weapons program has been backgrounded by the political debate over negotiations between the United States and the DPRK. Following the October 2002 meeting in Pyongyang, the United States and the DPRK rapidly ramped up the pressured nature of the situation. The United States announced the end of oil shipments to the DPRK, leading the DPRK to begin removing monitoring devices from its Yongbyon nuclear plant, and then in January 2003, North Korea withdrew from the NPT. During this time, Pyongyang insisted on bilateral negotiations with the United States, whereas the United States insisted on multilateral negotiations.

The posturing continued in February and March 2003, as the United States announced that it would deploy more forces to NEA to deter North Korea from making any rash moves. Pyongyang responded by test-firing a missile into the sea between Korea and Japan on the day of Roh Moo-hyun's inauguration as South Korean president and then intercepting a U.S. spy plane and shadowing it for twenty minutes. The United States followed through on its threat of military deployment by moving twenty-four bombers to Guam to put them within striking distance of North Korea. In mid-March, North Korea test-fired another missile, which commentators viewed as a provocative attempt to catalyze bilateral talks with the United States. The month of March ended with U.S.–ROK war games.

In mid-April, Pyongyang made a surprise announcement of its willingness to hold multilateral talks, if the United States is ready to make a bold switchover in its Korea policy for a settlement of the nuclear issue. As a *via media*, the United States and the DPRK met in Beijing for trilateral talks only ten days after Pyongyang's acceptance of an alternative to bilateral talks. The talks ended a day early, with the United States claiming that North Korea had both admitted the existence of completed nuclear weapons and made a proposal for giving up its nuclear program in exchange for unspecified "major concessions" from the United States. Despite North Korean complaints, the United States did not publicly respond to this offer, and the months of May and June passed without much movement.

At the first round of the six-party talks in Beijing in August 2003, the DPRK offered a "package solution" deal. The DPRK offered to revive the

Agreed Framework – without specifically referring to it – and to include a missile deal in exchange for the establishment of diplomatic relations with the United States and Japan, and the guaranteeing of economic cooperation between the DPRK and Japan and between the DPRK and the ROK. Pyongyang suggested that its dismantling of the nuclear program was contingent on a lessening of U.S. hostility, that a nonaggression treaty was the benchmark of this lessening of hostility, that such a treaty must be of binding legal force, and that action must be taken simultaneously – "word for word, action for action."[110] Kim Yong Il, the Vice Minister of Foreign Affairs and head of the DPRK delegation to the six-party talks, specified that the United States

> should also compensate for the loss of electricity caused by the delayed provision of light water reactors and complete their construction.... According to the order of simultaneous actions, the U.S. should resume the supply of heavy fuel oil, [and] sharply increase the humanitarian food aid.... According to this order, we will allow the refreeze of our nuclear facility and nuclear substance and monitoring and inspection of them from the time the US has concluded a non-aggression treaty with the DPRK and compensated for the loss of electricity. We will settle the missile issue when diplomatic relations are opened between the DPRK and the U.S. and between the DPRK and Japan. And we will dismantle our nuclear facility from the time the LWRs [light-water reactors] are completed.[111]

The North Koreans claimed that China, Russia, and South Korea were open to the package solution, whereas Japan and the United States remained focused on their own individual objectives.

To solve the nuclear standoff by taking account of North Korea's security concerns, the United States did explore the possibility of a multilateral security pact. Secretary of State Colin Powell said in October 2003, "It would be something that would be public, something that would be written, something that I hope would be multilateral."[112] Powell's staff was drafting sample agreements that he hoped would be acceptable to Pyongyang and would ease the impasse over its nuclear weapons programs. In October 2003, President Bush indicated for the first time that the United States would offer a multilateral security guarantee to be signed by Pyongyang's Northeast Asian neighbors and by

[110] See KCNA, "Keynote Speeches Made at Six-way Talks," August 29, 2003. Available at http://www.kcna.co.jp/item/2003/200308/news08/30.htm.

[111] See KCNA, "Keynote Speeches Made at Six-way Talks," August 29, 2003 at http://www.kcna.co.jp/item/2003/200308/news08/30.htm. On compensation for lost electricity, see also Harrison (2004).

[112] Agence France-Presse, "US Seeks Partners for Multilateral Security Pact with North Korea," October 11, 2003.

Washington. Pyongyang responded quickly with a cautiously positive reaction. Through its UN mission, North Korea said, "We are ready to consider Bush's remarks on the 'written assurances of non-aggression' if they are based on the intention to co-exist with the DPRK and aimed to play a positive role in realizing the proposal for a package solution on the principle of simultaneous actions."[113]

In mid-October 2003, the DPRK threatened to demonstrate its nuclear capabilities, and then in early December, Pyongyang presented a list of conditions that it viewed as prerequisites for the demolition of its nuclear program. The United States responded to these conditions with a demand that Pyongyang dismantle its nuclear program as a precursor to negotiations. This demand was an early exposition of the CVID requirement that the United States would unveil at the second round of six-party talks in February 2004.

In the third round of six-party talks, held in June 2004, the United States outlined a six-stage denuclearization process. First, the DPRK would make a unilateral declaration pledging to "dismantle all of its nuclear programs." Second, the parties involved in the talks would provide provisional multilateral security assurances, begin a study of the energy requirements of the DPRK, and begin a discussion of steps necessary to lift remaining economic sanctions and remove the DPRK from the List of State Sponsors of Terrorism. Third, "the parties would then conclude a detailed implementation agreement providing for the supervised disabling, dismantling, and elimination" of all DPRK nuclear programs – that is, both the HEU and the plutonium programs. Fourth, on conclusion of this agreement, "non-U.S. parties would provide heavy fuel oil to the DPRK." Fifth, during a three-month preparatory period, the DPRK would provide a complete listing of all nuclear activities, cease operations of these activities, and "permit the securing of all fissile material and the monitoring of fuel rods." Finally, after the dismantlement is completed, "lasting benefits to the DPRK" would result from the energy survey and the discussions on ending sanctions and the removal of the DPRK from the terrorist list.[114]

This proposal seemed like little more than a reformulation of the CVID mantra. North Korea was required to make the initial concessions without any guarantee of reciprocation from the United States. Whereas the requirements for the DPRK were quite specific, those for the United States were vague and contingent – the United States, for instance, would

[113] KCNA, October 25, 2003. Available at http://www.kcna.co.jp/item/2003/200310/news10/27.htm.

[114] "Dealing with North Korea's Nuclear Programs." Statement by James A. Kelly, Assistant Secretary of State for East Asian and Pacific Affairs, Senate Foreign Relations Committee, July 15, 2004.

not even participate in the new heavy fuel oil shipments.[115] The South Korean proposal from the third round, by way of contrast, gave Pyongyang more time to prepare for denuclearization, guaranteed progress toward normalization in response to dismantlement, and left the possibility of a nuclear solution to the DPRK's energy program – that is a revival of the Agreed Framework – open.

The third round of talks ended as inconclusively as the previous two, and with the U.S. presidential elections being held in November 2004, domestic U.S. politics trumped the holding of a new round of talks. After the reelection of George W. Bush, however, it looked liked new talks would come early in 2005. In January, North Korea said that it "would not stand against the U.S. but respect and treat it as a friend unless the latter slanders the former's system and interferes in its internal affairs."[116] Bush seemed to reciprocate this sentiment when he made only a brief mention of North Korean in his 2005 State of the Union address, saying that the United States was "working closely with the governments in Asia to convince North Korea to abandon its nuclear ambitions."

Caught in diplomatic gridlock, Pyongyang raised the ante of its own brinkmanship diplomacy with the February 10, 2005, statement that it had "manufactured nukes for self-defense to cope with the Bush administration's evermore undisguised policy to isolate and stifle the DPRK," and that it was therefore "compelled to suspend participation in the [Six-Party] talks for an indefinite period."[117] The Western media jumped on the fact that the announcement also contained North Korea's first public declaration that it had nuclear weapons. The February 10 statement generated a flurry of intensive "bi-multilateral" consultations, and China's preventive diplomacy with both Koreas reached the highest levels. As messages were exchanged between President Hu Jintao and Chairman Kim Jong Il, a visit by Hu to Pyongyang was scheduled for late 2005.[118] Meanwhile, there was also an intensification of diplomatic contact between Beijing and Seoul, with South Korea and all other parties looking for Beijing to find a way to reverse the DPRK position on the six-party talks. This softened the rhetorical posturing of the DPRK and the United States, and culminated in the fourth round of six-party talks in July and September 2005.

[115] On the problems of the six-stage plan from the third round of the six-party talks, see Harrison (2004).

[116] Quoted in ABC News Online, "N Korea to Resume Nuclear Talks," January 14, 2005. Available at http://www.abc.net.au/news/newsitems/200501/s1282279.htm.

[117] For an English text of the DPRK Ministry of Foreign Affairs statement of February 10, 2005, see KCNA, February 10, 2005. Available at http://www.kcna.co.jp/index-e.htm.

[118] The invitation was conveyed by DPRK Prime Minister Pak Pong Ju during his March visit to Beijing.

On July 9, 2005, North Korea finally agreed to return for a fourth round of the six-party talks later in the month.[119] The DPRK is showcasing this breakthrough not as a result of Chinese behind-the-scenes pressure but as due to direct bilateral "negotiations" between Assistant Secretary of State Christopher Hill of the United States (who replaced James Kelly as America's top negotiator at the six-party talks) and Kim Kye Gwan of the DPRK.[120] In fact, the first indication of Pyongyang's willingness to return soon to the six-party talks came on June 17, 2005, when Kim Jong Il held rare face-to-face, five-hour talks with South Korea's Unification Minister, Chung Dong Young. No date was set at that time. Tellingly, Kim Kye Gwan conveyed his government's definitive and date-specific decision to return to the six-party talks in the course of a three-hour dinner meeting a few weeks later with Christopher Hill, an event hosted by the Chinese in Beijing on the eve of a scheduled trip to Pyongyang by Tang Jiaxuan (state councilor and a former foreign minister) as part of Chinese efforts to bridge differences between the United States and the DPRK. However, the importance of China's behind-the-scenes warning that Washington would soon introduce a draft sanctions resolution in the UN Security Council – the so-called Plan B, which would corner Beijing in a lose–lose situation, thus diluting the threat of a Chinese veto – cannot be discounted.

To a certain extent, Pyongyang's decision to rejoin the six-party talks can be attributed to Chinese and South Korean mediation diplomacy that was aimed at providing a face-saving exit from the box of U.S.–DPRK mutual creation. The face-saving exit was particularly important in the wake of the Bush administration characterization of Kim as a "tyrant" and Condoleeza Rice's labeling of North Korea as an "outpost of tyranny." China, South Korea, and Russia have been prodding the Bush administration to stop using this kind of language, and to map out detailed economic and security incentives as *quid pro quo* for North Korea's nuclear disarmament. Indeed, the implicit withdrawal or suspension of the rhetoric in

119 Glenn Kessler, "North Koreas Agrees to Rejoin Talks," *Washington Post*, July 10, 2005, p. A01; Choe Sang-Hun, "South Korea Welcomes Return to Disarmament Talks," *International Herald Tribune*, July 10, 2005.

120 See "N. Korea, U.S. Could Spend More Time Alone Together," *Chosun Ilbo*, July 10, 2005. It should be noted in this connection that in the wake of the 1994 U.S.–DPRK Agreed Framework, the DPRK was determined to refute the notion that Beijing's behind-the-scenes diplomacy had anything to do with the Agreed Framework, which was quickly dubbed "the biggest diplomatic victory by the DPRK": "We held the talks independently with the United States on an independent footing, not relying on someone else's sympathy or advice, and the adoption of the DPRK-U.S. Agreed Framework is a fruition of our independent foreign policy, not someone's influence, with the United States finally accepting our proposal." See *Rodong Sinmun [Worker's Daily]* (Pyongyang), December 1, 1994.

the wake of the February 10 statement was important in Pyongyang.[121] The "words for words" and "action for action" approach that North Korea advocated as its negotiating stance and that China insinuated as group consensus in the chairman's statement at the end of the third round of six-party talks in June 2004 provided an exit with voice for Pyongyang and Washington.

In terms of the prospects for the talks themselves, it is a hopeful sign as far as format is concerned that Washington has not openly challenged Pyongyang's assertion that it would definitely return to "bilateral talks within the framework of six-party talks." A more flexible and pragmatic stance on the format is an important factor but not a decisive one. Substantively, however, Washington's refusal to improve the offer on the table from the previous round of talks – or even to combine its minimalist "not now but later down the road" offer with the rich and frontloaded package of incentives offered by Seoul as late as July 9, 2005[122] – probably led Seoul to unveiling in public three days later (July 12) its own proposed "energy-for-nuclear deal" for everyone to see and judge. Faced with this Marshall Plan–like announcement, Secretary of State Rice made a backpedaling response on July 13 that the Bush administration now planned to examine the South Korean proposal for its possible incorporation into the broader offer made at the third round of the six-party talks in June 2004. Why then did the Bush administration agree to sign on the Chinese draft of a Joint Statement despite the vehement opposition to any mention of a peaceful nuclear program during the first five days of the second phase of the fourth round of talks? Here is a list of reasons that fall into the category that the Chinese call "*Huo bu dan xing*" ("misfortunes never come singly"):

(1) There was no viable alternative given the failure of the policy of "tailored containment" in the past five years;
(2) China successfully mobilized "the coalition of the willing" in support of its *qiutong cunyi* Joint Statement, especially on the provision of a peaceful nuclear program (light-water reactor), with three in favor (China, South Korea, and Russia), one opposed (the United States), and one abstaining or split in its position between the two (Japan), creating a $3^1/_2$ and $1^1/_2$ situation (3 to 1, or perhaps 3.5 to 1.5 with Japan on the sidelines or close to the U.S. oppositional stand);

[121] See Joel Brinkley and David E. Sanger, "North Koreans Agree to Resume Nuclear Talks," *New York Times*, July 10, 2005, pp. 1, 11; Glenn Kessler, "Both Sides Bend to Restart N. Korea Talks," *Washington Post*, July 14, 2005, p. A20.

[122] See Joel Brinkley, "Rice Has No Plans to Improve Offer to North Korea in Arms Talks," *New York Times*, July 9, 2005, p. A3.

(3) China boxed the United States into a corner with a "yes or no" choice, forcing it to accept or else be blamed by the world community for the collapse of the critical fourth round of talks and presumably the failure of the six-party process;
(4) The Americans felt they could accept the Chinese draft of a Joint Statement subject to Washington's later backtracking via its selective and self-serving interpretations.

Sensing that the second-term Bush administration was suffering from multiple and multiplying disasters at home and abroad – a deepening quagmire in Iraq, another nuclear standoff with Iran, Hurricane Katrina, and a falling approval rating – Beijing increased pressure on Washington to either sign or take responsibility for a breakdown in the six-party talks. After two days of internal debates, President Bush gave the go-ahead on Sunday evening (September 18) to sign the Chinese-drafted Joint Statement. According to participants in the second session of the fourth round of talks (September 13–19), had President Bush decided to let the deal fall through, China was prepared to blame the United States for missing a chance to bring a diplomatic end to the confrontation.[123]

International relations theory casts doubt on the ability of multilateral international cooperation to solve the U.S.–DPRK nuclear standoff. International cooperation requires recognition of opportunities for the advancement of mutual interests, as well as corresponding policy coordination once these opportunities have been identified and recognized. As the number of actors increases, the likelihood of defection increases and the feasibility of sanctioning defectors diminishes. Furthermore, the costs of transactions and information rise in proportion to the multiplicity and complexity of each player's payoff structure and set of mutual interests, militating against any easy identification and realization of common interests in a given situation.[124] Charles Pritchard, the Bush administration's former top negotiator with North Korea, offered a blunt assessment and sharp critique of the administration's hardline policy toward North Korea, asserting that Pyongyang will not relinquish its nuclear weapons programs without more active *direct* U.S. engagement: "The idea that in a short period of time you can resolve this problem" in talks where diplomats from six countries sit down with twenty-four interpreters and try to make a deal without private consultations is "ludicrous."[125]

[123] Joseph Kahn and David E. Sanger, "U.S.-Korean Deal on Arms Leaves Key Points Open," *New York Times*, September 20, 2005.

[124] For an elaboration of the theoretical and policy implications, see the October 1985 special issue of *World Politics*, 38:1, especially Oye (1985).

[125] Quoted in Sonni Efron, "Ex-Envoy Faults U.S. on N. Korea," *Los Angeles Times*, September 10, 2003 (Internet version); see also Peter Slevin, "Former Envoy Presses North Korea Dialogue," *Washington Post*, September 9, 2003, p. A19.

More to the point, however, Pyongyang has little reason to trust Washington, given the sixty-year history of mutual distrust and hostility. "While in Washington the North Korean nuclear threat has been a major issue for the past decade," as Gavan McCormack reminds us, "in Pyongyang the U.S. nuclear threat has been the issue for the past fifty years. North Korea's uniqueness in the nuclear age lies first of all in the way it has faced and lived under the shadow of nuclear threat for longer than any other nation."[126] With the coming of the hardline Bush administration, Pyongyang has even more reason to distrust Washington, given the way the United States first appropriated North Korean national identity by making it a charter member of the "axis of evil" and then pursued an evil-state strangulation (regime change) strategy, although this strategy has proceeded in fits and starts due in no small measure to America's quagmire in Iraq, the first test case of the Bush Doctrine for the three charter members of the "axis of evil."

U.S.–ROK Alliance Relationship

U.S. relations with South Korea meanwhile seemed fairly consistent for the first decade of the post–Cold War era. The continued North Korean challenge and the continued U.S.–ROK alliance simply meant that there was little change in attitude. However, as South Korea opened to the North over the course of the late 1990s and early twenty-first century under Presidents Kim Dae Jung and Roh Moo-hyun, the ROK approach to Northeast Asian security drifted away from the U.S. approach, creating new tensions between the two allies and shifting the diplomatic scenario in a way that had not been anticipated by pundits and observers in the early 1990s.

The fact that the U.S.–ROK alliance has lasted fifty years is a testimonial to successful alliance management and abiding allied commitment. Alliances form, according to international relations theory, as a means of external balancing.[127] Alongside internal balancing through the aggregation of arms build-up and now defunct overseas territorial aggrandizement, they are one of three means of enhancing power and/or security. An alliance, therefore, is a means, not an end. When alliances dissolve, this is likely the result of changes in a state's identity (which leads to a shift in that state's strategy for power enhancement), in the nature of an external threat, in the perception of allied commitment and credibility, or in national interests and strategic preferences. Alliances are more

[126] McCormack (2004: 150). For a similar analysis of U.S. nuclear hegemony in Korea, see Hayes (1988); J. J. Suh (2006).

[127] For major analyses of alliances, see Liska (1962); Rothstein (1968); Altfeld (1984); Walt (1987, 1997); Snyder (1997).

likely to persist when there is a clear asymmetry of power (such that one state is the dominant state in the alliance), when they are highly institutionalized, or when the allied parties share a sense of common identity or similar political beliefs. Asymmetry of power, however, also raises the threat of either abandonment by the larger power or entrapment by the smaller state. Alliances are particularly vulnerable during times of rapid and turbulent change in global politics; those alliances that survive do so because leaders are willing to reduce uncertainty.[128] Three momentous transformations of our times – the "third wave" of global democratization, the end of the Cold War, and globalization – have profoundly altered both the contexts and conditions under which state and nonstate actors define and seek power enhancement and threat reduction, the primary *raison d'être* of alliances. The question is whether and how a Cold War alliance such as the U.S.–ROK alliance will endure or unravel – and if it endures, how it will rise to the challenges of the post–Cold War and post-9/11 world security order.

In 1953, when the alliance was forged, South Korea was a poor frontline domino state dependent on the United States for its survival and security. South Korea's rapid progress in its own economic and political development over the decades, however, has resulted in greater national confidence and a desire for a more equal and mutually respectful relationship with the United States. The end of the Cold War, accompanied by the triumph of South Korean President Roh Tae Woo's *Nordpolitik*, which led to normalization with Moscow in 1990 and with Beijing in 1992, gave South Korea space for more independence in both its identity and its foreign policy. Rather than continuing a foreign policy shaped by its status as a U.S. dependent, South Korea decided to develop a foreign policy in line with its new national identity as an NIC and an NDC. Evidence of this changed national identity came in 1999 when Seoul decided, largely out of deference to Beijing's sensitivity, not to join in the U.S. plan for TMD.

More generally, the U.S.–ROK alliance transitioned to some extent in the early 1990s from a Cold War military alliance to a security management system. As President Kim Dae Jung said, "U.S. forces stationed on the Korean peninsula and in Japan are decisive to the maintenance of peace and the balance of power not only on the peninsula but also in Northeast Asia."[129] However, there has been great debate about burden sharing between the two governments. The United States argues that the ROK wants to be an equal partner in decision making but is unwilling to make the corresponding financial and political commitments. In

[128] Haftendorn, Keohane, and Wallander (1999).

[129] Kim Dae Jung, "Address at the 54th Commencement Exercises of the Korean Military Academy," March 16, 1998. Available at http://www.bluehouse.go.kr/engpdown/031717485480316–1.html.

other words, the United States accuses the ROK of free-riding. The ROK, in contrast, accuses the United States of sharing the burden of paying for the alliance without sharing the power of the alliance. Such burden sharing without power sharing does not play well in Seoul's increasingly democratic and contentious domestic politics.

Until the early 1970s, the United States covered all costs for maintenance of the security presence in Korea. In the late 1970s, when the United States was contemplating troop withdrawal, it was able to convince Seoul to contribute to the support of U.S. forces in the ROK. From the early 1980s, the ROK committed to share maintenance costs for joint facilities, and by the early 1990s, increased its contribution to one-third of total base costs. In 1990, the ROK paid $330 million to support U.S. forces in Korea, and by 2002, the ROK was paying $490 million, an increase of $90 million from the previous year. In 2004, this number had increased to $623 million, and the United States requested a 9 percent increase for 2005.[130] South Korea's contributions as a percentage of its GDP and defense expenditure is said to exceed those of Germany and Japan.[131] According to 2000 data South Korea's share of "defense burden sharing" at 42 percent is higher than that of Germany (21 percent) but lower than that of Japan (79 percent).[132]

The special relationship between the United States and the ROK has been most threatened by a lack of agreement on the nature of the North Korean threat and on an appropriate conflict management approach. A vigorous policy debate rages in Washington and Seoul – and also in Tokyo – over how to assess the intents and capabilities of the DPRK. All-out invasion no longer appears to be the major threat from the north side of the DMZ, but rather the United States and the ROK must work out how to deal with limited acts of belligerence by the DPRK that are aimed at coercive bargaining. Although such pinpricks certainly raise concerns about escalation, they do not warrant all-out counterattack, and Pyongyang has played this high-stakes game adeptly so far. Under Kim Dae Jung, South Korea switched to the Sunshine Policy of opening up to the North, and Roh Moo-hyun has continued this opening more vigorously with his Policy of Peace and Prosperity. With the inter-Korean summit in June 2000, Kim Dae Jung called for the "dismantling of the Cold War structure" on the Korean peninsula, and although he also called for a continued U.S. presence on the Korean peninsula, some interpreted this phrase as a euphemism for a diminished role for the U.S.–ROK alliance. However, in 2001, the United States announced in the Quadrennial Defense Review its shift from a "threat-based" to a "capabilities-based"

[130] Gross (2004: 9). [131] J. Y. Chung (2003: 41).
[132] Ministry of National Defense (2003: 71).

model of assessing potential adversaries. Although in terms of conventional military, economic, domestic political, and allied capabilities the DPRK has become less of a threat, in other dimensions it is now judged by the United States as more of a threat. The continued pursuit and development of WMD, the use of brinkmanship negotiating tactics, and the threat of North Korean instability together increase the perception of a North Korean threat in Washington. Seoul, however, does not share this assessment.

To an unprecedented extent, the North Korea policies of Washington and Seoul have become out of sync with each other. The Bush administration's abandonment of Clinton-era policies led to a remarkable role reversal in the U.S.–ROK alliance relationship. More to the point, the Bush administration's approach can be said to have aided and abetted hardliners in Pyongyang, reviving Pyongyang's brinkmanship strategy during the 1993–94 nuclear crisis. Faced with such a threat, along with the U.S. decision to stop sending monthly heavy fuel supplies as stipulated by the Agreed Framework, Pyongyang's alleged revival of its nuclear program can hardly be surprising. From the perspective of Pyongyang's siege mentality, going nuclear is an essential move in its survival strategy. Coming as this did when South Korea was pursuing rapprochement with the DPRK, Bush administration policies came to be perceived as an obstacle to North–South reconciliation. These perceptions contributed in part to the failure of the March 2001 summit meeting between Bush and Kim Dae Jung.

The Bush administration then offended Kim's successor, Roh Moohyun, by welcoming his opponent in the 2002 presidential elections, Grand National Party (GNP) leader Lee Hoi-chang, to Washington and allowing him to see senior officials including Vice President Dick Cheney.[133] In September 2003, ROK Foreign Minister Yoon Young Kwan had a heated meeting with U.S. Secretary of State Colin Powel, demanding that the United States respond to the DPRK's call for a nonaggression pact or peace treaty and a plan for gradual improvements in economic relations in return for dismantling nuclear facilities. Yoon is said to have claimed that the ROK would not send any troops to aid the U.S. operation in Iraq unless the United States ceded ground on North Korea. Powell, according to several officials familiar with the exchange, curtly told him, "That is not how allies deal with each other."[134] The foreign minister was later forced to resign because of his inability or unwillingness to rein in the "pro-American" faction in the Ministry of Foreign Affairs and Trade.

133 See Snyder (2004). Being perceived as pro-American, however, likely hurt Lee's chances in the election.

134 David Sanger, "Intelligence Puzzle: North Korean Bombs," *New York Times*, October 14, 2003, p. A9.

Before his election, Roh Moo-hyun sent shockwaves through the U.S.–ROK alliance with streaks of populist rhetoric during the presidential campaign. He toned down his pronouncements after entering the presidential Blue House, but the United States remains wary, and the status of U.S. forces in Korea is likely to remain a sensitive issue for the remainder of Roh's presidency until 2008. As of 2004, however, Roh and the U.S. commanders in Korea had successfully overseen the relocation of U.S. bases to the south of Seoul and also the transfer of U.S. troops out of Korea to Iraq, not to mention Seoul's dispatch of some 3,000 South Korean troops to Iraq.

Even when the governments have been able to solve their tensions and cooperate, South Korean civil society, in recent years, has maintained a particular vigilance against the U.S. presence in South Korea. As part of popular grassroots pressures to minimize the negative externalities of the U.S. base presence, in 2002, more than 100 South Korean civic organizations joined together in a massive protest to voice their criticism of ROK–U.S. relations as symbolized and structured by the "unequal" Status of Forces Agreement (SOFA). They also sought to protest the behavior of U.S. troops stationed in Korea. Contention notably coalesced around the acquittal of two U.S. soldiers accused of killing two Korean teenagers in a June 2002 traffic accident. The object of these protests was not necessarily to end the alliance or provoke a withdrawal of U.S. forces but rather to seek compensation and a means of redressing grievances.

Katharine Moon refers to the "big tent" under which disparate anti-American groups and interests have gathered to share information, coordinate political action, and mobilize resources. Under this big tent, the anti-American movement includes not only left-leaning radical students, religious activists, the militant Korean Confederation of Trade Unions (KCTU), and the National Campaign for the Eradication of Crime by U.S. troops in Korea, but also law professionals, environmentalists, academics, peace activists, the conservative Federation of Korean Trade Unions (FKTU), leaders of mainstream NGOs, common villagers, local government officials, and even some National Assembly lawmakers. The overall aim has been to influence government policies – both South Korean and U.S. – and to address everyday issues touching common people's lives, including environmental safety, land usage, and violence against women. By providing an antagonist against which to unify, networks through which to build social capital, and entrance to the normally off-limits arena of foreign and security policy, the anti-American movement, according to Moon, has helped consolidate democracy in South Korea over the past decade.[135]

[135] See K. Moon (2003).

Despite the magnitude of the 2002 protests, South Korea is far from unified in its critique of the U.S.–ROK alliance. Although a Gallup poll in South Korea found that 76 percent of those in their twenties had negative attitudes toward the United States, only 26 percent of those older than fifty years did. Almost one out of every two South Koreans in their twenties favored the withdrawal of U.S. troops from the ROK, whereas the same opinion was held by only one out of ten South Koreans in their fifties. Similarly, the older generations had more negative opinions of North Korea than did the younger South Koreans.[136] A January 2004 poll found that 39 percent of South Koreans believed the United States to be the greatest threat to ROK security, whereas only 33 percent so labeled the DPRK.[137] An October 2004 *JoongAng Ilbo* poll – part of a global ten-country poll before the U.S. election – found that much of the dissatisfaction in the ROK with regard to the United States was directed at President George W. Bush. Whereas 65 percent of the 1,028 Koreans polled said they felt favorable toward Americans in general and 67 percent said it was important for the United States to play a leadership role on the world stage, 72 percent of the respondents felt unfavorable toward Bush. Among the ten countries participating in the survey, national antipathy for Bush was greater only in France and Spain than in Korea, and Koreans were proportionately the population in the survey most opposed to the Iraq war.[138] Among younger South Koreans, Bush is perceived as a gunslinger whose bellicose instincts are a greater danger to them than is Kim Jong Il's lust for nuclear arms.[139] According to Kim Young-hie, the *JoongAng Ilbo*'s editor-at-large, "Less a benevolent friend, the United States is seen as a hegemonic power that takes unilateral military actions without regard to the consequences. But the poll revealed that Koreans make a critical distinction between the state and the people."[140] Nonetheless, these widespread anti-American attitudes seem hardly conducive to alliance maintenance.

Regardless of civil society pressures, South Korea is ultimately constrained in the degree to which it can pursue an exit from the U.S.–ROK alliance. Without the security guarantee of the United States, the ROK would have to resort to internal balancing against the North Korean threat, and this almost certainly would require the development of nuclear weapons. Therefore, it remains more cost effective for Seoul to remain under the U.S. nuclear umbrella, even given the associated disadvantages. In addition, it is important to remember that South Korea and the United States remain active and vital economic partners, especially

136 See Cha (2003); S. J. Lee (2004).

137 Hong Yong-lim, "U.S. More Dangerous than NK? Most Seem to Think So," *Chosun Ilbo*, January 12, 2004.

138 *JoongAng Ilbo*, October 14, 2004.

139 Menon (2003: 7).

140 Kim Young-hie, "Why Koreans Favor Mr. Kerry," *JoongAng Ilbo*, October 14, 2004.

in the sectors that are important to Korea's growth and development as a mature industrialized economy.

One possible solution to the tensions between the United States and South Korea over the alliance is the regionalization of the alliance. A broadening of security commitments in East Asia so that the various burdens are shared by multiple countries might make for reduced bilateral tensions between the United States and South Korea. Regionalization would require a broadening of the goals of the alliance, however, and it quickly becomes unclear why the U.S.–ROK alliance would serve as a point of departure for a regional alliance. The public, for instance, increasingly fails to see the United States as the appropriate regional partner for South Korea, viewing China as Korea's "closest partner for the year 2006."[141] China's continued development into the regional economic focal point has intensified this belief. Because China's labor force has become so central for manufacturers of diverse national origins, Korea and other countries are willing to elevate economic prosperity above knee-jerk security concerns. This relationship with China amounts to a new, nonalliance-based organizational structure for regional stability and prosperity and therefore implicitly challenges American alliances as the critical guarantor of regional stability.

Economic and Functional Issues

U.S.–ROK Economic Relations

Over a period of twenty years, South Korea has become increasingly liberalized, reducing the protection of its domestic market. Its current tariff levels are comparable to those of other Organization for Economic Cooperation and Development (OECD) countries, and it has eliminated quantitative import restrictions on nearly all goods except rice and other agricultural goods. South Korea exports more than 40 percent of domestic production, making it the world's second largest exporter behind Japan.

Although the economic "miracle" that took place in South Korea was a homegrown phenomenon, the role of the United States in supporting the South Korean economy during the 1950s and 1960s cannot be undervalued. From 1946 to 1976, the United States provided $12.6 billion in economic and military aid to Korea, although when the costs of the U.S. military deployment are factored in, the total is closer to $1 billion per year. In the 1950s, South Korea was so dependent on American aid that many development agencies considered Korea to be a nightmare, an albatross, and a bottomless pit for resources. Korea used U.S. aid

[141] See J. H. Chung (2001: 784).

Table 5.2. U.S. Trade with North and South Korea, 1990–2004

Year	Exports to North Korea	Imports from North Korea	Total North Korean–U.S. Trade (Balance)	Change in North Korean–U.S. Trade	Exports to South Korea	Imports from South Korea	Total South Korean–U.S. Trade (Balance)	Change in South Korean–U.S. Trade
1990	0.03	0.0	0.03 (0.03)	N/A	16,946	19,446	36,392 (−2,500)	N/A
1991	0.1	0.1	0.2 (0.1)	+567%	18,890	18,560	37,450 (330)	+3%
1992	0.1	0.0	0.1 (0.1)	−50%	18,290	18,090	36,380 (200)	−3%
1993	2.0	0.0	2.0 (2.0)	+1900%	17,930	18,140	36,070 (−210)	−1%
1994	0.2	0.0	0.2 (0.2)	−90%	21,580	20,550	42,130 (1,030)	+17%
1995	11.6	0.0	11.6 (11.6)	+5700%	30,400	24,130	54,530 (6,270)	+29%
1996	0.5	0.0	0.5 (0.5)	−96%	33,305	21,670	54,975 (11,635)	+1%
1997	2.5	0.0	2.5 (2.5)	+400%	30,122	21,625	51,747 (8,497)	−6%
1998	4.4	0.0	4.4 (4.4)	+76%	20,403	22,805	43,208 (−2,402)	−17%
1999	11.3	0.0	11.3 (11.3)	+157%	24,922	29,475	54,397 (−4,553)	+26%
2000	2.7	0.1	2.8 (2.6)	−75%	29,242	37,611	66,853 (−8,369)	+23%
2001	0.5	0.0	0.5 (0.5)	−82%	22,376	31,211	53,587 (−8,835)	−20%
2002	25.1	0.1	25.2 (25.0)	+4940%	23,009	32,780	55,789 (−9,771)	+4%
2003	8.0	0.0	8.0 (8.0)	−68%	24,814	34,219	59,033 (−9,405)	+6%
2004	23.8	1.5	25.3 (22.3)	+218%	28,783	42,849	71,632 (−14,066)	+21%

Units: US$1 million.

Source: International Monetary Fund (1992: 247; 1993: 247; 1994: 265; 1995: 269; 1996: 275; 1997: 347; 1998: 280); MOFAT (1998: 396, 401; 1999: 481, 486; 2001: 497). Available at www.mofat.go.kr; KOTRA at www.kotra.or.kr; U.S. Department of Commerce; International Trade Administration at www.ita.doc.gov.

to finance commodity imports and thereby dampen inflationary pressure.[142] Despite repeated efforts by Washington to make aid more conditional, until the mid-1960s the majority of U.S. aid was given in grants rather than loans.[143]

Even though Seoul no longer depends on U.S. aid for its livelihood, the United States still has enormous economic importance to the ROK. As indicated in Table 5.2, trade between the two countries peaked at $67 billion in 2000. In 2003, the figure was $61 billion, and the United States slipped for the first time from being the largest export destination for Korean goods, giving way to China, which then became South Korea's largest overall trading partner in 2004. Still, South Korea's trade with the United States increased by 21 percent in 2004 over the previous year, from $59 billion in 2003 to an all-time high of $71.6 billion in 2004 – only $7.7 billion less than China's but $3.8 more than Japan's. Since the mid-1990s, South Korea has been the sixth or seventh largest trading partner of the United States in terms of total goods exchanged and is particularly important for U.S. agricultural exports. Even in 1998, following the AFC, the ROK's rank fell only to ninth. More specifically, South Korea is a market for U.S. agricultural products; it has consistently been the fourth largest agricultural market for the United States. The United States has usually run a trade deficit with South Korea, although it ran some trade surpluses in the mid-1990s just before and after the AFC. As Table 5.2 and Figure 5.1 show, since 1999, the average annual trade deficit has been around $9.17 billion.

The trade deficit is in some ways surprising, considering that the ROK consumes imported manufactures at a rate higher than the United States and three times the rate of Japan. In addition, the United States closely monitors Korean imports and is not afraid to launch antidumping cases against South Korea. Between 1980 and 2000, the United States averaged forty-two total antidumping actions per year against all trading partners. Currently, the ROK is subject to a remarkable fifteen U.S. antidumping orders; the International Monetary Fund (IMF) agreement with the ROK in the wake of the AFC forced Seoul to remove some of the offensive barriers to free trade. However, the Korean motor vehicle sector – the fourth largest in the world if Germany and France are counted as contributors to European Union production – accounts for nearly six percent of U.S. car sales. South Korea also exported significant amounts of steel to the United States following the AFC. In 2000, the Byrd Amendment to the annual agriculture bill redistributed antidumping duties to the steel industry and was therefore brought under suit in the WTO as an unfair trade practice. In 2001, the Bush administration tried to put tariffs in

[142] J. E. Woo (1991: 45–48). [143] J. E. Woo (1991: 79).

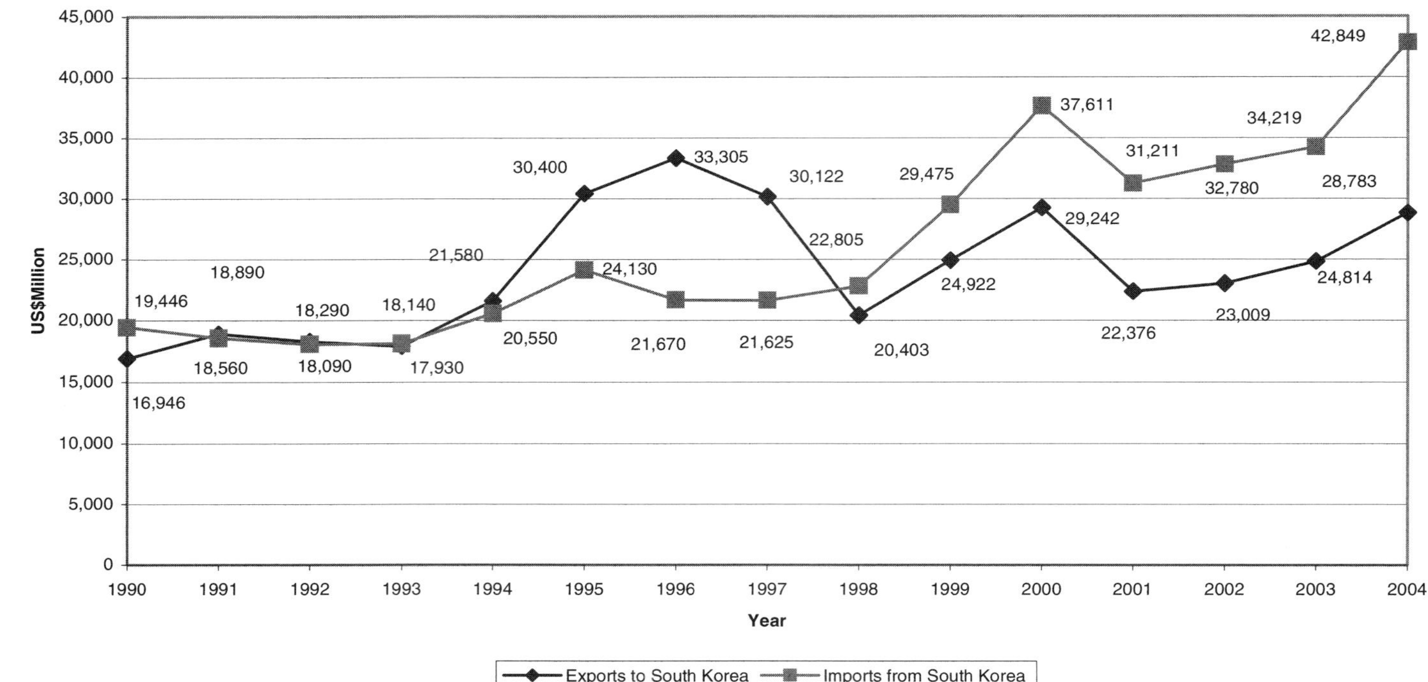

Figure 5.1. U.S. trade with South Korea, 1990–2004.
Source: International Monetary Fund (1992: 247; 1993: 247; 1994: 265; 1995: 269; 1996: 275; 1997: 347; 1998: 280); MOFAT (1998: 396,401; 1999: 481, 4862001: 497). Available at www.mofat.go.kr/ and KOTRA at www.kotra.or.kr.

place on steel imports to catalyze international negotiations over cutting world capacity; the WTO ruled against these tariffs, and the Bush administration, under threat of European Union (EU) retaliation, withdrew them at the end of 2003.

On the other side of the fence, the Clinton administration launched multiple antidumping actions against Korean steel companies in the late 1990s. Similarly, the United States and the European Union accused the ROK of propping up a semiconductor manufacturer to the detriment of U.S. and German firms, leading to a 2003 countervailing duty in the United States against chips from Hynix, the South Korean company. Because of Seoul's targeting of its telecommunications industry for growth, in April 2004 the U.S. Trade Representative named South Korea as a "key country of concern" in its annual report assessing the compliance of U.S. trading partners with international telecommunication agreements. U.S. officials also complain about discrimination against foreign competition in the automotive sector and protectionism in the agricultural sector. For example, only beginning in 1999 could Japan export cars to Korea, while Seoul controls the purchase, distribution, and end use of all imported rice under a WTO agreement that expired in 2005. Intellectual property rights also have been a cause of concern for the United States. In January 2004, Korea was elevated to the U.S. "priority watch list" regarding trade-related intellectual property rights (TRIPs), in part because of Seoul's alleged reluctance to prevent the growth of online music piracy and the continued piracy of U.S. motion pictures.[144]

The importance of the United States to South Korea's international economic relations might be said to be decreasing, if anything. In the late 1980s, the ROK was sending 40 percent of its manufacturing exports to the United States. This figure dropped to less than 20 percent by 2002, as South Korea increasingly exported to China and as the North American Free Trade Agreement (NAFTA) increased U.S.–Mexican trade at the expense of U.S. trade with the ROK. In 2003, China surpassed the United States as the primary destination of South Korean exports. During the early 1980s and late 1990s, the United States and Japan competed to be the number one exporter to Korea, but the trend for 2000 through 2003 shows Japan taking a clear lead as the key supplier of South Korea. Because much of the U.S.–ROK trade is intrafirm trade, this also means that the trade deficit is not so contentious as it once might have been, and the United States has shifted its gaze to concentrate on China as its crucial trade competitor.

The rise of China in NEA has meant increasing South Korean interest in some form of regional trade bloc, something that could adversely impact

[144] On ROK trade barriers, see Manyin (2004) and Noland (2004a).

Table 5.3. U.S.–South Korean FDI Relations, 1990–2004

Year	Amount of South Korean FDI into the United States.	Amount of South Korean FDI into the United States (Percent Change)	Amount of U.S. FDI into South Korea	Amount of U.S. FDI into South Korea (Percent Change)
1990	410	N/A	317	N/A
1991	450	+10%	297	−6%
1992	380	−16%	379	+27%
1993	416	+9%	341	−10%
1994	717	+72%	311	−9%
1995	1,402	+96%	645	+107%
1996	1,178	−16%	876	+36%
1997	1,195	+1%	3,190	+264%
1998	1,220	+2%	2,974	−7%
1999	1,810	+48%	3,739	+26%
2000	1,303	−28%	2,922	−22%
2001	1,837	+41%	3,889	+33%
2002	1,405	−24%	4,500	+16%
2003	730	−48%	1,200	−73%
2004	1,420	+95%	4,730	+294%

Units: US$1 million.
Source: Keum (1996: 581); MOFAT (1998: 406–07; 1999: 491, 493; 2001: 503, 505; 2002: 489, 491; 2003: 498–99); U.S. Embassy in Seoul available at http://seoul.usembassy.gov/wwwhe753.html; Export-Import Bank of Korea available at http://www.koreaexim.go.kr/kr/file/publication/200502_1.pdf.

U.S. interests. Japanese–Korean, Japanese–Korean–Chinese and ASEAN-Plus-Three[145] free trade areas have all been discussed, although little progress has been made on any of the three. Roh Moo-hyun has even discussed including North Korea in such a regional trade agreement as a means of enmeshing the DPRK in the global economy.

In the late 1990s, as shown in Table 5.3, an increasing amount of U.S. FDI went to South Korea. The reforms suggested by the IMF in the wake of the AFC included a liberalization of investment laws in the ROK. Until the late 1990s, South Korean prohibitions on FDI were akin to India's legendary limitations on foreign majority ownership. Whereas previously no foreign individual could own more than 5 percent of any company's outstanding shares, and foreign ownership overall in a Korean-headquartered company had to be less than 20 percent, after the crisis, in December 1997, these rules were relaxed such that the levels were 50 and 55 percent, respectively. This led to a massive uptick in FDI from the

[145] Association of South East Nations (ASEAN) plus China, Japan, and South Korea.

United States after the AFC, but this was a one-time event, and levels of FDI flows began to decline after 2001. Nonetheless, the United States remains the single largest investor in South Korea in terms of FDI stocks, although European investment flows have surpassed U.S. flows several times. Japan and China trail far behind both the United States and Europe in terms of inward FDI in South Korea. Overall, FDI to the ROK has fallen, and in 2002, the ROK ranked twenty-third out of thirty OECD countries in FDI inflows, although this rank appears to have improved to eighteenth in 2003, placing South Korea more in the middle of the pack.

Despite the relaxation on ownership rules, the ROK remains intimidating to investors from the United States and elsewhere. The most widely cited problem with investing in Korea, according to both firm-level surveys and complaints filed with the South Korean government, is labor market issues. In addition, South Korea is critiqued for not being transparent when it comes to accounting. In the Pricewaterhouse Coopers Opacity Index for 2001, South Korea ranked thirty-first out of thirty-five countries, making it more opaque than all but China, Indonesia, Russia, and Turkey. In addition, the ROK maintains some tax and regulatory controls that make it difficult for firms to return revenues to a foreign headquarters. Nonetheless, the ROK's rank in the annual A.T. Kearney FDI Confidence Index has continued to rise – from 21 in 2002 to 18 in 2003 – and its barriers have continued to fall, especially since the creation of the WTO. If South Korea could improve its labor market problems, increase its transparency, and relax some remaining restrictions on capital flows, it would likely increase its inward levels of FDI even more.[146]

The United States and the ROK worked for a number of years to achieve a bilateral investment treaty that would help increase FDI flows, but negotiations stopped in 1999. The major stumbling block to such a treaty is Korea's "screen quotas," which require that theaters fill 40 percent of their screen time with Korean movies. The United States – which also objects to such screen quotas in Canada and France – has made loosening and eventual elimination of the quotas preconditions for signing an investment treaty. As Figure 5.2 indicates, however, U.S. FDI into Korea has continued to grow despite the lack of a treaty. Although some in Congress have called for a bilateral free trade agreement between the two countries, those negotiations have never gotten off the ground. Although Korea would benefit relatively more in terms of GDP growth than the United States from such an agreement, both countries would reap positive benefits.[147] In 2004, the ROK established – with Chile – its first preferential trade agreement, and it is currently in negotiation with Japan and Singapore.

[146] Noland (2004a: 94–95). [147] Manyin (2004: 18–19).

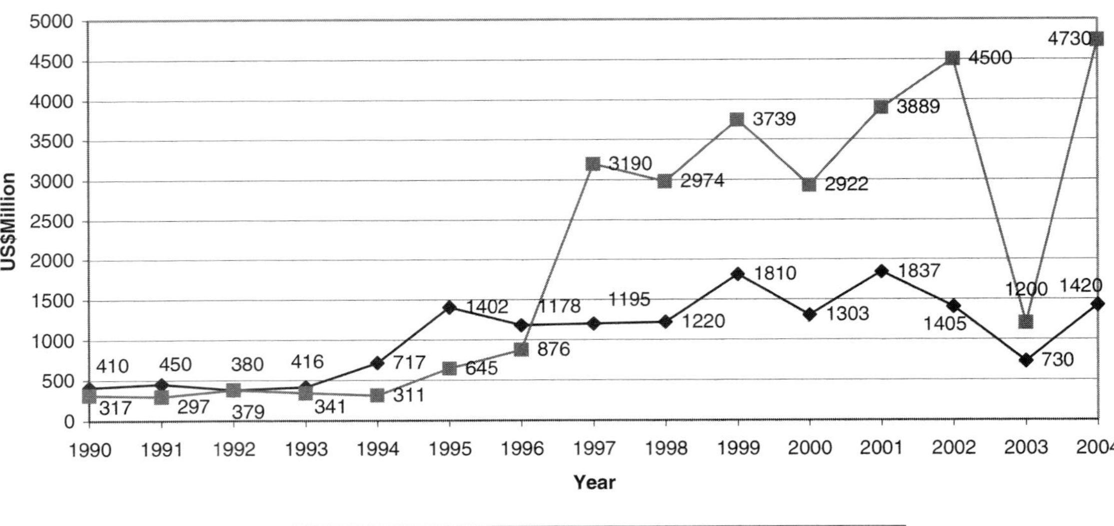

Figure 5.2. Amount of U.S.–South Korean FDI, 1990–2004.
Source: Keum (1996: 581); MOFAT (1998: 406–07; 1999: 491, 493; 2001: 503, 505; 2002: 489, 491; 2003: 498–99); U.S. Embassy in Seoul available at http://seoul.usembassy.gov/wwwhe753.html; Export-Import Bank of Korea available at http://www.koreaexim.go.kr/kr/file/publication/200502_1.pdf.

The risk of a slipping economic relationship between the United States and the ROK is in many ways a political risk. As South Korea is growing closer to China and Japan in its economic relations, there is also an increasing similarity of political opinion among the three when it comes to matters involving North Korea. Therefore, the decoupling of U.S. and South Korean economic interests might help facilitate the widening strategic differences between the two allies. Ultimately, though, U.S.–ROK economic relations are closer today than they were two decades ago. With increasing intraindustry trade, increasing services trade, expanding intercorporate penetration, and growing FDI, the relationship is evolving toward something more like the relationships that the United States maintains with most other rich OECD countries: bilateral interdependence is expanding. Given the ROK's additional trading partners, the relationship is less contentious and more mature.[148]

U.S.–ROK Sociocultural Interaction

The evolving relations between the United States and the ROK need to be seen in terms of a changing domestic culture in South Korea. Since the mid-1980s, a series of events has both reflected and effected a profound sociocultural transformation: the democratic revolution of the 1980s, the end of the Cold War, the advent of globalization and the information revolution, and the electoral victories of the progressive and populist candidates Kim Dae Jung and Roh Moo-hyun in December 1997 and December 2002, respectively. Since the end of the Cold War, South Korea has sought to enact a new national identity, freeing itself from the status of a frontline domino state dependent on the United States.

In the 1990s, over the course of consolidating democracy in South Korea, public perception shifted from seeing the United States as a liberator, protector, or benefactor to seeing South Korea as a geopolitical pawn in *Pax Americana.*[149] The end of the Cold War and South Korea's developing ties with Russia and China permitted South Koreans to express their deepening antagonism toward the United States more freely. Young Koreans involved in the student movement were more willing to speak their concerns regarding alliance burden sharing and the possibilities for peaceful relations with the DPRK.

[148] Noland (2004a: 100).

[149] The first surge of anti-Americanism had come in the early 1980s after the brutal suppression of the uprising in Kwangju. The United States was seen as complicit and was blamed for supporting the authoritarian South Korean regime. However, this sentiment had largely subsided by the time of democratic transition and consolidation in the late 1980s and early 1990s. See Shorrock (1986).

In addition, the United States in the early twenty-first century has done its part to antagonize South Korean citizens. When Bush labeled North Korea a member of the "axis of evil," South Koreans took great offense. The "evil" epithet was compounded by anti-American sentiments fueled by a Korean speed skater being stripped of his gold medal at the 2002 Winter Olympics for allegedly blocking a U.S. skater in the final lap of a race. In mid-February 2002, only a few weeks after the infamous "axis of evil" speech, the *New York Times* reported that even before Bush departed for a trip to Asia, the predominantly conservative South Korean press "was filled with denunciations of his inclusion of North Korea as part of the 'axis of evil,' protesting that Mr. Bush was undercutting years of diplomacy aimed at luring the Stalinist North out of its frightfully armed shell with economic incentives."[150] A 2002 poll indicated that 62 percent of South Koreans considered the "axis of evil" comment as "an excessive statement to escalate tensions in the Korean peninsula," whereas only 31 percent regarded it as "a proper statement to indicate the North Korean threat."[151]

In June 2002, two teenage girls on their way home from school were crushed by a U.S. armored vehicle on a narrow country road south of Seoul. The two soldiers in the vehicle were subsequently acquitted by a U.S. military court of all charges, including charges of negligent homicide and/or involuntary manslaughter. Nationwide protests broke out in response. Three days before the 2002 presidential election, on the night of December 14, more than 300,000 Koreans, holding votive candles and singing songs, rallied at no less than fifty-seven locations throughout the country, including at Seoul City Hall Plaza. They announced "the day of the restoration of national sovereignty," demanding a fair and equal partnership between Korea and the United States.[152]

Roh Moo-hyun's victory in the December 2002 election was due in part to his ability to capitalize on anti-U.S. sentiment and in part due to his innovative campaign. Online grassroots campaigning by young Korean "netizens" bypassed traditional conservative print media (e.g. *Chosun Ilbo, JoongAng Ilbo, Tong-A Ilbo*) to create websites that turned Roh into an Internet celebrity and organized voter registration campaigns. On election day when early returns showed Roh trailing, the wired generation launched a barrage of mobile phone and computer instant messaging to turn out voters.[153] Roh's victory, then, was linked directly to the changing sociocultural landscape in South Korea.

[150] David E. Sanger, "Allies Hear Sour Notes in 'Axis of Evil' Chorus," *New York Times*, February 17, 2002. See also Clay Chandler, "Koreans Voice Anti-American Sentiments," *Washington Post*, February 21, 2002.

[151] Larson and Levin (2004). [152] S. J. Han (2004: 164). [153] Lewis (2004: 194).

Can this truly be described as anti-Americanism? The answer is mostly no. As the Pew Global Attitude Project surveys have shown, anti-American sentiments have become a widespread and universal phenomenon under President George W. Bush's watch (Table 5.4). So-called anti-Americanism is really an expression of distaste for U.S. policies rather than a uniform opposition to Americans or the United States.[154] That said, however, opposition to U.S. policies or incidents would inevitably have some collateral damage to the image of the United States as a country or of its people.

In fact, after 60 years of alliance and interaction, there is a very close sociocultural link between South Korea and the United States. As Table 5.5 and Figure 5.3 indicate, around 700,000 South Koreans visit the United States each year. The number of Americans visiting South Korea has steadily increased since the early 1990s, and today, more than half a million people from the United States make the trip to Korea each year. The conventional wisdom is that South Korea has more Koreans holding American PhDs per capita than any non-U.S. country. These America-educated elites occupy leadership positions in higher education, government, the foreign service, religion, and sciences and arts. Virtually all South Korean ambassadors to the United States have received their PhDs from America's leading universities (e.g., Kim Kyong Won, Lee Hong Koo, Yang Sung Chul, Han Sung Joo, Hong Seok-hyun). The impact of their role and influence in the shaping of Korea's U.S. policy cannot be underestimated.

With English touted as the *lingua franca* of globalization and the passport to success, we see many anxious, well-endowed parents sending their young children to American preparatory schools or taking a wide range of short-cut options from the absurd (e.g., forcing tongue surgery to enable their children to speak without an accent) to the practical (e.g., sending their children to newly sprouting "English Villages" with intensified and simulated immersion, modeled after the famous Middlebury Foreign Language Summer School). The government has been supportive of this trend for young Koreans to study English.

Finally, the United States and South Korea are linked by the Korean diaspora. As indicated in Table 5.6, in 2003, the United States replaced China as the home to the largest number of overseas ethnic Koreans. An overwhelming majority of these immigrants to the United States are recent; the flow increased markedly after 1965 when Congress abolished the national origin quota system. However, because of the population's small size (less than 1 percent of the U.S. population) and lack of significant voting power, the political influence of these Koreans in the United

[154] See Cumings (2004).

Table 5.4. South Korean Attitudes Toward the United States, 2000–04 (percentage)

Date	Questions	Answers
10/25–11/18/2000 (*Tong-A Ilbo*)	Q-1: Do you like or dislike, or neither like nor dislike the United States?	1. Like (30.7) 2. Dislike (18.7) 3. Neither like nor dislike (50.6) 4. Do not know/No response
	Q-2: By which country do you feel most militarily threatened? Please select one country.	North Korea (53.7); Japan (20.7); United States (12.4); China (7.7); Russia (4.0)
	Q-3: Which country do you think will become the most influential in Asia in 10 years? Please select one country, regardless of whether it is an Asian country.	China (52.6); Japan (23.3); ROK (10.7); United States (8.1); Russia (2.1)
Late 2002 (Pew Research Center)	Q-1: How do you view United States?	Favorably (53); Unfavorably (44); No response (3)
	Q-2: What is the greatest danger to the world?	AIDs (24); Religious & Ethnic Hatred (28); Nuclear Weapons (30); Rich/Poor Gap (43); Pollution/Environment (73)
	Q-3: Do you favor or oppose U.S.-led war on terrorism?	Yes/Favor (24); No/Oppose (72)
01/05/2004 (Research & Research)	Q-1: What country do you consider as the biggest threat country to Korean security?	United States (39); North Korea (33); China (12); Japan (8)
October 2004 (*JoongAng Ilbo*)	Q-1: Do you have favorable view of Americans?	Favorable (65)
	Q-2: Do you have favorable or unfavorable view of President Bush?	Unfavorable (72)
	Q-3: Do you support George W. Bush or John Kerry as next president of the United States?	Support Bush (18); Support Kerry (68)
	Q-4: Was the United States right or wrong to invade Iraq?	Wrong to invade Iraq (85)

Source: "Multi-National Citizens' Poll on Current States Surrounding Korean Peninsula," *Tong-A Ilbo* (Seoul), December 4, 2000; *What the World Thinks in 2002* (Washington, DC: The Pew Research Center for the People & The Press, December 4, 2002); *Chosun Ilbo*, January 12, 2004; and *JoongAng Ilbo*, October 14, 2004.

Table 5.5. U.S.–ROK Exchange of Visitors, 1993–2004

Year	South Korean Visitors to United States	Percent Change	U.S. Visitors to South Korea	Percent Change	Total	Percent Change
1993	420,177	N/A	325,366	N/A	745,543	N/A
1994	576,741	+37%	332,428	+2%	909,169	+22%
1995	657,804	+14%	358,872	+8%	1,016,676	+12%
1996	839,573	+28%	399,300	+11%	1,238,873	+22%
1997	806,264	−4%	424,258	+6%	1,230,522	−1%
1998	425,330	−47%	405,735	−4%	831,065	−32%
1999	571,332	+34%	396,286	−2%	967,618	+16%
2000	719,227	+26%	458,617	+16%	1,177,844	+22%
2001	670,456	−7%	426,817	−7%	1,097,273	−7%
2002	692,407	+3%	459,362	+8%	1,151,769	+5%
2003	679,196	−2%	421,709	−8%	1,100,905	−4%
2004	700,000	+3%	570,000	+35%	1,270,000	+15%

Unit: Individuals.
Source: Korea National Tourism Organization. Available at http://www.knto.or.kr.

States is rather limited at the national level with one exception – Korean churches proved pivotal in pushing through the 2004 North Korean Human Rights Act.

U.S.–DPRK Economic Relations

Following North Korea's invasion of the South in June 1950, the United States imposed a nearly complete economic embargo on the DPRK. During the next four decades, the scope and specificity of U.S. sanctions steadily expanded, as Table 5.7 indicates. Article II of the U.S.–DPRK Agreed Framework of 1994 stated, "Within three months of the day of this Document, both sides will reduce barriers to trade and investment, including restrictions on telecommunications services, and financial transactions." In March 1995, the U.S. Department of Commerce approved the sale of 55,000 tons of corn to North Korea by a U.S. grain dealer, opening the door to U.S. exports to the DPRK. In the mid-1990s, Washington approved a number of transactions on a case-by-case basis, including telecommunications link-ups, tourist excursions, airline overflight payments, purchases of North Korean magnesite, and a grain-for-zinc barter deal.[155] Finally, in September 1999, almost 50 years after the

[155] See Eberstadt (1998c: 121).

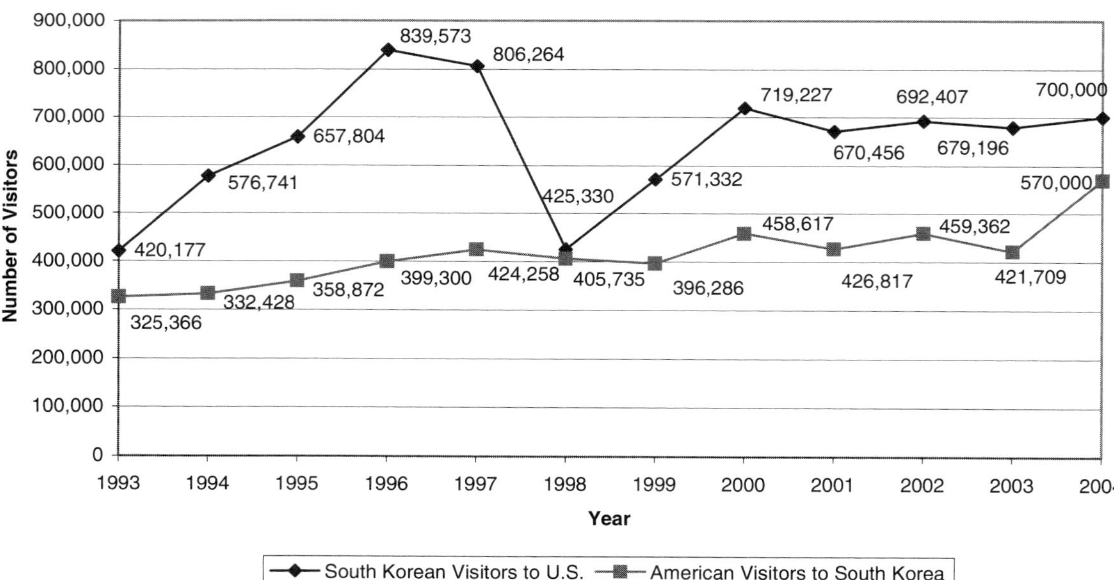

Figure 5.3. U.S.–South Korean exchange of visitors, 1993–2004.
Source: Korea National Tourism Organization. Available at http://www.knto.or.kr.

Table 5.6. Status of Overseas Ethnic Koreans in the United States in Comparative Terms (as of January 1, 2003)

	Japan	China	United States	Canada	Russia	Australia	Others	Total
Host country citizenship	260,168	1,967,285	682,264	67,232	549,943	17,876	23,024	3,567.792
Permanent residents	531,758	2,253	1,137,483	63,727	196	19,113	95,216	1,849,746
Sojourners	106,788	175,251	337,751	39,162	7,593	22,951	229,917	919,413
Total	898,714	2,144,789	2,157,498	170,121	557,732	59,940	348,157	6,336,951

Source: MOFAT (2004: 563).

Table 5.7. U.S. Sanctions Against North Korea, 1950–2004

Date	Related Law	Sanctions
01/28/1950	Export Control Act	Ban on exports to North Korea
12/17/1950	Trading with the Enemy Act	Freeze on North Korean assets in United States; announcement of the Overseas Assets Control Regulations, which virtually placed a total ban on trade and monetary transactions with North Korea
09/01/1951	Trade Agreement Extension Act	Prohibition against giving most-favored nation status to North Korea
08/01/1962	Foreign Assistance Act	Ban on grant of aid to North Korea
01/03/1975	Trade Act of 1974	Prohibition against giving Generalized System of Preferences benefits to North Korea
05/16/1975	Arms Export Control Act	Application of a comprehensive embargo on North Korea by U.S. Export-Import Bank
10/05/1986	Act of Ex-Im Bank	Prohibition against giving credits to North Korea by the U.S. Export-Import Bank
01/20/1988	Arms Export Control Act	Listed as a terrorism-supporting country, North Korea was subjected to bans on trade, grants by the Generalized System of Preferences, the sale of articles listed among the munitions control items, and aid and credits from the Export-Import Bank; U.S. instructions to vote against any international monetary institution's decision to grant aid to North Korea
04/04/1988	International Arms Trading Regulations (revised)	Ban on sales of defense industry materials and services as well as imports and exports with North Korea
03/06/1992	Munitions Control Items	Confirming North Korea was involved in giving missile technology to Iran and Syria, the United States banned the export of articles listed among the munitions control items and the government's contract with North Korea for two years; application of those bans on all activities of North Korea related to the manufacture of missiles, electronics, space aviation, and military aircraft
10/18/2004	North Korean Human Rights Act of 2004	In promoting human rights and freedom in North Korea, act calls for increased availability of nongovernment-controlled sources of information (e.g., radios) and daily 12-hour radio broadcasts into North Korea by Radio Free Asia and Voices of America and authorizes funding of US$2 million/year for fiscal years 2005–08; authorizes increased humanitarian aid once aid distribution according to internationally recognized humanitarian standards is ensured; authorizes $20 million/year for FY 2005–08 for humanitarian/legal assistance to North Korean refugees, orphans, and trafficking victims; also lists refugee/asylum eligibility for North Korean refugees

Source: Davis et al. (1994); Renneck (2003).

initial export embargo, President Bill Clinton announced that the United States would ease economic sanctions against North Korea affecting most trade and travel, thereby ending the longest-standing trade embargo in U.S. history. Many items that had previously required a license were now eligible for export without a license; certain items on the Commerce Control List (CCL) moved from a policy of denial status to case-by-case review.

Today, trade and related transactions are generally allowed for non–dual-use goods (dual-use goods are those that may have both civilian and military uses) if a set of overarching conditions are met. To lift all export controls applied to North Korea, Pyongyang first would have to be removed from the State Department list of countries supporting acts of international terrorism. The United States also cannot extend Normal Trade Relations status – formerly called Most-Favored Nation status – to North Korea because of the restrictions included in the 1951 Trade Agreement Extension Act that prohibited extending such status to communist states. Pursuant to the Trade Act of 1974, this lack of status also excludes the DPRK from the Generalized System of Preferences (GSP). U.S. citizens may, however, travel to North Korea, and there are no restrictions on the amount of money one may spend in transit or while there. Assets frozen prior to June 19, 2000 remain frozen.

Despite the easing of most trade restrictions, trade and investment between North Korea and the United States has remained virtually nonexistent and also highly politicized. As shown in Table 5.2, U.S.–DPRK trade is almost entirely one way: the U.S. exports moderate amounts of mostly agricultural goods to North Korea and imports virtually nothing from the DPRK. South Korea's trade with the United States in a single day in 2003 ($161 million) is more than two and one-half times greater than the combined total of North Korea's trade with the United States in a fourteen-year period (1990–2003). This mostly has to do with the DPRK's lack of export competitiveness. America's economic sanctions certainly denied Pyongyang access to the world's largest market, but North Korea has met with only limited success in selling its products in other markets where no sanctions existed. Nonetheless, on the issue of DPRK's export competitiveness, U.S. tariffs would be more important at this point than U.S. sanctions; the decision of some countries to consider Kaesong products under an ROK label is therefore critically important for the zone's success given such tariff barriers to North Korea's goods.

Perhaps far more damaging than U.S. sanctions against North Korea has been the repeated U.S. veto of North Korean membership in the keystone international financial institutions for multilateral aid (e.g., the Asian Development Bank, the IMF, the World Bank). This circumscription of DPRK membership in international organizations dates to the

November 1987 destruction of a KAL flight by a bomb planted by two North Korean agents. Following this incident, the United States placed North Korea on the list of countries supporting international terrorism, which, under the Export Administration Act of 1979, implied U.S. denial of trade, Beneficiary Developing Country status, the sale of items on the U.S. Munitions List, most foreign aid, Export-Import Bank funding, and support in international financial institutions. North Korea is particularly interested in changing its status so that it could effectively apply for membership in the World Bank and the IMF. The United States discussed the matter with South Korea and Japan in 2000, whereas South Korea supported North Korea's bid for this step toward normalization, Japan opposed a change in status until the matter of kidnapped Japanese citizens was resolved.[156]

The possibility of new international sanctions related to the second nuclear standoff remains present. When the IAEA condemned North Korea's reactivation of its nuclear weapons program in January 2003, it stopped short of referring the matter to the UN Security Council, a move that could have produced a new sanctions regime. North Korea has stated that any imposition of sanctions under the auspices of the United Nations will be considered an act of war.

In fact, it was revealed in early 2005 that the Bush administration had been developing strategies to choke off the DPRK's few sources of income, applying the tools used to interrupt the funding of Al Qaeda in the war on terrorism. A *New York Times* article described a "classified 'tool kit' of techniques" and "new instruments of pressure" that might be building blocks for "a broader quarantine of North Korea." The planning was allegedly a response to new illicit trafficking and counterfeiting by the DPRK undertaken to make up for lost missile sales and a crackdown on resource transfers from North Koreans living in Japan.[157]

Despite the extant prohibitions on economic interactions, since 1995, as Table 5.8 indicates, the United States has provided more than $1 billion in foreign assistance to the DPRK: about 60 percent in the form of food aid and about 40 percent in the form of energy assistance channeled through KEDO. Food aid amounting to more than 1.9 million tons has been channeled through the UN WFP. The $400 million U.S. contribution to KEDO funded approximately one-fourth of the KEDO program, whereas South Korea, Japan, the EU, and several other countries supplied the rest; $378 million went directly to the purchase of heavy fuel oil for North Korea as required by the Agreed Framework. The budget requests of

[156] Rennack (2003: 7–8).
[157] David E. Sanger, "U.S. Is Shaping Plan to Pressure North Koreans," *New York Times*, February 14, 2005, p. A1.

Table 5.8. U.S. Assistance to North Korea, 1995–2004

	Food Aid				
Calendar or Fiscal Year	Metric Tons	Commodity Value ($US Million)	KEDO Assistance ($US Million)	Medical Supplies ($US Million)	Total ($US Million)
1995	0	$0.0	$9.5	$0.2	$9.7
1996	19,500	$8.3	$22.0	$0.0	$30.3
1997	177,000	$52.4	$25.0	$5.0	$82.4
1998	200,000	$72.9	$50.0	$0.0	$122.9
1999	695,194	$222.1	$65.1	$0.0	$287.2
2000	265,000	$74.3	$64.4	$0.0	$138.7
2001	350,000	$102.8	$74.9	$0.0	$177.7
2002	207,000	$82.4	$90.5	$0.0	$172.9
2003	40,170	$33.6	$2.3	$0.0	$35.9
2004	60,000	N/A	$0.0	$0.0	N/A
TOTAL	**2,013,864**	**$648.8**	**$403.7**	**$5.2**	**$1,057.7**

Source: Manyin and Jun (2003: 1); Eberstadt (2004a: 34).

FY2004 and FY2005 from the Bush administration included no money for KEDO.[158]

Food aid to North Korea has generated its own debate in the United States. Some policy makers and commentators have called for it to be linked to broader foreign policy concerns, either by using the promise of food to encourage cooperation in security matters or by suspending food aid to trigger a collapse. Others, arguing that food should not be used as a weapon, have called for delinking humanitarian assistance from an overall policy toward the DPRK, either by providing food unconditionally or by conditioning it only on North Korea, allowing international relief groups greater freedom to distribute and monitor their aid. The provision of aid to North Korea has given Congress a vehicle to influence U.S. policy toward North Korea. Beginning in 1998, Congress included in the annual Foreign Operations Appropriations bill requirements that the president certify progress in nuclear and missile negotiations with North Korea before allocating money to KEDO operations.[159]

Although the Clinton administration claimed that food aid to North Korea was unconditional, it is clear that, in fact, during the 1990s the United States used food aid to secure North Korea's participation and increased cooperation in a variety of security-related negotiations.[160] The largest single U.S. pledge, more than 500,000 metric tons (MT) in 1999,

[158] Manyin and Jun (2003). [159] Manyin and Jun (2003: 5).
[160] See Natsios (2001); Noland (2000a: 182–91).

was provided as a *quid pro quo* for North Korea, allowing access to a suspected underground nuclear site at Kumchangri. Although the "food for talks" approach probably helped secure North Korea's participation in a number of talks, it did not appear to result in substantive changes in DPRK behavior. In June 2002, the Bush administration announced that future U.S. food aid would depend on North Korea's willingness to allow access of food donors to all areas of the country, a nationwide nutritional survey, and an improvement in monitoring food aid – conditions that other recipient countries meet. The administration demanded "verifiable progress." North Korea's failure to meet these conditions led the United States to reduce its 2003 aid to one-fifth of the 2002 level, with additional aid possible conditional on a better response by Pyongyang.[161]

There has always been an undercurrent of ambivalence in U.S. attitudes toward economic cooperation with the DPRK. On the one hand, an economically weak DPRK is inherently less capable of waging war and developing WMD than would be an economically strong DPRK, and from this perspective, the economic distress of the 1990s clearly altered the security balance in favor of the United States and the ROK. On the other hand, economic collapse in DPRK could potentially lead to highly destabilizing developments.

The latest movement in functional relations between the DPRK and the United States has been away from economic engagement and toward one-sided U.S. pressure on Pyongyang to improve its human rights record. The North Korean Human Rights Act, signed into U.S. law in October 2004, aims to promote human rights in North Korea and to provide humanitarian aid to North Korean citizens and refugees. The law allows the president to provide grants to private, nonprofit groups to support programs promoting human rights, democracy, rule of law, and the development of a market economy in North Korea. The president is enabled to spend at least $20 million a year until 2008 for humanitarian aid to North Korean citizens and refugees. The law also made refugees eligible for asylum in the United States. So antagonistic identities have been sharpened and accentuated by domestic identity politics in the United States, with the predictable negative consequence of adding another obstacle to reaching an agreement in the six-party talks in Beijing.

Conclusion

Emphasis on monocausal or single-factor explanations often obscures the dynamics at work in international politics. Regarding U.S. interactions with North and South Korea, there are many overlapping strands of

[161] Manyin and Jun (2003: 7).

causes and consequences. Because the United States has assumed such an important role – both historically and at the current moment – in the imaginations of both Korean states, it is crucial to look at how state interests in the triangle change in relation to the words and deeds of the other two states. Because of the taut sides and sharp angles of the Washington–Seoul–Pyongyang triangle, it is important to recognize that each of the three parties has a capacity to create self-fulfilling relations with the other two and that action and reaction are highly contingent.

The history of U.S.–Korean relations – especially U.S.–DPRK relations, stemming from the *General Sherman* incident to the recent standoffs over North Korea's nuclear pursuits – teaches us that the conflict between the United States and North Korea often goes beyond material power. First in the context of Western imperialists and the hermit kingdom and then in Cold War ideological rivalry, the U.S.–DPRK conflict has deep historical roots born in war and perpetuated for more than a half-century. The present conflict is not simply about nuclear weapons but rather about competing worldviews and perceptions of self and other. Rhetorically, it is as much about good and evil as about international security. The War on Terror that has followed from the September 11 attacks has involved a Manichean lens in which states are either with the United States or against it. Because of the history of conflict, the DPRK automatically made the "against the United States" list without even having to act.

Insofar as a "security dilemma" is a social structure composed of intersubjective understandings in which states have become so distrustful of each other that they define interests predominately in egotistical or self-help terms, it seems that the United States and North Korea have fomented mutually conflictive antagonistic identities.[162] The North Koreans have identified the United States as an imperialist state, and imperialism implies that the United States is an aggressive force in such a way as to deflect the sense of insecurity that feeds into North Korea's exaggerated sense of sovereignty and self-determination, which borders on isolationism. In addition, the North Korean guiding principle of *juche* – which suggests that the DPRK should be a stand-alone state in international relations – is in many ways constructed out of opposition to imperialist forces.

At first glance, it seems unclear how the United States could ever hope to break this condition. According to Chinese international security experts, the United States holds the two most important keys to resolving the North Korean problem in the name of peace or Korean reunification: the United States must step forward to end the state of hostility that has persisted since the earliest days of the Cold War and must simultaneously

[162] This definition of security dilemma is owed to Wendt (1992).

provide tangible assurances to North Korea that Washington does not seek the government's overthrow (regime change).[163] To consistently view and label Pyongyang as an enemy precludes any prospect of change in the socially constructed, hostile identity that prevails on the Korean peninsula. Following the lead of South Korea, which decided to drop the label of "enemy" from its annual Defense White Papers in characterizing North Korea, the United States should recognize the harmful role of such hostile identity discourse and strive to minimize it. Whereas the Clinton administration had formally moved away from the use of the term "rogue state," the Bush administration has brought it back into political currency and with direct reference to the DPRK. This was a step in the wrong direction.

Engagement with North Korea is a means of identity change for both the United States and North Korea. Engagement should entail constructive dialogue without divisive ideological discourse, mutual participation in international organizations, and normalization of relations. To deal more effectively with the problems that North Korea poses, it is better to bring Pyongyang into America's web of relations than to exclude it. Normalization of relations will be a crucial step in transforming the enemy identities that the two states are currently unable to break.

The added recent development that should encourage the United States to pursue more productive conversation with the DPRK is the way that Seoul has become frustrated with the continued security dilemma caused by U.S.–DPRK hostility. Again, it is impossible to look at this as moving only in one direction or the other. The ROK's identity – or perhaps evolving identities – was formed and protected by the U.S. occupation in the mid-1940s, by the U.S. involvement in the Korean War, and then by U.S. military and financial support throughout most of the remainder of the twentieth century. Yet, now the ROK has reached a stage of domestic economic and political maturity at which it is confident enough to begin identifying – at a cultural or national level – with the North Korean people. Therefore, when the South Korean people and the South Korean government see the United States operating in the nuclear talks with North Korea in such a way that they think North Korea is not receiving an honest deal, hostility against the United States increases. Likewise, when the United States is recognized as the cause of the division on the Korean peninsula, this contributes to South Korean popular opposition to the presence of U.S. troops, even though those U.S. troops have protected the southern half of the peninsula from forcible absorption into the North Korean system.

[163] Howard W. French, "Doubting U.S., China Is Wary of Korea Role," *New York Times*, February 19, 2005, pp. A1, A6.

In effect, there is a resurgence of national identity at the nation-state level, and the divided nation-state of Korea is watching its two halves officially move closer to one another, while the sixty-year protector and provocateur remains a target for both appeals and scorn from both of those halves, to greater and lesser degrees. The United States now risks provoking negative responses from both Korean states if it pursues the wrong path, and it risks losing its place on the Korean peninsula if it is not proactive enough. Not since the North Korean invasion of South Korea in 1950 after U.S. troops had left the peninsula has the question of the U.S. future on the peninsula been subject to so many possibilities and contingencies.

CHAPTER 6

The Future of the Two Koreas

> Men make their own history, but they do not make it just as they please; they do not make it under circumstances chosen by themselves, but under circumstances directly encountered, given, and transmitted from the past.
>
> – *Marx (1959: 320)*

> It was the best of times, it was the worst of times, it was the age of wisdom, it was the age of foolishness, it was the epoch of belief, it was the epoch of incredulity, it was the season of Light, it was the season of Darkness, it was the spring of hope, it was the winter of despair.
>
> – *Charles Dickens,* A Tale of Two Cities *(1859)*

To think about Korean unification in the post–Cold War era is to encounter a double paradox. Perhaps at no time since the end of World War II, when Korea was liberated and divided, has the prospect of Korean unification seemed closer, yet never has it been more distant. On the one hand, it is the weaker North Korea far more than the stronger South Korea that holds a master key to shaping the future of the divided Korean peninsula. On the other hand, the future of North Korea itself – if it will have any future – largely depends on the support of outside powers, most important, South Korea, China, the United States, Japan, and Russia, in that order. Accordingly, the prospect of Korean reunification is and becomes a function of North Korea's system dynamics, a complex and ongoing interplay of domestic reforms and external support. This suggests that there is an unusually large number of variables shaping the future of the divided Korean peninsula.

The present is evenly split between the past and the future – it is a part of the immutable past and the malleable future. How do we bridge the gap between empirical reality (the "is") and normative reality (the "ought")?

From what we know of the past, we develop our ideas for how the future should be. This chapter begins by assessing how the past and present affect the future, and then applies this thinking to the possibilities of peace and reunification on the Korean peninsula, including the specter of Northern collapse, the possibilities of reunification, and the variables and players affecting the trajectories this divided polity might take.

Bringing Future Studies Back In

The image of utopia as an alternative setting for human existence long has held sway over the imagination of the future. The common theme running through traditional utopian thinking from Plato through More, Bacon, Rousseau, Kant, Owen, and down to Marx is a prevision of an alternative human condition.[1] E. H. Carr gives a classic "realist" interpretation by juxtaposing "utopia" and "reality" as fundamentally opposed – the former being "the inclination to ignore what was and what is in contemplation of what should be," and the latter being "the inclination to deduce what should be from what was and what is." "The utopian," according to Carr, "believes in the possibility of more or less radically rejecting reality, and substituting his utopia for it by an act of will."[2] However, the concept of utopia as reflected in the writings of prominent contemporary futuristic thinkers is one of previsioning a desirable social order. Instead of dichotomizing utopia and reality as antinomies, the flow of historical reality is conceptualized in terms of ongoing dialogue and feedback between the actual and the potential.[3]

Utopian thinking is *ipso facto* anti–status quo. As Karl Mannheim observes, "Conservative mentality as such has no utopia."[4] It is Max Weber who argues for the power of utopian thinking in propelling society forward: "Certainly all historical experience confirms the truth – that man would not have attained the possible unless time and time again he reached out for the impossible."[5] It is utopian thinking that allows society to move past the notion of the inevitability of human suffering and to envision a more just and humane society.

In contrast, the terrors of the twentieth century – two global wars, totalitarianism, WMD – tempered the utopian project and gave birth to dystopian visions of the future. The future, instead of becoming a source of hope, has become an object of fear ("future shock") to be avoided, as manifested in the literary genre of dystopian (antiutopian) novels: Eugene Zamiatin's *We* – written but not published in the former Soviet

[1] See Manuel and Manuel (1979); Beres and Targ (1977). [2] Carr (1958: 11).
[3] S. S. Kim (1984: 302). [4] Mannheim (1968: 206).
[5] Cited in Gerth and Mills (1958: 128).

Union just three years after the Revolution – Aldous Huxley's *Brave New World* (1932), and George Orwell's *1984* (1949).

Despite wide variations in form and content, the utopian thinking that has evolved over the centuries still provides a rich source of insight to help unshackle our imaginations from the credo of the inevitability of human misery and to allow us to revision a more humane and just society. By affirming the possibility and desirability of alternative forms of human community, by stressing the mobilizing and liberating functions of faith, vision, and hope, and by defining values and facts in mutually complementary terms, the utopian tradition has made an important contribution to the dialectical synthesis of empirical and normative theory.

At the same time, the utopian tradition provides a poor guide for mapping strategies of change. Perhaps it was this problematic linkage between the present and the future that led Marx, for one, to lament that "philosophers only have interpreted the world in various ways; the point is to change it."[6] Whether looking backward to the Garden of Eden or looking forward to the resurrection of a City of God, a credible pathway from the present to the future has always been an elusive link in the utopian vision. Utopian thinking has also tended to be excessively preoccupied with harmony as a central value, projecting an image of a hermit society that seeks to isolate itself from the systemic constraints of the external world. Witness the extent to which the value of harmony (*he* in Chinese) was idealized and legitimized in the service of the hierarchical social order in the traditional Sinocentric world order in East Asia.[7]

The decline of utopian thinking and the accompanying dystopian sense of future shock were overtaken by a sudden explosion of future studies in the 1960s, and since that time, the field has seen a number of characteristic developments. With a new awareness of a highly complex and interdependent world with increasing perils and diminishing opportunities, there emerged in the late 1960s a new field of international relations known as "world order studies." From this new discipline, scholars such as Saul Mendlovitz, Richard Falk, Johan Galtung, and Ali Mazrui participated in the World Order Model Project, designing possible and preferable scenarios of alternative world futures, as well as some broad orientational guides for the transition process.[8] Rather than making point predictions about the shape of the future world, such future models endeavor to take account of possible contingencies and offer a range of outcomes that depend on the direction and possible interaction of key variables.

[6] Marx (1967: 402). [7] For a detailed discussion, see S. S. Kim (1979: 19–48).
[8] Mendlovitz (1975); Falk (1975); Galtung (1980); Mazrui (1976); Falk and Kim (1982); Falk, Kim, and Mendlovitz (1982, 1991).

At the same time, military research and development has been the "invisible hand" in the development of future studies. Government support of research and development, particularly the foundation of the RAND Project – now the RAND Corporation – in the United States at the end of World War II, catalyzed the emergence of a variety of future forecasting techniques (e.g., game theory, predictive statistical models, adaptive systems models).

Few of the global models from the 1960s, however, succeeded in predicting the major events of the 1970s: the global ecological movement, the oil crises, or the crisis of stagflation. Indeed, futuristic international relations research was replete with examples of erroneous predictions and glaring failures to anticipate major events.[9] Even fewer of their successors predicted the momentous structural transformations of 1989 to 1991. It is both surprising and revealing that structural realist theory, the most dominant international relations theory of the 1980s, proved to be so far off the mark, with so little power to predict the macrostructural changes in the international system, including the end of the Cold War and the demise of tripolarity and bipolarity.[10]

Many of these models failed because of their insistence on systemic stability, and although they were critiqued at the time for assumptions about the stability of economic and demographic growth rates and technological change, it was political change that truly derailed the projections. The crisis of socialism, the collapse of the Soviet Union, and the emergence of a single global economy showed just how wrong models could be.

Nonetheless, such models are important because their image of the future can be a powerful driver of human behavior. The way that the future is envisioned in the present determines actions in the present. For the citizens of Eastern Europe and the republics of the Soviet Union, the future was apparent from what they knew – in increasing amounts over the course of the 1980s – of life on the other side of the Iron Curtain. Therefore, they seized the opportunity to demand change. Whether the people of North Korea are similarly situated to demand change is debatable; Pyongyang has mastered the art of denying alternative envisionings of the future with its consistent presentation of a continual Manichean contest between *juche* socialism and U.S. imperialism.

Paradoxically, the most predictable quality of the future of humanity is its unpredictability.[11] Out of the variety of alternative images that are available to us and guide our actions today, some future will emerge.

[9] For a list of erroneous predictions, see S. S. Kim (1984: 317–18).

[10] See Deudney and Ikenberry (1991); Gaddis (1992/93); Kegley (1994); Kratochwil (1993); Lebow (1994); Lynn-Jones and Miller (1993).

[11] On this point, see S. S. Kim (1984: chap. 8).

What is crucial in this connection is that we not allow our biases to guide our analyses. This fault is most easily encountered simply by projecting continuity. As one scholar notes, "The projection of current trends into the future represents a vote of temporary approval for such trends."[12] In general, future models and scenarios reflect the conscious and subconscious projections of the analysts' dominant concerns, preferences, and histories, and these models and scenarios are products of a particular time and place in history.

The most ambitious projects can be labeled "normative forecasting": they offer a possible future and also undertake appropriate steps in pursuit of it. The Manhattan Project to build an atomic bomb, the Marshall Plan to rebuild Europe, and the Apollo Project to put a man on the moon are examples of normative forecasting and planning. Yet, these projects were not examples of participatory democracy and hardly took account of global needs. Beyond that, they had unanticipated consequences, whether hastening Soviet acquisition of the atomic bomb or hardening Cold War fault lines in Asia and Europe.

Regardless of whether future modeling projects are this ambitious, they are very often the product of developed Western countries. Because of constraints on resources and human capital, the developing world either fails to serve as a source of future forecasting, or it does not produce models and scenarios that the developed world is willing to accept as probable or informative. This has led to a glut of predictions involving the continuing spread of Western capitalism and democracy, and the continued benefits of technological – but not social or economic – innovation.[13]

The transition of the global order is ultimately a dialectic between preferred futures and the unfolding present. As globalization has expanded the interconnectedness of nations and peoples, more voices and visions have entered into the discourse about the future global order. At the same time, however, the demise of superpower competition has left the hegemonic United States as the actor uniquely placed to guide the development of the world system. Yet, how far the United States can go without a truly global coalition remains in doubt, and a single state such as North Korea has a striking ability to force the United States to delay, compromise, or abandon its plans for a particular region. Particularly important for forecasting future pathways is to look at the major role that very small decisions can play. Microdecisions being made today in Pyongyang, Seoul, and Washington – and also in Beijing, Moscow, and Tokyo – will have a large role in the way the future of NEA and the Korean peninsula plays out.

[12] Hampden-Turner (1970: 305). [13] Fukuyama (1992); Friedman (1999).

Paradoxically, the possibilities of shaping a preferred future are embedded in the inherent difficulties of prediction in social science inquiry. There are many reasons why prediction is so problematic, and so often off the mark, in international relations.[14] To begin with, we should be wary of any scientific claim for general laws in world politics because there are few laws that really command uncontested paradigmatic status and validity. Conceptual and methodological problems in establishing and validating general laws with predictive power abound: the unmanageably large number of known variables, the magnitude of the unknowns, the volatile nature of charged domestic politics, the resistance of available data to controlled laboratory experiment, the elusiveness of values and norms in quantitative analysis, and the complex and mysterious interaction between exogenous and endogenous factors.

History, despite what Francis Fukuyama would have us believe,[15] has not ended; it has been accelerating, even overheating, and often making a mockery of our expectations and predictions. Of course, at a time of such rapid and unpredictable change, it is easy to succumb to the fallacy of premature optimism or pessimism on the changing relationship between the future of North Korea and the future of the Korean peninsula or regional and global politics. As Robert Jervis reminds us, past generalizations can no longer provide a sure guide for the future if they are themselves no longer valid. To a significant degree, the flow of world politics has become contingent or path dependent because particular unexpected events can easily force world politics along quite different trajectories.[16] In other words, "past experience," whatever this may mean and even if not forgotten, can no longer serve as a reliable guide for the future.

Prediction of the exact shape of things to come in a post–Kim Il Sung North Korea is inherently problematic; it is like predicting the terminal point of a moving target on turbulent trajectory, subject to the competing and often contradictory domestic and external pressures that are characteristic of any state in an increasingly interdependent and interactive world. To predict the future of North Korea is also difficult because we cannot be certain about the relative weight of key variables in Pyongyang's informal politics and decision-making processes in the post–Kim Il Sung era.[17]

To say that North Korea's future is unpredictable is to say that its future is malleable, not predetermined. Herein lies the potential of external

[14] For further analysis and elaboration, see Choucri and Robinson (1978); S. S. Kim (1984: 301–42); Almond and Genco (1977); Jervis (1991/92).

[15] See Fukuyama (1989, 1992). [16] Jervis (1991/92: 42–45).

[17] For a detailed analysis of North Korea's informal politics, see S. S. Kim (2000c).

factors in reshaping North Korea's future in a preferred direction. Such a nondeterministic image of the future of the post–Kim Il Sung system opens up some space for the outside world to use whatever leverage it might have to help North Korean leaders opt for one futurible scenario or another in the coming years. State behavior is seldom determined by a single factor. State learning can rise in politics, especially at a time of national identity crisis, as an intervening variable providing "significant room for choice by publics and statesmen" in moving from here today to there tomorrow.[18]

In, Of, and By the Collapsist Scenario

In the context of the Korean peninsula, the question of future scenarios pertains to what are currently two separate Korean states. Despite a sixty-year history of division, only a few people argue that the division of Korea is a permanent phenomenon. With a population that for the most part is ethnically, linguistically, and historically homogenous, Korean unification has long been regarded as inevitable. If this is to be the future, however, there are a variety of contingent and path-dependent ways it can come about. One futurible, the unification-by-collapse scenario – also known as the unification-by-absorption scenario – has remained the dominant view underlying the debates about the future of the Korean peninsula.

The rapid succession of momentous changes in the international system from 1989 to 1991 – the crumbling of the Berlin Wall, German reunification, the end of the Cold War, and the demise of the Soviet Union and international communism – created the first wave of a global chorus that predicted that divided Korea was also heading inexorably toward reunification. Then came a second wave in the wake of the sudden death of North Korean President Kim Il Sung in July 1994, spreading famine, and the idling of North Korean factories; a flurry of predictions had North Korea either collapsing within six months or experiencing a German-style reunification by absorption within three years.[19] The U.S. Defense Department began planning with both Japan and South Korea for different contingencies of collapse. Even South Korean President Kim Young Sam (1993–98) jumped on the collapsist bandwagon, depicting North Korea as a "broken airplane" headed for a crash landing that would be followed by a quick reunification. In April 1996, as leaders of South Korea

[18] Jervis (1991/92: 40–41).

[19] See, for instance, Eberstadt (1994a, 1995b, 1997, 1999). For a detailed description of who's who espousing or free-riding the collapsist scenario in the latter half of the 1990s, see Noland (2004b: 12–16).

and the United States prepared to promote the Four-Party Peace Talks, they privately predicted that the collapse in the North could occur in as soon as two or three years. Likewise, the U.S.–DPRK Agreed Framework of 1994 was inked by the United States, if not by North Korea, on the assumption that North Korea's days were numbered. The fact that Kim Young Sam agreed for the ROK to take up a whopping 70 percent of the $4–$5 billion needed for the construction of two LWRs was also based on this assumption.

However, the argument for imminent unification via collapse and absorption depends on a set of unrealistic heroic assumptions: first, that North Korea would collapse or succumb to a peaceful reunification by absorption, without a big fight and without triggering another war; second, that North Korea's 1-million-strong troops would somehow disappear; third, that South Korea had both the will and the capacity to absorb a collapsing North Korea politically, militarily, economically, socially, and culturally; and fourth, that a united Korea would transform itself into a peaceful, democratic, and demilitarized state, voluntarily giving up its nuclear options and becoming a force for stability in NEA.[20]

The collapse-and-absorption argument has been marred by freewheeling conceptualization, right-leaning bias, and inattention to the evidence of the many obstacles and barriers to peaceful Korean reunification that are evident in the harsh realities on the ground. Despite these predictions of collapse, it has never been clear exactly what would collapse: the economy, the regime, the system, or the state? Most collapsist arguments commit the fallacy of premature economic reductionism, based on the misleading equation of economic breakdown with system or state collapse. Indeed, North Korea's resiliency since the mid-1990s and the regime's depth of psychological control over its citizens speak against an economic collapse that would yield a regime, system, or state collapse. Because of the black box of North Korean politics, it is difficult to determine whether regime or system collapse is possible without state collapse. Estimates of the likelihood of any of these are bound to vary widely.

When the collapsist theory was in vogue in the mid-1990s, it was widely (and wrongly) assumed that the collapse of the North Korean regime would *ipso facto* bring about German-style reunification by absorption into South Korea. For collapse and absorption to work successfully together, four characteristic assumptions would have to be true. First, the DPRK would have to collapse because of its economic difficulties and without a new Korean War. Second, the North Korean Army would have to agree to lay down its arms and abandon its command and control structures.

[20] Eberstadt (1997).

Third, the ROK would have to find the resources to politically, economically, socially, and culturally absorb the land and people of the DPRK. Finally, the reunified Korea would have to give up its nuclear holdings and demonstrate that it would be a force for stability in NEA. Because of the unlikelihood of all these assumptions being realized, Seoul, like Pyongyang, is hardly eager for a North Korean collapse, especially since the coming of the Kim Dae Jung government in February 1998 and of the Roh Moo-hyun government in February 2003, which has continued to pursue Kim Dae Jung's Sunshine Policy under the rubric of the Policy of Peace and Prosperity.

Central to the collapse-and-absorption argument is the popular perception that unification is the necessary and sufficient condition for securing a long peace on the Korean peninsula. Despite the primordial passions fueling so many state-making internal wars in so many trouble spots in the post–Cold War world, there is nothing intrinsically empowering or enduring about national "unity," especially if it is a hegemonic unity. The relevant example in this regard is not Germany but the two Yemens – Republican North Yemen and Marxist South Yemen – which were merged and unified in May 1990 only to erupt in civil war less than two years later.

Any collapse scenario, especially any that includes the demise of North Korea as a separate state, is unlikely for no other reason than the certainty that North Korea would not collapse without a fight or without generating a huge mess that no outside neighboring power would be willing or able to clean up. The various collapse scenarios often overlook the issue of how to deal with North Korea's 1-million-strong army. The peaceful accommodation or demobilization of the military in the North into a unified Korea would pose a problem of unprecedented magnitude, and this alone provides North Korea with unparalleled leverage to exercise its "collapse card."

Domestic, inter-Korean, and external (Northeast Asian) factors transmitted from the past are such that after more than a half-century of fratricidal politics, the two Koreas have become different nations, states, systems, societies, cultures, and identities. The notion of one homogeneous but divided nation-state waiting to be unified upon the removal of external sources of conflict is nothing more than ethnocentric romanticism cherished and exploited by hypernationalists in both Koreas. Of course, national unification has always remained an integral part of the Korean politics of competitive legitimation and delegitimation, the object of primordial passions, and the engine of the governmental-military-academic complexes in the North and South. Unification has become a kind of growth industry, siring myriad visions, strategies, and formulas for moving from here to there. The Korean War, which congealed the division originally imposed by the United States and the Soviet Union in

1945, was nothing less than Kim Il Sung's "magnificent obsession" gone awry, resulting in a fratricide that claimed more than 3 million lives and some 10 million separated families, apparently sealing the fate of Korea's divided polity: two separate, unequal, and incomplete nation-states on two divergent ideational and developmental trajectories.

There is little doubt that the North Korean leadership is overdetermined to use all available instruments of national military power to avert absorption by the South. Even without going nuclear, North Korea commands massive and forward-based forces deployed aggressively along the northern side of the peninsula's so-called DMZ. Moreover, North Korea is believed to have the world's third largest inventory of chemical weapons, as well as an impressive array of delivery systems. In this respect, Pyongyang's nuclear card and now its "missiles card" serve not only as a cost-effective strategic equalizer, but also as a cost-effective insurance policy for system maintenance.

Even if a system collapse were to occur, it would likely be violent and bloody, triggering internal civil violence rather than a peaceful reunification. Fearing the social, economic, political, and military costs of German-style unification, Seoul would prefer to intervene to set up a separate regime. This would serve to defuse the refugee "bomb" that would otherwise explode in the nation's capital, threatening to destroy its fragile democracy and its increasingly prosperous but vulnerable economy. Even before the advent of South Korea's financial crisis, in late 1997, a fundamental change in public attitudes and perceptions of the costs and benefits of national unification had already taken place. As South Koreans have learned about the megacrisis in the North with its massive famine, and as they have heard or read more about the international expectations for Korean reunification by absorption, they have become more worried that their own lives would change for the worse. Consequently, they have become more outspoken against unification by absorption. More South Koreans have hedged their bets on reunification, expecting the government to prefer that some kind of division remain between North and South, even after reunification, until the economic level of the North is raised. The costs of West Germany's incorporation of East Germany would pale in comparison with what South Korea would have to bear in absorbing North Korea.

The politics of fragmentation and regional antagonism in the South remain active despite or perhaps because of the remarkable transition to democracy in 1987. Since the founding of the ROK in 1948 there have been twelve declarations of martial law and emergency decrees, and several thousand industrial strikes. To add a collapsing North Korea with its regional antagonisms and a southward flood of several million poverty-stricken North Korean refugees seems a sure recipe for another fratricidal civil war and/or the end of Korean democracy. In all probability, the most desirable and feasible lesson to be drawn from the German experience is the model of "one Germany, two states" embodied in the 1972 Basic Treaty and actualized in the international relations of the two Germanys from 1972 to 1989.

To quicken Korean reunification by absorption would be to conflate and magnify the worst elements in two societies, separate systems, and diverging identities beyond the carrying capacity of a "united" Korea. Even under the most optimistic scenario – a peaceful reunification without too much bloodletting – a united Korea would most likely become hypernationalistic, posing a serious regional security challenge, potentially a very disruptive one. Given the absence of a Northeast Asian security community or regime, the disruptive or restructuring impact of Korean reunification on the stability of the region would also depend on a host of contingent factors, including the timing and method of reunification, the nature of the foreign policy of a united Korea, and the state of Northeast Asian international relations as symbolized and structured by the changing relationships among the Big Four.

Therefore, the opportunity for greater intra-Korean and inter-Korean reconciliation, rather than reunification by absorption, lies in the demise of great-power rivalry and the corresponding opening of more Korea-centric autonomous space. For the first time since the Korean division in 1945, it is now possible to speak of a new emerging consensus among the four major powers on the peaceful coexistence of the two Korean states – and identity differences – as part of the Korean solution and on the new inter-Korean detente as part of the Northeast Asian regional solution. Since the root causes of the conflict are more endogenous than exogenous, at least until the coming of the Bush administration in early 2001, resolution or abatement requires a "two-Koreas first" approach. No longer pawns on the great-power chessboard, the two Koreas now hold the key for mapping pathways toward a politics of reconciliation.

We now seem to be able to say that collapse is not the imminent outcome for North Korea. As Georgy Bulychev suggests, "The North Korean system was specifically designed by Kim Il Sung to withstand external pressures and to control and crush emerging internal challenges."[21] ROK President Roh Moo-hyun affirmed in April 2005, "The possibility of a sudden collapse of North Korea is remote, and the South Korean government has no intention to encourage it."[22] The Kim Jong Il regime has taken the minimum necessary steps to keep the state and economy afloat.

[21] Bulychev (2005).

[22] Ch'oe Hun and So' Myo-cha, "Roh Foresees No Collapse of North, Nor Hopes for It," *JoongAng Ilbo*, April 14, 2005.

To no small extent, this has included a series of (successful) appeals for international aid.

What must be recognized is that the future of the Korean peninsula is part of the future of the Northeast Asian system – indeed the global system. A system implies an ensemble of certain individual components (subsystems) that form a whole such that they both hold together (coherence) and change together (covariance). Changes in some subsystems produce changes in other parts of the system, but the system as a whole is greater than the sum of its individual parts, exhibiting characteristic properties and behaviors that are different from those of the parts. As long as the ensemble of individual subsystems is interconnected enough to affect the performance of the system as a whole, it is reasonable to treat the ensemble as a system.[23] In the present case, this is to say that the actions of the Big Four in NEA and in the world will condition, if not determine, how North and South Korea act, whereas North and South Korea's own actions will also help shape the future behaviors of the Big Four.

Conscious recognition of a system entails that there are a lot of moving parts and that making predictions will be difficult. When the butterfly flaps its wings in Moscow, what will happen in Seoul? Therefore, in what follows, a set of possible future scenarios for North Korea is listed; each is highly contingent such that there is little possibility of estimating the probability of its being the ultimate scenario for the Korean peninsula.

Alternative "Futurible" Scenarios

Since the mid-1990s, a dichotomist endgame debate on the future of the post–Kim Il Sung system – whether it will survive or collapse – has become a favorite sport that almost anyone, including North Korea's elite defectors, could play, and speculation has abounded.[24] This either/or endism debate needs to be enriched and broadened by the appreciation that the future of the post–Kim Il Sung system is not providentially predetermined but rather a product of selective human behavior.

Analytically, we can identify at least five futurible scenarios spanning the whole spectrum of the possible from one extreme to the other – system collapsing, system decaying, system maintaining, system reforming, and system transforming. Here, I focus on three of the most plausible futurible scenarios: maintenance, reform, or decay of the system. There

[23] On systems theory, see Jervis (1997).

[24] For a wide array of speculations and analyses on the future of post–Kim Il Sung North Korea, see B. J. Ahn (1994); Eberstadt (1993, 1997); Foster-Carter (1992, 1998); Moon and Kim (2001); B. C. Koh (1994); C. N. Kim (1996); K. W. Kim (1996); Y. S. Lee (1995); McCormack (1993); D. S. Suh (1993); Scalapino (1997).

is also a need to clarify briefly the temporal scope of futurible scenarios as the baseline for assessing any change or continuity. The future of North Korea may be divided into three time horizons: (1) the immediate future, viewed here as a one-year temporal horizon of immediate concern and focus (academic year, fiscal year, etc.); (2) the middle-range future, a five- to seven-year horizon of a longer-term project (e.g., a four-year college career, five-year electoral cycles in many democratic societies, or seven-year economic plans in socialist countries, including North Korea); and (3) the long-term futures, the thirty- to fifty-year horizon of dreamers, revolutionaries, and designers of world system transformation. As Harry Harding points out, most American analysis of North Korea in recent years has focused on the recent past and the immediate future, but it is North Korea's "longer-term future" that is ultimately more important than the issues of the recent past and the immediate future.[25] In the present section, the main focus is on the middle-range future – that is, the future of the post–Kim Il Sung system in 2010 or 2012.

As for the direction of change, it has several possible trajectories. The system-maintaining scenario, for instance, may continue unchanged in its current trajectory, or it may shift toward the system-reforming or system-degenerating trajectory. The three futurible scenarios should not be viewed as mutually exclusive because one can flow into another or vice versa.

System-Maintaining Scenario

The first futurible scenario for North Korea is that of system maintenance. Under this scenario, the Kim Jong Il regime will continue to command firm control of national ideology, identity, and polity. The objective is defensive, whereas the means are the everyday proclamation of the greatness of the *juche* ideology alongside the demonization of U.S. imperialism. Political reform is almost entirely out of the question if the desire of the North Korean regime is to maintain the current level of control and domination. Marcus Noland predicted in 1997 a system maintenance strategy of "muddling through": North Korea would make ad hoc adjustments as necessary and would rely on financial support from China and possibly South Korea and Japan.[26]

To finance the continuation of the regime as it currently exists, Pyongyang would probably have to explore the export of its missile and nuclear technologies, and continue its illicit counterfeiting and drug smuggling activities. It is unclear to what extent inter-Korean and international contacts can continue or expand under this scenario. It also is

[25] Harding (1995: 21–22). [26] Noland (1997).

unclear what role North Korea's nuclear bet plays in maintaining the current system. On the one hand, the probable existence of a nuclear deterrent may serve to keep the United States at bay in an era when Washington has made it known that it is not afraid to forcibly change regimes; on the other hand, the existence of the North Korean nuclear program directly draws U.S. attention to the peninsula.

System-Reforming Scenario

The second futurible scenario for North Korea is system reform. The most likely version of this scenario would be for Pyongyang to follow post-Mao China's path of economic opening and reform. This would involve some or all the following: a restructuring of the ownership system, the decollectivization of agriculture, a new system of economic decision making, the opening of new special economic zones, entry into keystone international economic institutions (e.g., the IMF, the World Bank, the Asian Development Bank, the WTO), normalization of relations with Washington and Tokyo, increasing inter-Korean economic cooperation, demobilization of parts of the KPA, and sending students to the United States and Japan for technical training.

China's record doubling of GDP per capita in a ten-year period should serve as inspiration to North Korea to follow this path. Yet, Pyongyang has issued mixed and contradictory signals and statements about post-Mao Chinese socialism. In six informal summit meetings between 1978 and 1991, Deng Xiaoping repeatedly urged Kim Il Sung to develop the economy through reform and opening. This only provoked Kim Il Sung's testy retort, "We opened, already," in reference to the Rajin-Sonbong Free Economic and Trade Zone.[27] In September 1993, however, Kim Il Sung reportedly told a visiting Chinese delegation that he admired China "for having achieved brilliant reforms and openness," while continuing to build "socialism with Chinese characteristics" and that the Chinese experience would become "an encouraging factor for us Koreans."[28] In a May 1999 meeting with Chinese Ambassador Wan Yongxiang in Pyongyang, Kim Jong Il is reported to have said that he supported Chinese-style reforms. In return, he asked Beijing to respect "Korean-style socialism."[29]

The North Korean pronouncement in January 2001 on the need for "new thinking" to adjust ideological perspectives and work ethics to

[27] Economist Intelligence Unit (EIU), *Country Report: South Korea and North Korea* (1st Quarter, 1999), p. 40.
[28] *North Korean News*, No. 702 (September 27, 1993), p. 5. [29] AFP, July 16, 1999.

promote the "state competitiveness" required in the new century[30] – accompanied by Kim Jong Il's second "secret" visit to Shanghai in less than eight months (January 15–20, 2001) for an extensive personal inspection of "capitalism with Shanghai characteristics" – prompted a flurry of wild speculation about *juche* being Shanghaied and North Korea becoming a "second China." With an *ex cathedra* statement to his National Security Council, President Kim Dae Jung took the lead on this "second China" theme, declaring that Kim Jong Il's visit to Shanghai "shows that North Korea is deeply interested in the Chinese-style reform and open-door policy and that it is trying to become a second China." He is also reported to have ordered his cabinet to brace for a "considerable degree of change."[31]

Despite North Korea's seeming determination to undertake economic reform and the popular perception that Chinese-style reform and opening is the most promising way, there are at least five major obstacles. First, China's reform and opening came about during the heyday of the revived Cold War when anti-Soviet China enjoyed and exercised its maximum *realpolitik* leverage, as was made evident, for instance, in Beijing's easy entry into the World Bank and IMF in May 1980. When China started its economic reforms, it was already substantially down the path to political normalization with the United States and therefore could also economically cooperate with the United States. However, Pyongyang's unwillingness to meet the minimum necessary transparency standards, its placement on the U.S. list of states supporting terrorism, and Japanese opposition stemming from unresolved abduction issues have blocked the government's membership into the keystone international financial institutions (e.g., the IMF, the World Bank, the Asian Development Bank).

Second, China's economic reforms were tied to a political changing of the guard: the ascendancy of Deng Xiaoping as the new paramount leader in December 1978 with the purging of the Gang of Four and Mao's designated heir apparent Huo Guofeng. Despite much speculation to the contrary, Kim Jong Il seems firmly positioned to remain in power and even to name his successor in the Kim dynasty. Third, unlike post-Mao China, North Korea does not have rich, famous, and enterprising overseas Koreans to generate the level of FDI that China attracted in the 1980s. Fourth, the agriculture-led reform process we have seen in East Asian transitional economies may simply not be available to North

30 See "21 seki nun koch'anghan chonpyon ui seki, ch'angcho ui seki ita" (The Twenty-First Century Is a Century of Great Change and Great Creation), *Rodong Sinmun [Worker's Daily]*, January 4, 2001, p. 2; "Motun muncherul saeroun kwanchom kwa noppieso poko pulo nakacha" (Let Us See and Solve All Problems from a New Viewpoint and a New Height), editorial, *Rodong Sinmun [Worker's Daily]*, January 9, 2001, p. 1.

31 Chanda (2001: 26).

Korea, due to the very different initial conditions, which resemble East European economies or the former Soviet Union more than China or Vietnam.

A fifth obstacle has to do with Pyongyang's catch-22 identity dilemma. To save the *juche* system would require destroying important parts of it and would also require considerable opening to and help from its capitalist southern rival. Yet, to depart from the ideological continuity of the system that the Great Leader Kim Il Sung ("the father of the nation") created, developed, and passed onto the son is viewed not as a survival necessity but as an ultimate betrayal of *raison d'état.* As Noland puts it, "why be a third-rate South Korea when one can head south and become the real thing?"[32]

Even if North Korea does undertake sufficient economic reforms to join the world economy, it will find itself in a highly competitive economic region. Whereas the Asian Tigers had not yet blossomed when China began reforming, today Japan, South Korea, Malaysia, Singapore, Taiwan, and the PRC itself all offer possibly fierce competition for any North Korean export strategy. The Kim Jong Il regime is also likely to be wary of the creeping pluralization if not liberalization that accompanied – and has continued to accompany – economic liberalization in China. The 1989 Tiananmen carnage is symbolic of the tensions that exist in the reforming of a socialist state, and North Korea is all too aware of them. Even if a strategy of systemic reform were undertaken by North Korea, it is likely that a democratic spark such as that of Beijing in 1989 would result in a quick reversion to the strategy of system maintenance.

Nonetheless, there has been some evidence of North Korea preferring the system reform strategy. In 1991, the DPRK established the Rajin-Sonbong Free Economic and Trade Zone, which has since become the Rajin-Sonbong Free Economic Zone.[33] Pyongyang also agreed to participate in the TRADP and recently created the Sinuiju Special Autonomous Region (SAR) on the Chinese border and the Kaesong Industrial Zone for cooperating with South Korea. Between 1992 and 2000, the DPRK wrote forty-seven new laws on foreign investment, and a September 1998 constitutional revision mentions "private property," "material incentives," and "cost, price and profit" in a document that otherwise reads like an orthodox manifestation of the DPRK's *juche* philosophy.[34] During his visit to Shanghai in January 2001, Kim Jong Il highly praised the Chinese developmental model of reform and opening (with Shanghai characteristics). In the summer of 2002, the DPRK adjusted its system of controlled prices, devalued the won, raised wages, adjusted the rationing system, opened a "socialist goods trading market," gave farmers a type of property right

[32] Noland (2002: 182). [33] Cotton (1998). [34] See Noland (2001).

regarding the cultivation of particular parcels of land, and extended laws for special economic zones.[35]

Particularly significant to the issue of cultural and system reform in the DPRK, but not sufficiently acknowledged, is the identity-changing or identity-redefining role of North Korea's returning refugees in the slow-motion transformation of North Korean society. The refugees returning home from Northeast China now constitute the first statistically significant group of North Koreans to have acquired firsthand life experience in the near abroad. They were witness to the fact that life in relatively poor Northeast China is far more plentiful than the "socialist paradise" at home, and South Korea's prosperity was made amply evident by the presence of South Korean humanitarian NGOs, tourists, businesspeople, and Christian missionaries in the region. The returning refugees are too numerous to be silenced, suppressed, or imprisoned.[36]

Still, North Korea's ability or willingness to live and let live with identity differences with the South in the course of taking such a system-reforming strategy remains an open question subject to further research, although some indications are provided in the form of growing inter-Korean exchange and functional cooperation. With serious reforms launched in mid-2002, the datapoints for testing this hypothesis still appear insufficient to draw any firm conclusions.

System-Decaying Scenario

The third futurible scenario for North Korea is system decay. If the North Korean *juche* system remains rigid in both theory and practice, the most likely scenario might be one of systemic decay, in which Pyongyang would be unable to make even the necessary adjustments for system maintenance, meaning that the economy would continue to decline with the famine situation steadily worsening. This scenario predicts food riots and a spiral into outright civil conflict. Catalysts for this scenario could include a string of top political or military defections from North Korea, a sudden halt after embarking on an economic reform path whereby citizens with a new taste of prosperity suddenly turn against the state, or a miscalculation in the ongoing brinkmanship game with the United States such that Washington decides to strike militarily against North Korea.

If the system decay scenario were to come to fruition, it might lead quickly to a situation of system collapse. North Korea's economic system seems so completely fragile as to hearken the quick arrival of a precipice of collapse in the event of accelerating system decay. Yet, in contrast, the example of the so-called "fourth world" countries of sub-Saharan Africa

[35] See Noland (2003). [36] Lankov (2004b: 872).

demonstrates that states can limp along with zero or negative growth rates for years, particularly if international aid is providing a lifeline. Even small levels of political instability should not necessarily be seen as indicative of coming system collapse. Hwang Jang-yop, for instance, warned against the danger of reading too much into his defection: "The republic [North Korea] is in economic difficulty but it remains politically united and there's no danger of its collapse."[37] This prediction made in early 1977 has held true so far. In addition, North Korea is not lacking for state capacity or military strength, and it has employed and will continue to employ both in pursuit of its survival.

Predictions of collapse ran rampant upon the death of Kim Il Sung. Many in Japan, South Korea, and the United States predicted that North Korea would collapse within six months or, from the more cautious pundits, that it would last for three years at best; they believed that collapse would be accompanied by a German-style reunification by absorption. (Some argued in a contrary fashion that there was "no reliable theory linking economic distress or deprivation to political change."[38]) A 1995 RAND study conducted by Charles Wolf optimistically proposed that a unified Korea would have a $2 trillion GDP by 2015 – about five times the ROK GDP in 1994.[39] Karen Elliott House argued in the *Wall Street Journal* that the United States should "cease seeking to prop up Pyongyang and let its inevitable collapse come sooner than later."[40] Nicholas Eberstadt, writing in *Foreign Affairs,* went further and called for a proactive policy of hastening the collapse of the DPRK and thereby "hastening Korean reunification."[41] However, some suggested that if North Korea truly did begin moving down the pathway of system decay toward system collapse, there would need to be a new scenario of system rescue involving a massive financial bailout by Seoul, Tokyo, Washington, and possibly Beijing, with additional assistance from the UN, the World Bank, and possibly the IMF.

In terms of futurible scenarios for reunification, the one that has been most talked about at official inter-Korean levels is a proposal for a federation of the two Korean states. Pyongyang has proposed that the two Koreans be joined together in a Democratic Confederal Republic of Koryo, whereas Seoul has proposed a Korean National Community. Both proposals preserve the two separate political systems and implicitly believe that unification is possible and most desirable if one's own system and one's own national identity not only survives, but also dominates.

37 Cited in *Far Eastern Economic Review* (February 27, 1997), p. 15.
38 Noland (1997: 106). 39 Wolf et al. (1995: 7–8).
40 Karen Elliott House, "Let North Korea Collapse," *Wall Street Journal*, February 21, 1997, p. A14.
41 Eberstadt (1997).

Pyongyang, therefore, desires a class-based *juche* state and has emphasized preconditions such as the legalization of communist parties and the establishment of a "progressive government" in the South before further steps toward reunification can be made. Seoul, in contrast, speaks of liberal democracy and has advocated a proportional representation voting system for any national bodies that would take advantage of the ROK's two-to-one population ratio over the North. Whereas Seoul is willing to work step-by-step toward reunification, Pyongyang would prefer to deal with outstanding issues on a package basis. Ironically, however, whereas Seoul favors nationwide elections for any confederal bodies, Pyongyang would prefer a series of political conferences.

Unification by war, however, is a scenario that both Pyongyang and Seoul seem to have ruled out. For Pyongyang, in particular, this effectively precludes unification on its terms. Without the military option, the DPRK will not be able to bring about its style of Korean reunification. In addition, North Korea's accumulation of nuclear weapons has increased the danger of any sort of scenario involving armed conflict. The ROK has worked to reduce the possibility of any outbreak of armed conflict, tolerating to some extent DPRK pinprick provocations and warning against U.S. preemptive strikes against North Korea as a violation of the current Korea–U.S. Combined Forces Command structure.[42]

With both the federation approach and reunification by war seeming unlikely, what seems most probable is a "peace by pieces" approach, and this possibility is explored further in the final section of this chapter, whereas the next section tracks and explains the different variables – at the local, inter-Korean, dyadic, and international levels – that make one scenario more likely than another.

Toward Synergistic Interactive Explanations

Given these different possible future scenarios for the Korean peninsula and Korean reunification, the important question is which scenario we can expect to see realized. To explain the likelihood of various scenarios and the probability of one occurring over another, we must look at the different variables that will explain particular contingencies and path dependencies. In the case of Korean reunification, this means looking at the domestic politics of both North and South Korea, inter-Korean politics, the international politics of NEA, and global politics as actors at and across all four levels have a role to play in determining how inter-Korean politics and the politics of Korean reunification will develop. As

[42] "ROKG Ministers Answer Questions on Security, Diplomacy, Unification to Parliament," *Chosun Ilbo*, November 14, 2004.

has been described throughout this book, identity politics at the local, inter-Korean, regional, and global levels have been inextricably linked and intermingled, even as the import of international identity politics among the Big Four has been filtered by the particularistic interests of political elites in the two Koreas.[43]

The Local Level

The two half-Koreas on the divided peninsula have used the politics of national identity mobilization in often violent ways in attempts to maximize their exclusive security and legitimacy. The politics of competitive legitimation and delegitimation started in 1945 from the same cultural and historical baseline, and then developed in very different ways under the sponsorship of the two competing Cold War superpowers. National reunification has always remained an integral part of this political rhetoric, the object of primordial passions and the engine of governmental-military-academic complexes in both the North and the South. As a case in point, the two Koreas cannot even agree on what to call "Korea" in Korean – it is *Chosun* in the North and *Hankuk* in the South. One of the fundamental obstacles to peace and unification on the divided Korean peninsula is the fact that each Korean state has defined itself – its national identity – in so many ways in opposition to the other Korean state.[44]

Today, in North Korea, the legitimacy of the DPRK as a state is under question: can Pyongyang continue to provide the basic human needs that define a state as internally sovereign?[45] The collapsist scenarios regarding North Korea have revolved around the DPRK's economic woes. Suffering from the systemic problems that have plagued all socialist state-run economies, North Korea's economic health has deteriorated further because of the interruption or reduction of foreign trade, poor harvests leading to famine conditions, allocation of resources to maintenance of the military, and the use of scarce resources for grandiose projects glorifying the Kim family state. Between 1990 and 1995, the North Korean economy contracted by one-fourth, and in 1992, the government urged citizens to eat only two meals per day. In the summer of 1995, after flash floods ruined agricultural crops, the DPRK made an unprecedented appeal to international aid agencies and bilateral donors for food aid.

Marcus Noland estimates that "fixing" the North Korean economy to generate rising living standards would cost about $2 billion annually, half

[43] C. S. Chun (2001: 143).
[44] Grinker (1998: 8–9); Bleiker (2004); S. S. Kim (1991); Gills (1996).
[45] On internal versus external sovereignty, see Jackson (1990).

of which would be for recurrent flow consumption expenditures and the other half for industrial and infrastructural investments.[46] In July 2002, the Kim Jong Il regime deviated from a strict system maintenance scenario by changing prices, wages, and the value of the currency and by allowing more formalized markets in North Korea. The future actions of North Korea will be determined in large part by how secure the regime feels in its ability to manage its economic situation on its own. So far, North Korea has erred on the side of isolationism and autarky.

It is estimated that the monetary cost of rescuing a collapsing North Korean economy would be between $250 billion and $3.5 trillion,[47] although such figures are little more than shots in the dark given the absence of reliable statistics on North Korea and the uncertainties regarding the domestic and external factors involved in Korean reunification. Indeed, the focus of research and debate in South Korea on reunification has shifted subtly but significantly from questions on how to achieve it to more sobering and rational cost–benefit calculations.[48] In 1997, Marcus Noland estimated a $1 trillion price tag if the main goal was to prevent mass migration from the northern part of the peninsula and the main means was massive capital investment.[49] In a later general equilibrium model, Noland and coauthors suggested that a high level of North–South migration might limit the amount of investment needed in the North and thereby provide a superior outcome for a reunified Korea.[50]

The closest comparison case is reunified Germany, where unification euphoria in West Germany quickly degenerated into despair and recrimination as West German subsidies bound for East Germany ballooned to $100 billion annually, whereas East Germany experienced an unprecedented rise in unemployment, social alienation, and rates of death and suicide. Approximately $650 billion was transferred from West to East Germany; these transfers made up 63 and 95 percent of East German GDP in 1991 and 1992, respectively.[51] In September 1998, Chancellor Helmut Kohl, the reunifier of Germany, was voted out of office – his singular achievement had become one of the causes of his electoral defeat. German one-nation identity proved itself to be a slender reed rather than a solid foundation for the politics of national reconstruction.

Nonetheless, in almost every dimension, South Korea is no West Germany, North Korea is no East Germany, and the German precedent – where no fratricidal war had occurred – is not the perfect analogue for the

[46] Noland (2000b).
[47] Ch'oe Hun and So' Myo-cha, "Roh Foresees No Collapse of North, Nor Hopes for It," *JoongAng Ilbo*, April 14, 2005. See also "Costs of Unifying Koreas Put at $200 Billion to $2 Trillion," *The Korea Herald* (Seoul), June 29, 1996, p. 1.
[48] Lee and Hong (1997). [49] Noland (1997: 113).
[50] Noland, Robinson, and Liu (1998). [51] Y. S. Lee (2002).

Table 6.1. Comparison of Major Economic Indexes of North and South Korea, 2004

Sector/Category	Unit	North Korea (A)	South Korea (B)	A:B
Population	1 million	22.7	48.1	1:2.1
Nominal GNI	$ billion	20.8	681.0	1:33
Per capita GNI	$	914	14,162	1:15.5
GDP growth rate (2004)	%	2.2	4.6	1:2.0
Total foreign trade volume	$ billion	2.86	478.3	1:167
Exports		1.02	253.8	1:249
Imports		1.84	224.46	1:122
Trade balance	$ million	–820	29,340	
Trade as percentage of GNI	%	13.8	70.0	1:5.1
Scale of assessments for UN budget	%	0.010	1.796	1:180
Industrial structure	%			
Service		32.3	55.5	1:1.7
Mining and manufacturing		27.2	29.1	1:1.1
Construction		9.3	9.3	1:1
Agriculture, forestry, and fishing		26.7	3.7	1:0.14
Electricity, gas, and water		4.4	2.4	1:0.5
Coal production	1 million tons	22.8	3.2	1:0.14
Power generation capicity	1 million kw	7.7	60.0	1:7.7
Power generation	100 million kwh	206	3,421	1:16.6
Cruide oil import	10,000 bbl	390.0	82,579	1:212

Source: ROK Ministry of Unification and UN Doc. A/RES/58/1B.

Korean peninsula (Table 6.1). The Iron Curtain in Germany was far more permeable than is the thirty-eighth parallel: East Germans tuned into West German radio and television, and, beginning in the 1970s, between 1.1 and 1.6 million East Germans visited the West each year, whereas 1.2 to 3.1 million West Germans traveled in the opposite direction.[52] ROK President Roh Moo-hyun was clear: "Korea's unification process will be fairly different from Germany's."[53]

For South Korean citizens, the effects of reunification would be highly differential. Nontraded goods sectors, such as construction, would be able to take advantage of the new demand coming from North Korea. Noland suggests an interesting trajectory of South Korean economic development that could emerge from a massive investment package given to the

[52] Bleiker (2004: 57).
[53] "Roh Opposes Sanctions on North Korea," *Chosun Ilbo*, April 14, 2005.

North. He suggests that investment in North Korea would yield profits to owners of capital in the South, which would shift the distribution of income away from labor and toward capital. In addition, the income distribution among different classes of labor would shift toward more highly skilled classes of labor.[54]

More difficult to calculate than the economic impact of North Korean collapse and/or reunification is the social impact. Although much is made of the ethnic homogeneity among North and South Koreans – Roy Richard Grinker refers to this as a "master narrative of homogeneity," presuming that unification will immediately recover the lost national unity and identity[55] – the truth is that the degree of similarity is difficult to assess. After sixty years behind a Stalinist curtain of near-absolute control, how similar in actuality are North Koreans to their alleged brethren in the South? Whereas South Koreans are cosmopolitan and technologically adept, North Koreans are sheltered and uninformed about both global events and new lifestyle developments. As has happened to East Germans, North Koreans likely would be relegated to a second-class status in a unified Korea, and the 2 to 3 million members of the military and the nomenklatura would need to be retrained and deideologized.[56] Neoconservative critics, in fact, contend that a belief in some sort of eternal consanguinity has led to poor policy decisions in the ROK.[57] Recognizing the differences that have developed between them and North Koreans, 78.5 percent of South Koreans polled in a 1995 survey advocated unification only after the recovery of "national homogeneity," whereas only 9.5 percent favored immediate reunification.[58] In general, evidence suggests that, despite the strong emotional appeal of reunification, enthusiasm quickly wanes when the costs are considered.

Since the end of the Cold War, South Korea has had to absorb an increasing number of North Korean defectors. Whereas only 607 North Koreans defected to the ROK before 1989, that number doubled in 2003 alone. In July 2004, the ROK airlifted nearly 460 North Korean refugees from Vietnam, the largest defection since the Korean War. As of September 2004, some 6,300 North Koreans have defected, and the ROK government has supported them with more than $65 million of funding.[59] One of the most symbolic manifestations of diverging Northern and Southern identities is the extreme difficulty that most North Korean defectors encounter, despite being offered generous financial aid, job training, and other assistance in the South.[60] North Korean defectors

[54] Noland (2002). [55] Grinker (1998: 4). [56] Bulychev (2005).
[57] For example, Eberstadt (2004b: 432–33). [58] Sejong Institute (1995: 70).
[59] Seo Dong-shin, "Number of NK Defectors in South Exceeds 5,000," *The Korea Times*, September 7, 2004.
[60] W. Y. Lee (1997); I. J. Yoon (2001: 14); Bulychev (2005); Bleiker (2005: xliii).

have had difficulty dealing with the competitive nature of a market society, with handling money and with making wise choices among competing goods. They have found that their North Korean education was insufficient given the computer skills, grasp of English, and knowledge of Chinese written characters that are needed in South Korea.[61] These experiences set a poor precedent for the integration of their former countrypersons.

It is particularly revealing that defectors from the North suffer far more from psychological problems than do immigrant workers from other countries. Many defectors criticize South Korean society and its people for being "closed" and "selfish." Defectors form the North "unanimously agree that the vast majority of North Koreans harbored great love and respect for Kim Il Sung as the man who freed them from the Japanese, defeated the Americans in the Korean War, and built the foundations of the national economy." Equally revealing, though, is the fact that most defectors have no difficulties adjusting to the political dimensions of the South Korean system.[62]

The revealed identity differences between North and South Korea are not without precedent in Germany. Lothar de Mazière, East Germany's first freely elected prime minister, once said, "Every day we are surprised anew that 45 years of separation had a greater impact upon us than we thought it had when the Wall came down." A common experience among East Germans was the realization that they had a common identity as East Germans.[63] At the local level at least, this may be more so with the two Koreas than the two Germanys, given the longstanding in-country regionalism and contentious regional identity politics in South Korea.

The Inter-Korean Dyadic Level

For nearly two decades after the "end" of the Korean War, the two Korean states talked about and sometimes acted out their competing unification visions only in the context of the overthrow or replacement of one national identity by the other. After the Nixon-in-China shock and the ensuing Sino–American rapprochement in the early 1970s, the two Koreas experienced three short cycles of inter-Korean dialogue and détente. Beginning in August 1971, there was a series of seven Red Cross talks held alternately in Pyongyang and Seoul over two years. With these talks ongoing, North and South Korea produced a joint communiqué in which they both agreed to uphold three principles: (1) unification achieved through independent efforts; (2) unification achieved through peaceful means; and (3) national unity sought by transcending

[61] Bleiker (2004: 43–44). [62] Bleiker (2004: 44). [63] Bleiker (2004: 50).

differences in ideas, ideologies, and systems. The second cycle of talks, running from September 1984 through February 1986, involved a flurry of contacts and exchanges in various functional and humanitarian fields and reaffirmed the three principles of unification. The third cycle, which began in 1988, inspired in part by changes in international identity politics linked with the end of the Cold War, was more promising than the first two. It jumpstarted inter-Korean trade, guided the entry of the two Koreas into the United Nations as two separate but equal member states, and led to the drafting of two documents: the North–South Basic Agreement (officially known as "Agreement on Reconciliation, Nonaggression, and Exchanges and Cooperation between the South and the North") and the "Joint Declaration of the Denuclearization of the Korean Peninsula." The two historic accords were signed by the ROK prime minister and the DPRK premier, and then entered into force on February 19, 1992.

The Basic Agreement stipulates that "the two sides shall endeavor together to transform the present state of armistice into a solid state of peace between the South and the North and shall abide by the present Military Armistice Agreement (of July 27, 1953) until such a state of peace has been realized" (Article 5). The Joint Declaration of the Denuclearization of the Korean Peninsula of 1992 stipulates in peremptory language that "the South and the North shall not test, manufacture, produce, receive, possess, store, deploy or use nuclear weapons." Since the early 1990s, these historic accords have been breached more than they have been observed or implemented, as the DPRK made clear with the revelations that sparked the nuclear standoff in late 2002.

With Kim Dae Jung's inauguration as ROK president in February 1998, South Korea initiated the Sunshine Policy of opening to North Korea with a pledge not to undermine or absorb the DPRK. The Sunshine Policy was based in part on explicit recognition of the fact that undermining the DPRK is simply not a viable policy option because of the disorder and destruction that would follow from a Northern collapse. There was no specific formula for the implementation of the policy; it was a "policy toward the North" rather than a "unification formula."[64] The twin pillars of the policy were the separation of politics from economics and the use of the principle of flexible reciprocity.[65] As Marcus Noland observes, the Sunshine Policy aimed to create "a set of interdependencies that in the long run would discourage the North from external aggression and perhaps even promote the internal transformation of the regime."[66] President Kim Dae Jung's repeated pledges and pronouncements that the South has no intention "to undermine or absorb North Korea," speaking to one of the remaining key fears in Pyongyang, stand out as one of the

[64] Y. S. Yang (1998: 48). [65] Y. S. Yang (1998: 48). [66] Noland (2000a: 113).

most significant steps toward accepting identity difference as an integral part of the peace process.[67]

The Sunshine Policy created the appropriate conditions – both in South Korea and in North Korea – for the historic inter-Korean summit of June 13–15, 2000, which saw President Kim Dae Jung and Chairman Kim Jong Il embrace each other before domestic and global television audiences. The summit gave rise to many predictions about the imminent reunification of Korea. Although the two Kims symbolically signaled their acceptance of each other's legitimacy through their actions at the summit, neither of them enunciated a belief that reunification would be coming in the near future. Kim Dae Jung, in fact, predicted that it would take twenty to thirty years for the divided Korean peninsula to achieve national unification, even as North Korea declared for the first time that "the issue of unifying the differing systems in the North and the South as one *may be left to posterity to settle slowly in the future*."[68]

But the significance of the summit should not be underrated. It was all about mutual recognition and legitimation, and it succeeded in finally bringing the two Koreas down from their hegemonic unification dreamlands to acceptance of the possibility of peaceful coexistence as two separate states. The single greatest accomplishment of the summit was to put an end – albeit perhaps only a temporary one – to the fratricidal politics of competitive legitimation and delegitimation. This change may have been limited in domain as well. The Joint Declaration produced by the summit was conspicuously silent on security and military issues, in effect anointing economic relations as the practical pathway for the development of inter-Korean relations. The fourth article of the document used the term "national economy," apparently assuming an eventual integration of North and South Korean economies.[69] Since the 2000 summit meeting, more than twenty-five agreements have been signed between the two Koreas, as listed in Table 6.2.

Trade with South Korea is in general *de facto* economic aid for North Korea, and the ROK has become one of the major sources of hard currency in the DPRK.[70] Beginning in the early 1990s with small exchanges of goods, since 2002, South Korea has become and has remained the North's second largest trading partner, surging ahead of Japan. Trade, which was essentially the functional cornerstone of Kim Dae Jung's Sunshine Policy, has continued despite nuclear tensions, naval provocations, and short-range missile testing by the DPRK. Over the course of Kim Dae Jung's presidency, trade increased threefold, moving from $221 million in 1998 to $721 million in 2003.

[67] Bleiker (2005: xliii).
[68] *Rodong Sinmun [Worker's Daily]*, June 25, 2000, p. 6; emphasis added.
[69] C. I. Moon (2002: 231–32). [70] See Kim and Winters (2004).

Table 6.2. Chronology of Inter-Korean Agreements, 1972–2005 (as of August 2005)[a]

No.	Date[b]	Place	Agreement
1	07/04/72		South–North Joint Communiqué of July 4, 1972
2	12/13/91		Agreement on Reconciliation, Nonaggression, and Exchanges and Cooperation Between South and North Korea (the Basic Agreement)
3	01/20/92		Joint Declaration of the Denuclearization of the Korean Peninsula
4	02/19/92		Agreement on Composition and Operation of Subcommittees from South–North High-Level Negotiations
5	03/19/92		Agreement on Establishment and Operation of a South–North Joint Nuclear Control Commission
6	05/07/92		Agreement Regarding the Establishment and Operation of a South–North Joint Military Commission
7	05/07/92		Agreement Concerning the Establishment and Operation of South–North Liaison Offices
8	05/07/92		Agreement on the Establishment and Operation of a South–North Joint Commission for Exchanges and Cooperation
9	09/17/92		Agreement on Composition and Operation of a South–North Joint Reconciliation Commission
10	09/17/92		Protocol on Implementation and Observance of Chapter 3, South–North Exchanges and Cooperation, of the Agreement on Reconciliation, Nonaggression and Exchanges and Cooperation
11	09/17/92		Protocol on Implementation and Observance of Chapter 2, Nonaggression, of the Agreement on Reconciliation, Nonaggression and Exchanges and Cooperation
12	09/17/92		Protocol on Implementation and Observance of Chapter 1, Reconciliation, of the Agreement of Reconciliation, Nonaggression and Exchanges and Cooperation
13	06/28/94		Agreement for Holding of a Summit Meeting between South and North Korea
14	07/02/94		Agreement of the Procedure for Holding a Summit Meeting between South and North Korea
15	04/08/00	Pyongyang	South–North Agreement (on Summit Meeting)

16	05/18/00	Panmunjom	Agreement on Working Procedures for Implementing the April 8 South–North Agreement on Inter-Korean Summit
17	06/15/00	Pyongyang	South–North Joint Declaration
18	06/30/00	Mt. Kumgang	Agreement to Exchange Visits by Separated Families, Establish and Operate a Reunion Center and Repatriate Unconverted Long-Term Prisoners
19	12/16/00	Pyongyang	Agreement on Procedures for Resolution of Commercial Disputes between the South and the North
20	12/16/00	Pyongyang	Agreement on Prevention of Double Taxation of Income between the South and the North
21	12/16/00	Pyongyang	Agreement on Clearing Settlement between the South and the North
22	12/16/00	Pyongyang	Agreement on Investment Protection between the South and the North
23	08/28/02	Mt. Kumgang	Agreement on North Korea's Participation in Pusan Asian Games (Asiad)
24	08/30/02	Seoul	Agreement at Second Meeting of the Inter-Korean Economic Cooperation Promotion Committee
25	09/08/02	Mt. Kumgang	Agreement at Fourth Inter-Korean Red Cross Meeting
26	09/17/02	Mt. Kumgang	Agreement on Provision of Materials for Inter-Korean Linkage
27	09/17/02	Mt. Kumgang	Agreement Reached at First Round of Working-Level Talks on Inter-Korean Railways and Highways
28	11/09/02	Pyongyang	Agreement at Third Inter-Korean Economic Cooperation Promotion Committee
29	01/22/03	Mt. Kumgang	Agreement Made at Third South–North Korean Red Cross Working-Level Contact
30	01/25/03	Pyongyang	Agreement Made at Second Meeting of Working-Level Consultations on the Connection of South–North Railways and Roads
31	01/27/03	Panmunjom	Interim Military Guarantee Agreement for the Use of Temporary Roads between South–North Control Zones in the Eastern and Western Coastal Districts
32	05/23/03	Pyongyang	Agreement reached at end of Fifth Meeting of Inter-Korean Economic Cooperation Promotion Committee
33	06/09/03	Kaesong	Agreement on Connection of Inter-Korean Rails and Roads
34	07/04/03	Munsan	Third Meeting Agreement on Connection of Inter-Korean Rails and Roads
35	07/31/03	Kaesong	Agreement of Second Meeting of Inter-Korean Consultation on Economic Cooperation System
36	08/28/03	Seoul	Agreement reached at end of Sixth Meeting of the South–North Economic Cooperation Promotion Committee

(cont.)

Table 6.2. (cont.)

No.	Date[b]	Place	Agreement
37	10/28/03	Kaesong	Agreement of Seventh Working-Level Contact on Connection of Inter-Korean Railways and Roads
38	11/08/03	Pyongyang	Agreement of Seventh Meeting of Inter-Korean Economic Cooperation Promotion Committee
39	11/21/03	Mt. Kumgang	Agreement from Second Inter-Korean Red Cross Talks
40	12/05/03	Sokcho	Agreement at Eighth Working-Level Contact for the Inter-Korean Railroads and Road Reconnections
41	03/05/04	Seoul	Agreement at Eighth Meeting of the Inter-Korean Economic Cooperation Promotion Committee
42	06/05/04	Pyongyang	Official Signature and Exchange of the Inter-Korean Maritime Agreement and Subsequent Agreement (June 5, 2004)
43	07/12/05	Seoul	Agreement at Tenth Meeting of the Inter-Korean Economic Cooperation Promotion Committee (July 12, 2005)
44	07/27/05	Kaesong	Agreement from First Round of the Consultative Meeting of Inter-Korean Working-Level Fishery Cooperation (July 17, 2005)
45	07/30/05	Kaesong	Agreement from Fifth Working-Level Consultative Meeting on Inter-Korean Road and Railway Reconnection (July 30, 2005)
46	08/05/05	Panmunjom	Nine Agreements on Inter-Korean Economic Cooperation to Come into Effect (August 5, 2005)
47	08/19/05	Kaesong	Agreement at First Round of the Inter-Korean Agricultural Economic Cooperation (August 19, 2005)

[a] Agreements between DPRK and KEDO (of which the ROK is a member), as well as numerous "joint press statements," are excluded.
[b] Date signed or entered into force.
Source: The ROK Ministry of Unification. Available at http://www.unikorea.go.kr.

One of the key components of this trade is processing-on-commission (POC) trade, in which South Korean companies export raw materials to the DPRK and then import finished or semifinished products. This type of trade involves the creation of new jobs in North Korea, some degree of technology transfer, a fair amount of investment in the North from the South, and, most important, direct contact between North and South Koreans. Many of the POC plants that have been established use South Korean machinery and supervisors. By 2003, South Korean companies were making shoes, beds, television sets, and men's suits in the North.[71]

In addition, since the mid-1990s, Seoul has increased its flows of "nontransactional" trade, which is the exchange of noncommercial goods, such as those used in the KEDO reactor projects or for humanitarian aid. Nontransactional trade began in 1995 and has increased to such a degree that it is almost as great as transactional trade. Overall, these increased trading relations are part of a program led by the ROK but accepted by the DPRK to create functional linkages between North and South in the interest of managing conflict, maintaining peace, and catalyzing eventual reunification.[72]

There have been important limitations to the amount of economic contact between North and South Korea. Pyongyang's lack of hard currency reserves means that it cannot import as much as it otherwise might from the ROK, and because of the state's control of the economy and the general poverty in the country, there are no free domestic markets for South Korean products. Although the DPRK has expanded the number of citizens that it sends abroad to study economics and business and has passed some important economic reform legislation, South Korean investors remain frightened about the safety and profitability of their investments in the North. For instance, in November 2000, DPRK officials denied Hansung Shipping vessels entry to the port of Nampo, even though that shipping line carried 90 percent of all North–South POC trade at the time.[73]

In addition, cultural and social exchanges – visits to Mt. Kumgang and family reunions – have not been as revolutionary as some had hoped. Although spectacular media events, they have not spawned the type of lasting connections between North and South Koreans that can be considered true functional linkages. Although since its opening in November 1998, the Mt. Kumgang project has increased the number of South Koreans who travel to the North, it has done so at great financial cost to Hyundai and without allowing sustained interaction between

[71] James W. Brooke, "Quietly, North Korea Opens Markets," *New York Times*, November 19, 2003, pp. W1, W7.

[72] Ministry of Unification (2005).

[73] Y. S. Dong (2001: 90–91).

South Korean tourists and their North Korean hosts. Likewise, the family reunions are symbolically important and emotionally moving, yet the meetings are brief, occur only once, and do not include mechanisms for future contact. At the current rate, most of the 122,000 elderly South Koreans who have applied to participate will die before given the opportunity, as some 20,000 already have.[74]

Although trade numbers may be growing and increasingly impressive, it is investment that will make the most difference in terms of the North Korean economy and in terms of economic relations fostering peace on the peninsula.[75] Although the DPRK promulgated, congruent with the launch of the Sunshine Policy in the South, its 1998 constitution and three subsequent laws focused on external economic cooperation – the Foreign Equity Law, the Contractual Joint Venture Law, and the Foreign Enterprises Law – laws on taxation of foreign investment, control over foreign exchange, the role of foreign banks, leasing of land, and customs are in many ways discordant with the *juche* philosophy that undergirds the DPRK's national identity.[76] Conversely, they are of questionable attraction for South Korean companies. For example, a Hyundai-financed greenhouse in North Korea belongs not to Hyundai but to the DPRK, which also claims 40 percent of the produce grown there for state use.[77] According to a Korean Development Institute survey, of 672 companies that started doing business in the DPRK in 2000 or 2001, only 171 were still involved in North Korea in November 2001, and only one-third of the 115 firms who responded said that they were making a profit in their Northern ventures.[78]

Many aspects of inter-Korean economic relations remain uncertain. The investment atmosphere could change entirely if the new Kaesong Industrial Complex in North Korea takes off; it has already attracted attention from a number of small and medium-size companies in South Korea. The reconnection of roads and railways between the two countries – what President Kim Dae Jung characterized as the *de facto* unification – will reduce the transaction costs of trade and embed both countries in a larger trading system. Pyongyang has recognized the essential need to open itself to foreign economic agents and has undertaken legal reform to encourage investment and trade. South Korea is the most likely source of the funding that can revitalize or at least stabilize the DPRK's economy.

Despite the simmering nuclear standoff, a bus leaves Seoul every working day to bring South Korean managers and supervisors to the Kaesong

[74] Foster-Carter (2003). [75] See Kim and Winters (2004). [76] See E. Y. J. Lee (2000).
[77] Anthony Faiola, "A Crack in the Door in N. Korea," *Washington Post*, November 24, 2003, p. A10.
[78] Tait (2003: 311).

Industrial Complex just north of the DMZ, where together with North Korean workers they produce kitchenware and clothing for sale in South Korean marketplaces (they are not yet sold in North Korea). What many realists dismissed as beyond the realm of possibility only a few years ago is now happening as raw materials and finished products are passing along and through what was once considered a major invasion route.[79] Such "peace by pieces" functional cooperation provides ways of living with rather than fighting about identity differences on the divided Korean peninsula.

The Regional Level and the Roles of the Big Four

There are three main possibilities for the position of a unified Korea in East Asia.[80] The conventional view is that a unified Korean government will be a key actor in the region and will be more independent of U.S. influence. The vision of "armed neutrality" sees a united Korea as enmeshed in the NEA regional economy and allied with no one in particular. A third possibility is that the economic and military capabilities of a united Korea would make it a prominent regional power. The reactions of China, Japan, Russia, and the United States to the possibility of Korean unification is conditioned on the relatively likelihood of each scenario. Given the difficulty of estimating these future probabilities, the Big Four must prepare contingent strategies and attempt to diagnose the likely future of the Korean peninsula based on its variegated past and dynamic present.

The Role of China

Anticipation of a Korean reunification by Southern absorption or by system collapse in the North has found its way into China's foreign policy thinking and behavior. Nonetheless, it is important to recognize that China's thinking on Korean unification, far from being cast in stone, has mutated along with the evolution of the domestic, Northeast Asian regional, and global situations – including perhaps most important the state of Sino–American relations. In the early twenty-first century, China has emerged as a formidable regional power, enjoying its most benign external security environment in modern times, while casting a long shadow over the security calculus of every neighboring state. Of the four great powers, only China maintains good comprehensive relations with both North and South Korea, and it does so by using low-key, conservative tactics.

[79] Feffer (2005). [80] V. D. Cha (1997).

Before ROK normalization, the litmus test by which Seoul assessed Beijing's Korea policy was the degree to which China supported either (1) Korean unification North Korean style, or (2) peace and stability on the peninsula (i.e., the peaceful coexistence of the two Koreas). Only with the formal normalization decision in 1992 did China come to be viewed in Seoul as favoring the status quo.[81] For Pyongyang, any slight deviation by Beijing from its rigid unification formula, actual or perceived, at least until the 2000 inter-Korean summit, was deeply resented as allied abandonment and socialist betrayal.

In 1993, Chen Qimao, a leading Chinese international relations scholar and former president of the Shanghai Institute of International Studies, stated China's position on the Korean unification issue in the following terms:

> China supports President Kim Il Sung's plan to reunify North and South Korea in a Confederal Republic of Koryo under the principle of "one country, one nation; two systems, two governments." This is not only because of China's traditional friendship with North Korea but also because the Chinese leadership believes this policy meets *the current situation* of Korea and supports Korea's national interest as well as the peace and stability of the region. By contrast, *a dramatic change* – which would be very dangerous and could easily turn into a conflict, even a war – would be a disaster for the Korean nation. Further, it would threaten not only China's security but the security of the entire Asia-Pacific region and even the world as well.[82]

China was expressing a desire to have its Korean unification cake and eat it, too, by supporting the peaceful coexistence of the two Koreas under the guise of Kim Il Sung's confederal formula, while opposing any "dramatic change" (i.e., a German-style Korean reunification) as the most preferable and feasible way of maintaining the peace and stability on the Korean peninsula. Chinese Korea watchers tend to be conservative about Korean unification, hoping that the status quo can be maintained for a considerable period of time.[83] China very easily can be seen as having a deep enough desire to keep the North Korean state from collapsing such that Chinese intervention is likely in the event that the DPRK truly approaches system collapse.

What heightened Beijing's security concerns and its opposition to the unification-by-absorption scenario was its perception of U.S. strategy. "To put it bluntly," one pro-PRC newspaper in Hong Kong wrote, "the United States wants to . . . topple the DPRK, and this is a component of U.S. strategy to carry out peaceful evolution in the socialist countries." The United States "will practice a strategy of destruction against North Korea . . . with

[81] V. D. Cha (1999b). [82] Q. Chen (1993a: 70); emphasis added. [83] Y. H. Park (1998).

the aim of enabling South Korea to gobble up North Korea, like West Germany gobbling up East Germany."[84] With the improvement of Sino–American relations in the late 1990s, such anti-American assessments of the Korean situation seemed to subside by the latter part of 1997, especially in the wake of President Jiang Zemin's state visit to the United States, although China's hardliners have remained wedded to the notion that America's prounification policy is an integral part of America's policy of containment toward China.

Although Beijing's status quo antiunification policy does serve to maximize China's leverage as a balancer in Northeast Asian politics, China also genuinely fears that North Korea could come to feel cornered and see no choice but to fight back, triggering a regional war at the very least. Beijing does not doubt that Pyongyang would fight rather than succumb to German-style hegemonic unification. The use of nuclear weapons in such a war would affect North and South Korea more than China.[85] Even if the system in the North simply collapsed, moreover, it would be likely to trigger a bloody civil war rather than immediate absorption by the South. Any sort of disruptive reunification process and certainly any sort of new Korean War is particularly unappealing to China because of the ramifications for China's economy. International anxiety about instability in NEA would entail tremendous financial costs for China and might put a halt to the Chinese economic juggernaut.[86] An alternative scenario in which the North Korean economy would decline apace could hardly be comforting to China. Fearing the ideological and geostrategic consequences of a united Korea, Beijing might intervene to rescue a DPRK on the verge of collapse as a way of maintaining a strategic shield in the northern half of the Korean peninsula or as a way of arresting a massive exodus of refugees.

Even if we accept the possibly heroic assumption that Korean reunification will come about peacefully, neither igniting a civil war nor generating a massive refugee exodus, Beijing would still have to cope with a wide range of territorial disputes over fisheries and mineral and oil or gas deposits in the Yellow Sea, some of which are already on the Sino–ROK negotiations agenda. China's security dilemma today is not only ethnonationally charged, but also geostrategically entangled because more than 80 million members of minority nationalities (or about 8 percent of the total PRC population) reside in strategically sensitive but politically "autonomous" regions that account for roughly 64 percent of Chinese territory. The PRC lives in fear of the non-Han peoples in Xinjiang,

[84] See *Hsin Pao* (Hong Kong), April 8, 1994, p. 24, in *FBIS-China*, April 12, 1994, pp. 13–15; and *Hsin Pao*, June 24, 1994, 25, in *FBIS-China*, June 24, 1994, pp. 7–8, quotations on 14 and 7, respectively.

[85] Eberstadt (2004b: 434). [86] Eberstadt (2004b: 447).

Inner Mongolia, and Tibet refusing to allow their national identities to be misappropriated. What would a united and nationalistically charged Korea do about its historical territorial claims along the Sino–Korean border or in the northeastern provinces? Organizations such as Damui (Reclaim) in South Korea, with more than 50,000 members, are advancing the irredentist claim: "Manchuria was ours but was taken away [and] . . . maybe, one day, it'll be ours again." Damui's activities have already provoked Beijing's strong protests, and Seoul has acknowledged the need to curb such activities.[87]

A new unified Korea would lead to a new geostrategic landscape in the region, we are told, fundamentally changing Korea's foreign relations with the four major powers and making the "power struggle and economic competition in the region more apparent and more intense."[88] Some Chinese analysts have even compared the nationalism of a rising Korea with that of Japan more than a half-century ago: Korea "may follow Japan to gradually reveal the isolationist and radical characteristics of its nationalism. The self-swelling and arrogance of the irrational feelings of [Korean] nationalism have yet to be truly tested and challenged. . . . Thus, people are commonly worried that it may be very difficult to be sure about what the Koreans want to do, if the Korean peninsula is unified to be a stronger and richer nation."[89]

Some Chinese analysts have nonetheless given some thought to various endgame scenarios. According to one scholar, China's ultimate concern is not who will be the next "Great Leader" in Pyongyang but "whether the DPRK will remain as a stable and friendly buffer state."[90] One scenario envisions factional infighting in a collapsed North Korea, with one faction seeking help from the United States and/or South Korea and another seeking help from China. In such an event, according to Eric McVadon, who conducted extensive interviews with Chinese military officers, "Beijing would reject the appeal and urge Washington and Seoul to do the same. If Beijing's bilateral urging was insufficient, and it appeared that the United States and/or the ROK were ready to accede to the request, China would ask that the UN Security Council step in to prevent the movement of United States or ROK forces into the North."[91] Viewed in this light, there can be no doubt that President Kim Dae Jung's Sunshine Policy, especially the pledge not to undermine or absorb North Korea, was music to Chinese geopolitical and geostrategic ears.

Ultimately, China is not opposed to Korean reunification provided, we are told, that (1) it comes about gradually and peacefully; (2) it is a negotiated unification between the two Koreas, not a hegemonic unification

[87] Kreisberg (1996: 84–85). [88] F. Wang (1999: 181). [89] F. Wang (1999: 181). [90] X. Yi (1995: 133). [91] McVadon (1999: 287).

by absorption; and (3) a unified Korea does not harm or threaten China's security or national interests. "China will use her influence to strive for the peaceful unification of Korea, and to keep unified Korea as a friendly, or at best, *neutral* neighbor."[92] A united Korea would be expected, moreover, to be drawn within China's economic and military sphere; China should help shape developments in Korea, not merely follow the lead of the United States and Japan.[93] What is missing here is any ideological or identity-related imperative for the reunification of Korea under the leadership of a socialist ally. On the contrary, the maintenance of domestic stability – the successful establishment of a "well-off society" (*xiaokang shehui*) – as the single greatest challenge takes precedence over reunification, which is now defined as a goal to be achieved eventually, peacefully, gradually, and without outside interference.

Perhaps the single greatest contribution Beijing has made is to drive home the notion that North Korea is no banana republic that will collapse quietly without a big fight or without creating a huge problem for neighboring powers. Here, more than in any other issue area, China has played a major role in Korean affairs by not only providing diplomatic and economic support to the DPRK, but also by making clear to Seoul, Washington, and Tokyo that it is in the now common interest of all to promote the peaceful coexistence of the two Korean states on the peninsula rather than cope with the turmoil, chaos, and massive exodus of refugees that would follow in the wake of system collapse in the North. Such a system-maintaining scenario is and becomes the best/worst option for lack of a better alternative.

In short, China currently sees in the prospect of Korean reunification far more dangers than opportunities. A unified Korea would remove the DPRK as China's geostrategic *cordon sanitaire* and would deprive Beijing of the utility of using the Korean issue to advance its own national interests across the board, including in its dealings with the United States. Korean unification would also diminish Beijing's leverage in Korean and world affairs, would mean a more lonely and antisocialist world with one less socialist regime, would spew more refugees into northeastern provinces, and would trigger Japanese rearmament if the United States were to withdraw military forces from Korea.

The Role of Russia

Post-Soviet Russia's geostrategic power has declined in both absolute and relative terms, and the country has come to play only a minor role in Northeast Asian affairs. Furthermore, Korean reunification would seem

[92] G. Zhao (1997: 82). [93] J. Cai (1996: 200).

to pose much less of a challenge to Russia, compared with the other members of the Big Four. Moscow can look forward with equanimity to a unified Korea, having the least to lose politically, militarily, or economically from unification. In an acentric world, balance-of-power considerations suggest that a unified Korea would be a better defender of freedom of the seas than a weak and divided Korea dominated by China or Japan; that historic Korean animosity toward Japan and suspicion of China would prompt it to cultivate closer relations with Russia; and that, as a major industrial producer, a unified Korea would find a natural complementariness in Russia's markets, especially those for energy and raw materials.[94]

For Russia, however, support for unification does not mean support for the usual scenario of collapse in which the ROK absorbs the DPRK. Unification by North Korean collapse would be detrimental to Russian interests in border security and regional economic development. Nonetheless, Russian leaders often claim that only Russia among the Big Four supports *peaceful* Korean unification and also point out that Russia and Korea have never been at war. According to Alexander Zhebin, a leading Koreanist in Moscow, the security of Russia's Far East, its economic interests, and its support for peaceful Korean reunification are all inextricably linked:

> The security of Russia's Far Eastern regions and their populations depends on how events in Korea will develop. In the event of a US-DPRK military conflict, radioactive clouds from Korean Chernobyls (it is necessary to include more than 10 South Korean atomic power plants that might be destroyed) and streams of Korean refugees would possibly not reach America's Pacific coast, but they would surely get to Russia. And perhaps the US maps for targeting their cruise missiles will once again happen to be "out of date," as happened when the Chinese Embassy in Belgrade was bombed during the war over Kosovo. The military option is unacceptable to Moscow, because it would pose a direct threat to Russia's security. . . . Military conflict might also shatter hopes for the implementation of international oil, gas, transport, and other projects in Northeast Asia that are part of Russian plans for the social and economic development of its Far East.[95]

Much of Russia's diplomatic maneuvering in the early 1990s was couched in terms of aiding Korean reunification. But more truthfully the Kremlin at that time might have been expecting the DPRK to collapse along the lines of the Soviet empire. Moscow's downgraded relations with Pyongyang meant that Russia lacked sufficient influence in North Korea to play a mediating role. During the mid-1990s, a number of prominent Russian communists visited the DPRK at the invitation of the North Korean leadership, and these visitors expressed general admiration for Kim Jong Il. The North Korean leader kept asking his visitors what had

[94] Rubinstein (1997: 161–62). [95] Zhebin (2005: 148).

prompted Gorbachev "to choose the wrong way" and offered his own opinion that it was a case of high treason through which "Gorbachev and his henchmen on purpose destroyed the socialist system and the great state."[96]

Since the mid-1990s, Russian leaders have used bilateral meetings with ROK and DPRK leaders to enhance Russia's role in conflict resolution on the Korean peninsula. Kim Dae Jung endorsed this role in a May 1999 visit to Moscow, and Russian President Boris Yeltsin reiterated his support for growing contact between the North and the South.[97] Russia was pleased by the surprise June 2000 inter-Korean summit and hailed it as a major breakthrough, although there was some speculation among Russian analysts that Pyongyang was hoping mostly to extract concessions from the United States through the summit.[98] There is also speculation among external analysts that Russia's real interest in the Korean peninsula relates to its desire to have increased political and diplomatic cachet in Beijing, Tokyo, and Washington.[99]

Russia generally expressed significant support for Kim Dae Jung's Sunshine Policy. Analysts saw it as a means of improving the external environment of North Korea such that the regime might feel more at ease considering reunification. These Russian analysts believe that the DPRK, after embarking on reforms, may reap a quick harvest because of foreign aid, investment, technical assistance, and other opportunities.[100] China and Vietnam should serve as encouragement to Pyongyang in this regard. The conclusion of Russian Korea watchers is that Kim Jong Il's regime remains firmly in power but that permanent economic crisis, the maturation of the postrevolutionary generation, and the increased flow of information from abroad all contribute to a ticking time bomb that is bound to explode. Because a precipitous reunification is not desirable, Russia believes that the international community should consider the prospect of long-term coexistence of the two states and that a relatively secure and confident North Korea will prove a partner for dialogue and reform, rather than an isolated country under the burden of sanctions.[101] From the other side of the DMZ, and for the same reasons, South Korean officials supported the signing of a new Russo–DPRK treaty in 2000 and said it would have no averse impact on Russo–ROK relations.[102]

In terms of security, Russia does not worry about the possibility of Japan or China achieving a predominant position in a unified Korea; this perhaps is why Moscow takes an interest in being an intermediary

[96] The DPRK Report, NAPSNET, No. 10, p. 1. [97] Wishnick (2004).
[98] See The DPRK Report, NAPSNET, No. 23, April 2000, p. 2.
[99] Eberstadt (2004b: 430). [100] The DPRK Report, NAPSNET, No. 12, May 1998, p. 6.
[101] Torkunov (2003: 46). [102] Wishnick (2004).

for reunification talks. In fact, it is likely that Russia views a unified Korea as a counterbalance to potential threats from Japan or China. Along these same lines, however, Russia perhaps should be worried that Korean reunification would bring about an increase in Japanese armament, even Japanese nuclearization. There is the definite potential for a security dilemma atmosphere between Japan and Korea in which a unified Korea might ally with Russia as protection – indeed nuclear protection – against Japan, but with the consequence of increasing hostility in the region. To avoid such a scenario, an arrangement wherein the Big Four would conclude an international agreement guaranteeing unified Korea's independence and integrity has been proposed.[103] Such an arrangement would, however, be dependent on the balance of power among the guarantors and questionable collective security mechanisms.

Russia favors a gradual process of Korean unification in which the two Korean states pursue long-term peaceful coexistence with neither the ROK nor the United States attempting to change North Korea's behavior or seeking North Korea's collapse. Then, Korean unification can be achieved through peaceful means where Seoul and Pyongyang negotiate on an equal footing.[104] Following his July 2000 summit with Kim Jong Il, Russian President Vladimir Putin said that reunification should take place on the basis of the June 2000 joint declaration in an atmosphere of peace and stability. In steadfastly promoting Korean reunification, Russia opens the door to North Korean attempts at exploitation. Pyongyang will undoubtedly attempt to write off its nearly $4 billion in debt to Moscow, to obtain Russian assistance for the modernization of Soviet-built industries, and to acquire Russian-made weapons on easy terms as conditions for reunification talks with Seoul.

The Role of Japan

Japan remains an enigmatic economic power in search of an appropriate national identity and role conception. Japan has an inordinate stake in the outcome of a Korean reunification but, because of historical-cum-national-identity issues, is limited in the role that it can play. Whatever form a unified Korea might take, its political and economic system, its strategic choices and posture, and its relations with other major regional and global powers – especially China and the United States – will impact and shape Japan's security and prosperity. This may well explain Japan's Janus-faced approach to Korean unification. As Richard Halloran put it, "Tokyo goes through the motions of supporting reunification but that is '*tatemae*,' or façade. The '*hone*,' or reality, is that few Japanese would like

[103] S. H. Joo (2003). [104] S. H. Joo (2003).

to see Korea unified even though it would be politically incorrect to say so in public."[105]

The Japanese government was rather indifferent to Korean unification throughout the 1950s and 1960s. But since the 1970s, *faute de mieux*, Tokyo began to favor status quo on the Korean peninsula, a position at the time very much congruent with American policy. A combination of Japanese guilt and Korean *han* (unredeemed resentment) related to Japan's past colonial injustices has led Tokyo to take a relatively safe and passive position on inter-Korean relations. In a 1995 survey of Japanese Korea experts, more than one-third had an objection to Korean reunification – a larger proportion of experts than in China.[106] Japanese popular opinion holds that reunification is unlikely (37 percent of respondents to one survey in the mid-1990s said that it was ten or more years away) or completely impossible (28 percent of survey respondents suggested this).[107]

It is also unclear what type of leverage Japan commands in shaping the future of the Korean peninsula. Although it has made efforts in recent years to tie economic and aid policy to developments on the Korean peninsula, in many ways Tokyo has almost no role to play in the central unification issues, such as a North–South dialogue process, burgeoning North–South trade, arms control and disarmament of the peninsula, and the conclusion of a peace treaty.[108]

With continuing uncertainties on the Korean peninsula, lingering questions about the U.S.–DPRK nuclear confrontation, increasing anti-Americanism (or more precisely, anti-Bushism) in South Korea, and increasing rightward shifts in Japan, however, it is all but certain that Tokyo will be both pushed and pulled to take a more assertive posture in inter-Korean affairs. This is particularly true in the security domain, which raises questions about Japan's self-image as a "civilian power" and has obvious implications for Japan's role in Korean reunification, if and when it occurs.[109] But it is also true in the economic domain, where there has been significant Japanese surprise at the strength and degree of inter-Korean trade, as Seoul has surged ahead of Tokyo as Pyongyang's second largest trading partner.

The mutual distrust and enmity between Korea and Japan stemming from the burden of history give rise to a wide range of opinions and perspectives on Japan's role in or attitude toward a unified Korea. At one extreme Kenichi Takemura, a television commentator, author, and self-styled "internationalist," flatly declared in 1990 his pessimistic, realist prognostication of what Korean reunification would bring

[105] Halloran (1997: 216). [106] Y. S. Lee (1995: 13).
[107] *The White Paper of National Opinion Survey for Korea, Japan, and China* (Seoul: KBS & Yonsei University, 1996), p. 435.
[108] Yamaji (2004). [109] On Japan as a "civilian power," see Funabashi (1991/92).

about: "An all-out invasion of Japan by Korea is inevitable if Korea is reunified . . . therefore it is in Japan's best interest to help North Korea economically so the Korean peninsula remains divided as now."[110] Takemura clearly beefs up the long-standing strategic axiom of Korea being "a dagger pointed at the heart of Japan," although aggression has historically come from China rather than from Korea itself.

At the other extreme of the spectrum, Victor D. Cha rejects what he calls "the conventional wisdom" – that is, that a united Korea would be more independent of American influence, would further consolidate Sino–Korean relations, and would vent negatively toward Japan. Cha's "quasialliance" argument is that Sino–Korean relations would quickly deteriorate in tandem with a rapid improvement in Japan–Korean relations due to the imperative of Japan–Korean security cooperation in the face of a diminished U.S. presence and the economic fundamentals of unification.[111] Masashi Nishihara, the president of Japan's National Defense University, claims that "Japan seeks a united Korea that is friendly to Tokyo and Washington, that is economically viable and politically open, and that will allow token U.S. presence to remain."[112]

In general, Japan's policy toward Korean reunification appears to be shifting and path dependent. For instance, a combination of trepidation regarding Korean reunification and the nuclear weapons and missile threats from the North caused Japan to stand up and take notice of the tides of inter-Korean relations in the late 1990s. Within Japan today, a collapsist school favors the scenario of unification by absorption, whereas a survival school advocates unification by consensus.[113] It is the interplay between these two schools of thought in the context of a changing international environment that will yield most current Japanese thinking on Korean reunification. A unified Korea that shares Japan's democratic and economic systems would help maintain long-term stable bilateral relations, address frictions and disputes between the two countries in a practical manner, and further build confidence and trust between the two countries for greater economic and cultural exchanges and cooperation. Japan definitely does not want to see a unified Korea in possession of offensive weapons that could threaten Japan, such as medium-range ballistic missiles, long-range bombers, blue water naval capability, or, above all, nuclear weapons. If a unified Korea possessed such weapons, Japan could view this as a potential threat and take preventive countermeasures. After all, in the 1991–92 ROK Defense White Paper, Japan was treated as a hypothetical enemy, and when the Tokdo/Takeshima Islands issue surfaced in February 1995, Seoul undertook military exercises in the

[110] Quoted in *Far Eastern Economic Review* (Hong Kong), January 31, 1991, p. 31.
[111] V. D. Cha (1997: 82–86; 2000a).
[112] Quoted in Armacost and Pyle (2001: 126). [113] T. Y. Paek (1999).

seas near the islands. However, the unification of Korea would remove a major destabilizing factor in NEA and therefore contribute to peace and stability.[114] The South Korean public, however, has little faith that Japan will aid reunification. A mid-1990s survey found that 79.5 percent of Korean respondents believed that Japan would implicitly obstruct reunification, and only 5.7 percent of them believed that Japan would strongly support it.[115]

The best policy approach for realizing a desirable outcome for a unified Korea would be, it seems, to keep close trilateral policy coordination among Japan, the ROK, and the United States before, during, and after unification.[116] After all, the postunification defense posture of a unified Korea will be affected by its threat perception, which is difficult to predict without knowing the overall international situation during the postunification period. However, threat perception can be affected by biases or preconceptions, and given historical fears and antipathy toward Japan, this does not bode well for relations between a united Korea and Japan.

Masao Okonogi, Japan's foremost Korea expert, argues that many Japanese worry about a rise of extreme nationalism directed against Japan in a unified Korea. The possibility of a unified Korea turning to China to counter Japan cannot be denied. Following a November 1995 summit at which Presidents Kim Young Sam and Jiang Zemin took a unified stance in criticizing Japan, possibilities for PRC–ROK collaboration were reported in the Japanese and Korean media.[117] Likewise, Sino–Korean opposition to Japanese textbooks has been a similar cause for concern in Tokyo.

Japan is also worried about a possible flow of North Korean refugees in the wake of reunification. Currently, Japan takes very few refugees and concentrates on providing support through the United Nations. Recently, the Japanese government has put "dozens" of Japanese citizens – Japanese spouses of North Korean nationals who fled North Korea to China and want to return to Japan – under its protection but has stayed quiet about its activities out of consideration for China, which is effectively violating its 1986 repatriation agreement with North Korea. Officially, the Japanese government does not accept seekers of political asylum and does not issue travel documents to allow travel to Japan to apply for refugee status.[118] It is not clear what Japan would do if it suddenly were faced with waves of North Korean "boat people" or with North Korean citizens suddenly claiming Japanese ancestry for the purpose of emigration.

The uncertainty facing Japan regarding Korean reunification limits Japan's ability to take a clear stance on the issue, which in turn leads to a popular belief in South Korea that Japan is opposed to reunification.

114 Okonogi (2000: 129). 115 T. Y. Paek (1999: 43–44). 116 Yamaji (2004).
117 Okonogi (2000: 129). 118 Samuels (2004: 327).

Although Japan has much to gain from a reunified Korea that would remove the North Korean threat, promote regional integration, and offer new opportunities for Japanese investment in the modernization of North Korea, Tokyo is also concerned about the possibility of national identity conflict and of a Sino–Korean integration that would exclude Japan. At the moment, Japan is losing leverage with North Korea because of declining trade relations and therefore is losing one of its points of entry to the discourse on Korean reunification. Japanese aid could, however, play a very large role in the Korean reunification process and could even play a role in facilitating or stimulating inter-Korean dialogue. Therefore, neither the Japanese nor the Koreans should discount the possibility of a proactive role for Tokyo in reunification. But the creation of such a role will undoubtedly require significant effort to get past the national identity issues that plague both ROK–Japan and DPRK–Japan relations and that are consequently primed to plague relations between Japan and a united Korea as well.

The Role of the United States

When looking at the role of the United States in the realm of Korean reunification, it is worth repeating Selig Harrison's argument that "in North Korea and South Korea alike, it is an article of faith that the United States deserves the principal blame for the division of the peninsula and thus has a special responsibility for helping to restore national unity."[119] Although it is unclear whether there is a sense of guilt among U.S. policy makers for the enduring division, in a mid-1990s four-nation survey of NEA experts in China, Japan, Russia, and the United States, the United States showed the most support for Korean reunification.[120] What is clear is that the United States has the power to facilitate or hinder reunification. However, despite the suggestive stance of U.S.-based experts, never has the U.S. government either taken or pursued a clear position on Korean reunification.

During the long Cold War years, the predominant concern and objective was to deter Kim Il Sung from realizing his "magnificent obsession" of accomplishing Korean reunification by force. With the demise of the bipolar order, however, the situation became complicated as reunification seemed to become a more likely possibility. It also became complicated because, as compared with the relative simplicity of the Cold War, North Korea's behavior in the post–Cold War era confronted Washington with more complex and multifaceted challenges, such as the development of WMD and the threat of internal implosion or external explosion. The

[119] Harrison (2002: 102). [120] Y. S. Lee (1995: 13).

focus of U.S. concern regarding Korea shifted from the containment of communism to regional and peninsular peace and stability. This has ironically led the United States to be seen in the post–Cold War period as playing the unusual role of "honest broker" for the resolution of the Korean conflict, without taking a firm position on reunification, without ending its alliance with South Korea, without removing its troops from the Korean peninsula, and without normalizing its relations with North Korea.

There is no explicit U.S. policy on Korean reunification. A policy of muddling through – hoping to avoid disaster but taking only limited actions to prevent it – is a recurring theme in U.S. attitudes toward the North Korean question. The evolution of U.S. policy toward North Korea can therefore serve as a proxy for understanding the implicit U.S. policy on Korean reunification.

The long-standing official U.S. policy was to support the peaceful reunification of the peninsula under conditions acceptable to the Korean people. During the 1990s, senior government officials reiterated that U.S. policy is to "build a durable peace on the peninsula as a key contributor to regional stability and to facilitate progress by the Korean people... toward national reunification."[121] In the early 1990s, however, for the first time since the Korean War (and particularly in the wake of German reunification), it became common to hear and even faddish to assert in the United States that Korean reunification by Southern absorption was inevitable. This trend intensified in the wake of Kim Il Sung's death in July 1994, as many experts in Seoul and Washington predicted that North Korea would soon collapse.[122] This euphoria surrounding the idea of North Korean collapse is what led the Clinton administration to sign on to the 1994 Agreed Framework, despite the likely domestic political difficulties of implementing its clauses, specifically the $4.5 billion LWR component. This phase of anticipating North Korean collapse and Korean reunification lasted from 1994 until the North Korean missile test of 1998 sparked a new initiative in U.S. policy toward North Korea.

One prominent book during this first phase of post–Cold War attitudes toward reunification was Nicholas Eberstadt's *The End of North Korea*.[123] In earlier work, Eberstadt had argued that the North was likely to implode soon because its economy was deteriorating even as its WMD were accumulating. He called for rapid reunification, such as in the German case, in the hope that this would spur economic growth and reduce regional tensions. He argued that Western governments needed to stop coddling Pyongyang, even at the risk of offending China or Russia, and he called

[121] Quoted in Drennan (1998b: 167–68).
[122] McDevitt (2001: 256); Noland (2004b: 12–19). [123] Eberstadt (1999).

for the United States to underwrite the security of a united Korea and for Japan to underwrite its finances.[124] Others argued against this dual optimism about collapse and reunification, asserting that not only could North Korea stagger on for years without imploding, but also that, in the event of reunification, it was likely to cost Seoul upward of $1 trillion for a period of ten to twenty-five years.[125]

In his most recent writings, Eberstadt has changed his tune again. He now acknowledges that "the extraordinary complexity of the phenomena under consideration, the independent and unpredictable nature of the human agency at their center, and the ultimately irresolvable problem of asymmetries of information," consign the endeavor of predicting the DPRK's collapse "to the realm of art."[126] Eberstadt suggests a scenario-building approach, similar to the one suggested here.[127]

One thing that Eberstadt's collapsist school failed to realize is that Kim Il Sung's death may actually have created a more stable DPRK. Kim Jong Il's North Korea differs from that of his father, when the dream of unification involved the absorption of South Korea. As Georgy Bulychev suggests, "Kim Jong Il . . . is neither Nero nor Louis XIV – he thinks about 'après moi' and wants to keep the state in place, but he also understands that it is impossible to do this without change."[128] In this context, a change in the regime's strategic paradigm, rather than the change of the regime itself, looks more and more like the proper resolution to the broad concerns about North Korea's future.

With the 1998 missile test signaling the need to discuss with the DPRK the future of North Korea, the Perry Report, issued in October 1999, initiated the second phase of implicit U.S. policy toward Korean reunification by noting the centrality of the Agreed Framework and calling for a two-track approach of step-by-step comprehensive engagement and normalization with a concurrent posture of deterrence. This short-lived second phase was one of active engagement, in which it appeared that the United States might be willing to address some of the issues – normalization and security – that would facilitate engaged dialogue between Seoul and Pyongyang on reunification. The logic of this deterrence-plus policy was to neither prop up the North Korean system nor seek its collapse, but instead to promote a process of dialogue and confidence building that moved beyond mere deterrence. With the deterrence-plus policy came a shift from a reactive stance to a more active role in the management of inter-Korean affairs.

During this period, there was an alignment of U.S. and ROK views on reunification. The U.S. troop presence in Korea and President Kim Dae

[124] Eberstadt (1997). [125] Noland (1997). [126] Eberstadt (2004a: 24).
[127] Eberstadt (2004b: 429). [128] Bulychev (2005).

Jung's public declaration on several occasions that U.S. troops should remain even after the two Koreas are unified became symbols of allied credibility, resolve, and commitment. As Kim Dae Jung explained, "The U.S. forces stationed on the Korean peninsula and in Japan are decisive to the maintenance of peace and balance of power not only on the peninsula but also in Northeast Asia."[129] The official response from the United States was as follows:

> The U.S. welcomes the public statements of ROK President Kim Dae Jung affirming the value of the bilateral alliance and the U.S. military presence even after reunification of the Korean peninsula. The U.S. strongly agrees that our alliance and military presence will continue to support stability both on the Korean peninsula and throughout the region after North Korea is no longer a threat.[130]

At the same time, there emerged a consensus in South Korean and U.S. intelligence communities that North Korea could muddle through for at least another fifteen years.

The third phase of implicit U.S. policy toward Korean reunification inaugurated under George W. Bush is one of hesitantly catalyzing regime change. Neoconservatives aiming to remake the world are tempted to argue for preemptive strategic action – either unilateral or collective – aimed at causing regime change, dismantling North Korea, and creating a new, unified Korea under U.S. guidance.[131] The failure to implement regime change easily in Iraq, however, has contributed to a slowing of any such virulent policy. The third phase, in fact, has come to resemble the muddling through of the early phase of U.S.–DPRK relations. The United States seems content to see moves toward inter-Korean rapprochement as an interim means to deal with the nuclear crisis; then it wants the peace process to move back to a status quo of long-term, open-ended negotiations that may some day lead to Korean coexistence, followed by reconciliation and perhaps reunification. The United States

[129] Address by Kim Dae Jung at the 54th Commencement Exercises of the Korean Military Academy, March 16, 1998. Available at http://www.bluehouse.go.kr/engpdown/031717485480316-1.

[130] U.S. Department of Defense, Office of International Security Affairs, *United States Security Strategy for the East Asia-Pacific Region 1998* (Washington, DC: U.S. Department of Defense, Nov. 1998) p. 62.

[131] Olsen (2003: 87). On public calls for a more active policy toward North Korea and Korean unification, see Michael Judge, "North Korea's Dr. Evil," *Wall Street Journal*, October 15, 2002; "Pyongyang's Nuclear Blackmail," *Wall Street Journal*, October 18, 2002; Chuck Downs, "Kim Jong-il: Unfit Even for Dictatorship," *Wall Street Journal*, October 21, 2002; Bill Gertz, "Lawmakers Ask Bush to End Accord," *Washington Times*, October 31, 2002; "Kim Jong-il's Sunset," *Far Eastern Economic Review*, November 7, 2002; and James T. Hackett, "North Korea Ripe for Change," *Washington Times*, December 2, 2002.

is, in other words, more than content to see the Korean peace process remain a slow sequence of talks and is likely to facilitate this incrementalism by dragging its feet whenever it is possible to do so discreetly. This tacit reluctance aids contemporary U.S. policy goals by retaining a North Korean adversary that provides a rationale for keeping U.S. armed forces deployed on the Korean peninsula and for creating NMD and TMD systems.[132]

This muddling through is risky but certainly superior to a strategy of regime change that could lead to collapse via armed conflict. The process of encouraging a reunification-via-collapse scenario is dangerous because it would almost certainly entail the ROK military undertaking a major role in the administration, pacification, and reconstruction of the North, thrusting it into a political role that it has not had since the transition to democracy in South Korea. An unstable, undemocratic, united Korea emerging as a result of DPRK collapse is a real possibility. Therefore, short of a renewal of the Korean War, reunification via collapse is, for all but the hardest of the hardliners, the least desirable outcome.

In addition, it is unclear whether the U.S. military is ready for such a scenario if it were to emerge. In the event of collapse, current forces stationed in South Korea would have to assume very different roles and missions, potentially on a fairly abrupt basis and almost certainly including humanitarian missions. The military would likely be involved in reconstruction of the northern Korean economy and infrastructure, and would certainly be involved in dismantling North Korean WMD.[133] Coordination – possibly collaboration – with the Chinese PLA also would be a necessary skill for U.S. forces in a reunified Korea. Finally, the U.S. Army would need to enhance its intelligence collection and analysis capabilities across a broader spectrum of issues to deal with the new contingencies of collapse. Particularly dangerous collapse scenarios involve collapse through internal or external war and collapse that leads to rogue operations by the DPRK military.[134]

If the U.S. military were to be a major player in reunification, this might lead to resentment on the part of South Korea. "The clashing US and South Korean approaches can be explained," as John Feffer observes, "by the way they view an ideal reunification process. The way communist states collapsed in Europe led Americans to expect that states reunify with a bang, not a whisper."[135] For instance, the ROK is unlikely to want to pay for the use of U.S. troops in reunification efforts. It is even possible that growing anti-U.S. sentiment in South Korea might serve to inhibit reunification by driving the United States into a position of opposition on the

[132] Olsen (2003: 88–89). [133] Haselden (2002/03: 122–23).
[134] Pollack and Lee (1999: 93–98); Mitchell (2002/03: 133). [135] Feffer (2005).

reunification issue.[136] Were Korea to unify, it could be financially expensive for the United States, could lead to a loss of U.S. strategic access to and leverage over Korea, and could adversely affect U.S.–PRC relations. Therefore, it might not take much to push the United States into opposition. In addition, reunification could prove damaging to the U.S.–Japan relationship because of Korea's role as a geopolitical buffer and because of Japanese anxieties about Korea's postreunification potentials. The Japan factor is arguably the most important criterion that could lead to U.S. opposition to reunification.[137] If the United States does oppose Korean unification, Washington could undertake a more subversive form of opposition by publicly doubting the viability of reunification.[138]

The best strategy for reunification is one that involves reconciliation between North and South Korea. Reunification that is not preceded by a significant degree of reconciliation could prove disastrous. Emphasizing reconciliation is essentially a matter of recognizing priorities. Although reunification without reconciliation could be a prescription for disaster, reconciliation without reunification still represents significant progress; it would benefit all parties and is entirely compatible with U.S. interests in the region and on the peninsula.[139] Unfortunately, whereas the engagement phase of the late 1990s may or may not have helped catalyze the June 2000 inter-Korean summit, the regime change phase of the Bush administration has created a situation in which South Korea seems to lack U.S. support to pursue reconciliation and might even put itself at odds with its ally if it does so.

Currently, the United States maintains a high level of interest in North Korea because of Pyongyang's development of nuclear weapons. If the United States and North Korea can successfully resolve the nuclear weapons issue, it is unclear in what direction the relationship between these two countries would develop. Perhaps more important is the apparent North Korean belief that abandonment of the nuclear program implies abandonment of the only thing that is keeping the United States from implementing a policy of forcible regime change in the DPRK. That is to say, the U.S. desire to alter the future alignment of power in NEA by taking away North Korea's nuclear program only inspires North Korea to hold on more tightly to its nuclear weapons as a deterrent against U.S. action. This suggests a status quo trajectory of nuclear contention for years to come.

The Global Community

As the first truly global organization in all human history, the United Nations provides the most legitimate institutional expression of the idea

[136] Mitchell (2002/03: 129–30). [137] Olsen (2003: 86). [138] Olsen (2003: 87).
[139] Drennan (1998b: 174–75).

of a global community, helping facilitate, however imperfectly, the global conscious-raising, consensus-building, standard-setting, and law-making processes to deal with multitudes of problems concerning global peace and security, global development, global human rights, and global environmental protection. The United Nations began its life as a successor to the League of Nations with much promise. It was representative of the most ambitious attempt yet to create a single global community where all states had a voice. However, because of global geopolitical dynamics, the United Nations transitioned from being a meeting place for one global community to being a battleground for the two and then three Cold War blocs, as the First, Second, and Third Worlds each did their best to manipulate the world organization to their own nationalistic ends. The so-called UN crisis can be understood mainly as a crisis of *national* policy in the *global* organization. Indeed, the fundamental challenge for the United Nations will be how to stay relevant and viable as a global yet statecentric organization in a globalizing and fragmenting world where the competing and often mutually conflicting claims of state sovereignty and humanitarian intervention are vying for primacy.

The Quest for International Legitimation

In regard to the politics of divided Korea, no other global institution matches the importance of the United Nations. It is there that Seoul and Pyongyang, having searched the world over for a forum, can readily find an arena commanding global audiences and global primetime in their long march to absolute one-nation international legitimation. If national identity changes through processes of social interaction in international institutions, as social constructivists argue, then the United Nations more than any other international intergovernmental organization provides a social and institutional context to explore change and continuity in the identity politics of the two Koreas.

UN membership, which increased from 51 in 1945 to 191 in 2003, has come to be viewed as the imprimatur of international recognition and legitimation – a national identity badge, as it were – that no self-respecting country, especially divided or breakaway ones, could do without (Table 6.3). For many Third World states and ministates, UN membership is not only the locus of shortest and cheapest forum shopping, but also the most important catalyst for diplomatic recognition by more states. For the two Korean states, locked in their zero-sum game of competitive legitimation and national identity mobilization over the years, this necessarily implies that the UN has been a prime global battleground.

Given that national identity is a relationship, not a possession, it is important to look at how each Korean state has chosen to present its national role conception and role performance within the global

Table 6.3. UN Membership and Two Koreas' Recognition Race, 1945–2005

Month/Year	Countries Recognizing DPRK	Countries Recognizing ROK	Countries Recognizing Both Koreas	Countries Recognizing Only DPRK	Countries Recognizing Only ROK	Countries with UN Membership
1945	N/A	N/A	N/A	N/A	N/A	51
1948	8	0		8		58
1950	12	6		12	6	60
1955	12	6		12	6	60
1959	14	15		14	15	82
1962	16	54		16	54	110
1965	23	73		23	73	117
1970	35	81		35	81	127
1976	93	96	49			147
1980	102	115	64	38	51	154
1985	103	126	69	34	57	159
1990	109	146	90	19	56	160
1992	127	169	117	10	52	179
1995	132	180	126	5	54	185
1999	135	183	131			189
2003	153	186	150	3	36	191
2005	155	186	152	3	34	191

Source: Adapted from the Research Institute for National Unification, *Nampukhan gukyok chuse pigyo yonku* [*A Comparative Study of the Trends in the National Power of South and North Korea*] (Seoul: Research Institute for National Unification, December 1993), pp. 547–48; the Board of Unification, *Pukhan kaeyo > 95* [*Synopsis on North Korea > 95*] (Seoul: Tongilwon, December 1995), pp. 450–57; UN Press Release, ORG/1156 (19 January 1993); ROK Ministry of Unification. Available at http://www.unikorea.go.kr.

community, specifically as symbolized and structured by the UN system in general and the UN General Assembly in particular.[140] For both Koreas, UN membership has largely been used as a means to the ends of self-affirmation and embarrassment of the other. As argued in Chapter 1, national identity enactment entails an ongoing negotiating (social interaction) process through the cycles of international life to enhance physical and psychological survival, security, and well-being, in the course of which the self attempts to secure an identity that others do not bestow, whereas others attempt to bestow an identity that the self does not appropriate. Nothing better illustrates this than the long struggle of each of the two Koreas to have its own one-nation identity accepted by the global community.

A historical turnabout occurred on September 17, 1991, the first day of the (forty-sixth) annual session, when the UN General Assembly admitted the DPRK and the ROK as the 160th and 161st member states.[141] This milestone was made possible by what had already occurred in the Security Council five weeks earlier. Indeed, the 3001st meeting of the Security Council on August 8, 1991 may well be remembered as one of the most remarkable events or nonevents in the annals of global high politics in the world organization. On this day, the Security Council devoted only five minutes – between 11:30 am and 11:35 am EST to be exact – to finally crossing the Rubicon on divided Korea. Without any debate, the council unanimously adopted the report of the Committee on the Admission of New Members concerning the applications of the two Koreas for UN membership.

Equally revealing is the rather unusual manner of the action. The two separate membership applications were merged into a single draft resolution, and the council decision (and recommendation to the UN General Assembly) was adopted without a vote as Resolution 702 (1991).[142] The brevity of the Security Council action merely underscored the consensus of the Perm Five (P-5) to accept the two separate membership applications as a package deal to prevent the intrusion of the zero-sum style inter-Korean politics, even as the decision itself was touted as consonant with the principle of universality, and as such, as the triumph of both Koreas in their quest for international legitimation. That a collective decision could be made in 1991 to perform diplomatic surgery as delicate as separating the Korean conjoined twins is another testimonial to the virtuous circle of UN rejuvenation in the early post–Cold War years.

[140] For analyses of the two Koreas' UN diplomacy, see S. S. Kim (1997c); C. Y. Pak (1995); Y. W. Kihl (1998); B. C. Koh (2000); S. W. Lee (2004).
[141] UN General Assembly Resolution 46/1 (September 17, 1991).
[142] UN Doc., S/PV. 3001 (August 8, 1991).

Yet, far from accepting its UN membership as a diplomatic triumph or even as a grand bargain for state security and survival, Pyongyang reacted to the process in a way that was defensive and despondent to a fault. The statement of the DPRK Foreign Ministry – dated May 27, 1991 – and submitted to the Security Council reversing its long-standing opposition to the simultaneous dual-entry formula, acknowledges in a bitter tone Pyongyang's national identity entrapment dilemma:

> Taking advantage of the rapid changes in the international situation, the south Korean authorities are committing the never-to-be condoned treason to divide Korea into two parts... by trying to force their way into the United Nations.... As the south Korean authorities insist on their unilateral United Nations membership, if we leave this alone, important issues related to the interests of the entire Korean nation would be dealt with in a biased manner on the United Nations rostrum and this would entail grave consequences. We can never let it go that way. The Government of the Democratic People's Republic of Korea has *no alternative but to enter the United Nations at the present stage as a step to tide over such temporary difficulties created by the south Korean authorities.*[143]

To better understand North Korea's one-nation identity angst, it is essential to step back a little and reassess the changes that have occurred over the years in the UN's role, especially in relation to the "Korean question" in its many contentious and mutating manifestations. Because direct negotiations with the Soviet Union on the Korean independence-cum-reunification question had failed to produce agreement, the United States reached the conclusion in 1947 that the United Nations was the only remaining forum for the Korean reunification issue. Despite the opposition from the Soviet Union, the United Nations adopted on November 14, 1947, a U.S.-sponsored draft resolution that called for the establishment of UNTCOK to facilitate, monitor, and supervise the (May 10, 1948) general elections in (South) Korea. On August 15, the new ROK was formally inaugurated in Seoul, and four months later the UN General Assembly adopted another American draft resolution – Resolution 195 (III) of December 12, 1948 – which declared

> that there has been established a lawful government (the Government of the Republic of Korea) *having effective control and jurisdiction over that part of Korea where the Temporary Commission was able to observe and consult* and in which the great majority of the people of all Korea reside; that this Government is based on elections which were a valid expression of the free will of the electorate of that part of Korea and which were observed by the Temporary Commission; and that this is the only such Government in Korea.[144]

143 UN Doc. S/22642 (June 3, 1991), p. 4; emphasis added.

144 UN Doc. GAOR, 187th Meeting, December 12, 1948, Resolution 195 (III), "The Problem of the Independence of Korea," pp. 25–27; quote at p. 25; emphasis added.

This resolution may be considered as an opening salvo in the United Nations' involvement in the so-called Korean issue. Taking advantage of the lack of clarity of the resolution,[145] South Korea lost no time in advancing its claim that the ROK was the only legal national government in Korea, thus providing "the decisive occasion for the ROK to determine the formula of the unification of Korea under United Nations supervision."[146] For ROK President Syngman Rhee, unification was nothing less than "territorial restoration," even as he repeatedly issued clarion calls to reunify the country peacefully if possible and by force if necessary.[147] In the North, however, on August 25, a Supreme People's Council was "elected" with Kim Il Sung as its chairman, and on September 9, this group proclaimed the establishment of the DPRK and claimed jurisdiction over all Korea. In short, by the fall of 1948, liberated and divided Korea formally ceased to be a unified nation-state.

Early in 1949, first the ROK and then the DPRK applied for UN membership; the outcome in the Security Council was predictable. In the following decade, South Korea reapplied several times, whereas North Korea did so once and then signed on to a 1957 Soviet dual-membership proposal. South Korea benefited from the competition in the UN arena because it was repeatedly cited as the sole legitimate government on the Korean peninsula, while facing the Soviet minority veto each time. In 1960, as indicated in Table 6.3, fifty-six governments recognized Seoul, whereas only fifteen recognized Pyongyang. North Korea, meanwhile, had sunk so low as to accept the plan for separate admission, although it was not implemented. The DPRK was concerned through the 1960s, mostly with maintaining sovereignty and legitimacy at home.

The 1970s, however, stand out as *la belle époque* of Pyongyang's engagement in the politics of competitive legitimation. South Korea found itself challenged by a changing international milieu, marked by East–West détente, Sino–American rapprochement, the American defeat in Indochina, drawdowns of U.S. troops from Korea, the entry of the PRC into the United Nations, and the rise of the Third World as a collective

[145] One interpretation, preferred by the successive governments in South Korea, is that the UN General Assembly has recognized only one government in Korea as meeting the criteria of a lawful government, namely, the ROK government; hence, the latter is the "only lawful government" on the Korean peninsula as a whole. Another interpretation, which is viewed as more plausible by disinterested parties, is that the UN General Assembly has recognized the ROK government as the only "lawful government" that meets two key conditions: (1) "having effective control and jurisdiction over that part of Korea where the UNTCOK was able to observe [elections] and consult [with the people concerned]," that is to say, the U.S. occupation zone in the South; and (2) being "based on elections which were a valid expression of the free will of the electorate of [the same part of Korea]." Revealing enough, it is this latter interpretation that Tokyo has embraced in its normalization negotiations with Seoul in 1965.

[146] S. J. Kim (1976: 36). See also C. Y. Pak (1995: 613). [147] S. J. Kim (1976: 37).

global actor calling for a New International Economic Order (NIEO). Pyongyang began actively recruiting members of the nonaligned movement to support its quest for absolute legitimation at the United Nations.

By 1973, both Koreas had established an observer mission to the United Nations in New York, and the ROK moved to adopt the German formula (admission as separate member states), but Pyongyang rejected this out of hand and called for the formation of a "Confederal State of Koryo" that would be a transitional step toward reunification. Kim Il Sung said, "If the North and the South want to enter the United Nations before unification, they should enter as one state at least under the name of the Confederal Republic of Korea."[148]

Yet, rather than leading to entry for both states or even one state, this chain of events led to a strange denouement in 1975 when the General Assembly adopted two contradictory resolutions on the same day, one pro-ROK (Resolution 3390A) by a vote of 59–51 with 29 abstentions and the other pro-DPRK (Resolution 3390B) by a vote of 54–43 with 42 abstentions. The DPRK, ignoring the pro-ROK resolution, pronounced the pro-DPRK statement to be "an epochal event" and "a great turning point" in the history of UN politics. In fact, however, the 1975 debate merely forced the world organization to recognize and legitimize the reality of the two separate governments and states on the Korean peninsula. Pyongyang thereafter rather abruptly dropped the UN issue. By mid-1976, a nearly equal number of countries recognized each Korean state, and more than half of these recognized both (Table 6.3). Neither Seoul nor Pyongyang retaliated against those countries engaging in dual recognition.

In the 1980s, however, North Korea suffered a series of diplomatic setbacks. The Third World quest for the NIEO exhausted itself, and U.S. hegemony in the United Nations returned. The hosting of numerous *juche* conferences and symposia in North Korea paled in comparison to Seoul's hosting of the Interparliamentary Union conference in 1983, the World Bank/IMF annual meetings in 1985, the Asian Games in 1986, and, most important, the Summer Olympic Games in 1988. Pyongyang's global search for Olympic boycotters solicited only Cuba to abstain. The 1983 Rangoon bombing and the 1987 midair sabotage of a KAL jetliner painted Pyongyang as a vicious violator of international norms. Sensing the changing tides, the DPRK reoffered Kim Il Sung's proposal for joint membership as a single confederal unit. But there was no precedent for this because the United Nations, despite its name, admits states, not nations or confederations. At home, Pyongyang remained adamant in its rhetoric, describing the dual-entry proposal as "a criminally splittist act" and asserting that "the United States... has authored the splittist

[148] *People's Korea,* June 27, 1973.

idea . . . in order to achieve their goal of keeping south Korea forever under their control."[149]

On March 8, 1991, South Korea made a decisive shift from secret to open diplomacy, declaring publicly that Seoul would apply for UN membership in 1991. Seoul then announced a 36-nation tour by its current and former prime and foreign ministers to drum up support for simultaneous entry if possible and unilateral entry if necessary. Without explicit support from Beijing, Seoul was banking on the notion that China would not dare risk its international reputation and economic interests by casting a solo veto. This gamble paid off, or rather the issue became moot, when Pyongyang dramatically reversed its long-standing party line on May 27 and jump-started its own application for separate UN membership.

The United Nations' management of the four major Cold War membership and national identity cases in the twenty-year period (1971–91) – indeed, the four major fault lines of Cold War politics – suggests the outer possibilities and limitations of its potential role in Korean reunification. With the Cold War, major membership problems relating to the divided polities of China, Germany, Vietnam, and Korea began plaguing the United Nations. Each has since been cleared off the agenda. In 1971, thanks to U.S.–China rapprochement, Beijing was recognized as the appropriate holder of China's UN seat, and Taipei was forced to give up its seat at the table. The problem of the existence of two German states was resolved first in 1973 through their simultaneous admission to the United Nations, and then in 1990 through the reunification of Germany. In 1977, two years after the takeover of South Vietnam by North Vietnam, a single Vietnam was granted membership. Finally, in 1991, through a process of simultaneous admission, both North and South Korea became members of the United Nations.

If Korean reunification is defined as a specific event or outcome, the United Nations' role is indirect and limited to *ex post facto* legitimation of what had already been settled by war, absorption, or consent outside the world organization. However, if Korean reunification is defined as the ongoing peace or reconciliation process, the United Nations has an important role to play. This is what President Kim Dae Jung called "*de facto* Korean unification" through which people, goods, and services can move freely across the DMZ, using the newly reconnected inter-Korean railways and roads without any prior *de jure* unification.[150] By accepting and legitimizing North and South Korea as two separate but equal member states, the United Nations has expanded the possibility of both Koreas peacefully coexisting and cooperating inside and outside the world organization. Herein lies the United Nations' socialization role in

[149] *Rodong Sinmun [Worker's Daily]*, May 18, 1991. [150] C. I. Moon (2005: 8–9).

member states' identity politics, as states change or adjust their national identities in the course of their social interaction processes and gradually internalize the ineluctable truth that the world organization is and becomes a world of many national identities and that the peaceful coexistence of identity differences is *modus operandi.*

However, the United Nations' involvement in the Korean War did little to enhance UN prestige or effectiveness during the Cold War. Despite the critical role the United Nations played in the prevention of Kim Il Sung's "magnificent obsession" with Korean reunification by force, in the end the United Nations' collective security system, as embodied in Chapter VII enforcement provisions, emerged far more weakened than strengthened. The fact that the United Nations did not have a prominent role in managing or resolving some of the major conflicts that wracked Asia during the Cold War is in no small measure due to the controversies and legacies generated by the United Nations' involvement in the Korean War.[151] In addition, the presence of the Big Four in the region with interests of their own in managing conflict, a widespread perception and suspicion that the UN system (especially the Security Council) and the international financial institutions are tools of powerful Western states, and a strong attachment to the norms of state sovereignty and noninterference are additional factors working against the United Nations' involvement in most East Asian regional conflicts or disputes. Some exceptions are UN peacemaking operations in Cambodia (UN Transitional Authority in Cambodia [UNTAC]) and East Timor (UN Transitional Administration in East Timor [UNTAET]), as well as the UN Mission of Support in East Timor [UNMISTET]).[152] At the same time, one of the defining and discouraging characteristics of the UN system of conflict management has been its inability or unwillingness to manage conflicts in their early, upstream stages before they reach the downstream, crisis stage. The United Nations has largely been preoccupied with reacting to full-blown crises rather than managing emerging conflicts.[153]

Although the ROK has been more active than the DPRK in joining international organizations, it has not solicited them to play a more active role in Korean reunification or the peace process. Seoul has preferred to coordinate directly with its ally the United States. At the end of the day, the United Nations and other international organizations have played a limited role – and often an indirect one – in the inter-Korean peace process. Still, the United Nations has performed a vital normative function as "the provider of normative and legal frameworks that constrain

[151] See Stueck (1995: 370). For an excellent discussion about the United Nations' marginal and indirect role in managing violent conflicts in Asia, see Foot (2003).
[152] Foot (2003: 312). [153] See S. S. Kim and A. Kim (2004: 987).

certain forms of state behaviors – and as an arena where interests can be exposed, legitimized, or delegitimized."[154]

International Humanitarian Assistance

On the ground in the DPRK, the United Nations has played an indispensable role in addressing the North Korean famine and resulting deaths variously estimated between 1 million (roughly 5 percent of the population)[155] to 2.5 million (11 percent of the population).[156] In issuing an urgent appeal for emergency UN aid in 1995, the DPRK government for the first time allowed a UN Assessment Mission – representing the UN Department of Humanitarian Affairs, the UNDP, the World Health Organization (WHO), UNICEF, the WFP, and the Food and Agriculture Organization (FAO) – into the country to assess damages. After several on-site assessments, the United Nations, and especially the WFP, responded in November with food relief – an initial shipment of 5,140 tons of rice for distribution among 500,000 people left destitute by summer floods. By December, the reclusive and sovereignty-bound North Korea was now cooperating more willingly than ever before with multilateral aid officials, taking them to the disaster-stricken hinterlands away from the Potemkin Village of Pyongyang. As a result, WFP aid workers were able to send back to their home offices eyewitness accounts of all the signs of spreading famine and starvation: in certain areas, children could be found at less than 80 percent of their average target weight for their height. However, because of Pyongyang's international reputation as a swollen garrison state, and the fact that all foreign television and print media had been denied access to North Korea, there was a tepid international response to the famine. As shown in Table 6.4, UN Consolidated Inter-Agency Humanitarian Assistance for the DPRK from July 1996 to December 2004 amounts to $1.49 billion, about 65 percent of funds requested. The WFP targeted the food assistance to the most vulnerable population groups, including the youngest children and pregnant and nursing women, and contributed to saving lives and improving the nutritional status of many in North Korea.

The UN appeal served to legitimize and justify the participation of the United States, Japan, and South Korea, overcoming the domestic political difficulties in those countries associated with providing aid to North Korea. Since 1995, the WFP has delivered almost 4 million metric tons of food aid, mostly cereals, to the DPRK. Table 6.3 shows how the United Nations' aid has come to an annual average of 67 percent of the DPRK's requests. The WFP has also identified the urban population to

[154] Foot (2003: 340). [155] Haggard and Noland (2005: 8). [156] Natsios (2001: 215).

Table 6.4. UN Consolidated Interagency Humanitarian Assistance Appeals for DPRK, 1996–2004

Appeal Timeframe	Funds Requested ($US Million)	Contributions ($US Million)	Percentage of Needs Covered
07/1996–03/1997	43.6	34.4	79%
04/1997–03/1998	184.4	158.4	86%
01/1998–12/1998	383.2	215.9	56%
01/1999–12/1999	292.1	189.9	65%
01/2000–12/2000	313.8	153.1	49%
01/2001–12/2001	384.0	248.0	65%
01/2001–12/2002	246.8	220.0	89%
01/2001–12/2003	229.4	133.1	58%
01/2001–12/2004	208.8	125.2	60%
TOTAL	2286.1	1478.0	N/A

Source: UN Office for the Coordination of Humanitarian Affairs, Geneva, Switzerland. Available at http://ocha.unog.ch/fts/analysis/index.asp?action=1&var=appeal_title&dir=asc.

be quite vulnerable because urban households have less access to food due to the lower rations received through the public distribution system (PDS) as compared with those issued at cooperative farms. Because of the 2002 economic reforms in the DPRK, the population has experienced skyrocketing food prices; households now spend an average of 65 percent of their income on food, including their government ration.[157]

In fact, the food crisis seemed to be rearing its head once again. The WFP announced in 2004 that the vast majority of North Koreans were in dire need of outside help. From late 2004 to early 2005, nearly 1 million elderly citizens and 600,000 children in North Korea stopped receiving cooking oil rations. Another 2.5 million North Koreans were expected to see their rations cut in the summer.[158] However, to feed these people, the WFP depends on international contributions to continue its program in North Korea. As Table 6.5 indicates, Japan (23%), the ROK (14%), and the United States (11%) are the three most important contributors, and it is always possible that geopolitical disputes with North Korea could drive these countries to decrease their contributions.

This involvement in the North Korean famine has led to a wealth of new information about North Korea, given the number of surveys and studies conducted by UN organs. In 2002, UNICEF and the WFP conducted a nutrition survey, and in 2003, the WFP released a set of household food

[157] World Food Programme (2005a, 2005b).
[158] "N. Korea Desperately in Need of Food Aid: WFP," *Chosun Ilbo*, April 26, 2005.

Table 6.5. WFP's Food Aid Operational Requirements in DPRK, January 1, 2004–June 30, 2005 (as of May 18, 2005)

WFP Appeal	U.S. Dollars 171,177,896		Metric Tons (MT) 481,190	
Donor	Resource Level (US$)	Percentage of Total	Purchase Requests Raised (in MT)	Percentage of Total
Australia	6,548,690	3.83	17,875	3.71
Canada	4,321,970	2.52	6,639.1	1.38
Cuba	570,000	0.33	2,500	0.52
EUR Commission	5,510,579	3.22	12,343.5	2.57
Finland	390,179	0.23	518	0.11
Germany	2,784,788	1.63	9,419	1.96
Ireland	932,836	0.54	1,210	0.25
Italy	3,610,109	2.11	5,243.5	1.09
Japan	39,546,665	23.10	131,487	27.33
Republic of Korea	23,385,414	13.66	100,000	20.78
Luxembourg	808,166	0.47	2,000	0.42
New Zealand	523,249	0.31	825	0.17
Norway	1,759,989	1.03	2,641	0.55
Private donors	123,481	0.07	102	0.02
United States	19,025,900	11.11	50,000	10.39
Multilateral total received	118,120,986		371,155.0	
Percentage against appeal	69%		77%	
Shortfall	53,056,910		110,035.2	
Percentage shortfall	31%		23%	

Source: WFP Resourcing Update on the DPRK.

economy analyses. The FAO and the WFP fielded a joint Crop and Food Supply Assessment Mission in September and October 2004. Anthropometric surveys were carried out in 1998 and 2002. The UN Environmental Program carried out the first ever State of the Environment report of the DPRK in 2003.[159]

These studies have indicated the successfulness of the various food aid programs from the 1990s. The 2004 Nutrition Survey suggested an improvement in nutritional status among small children since the last survey in 2002.[160] Because of the WFP's policy of "no access, no food," food distribution affects 154 of 203 counties/districts in the DPRK, accounting for 83 percent of the country's civilian population. The WFP has periodically stopped distribution to provinces where it has not been allowed

[159] UNEP (2003). [160] World Food Programme (2005a).

to monitor the outlay of food. Because of new constraints imposed on the humanitarian community in late 2004, the WFP had to reduce its international monitoring staff from fifteen to ten during 2005. However, WFP maintained its main office in Pyongyang and five suboffices located in Sinuiju, Wonsan, Hamhung, Chongjin, and Hyesan. With these six offices, the WFP by far has the greatest geographical coverage of any international organization working in the DPRK. In a surprise move in the fall of 2005, North Korea requested that all international aid organizations leave the country because of alleged political interference by the United States. The United Nations opened negotiations with Pyongyang to try to reach an agreement that would allow continued disbursement of food aid, but the ultimate outcome is unclear.

Multilateral Development Aid

When it comes to global economic development, the ROK is a supplier of multilateral development aid, whereas the DPRK is a recipient of such aid. In his 1993 speech before the General Assembly, ROK Foreign Minister Han Sung-joo underscored the need for "a substantial increase in development resources" and encouraged developed countries to "enhance their efforts in this area."[161] Nonetheless, although the ROK has seen its dues payments to the United Nations increase, it has not increased its total level of official development assistance (ODA), which remains less than the 0.7 percent of GDP target set by the United Nations. However, to be fair, this is in part because the aid that the ROK sends to the DPRK is not counted in its ODA numbers. Similarly, because of U.S. and Japanese objections, the DPRK has not been able to benefit from developmental aid from the World Bank or the Asian Development Bank. The UNDP therefore remains the best hope for developmental aid reaching North Korea because it is more difficult for the United States, Japan, or other countries to interfere with UNDP aid for political reasons. Nonetheless, the UNDP is itself cautious about the prospects of providing money to a DPRK with unknown nuclear and military ambitions. Recently, the UNDP did decide to extend the life of the TRADP through 2015.[162]

Since the establishment of the UNDP country office in Pyongyang in 1980, a strong environmental partnership has been forged between the DPRK government and the UNDP. The environment was considered a major priority area in the first (1997–2000) and second (2001–03) Country Cooperation Frameworks, which serve as the basis for the UNDP's involvement with the DPRK.

161 Quoted in B.C. Koh (2000: 202).
162 "UNDP Extends River Project in N. Korea, China by a Decade," Yonhap, April 27, 2005.

The United Nations and Inter-Korean Reconciliation

In the 1990s, few knew what the United Nations would hold in store for North and South Korea. Would their joint membership mollify or exacerbate the politics of competitive legitimation and delegitimation? Would the organization's new imprimatur in the post–Cold War world of globalization help reduce the Cold War dynamics on the Korean peninsula? Fifteen years later, it seems that neither overly optimistic nor overly pessimistic predictions have come true.

Both North and South Korea have followed into the post–Cold War world the trajectories that they were on from the 1980s until at least 2000. South Korea has embraced globalization and has expanded its interest in multilateral cooperation. It pays large UN dues, participates in UN leadership roles, speaks in favor of UN peacekeeping, has signed onto many major international agreements and participated in international conferences, has tried to expand cooperation on environmental issues, and has called for more multilateral developmental aid. North Korea, in contrast, has preferred to continue its autarkic orientation, using the United Nations as a sounding board for speeches on state sovereignty and *juche* self-reliance. At the same time, North Korea has accepted aid from various parts of the UN system for famine relief and, to a lesser extent, economic development.

With the 2000 inter-Korean summit meeting, the tone and style of the two Koreas' multilateral diplomacy in the world organization changed. For the first time in the checkered history of the "legitimacy war" inside and outside the United Nations, Seoul and Pyongyang jointly sponsored a draft resolution, which the General Assembly then adopted unanimously – without a vote – on October 31, 2000: General Assembly Resolution A/55/11, "Peace, Security and Reunification on the Korean peninsula." Revealingly, this resolution reflected Seoul's position by prioritizing peace over reunification. Nonetheless, North Korea's State of the World message delivered by Ambassador Li Hyong Chol on September 15, 2000, singled out "independence as our life and soul. The idea of independence runs through [the] domestic and foreign policies and lines of the Government of the Democratic People's Republic of Korea. . . . The summit meeting and the resulting joint declaration represent a historic milestone, marking a turning-point in achieving the cause of independent reunification of our nation."[163]

Although the United Nations is likely to continue to play a role in North Korea and although the two Korean states are likely to continue to play their roles in the United Nations, it seems that the major catalysts for Korean reunification and for moderation in the Korean security system

[163] UN Doc. A/55/PV.17 (September 15, 2000), p. 26.

will come from intra-Korean and bilateral sources. The intra-Korean summit of June 2000 and the working-level meetings that have followed in its wake occurred independently of the United Nations. Because of China's veto threat, the six-party talks have progressed or stalled independently of the United Nations. Although the United Nations does have certain roles to play on the Korean peninsula, compared with those of the United States, China, and the two Korean states themselves, they hardly seem to be the leading ones.

Although the United Nations – and specifically the question of Korean membership in that body – has played a role in the politics of competitive legitimation and delegitimation on the Korean peninsula, the majority of relevant factors for Korean reunification are captured at the local, inter-Korean, and dyadic levels. Before the eruption of the 2002–03 nuclear stand-off, North Korea was building relations with the IMF, the World Bank, and the Asian Development Bank. The DPRK has also been involved with a set of international organizations and NGOs providing food aid for the past ten years. Shin-wha Lee notes the major success of incorporating the DPRK into the ARF (ASEAN Regional Forum), described in the world media as the "beginning of the end of North Korea's isolation."[164] Yet, none of these organizations are actively crafting a reunification strategy or pushing North Korea in one direction or another.

One suggestion has been "an internationally sponsored Marshall Plan for North Korea." According to Georgy Bulychev, such a program would need to avoid suspicions of being aimed at regime change – even by way of a "velvet revolution" – and should provide instead for the gradual transformation of the current political elite. As compared with collapsist predictions, the program should include multiple stages and be implemented over a period that could exceed ten or fifteen years.[165]

Will the Two Koreas Become One?

The most obvious question – how long the post–Kim Il Sung system will survive and in what shape or form – has no simple answer. The interplay between North Korea and the outside world is highly complex, variegated, and even confusing. What complicates our understanding of the shape of things to come in North Korea is that all countries involved have become moving targets on turbulent trajectories subject to competing and often contradictory pressures and forces. What is the future of the Chinese, Japanese, and Russian economies? What is the future of the Chinese Communist Party? How stable is South Korean democracy? How stable is the U.S.–Japan alliance? How much aid will the South Korean public

[164] S. W. Lee (2004: 180). [165] Bulychev (2005).

provide to North Korea? The answers to these questions and others like them imply the range of possibilities for what might become of North Korea.

To bring about a long peace and reunification – a scenario of unification by consensus – is to require that the two Koreas, especially the stronger and more stable South, take a series of small but practical steps toward the creation of a "working peace system."[166] Although committed to a democratic and peaceful reunification as the ultimate end, such a functional approach proceeds from the premises (1) that national unification per se does not automatically bring about peace, power, prosperity, and democracy; (2) that Korean reunification without prior inter-Korean reconciliation – indeed without a prior working peace system – may be a sure recipe for catastrophe for all; and (3) that the two Koreas must first initiate the politics of regional reconciliation with changes at home and then start the functional peace process by discussing areas of mutual interest on which they can most readily reach agreement.

The working peace system is premised on and proceeds from the acceptance of identity differences that all social and economic actors in both Koreas will come together based on what unites them. Such a functional approach, starting in the area of economics, could provide the desired popular pressure or spillover effects to keep the on-again, off-again inter-Korean dialogue alive, while stimulating the opening of more and more channels of communication and exchanges in related areas. A system of multiple functional channels is what is meant in functional international theory by "peace by pieces": pieces that can be seen as constituting organic elements of gradual social and economic integration of the two Koreas lead gradually to a working peace system.

Civil war analysts who use incentive-based strategic bargaining approaches to study the end of intrastate wars have recognized a three-step process by which such wars draw to a conclusion: negotiation, settlement, and implementation. Each step implies that the two parties have reached a particular conclusion: (1) to discuss a compromise settlement seriously, (2) to accept a final peace agreement and a new postconflict order, and (3) to carry out the actual agreement. The two Koreas will neither seriously consider nor conclude a peace agreement unless there are exogenous changes that make maintenance of the status quo unacceptable because "negotiated reunification does not occur during periods of stability and prosperity, but rather during periods when both states are faced with crisis conditions that make the status quo division too costly to maintain."[167] As the ROK remains relatively stable and prosperous – despite the Asian Financial Crisis of 1997–98 and President Roh Moo-hyun's impeachment of mid-2004 – and the DPRK has developed coping

[166] For classical functionalism, see Mitrany (1966). [167] A. Kim (2004: 210).

mechanisms for dealing with instability and its lack of prosperity, the possibility of the two states overcoming their desire for regime maintenance with any sort of grand compromise solution might seem slim. Therefore, the policy of going step by step to make a series of functional linkages and network connections seems preferable.

To identify appropriate functional linkages, a conflict management analysis is a useful tool. If inter-Korean relations are approached through a conflict management lens, several avenues of optimism emerge. Using a conflict management approach requires dispelling several misperceptions: (1) that all conflicts are inherently bad or dangerous and as such should be eliminated or resolved, (2) that there is a single-level or single-factor solution to all armed conflicts or security dilemmas, and (3) that diagnosis and prescription are always matched. This approach is one of the ways of organizing thought on the past and present with an eye toward creating a more peaceful future.

The conflict management approach has come into vogue in the study of international relations because of the confluence of a number of factors. First, there has been a shift away from conventional concerns about great-power wars and superpower rivalry toward a greater focus on intrastate conflicts and state-making identity wars. Second, there has been a shift away from systemic-level variables toward dyadic-level interaction variables. Third, there has been a shift toward a more dynamic and process-oriented conceptualization of international conflict. Finally, there has been a shift from monocausal or single-factor explanations toward a multifaceted and multidimensional approach to conflict analysis and management.[168]

It follows that evidence of effective conflict management is likely to include partnerships between and among the different types of actors at several levels. No single actor – the United Nations, regional organizations, great powers, or NGOs – possesses the necessary resources, skills, and strategies for the successful prevention, containment, or resolution of a complex armed conflict, such as the one lingering on the Korean peninsula. More than one set of intervention strategies or response mechanisms may be necessary to address sources of conflict at different levels of analysis. Given the Korean peninsula's place in regional and global affairs, both the inter-Korean conflict and the extrapeninsular conflict will need to be addressed.

Nicholas Eberstadt recently suggested that the standoff over the North Korean nuclear issue might be an unstable equilibrium that is, in fact, creating increasing room for North Korean nuclear expansion. It is unclear how long such an equilibrium might last: one year, five years, ten years, or more? The open question then is what might cause a shift in the

[168] S. S. Kim and A. Kim (2004).

equilibrium. Revolt of some sort in the DPRK and external intervention seem the two likely candidates.[169] Although there is a lot of resistance to a negotiated settlement to the nuclear crisis, even Eberstadt is willing to concede that "when all is said and done, a negotiated final settlement to the North Korean nuclear crisis improves the immediate- and medium-term security environment for all of the DPRK's neighbors, almost irrespective of the price exacted for the deal," although he suggests that Pyongyang is unlikely to accept a deal.[170]

The way the outside world – Seoul, Beijing, Moscow, Tokyo, and Washington – responds to Pyongyang is closely keyed to the way North Korea responds to the outside world. North Korea's unpredictable future is malleable rather than predetermined. This nondeterministic image of the future of the post–Kim Il Sung system opens up some space for the outside world to use whatever leverage it might have to help North Korean leaders opt for one futurible scenario or another in the coming years. That said, however, the Big Four "can impose a set of constraints and opportunities, but they cannot dictate the nature and direction of Korean unification."[171]

Ultimately, the peace-by-pieces approach is not limited to the Korean peninsula. Rather, it will involve the active participation of the Big Four that historically has been involved in Korean affairs. Although the participation of the United Nations in resolving the conflict on the Korean peninsula has been limited so far, there may be an increasing role for international organizations and international NGOs. Although it is at the local level and the inter-Korean level where the final decisions about the future pathways of the two Korean states should be made, they will be made with consideration of external actors, and these external actors thus have a major role to play in determining the direction of Korean rapprochement and reunification.

More than a quarter-century ago, astronaut Frank Borman had to travel some 240,000 miles to the moon to enact from Spaceship Apollo 8 a global human identity, "From out there it really is 'one world'." Today, the two Korean states truly exist in a global village on earth, thanks to the forces of globalization sweeping over the world, thinking globally but acting locally. Most ironic and revealing in the final analysis is that the reunification drive of the two Koreas resembles a Taoist paradox: doing less and less is really achieving more and more. To hold together different parts of a whole, one must first let them go their separate ways.

[169] Eberstadt (2004b: 438). [170] Eberstadt (2004b: 441). [171] C. I. Moon (2005: 10).

References

Acharya, Amitav (2003/04) "Will Asia's Past Be Its Future?" *International Security*, 28(3), 149–64.

Acheson, Dean G. (1950) "Crisis in Asia: An Examination of United States Policy," *Department of State Bulletin*, January 23, pp. 111–18. (Originally delivered on January 12, 1950 at the National Press Club.)

Ahn, Byung-Joon (1994) "Korea's Future After Kim Il Sung," *Korea and World Affairs*, 18(3), 442–72.

Ahn, Byung-min (2004) "ROK-Russia Summit to Boost Railway Link Project," *The Korea Times*, September 21.

Akaha, Tsuneo (2002) "Japan's Policy Toward North Korea: Interests and Options," in Tsuneo Akaha, ed., *The Future of North Korea*, New York: Routledge, pp. 77–94.

Alagappa, Muthiah (1998) "Introduction," in Muthiah Alagappa, ed. *Asian Security Practice: Material and Ideational Influences*, Stanford, CA: Stanford University Press, pp. 1–24.

Alagappa, Muthiah (2003) "Preface," in Muthiah Alagappa, ed. *Asian Security Order: Instrumental and Normative Features*, Stanford, CA: Stanford University Press, pp. ix–xv.

Almond, Gabriel A. and Stephen J. Genco (1977) "Clouds, Clocks, and the Study of Politics," *World Politics*, 29(4), 489–522.

Altfeld, Michael F. (1984) "The Decision to Ally: A Theory and Test," *Western Political Quarterly*, 37(4), 523–44.

Angell, Norman (1913) *The Great Illusion: A Study of the Relation of Military Power in Nations to Their Economic and Social Advantage*, 4th ed., New York: G. P. Putnam's Sons.

Armacost, Michael H. and Kenneth B. Pyle (2001) "Japan and the Unification of Korea: Challenges for U.S. Policy Coordination," in Nicholas Eberstadt and Richard J. Ellings, eds., *Korea's Future and the Great Powers*, Seattle: University of Washington Press, pp. 125–63.

Armstrong, Charles K. (1998) "'A Socialism of Our Style': North Korean Ideology in a Post-Communist Era," in Samuel S. Kim, ed., *North Korean Foreign Relations in the Post-Cold War Era*, New York: Oxford University Press, pp. 32–53.

Armstrong, Charles K. (2001) "The Nature, Origins, and Development of the North Korean State," in Samuel S. Kim, ed., *The North Korean System in the Post-Cold War Era*, New York: Palgrave, pp. 39–63.

Armstrong, Charles K., Gilbert Rozman, Samuel Kim, and Stephen Kotkin, eds. (2006) *Korea at the Center: Dynamics of Regionalism in Northeast Asia*, Armonk, NY: M. E. Sharpe.

Arreguin-Toft, Ivan (2001) "How the Weak Win Wars: A Theory of Asymmetric Conflict," *International Security*, 26(1), 93–128.

Auster, Bruce B. and Kevin Whitelaw (2003) "Upping the Ante for Kim Jong Il: Pentagon Plan 5030, A New Blueprint for Facing Down North Korea," *U.S. News & World Report*, July 21, p. 21.

Axelrod, Robert (1984) *The Evolution of Cooperation*, New York: Basic Books.

Bacevich, Andrew (2002) *American Empire: The Realities and Consequences of U.S. Diplomacy*, Cambridge, MA: Harvard University Press.

Bajanov, Evgeny (1995) "Assessing the Politics of the Korean War, 1949–51," *Bulletin of Cold War International History Project*, 5.

Baldwin, David A. (1979) "Power Analysis and World Politics: New Trends Versus Old Tendencies," *World Politics*, 31, 161–94.

Baldwin, David A., ed. (1993) *Neorealism and Neoliberalism: The Contemporary Debate*, New York: Columbia University Press.

Barber, Benjamin R. (1995) *Jihad vs. McWorld: How the Planet is Both Falling Apart and Coming Together and What This Means for Democracy*, New York: Times Books.

Barber, Benjamin R. (2003) *Fear's Empire: War, Terrorism, and Democracy*, New York: Norton.

Barry, Mark Philip (1996) *Contemporary American Relations with North Korea: 1987–1994*, PhD dissertation, Woodrow Wilson Department of Government and Foreign Affairs, University of Virginia, Charlottesville.

Barston, Ronald P. (1971) "The External Relations of Small States," in August Schou and Arne Olav Bruntland, eds., *Small States in International Relations*, Stockholm: Almqvist & Wiskell, pp. 39–56.

Bazhanov, Evgeny P. (2000a) "Russia's Policies Toward the Two Koreas," in Wonmo Dong, ed., *The Two Koreas and the United States*, Armonk, NY: M. E. Sharpe, pp. 147–65.

Bazhanov, Evgeny P. (2000b) "Russian Views of the Agreed Framework and the Four-Party Talks," in James Clay Moltz and Alexander Y. Mansourov, eds., *The North Korean Nuclear Program: Security, Strategy and New Perspectives from Russia*, New York: Routledge, pp. 219–35.

Bazhanov, Evgeny P. (2006) "Korea in Russia's Post Cold War Regional Political Context," in Charles K. Armstrong, Gilbert Rozman, Samuel S. Kim, and Stephen Kotkin, eds., *Korea at the Center: Dynamics of Regionalism in Northeast Asia*, Armonk, NY: M. E. Sharpe, pp. 214–26.

Bazhanov, Evgeny and Natalya Bazhanov (1994) "The Evolution of Russian-Korean Relations," *Asian Survey*, 34(9), 789–98.

Bedeski, Robert E. (1995) "Sino-Korean Relations: Triangle of Tension, or Balancing a Divided Peninsula?" *International Journal*, 50, 516–38.

Bell, Daniel, ed. (1967) *Toward the Year 2000: Work in Progress*, Boston: Beacon Press.

Beres, Louis Rene and Harry R. Targ (1977) *Constructing Alternative World Futures: Reordering the Planet*, Cambridge, MA: Schenkman.

Berger, Thomas U. (1993) "From Sword to Chrysanthemum: Japan's Culture of Anti-Militarism," *International Security*, 17(4), 119–50.

Berger, Thomas U. (2000) "Set for Stability? Prospects for Conflict and Cooperation in East Asia," *Review of International Studies*, 26(3), 405–28.

Berger, Thomas U. (2003) "The Construction of Antagonism: The History Problem in Japan's Foreign Relations," in G. John Ikenberry and Takashi Inoguchi, eds. *Reinventing the Alliance: US-Japan Security Partnership in an Era of Change*, New York: Palgrave Macmillan, pp. 63–88.

Berger, Thomas U. (2004) "Japan's International Relations: The Political and Security Dimensions," in Samuel S. Kim, ed., *The International Relations of Northeast Asia*, Boulder, CO: Rowman & Littlefield, pp. 135–69.

Berger, Thomas U. (2005a) "The Politics of Memory in Japanese Foreign Relations," Unpublished manuscript, Department of International Relations, Boston University, Boston.

Berger, Thomas U. (2005b) "Of Shrines and Hooligans: The Structure of the History Problem in East Asia after 9/11," Unpublished manuscript, Department of International Relations, Boston University, Boston.

Betts, Richard K. (1993/94) "Wealth, Power, and Instability: East Asia and the United States After the Cold War," *International Security*, 18(3), 34–77.

Bin, Yu (2004) "China-Russia Relations: Presidential Politicking and Proactive Posturing," *Comparative Connections* [Online], 6(1), 125–36. Available at http://www.csis.org/media/csis/pubs/0401q.pdf.

Binder, Leonard, et al., eds. (1971) *Crises and Sequences in Political Development*, Princeton, NJ: Princeton University Press.

Bleiker, Roland (2004) "Identity, Difference, and the Dilemmas of Inter-Korean Relations: Insights from Northern Defectors and the German Precedent," *Asian Perspective*, 28(2), 35–63.

Bleiker, Roland (2005) *Divided Korea: Toward a Culture of Reconciliation*, Minneapolis: University of Minnesota Press.

Bloom, William (1990) *Personal Identity, National Identity and International Relations*, New York: Cambridge University Press.

Boot, Max (2001) "The Case for American Empire," *The Weekly Standard*, 7(5), 27.

Bridges, Brian (1993) *Japan and Korea in the 1990s: From Antagonism to Adjustment*, Bookfield, VT: Edward Elgar.

Brooks, Stephen G. and William C. Wohlforth (2000/01) "Power, Globalization, and the End of the Cold War: Reevaluating a Landmark Case for Ideas," *International Security*, 25(3), 5–53.

Brzezinski, Zbigniew (1997) *The Grand Chessboard: American Primacy and Its Geostrategic Imperatives*, New York: Basic Books.

Bueno de Mesquita, Bruce and David Lalman (1992) *War and Reason: Domestic and International Imperatives*, New Haven, CT: Yale University Press.

Bull, Hedley (1977) *The Anarchical Society: A Study of Order in World Politics*, New York: Columbia University Press.

Bulychev, Georgy (2005) "A Long-Term Strategy for North Korea," *Japan Focus* [Online], February 15. Available at http://japanfocus.org/article.asp?id=222.

Burrows, William E. and Robert Windrem (1994) *Critical Mass: The Dangerous Race for Superweapons in a Fragmenting World*, New York: Simon & Schuster.

Buruma, Ian (1994) *The Wages of Guilt: Memories of War in Germany and Japan*, New York: Farrar, Straus and Giroux.

Buzan, Barry (1991) *People, States and Fear: An Agenda for International Security Studies in the Post-Cold War Era*, 2nd ed., Boulder, CO: Lynne Rienner.

Buzan, Barry and Gerald Segal (1994) "Rethinking East Asian Security," *Survival*, 36(2), 3–21.

Buzan, Barry and Rosemary Foot, eds. (2004) *Does China Matter? A Reassessment*, London: Routledge.

Buzo, Adrian (1999) *The Guerilla Dynasty: Politics and Leadership in North Korea*, Boulder, CO: Westview Press.

Cai, Jianwei, ed. (1996) *Zhongguo da zhanlue: lingdao shijie da lantu* [*China's Grand Strategy: A Blueprint for World Leadership*], Haikou, China: Hainan chubanshe.

Calder, Kent C. (1988) *Crisis and Compensation*. Princeton, NJ: Princeton University Press.

Calder, Kent C. (1989) "The North Pacific Triangle: Sources of Economic and Political Transformation," *Journal of Northeast Asian Studies*, 8, 3–17.

Carr, E. H. (1958) *The Twenty Years' Crisis 1919–1939: An Introduction to the Study of International Relations*, New York: St. Martin's Press.

Carter, Ashton B. and William J. Perry (1999) *Preventive Defense: A New Security Strategy for America*, Washington, DC: Brookings Institution Press.

Cha, Victor D. (1997) "Korean Unification: The Zero-Sum Past and the Precarious Future," *Asian Perspective*, 21(3), 63–92.

Cha, Victor D. (1999a) *Alignment Despite Antagonism: The United States-Korea-Japan Security Triangle*, Stanford, CA: Stanford University Press.

Cha, Victor D. (1999b) "Engaging China: Seoul-Beijing *Détente* and Korean Security," *Survival*, 41, 73–98.

Cha, Victor D. (2000a) "Japan's Grand Strategy on the Korean Peninsula: Optimistic Realism," *Japanese Journal of Political Science*, 1(2), 249–74.

Cha, Victor D. (2000b) "The Security Domain of South Korea's Globalization," in Samuel S. Kim, ed., *Korea's Globalization*, New York: Cambridge University Press, 2000, pp. 217–41.

Cha, Victor D. (2001a) "Japan-Korea Relations: Ending 2000 with a Whimper, Not a Bang," *Comparative Connections* [Online], 2(4), 88–93. Available at www.csis.org/media/csis/pubs/0401q.pdf.

Cha, Victor D. (2001b) "Japan-Korea Relations: History Haunts, Engagement Dilemmas" *Comparative Connections* [Online], 3(1), 104–12. Available at www.csis.org/media/csis/pubs/0101q.pdf.

Cha, Victor D. (2001c) "Japan–Korea Relations: Quicksand," *Comparative Connections* [Online], 3(3): 101–07. Available at www.csis.org/media/csis/pubs/0103q.pdf.

Cha, Victor D. (2003) "South Korea: Anchored or Adrift?" in Richard J. Ellings and Aaron L. Friedberg, eds. *Strategic Asia 2003–04: Fragility and Crisis*, Seattle: The National Bureau of Asian Research, pp. 109–30.

Cha, Victor D. and David C. Kang (2003) *Nuclear North Korea: A Debate on Engagement Strategies*, New York: Columbia University Press.

Chace, James (2002) "Imperial America and the Common Interest," *World Policy Journal*, Spring, 1–9.

Chanda, Nayan (2001) "Kim Flirts with Chinese Reform," *Far Eastern Economic Review*, February 8, 26.

Chang, Iris (1997) *The Rape of Nanking: The Forgotten Holocaust of World War II*, New York: Penguin.

Chang, Parris H. (1993) "Beijing's Policy Toward Korea and PRC-ROK Normalization of Relations," in Manwoo Lee and Richard W. Mansbach, eds., *The Changing Order in Northeast Asia and the Korean Peninsula*, Seoul: The Institute for Far Eastern Studies, Kyungnam University, pp. 155–72.

Chang, Sung-hwan (1974) "Russian Designs on the Far East," in Taras Hunszak, ed., *Russian Imperialism from Ivan the Great to the Revolution*, New Brunswick, NJ: Rutgers University Press.

Chen, Qimao (1993a) "The Role of the Great Powers in the Process of Korean Reunification," in Amos A. Jordan, ed., *Korean Unification: Implications for Northeast Asia*, Washington, DC: Center for Strategic and International Studies, pp. 59–79.

Chen, Qimao (1993b) "New Approaches in China's Foreign Policy: The Post-Cold War Era," *Asian Survey*, 33(3), 237–51.

Chicago Council on Foreign Relations (2004) *Global Views 2004: Comparing South Korean and American Public Opinion and Foreign Policy*, Chicago: Chicago Council on Foreign Relations.

Cho, Soon Sung (1967) *Korea in World Politics 1940–1950: An Evaluation of American Responsibility*, Berkeley: University of California Press.

Choucri, Nazli and Thomas Robinson, eds. (1978) *Forecasting in International Relations*, San Francisco: Freeman.

Christensen, Thomas J. (1992) "Threats, Assurances, and the Last Chance for Peace: The Lessons of Mao's Korean War Telegrams," *International Security*, 17(1), 122–54.

Christensen, Thomas J. (1996) *Useful Adversaries: Grand Strategy, Domestic Mobilization, and Sino-American Conflict, 1947–1958*, Princeton, NJ: Princeton University Press.

Christensen, Thomas J. (2001) "Posing Problems Without Catching Up: China's Rise and Challenges for U.S. Security Policy," *International Security*, 25(4), 5–40.

Chufrin, Gennady, ed. (1999) *Russia and Asia: The Emerging Security Agenda*, New York: Oxford University Press.

Chun, Chae-sung (2001) "The Cold War and Its Transition for Koreans: The Meaning from a Constructivist Viewpoint," in Chung-in Moon, Odd Arne Westad, and Gyoo-hyoung Kahng, eds., *Ending the Cold War in Korea: Theoretical and Historical Perspectives*, Seoul: Yonsei University Press, pp. 115–45.

Chun, Hae-jong (1968) "Sino-Korean Tributary Relations in the Ch'ing Period," in John K. Fairbank, ed., *The Chinese World Order: Traditional China's Foreign Relations*, Cambridge, MA: Harvard University Press, pp. 90–111.

Chun, Hongchan and Charles E. Ziegler (1997) "The Russian Federation and South Korea," in Stephen J. Blank and Alvin Z. Rubinstein, eds., *Imperial Decline: Russia's Changing Role in Asia*, Durham, NC: Duke University Press, pp. 185–210.

Chun, In Young (1977) *North Korea and the United States, 1955–1972: A Study of North Korea's Hostility Toward the United States*, PhD dissertation, University of Cincinnati, Cincinnati, OH.

Chung, Chong-wook (1999) "Limitations of South Korea-China Military Cooperation," *Korea Focus*, 7(5), 97–9.

Chung, Jae Ho (1993) "The Political Economy of South Korea-China Bilateralism: Origins, Progress, and Prospects," in Ilpyong Kim and Hong Pyo Lee, eds., *Korea and China in a New World: Beyond Normalization*, Seoul: The Sejong Institute, pp. 257–309.

Chung, Jae Ho (2001) "South Korea Between Eagle and Dragon: Perceptual Ambivalence and Strategic Dilemma," *Asian Survey*, 41(5), 777–96.

Chung, Jin-Young (2003) "Cost Sharing for USFK in Transition: Whither the ROK-U.S. Alliance?" in Donald W. Boose, Jr., Balbina Y. Hwang, Patrick Morgan, and Andrew Scobell, eds., *Recalibrating the U.S.-Republic of Korea Alliance*, Carlisle, PA: Strategic Studies Institute, U.S. Army War College, pp. 35–53.

Clough, Ralph (1987) *Embattled Korea: The Rivalry for International Support*, Boulder, CO: Westview Press.

Connor, Walker (1978) "A Nation Is a Nation, Is a State, Is an Ethnic Group, Is a . . . ," *Ethnic and Racial Studies*, 1(4), 377–400.

Connolly, William E. (1991) *Identity/Difference: Democratic Negotiations of Political Paradox*, Ithaca, NY: Cornell University Press.

Cotton, James (1998) "The Rajin-Sonbong Free Trade Zone Experiment: North Korea in Pursuit of New International Linkage," in Samuel S. Kim, ed., *North Korean Foreign Relations in the Post-Cold War Era*, New York: Oxford University Press, pp. 212–34.

Council on Foreign Relations (1999a, July) *U.S. Policy Toward North Korea: A Second Look* [Online], Task Force Report No. 24, New York: Council on Foreign Relations Press. Available at http://www.cfr.org/publication.html?id=3205.

Council on Foreign Relations (1999b, October) *Safeguarding Prosperity in a Global Financial System: The Future International Financial Architecture*, Task Reforce Report No. 25, New York: Council on Foreign Relations Press.

Council on Foreign Relations (2003) *Meeting the North Korean Nuclear Challenge: Report of an Independent Task Force Sponsored by the Council on Foreign Relations*, New York: Council on Foreign Relations Press.

Crocker, Chester A., Fen Osler Hampson, and Pamela Aall (2004) *Taming Intractable Conflicts: Mediation in the Hardest Cases*, Washington, DC: United States Institute of Peace Press.

Cruz, Consuelo (2000) "Identity and Persuasion: How Nations Remember Their Pasts and Make Their Futures," *World Politics*, 52(3), 275–312.

Cumings, Bruce (1981) *The Origins of the Korean War: Liberation and the Emergence of Separate Regimes 1945–1947*, Princeton, NJ: Princeton University Press.

Cumings, Bruce (1984) "The Political Economy of China's Turn Outward," in Samuel S. Kim, ed., *China and the World: Chinese Foreign Policy in the Post-Mao Era*, Boulder, CO: Westview Press, pp. 235–65.

Cumings, Bruce (1990) *The Origins of the Korean War, Vol. II: The Roaring of the Cataract 1947–1950*, Princeton, NJ: Princeton University Press.

Cumings, Bruce (1997) *Korea's Place in the Sun*. New York: W. W. Norton.

Cumings, Bruce (2004) "Anti-Americanism in the Republic of Korea," *Joint U.S.-Korea Academic Studies*, 14, 205–29.

Davis, Zachary S., Larry A. Niksch, Larry Q. Nowels, Vladimir N. Pregelj, Rinn-Sup Shinn, and Robert G. Sutter (1994) "Korea: Procedural and Jurisdictional Questions Regarding Possible Normalization of Relations with North Korea," Congressional Research Service, Report for Congress 94–933, November 29.

Denisov, V. I. (1997) "Russia and the Problem of Korean Unification," in Tae-Hwan Kwak, ed., *The Four Powers and Korean Unification Strategies*, Seoul: Institute for Far Eastern Studies, pp. 35–47.

Deng, Yong and Fei-Ling Wang, eds. (2005) *China Rising: Power and Motivation in Chinese Foreign Policy*, Lanham, MD: Rowman & Littlefield.

Desch, Michael C. (1998) "Culture Clash: Assessing the Importance of Ideas in Security Studies," *International Security*, 23(1), 141–70.

Deudney, Daniel and G. John Ikenberry (1991) "Soviet Reform and the End of the Cold War: Explaining Large-Scale Historical Change," *Review of International Studies* 17, 225–50.

Deutsch, Karl W. (1967) *Political Community and the North Atlantic Area,* New York: Greenwood Press.

Deutsch, Karl W. (1988) *The Analysis of International Relations,* Englewood Cliffs, NJ: Prentice Hall.

Dittmer, Lowell (1992) *Sino-Soviet Normalization and Its International Implications,* Seattle: University of Washington Press.

Dittmer, Lowell (2004) "The Emerging Northeast Asian Regional Order," in Samuel S. Kim, ed. *The International Relations of Northeast Asia.* Lanham, MD: Rowman & Littlefield, pp. 331–62.

Dittmer, Lowell and Samuel S. Kim (1993a) "In Search of a Theory of National Identity," in Lowell Dittmer and Samuel S. Kim, eds., *China's Quest for National Identity,* Ithaca, NY: Cornell University Press, pp. 1–31.

Dittmer, Lowell and Samuel S. Kim, eds. (1993b) *China's Quest for National Identity,* Ithaca, NY: Cornell University Press.

Dong, Wonmo (2000) *The Two Koreas and the United States,* Armonk, NY: M. E. Sharpe.

Dong, Yong-seung (2001) "After the Summit: The Future of Inter-Korean Economic Cooperation," *East Asian Review,* 13(2), 75–96.

Doyle, Michael (1983a) "Kant, Liberal Legacies, and Foreign Affairs," *Philosophy and Public Affairs,* 12, 205–35.

Doyle, Michael (1983b) "Kant, Liberal Legacies, and Foreign Affairs, Part 2," *Philosophy and Public Affairs,* 12, 323–53.

Drake, Frederick C. (1984) *The Empire of the Seas: A Biography of Rear Admiral Robert Wilson Shufeldt, USN,* Honolulu: University of Hawaii Press.

Drennan, William (1998a, October) "Special Report No. 38: Mistrust and the Korean Peninsula: Dangers of Miscalculation," Washington, DC: U.S. Institute for Peace. Available at http://www.usip.org/pubs/specialreports/early/sr_korea.html.

Drennan, William (1998b) "The U.S. Role in Korean Reunification," *Korea and World Affairs,* 22(2), 159–76.

Eberstadt, Nicholas (1993) "North Korea: Reform, Muddling Through, or Collapse?" *NBR Analysis,* 4(3), 5–16.

Eberstadt, Nicholas (1994a) "Reform, Muddling Through, or Collapse?" in Thomas H. Henriksen and Lho Kyong-soo, eds., *One Korea?,* Stanford, CA: Hoover Institution Press.

Eberstadt, Nicholas (1994b) "Inter-Korean Economic Cooperation: Rapprochement Through Trade?" *Korea and World Affairs,* 18, 642–61.

Eberstadt, Nicholas (1994c) "Demographic Shocks After Communism: Eastern Germany, 1989–93," *Populations and Development Review,* 20, 137–52.

Eberstadt, Nicholas (1995a) "China's Trade with the DPRK, 1990–1994: Pyongyang's Thrifty New Patron," *Korea and World Affairs,* 19, 665–85.

Eberstadt, Nicholas (1995b) *Korea Approaches Reunification,* Armonk, NY: M. E. Sharpe.

Eberstadt, Nicholas (1995c) "China's Trade with the DPRK 1990–1994," *Korea and World Affairs,* 19, 665–85.

Eberstadt, Nicholas (1996) "How Much Money Goes from Japan to North Korea?" *Asian Survey,* 36, 523–42.

Eberstadt, Nicholas (1997) "Hastening Korean Unification," *Foreign Affairs,* 76(2), 77–92.

Eberstadt, Nicholas (1998a) "North Korea's Unification Policy: 1948–1996," in Samuel S. Kim, ed., *North Korean Foreign Relations in the Post-Cold War Era,* New York: Oxford University Press, pp. 235–57.

Eberstadt, Nicholas (1998b) "North Korea's International Trade in Capital Goods, 1970–1995: Indications from Mirror Statistics," *Journal of East Asian Affairs*, 13, 165–223.

Eberstadt, Nicholas (1998c) "U.S.-North Korea Economic Relations: Indications from North Korea's Past Trade Performance," in Tong Whan Park, ed., *The U.S. and the Two Koreas: A New Triangle*, Boulder, CO: Lynne Rienner, pp. 119–46.

Eberstadt, Nicholas (1999) *The End of North Korea*, Washington, DC: American Enterprise Institute.

Eberstadt, Nicholas (2004a) "The Persistence of North Korea," *Policy Review*, 127, 23–48.

Eberstadt, Nicholas (2004b) "Korean Scenarios Alternative Futures for the Korean Peninsula," in Ashley J. Tellis and Michael Wills, eds., *Strategic Asia 2004–05: Confronting Terrorism in the Pursuit of Power*, Seattle: National Bureau of Asian Research, pp. 428–55.

Eberstadt, Nicholas and Richard J. Ellings, eds. (2001) *Korea's Future and the Great Powers*, Seattle: University of Washington Press.

Eckert, Carter J. (1991) *Offspring of Empire: The Koch'ang Kims and the Colonial Origins of Korean Capitalism, 1876–1945*. Seattle: University of Washington Press.

Eckert, Carter, Ki-Baik Lee, Young Lew, Michael Robinson, and Edward W. Wagner (1991) *Korea Old and New: A History*, Cambridge, MA: Harvard University Press.

Eland, Ivan (2002) "The Empire Strikes Out: The 'New Imperialism' and Its Fatal Flaws," *Policy Analysis*, 459, 1–27.

Ellings, Richard J. and Aaron L. Friedberg, eds. (2002) *Strategic Asia 2002–03: Asian Aftershocks*, Seattle: National Bureau of Asian Research.

Ellison, Herbert J. (2001) "Russia, Korea, and Northeast Asia," in Nicholas Eberstadt and Richard J. Ellings, eds., *Korea's Future and the Great Powers*, Seattle: University of Washington Press, pp. 164–87.

Elman, Miriam Fendius (1995) "The Foreign Policies of Small States: Challenging Neorealism in Its Own Backyard," *British Journal of Political Science*, 25, 171–217.

Erikson, Erik H. (1946) "Ego Development and Historical Change," *Psychoanalytic Study of the Child*, 2, 359–96.

Erikson, Erik H. (1956) "The Problem of Ego Identity," *Journal of the American Psychoanalytic Association* 4, 56–121.

Erikson, Erik H. (1959) "Identity and the Life Cycle: Selected Papers by Erik H. Erikson," *Psychological Issues*, 1, 1–171.

Erikson, Erik H. (1963) *Childhood and Society*, 2nd ed., New York: Norton.

Erikson, Erik H. (1965) *The Challenge of Youth*, Garden City, NY: Doubleday, Anchor.

Erikson, Erik H. (1968) "Identity and Identity Diffusion," in Chad Gordon and Kenneth J. Gergen, eds., *The Self in Social Interaction*, New York: Wiley, pp. 197–205.

Erikson, Erik H. (1974) *Dimensions of a New Identity*, New York: Norton.

Fairbank, John K., ed. (1968) *The Chinese World Order: Traditional China's Foreign Relations*, Cambridge, MA: Harvard University Press.

Falk, Richard A. (1975) *A Study of Future Worlds*, New York: Free Press.

Falk, Richard A. (2003, March 24) "Will the Empire Be Fascist?" Available at http://www.transnational.org/forum/meet/2003/Falk_FascistEmpire.html.

Falk, Richard A. and Samuel S. Kim (1982) *An Approach to World Order Studies and the World System,* New York: Institute for World Order.

Falk, Richard A., Samuel S. Kim, and Saul H. Mendlovitz, eds. (1982) *Studies on a Just World Order, Vol. I: Toward a Just World Order,* Boulder, CO: Westview Press.

Falk, Richard A., Samuel S. Kim, and Saul H. Mendlovitz, eds. (1991) *Studies on a Just World Order, Vol. III: The United Nations and a Just World Order,* Boulder, CO: Westview Press.

Feffer, John (2003) *North Korea South Korea: U.S. Policy at a Time of Crisis.* New York: Seven Stories Press.

Feffer, John (2005) "Korea's Slow-Motion Reunification," Policy Forum Online 05–53A: June 28, 2005. Available at http://www.nautilus.org/fora/security/0553Feffer.html.

Feffer, John (2006) "Grave Threats and Grand Bargains: The United States and Regional Order in Northeast Asia," in John Feffer, ed. *The Future of U.S.-Korean Relations,* New York: Routledge, pp. 178–99.

Ferguson, Joseph (2003) "Russia's Role on the Korean Peninsula and Great Power Relations in Northeast Asia: Ramifications for the U.S.-ROK Alliance," *NBR Analysis,* 14(1), 1–14.

Ferguson, Niall (2004) *Colossus: The Price of America's Empire,* New York: Penguin Press.

Foot, Rosemary (2003) "The UN System as a Pathway to Security in Asia: A Buttress, Not a Pillar," in Muthiah Alagappa, ed. *Asian Security Order: Instrumental and Normative Features,* Stanford, CA: Stanford University Press, pp. 311–45.

Foster-Carter, Aidan (1992) *Korea's Coming Unification,* Economist Intelligence Unit M2, London: Economist Intelligence Unit.

Foster-Carter, Aidan (1994) "Korea: Sociopolitical Realities of Reuniting a Divided Nation," in Thomas H. Hendricksen and Lho Kyong-soo, eds., *One Korea?* Stanford, CA: Hoover Institution Press, pp. 31–47.

Foster-Carter, Aidan (1998) "Regime Dynamics in North Korea: An European Perspective," in Chung-in Moon, ed. *Understanding Regime Dynamics in North Korea: Contending Perspectives and Comparative Implications,* Seoul: Yonsei University Press, pp. 113–39.

Foster-Carter, Aidan (2003) "North Korea–South Korea Relations: Symbolic Links, Real Gaps," *Comparative Connections* [Online], 5 (2), 91–100. Available at http://www.csis.org/media/csis/pubs/0302q.pdf.

Friedberg, Aaron L. (1993/94) "Ripe for Rivalry: Prospects for Peace in a Multipolar Asia," *International Security,* 18(3), 5–33.

Friedberg, Aaron L. (2000) "Will Europe's Past Be Asia's Future?" *Survival,* 42(3), 147–59.

Friedman, Thomas (1999) *The Lexus and the Olive Tree,* New York: Farrar Straus Giroux.

Fukuyama, Francis (1989) "The End of History?" *National Interest,* Summer, 3–18.

Fukuyama, Francis (1992) *The End of History and the Last Man,* New York: Free Press.

Funabashi, Yoichi (1991/92) "Japan and the New World Order," *Foreign Affairs,* 70(5), 58–74.

Gaddis, John Lewis (1992/93) "International Relations Theory and the End of the Cold War," *International Security,* 17(3), 5–58.

Galtung, Johan (1976) "On the Future, Future Studies and Future Attitudes," in H. Ornauer, H. Wiberg, A. Sicinski, and J. Galtung, eds., *Images of the*

World in the Year 2000: A Comparative Ten Nation Study, Atlantic Highlands, NJ: Humanities Press, pp. 3–21.
Galtung, Johan (1980) *The True Worlds: A Transnational Perspective*, New York: Free Press.
Garrett, Banning and Bonnie Glaser (1995) "Looking Across the Yalu: Chinese Assessments of North Korea," *Asian Survey*, 35(6), 528–45.
Garver, John W. (1998) "Sino-Russian Relations," in Samuel S. Kim, ed., *China and the World: Chinese Foreign Policy Faces the New Millennium*, Boulder, CO: Westview Press, pp. 114–32.
Gellner, Ernest (1983) *Nations and Nationalisms*, Ithaca, NY: Cornell University Press.
George, Alexander L. (1993) *Bridging the Gap: Theory and Practice in Foreign Policy*, Arlington, VA: U.S. Institute of Peace Press.
Gerth, H. H. and C. Wright Mills, eds. (1958) *From Max Weber: Essays in Sociology*, New York: Oxford University Press.
Gills, Barry K. (1996) *Korea Versus Korea: A Case of Contested Legitimacy*, New York: Routledge.
Gilpin, Robert (1981) *War and Change in World Politics*, New York: Cambridge University Press.
Goldstein, Avery (2005) *Rising to the Challenge: China's Grand Strategy and International Security*, Stanford, CA: Stanford University Press.
Goncharov, Sergei N., John W. Lewis, and Xue Litai (1993) *Uncertain Partners: Stalin, Mao, and the Korean War*, Stanford, CA: Stanford University Press.
Gong, Gerrit W., ed. (1996) *Remembering and Forgetting: The Legacy of War and Peace in East Asia*, Washington, DC: Center for Strategic and International Studies.
Gorbachev, Mikhail (1987) *Realities and Guarantees for a Secure World*, Moscow: Novosti Press Agency.
Good Friends (1999) "The Report on Daily Life and Human Rights of North Korean Food Refugees in China" [Online]. Available at http://www.jungto.org/gf.
Green, Michael (1997) "North Korean Regime Crisis: U.S. Perspectives and Responses," *Korean Journal of Defense Analysis*, 9, 7–25.
Green, Michael (2000, July 31) "Why Tokyo Will Be a Larger Player in Asia," Northeast Asia Peace And Security Network Special Report.
Green, Michael (2001) *Japan's Reluctant Realism: Foreign Policy Challenges in an Era of Uncertain Power*, New York: Palgrave.
Grimes, William W. (2000) "Japan and Globalization: From Opportunity to Restraint," in Samuel S. Kim, ed., *East Asia and Globalization*, Lanham, MD: Rowman & Littlefield, pp. 55–79.
Grinker, Roy Richard (1998) *Korea and Its Futures: Unification and the Unfinished War*, New York: St. Martin's Press.
Gross, Donald G. (2005) "U.S.–Korea Relations: South Korea Confronts U.S. Hardliners on North Korea," *Comparative Connections* [Online], 6(4), 47–57. Available at http://www.csis.org/media/csis/pubs/0404q.pdf.
Gurtov, Melvin (1994) "The Future of China's Rise," *Asian Perspective*, 18(1), 109–28.
Gurtov, Melvin (2002) "Common Security in North Korea: Quest for a New Paradigm in Inter-Korean Relations," *Asian Survey*, 42(3), 397–418.
Gurtov, Melvin and Peter Van Ness, eds. (2005) *Confronting the Bush Doctrine: Critical Views from the Asia-Pacific*. London and New York: RoutledgeCurzon.

Ha, Yong Chool (1994) "Russo-North Korean Relations in Transition," in Doug Joong Kim, ed., *Foreign Relations of North Korea During Kim Il Sung's Last Days,* Seoul: Sejong Institute, pp. 331–55.

Haas, Ernst (1986) "What Is Nationalism and Why Should We Study It?" *International Organization,* 40, 707–44.

Habeeb, William (1988) *Power and Tactics in International Negotiation: How Week Nations Bargain with Strong Nations,* Baltimore: The Johns Hopkins University Press.

Habermas, Jürgen (1973) *Legitimation Crisis,* Thomas McCarthy, trans., Boston: Beacon.

Habermas, Jürgen (1994) "Citizenship and National Identity," in Bart van Steenbergen, ed., *The Condition of Citizenship,* London: Sage, pp. 20–35.

Haftendorn, Helga, Robert O. Keohane, and Celeste A. Wallander, eds. (1999). *Imperfect Unions: Security Institutions over Time and Space.* New York: Oxford University Press.

Haggard, Stephan (1990) *Pathways from the Periphery: The Politics of Growth in the Newly Industrializing Countries,* Ithaca, NY: Cornell University Press.

Haggard, Stephan and Marcus Noland (2005) *Hunger and Human Rights: The Politics of Famine in North Korea,* Washington, DC: U.S. Committee for Human Rights in North Korea.

Haggard, Stephan, David Kang, and Chung-in Moon (1997) "Japanese Colonialism and Korean Development: A Critique," *World Development,* 25(6), 867–81.

Hahm, Chaibong and Kim Seog-gun (2001) "Remembering Japan and North Korea: The Politics of Memory in South Korea," in Gerrit W. Gong, ed., *Memory and History in East and Southeast Asia: Issues of Identity in International Relations,* Washington, DC: CSIS Press, pp. 101–12.

Hall, Rodney Bruce (1999) *National Collective Identity: Social Constructs and International Systems,* New York: Columbia University Press.

Halloran, Richard (1997) "Korean Reunification and the United States: A Futuristic and Speculative Assessment," in Dalchoong Kim and Chung-in Moon, eds. *History, Cognition, and Peace in East Asia,* Seoul: Yonsei University Press, pp. 215–33.

Hampden-Turner, Charles (1970) *Radical Man,* Cambridge, MA: Schenkman.

Han, Sang-Jin (2004) "Korea and U.S. Culture: Cultural Interaction from a Korean Perspective," *Pacific Partners: Korean-American Relations in the Twenty-first Century.* Proceedings of the Conference on Enhancing the Partnership Between Korea and the United States in the Twenty-First Century, The Center for Korean Studies, University of Hawaii, Manoa.

Han, Sung-Joo (1993) "Fundamentals of Korea's New Diplomacy," *Korea and World Affairs,* 17(2), 227–45.

Han, Sung-Joo (1995) *Segyehwa sidae ui Hankuk Oeykyo* [*Korean Diplomacy in an Era of Globalization*], Seoul: Chisik Sangyopsa.

Han, Sung-Joo (1999) *Samkak kwankyae ui taetong: Mikuk, Chungkuk kuriko Hanpanto* [*The Quickening of a Triangular Relations: The United States, China, and the Korean Peninsula*], *Kyekan Sasang* [*Quarterly Thought*], 11, 29–70.

Handel, Michael (1981) *Weak States in the International System,* London: Frank Cass.

Hao, Yufan and Zhai Zhihai (1990) "China's Decision to Enter the Korean War: History Revisited," *The China Quarterly,* 121, 94–115.

Harding, Harry (1995) "The New Regime in North Korea and Its Future: Principal Scenarios," in *The Future of North Korea: Implications for the Korean Peninsula and*

Northeast Asia, Seoul: The Institute of Foreign Affairs and National Security, pp. 21–37.

Harrison, Selig (1996) *Japan's Nuclear Future: The Plutonium Debate and East Asian Security*, Washington, DC: Carnegie Endowment for International Peace.

Harrison, Selig (1998a) "North Korea from the Inside Out," *Washington Post*, 21 June, p. C01.

Harrison, Selig (1998b) "U.S. Policy Toward North Korea," in Dae-Suk Suh and Chae Jin Lee, eds., *North Korea After Kim Il Sung*, Boulder, CO: Lynne Rienner, pp. 61–83.

Harrison, Selig (2002) *Korean Endgame: A Strategy for Reunification and U.S. Disengagement*, Princeton, NJ: Princeton University Press.

Harrison, Selig (2004) *Ending the North Korean Nuclear Crisis: A Proposal by the Task Force on U.S. Korea Policy*, Chicago: The Center for International Policy and the Center for East Asian Studies, University of Chicago.

Harrison, Selig (2005a) "Did North Korea Cheat?" *Foreign Affairs*, 84(1), 99–110.

Harrison, Selig (2005b) "Harrison Replies," *Foreign Affairs* 84(2), 146–48.

Hart, Tom (2001) "The PRC-DPRK Rapprochement and China's Dilemma in Korea," *Asian Perspective*, 25(3), 247–59.

Hart-Landsberg, Martin (1998) *Korea: Division, Reunification, and U.S. Foreign Policy*, New York: Monthly Review Press.

Haselden, Carl E. (2002/03) "The Effects of Korean Unification on the U.S. Military Presence in Northeast Asia," *Parameters*, Winter, 120–32.

Hauner, Milan (1992) *What Is Asia to Us? Russia's Asian Heartland Yesterday and Today*, London: Routledge.

Hayes, Peter (1988) "American Nuclear Hegemony in Korea," *Journal of Peace Research*, 25(4), 351–64.

Hayes, Peter (1991) *Pacific Powderkeg: American Nuclear Dilemmas in Korea*, Lexington, MA: Lexington Books.

Hayes, Peter (1993b) "The Republic of Korea and the Nuclear Issue," in Andrew Mack, ed., *Asian Flashpoint*, Canberra, Australia: Allen & Unwin, pp. 51–83.

Hayes, Peter (1994c) "Should the United States Supply Light-Water Reactors to Pyongyang?" *The Korean Journal of Defense Analysis*, 6, 179–221.

Hayes, Peter (2003) "Bush's Bipolar Disorder and the Looming Failure of Multilateral Talks with North Korea," *Arms Control Toda*, 33(8), 3–6.

Hayes, Peter, Lyuba Zarsky, and Walden Bello (1986) *American Lake: Nuclear Peril in the Pacific*, New York: Penguin Books.

Held, David (1995) *Democracy and the Global Order: From the Modern State to Cosmopolitan Governance*, Stanford, CA: Stanford University Press.

Heginbotham, Eric and Richard Samuels (1998) "Mercantile Realism and Japanese Foreign Policy," *International Security*, 22(4), 171–203.

Henderson, Gregory (1974). "Korea," in Gregory Henderson, Richard Ned Lebow, and John G. Stoessinger, eds. *Divided Nations in a Divided World*, New York: McKay, pp. 43–96.

Hicks, George (1997) *Japan's War Memories: Amnesia or Concealment?* Aldershot: Ashgate.

Hirschman, Albert O. (1980) *National Power and the Structure of Foreign Trade*, Exp. ed., Berkeley: University of California Press.

Hoffmann, Stanley (2003) "The High and the Mighty: Bush's National-Security Strategy and the New American Hubris," *The American Prospect*, January 13, 28–31.

Holsti, K. J. (1996) *The State, War, and the State of War*, New York: Cambridge University Press.

Hong, Soon-young (1999) "Thawing Korea's Cold War: The Path to Peace on the Korean Peninsula," *Foreign Affairs*, 78, 8–12.

Hoover, Kenneth R. (1975) *A Politics of Identity: Liberation and the Natural Community*, Urbana: University of Illinois Press.

Hopf, Ted (1998) "The Promise of Constructivism in International Relations Theory," *International Security*, 23(1), 171–200.

Hopf, Ted (2002) *Social Construction of International Politics: Identities and Foreign Policies*, Ithaca, NY: Cornell University Press.

Hosking, Geoffrey (1997) *Russia: People and Empire*, Cambridge, MA: Harvard University Press.

Howard, Michael (1979) "War and the Nation-State," *Daedalus*, 108(4), 101–10.

Hu, Weixing (1995) "Beijing's Defense Strategy and the Korean Peninsula," *Journal of Northeast Asian Studies*, 14, 50–67.

Hughes, Christopher W. (1999) *Japan's Economic Power and Security: Japan and North Korea*, New York: Routledge.

Huntington, Samuel (1991) *The Third Wave: Democratization in the Late Twentieth Century*, Norman: University of Oklahoma Press.

Huntington, Samuel (1996) *The Clash of Civilizations and the Remaking of World Order*, New York: Simon & Schuster.

Huntington, Samuel (1999) "The Lonely Superpower," *Foreign Affairs*, 78(2), 35–49.

Hwang, Eui-gak (1993) *The Korean Economies*, Oxford: Clarendon Press.

Hwang, Jang Yop (1998) *Pukhan ui chinsil kwa hwi* [*North Korea's Truth and Lies*], Seoul: Institute of National Unification Policy.

Hwang, Jang Yop (1999) *Nanun yoksaui chili rul poattda* [*I Have Witnessed Historical Truth*], Seoul: Hanul.

Ignatieff, Michael (2003a) "The Burden," *New York Times Magazine*, January 5, pp. 22–27, 50–54.

Ignatieff, Michael (2003b) "The Challenges of American Imperial Power," *Naval War College Review*, 56(2), 53–63.

Ikenberry, G. John (2004) "Illusions of Empire: Defining the New American Order," *Foreign Affairs*, 83(2), 144–54.

Ikenberry, G. John and Michael Mastanduno (2003a) *International Relations Theory and the Asia-Pacific*, New York: Columbia University Press.

Ikenberry, G. John and Michael Mastanduno (2003b) "Conclusion: Images of Order in the Asia-Pacific and the Role of the United States," in G. John Ikenberry and Michael Mastanduno, eds., *International Relations Theory and the Asia-Pacific*, New York: Columbia University Press, pp. 421–39.

International Institute for Strategic Studies (IISS) (1997) "Armed Conflicts and Fatalities 1945–1994," *The Military Balance, 1997–1998*, London: IISS.

International Institute for Strategic Studies (IISS) (2001) *The Military Balance, 2001–2002*. London: IISS.

International Institute for Strategic Studies (IISS) (2002) *The Military Balance, 2002–2003*. New York: Oxford University Press.

International Institute for Strategic Studies (IISS) (2004) *The Military Balance, 2004–2005*, New York: Oxford University Press.

International Institute for Strategic Studies (IISS) (2005) *The Military Balance, 2005–2006*. New York: Oxford University Press.

International Monetary Fund (IMF) (1992) *1992 Direction of Trade Yearbook*, Washington, DC: IMF.

International Monetary Fund (IMF) (1993) *1993 Direction of Trade Yearbook*, Washington, DC: IMF.

International Monetary Fund (IMF) (1994) *1994 Direction of Trade Yearbook*, Washington, DC: IMF.

International Monetary Fund (IMF) (1995) *1995 Direction of Trade Yearbook*, Washington, DC: IMF.

International Monetary Fund (IMF) (1996) *1996 Direction of Trade Yearbook*, Washington, DC: IMF.

International Monetary Fund (IMF) (1997) *1997 Direction of Trade Yearbook*, Washington, DC: IMF.

International Monetary Fund (IMF) (1998) *1998 Direction of Trade Yearbook*, Washington, DC: IMF.

Hahm, Chaibong and Seog-gun Kim (2001). "Remembering Japan and North Korea: The Politics of Memory in South Korea," in Gerrit W. Gong, ed., *Memory and History in East and Southeast Asia: Issues of Identity in International Relations*. Washington, DC: CSIS Press, pp. 101–12.

Jackson, Robert H. (1990) *Quasi-States: Sovereignty, International Relations, and the Third World*, New York: Cambridge University Press.

Japan Ministry of Foreign Affairs (2004) *Diplomatic Bluebook 2004*. Tokyo: Government of Japan. Available at http://www.mofa.go.jp/policy/other/bluebook/2004/index.html.

Jepperson, Ronald L, Alexander Wendt, and Peter J. Katzenstein (1996) "Norms, Identity, and Culture in National Security," in Peter J. Katzenstein, ed., *The Culture of National Security: Norms and Identity in World Politics*, New York: Columbia University Press, pp. 33–75.

Jervis, Robert (1976) *Perceptions and Misperceptions in International Politics*, Princeton, NJ: Princeton University Press.

Jervis, Robert (1980) "The Impact of the Korean War on the Cold War," *Journal of Conflict Resolution*, 24, 563–92.

Jervis, Robert (1991/92) "The Future of World Politics: Will It Resemble the Past?" *International Security*, 16(3), 39–73.

Jervis, Robert (1997) *System Effects: Complexity in Political and Social Life*, Princeton, NJ: Princeton University Press.

Jervis, Robert (2002) "Theories of War in an Era of Leading-Power Peace," *American Political Science Review*, 96(1), 1–14.

Ji, You (2001a) "China and North Korea: A Fragile Relationship of Strategic Convenience," *Journal of Contemporary China*, 10(28), 387–98.

Ji, You (2001b) "The PLA, the CCP and the Formulation of Chinese Defense and Foreign Policy," in Yongjin Zhang and Greg Austin, eds., *Power and Responsibility in Chinese Foreign Policy*, Canberra, Australia: Asia Pacific Press, pp. 105–131.

Jia, Hao and Zhuang Qubing (1992) "China's Policy Toward the Korean Peninsula," *Asian Survey*, 32(12), 1137–56.

Johnson, Chalmers (2004) *The Sorrows of Empire: Militarism, Secrecy, and the End of the Republic*, New York: Metropolitan Books.

Johnson, Chalmers (2005) "The Real 'China Threat'," *Asia Times* [Online], March 19. Available at http://www.atimes.com/korea.html.

Johnston, Alastair Iain (1995) *Cultural Realism: Strategic Culture and Grand Strategy in Chinese History*, Princeton, NJ: Princeton University Press.

Johnston, Alastair Iain (1998) "China's Militarized Interstate Dispute Behaviour 1949–1992: A First Cut at the Data," *China Quarterly*, 153, 1–30.

Johnston, Alastair Iain (2003) "Socialization in International Institutions: The ASEAN Way and International Relations Theory," in G. John Ikenberry and Michael Mastanduno, eds., *International Relations Theory and the Asia-Pacific*, New York: Columbia University Press, pp. 107–62.

Johnston, Alastair Iain (2004) "China's International Relations: The Political and Security Dimensions," in Samuel S. Kim, ed., *The International Relations of Northeast Asia*, Lanham, MD: Rowman & Littlefield, pp. 65–100.

Johnston, Alastair Iain and Paul Evans (1999) "China's Engagement with Multilateral Security Institutions," in Alastair Iain Johnston and Robert S. Ross, eds., *Engaging China: The Management of an Emerging Power*, New York: Routledge, pp. 235–72.

Johnston, Alastair Iain, Rawi Abdelai, Yoshiko Herrera, and Terry Martin (2001). "Treating Identity as a Variable," Paper presented at the annual meeting of the American Political Science Association, San Francisco, CA, August 30–September 2.

Joo, Seung-ho (1998) "Russia and Korea," in Bae-ho Hahn and Chae-jin Lee, eds., *The Korean Peninsula and the Major Powers*, Seoul: The Sejong Institute.

Joo, Seung-ho (2000a) "DPRK-Russian Rapprochement and Its Implications for Korean Security," *International Journal of Korean Unification Studies*, 6, 193–223.

Joo, Seung-ho (2000b) *Gorbachev's Foreign Policy Toward the Korean Peninsula, 1985–1991*, Lewiston, NY: Edwin Mellon.

Joo, Seung-ho (2001) "The New Friendship Treaty Between Moscow and Pyongyang," *Comparative Strategy*, 20(5), 467–82.

Joo, Seung-ho (2003) "Russia and the Korean Peace Process," in Tae-Hwan Kwak and Seung-Ho Joo, eds., *The Korean Peace Process and the Four Powers*, Burlington, VT: Ashgate, pp. 143–70.

de Jourvenal, Bertrand (1967) *The Art of Conjecture*, New York: Basic Books.

Jungk, Robert and Johan Galtung, eds. (1969) *Mankind 2000*, London: Allen & Unwin.

Kagan, Robert (1998) "The Benevolent Empire," *Foreign Policy*, 111, 24–35.

Kagan, Robert and William Kristol, eds. (2002) *Present Dangers: Crisis and Opportunity in American Foreign and Defense Policy*, San Francisco: Encounter Books.

Kahn, Herman and Anthony Wiener (1967) *The Year 2000: A Framework for Speculation on the Next Thirty-Three Years*, New York: Macmillan.

Kang, C. S. Eliot (2004) "Japan in Inter-Korean Relations," in Samuel S. Kim, ed., *Inter-Korean Relations: Problems and Prospects*, New York: Palgrave Macmillan, pp. 97–116.

Kang, C.S. Eliot and Yoshinori Kaseda (2000) "Japanese Security and Peace Regime on the Korean Peninsula," *International Journal of Korean Unification Studies*, 9(1), 117–35.

Kang, David C. (2005a) "Japan–Korea Relations: History Impedes the Future," *Comparative Connections* [Online], 7(1), 123–32. Available at http://www.csis.org/media/csis/pubs/0501q.pdf.

Kang, David C. (2005b) "Japan: U.S. Partner or Focused on Abductees?" *The Washington Quarterly*, 28(4), 107–17.

Kang, David C. and Ji-Young Lee (2005) "Japan–Korea Relations: Little Progress on North Korea or History Dispute," *Comparative Connections* [Online], 7(2), 133–42. Available at http://www.csis.org/media/csis/pubs/0502q.pdf.

Kapstein, Ethan B. (1995) "Is Realism Dead? The Domestic Sources of International Politics," *International Organization*, 49(4), 751–74.

Katzenstein, Peter J., ed. (1996) *The Culture of National Security: Norms and Identity in World Politics*, New York: Columbia University Press.

Katzenstein, Peter J. and Nobuo Okawara (2001/02) "Japan, Asia-Pacific Security, and the Case of Analytical Eclecticism," *International Security*, 26(3), 153–85.

Kegley, Charles W. Jr. (1994) "How Did the Cold War Die? Principles for an Autopsy," *Mershon International Studies Review*, 38, 11–41.

Kegley, Charles W, Jr. (1995) *Controversies in International Relations Theory: Realism and the Neoliberal Challenge*, New York: St. Martin's Press.

Kennedy, Paul (1993) *Preparing for the Twenty-First Century*, New York: Random House.

Kennedy, Paul, Richard Perle, and Joseph S. Nye, Jr. (2003) "The Reluctant Empire: In a Time of Great Consequence," *Brown Journal of World Affairs*, 10(1), 11–31.

Keohane, Robert O. and Joseph S. Nye (1977) *Power and Interdependence*, Boston: Little, Brown.

Keohane, Robert O. (1984) *After Hegemony: Cooperation and Discord in the World Political Economy*, Princeton, NJ: Princeton University Press.

Keum, Hieyeon (1996) "Normalization and After: Prospects for the Sino-South Korean Relations," *Korean and World Affairs*, 20, 572–80.

Khong, Yuen Foong (1987) "The Lessons of Korea and the Vietnam Decisions of 1965," in Charles F. Hermann, Charles W. Kegley, Jr., and James N. Rosenau, eds., *New Directions in the Study of Foreign Policy*, Boston: Allen & Unwin, pp. 302–49.

Khong, Yuen Foong (1992) *Analogies at War: Korea, Munich, Dien Bien Phu, and the Vietnam Decisions of 1965*, Princeton, NJ: Princeton University Press.

Kihl, Young Whan (1998) "North Korea and the United Nations," in Samuel S. Kim, ed., *North Korean Foreign Relations in the Post-Cold War Era*, New York: Oxford University Press, pp. 258–79.

Kihl, Young Whan and Peter Hayes, eds. (1997) *Peace and Security in Northeast Asia: The Nuclear Issue and the Korean Peninsula*, Armonk, NY: M. E. Sharpe.

Kim, Abraham (2004) "The Challenges of Peacefully Reunifying the Korean Peninsula," in Samuel S. Kim, ed., *Inter-Korean Relations: Problems and Prospects*, New York: Palgrave, pp. 197–218.

Kim, C. I. Eugene and Han-Kyo Kim (1967) *Korea and the Politics of Imperialism, 1876–1910*, Berkeley: University of California Press.

Kim, Choong-Nam (1996) "The Uncertain Future of North Korea: Soft Landing or Crash Landing?" *Korea and World Affairs*, 20(4), 623–36.

Kim, Dalchoong and Chung-in Moon, eds. (1997) *History, Cognition, and Peace in East Asia*, Seoul: Yonsei University Press.

Kim, Hakjoon (1990) "International Trends in Korean War Studies: A Review of the Documentary Literature," *Korea and World Affairs*, 14(2), 326–46.

Kim, Hakjoon (1993) *Korea's Relations with Her Neighbors in a Changing World*, Elizabeth, NJ: Holly.

Kim, Hakjoon (1994) "Russian Archives on Origins of Korean War," *Korea Focus*, 2(2), 22–31.

Kim, Hong Nack (1998). "Japan in North Korean Foreign Policy," in Samuel S. Kim, ed., *North Korean Foreign Policy in the Post-Cold War Era*, New York: Oxford University Press, pp. 116–39.

Kim, Hong Nack (2006) "Japanese-North Korean Relations Under the Koizumi Government," in Hong Nack Kim and Young Whan Kihl, eds., *North Korea: The Politics of Regime Survival,* Armonk, NY: M. E. Sharpe, pp. 161–82.

Kim, Ilpyong J. (1994) "The Soviet Union/Russia and Korea: Dynamics of 'New Thinking,'" in Young Whan Kihl, ed., *Korea and the World: Beyond the Cold War,* Boulder, CO: Westview Press, pp. 83–95.

Kim, Jungwon Alexander (1975) *Divided Korea: The Politics of Development, 1945–72,* Cambridge, MA: Harvard University Press.

Kim, Key-Hiuk (1980) *The Last Phase of the East Asian World Order,* Berkeley: University of California Press.

Kim, Kyung-won (1996) "No Way Out: North Korea's Impending Collapse," *Harvard International Review,* 18(2), 22–71.

Kim, Samuel S. (1976) "The Developmental Problems of Korean Nationalism," in Se-Jin Kim and Chang-hyun Cho, eds., *Korea: A Divided Nation,* Silver Spring, MD: The Research Institute on Korean Affairs, pp. 10–37.

Kim, Samuel S. (1979) *China, the United Nations, and World Order,* Princeton, NJ: Princeton University Press.

Kim, Samuel S. (1980/81) "United States Korean Policy and World Order," *Alternatives: A Journal of World Policy,* 6, 419–52.

Kim, Samuel S. (1984) *The Quest for a Just World Order,* Boulder, CO: Westview Press.

Kim, Samuel S. (1991) "North Korea and the Non-Communist World: The Quest for National Identity," in Chong-Sik Lee and Se-Hee Yoo, eds., *North Korea in Transition,* Berkeley: Center for Korean Studies, Institute of East Asian Studies, University of California at Berkeley, pp. 17–42.

Kim, Samuel S. (1992) "China as a Regional Power," *Current History,* 91, 247–52.

Kim, Samuel S. (1995) "North Korea in 1994: Brinkmanship, Breakdown and Breakthrough," *Asian Survey,* 35(1), 13–27.

Kim, Samuel S. (1997a) "China as a Great Power," *Current History,* 96, 246–51.

Kim, Samuel S. (1997b) "Puk-Mi hyopsang kwa Pukhan ui chunryak" [DPRK-US Negotiations and North Korea's Strategy], in Kwak Tae-hwan, ed., *Pukhan ui Hyopsang Chunryak kwa NamPukhan Kwangkye* [*North Korea's Negotiating Strategy and South-North Relations*], Seoul: Institute of Far Eastern Studies, Kyungnam University, pp. 163–86.

Kim, Samuel S. (1997c) "North Korea and the United Nations," *International Journal of Korean Studies,* 1, 77–105.

Kim, Samuel S. ed. (1998a) *North Korean Foreign Relations in the Post-Cold War Era,* New York: Oxford University Press.

Kim, Samuel S. (1998b) "In Search of a Theory of North Korean Foreign Policy," in Samuel S. Kim, ed., *North Korean Foreign Relations in the Post-Cold War Era,* New York: Oxford University Press, pp. 3–31.

Kim, Samuel S. (1998c) "Chinese Foreign Policy in Theory and Practice," in Samuel S. Kim, ed. *China and the World: Chinese Foreign Policy Faces the New Millennium.* Boulder, CO: Westview Press, pp. 3–33.

Kim, Samuel S. (1999) "China and the United Nations," in Elizabeth Economy and Michel Oksenberg, eds., *China Joins the World: Progress and Prospects,* New York: Council on Foreign Relations Press, pp. 42–89.

Kim, Samuel S. (2000a) "Korea and Globalization (Segyehwa): A Framework for Analysis," in Samuel S. Kim, ed., *Korea's Globalization,* New York: Cambridge University Press, pp. 1–28.

Kim, Samuel S. (2000b) "Korea's Globalization Drive: Promise Versus Performance," in Samuel S. Kim, ed., *Korea's Globalization*, New York: Cambridge University Press, pp. 242–81.

Kim, Samuel S. (2000c) "North Korean Informal Politics," in Lowell Dittmer, Haruhiro Fukui, and Peter N. S. Lee, eds. *Informal Politics in East Asia*, New York: Cambridge University Press, pp. 237–68.

Kim, Samuel S., ed. (2000d) *East Asia and Globalization*, Lanham, MD: Rowman & Littlefield.

Kim, Samuel S. (2001) "The Making of China's Korea Policy in the Era of Reform," in David M. Lampton, ed. *The Making of Chinese Foreign and Security Policy in the Era of Reform*. Stanford, CA: Stanford University Press, pp. 371–408.

Kim, Samuel S. (2004a) "Introduction: Managing the Korean Conflict," in Samuel S. Kim, ed., *Inter-Korean Relations: Problems and Prospects*, New York: Palgrave Macmillan, pp. 1–20.

Kim, Samuel S. (2004b) "China's New Role in the Nuclear Confrontation," *Asian Perspective*, 28(4), 147–84.

Kim, Samuel S. (2004c) "China in World Politics," in Barry Buzan and Rosemary Foot, eds., *Does China Matter? A Reassessment*, New York: Routledge, pp. 37–53.

Kim, Samuel S. (2004d) "Regionalization and Regionalism in East Asia," *Journal of East Asian Studies*, 4(1), 39–67.

Kim, Samuel S. ed. (2004e) *The International Relations of Northeast Asia*. Lanha, MD: Rowman & Littlefield.

Kim, Samuel S. and Lowell Dittmer (1993) "Whither China's Quest for National Identity?" in Lowell Dittmer and Samuel S. Kim, eds., *China's Quest for National Identity*, Ithaca, NY: Cornell University Press, pp. 237–90.

Kim, Samuel S. and Abraham Kim (2004) "Conflict Management," in Mary Hawkesworth and Maurice Kogan, eds., *Encyclopaedia of Government and Politics*, 2nd ed., Vol. 2, New York: Routledge, pp. 980–93.

Kim, Samuel S. and Matthew S. Winters (2004) "Inter-Korean Economic Relations," in Samuel S. Kim, ed., *Inter Korean Relations: Problems and Prospects*, New York: Palgrave Macmillan, pp. 57–80.

Kim, Taeho (1997) "Korean Views on the Taiwan-PRC Relations and the Japan Factor," in James R. Lilley and Chuck Downs, eds., *Crisis in the Taiwan Strait*, Washington, DC: National Defense University Press, pp. 303–25.

Kim, Taeho (1999) "Strategic Relations Between Beijing and Pyongyang: Growing Strains amid Lingering Ties," in James R. Lilley and David Shambaugh, eds., *China's Military Faces the Future*, Armonk, NY: M. E. Sharpe, pp. 295–321.

Koh, Byung Chul (1984) *The Foreign Policy Systems of North and South Korea*, Berkeley: University of California Press.

Koh, Byung Chul (1985) "China and the Korean Peninsula," *Korea and World Affairs*, 9, 264–79.

Koh, Byung Chul (1994) "Prospects for Change in North Korea," *Korean Journal of National Unification*, 3, 237–55.

Koh, Byung Chul (1998) "Japan and Korea," in Bae-ho Hahn and Chae-jin Lee, eds. *The Korean Peninsula and the Major Powers*, Seoul: Sejong Institute, pp. 33–68.

Koh, Byung Chul (2000) "*Segyehwa*, the Republic of Korea, and the United Nations," in Samuel S. Kim, ed., *Korea's Globalization*, New York: Cambridge University Press, pp. 196–216.

Koh, Byung Chul, Se Jin Kim, Jae Kyu Park, Young-Ho Lee, and Chang-Yoon Choi (1977) *Pukhan Oekyo-ron* [*On North Korea's Foreign Policy*], Seoul: Kyungnam University Press.

Kohli, Atul (1994) "Where Do High Growth Political Economies Come From? The Japanese Lineage of Korea's 'Developmental State,'" *World Development*, 22(9), 1269–93.

Kortunov, Sergei (2003) "Russia's National Identity: Foreign Policy Dimension," *International Affairs* [Moscow], 49(4), 97–106.

Koo, Youngnok (1995) *Hankuk ui Kukka yiyik* [*Korea's National Interest*], Seoul: Pommunsa.

Kovrigin, Evgenii (2003) "The Russian Federation and the Two Korean States: Economic Cooperation the Early 21 Century," *The Seinan Law Review* 35 (3–4), 95–128.

Kowert, Paul A. (1998) "Agent Versus Structure in the Construction of National Identity," in Vendulka Kubalkova, Nicholas Onuf, and Paul Kowert, eds., *International Relations in a Constructed World*, Armonk, NY: M. E. Sharpe, pp. 101–22.

Kowert, Paul A. (1999) "National Identity: Inside and Out," *Security Studies*, 8, 1–34.

Kratochwil, Friedrich (1993) "The Embarrassment of Changes: Neo-Realism as the Science of Realpolitik Without Politics," *Review of International Studies*, 19, 63–80.

Krause, Jill and Neil Renwick, eds. (1996) *Identities in International Relations*, New York: St. Martin's Press.

Krauthammer, Charles (1991) "The Unipolar Moment," *Foreign Affairs*, 70, 24–33.

Krauthammer, Charles (2001) "The American Empire and the Islamic Challenge," *The Weekly Standard*, 7(9), 25.

Kreisberg, Paul H. (1996) "Threat Environment for a United Korea: 2010," *Korean Journal of Defense Analysis*, 8, 84–85.

Kupchan, Charles A. (2002) *The End of the American Era: U.S. Foreign Policy and the Geopolitics of the Twenty-First Century*, New York: Knopf.

Lampton, David M. and Richard Daniel Ewing (2004) *The U.S.-China Relationship Facing International Security Crises: Three Case Studies in Post-9/11 Bilateral Relations*, Washington, DC: The Nixon Center.

Laney, James T. (1996) "North and South Korea: Beyond Deterrence," Speech delivered to the Asia Society Corporate Conference, Seoul, Korea, May 11.

Lankov, Andrei (2004a) "Cold War Alienates Seoul, Moscow," *The Korea Times*, September 17 [Online] Available at http://times.hankooki.com.

Lankov, Andrei (2004b) "North Korean Refugees in Northeast China," *Asian Survey*, 44(6), 856–73.

Lardy, Nicholas (2002) *Integrating China into the Global Economy*, Washington, DC: Brookings Institution Press.

Larson, Eric, Norman Levin, Seonhae Baik and Bogdan Savych (2004) *Ambivalent Allies?: A Study of South Korean Attitudes Toward the U.S.* Santa Monica, CA: Rand Corporation, March.

Lebow, Richard Ned (1981) *Between Peace and War: The Nature of International Crisis*, Baltimore: The Johns Hopkins University Press, pp. 57–97.

Lebow, Richard Ned (1994) "The Long Peace, the End of the Cold War, and the Failure of Realism," *International Organization*, 48, 249–78.

Lee, Chae-jin (1996) *China and Korea: Dynamic Relations*, Stanford, CA: Hoover Institution Press.

Lee, Chae-jin (1998a) "The Evolution of China's Two Korea Policy," in Bae-ho Hahn and Chae-jin Lee, eds., *The Korean Peninsula and the Major Powers*, Seoul: Sejong Institute, pp. 115–46.

Lee, Chae-jin (1998b) "China and North Korea," in Dae-sook Suh and Chae-jin Lee, eds., *North Korea After Kim Il-Sung*, Boulder, CO: Lynne Rienner, pp. 165–209.

Lee, Changsoo and George De Vos (1981) *Koreans in Japan: Ethnic Conflict and Accommodation*, Berkeley: University of California Press.

Lee, Chong-sik (1963) *The Politics of Korean Nationalism*, Berkeley: University of California Press.

Lee, Chong-sik (1985) *Japan and Korea: The Political Dimension*, Stanford, CA: Hoover Institution Press.

Lee, Eric Yong-Joong (2000) "Development of North Korea's Legal Regime Governing Foreign Business Cooperation: A Revisit Under the New Socialist Constitution of 1998," *Northwestern Journal of International Law and Business*, 21(1), 199–242.

Lee, Jong Seok (2001) *PukHan-Chungkuk Kwan Kyae 1945–2000 [DPRK-PRC Relations, 1945–2000]*. Seoul: Jungsim.

Lee, Shin-wha (1999a) "Preventing Refugee Crisis: A Challenge to Human Security," *Asian Perspective*, 23, 133–54.

Lee, Shin-wha (1999a) "Responses to North Korean Food Refugees," *Security Dialogue* 30, 122–24.

Lee, Shin-wha (1999b) "A Number of People in Limbo," *Vantage Point*, May, 22–25.

Lee, Shin-wha (2004) "International Organizations and the Inter-Korean Peace Process: Traditional Security Versus Nontraditional Security," in Samuel S. Kim, ed., *Inter-Korean Relations: Problems and Prospects*, New York: Palgrave Macmillan, pp. 175–96.

Lee, Sook-Jong (2004) "The Roots and Patterns of Anti-Americanism in Korean Society: A Survey-Based Analysis," *Joint U.S.-Korea Academic Studies*, 14, 183–204.

Lee, Won Sul (1982) *The United States and the Division of Korea, 1945*, Seoul: Kyunghee University Press.

Lee, Woo-young (1997) "Northern Defectors in South Korea," *Korea Focus*, 5(3), 31–40.

Lee, Young-sun (1995) "Is Korean Reunification Possible?" *Korea Focus*, 3(3), 5–21.

Lee, Young-sun (1997) "Kim Jong-Il and Economic Reform: Myth and Reality," *Korea Focus*, 5(6), 70–83.

Lee, Young-sun (2002) "The Cost and Financing of Korean Unification," in Sung-Hee Jwa, Chung-in Moon, and Jeong-Ho Roh, eds., *Constitutional Handbook on Korean Unification*, Part III, Seoul: Korea Economic Research Institute, pp. 1125–61.

Lee, Young-sun and Yong-Pyo Hong (1997) "Unified Korea and New Strategies for National Survival," in Dalchoong Kim and Chung-in Moon, eds., *History, Cognition, and Peace in East Asia*, Seoul: Yonsei University Press, pp. 177–99.

Legvold, Robert (1999) "The Three Russias: Decline, Revolution, and Reconstruction," in Robert Pastor, ed., *A Century's Journey: How the Great Powers Shape the World*, New York: Basic Books, pp. 139–90.

Levin, Norman D. (1997) "What if North Korea Survives?" *Survival*, 39, 156–74.

Levy, Jack (2001) "Theories of Interstate and Intrastate War: A Levels-of-Analysis Approach," in Chester A. Crocker, Fen Osler Hampson, and Pamela Aall, eds., *Turbulent Peace: The Challenges of Managing International Conflict*, Washington, DC: United States Institute of Peace Press, pp. 3–27.

Lewis, John Wilson and Xue Litai (1988) *China Builds the Bomb*, Stanford, CA: Stanford University Press.

Lewis, Peter (2004) "Broadband Wonderland," *Fortune*, 20, 191–98.
Li, Vladimir F. (2000a) "North Korea and the Nuclear Nonproliferation Regime," in James Clay Moltz and Alexandre Y. Mansourov, eds., *The North Korean Nuclear Program*, New York: Routledge, pp. 138–55.
Li, Vladimir F. (2000b) *Rossiya I Koreya v geopolitike evraziiskogo vostoka (xx vek)* [*Russia and Korea in the Geopolitics of the Eurasian East (20th century)*], Moscow: Nauchnaya Kniga.
Liska, George (1962) *Nations in Alliance: Limits of Interdependence*, Baltimore: The Johns Hopkins University Press.
Litwak, Robert (2000) *Rogue States and U.S. Foreign Policy*. Baltimore: The Johns Hopkins University Press.
Litwak, Robert (2001) "What's in a Name? The Changing Foreign Policy Lexicon," *Journal of International Affairs*, 54(2), 375–92.
Litwak, Robert (2003) "Non-Proliferation and the Dilemmas of Regime Change," *Survival*, 45(4), 7–32.
Liu, Jinzhi and Yang Huaisheng, eds. (1994) *Zhongguo dui Chaoxian he Hanguo zhengci wenjian huibian 5 (1974–1994)* [*A Collection of Documents on China's Policy toward the Democratic People's Republic of Korea and the Republic of Korea, Vol. 5 (1974–1994)*], Beijing: Zhongguo shehui kexue chubanshe.
Liu, Ming (2003) "China and the North Korean Crisis: Facing Test and Transition," *Pacific Affairs*, 76(3), 347–73.
Lynn-Jones, Sean and Steven Miller, eds. (1993) *The Cold War and After: Prospects for Peace*, Cambridge, MA: MIT Press.
Macdonald, Donald Stone (1992) *U.S-Korean Relations from Liberation to Self-Reliance: The Twenty-Year Record: An Interpretative Summary of the Archives of the U.S. Department of State for the Period 1945 to 1965*, Boulder, CO: Westview Press.
Mack, Andrew (1975) "Why Big Nations Lose Small Wars: The Politics of Asymmetric Conflict," *World Politics*, 27(2), 175–200.
Mack, Andrew (1993) "The Nuclear Crisis on the Korean Peninsula," *Asian Survey*, 33, 339–59.
Mallaby, Sebastian (2002) "The Reluctant Imperialist: Terrorism, Failed States and the Case for American Empire," *Foreign Affairs*, 81(2), 2–7.
Mann, James (2004) *Rise of the Vulcans: The History of Bush's War Cabinet*, New York: Viking.
Mann, Michael (2003) *Incoherent Empire*, New York: Verso.
Mannheim, Karl (1968) *Ideology and Utopia*, New York: Harcourt, Brace & World.
Manning, Robert (1999) "The Enigma of the North," *Wilson Quarterly*, 23, 72–80.
Manning, Robert (2002) "United States-North Korean Relations: From Welfare to Workfare?" in Samuel S. Kim and Tai Hwan Lee, eds., *North Korea and Northeast Asia*, Lanham, MD: Rowman & Littlefield, pp. 61–88.
Mansourov, Alexandre Y. (1995) "The Origins, Evolution, and Current Politics of the North Korean Nuclear Program," *Nonproliferation Review*, 2(3), 25–38.
Mansourov, Alexandre Y. (2000a) "The Natural Disasters of the Mid-1990s and the Their Impact on the Implementation of the Agreed Framework," in James Clay Moltz and Alexandre Y. Mansourov, eds., *The North Korean Nuclear Program*, New York: Routledge, pp. 76–90.
Mansourov, Alexandre Y. (2000b) "North Korea's Negotiations with the Korean Peninsula Energy Development Organization (KEDO)," in James Clay Moltz and Alexandre Y. Mansourov, eds., *The North Korean Nuclear Program*, New York: Routledge, pp. 156–70.

Mansourov, Alexandre Y. (2004) "Kim Jong Il Re-Embraces the Bear, Looking for the Morning Calm: North Korea's Policy Toward Russia Since 1994," in Byung Chul Koh, ed., *North Korea and the World: Explaining Pyongyang's Foreign Policy*, Seoul: Kyungnam University Press, pp. 239–84.

Manuel, Frank E. and Fritzie P. Manuel (1979) *Utopian Thought in the Western World*, Cambridge, MA: Harvard University Press.

Manyin, Mark E. (2003, November 26) "Japan-North Korean Relations: Selected Issues," Washington, DC: Congressional Research Service.

Manyin, Mark E. (2004, July 1) "South Korea-U.S. Economic Relations: Cooperation, Friction, and Future Prospects," CRS Report for Congress, Washington, DC: Congressional Research Service.

Manyin, Mark E. and Ryun Jun (2003, March 17) "U.S. Assistance to North Korea," Report to Congress, Washington, DC: Congressional Research Service.

Mao, Zedong (1965) *Selected Works of Mao Tse-Tung*, Vol. 1, Beijing: Foreign Languages Press.

Marx, Karl (1959) "The 18th Brumaire of Louis Napoleon," in Lewis Feuer, ed., *Basic Writings on Politics and Philosophy: Karl Marx and Friedrich Engels*, New York: Doubleday.

Marx, Karl (1967) *Writings of Young Marx on Philosophy and Society*, Lloyd D. Easton and Kurt H. Guddat, trans. and eds., Garden City, NY: Anchor Books.

Matray, James Irving (1985) *The Reluctant Crusade: American Foreign Policy in Korea, 1941–1950*, Honolulu: University of Hawaii Press.

Mazrui, Ali A. (1976) *A World Federation of Cultures: An African Perspective*, New York: Free Press.

McCormack, Gavan (1993) "Kim Country: Hard Times in North Korea," *New Left Review*, 198, 21–48.

McCormack, Gavan (2004) *Target North Korea: Pushing North Korea to the Brink of Nuclear Catastrophe*, New York: Nation Books.

McDevitt, Michael (2001) "The Post-Korean Unification Security Landscape and U.S. Security Policy in Northeast Asia," in Nicholas Eberstadt and Richard Ellings, eds., *Korea's Future and the Great Powers*, Seattle: University of Washington Press, pp. 251–96.

McVadon, Eric A. (1999) "Chinese Military Strategy for the Korean Peninsula," in James R. Lilley and David Shambaugh, eds., *China's Military Faces the Future*, Armonk, NY: M. E. Sharpe, pp. 271–94.

Mearsheimer, John (2001) *The Tragedy of Great Power Politics*, New York: Norton.

Mendlovitz, Saul H., ed. (1975) *On the Creation of a Just World Order*, New York: Free Press.

Menon, Rajan (2003) "The End of Alliances," *World Policy Journal*, 20(2), 1–20.

Merton, Robert K. (1949) *Social Theory and Social Structure: Toward the Codification of Theory and Research*, Glencoe, IL: Free Press.

Meyer, Peggy Falkenheim (2005) "Russo-North Korean Relations," Paper presented at the International Council for Korean Studies Conference 2005, Arlington, VA, August 5–6.

Meyer, Peggy Falkenheim (2006) "Russo-North Korean Relations Under Kim Jong Il," in Young Whan Kihl and Hong Nack Kim, eds., *North Korea: The Politics of Regime Survival*, Armonk, NY: M. E. Sharpe, pp. 203–14.

Michael, Franz H. and George E. Taylor (1964) *The Far East in the Modern World*, Rev. ed., New York: Holt, Rinehart and Winston.

Ministry of Foreign Affairs (MOFA) (1979), *Han'guk oegyo 30-nyôn* [*Thirty Year Diplomacy of the ROK*], Seoul: MOFA.

Ministry of Foreign Affairs (MOFA) (1997) *Oekyo paekso 1997* [*Diplomatic White Paper 1997*], Seoul: MOFA.

Ministry of Foreign Affairs and Trade (MOFAT) (1998) *HanChung kwankye hyunhwang mit choekun Chungkuk chungse* [*The State of ROK-PRC Relations and Recent Chinese Affairs*], Seoul: MOFAT.

Ministry of Foreign Affairs and Trade (MOFAT) (1999) *Oekyo paekso 1998* [*Diplomatic White Paper 1998*], Seoul: MOFAT.

Ministry of Foreign Affairs and Trade (MOFAT) (2000) *Oekyo paekso 1999* [*Diplomatic White Paper 1999*]. Seoul: MOFAT.

Ministry of Foreign Affairs and Trade (MOFAT) (2001) *Oekyo paekso 2000* [*Diplomatic White Paper 2000*]. Seoul: MOFAT.

Ministry of Foreign Affairs and Trade (MOFAT) (2002) *Oekyo paekso 2001* [*Diplomatic White Paper 2001*]. Seoul: MOFAT.

Ministry of Foreign Affairs and Trade (MOFAT) (2003) *Oekyo paekso 2002* [*Diplomatic White Paper 2002*]. Seoul: MOFAT.

Ministry of Foreign Affairs and Trade (MOFAT) (2004) *Oekyo paekso 2003* [*Diplomatic White Paper 2003*]. Seoul: MOFAT.

Ministry of Foreign Affairs and Trade (MOFAT) (2005) *Oekyo paekso 2004* [*Diplomatic White Paper 2004*]. Seoul: MOFAT.

Ministry of National Defense (MND) (2000) *2000 Defense White Papers*, Seoul: MND.

Ministry of National Defense (MND) (2003) *ROK-US Alliance and USFK*, Rev. Edition, Seoul: MND.

Ministry of National Defense (MND) (2005) *2004 Defense White Paper*, Seoul: MND.

Ministry of Unification (MOU) (2003a, February) *Tong'il paekso 2003* [*Unification White Paper 2003*]. Seoul: MOU.

Ministry of Unification (MOU) (2003b, December) *2004 PukHan Kaeyo* [*2004 North Korean Synopsis*]. Seoul: MOU.

Ministry of Unification (MOU) (2004, February) *Tong'il paekso 2004* [*Unification White Paper 2004*]. Seoul: MOU.

Ministry of Unification (MOU) (2005, February) *Tong'il paekso 2005* [*Unification White Paper 2005*]. Seoul: MOU.

Mitchell, Derek (2002/03) "A Blueprint for U.S. Policy Toward a Unified Korea," *Washington Quarterly*, 26(1), 23–137.

Mitrany, David (1966) *A Working Peace System*, Chicago: Quadrangle.

Moon, Chung-in (1991) "International Quasi-Crisis: Theory and a Case of Japan-South Korean Bilateral Friction," *Asian Perspective*, 15(2), 99–123.

Moon, Chung-in (1996) *Arms Control on the Korean Peninsula*, Seoul: Yonsei University Press.

Moon, Chung-in (2002) "Sustaining Inter-Korean Reconciliation: North-South Korea Cooperation," *Joint U.S.-Korea Academic Studies*, 12, 225–50.

Moon, Chung-in (2005) "Rethinking Korean Unification and the Future of North Korea," *Korea and World Affairs*, 29(1), 7–25.

Moon, Chung-in, Masao Okonogi, and Mitchell B. Reiss, eds. (2000) *The Perry Report, the Missile Quagmire, and the North Korean Question: The Quest of New Alternatives*, Seoul: Yonsei University Press.

Moon, Chung-in, Odd Arne Westad, and Gyoo-hyoung Khang, eds. (2001) *Ending the Cold War in Korea: Theoretical and Historical Perspectives*, Seoul: Yonsei University Press.

Moon, Chung-in and Yongho Kim (2001) "The Future of the North Korean System," in Samuel S. Kim, ed. *The North Korean System in the Post-Cold War Era*, New York: Palgrave, pp. 221–58.

Moon, Katharine H. S. (2000) "Strangers in the Midst of Globalization: Migrant Workers and Korean Nationalism," in Samuel S. Kim, ed., *Korea's Globalization*, New York: Cambridge University Press, pp. 147–69.

Moon, Katharine H. S. (2003) "Korean Nationalism, Anti-Americanism, and Democratic Consolidation," in Samuel S. Kim, ed., *Korea's Democratization*, New York: Cambridge University Press, pp. 135–58.

Moore, Barrington, Jr. (1978) *Injustice: The Social Bases of Obedience and Revolt*, White Plains, NY: M. E. Sharpe.

Morrison, Charles E. and Astri Suhrke (1979) *Strategies of Survival: The Foreign Policy Dilemmas of Smaller Asian States*, New York: St. Martin's Press.

Myers, Ramon and Mark Peattie, eds. (1984) *The Japanese Colonial Empire, 1895–1945*, Princeton, NJ: Princeton University Press.

Nam, Kwang-sik (2004) "Keeping Mum on China's Claim," *Vantage Point*, 27(9), 15–19.

Nanto, Dick K. and Emma Chanlett-Avery (2005, February 9) *The North Korean Economy: Background and Policy Analysis*, Washington, DC: Congressional Research Service.

Natsios, Andrew (2001) *The Great North Korean Famine*, Washington, DC: U.S. Institute of Peace Press.

Neustadt, Richard E. and Ernest R. May (1986) *Thinking in Time: The Uses of History for Decision-Makers*, New York: Free Press.

Niksch, Larry A. (1992) "North Korea's Nuclear Weapons Program," CRS Issue Brief. Washington, DC: Congressional Research Service.

Niksch, Larry A. (1994a) "Comprehensive Negotiations with North Korea: A Viable Alternative for a Failed U.S. Strategy," *Korea and World Affairs*, 18, 250–72.

Niksch, Larry A. (1994b) "Opportunities and Challenges in Clinton's Confidence-Building Strategy Towards North Korea," *The Korean Journal of Defense Analysis*, 6, 145–56.

Niou, Emerson and Peter Ordeshook (1994) "Less Filling, Tastes Great: The Realist-Neoliberal Debate," *World Politics*, 46, 209–34.

Noland, Marcus (1997) "Why North Korea Will Muddle Through," *Foreign Affairs*, 76(4), 105–18.

Noland, Marcus, ed. (1998) *Economic Integration of the Korean Peninsula*, Washington, DC: Institute for International Economics.

Noland, Marcus (2000a) *Avoiding the Apocalypse: The Future of the Two Koreas*, Washington, DC: Institute for International Economics.

Noland, Marcus (2000b) "The Economics of Korean Unification," [Online], Washington, DC: Institute for International Economics. Available at http://www.iie./publications/papers/paper.cfm?ResearchID=364.

Noland, Marcus (2001) "Economic Strategies for Reunification," in Nicholas Eberstadt and Richard J. Ellings, eds., *Korea's Future and the Great Powers*, Seattle: The National Bureau of Asian Research and University of Washington Press, pp. 191–228.

Noland, Marcus (2002) "North Korea's External Economic Relations: Globalization in 'Our Own Style'," in Samuel S. Kim and Tai Hwan Lee, eds., *North Korea and Northeast Asia*, Lanham, MD: Rowman & Littlefield, pp. 165–93.

Noland, Marcus (2003, July) "Famine and Reform in North Korea," Institute for International Economics Working Paper, WP 03–5, July.

Noland, Marcus (2004a) "The Strategic Importance of U.S.-Korea Economic Relations," *Joint U.S.-Korea Academic Studies*, 14, 79–102.

Noland, Marcus (2004b) *Korea After Kim Jong-il,* Washington, DC: Institute for International Economics.

Noland, Marcus, Sherman Robinson, and Li Gang Liu (1998) "The Costs and Benefits of Korean Unification," *Asian Survey,* 38, 801–14.

North Korea Advisory Group (1999), "Report to the Speaker, U.S. House of Representatives," November.

Norton, Anne (1988) *Reflections on Political Identity,* Baltimore: The Johns Hopkins University Press.

Nye, Joseph S., Jr. (1974) "Transnational Relations and Interstate Conflicts: An Empirical Analysis," *International Organization,* 28, 961–96.

Nye, Joseph S., Jr. (1988) "Neorealism and Neoliberalism," *World Politics,* 40, 235–51.

Nye, Joseph S., Jr. (1990) *Bound to Lead: The Changing Nature of American Power,* New York: Basic Books.

Nye, Joseph S., Jr. (1995) "East Asian Security: The Case for Deep Engagement," *Foreign Affairs,* 74(4), 90–102.

Nye, Joseph S., Jr. (2004) *Soft Power: The Means to Success in World Politics,* New York: Public Affairs.

Oberdorfer, Don (1997) *The Two Koreas: A Contemporary History,* Reading, MA: Addison-Wesley.

Oh, Kongdan and Ralph Hassig (1999) "North Korea Between Collapse and Reform," *Asian Survey,* 39(2), 287–309.

Oh, Kongdan and Ralph Hassig (2000) *North Korea Through the Looking Glass.* Washington, DC: Brookings Institution Press.

O'Hanlon, Michael and Mike Mochizuki (2003) *Crisis on the Korean Peninsula: How to Deal with a Nuclear North Korea,* New York: McGraw-Hill.

Okonogi, Masao (2000) "The North Korean Crisis and Japan's Choice," in Wonmo Dong, ed., *The Two Koreas and the United States,* Armonk, NY: M. E. Sharpe, pp. 119–29.

Olsen, Edward A. (2003) "The United States and the Korean Peace Process," in Tae-Hwan Kwak and Seung-Ho Joo, eds., *The Korean Peace Process and the Four Powers,* Burlington, VT: Ashgate, pp. 76–97.

Ornauer, Helmut, et al., eds. (1976) *Images of the World in the Year 2000: A Comparative Ten Nation Study,* Atlantic Highlands, NJ: Humanities Press.

Oye, Kenneth A. (1985) "Explaining Cooperation Under Anarchy: Hypotheses and Strategies," *World Politics,* 38, 1–24.

Paek, Tae-youl (1999) "Korean Unification and Japan's Foreign Policy," in Lee Young-Sun and Masao Okonogi, eds., *Japan and Korean Unification,* Seoul: Yonsei University Press, pp. 33–50.

Paige, Glenn D. (1968) *The Korean Decision: June 24–30, 1950,* New York: The Free Press.

Pak, Chi Young (1995) "Korea and the United Nations," *Korea and World Affairs,* 19(4), 612–31.

Park, Han S. (1998) "Human Needs, Human Rights, and Regime Legitimacy: The North Korean Anomaly," in Moon Chung-in, ed., *Understanding Regime Dynamics in North Korea,* Seoul: Yonsei University Press, pp. 221–35.

Park, Jung Sun (2006) "The Korean Wave: Transnational Cultural Flows in Northeast Asia," in Charles K. Armstrong, Gilbert Rozman, Samuel S. Kim, and Stephen Kotkin, eds., *Korea at the Center: Dynamics of Regionalism in Northeast Asia,* Armonk, NY: M. E. Sharpe, pp. 244–56.

Park, Young-ho (1998) "International Perceptions of Korean Unification Issues," *Korea Focus*, 6(1), 72–80.

Pastor, Robert (1999) "The Great Powers in the Twentieth Century: From Dawn to Dusk," in Robert A. Pastor, ed., *A Century's Journey: How the Great Powers Shape the World*, New York: Basic Books, pp. 1–31.

Paul, T. V. (1994) *Asymmetric Conflicts: War Initiation by Weaker Powers*, New York: Cambridge University Press.

Paviatenko, Viktor N. (1999) "Russian Security in the Pacific Asian Region: The Dangers of Isolation," in Gilbert Rozman, Mikhail G. Nosov, and Koji Watanabe, eds., *Russia and East Asia: The 21st Century Security Environment*, Armonk, NY: M. E. Sharpe, pp. 44–59.

Perry, William (1999) "Review of United States Policy Toward North Korea: Findings and Recommendations." Available at http://www.state.gov/www/regions/eap/991012_northkorea_rpt.html.

Perry, William (2002) "The United States and the Future of East Asian Security: – Quo Vadis?" in Keun-Min Woo, ed., *Building Common Peace and Prosperity in Northeast Asia*, Seoul: Yonsei University Press, pp. 119–29.

Podberezsky, Igor V. (1999) "Between Europe and Asia: The Search for Russia's Civilizational Identity," in Gennady Chufrin, ed., *Russia and Asia: The Emerging Security Agenda*, New York: Oxford University Press, pp. 33–51.

Pollack, Jonathan D. (2003) "The United States, North Korea, and the End of the Agreed Framework," *Naval War College Review*, 56(3), 11–49.

Pollack, Jonathan and Lee Chung-min (1999) *Preparing for Korean Unification*, Santa Monica, CA: RAND.

Powell, Robert (1991) "Absolute and Relative Gains in International Relations," *American Political Science Review*, 85(4), 1303–20.

Powell, Robert (1994) "The Neorealist-Neoliberal Debate," *International Organization*, 48(2), 313–44.

Prizel, Ilya (1998) *National Identity and Foreign Policy: Nationalism and Leadership in Poland, Russia and Ukraine*, New York: Cambridge University Press.

Putin, Vladimir (2003) "A State of the Nation Address to the Federal Assembly of the Russian Federation (Moscow, May 16, 2003)," *International Affairs* (Moscow), 49(4), 1–17.

Putnam, Robert (1988) "Diplomacy and Domestic Politics: The Logic of Two-Level Games," *International Organization*, 42, 427–60.

Ravenhill, John (2002) "A Three Bloc World? The New East Asian Regionalism," *International Relations of the Asia-Pacific*, 2(2), 167–95.

Reiss, Mitchell B. and Robert L. Gallucci (2005) "Responses: Red-Handed: The Truth About North Korea's Weapons Program," *Foreign Affairs*, 84(2), 142–45.

Rennack, Dianne (2003, January 24) "North Korea: Economic Sanctions," Report for Congress, Washington, DC: Congressional Research Service.

Rice, Condoleeza (2000) "Promoting the National Interest," *Foreign Affairs*, 79(1), 45–62.

Risse-Kappen, Thomas (1994) "Ideas Do Not Float Freely: Transnational Coalitions, Domestic Structures, and the End of the Cold War," *International Organization*, 48(2), 185–214.

Roh, Tae Woo (1992) *Korea in the Pacific Century: Selected Speeches 1990–1992*, Lanham, MD: University Press of America.

Rose, Gideon (1998) "Neoclassical Realism and Theories of Foreign Policy," *World Politics*, 51, 144–72.

Rosecrance, Richard and Arthur A. Stein, eds. (1993) *The Domestic Bases of Grand Strategy*, Ithaca, NY: Cornell University Press.

Rosenau, James N. (1987) "Toward Single-Country Theories of Foreign Policy: The Case of the USSR," in Charles Hermann, Charles W. Kegley, and James Rosenau, eds., *New Directions in the Study of Foreign Policy*, Winchester, MA: Allen & Unwin, pp. 53–74.

Rosenau, James N. (1990) *Turbulence in World Politics: A Theory of Change and Continuity*, Princeton, NJ: Princeton University Press.

Rosenau, James N. (1994) "China in a Bifurcated World: Competing Theoretical Perspectives," in Thomas W. Robinson and David Shambaugh, eds., *Chinese Foreign Policy: Theory and Practice*, New York: Oxford University Press, pp. 524–51.

Rosenau, James N. (1996) "The Dynamics of Globalization: Toward an Operational Formulation," *Security* Dialogue, 27(3), 247–62.

Rothstein, Robert L. (1968) *Alliances and Small Powers*, New York: Columbia University Press.

Roy, Dennis (1998) "North Korea as an Alienated State," *Survival*, 38(4), 22–36.

Rozman, Gilbert (2002a) "Japan's Quest for Great Power Identity," *Orbis*, 46(1), 73–91.

Rozman, Gilbert (2002b) "Japan and South Korea: Should the U.S. Be Worried About Their New Spat in 2001?" *Pacific Review*, 15(1), 1–28.

Rozman, Gilbert (2002, May) "South Korean Identity: In Search of National Pride, East Asian Regionalism and a Role in Globalization," Unpublished manuscript, Department of Sociology, Princeton University.

Rozman, Gilbert (2003) "Japan's North Korean Initiative and U.S.-Japanese Relations," *Orbis*, 47(3), 527–39.

Rozman, Gilbert (2004) *Northeast Asia's Stunted Regionalism: Bilateral Distrust in the Shadow of Globalization*, Cambridge: Cambridge University Press.

Rozman, Gilbert, Mikhail G. Nosov, and Koji Watanabe, eds. (1999) *Russia and East Asia: The 21st Century Security Environment*, Armonk, NY: M. E. Sharpe.

Rubinstein, Alvin Z. (1997) "Russia's Relations with North Korea," in Stephen Blank and Alvin Rubenstein, eds., *Imperial Decline: Russia's Changing Role in Asia*, Durham, NC: Duke University Press, pp. 155–84.

Ruggie, John Gerard (1998) "What Makes the World Hang Together? Neo-utilitarianism and the Social Constructivist Challenge," *International Organization*, 52(4), 855–85.

Russett, Bruce (1993) *Grasping the Democratic Peace: Principles for a Post-Cold War World*, Princeton, NJ: Princeton University Press.

Russett, Bruce and John Oneal (2001) *Triangulating Peace: Democracy, Interdependence, and International Organizations*, New York: Norton.

Samuels, Richard J. (2004) "Payback Time: Japan-North Korea Economic Relations," in Ahn Choong-yong, Nicholas Eberstadt, and Lee Young-sun, eds., *A New International Engagement Framework for North Korea? Contending Perspectives*, Washington, DC: Korean Economic Institute of America, pp. 317–33.

Scalapino, Robert (1997) "North Korea at a Crossroads," Essays in Public Policy No. 73, Stanford, CA: Hoover Institution, Stanford University, pp. 1–18.

Scalapino, Robert A. and Chong-sik Lee (1972) *Communism in Korea, Part I: The Movement*, Berkeley: University of California Press.

Schell, Jonathan (2003) "America's Vulnerable Imperialism," *YaleGlobal*, November 24. Available at http://yaleglobal.yale.edu/display.article?id=2873.

Scholte, Jan Aart (1996) "Globalisation and Collective Identities," in Jill Krause and Neil Renwick, eds. *Identities in International Relations,* New York: St. Martin's Press, pp. 38–78.

Schou, August and Arne Olau Brundland, eds. (1971) *Small States in International Relations,* Stockholm: Almqvist & Wiskell.

Schweller, Randall (1998) *Deadly Imbalances: Tripolarity and Hitler's Strategy of World Conquest,* New York: Columbia University Press.

Scobell, Andrew (2004a, March) *China and North Korea: From Comrades-in-Arms to Allies at Arm's Length,* Strategic Studies Institute Monograph, Carlisle, PA: U.S. Army War College.

Scobell, Andrew (2004b) "China and Inter-Korean Relations: Beijing as Balancer," in Samuel S. Kim, ed. *Inter-Korean Relations: Problems and Prospects,* New York: Palgrave Macmillan, pp. 81–96.

Scobell, Andrew (2005, July) *North Korea's Strategic Intentions,* Strategic Studies Institute Monograph, Carlisle, PA: U.S. Army War College.

Sejong Institute (1995) *'95 Kukmin uisik chosa* [*Survey of National Consciousness, 1995*], Seoul: Sejong Institute.

Sejong Institute (1997) *Korea's National Strategy: Agenda Setting for the 21st Century,* Seoul: Sejong Institute.

Seymour, James D. (2005) "China: Background Paper on the Situation of North Koreans in China," A Writenet Report, Commissioned by United Nations High Commissioner for Refugees, Protection Information Section (DIP). January. Available http://www.unhcr.ch/cgi-bin/texis/vtx/home/opendoc.pd?tbl=RSDCOI&id=4231d11d4.

Seymour, James D. (2006) "The Exodus: North Korea's Out-Migration," in John Feffer, ed., *The Future of U.S.- Korean Relations,* New York: Routledge, pp. 130–59.

Shambaugh, David (2003) "China and the Korean Peninsula: Playing for the Long Term," *The Washington Quarterly,* 26(2), 43–56.

Shambaugh, David (2004/05) "China Engages Asia: Reshaping the Regional Order," *International Security,* 29(3), 64–99.

Shambaugh, David, ed. (2006) *Power Shift: China and Asia's New Dynamics,* Berkeley: University of California Press.

Shen, Jiru (2003) "Weihu DongBeiYa anquan de dangwu zhili [The Urgent Task of Preserving Peace in Northeast Asia]," *Shijie jingji yu zhengshi* [*World Economics and Politics*], 9, 53–58.

Shi, Yinhong (2003) "How to Understand and Deal with the DPRK Nuclear Crisis," *Ta Kung Pao* (Hong Kong), January 15, p. A11 (trans. FBIS-CHI-2003-0115, January 16, 2003).

Shim, Jae Hoon (1999) "A Crack in the Wall," *Far Eastern Economic Review,* 29 April, 10–12.

Shin, Gi-Wook and Paul Yunsik Chang (2004) "The Politics of Nationalism in U.S.-Korean Relations," *Asian Perspective,* 28(4), 119–45.

Shorrock, Tim (1986) "The Struggle for Democracy in South Korea in the 1980s and the Rise of Anti-Americanism," *Third World Quarterly,* 8(4), 1195–1218.

Sigal, Leon V. (1997) "Who is Fighting Peace in Korea? An Undiplomatic History," *World Policy Journal,* 24, 44–58.

Sigal, Leon V. (1998) *Disarming Strangers: Nuclear Diplomacy with North Korea,* Princeton, NJ: Princeton University Press.

Sigal, Leon V. (2000) "Negotiating an End to North Korea's Missile Making," *Arms Control Today,* 30(5), 3–7.

Snyder, Glenn H. (1997) *Alliance Politics*, Ithaca, NY: Cornell University Press.

Snyder, Jack (1984/85) "Richness, Rigor, and Relevance in the Study of Soviet Foreign Policy," *International Security*, 9(3), 89–108.

Snyder, Jack (2004) "One World, Rival Theories," *Foreign Policy* 145, 52–62.

Snyder, Scott (1997) "North Korea's Decline and China's Strategic Dilemma. Special Report," Washington, DC: U.S. Institute of Peace.

Snyder, Scott (1999) *Negotiating on the Edge: North Korean Negotiating Behavior*, Washington, DC: U.S. Institute of Peace Press.

Snyder, Scott (2000) "Pyongyang's Pressure," *Washington Quarterly*, 23, 163–70.

Snyder, Scott (2000/01) "North Korea's Challenge of Regime Survival: Internal Problems and Implications for the Future," *Pacific Affairs*, 73(4), 517–33.

Snyder, Scott (2003a) "China–Korea Relations: Beijing in the Driver's Sear? China's Rising Influence on the Two Koreas," *Comparative Connections* [Online], 4(4): 95–101. Available at http://www.csis.org/media/csis/pubs/0204q.pdf.

Snyder, Scott (2003b) "China–Korea Relations: A Turning Point for China?" *Comparative Connections* [Online], 5(2): 101–07. Available at http://www.csis.org/media/csis/pubs/0302q.pdf.

Snyder, Scott (2003c) "China–Korea Relations: Middle Kingdom Diplomacy and the North Korean Nuclear Crisis," *Comparative Connections* [Online], 5(3): 113–18. Available at http://www.csis.org/media/csis/pubs/0303q.pdf.

Snyder, Scott (2004) "China–Korea Relations: No Shows, Economic Growth, and People Problems," *Comparative Connections* [Online], 5(4): 111–17. Available at http://www.csis.org/media/csis/pubs/0304q.pdf.

Snyder, Scott(2005) "China–Korea Relations: Six-Party Success and China's Peninsular Diplomacy," *Comparative Connections* [Online], 7(3): 109–16. Available at http://www.csis.org/media/csis/pubs/0503q.pdf.

Snyder, Scott, Ralph A. Cossa, and Brad Glosserman (2005) "The Six-Party Talks: Developing a Roadmap for Future Progress," *Issues & Insights* 5(8): 1–28.

Sokov, Nikolai (2002) "A Russian View of the Future Korean Peninsula," in Tsuneo Akaha, ed., *The Future of North Korea*, New York: Routledge, pp. 129–46.

Song, Dexing (1998) "Lengzhan hou DongbeiYa anquan xingshe de bianhua [Changes in the Post-Cold War Northeast Asian Security Situation]," *Xiandai guoji guanxi* [*Contemporary International Relations*], 9, 34–38.

Sprout, Harold and Margaret Sprout (1971) *Toward a Politics of the Planet Earth*, New York: Van Nostrand Reinhold.

Spurr, Russell (1988) *Enter the Dragon: China's Undeclared War Against the U.S. in Korea, 1950–1951*, New York: Newmarket Press.

Stockholm International Peace Research Institute (SIPRI) (2001) *SIPRI Yearbook 2001: Armaments, Disarmament and International Security*, New York: Oxford University Press.

Stockholm International Peace Research Institute (SIPRI) (2002) *SIPRI Yearbook 2002: Armament, Disarmament and International Security*, New York: Oxford University Press.

Stockholm International Peace Research Institute (SIPRI) (2004) *SIPRI Yearbook 2004: Armaments, Disarmament and International Security*, New York: Oxford University Press.

Stockholm International Peace Research Institute (SIPRI) (2005) *SIPRI Yearbook 2005: Armaments, Disarmament and International Security*, New York: Oxford University Press.

Stueck, William (1995) *The Korean War: An International History*, Princeton, NJ: Princeton University Press.

Suh, Dae-Sook (1967) *The Korean Communist Movement 1918–1948*, Princeton, NJ: Princeton University Press.

Suh, Dae-Sook (1988) *Kim Il Sung: The North Korean Leader*, New York: Columbia University Press.

Suh, Dae-Sook (1993) "The Prospects for Change in North Korea," *Korea and World Affairs*, 17(1), 5–20.

Suh, Jae-Jung (2006) "Imbalance of Power, Balance of Asymmetric Terror: Mutual Assured Destruction (MAD) in Korea," in John Feffer, ed., *The Future of U.S.-Korean Relations*, New York: Routledge, pp. 64–80.

Suny, Ronald Grigor (1999/2000) "Provisional Stabilities: The Politics of Identities in Post-Soviet Eurasia," *International Security*, 24(3), 139–78.

Sutter, Robert (2005) *China's Rise in Asia: Promises and Perils*, Lanham, MD: Rowman & Littlefield.

Tait, Richard (2003) "Playing by the Rules in Korea: Lessons Learned in the North-South Economic Engagement," *Asia Survey*, 43(2), 305–28.

Takahashi, Kosuke (2005) "Japan-South Korea Ties on the Rocks," *Japan Focus*, March 28.

Tamamoto, Masaru (1991) "Japan's Uncertain Role," *World Policy Journal*, 8, 584–85.

Tanter, Raymond and Richard H. Ullman, eds. (1972) *Theory and Policy in International Relations*, Princeton, NJ: Princeton University Press.

Thomas, W. I. (1928) *The Child in America*, New York: Knopf.

Thucydides (1978) *The Peloponnesian War*, Rex Warner, trans., New York: Penguin.

Todd, Emmanuel (2003) *After the Empire: The Breakdown of the American Order*, New York: Columbia University Press.

Toloraya, Georgi (2002) "Russia and North Korea," in Tsuneo Akaha, ed., *The Future of North Korea*, New York: Routledge, pp. 147–56.

Toloraya, Georgi (2003a) "Korean Peninsula and Russia," *International Affairs (Moscow)*, 49(1), 24–34.

Toloraya, Georgi (2003b) "President Putin's Korea Policy," *The Journal of East Asian Affairs*, 17(1), 23–51.

Tolz, Vera (1998) "Conflicting 'Homeland Myths' and Nation-State Building in Postcommunist Russia," *Slavic Review* 57 (2), 267–94.

Torkunov, A. (2003) "The Korean Issue," *International Affairs (Moscow)*, 49(4), 37–47.

Truman, Harry S. (1955), *Memoirs Vol. 1: Year of Decisions*, Garden City, NY: Doubleday.

United Nations Development Programme (UNDP) (1999) *Human Development Report 1999*, New York: Oxford University Press.

United Nations Development Programme (UNDP) (2004) *Human Development Report 2004*, New York: Oxford University Press.

United Nations Development Programme (UNDP) (2005). *Human Development Report 2005*, New York: Oxford University Press.

United Nations Environment Programme (UNEP) (2003) *State of the Environment DPR Korea 2003* [Online]. Available at http://www.unep.org/PDF/DPRK_SOE_Report.pdf.

United States Department of Defense (1990) *A Strategic Framework for the Asian Pacific Rim: Looking Towards the Twenty-first Century*, Washington, DC: Department of Defense.

United States Department of Defense (2001) *Quadrennial Defense Review Report (QDRR 2001)*, September 30, p. 2. Available at http://www.defenselink.mil/pubs/qdr2001.pdf.

Vasquez, John (1987) "Foreign Policy, Learning, and War," in Charles F. Hermann, Charles W. Kegley, Jr., and James N. Rosenau, eds., *New Directions in the Study of Foreign Policy*, Boston: Allen & Unwin, pp. 366–83.

Vasquez, John (1992) "World Politics Theory," in Mary Hawkesworth and Maurice Kogan, eds., *Encyclopedia of Government and Politics*, Vol. 2, New York: Routledge, pp. 839–61.

Verba, Sidney (1971) "Sequences and Development," in Leonard Binder et al., eds., *Crises and Sequences in Political Development*, Princeton, NJ: Princeton University Press.

Vital, David (1967) *The Inequality of States: A Study of the Small Power in International Relations*, New York: Oxford University Press.

Vorontsov, Alexander (2002) "Russia and the Korean Peninsula: Contemporary Realities and Prospects," *Far Eastern Affairs*, 30(3).

Wada, Haruki (1992) *Kim Il-song kwa Manchu hanil chonchaeng* [*Kim Il Sung and the Manchurian Resistance War Against Japan*], Yi Chong-sok, trans., Seoul: Ch'angchak kwapi pyongsa.

Wallander, Celeste (1996) "The Sources of Russian Conduct: Theories, Frameworks, and Approaches," in Celeste Wallander, ed., *The Sources of Russian Foreign Policy after the Cold War*, Boulder, CO: Westview Press, pp. 1–20.

Wallensteen, Peter and Karin Axell (1993) "Armed Conflict at the End of the Cold War, 1989–92," *Journal of Peace Research*, 30, 331–46.

Wallensteen, Peter and M. Sollenberg (2001) "Armed Conflict, 1989–2001," *Journal of Peace Research*, 38(5), 629–44.

Walt, Stephen M. (1987) *The Origin of Alliances*, Ithaca, NY: Cornell University Press.

Walt, Stephen M. (1997) "Why Alliances Endure or Collapse," *Survival*, 39(1), 156–79.

Walt, Stephen M. (1998) "International Relations: One World, Many Theories," *Foreign Policy*, 110, 29–46.

Waltz, Kenneth N. (1959) *Man, the State and War*, New York: Columbia University Press.

Waltz, Kenneth N. (1979) *Theory of International Politics*, Reading, MA: Addison-Wesley.

Waltz, Kenneth N. (1997) "Evaluating Theories," *American Political Science Review*, 91(4), 913–17.

Wang, Fei-Ling (1998) "China and Korean Unification: A Policy of Status Quo," *Korea and World Affairs*, 22, 177–98.

Wang, Fei-Ling (1999) "Joining the Major Powers for the Status Quo: China's Views and Policy on Korean Reunification," *Pacific Affairs*, 72, 167–85.

Wang, Jianwei (2003) "Territorial Disputes and Asian Security: Sources, Management, and Prospects," in Muthiah Alagappa, ed., *Asian Security Order: Instrumental and Normative Features*, Stanford, CA: Stanford University Press, pp. 380–423.

Wang, Jisi (2005) "China's Search for Stability with America," *Foreign Affairs* 84(3), 39–48.

Wang, Yizhou (1999) "Mianxiang ershi shiji de Zhongguo waijiao: sanzhong xuqiu de xunqiu jiqi pinghem [China's Diplomacy for the 21st Century: Seeking and Balancing Three Demands]," *Zhanlue yu guanli* [*Strategy and Management*], 6, 18–27.

Wang, Yizhou, ed. *Construction Within Contradictions: Multiple Perspectives on the Relationship Between China and International Organizations,* Beijing: China Development Publishing House.

Weathersby, Kathryn (1995) "To Attack, or Not to Attack? Stalin, Kim Il Sung, and the Prelude to War," *Bulletin of Cold War International History Project,* 5, 1–9.

Weathersby, Kathryn (1996) "New Russian Documents on the Korean War: Introduction and Translations," *Bulletin of Cold War International History Project,* 6–7, 30–84.

Weathersby, Kathryn (1999) "The Korean War Revisited," *The Wilson Quarterly,* 23(3), 91–95.

Weber, Max (1968) *From Max Weber: Essays in Sociology,* in H. H. Gerth and C. Wright Mills, eds., New York: Oxford University Press.

Weigert, Andrew, J. Smith Teitge, and Dennis W. Teitge (1986) *Society and Identity: Toward a Sociological Psychology,* Cambridge: Cambridge University Press.

Weiner, Michael (1994) *Race and Migration in Imperial Japan,* New York: Routledge.

Wendt, Alexander (1987) "The Agent-Structure Problem in International Relations Theory," *International Security,* 41, 335–70.

Wendt, Alexander (1992) "Anarchy Is What States Make of It: The Social Construction of Power Politics," *International Organization,* 46, 391–425.

Wendt, Alexander (1994) "Collective Identity Formation and the International State," *American Political Science Review,* 88, 384–96.

Wendt, Alexander (1995) "Constructing International Politics," *International Security,* 20(1), 71–81.

Wendt, Alexander (1999) *Social Theory of International Politics,* New York: Cambridge University Press.

Whiting, Allen S. (1989) *China Eyes Japan,* Berkeley: University of California Press.

Williams, William Appleman (1961) *The Tragedy of American Diplomacy,* Rev. ed., New York: Delta Books.

Williams, William Appleman (1980) *Empire as a Way of Life,* New York: Oxford University Press.

Wishnick, Elizabeth (2001a) "Review of *Rossiia I Koreia v geopolitike evrazeiskogo vostoka [Russia and Korea in the Geopolitics of the Eurasian East]* by Vladimir Li," Northeast Asia Peace and Security Network, Special Report.

Wishnick, Elizabeth (2001b) *Mending Fences: Moscow's China Policy from Brezhnev to Yeltsin,* Seattle: University of Washington Press.

Wishnick, Elizabeth (2002) "Russian-North Korean Relations: A New Era?" in Samuel S. Kim and Tai Hwan Lee, eds., *North Korea and Northeast Asia,* New York: Rowman & Littlefield, pp. 139–62.

Wishnick, Elizabeth (2004) "Russia in Inter-Korean Relations," in Samuel S. Kim, ed., *Inter-Korean Relations: Problems and Prospects,* New York: Palgrave Macmillan, pp. 117–38.

Wit, Joel S., Daniel B. Poneman, and Robert L. Gallucci (2004) *Going Critical: The First North Korean Nuclear Crisis,* Washington, DC: Brookings Institution Press.

Wohlforth, William C. (1993) *The Elusive Balance: Power and Perceptions During the Cold War,* Ithaca, NY: Cornell University Press.

Wohlforth, William C. (1994/95) "Realism and the End of the Cold War," *International Security,* 19(2), 91–129.

Wohlforth, William C. (1999) "The Stability of a Unipolar World," *International Security,* 24(1), 5–41.

Wolf, Charles, Jr. (1995) *Long-Term Economic and Military Trends, 1994–2015: The United States and Asia*, Santa Monica, CA: RAND.
Wolf, Charles, Jr. (1997) "Asia in 2015," *Wall Street Journal*, 20 March, p. A16.
Wolf, Charles, Jr. and Kamil Akramov (2005) *North Korean Paradoxes: Circumstances, Costs, and Consequences of Korean Unification*, Santa Monica, CA: Rand.
Woo, Jung-En (1991) *Race to the Swift*, New York: Columbia University Press.
Woodruff, David (1999) *Money Unmade: Barter and the Fate of Russian Capitalism*, Ithaca, NY: Cornell University Press.
World Bank (1991) *World Development Report 1991*, New York: Oxford University Press.
World Bank (1996) *World Development Report 1996*, New York: Oxford University Press.
World Bank (1997) *World Development Report 1997*, New York: Oxford University Press.
World Bank (1999) *World Development Report 1998/99*, New York: Oxford University Press.
World Bank (2001) *World Development Report 2000/2001*, New York: Oxford University Press.
World Bank (2002) *World Development Report 2002*, New York: Oxford University Press.
World Bank (2003a) *World Development Report 2003*, New York: Oxford University Press.
World Bank (2003b) *World Development Report 2004*, New York: Oxford University Press.
World Bank (2004) *World Development Report 2005*, New York: Oxford University Press.
World Bank (2005) *World Development Report 2006*, New York: Oxford University Press.
World Food Programme (2005a) "WFP DPR Korea EMOP 10141.3 Emergency Food World Food Programme Assistance to Vulnerable Groups." Available at http://www.wfp.org/operations/current_operations/project_docs/101413.pdf).
World Food Programme (2005b) "Update on Korea, Democratic Republic," May 18.
Yamaji, Hideki (2004) "Policy Recommendations for Japan: Unification of the Korean Peninsula," Washington, DC: The Brookings Institution, Center for Northeast Asian Policy Studies.
Yan, Xuetong (1995) "Lengzhan hou Zhongguo de duiwai anquan zhanlüe [China's post-Cold War External Security Strategy]," *Xiandai guoji guanxi* [*Contemporary International Relations*], 8, 23–29.
Yan, Xuetong and Li Zhongcheng (1995) "Zhanwang xia shiji chu guoji zhengzhi [Prospects for International Politics in the Beginning of the Next Century]," *Xiandai guoji guanxi* [*Contemporary International Relations*], 6, 2–8.
Yang, Chengxu (1994) "Dui Dong Ya anquan wenti de fenxi [An Analysis of the East Asian Security Problem]," *Guoji wenti yanjiu* [*International Studies*], 3, 19–22.
Yang, Sang Chul and Kang Hak Suk (1995) *Pukhan Oekyo Chongchaek* [*North Korean Foreign Policy*], Seoul: Seoul Press.
Yang, Seung Ham, Woosang Kim, and Yongho Kim (2004) "Russo-North Korean Relations in the 2000s: Moscow's Continuing Search for Regional Influence," *Asian Survey*, 44(6), 794–814.

Yang, Young Shik (1998) "Kim Dae-jung Administration's North Korea Policy," *Korea Focus,* 6(6), 48–62.

Yi, Xiaoxiong (1995) "China's Korea Policy: From 'One Korea' to 'Two Koreas,'" *Asian Affairs,* 22(2), 119–39.

Yoon, In-Jin (2001) "North Korean Defectors Abroad and in South Korea," *Development and Security,* 30(1), 1–26.

Yoon, Tae-Ryong (2006) *Fragile Cooperation: Net Threat Theory and Japan-Korea-U.S. Relations,* PhD dissertation, Department of Political Science, Columbia University, New York, New York.

Yu, Shaohua (1997) "Chaoxian bandao xingshi de fazhan yu qianjing [The Evolving Situation and Future Prospects of the Korean Peninsula]," *Guoji wenti yanjiu [International Studies]*, 4, 12–16.

Yufan, Hao and Zhai Zhihai (1990) "China's Decision to Enter the Korean War: History Revisited," *The China Quarterly,* 121, 94–115.

Zacek, Jane Shapiro (1998) "Russia in North Korean Foreign Policy," in Samuel S. Kim, ed., *North Korean Foreign Relations,* Hong Kong: Oxford University Press.

Zakaria, Fareed (1998) *From Wealth to Power: The Unusual Origins of America's World Role,* Princeton, NJ: Princeton University Press.

Zhang, Aiping (1994) *Zhongguo Renmin Jiefang Jun [China's People's Liberation Army]*, Vol. 1, Contemporary China Series, Beijing: Dangdai Zhongguo Chubanshe.

Zhang, Xiaoming (1998) "The Korean Peninsula and China's National Security: Past, Present, and Future," *Asian Perspective,* 22, 259–72.

Zhao, Gancheng (1997) "China's Korea Unification Policy," in Tae-Hwan Kwak, ed., *The Four Powers and Korean Unification Strategies,* Seoul: Institute for Far Eastern Studies, Kyungnam University, pp. 59–86.

Zhebin, Alexander (2005) "The Bush Doctrine, Russia, and Korea," in Mel Gurtov and Peter Van Ness, eds., *Confronting the Bush Doctrine: Critical Views from the Asia-Pacific,* New York: Routledge Curzon, pp. 130–52.

Zou, Yunhua (1998) "The Relationship Between TMD and the Global and Regional Security," *Guoji wenti yanjiu [International Studies]*, 1, 27–29.

Index